Philosophical Dialogues

Arne Næss and the
Progress of Ecophilosophy

Edited by
Nina Witoszek and Andrew Brennan

ROWMAN & LITTLEFIELD PUBLISHERS, INC.
Lanham • Boulder • New York • Oxford

ROWMAN & LITTLEFIELD PUBLISHERS, INC.

Published in the United States of America
by Rowman & Littlefield Publishers, Inc.
4720 Boston Way, Lanham, Maryland 20706

12 Hid's Copse Road
Cumnor Hill, Oxford OX2 9JJ, England

Layout and Laserset by Lukács Info, Oslo, Norway
Illustrations by Sigmund Kvaløy Sætreng
Photo by Paul Kashap

British Library Cataloguing in Publication Information Available

Library of Congress Cataloging-in-Publication Data

Philosophical dialogues : Arne Næss and the progress of ecophilosophy /
    edited by Nina Witoszek and Andrew Brennan.
        p. cm.
    Includes bibliographical references.
    ISBN 0-8476-8928-X (hardcover : alk. paper). — ISBN 0-8476-8929-8
(pbk. : alk. paper)
        1. Deep ecology—Philosophy. 2. Environmental ethics. 3. Næss, Arne.
    I. Witoszek, Nina. II. Brennan, Andrew.
    GE195.P53   1998
    179'.1—dc21   98-24368
                                                                CIP
Printed in the United States of America

Contents

v

List of Figures

Preface

Dialogue—one of the most fetishized concepts of our time—is much easier to talk about than to implement as a modus operandi. All too often the ostensibly pluralist and dialogic turns out to be a discreetly disguised exercise in the monologic imagination: a cult, a school, an ordinance, the Word of the Father. In the pages that follow we have tried to register what we consider to be one of the more genuine and seminal intellectual dialogues of the latter part of the twentieth century. Its instigator is the Norwegian philosopher Arne Næss; its concern is the fate of the planet.

More than thirty years have passed since Næss first broached the main premises of the deep ecological project. Seldom has such a laconic—and open-ended—statement provoked such an avalanche of response and spurred so many initiatives. How to account for this? After all, here was a daring, radical vision of social change being propounded at the very twilight of utopias. Its magnetism derived not merely from its appeal to an unspent idealism but, first of all, from its sheer common-sense formulation of the roots of and remedies to environmental crisis.

Despite the myriad of explications and anthologies of Næss's thought, none has hitherto presented the ways in which deep ecology matured and mutated through dialogical confrontation and polemic. All too often nonspecialist scholars and commentators, unaware of the growth and development that has taken place within ecophilosophy over the last thirty years, draw on or refer to isolated pronouncements or materials published during the movement's infancy. During this period Næss not only attempted to address emerging postmodern and feminist perspectives but to rethink his own vision and methodology in the light of critique and controversy.

Hence this volume, although celebratory, is not a piece of hagiography. On the contrary, it attempts to bring together the most significant—and hard hitting—exchanges between Næss and his interlocutors. Some have been hitherto unpublished, other difficult of access because they took place in television studios or in the depths of Norwegian forest.

The book is dialogic in a triple sense. First, it tries to show the sheer breadth of Næss's engagement with other thinkers. They range from encounters with Sir Alfred Ayer and Paul Feyerabend, through exchanges with ecofeminists such as Karen Warren, to polemics with Indian intellectuals such as Ramachandra Guha. In a real sense, dialogue and confrontation remain Næss's element. Even as we go to print close to his eighty-fifth birthday, he has been excitedly taking up the challenges presented by some of his opponents in this volume, rethinking his position and preparing further responses.

Second, to bring this work up to date and to introduce a fresh perspective on earlier exchanges, we have invited a number of significant scholars in the field of environmental philosophy to comment briefly on crucial areas of concern. How does deep ecology rate at the end of the twentieth century? Is it, as some claim, a spent force or does it remain at the cutting edge of ecological thought as we enter the new millennium?

Third, the latent scenario in this book is that of a Platonic symposium, with Næss cast in his favorite role of Socrates. Like Socrates, Næss has always wanted to be a "respectable pest." This book goes some way towards illustrating his achievements in this regard. Recall the famous feast, where a lively debate on the nature of love is broken up by the entrance of the drunken Alcibiades. Socrates's pupil first extols his master and then asks him for guidance. Socrates, however, evades both Alcibiades's advances and his desire to turn him into a guru. In the subsequent confrontation, Alcibiades is all emotional commitment, a shard of a "broken timber of humanity"—set over against Socrates's stoic sang-froid. The feast ends in the philosopher's triumph: Socrates maintains his sobriety to the end of the revels, then throws himself into a totally different debate where he puts everybody to sleep, and finally goes off to swim in the Leykon and pursue his daily routines.

For some readers, Næss's "symposium" may well exhibit a similar anticlimax. Næss's engagement in the search for the truth, his passionate interest in the moral improvement of the world, and his exquisite debating stamina forever clash with his ultimately skeptical, even playful detachment from the pedantries, intensities, and insincerities of academic debate.

Næss's "progress" is intriguing. His green writings sprouted from logical empiricism and the Vienna Circle—a dry and seemingly infertile ground. Consider his earlier texts on language, or the philosophy of Spinoza, and compare these with his later polemical and morally engaged writings. What a metamorphosis! The desert cacti have come to blossom. Challenge and provocation enter the titles of his articles. The style becomes more engaged and combative. A green *homo ludens* replaces a gray *homo pedanticus*.

The method, however, stays the same: Næss's basic philosophical equipment is still that of the logical empiricist. Ecosophy T is laid out as a series of prescriptions that could be endorsed by an emotivist. The deduction of actions from underlying principles is set out as if in a textbook of empiricist philosophy of science. The famous apron diagram has a Hempelian flavor, reminding us that Næss is no stranger to the deductive-nomological method. How striking, that this Spartan approach should produce such a flourishing of ideas, controversy, and new moral demands.

This flourishing, we propose, is not simply a consequence of the urgency of Næss's thought its timing or phrasing. It is equally a response to the poetics of ambiguity that characterize his later work. As Harold Glasser has noted:

> Following the zetetic skeptic tradition [Næss] eschews dogma by asserting that his own work is searching, "on the way," it is necessarily fragmentary and ever amenable to improvements, modifications and elaborations. Caveats aside,

Næss's penchant for revising can make it difficult to pin down his interpretation of particular elements of the deep ecology approach.[1]

Næss claims that the open texture and methodological vagueness of his work have been a semantic device which encourages widespread acceptance of deep ecology. Even if this is true, the present volume illustrates that Næss's work has provoked an unprecedented philosophical argument and attracted multiple interpretations. What is included here is only a sample of a larger colloquium between Næss, his apologists and critics.[2] A number of interlocutors and long-time collaborators had to be omitted because their exchanges with him, however enriching for Næss's thought, belong to the genre of exegesis rather than polemics. This applies, for example, to the significant body of work produced by David Rothenberg and by many of Næss's Norwegian students and collaborators.

The essays and comments which follow speak for themselves, making further introductions unnecessary. They record an astonishing moment in the history of western philosophy; its premises threatened to unhinge centuries of value theory based on the idea of humans as the only entities which possess moral worth in their own right. Like any genuinely subversive philosophy which has inspired a movement and a wide following from politicians to poets, Næss's vision has been subject to a gentle rebuttal, if not to side-tracking, by mainstream philosophers.

An unsympathetic observer might wonder if the deep ecology platform sets out an effective political agenda. One might also question the dubious nature of some environmental movements claiming their credentials from the deep platform (see for example the section on "schisms" in this volume). Finally, one might object that the core preoccupations of the followers of deep ecology are too narrowly fixed on the forest, the mountain, and other wild places. Næss's disciples have neglected, for the most part, the habitats in which the majority of humans live and act: the city, the savannah and the shores of seas and lakes.

So much for reservations. Despite their undoubted force, the exchanges printed here go some way towards addressing them. They illustrate that Næss has never stood still: he has come increasingly to recognize that his own vision is only part of a larger agenda of moral and political concern, embracing the situation of women, the prospects for peace, and the advancement of human rights. Today's deep ecology may have lost some of its earlier spikiness. But this represents a change to an ever more open and dialogic stance.

Leszek Kolakowski, a philosopher who has advocated the praise of inconsistency, talks about a "chronic conflict in philosophy, which seems to be able to marshal its history: the conflict between the quest for the absolute and a flight from it, between fear of oneself and fear of losing oneself in the very principle, in which sustenance is hoped for." Kolakowski divides all philosophers into priests and jesters. The jester is the eternal *puer*, a skeptical observer of social order: active, critical, questioning all that appears self-evident; he embodies imagination, pluralism, individuality, playfulness, relishes the tensions between ideals, and enjoys exploring the future, the possible, the hopeful. The priest is the *senex*, a conservative who believes in a harmonious system of values; he guards the absolute, defends the past, orthodoxy, tradition and sanctity. "The priest and the jester both violate the mind; the priest with the garrote of catechism, the fool with the needle of mockery."[3]

Næss confounds this dichotomy. As this volume will show, in his dialogic vision the priest and the jester constantly exchange roles, defy one another—and their critics. A skeptical priest and a pious jester are joined in a paradoxical alliance.

Notes

[1] Harold Glasser, "Demystifying the Critiques of Deep Ecology," in *Rethinking Deep Ecology*, Nature and Humanities Series, ed. Nina Witoszek (Oslo: Center for Development and the Environment, 1996), 93–94.

[2] Papers reprinted in the present volume have been left as close to their original form as possible. In particular, no attempt has been made to rewrite articles so as to remove gender uses of "man" and "he" in application to persons in general.

[3] Leszek Kolakowski, "The Priest and the Jester," in *Stalinism and Beyond*, trans. Jane Zielonko Peel (London: Paladin Books, 1971), 124, 127.

Acknowledgments

The publication of this volume has been made possible thanks to the support and financial assistance of the Center for Development and the Environment at Oslo University and the Schweisfurth Foundation in Munich.

We are grateful to Kit Fai Næss, Jon Wetlesen, Per Ariansen and Bayard Catron for their imaginative suggestions at the early planning stages of this volume in 1995. We should also add that the final shape of *Philosophical Dialogues* benefited greatly from comments and suggestions of Alan Drengson, Harold Glasser, Patsy Hallen, Pat Sheeran and Arne Næss himself. The dialogic form of the volume has been enhanced by the willingness of a number of leading scholars and writers in the field to comment on the existing exchanges.

We are especially grateful to Lóránd Lukács Jr. for his generous graphic and technical assistance in the preparation of this volume. The enormous task of typing and formatting the debates has been eased by the contributions of Kit Fai Næss, Peder Anker, Yeuk-Sze Lo and Pål Deberitz. We also owe a special debt to Sigmund Kvaløy, Arne Næss's long time collaborator, for his illustrations which adorn our book.

Finally, we are grateful to the publishers of those articles which originally appeared elsewhere for permission to reprint them in the present volume.

Chapter 1 is reprinted from Arne Næss, "The Shallow, the Deep, Long-Range Movements: A Summary," *Inquiry* 16 (1973): 95–100. Reprinted with permission from *Inquiry*. © Scandinavian University Press.

Chapter 2 is reprinted from Arne Næss and George Sessions, "The Deep Ecology Platform." Printed with permission from Arne Næss and George Sessions. © Arne Næss and George Sessions.

Chapter 3 is reprinted with minor revisions from *Reflexive Water: The Basic Concerns of Mankind*, ed. Fons Elders (London: Souvenir Books, 1974), 13–68. Reprinted with permission from Souvenir Press. © Souvenir Press Ltd.

Chapter 4 is reprinted from Arne Næss, "Ayer on Metaphysics: A Critical Commentary by a Kind of Metaphysician," *The Philosophy of A. J. Ayer*, ed. Lewis Edwin Hahn (Chicago: Open Court, 1992), 329–340. Reprinted with permission from Open Court Publishers. © The Library of Living Philosophers.

Chapter 5 is reprinted from Alfred J. Ayer, "A Reply to Arne Næss," published in *The Philosophy of A. J. Ayer*, ed. Lewis Edwin Hahn (Chicago: Open Court, 1992), 340–346. Reprinted with permission from Open Court Publishers. © The Library of Living Philosophers.

Chapter 8 is reprinted with minor revisions from Arne Næss, "Paul Feyerabend: A Green Hero?" *Beyond Reason*, ed. G. Munevar (Dordrecht: Kluwer, 1991), 403–416. Reprinted with permission from Kluwer Academic Publishers. © Kluwer Academic Publishers.

Chapter 11 is reprinted with minor revisions from Genevieve Lloyd, "Spinoza's Environmental Ethics," *Inquiry* 23 (1980): 293–311. Reprinted with permission from *Inquiry*. © Scandinavian University Press.

Chapter 12 is reprinted with minor revisions from Arne Næss, "Environmental Ethics and Spinoza's Ethics: Comments on Genevieve Lloyd's Article," *Inquiry* 23 (1980): 313–325. Reprinted with permission from *Inquiry*. © Scandinavian University Press.

Chapter 14 is reprinted with minor revisions from Richard Watson, "A Critique of Anti-Anthropocentric Biocentrism," *Environmental Ethics* 5 (Fall, 1983): 245–256. Reprinted with permission from Richard A. Watson. © Richard A. Watson.

Chapter 15 is reprinted with minor revisions from Arne Næss, "A Defense of the Deep Ecology Movement," *Environmental Ethics* 6 (Fall, 1984): 265–270. Reprinted with permission from Arne Næss. © Arne Næss.

Chapter 16 is reprinted with minor revisions from William C. French, "Against Biospherical Egalitarianism," *Environmental Ethics* 17 (Spring, 1995): 39–57. Reprinted with permission from William C. French. © William C. French.

Chapter 19 is reprinted with minor revisions from Warwick Fox, "Deep Ecology: A New Philosophy of Our Time?" *The Ecologist* 14 (1984): 194–200. Reprinted with permission from *The Ecologist*. © *The Ecologist*.

Chapter 20 is reprinted with minor revisions from Arne Næss, "Intuition, Intrinsic Value, and Deep Ecology," *The Ecologist* 14 (1984): 201–203. Reprinted with permission from *The Ecologist*. © *The Ecologist*.

Chapter 21 is reprinted with minor revisions from Arne Næss, "On Guiding Stars of Deep Ecology": Warwick Fox's Response to Næss's Response to Fox," *The Ecologist* 16 (1984): 203–204. Reprinted with permission from *The Ecologist*. © *The Ecologist*.

Chapter 23 is reprinted with minor revisions from Peter Reed, "Man Apart: An Alternative to the Self-Realization Approach," *Environmental Ethics* 11 (Spring, 1989): 53–69. Reprinted with permission from *Environmental Ethics*. © *Environmental Ethics*.

Chapter 24 is reprinted with minor revisions from Arne Næss, "'Man Apart' and Deep Ecology: A Reply to Reed," *Environmental Ethics* 12 (summer, 1989): 185–192. © Arne Næss.

Chapter 26 is reprinted from Kirkpatrick Sale, "Deep Ecology and Its Critics," *The Nation* (May 14, 1998): 670–674. Reprinted with permission from *The Nation* magazine. © The Nation Company, L. P.

Chapter 27 is reprinted with minor revisions from Arne Næss, "A European Looks at North American Branches of the Deep Ecology Movement," *The Trumpeter* 5:2 (Spring, 1988): 75–76. Reprinted with permission from *The Trumpeter*. © *The Trumpeter*.

Chapter 31 is reprinted with minor revisions from Ariel Salleh, "Class, Race, and Gender Discourse in the Ecofeminism/Deep Ecology Debate," *Envi-*

ronmental Ethics 15 (Fall, 1993): 225–244. Reprinted with permission from Ariel Salleh. © Ariel Salleh.

Chapter 35 is reprinted from Murray Bookchin, "Social Ecology versus Deep Ecology," *Green Perspectives, Newsletter of the Green Program Project* 4/5 (Summer, 1987). Reprinted with permission from Murray Bookchin. © Murray Bookchin.

Chapter 40 is reprinted with minor revisions from Ramachandra Guha, "Radical American Environmentalism and Wilderness Preservation: A Third World Critique," *Environmental Ethics* 11 (1989): 71–83. Reprinted with permission from Ramachandra Guha. © Ramachandra Guha.

Chapter 43 is reprinted with minor revisions from Arne Næss and Ivar Mysterud, "Philosophy of Wolf Policies (I): General Principles and Preliminary Exploration of Selected Norms," *Conservation Biology* 1 (1987): 23–34. Reprinted with permission from *Conservation Biology*. © *Conservation Biology*.

Chapter 44 is reprinted with minor revisions from Harold Glasser, "Næss's Deep Ecology Approach and Environmental Policy," *Inquiry* 39 (1996): 157–187. Reprinted with permission from *Inquiry*. © Scandinavian University Press.

Chapter 46 is reprinted with minor revisions from *Worldviews: Environment, Culture, and Religion*. Reprinted with permission from *Worldviews*. © White Horse Press.

Arne Næss in southern Chile, 1994. Photo courtesy of Doug Tompkins.

Part I

Philosophical Systems and Systems of Philosophy

Figure 1. The Ecophilosopher.

Chapter 1

The Shallow and the Deep, Long-Range Ecology Movements: A Summary

Arne Næss

The emergence of ecologists from their former relative obscurity marks a turning point in our scientific communities. But their message is twisted and misused. A shallow, but presently rather powerful movement, and a deep, but less influential movement, compete for our attention. I shall make an effort to characterize the two.

I. The Shallow Ecology Movement

Fight against pollution and resource depletion. Central objective: the health and affluence of people in the developed countries.

II. The Deep Ecology Movement

(1) Rejection of the man-in-environment image in favor of *the relational, total-field image.* Organisms as knots in the biospherical net or field of intrinsic relations. An intrinsic relation between two things A and B is such that the relation belongs to the definitions or basic constitutions of A and B, so that without the relation, A and B are no longer the same thing. The total-field model dissolves not only the man-in-environment concept, but every compact thing-in-milieu concept—except when talking at a superficial or preliminary level of communication.

(2) *Biospherical egalitarianism* in principle. The "in principle" clause is inserted because any realistic praxis necessitates some killing, exploitation, and

3

suppression. The ecological field-worker acquires a deep-seated respect, or even veneration, for ways and forms of life. He reaches an understanding from within, a kind of understanding that others reserve for fellow men and for a narrow section of ways and forms of life. To the ecological field-worker, *the equal right to live and blossom* is an intuitively clear and obvious value axiom. Its restriction to humans is an anthropocentrism with detrimental effects upon the life quality of humans themselves. The quality depends in part upon the deep pleasure and satisfaction we receive from close partnership with other forms of life. The attempt to ignore our dependence and to establish a master-slave role has contributed to the alienation of man from himself.

Ecological egalitarianism implies the reinterpretation of the future-research variable, "level of crowding," so that general mammalian crowding and loss of life-equality is taken seriously, not only human crowding. (Research on the high requirements of free space of certain mammals has, incidentally, suggested that theorists of human urbanism have largely underestimated human life-space requirements. Behavioral crowding symptoms, [neuroses, aggressiveness, loss of traditions, etc.] are largely the same among mammals.)

(3) *Principles of diversity and of symbiosis.* Diversity enhances the potentialities of survival, the chances of new modes of life, the richness of forms. And the so-called struggle for life, and survival of the fittest, should be interpreted in the sense of the ability to coexist and cooperate in complex relationships, rather than the ability to kill, exploit, and suppress. "Live and let live" is a more powerful ecological principle than "Either you or me."

The latter tends to reduce the multiplicity of kinds of forms of life, and also to create destruction within the communities of the same species. Ecologically inspired attitudes therefore favor diversity of human ways of life, of cultures, of occupations, of economies. They support the fight against economic and cultural, as much as military, invasion and domination, and they are opposed to the annihilation of seals and whales as much as to that of human tribes and cultures.

(4) *Anti-class posture.* Diversity of human ways of life is in part due to (intended or unintended) exploitation and suppression on the part of certain groups. The exploiter lives differently from the exploited, but both are adversely affected in their potentialities of self-realization. The principle of diversity does not cover differences due merely to certain attitudes or behaviors forcibly blocked or restrained. The principles of ecological egalitarianism and of symbiosis support the same anti-class posture. The ecological attitude favors the extension of all three principles to any group conflicts, including those of today between developing and developed nations. The three principles also favor extreme caution toward any over-all plans for the future, except those consistent with wide and widening classless diversity.

(5) Fight against *pollution and resource depletion.* In this fight ecologists have found powerful supporters, but sometimes to the detriment of their total stand. This happens when attention is focused on pollution and resource depletion rather than on the other points, or when projects are implemented which reduce pollution but increase evils of other kinds. Thus, if prices of life necessi-

ties increase because of the installation of anti-pollution devices, class differences increase too. An ethics of responsibility implies that ecologists do not serve the shallow, but the deep ecological movement. That is, not only point (5), but all seven points must be considered together.

Ecologists are irreplaceable informants in any society, whatever their political color. If well organized, they have the power to reject jobs in which they submit themselves to institutions or to planners with limited ecological objectives. As it is now, ecologists sometimes serve masters who deliberately ignore the wider perspectives.

(6) *Complexity, not complication.* The theory of ecosystems contains an important distinction between what is complicated without any "Gestalt" or unifying principles—we may think of finding our way through a chaotic city—and what is complex. A multiplicity of more or less lawful, interacting factors may operate together to form a unity, a system. We make a shoe or use a map or integrate a variety of activities into a workaday pattern. Organisms, ways of life, and interactions in the biosphere in general exhibit complexity of such an astoundingly high level as to color the general outlook of ecologists. Such complexity makes thinking in terms of vast systems inevitable. It also makes for a keen, steady perception of the profound human ignorance of biospherical relationships and therefore of the effect of disturbances.

Applied to humans, the complexity-not-complication principle favors division of labor, *not fragmentation of labor.* It favors integrated actions in which the whole person is active, not mere reactions. It favors complex economies, an integrated variety of means of living. (Combinations of industrial and agricultural activity, of intellectual and manual work, of specialized and nonspecialized occupations, of urban and non-urban activity, of work in city and recreation in nature with recreation in city and work in nature.)

It favors soft technique and "soft future-research," less prognosis, more clarification of possibilities. More sensitivity toward continuity and live traditions, and more importantly, towards our state of ignorance.

The implementation of ecologically responsible policies requires in this century an exponential growth of technical skill and invention but in new directions, directions that today are not consistently and liberally supported by the research policy organs of our nation-states.

(7) *Local autonomy and decentralization.* The vulnerability of a form of life is roughly proportional to the weight of influences from afar, from outside the local region in which that form has obtained an ecological equilibrium. This lends support to our efforts to strengthen local self-government and material and mental self-sufficiency. But these efforts presuppose an impetus towards decentralization. Pollution problems, including those of thermal pollution and recirculation of materials, also lead us in this direction, because increased local autonomy, if we are able to keep other factors constant, reduces energy consumption. (Compare an approximately self-sufficient locality with one requiring the importation of foodstuffs, materials for house construction, fuel, and skilled labor from other continents. The former may use only five percent of the energy

used by the latter.) Local autonomy is strengthened by a reduction in the number of links in the hierarchical chains of decision. (For example, a chain consisting of a local board, municipal council, highest sub-national decision-maker, a state-wide institution in a state federation, a federal national government institution, a coalition of nations, and of institutions, e.g., EEC top levels, and a global institution, can be reduced to one made up of a local board, nation-wide institution, and global institution.) Even if a decision follows majority rule at each step, many local interests may be dropped along the line, if it is too long.

Summing up then, it should, first of all, be borne in mind that the norms and tendencies of the Deep Ecology movement are not derived from ecology by logic or induction. Ecological knowledge and the lifestyle of the ecological field-worker have *suggested, inspired, and fortified* the perspectives of the Deep Ecology movement. Many of the formulations in the above seven-point survey are rather vague generalizations, only tenable if made more precise in certain directions. But all over the world the inspiration from ecology has shown re-markable convergences. The survey does not pretend to be more than one of the possible condensed codifications of these convergences.

Secondly, it should be fully appreciated that the significant tenets of the Deep Ecology movement are clearly and forcefully *normative*. They express a value priority system only in part based on results (or lack of results, see point 6) of scientific research. Today, ecologists try to influence policy-making bodies largely through threats, through predictions concerning pollutants and resource depletion, knowing that policy-makers accept at least certain minimum norms concerning health and just distribution. But it is clear that there is a vast number of people in all countries, and even a considerable number of people in power, who accept as valid the wider norms and values characteristic of the Deep Eco-logy movement. There are political potentials in this movement which should not be overlooked and which have little to do with pollution and resource deple-tion. In plotting possible futures, the norms should be freely used and elabo-rated.

Thirdly, insofar as ecology movements deserve our attention, they are ecophi-losophical rather than ecological. Ecology is a limited science which makes use of scientific methods. Philosophy is the most general forum of debate on fundamentals, descriptive as well as prescriptive, and political philosophy is one of its subsections. By an *ecosophy* I mean a philosophy of ecological harmony or equilibrium. A phi-losophy is a kind of *sophia* wisdom, is openly normative; it contains both norms, rules, postulates, value priority announcements and hypotheses concerning the state of affairs in our universe. Wisdom is policy wisdom, prescription, not only scientific description and prediction.

The details of an ecosophy will show many variations due to significant dif-ferences concerning not only "facts" of pollution, resources, population, etc., but also value priorities. Today, however, the seven points listed provide one uni-fied framework for ecosophical systems.

In general systems theory, systems are mostly conceived in terms of causally or functionally interacting or interrelated items. An ecosophy, however, is more like a system of the kind constructed by Aristotle or Spinoza. It is expressed verbally as a set of sentences with a variety of functions, descriptive and prescriptive. The basic relation is that between subsets of premises and subsets of conclusions, that is, the relation of derivability. The relevant notions of derivability may be classed according to rigor, with logical and mathematical deductions topping the list, but also according to how much is implicitly taken for granted. An exposition of an ecosophy must necessarily be only moderately precise, considering the vast scope of relevant ecological and normative (social, political, ethical) material. At the moment, ecosophy might profitably use models of systems, rough approximations of global systematizations. It is the global character, not preciseness in detail, which distinguishes an ecosophy. It articulates and integrates the efforts of an ideal ecological team, a team comprising not only scientists from an extreme variety of disciplines, but also students of politics and active policy-makers.

Under the name of *ecologism* various deviations from the deep movement have been championed—primarily with a one-sided stress on pollution and resource depletion, but also with a neglect of the great differences between under- and over-developed countries in favor of a vague global approach. The global approach is essential, but regional differences must largely determine policies in the coming years.

Notes

This chapter is reprinted with minor revisions from a summary of an introductory lecture at the World Future Research Conference, Bucharest, 3–10 September 1972. Published in *Inquiry* 16 (1973): 95–100. The original paper was confiscated by the Ceaușesku-regime, and, doubtlessly, it preserved somewhere in the archives in Bucharest. Arne Næss comments, "I found some years later that the seven points made the deep ecology movement too narrow—a kind of sect. Also, the word 'equal intrinsic value' should be cut out in favor of 'some intrinsic value.'"

Chapter 2

The Deep Ecology Platform

Arne Næss and George Sessions

1. The flourishing of human and nonhuman life on earth has intrinsic value. The value of nonhuman life forms is independent of the usefulness these may have for narrow human purposes.
2. Richness and diversity of life forms are values in themselves and contribute to the flourishing of human and nonhuman life on earth.
3. Humans have no right to reduce this richness and diversity except to satisfy vital needs.
4. Present human interference with the nonhuman world is excessive, and the situation is rapidly worsening.
5. The flourishing of human life and cultures is compatible with a substantial decrease of the human population. The flourishing of nonhuman life requires such a decrease.
6. Significant change of life conditions for the better requires changes in policies. These affect basic economic, technological, and ideological structures.
7. The ideological change is mainly that of appreciating life quality (dwelling in situations of intrinsic value) rather than adhering to a high standard of living. There will be a profound awareness of the difference between big and great.
8. Those who subscribe to the foregoing points have an obligation directly or indirectly to participate in the attempt to implement the necessary changes.

Notes

"The Deep Ecology Platform" has been cited in numerous studies by Næss. See, for example, A. Næss, "Will the Defenders of Nature Please Rise?" *Conservation Biology*, ed. M. E. Saulé (Sinauer Associates Inc., 1986), 504–515.

Chapter 3

The Glass Is on the Table: The Empiricist versus Total View

Arne Næss, Alfred Ayer, and Fons Elders

ELDERS: Ladies and gentlemen, I would like to welcome you to a debate which will, I suppose, be of interest in many respects. I would like to lose as little time as possible in beginning this philosophical contest, in which you will see an avid football fan, Sir Alfred, and a lover of boxing and alpinism, Arne Næss, debating with each other on central issues of their own philosophies. First of all, we have to discover what kinds of philosophical views both philosophers have. Sir Alfred and Mr. Næss, would you each explain to the audience what you consider to be your tasks as philosophers? Sir Alfred?

AYER: Well, I suppose to try to answer a certain quite specific range of questions that are classified as philosophical questions—and are very much the same questions that, I think, have been asked since the Greeks, mainly about what can be known, how it can be known, what kind of things there are, how they relate to one another.

In general, I would think of philosophy as an activity of questioning accepted beliefs, trying to find criteria and to evaluate these criteria; trying to unearth the assumptions behind thinking, scientific thinking and ordinary thinking, and then trying to see if they are valid. In practice this generally comes down to answering fairly concrete specific questions.

And I hope, in a sense, to finding the truth.

ELDERS: And you, Mr. Næss?

NÆSS: Well, I see it a little differently, I think, because I would rather say that to philosophy belong the most profound, the deepest, and the most fundamental problems. They will change very little, and they have not changed much over the last two thousand years. So we have different conceptions of philosophy, but we agree that the epistemological question, "what can we know?" and the ontological one, "what main kinds of things are there?" belong to philosophy. As I see it, they are among the most profound questions we can ask.

AYER: Yes, but how do you measure the profundity of a problem? I mean, a problem may often look quite trivial and then turn out to be profound. In a sense, you try to answer what you're puzzled by. Now this may be something very profound, it may even look quite superficial, then turn out to be profound.

NÆSS: How do we measure? Well, that's one of the most profound questions of all. How do we know? I suppose it will vary with cultural and social circumstances. It involves fundamental valuations, not only investigations of fact or logic.

ELDERS: Sir Alfred, would you give an outline of a skeptic?

AYER: Well, I was going to talk about this. It seems to me that, perhaps not so much in ancient philosophy, but certainly in modern philosophy since Descartes, a lot of problems have arisen out of a certain very characteristic skeptical argument. I should say that a skeptic is always someone who questions one's right to make certain assumptions—often assumptions about the existence of certain kinds of things—on the ground of their going beyond the evidence.

I mean, a very obvious and classical example would be skepticism about other minds. People will say, well, all you observe is other people's behavior; all you observe is their actions, the expressions on their faces. How do you know that anything goes on behind? How do you know that everybody isn't a robot, or whatever? And so you get skepticism also tied up with a certain neurosis, I think. It has also a certain emotional tone.

Or again take the classical example of the skepticism of David Hume, the skepticism about induction. Hitherto, when you lit a cigarette, it would smoke, and so on; when you have walked on the floor it has supported you. How do you know that this will happen in the future? How can you extrapolate from past evidence to future occurrences? And then you are proving that the argument is, in a sense, circular, always presupposing something that you can't justify. And a lot of philosophy comes out as the posing of arguments of this kind and the attempts to find replies to them. And you could even characterize different sorts of philosophy by their different ways of meeting the skeptic. Now, I think one mark of a philosopher, why I think that Arne Næss is a profound philosopher, is to take skepticism seriously. Would you?

ELDERS: But in *The Problem of Knowledge* you are quite critical about skepticism.

AYER: I think I rather cheated in *The Problem of Knowledge*. It seems to me that I gave skepticism a good run, and then in the end somehow some little strong John Bull common sense came out in me and I took away from the skeptic the victory he had won, like a referee in a boxing match.

NÆSS: [. . .] I'm sorry to say but in some ways I feel miserable to be defending skepticism now, because there is a very tragic conflict between the attitude I hold in my integrated and concentrated moments, which is more or less skeptical, and the requirements of consistent action. For instance, when we believe that we really must do something about some terribly pressing problem, we must somehow narrow down our perspective. The vast plurality of possible worlds—and how do we know in which world we live—are suddenly not only irrelevant, but contemplation of them undermines the willingness and capacity to act. Most people are only willing to act forcefully and consistently when they have a belief in the truth and close their minds to all else.

AYER: But I should have thought this was a field in which a certain kind of skepticism anyhow was very desirable and fruitful. It's very healthy indeed not to listen to the rhetoric about democracy, but to look at the facts. Look and see what actually happens: see how people live their lives, see what is actually done in the law courts, look behind the words to realities. This is in a sense a formal skepticism, although you're not skeptical about the words that we use to mark them with. And I would think there that your approach is thoroughly skeptical and at the same time constructive in this field.

NÆSS: Yes, it's desirable that people should be like you in this way, but mostly they seem not to be like that. The students say that we must get rid of particular textbooks of Næss because they undermine convictions and will undermine collective action now and over the next five years. And this is real; it is a tragedy, because they need rhetoric and dogmatism, I think. Scepticism breeds passivity. I do not feel that way, but the students do.

ELDERS: But, Sir Alfred, if you are stressing this point of the relationships between certain philosophical schools on one hand and certain values on the other hand, do you see any relation between your empiricism and your role as director of the Humanist Movement in Great Britain?

AYER: Yes, I see some relation. I don't see a relation in the sense that I would be able to deduce my political or my social views from any set of metaphysical or epistemological principles. I don't think that, in this sense, I have a coherent system or that there can be one. But of course I think that there is some relation, inasmuch that if one has an empirical, even skeptical temper of mind, then one will be hostile to rhetoric, or at least one will look for the facts behind the rhetoric.

I've been a humanist, for example, partly because I could see no reason to believe in the existence of God. And therefore I would be opposed to people who not only maintained this, but also based political or social programs on it.

I would be a humanist in as much as I think I would be professionally opposed to humbug of any kind: the kind of humbug that you too often find in people in power, in judges and people of that sort. And, in a sense, I would expect an empirical philosopher to be radical, although if one looks at history, this isn't always so: Hume, who was the greatest of all empiricists, was in fact, if anything, a Tory. This was partly because of his skepticism. He was so skeptical about schemes of human improvement.

ELDERS: Like Schopenhauer.

AYER: Yes. But in general it has certainly been true in the last century or so that there has been a close association, so close an association between empiricism and radicalism that it couldn't entirely be an accident. But I think it's a matter of a certain habit of mind, a certain critical temper in the examination of political and social as well as philosophical questions, that is responsible for this, rather than some deduction from first principles.

ELDERS: Yes, but these are not really arguments, but merely a piece of history.

AYER: I'm giving you an explanation. You asked me what I thought the connection was, and I . . .

ELDERS: The historical explanation. But we're talking now on the level of arguments about the relation between empiricism and humanism.

AYER: But it's slightly more than this, because I think a certain habit of mind, a certain critical temper that you would develop if you did philosophy in the sort of way that Næss and I do it, would on the whole tend . . . after all, you bring the same intelligence to bear on any of a wide range of problems, even though they aren't necessarily the same problems, and this would, I think, tend to have the effect of making you a liberal radical in social and political questions. This would be more than just an historical accident, as it might be if I happened to be both Protestant and have brown eyes; it's not as accidental as that. There is, I think, some causal connection of a very close kind.

But I don't think that I can, from any kind of empiricist premises, deduce a political program. I mean, you can't get rabbits out of hats that don't contain them. Do you agree?

NÆSS: Well, no! First of all, you expect that as philosophers we should somehow be able to deduce them, whereas I would say our responsibility is to connect our views—our ethical and epistemological as well as our political views—in a fairly decent way so that we get a coherent whole. The connections may be looser than ordinary scientific connections, looser than deductions. I think we disagree here on how we conceive of our roles as philosophers. I consider myself a philosopher when I'm trying to convince people of nonviolence, consistent nonviolence whatever happens. That is a fairly fantastic doctrine, considered descriptively or empirically. I must therefore make clear, to others and myself what kind of normative principles I also make use of, and derive from them the special norms and hypotheses characteristic of Gandhian strategy of conflict behavior. I think I believe in the ultimate unity of all living beings. This is a very vague and ambiguous phrase, but I have to rely on it. It is a task for analytical philosophy to suggest more precise formulations. Because I have such principles, I also have a program of action, the main outline of which is part of my philosophy. So I might suddenly try to win you over to consistent nonviolence and to persuade you to join some kind of movement—and this in spite of my not believing that I possess any guarantee that I have found any truths.

AYER: I can see you might indeed try to persuade me of this, but I don't think you'd persuade me of these methods. The ultimate unity of living things: I mean . . .

ELDERS: Is this metaphysics, in your opinion?

AYER: Well it could be an ordinary scientific statement. In fact it would include not only living things but also inanimate things, if they were all made of atoms; in this sense they are homogeneous. Then I suppose there is more homogeneity between organic things, although the difference between organic and inorganic is so slight.

It doesn't seem to me that on any scientific basis of this sort, one is going to build an ethical view. After all, civil wars take place, and the people who fight each other in them don't deny that they're each human beings and even belong to the same nation: but it doesn't stop the fighting.

So, in fact, this alone is not going to be sufficient. You have to put up some moral principle, which is not going to be deducible from any factual or metaphysical one; that it is wrong to take life of any kind. But do you then extend this to all life, mosquitoes and the like, or just human life? I'm not saying this ironically: I think that it's a perfectly defensible position to be vegetarian and so on—I'm not, but I think . . .

ELDERS: But will you try, Mr. Næss, to give the metaphysical foundation for your belief in nonviolence, about which we can speak later? We are still at the level of principles and arguments for or against metaphysics.

AYER: And it's partly political too, isn't it? It's not just metaphysical. How well Gandhi did against the British, he would have done less well against the Nazis.

NÆSS: Yes, metaphysical and political and anthropological, all at once, all in one: therefore systems are unavoidable. Gandhi as a leader in Germany? Perhaps one million Jews killed before 1938, none after. He advised resistance, not submission. The metaphysical principle here of course belongs more to the Indian than to the European tradition.

AYER: Yes, I would say so.

NÆSS: But the ecological movement may change the European tradition. The formulation "all living beings are ultimately one," is neither a norm nor a description. The distinction between descriptions and norms and even imperatives can be put in afterwards, semantically speaking. It is the kind of utterance you make in support of something I would call an intuition, by which I do not mean that it is necessarily true. In moments of concentration you are aware of vast perspectives: yes, that is the thing, ultimately life is one!

And then you start to ask yourself how you can argue for this and what does it mean; and at this moment you need a norm, a system of ethics and an ontology and plenty of hypotheses in many fields covered by the sciences. And you say: a mosquito and myself are obviously not biologically the same, so I must mean something different from it. For instance, something like: if I hurt you, I hurt myself. My self is not my ego, but something capable of immense development. Think of a picture from the war: a young man is just going to throw a grenade and there is another young man, the so-called enemy, very similar to him, also intending to do the same at exactly the same moment. It's a case of "him or me," but they are also obviously aware of the fact that they are the same kind of being and that to throw grenades at each other is really nonsense. They are one.

AYER: Well, I share your moral sentiments, but I think what you've been saying is very largely just false. It's like the schoolmaster who is going to beat the boy and says, "This is going to hurt me more than it'll hurt you." That's an absolute lie. It isn't going to hurt the schoolmaster at all—on the contrary, in only too many cases it's going to give him pleasure.

NÆSS: The boy also if he's a masochist.

AYER: The boy also if he's a masochist, yes. But, in fact, what you are saying simply isn't true. I mean, not only a mosquito, and I but even you and I are not one. Of course, if I sympathize with you and you are hurt I shall be sorry, but I shan't be hurt in the same way. It's indeed true, empirically true, that to a rather limited extent human beings sympathize with one another; with people they know and like, and people they feel in some way close to. But to say that they're one is in any literal sense just false. I'm not identical with you, and it would be a terrible thing if I were, in a way. [Laughter.] I mean, this discussion would be very difficult.

ELDERS: Or it would be much more easy.

AYER: Ah, well, yes, it would be. It would be even more solipsistic than it sometimes tends to become.

ELDERS: Growing more and more together.

AYER: It seems to me that clearly, if one takes these things literally, they're false; and therefore you take them metaphorically. Now, it's just when you take them metaphorically that they become moral principles of a perfectly respectable kind that you ought to treat other people as though they . . . mean, if you like, as in the Christian way of thinking . . . I mean, deal with other people as you wish them to deal with you. They wouldn't necessarily have the same tastes, but in a sense one should treat other people as if they were as important to you as yourself. This is a perfectly good moral principle. But why pretend that we are identical when we are not?

ELDERS: Now you need some whisky, Mr. Næss?

NÆSS: No, no. You are too rash.

AYER: He doesn't want to identify with me too much, does he?

NÆSS: Too rash, you are too rash. First of all, there is no definite literal sense of an utterance like this in relation to its metaphorical sense. You have to analyze it from a great many points of view. Its so-called literal meaning is hardly exemplified in any available text; what is the literal sense of the identity of all living beings?

AYER: Well, I mean it in the sense in which the evening star is identical with the morning star; in the sense in which the Young Pretender is identical with Charles Edward Stuart; in the sense in which the author of *Pickwick* is identical with the author of *Oliver Twist*: this is what I would call the literal sense of identity. Now it's up to you since you're not using it in that sense, to define a sense in which you are using it.

NÆSS: That's right.

AYER: And now I subside.

NÆSS: Good. That's better. [Laughter.] Have patience!

When we say that we are the same, three concepts may profitably be interconnected. The ego, the self with a small s, and then this great Self, with a capital S, the atman, which you hear so much about in Indian philosophy, but also, of course, in certain Western traditions. If you as a boy had had a very much wider development, your self, what you take to be part of you, would not only include your body, it would include everything that's yours, so to speak; so what is yours would have been much wider.

This justifies the tentative introduction of an entity, the Self, with a capital S, the power of which gradually increases. You might still say your limits are those of your body, but there you would have to include units of your central nervous system such as, for instance, those corresponding to the Milky Way and the Andromeda nebula in so far as you have sensuous or other bodily interactions with them.

And in this kind of philosophy they ultimately believe that human beings can develop in such a way, that in a sense their selves include the other selves in a certain way.

AYER: But in what sense? In what sense does my self include Fons? Or could it ever, however much I thought of him?

NÆSS: Now you are too impolite. Fons is not utterly different.

ELDERS: I should like that.

AYER: I'm sorry, but I don't know, I . . . Fons would like it.

NÆSS: Philosophy is just this; that you develop something that I've started and gradually you introduce preciseness from different directions. Then you breathe three times, reinforce your intuition, and go a little further towards precision. But there is no hurry; this process will take a long time. And of course sometimes intuitions vanish for some of us, for instance, those of "absolute movement" or of an absolute "voice of conscience."

I suppose you would say that the limits of the self gradually increase from infancy to puberty; and the sense in which it increases is, I would say, what you are concerned about. What you identify yourself with . . . the norms you internalize.

AYER: Ah! Now that's, yes . . .

NÆSS: And concern in the sense in which you say "my"! You use the possessive term, my—my mother, for instance.

ELDERS: I think in a biological sense we form a chain of divisions; so for example, in this sense, you can use the meaning of the greater Self, against the small self or ego.

NÆSS: Yes, biologically we are just centers of interactions in one great field.

AYER: But why put things in a portentous way when they can be put in a simple way? Why not say that as you grow older you come to comprehend more things; your knowledge perhaps increases, and then after a certain point, I'm afraid diminishes again. But up to a point it increases. Perhaps your range of sympathy is greater; perhaps you identify with more things and sometimes again with less.

Again, one can't always generalize; some people differ in this respect, some people narrow themselves in the sense of concentrating more on themselves. When one has a fairly precise method, a precise way of describing all these facts, why does one have to make such portentous statements about one's self expanding and including everything. It sounds romantic, but it's quite superfluous when what you mean can be put quite definitely: that these things happen, and these things are empirically testable. I would say that what you're describing is true of some people, not of others.

NÆSS: Well, what is portentous depends on at which university you are studying.

AYER: Portentous. I did not say pretentious, that would have been rude. I said portentous.

NÆSS: I meant portentous also: and that depends on the university. If you had been at Oxford or Cambridge at the time of Wittgenstein, it would have been a different thing than what it was at the time of Bradley and of the Hegelians. Trivialism is portentous if carried to extremes. But let us go back to the belief in the pervasiveness of the "I." Well, people then used certain terms about which we now would say "Oh, my God, don't be so portentous." So this is completely relative, I think. There are a million things to be said: must they all begin with "I?" Spinoza introduces the "I" in part two, not in part one, of his system. Do we have a definite ego all the time? Isn't that a weird construction? A Cartesian prejudice? "I developed from this to that" or "Now I am developing more in this direction" or "I was very different when I was thirteen from when I was twelve," and so on—I, I, I!

Must we think that there is such an entity? I wouldn't simply think there is a definite entity there. Without this skepticism I would not feel "all living things are ultimately one" to be a good slogan.

AYER: I don't think I disagree with you there. I certainly don't want to postulate any sort of Cartesian substance anything, of which the ego could be a name. I'm very puzzled about this, I don't at all know the answer to it, but I'm inclined to think that you can't define a personal identity except in terms of the identity of the body.

But of course, if that's right, if you can only define personal identity in terms of bodily identity, then your thesis that one's identity could include other people would become false, except if some kind of bodily identification were to take place. I'm not very positive about this, but let us take, say, the relation between you and me. We're about the same age, your self and my self are sitting here now and two small boys went to school so many years ago. Now clearly there is a physical relation, in the sense that there is a spatio-temporal continuity between these bodies and those ones and there are also certain causal connections. I mean that what we are thinking now is causally dependent upon what happened to those bodies then. Whether there is more than this I would be inclined to dispute except for memory but that again could be held to be a function of physical stimuli.

So I'm inclined, I think, to equate personal identity with bodily identity, but I'm not sure about this.

But even if this equation were shown to be wrong, as it easily might be, I wouldn't want a Cartesian substance. I would want something like a Humean theory of a series of experiences linked by memory and the overlapping of consciousness and so on, so that in this sense I don't want to attach too much importance to the I.

But I think I wanted to say that in whatever way you define the series of experiences which are properly called mine, they are always exclusive of those properly called yours. I don't think that series of experiences from different persons can logically intersect. Although paranormal psychology might produce phenomena that one might want to describe in this sort of way, I don't want to be at all dogmatic about this.

NÆSS: I'm genuinely glad to hear this. I agree concerning the term "experience." Its logic is subjective: insisting on using that term, you are caught in the same trap as Hume.

Perhaps before the year 3000 there will be "hardware" people, let us say people who have abandoned their brains, taking in computers instead. Collectivists may prefer this: it might herald the end of egos. But it couldn't be quite the end, and is perhaps not central to what we are speaking about. More central is the fact that, as a philosopher, I think I have a kind of total view, which would include logic, epistemology, and ontology, but also evaluations, and that I do not escape from the relevance of them at any moment. When I'm saying who I am, so to speak, I cannot avoid indicating what kind of evaluations I make, what kind of priorities or values I have, etc. And there it seems to me that we get into a metaphysical area, a "portentous" area, because only there do we realize just how many different conceptions of fact and experience are possible.

I have a feeling that the empiricism that I suspect you are inclined to accept is too narrow, in the sense that you do not admit a commitment to statements which are untestable empirically. I am inclined to say, "your thinking is too narrow." Would this hurt you slightly? If I hurt you I hurt myself, which means that if, for instance, I now said something to you and the next moment I thought that it had been unfair of me to say that when I realized that it had hurt you somehow—not that you couldn't easily win an argument—but if it had hurt you, I would have a moment of identification. Phenomenologically there would be "one" hurt, which was not yet "my" experience. I expect you now to jump into psychology and say that when you identify yourself with somebody else this is a matter of psychology, not philosophy, and that we have the empirical evidence from more or less good experiments which can show us to what extent we identify with each other. It has no ontological consequences. If A identifies with B, he remains A.

But for me it is more a question of what in German they would call *Einstellung*; it's something that is not reducible to empirical psychology, because whatever the psychologists find, I would stick to it probably. They are committed to a definite conceptual framework from the very beginning.

AYER: Yes, I wasn't going to take that move, because I don't think these labels matter all that much: these are classifications for librarians. I think we should be free to say what we like in every field if we like. I was rather going to take up what you said earlier about this question of who I am. I think when I was arguing before I was using it more in what could be called a "passport" sense; for example, who is Arne Næss? I would say that he is someone who answers to such and such a description, whereas you were clearly using it in a wider sense than this. You were meaning by "who am I?" something, which has to do with your own conception of yourself. When you said that hurting me would hurt you, this means that it would in some way be injurious not to your identity as the passport Arne Næss, but injurious to your conception of yourself, injurious to the sort of man you like to think of yourself as being. And possibly also if you hurt me it would have repercussions on your own character, and therefore in this sense you've injured yourself. You wouldn't literally feel the pain that I felt, but you would be damaging yourself; which means that you are, in a certain sense, identifying with me, because you regard it as part of your conception of yourself that you don't gratuitously or voluntarily or deliberately hurt other human beings.

Now there seems to be no quarrel here whatsoever. But I think that if there is a difference between us, it is that I make a sharper distinction than you do between what's descriptive and what's normative. I would say that this was simply an announcement of what rightly, to put it in this way, could be called a policy.

I mean, it is perhaps not quite right, it's somehow not so deliberate as that, and it's more important to you than that. But this is a form of life that you're adopting, and something that goes very deep, and you put this forward, if you like, for me either to imitate you or disagree with you.

But, I think that a mistake could only arise, and I should only have a quarrel with you, if you tried to prove it by deducing it from what masqueraded as a statement of fact. If you accept what I have just said as what you mean by "you and I are one" or "you identify with me," then we are talking in sympathy. It's only if you say that you have this policy because, and then make this appear as a factual statement, that we then quarrel on intellectual grounds.

ELDERS: So, in fact, the central question is the relationship between metaphysics and morality.

NÆSS: A norm or a moral injunction should not masquerade as a description; but neither should a statement involving description, for instance factual description, masquerade as a norm. "All living beings are ultimately one" admits partial interpretations or analyses in various directions, descriptive and normative. None seem to be exhaustive, which is typical of good old metaphysical formulae.

Incidentally, the distinction between fact and norm, or injunction, is ultimate: it is not that I think the norms are less normative, but that the descriptions are less descriptive. Description presupposes, for instance, a methodology of description. A methodology includes at least one postulate, at least one rule. A change of postulates and rules changes the description. This makes the notion of description as opposed to norm a little shaky: therefore I no longer use the term fact. It suggests independence of postulates and rules.

ELDERS: There we go, Sir Alfred.

NÆSS: I am sorry, I would feel badly if you were to take me as just a Heideggerian or some kind of . . .

AYER: No, no, on the contrary, I mean, I wouldn't . . .

NÆSS: I'm not so sure I'm not. I'm quite near Heidegger in a certain sense.

AYER: Nonsense, nonsense, nonsense!

NÆSS: Yes, we are *Geworfen.* I feel very much that I have been thrown into the world, and that I am still being thrown.

AYER: Now why do yourself this injustice? Why spoil it? Now leave him out, keep him out. How do you know we are thrown into existence? You may have had a very difficult birth for all you remember.

NÆSS: We probably agree that a dogmatic view of all things lacks value, even if it were possible to work it out. But implicitly we pretend to coherence, implicitly we pretend to have methods of how to establish views empirically or otherwise. In short, we implicitly pretend to have views relevant to whatever we say. And those views are personal, not something found in libraries.

I'm inviting you to let us get hold of more of you; and not psychologically or socially, as Mr. So-and-So or Sir So-and-So, but to get to know how you perceive the world, its relation to yourself, the basic features of the condition of man as you experience them.

And I call this philosophy a total view.

AYER: Oh, no, no, no.

NÆSS: Now you try to take that back?

AYER: No I don't take it back. Let me put it this way. I don't think that the term "total philosophy" . . .

NÆSS: Total view.

AYER: . . . has any very useful application. What would having a total philosophy imply? In what way, in what concrete way, do we differ? I mean, I also have opinions about politics, ethics, aesthetics and express them and act on them. But these are not part of a total philosophy in your sense. How would I have to change, either in these opinions or in the meta-language, in order to have a total philosophy in your sense?

ELDERS: May I try to formulate a question by which you could perhaps illustrate your point of view? Does your offensive nonviolence, Mr. Næss, imply that you would prefer to be killed by someone else rather than kill someone else? Is it part of your philosophy?

NÆSS: It would be more than a preference, actually. It might be that I would prefer to kill the other person, but I value the preference negatively. Norms have to do with evaluations, with pretensions to objectivity, rather than preferences. Let me formulate it thus: I hope I would prefer to be killed by someone else rather than to kill, and I ought to prefer it.

ELDERS: And this is a part of your philosophy?

NÆSS: Yes. And it has empirical, logical, methodological, ontological, etc., ramifications, like other philosophical issues. It belongs to a greater unity of opinions which in part are derived from certain principles of descriptive and normative kinds.

ELDERS: And how is it for you, Sir Alfred?

AYER: I should, I think, disagree. Although it's a very difficult question I can imagine situations certainly in which I should prefer to kill someone rather than be killed by them, in which I should in fact try to kill someone rather than allow him to kill me.

After all we were both, I assume, in the war and there these situations arose. But I don't see in fact how this fits in. Because supposing I gave a different answer from the answer that he gave or indeed suppose I gave the same one, how would this in either case be part or not be part of a total philosophy?

It might of course in some situations be an extremely important concrete moral question; but what I am denying when I reject that sort of philosophy is that the way either of us answers a question of this kind has any relation, any logical relation, to our views, for example, on probability or on the theory of knowledge, or on the mind-body question, even on such questions as the freedom of the will. Whatever our theoretical views about the freedom of the will, I can't see that they would settle a question of this kind one way or the other. I mean, we might both be determinists in theory and yet take different views about this; or we might one of us believe in free will, the other in determinism and take the same view. When I was skeptical and said you shouldn't have this total philosophy, what I meant was that I can't see what the links are supposed to be to make the totality.

But of course I have opinions on all these matters and very strong ones, although in this particular case I think I would probably dissent from you. I think I'm not a total pacifist. I haven't been in the past, and I think I can imagine circumstances in which I shouldn't be in the future. I think if something like the Nazis were to reappear, I would want to defend myself against them as I did then.

NÆSS: There is a relation between not wanting to kill somebody else, even in a fight, and epistemology; because any question which you answer implies a methodology. And this also holds good for the question "Would you prefer to be killed rather than to kill?" In order to answer this I must have a kind of methodology to find out whether I would. All fields of inquiry are interrelated, therefore we implicitly must pretend to cover them all when giving any answer whatsoever. We presuppose a total survey from mathematics to politics.

AYER: May I put this concretely? Suppose that either you or I held a physicalist view of human beings, something like Gilbert Ryle's *The Concept of Mind.* Suppose you were a behaviorist and thought of the mind as the ghost in the machine and so on, do you think that this would then entail an answer one way or the other to your question? Do you think that Ryle, for example, is in some way logically committed to giving a different answer to this question from the one that you would give?

NÆSS: No, I don't think it would entail this. But I think that certain views cohere more or less and that it's the business of a philosopher today to try out to what extent they cohere; to what extent they're not only logically consistent, for that would leave us too free, but also coherent in their nonlogical aspects.

AYER: Do you think that this view of the mind would even favor one answer to this moral question more than another? I mean, could you deduce simply from Ryle's book, other than psychologically, even in a semi-logical way, what moral position, what view he would take on this moral question?

NÆSS: I think that if you made different combinations of interpretations, it favors, so to speak statistically, the acceptance of violence. But we would be capable of reconstructing it in such a way that it would not favor violence. And this is an important thing. A book like Ryle's leaves things implicit: presuppositions, postulates, methodological rules. No single, definite set can be said to be presumed, therefore there will be a plurality of interpretations and a plurality of reconstructions.

And I agree with you, it is too easy to talk about a total view and to say, "I have one." I detest questions like "What is your total view?"

AYER: Yes.

NÆSS: Yes.

AYER: Well, there you see how much I sympathize with you.

NÆSS: We cannot have a total view in the sense that we are somehow inescapably linked to certain definite opinions; nor can we behave like a general surveying an army of possible views and pick out some, saying these are my views—the relationship between ourselves and our views is too intimate.

AYER: I should have thought, in fact, that your general philosophical position, with which I sympathize, went entirely the opposite way, and that the tendency would be to see each question independently on its own merits; not to feel that you were committed by your answer to this one, by any answer to that one.

NÆSS: Not any longer.

AYER: Not any longer?

NÆSS: No, because I feel that as a philosopher I am an acting person, not an abstract researcher. Even this discussion is not really some kind of a contemplative affair; it is also a kind of continuous action all the time.

AYER: Indeed, indeed. In certain things you then require more coherence in action than you do in theory. You don't mind your theories being incoherent, but you want your actions to be coherent.

NÆSS: In research I tend to adopt an almost playful attitude in the sense of looking at and pleasurably contemplating more combinations of views than anybody else. More kinds of common sense even! But as an acting person I take a stand, I implicitly assume very many things, and with my Spinozist leanings towards integrity—being an integrated person as the most important thing—I'm now trying to close down on all these vagaries. I am inviting you to do the same.

AYER: But, why should I . . .

NÆSS: As a person you may have such a high level of integration that if you took some years off and tried to meditate a little more, you would be able to articulate some of your basic evaluations. These are more than inclinations; Jaspers calls them *Einstellungen*. They determine or at least express an important part of what would be your total view.

AYER: It's not a prospect that I find at all desirable. Failure to be articulate has never been my problem, I think.

NÆSS: I think so.

AYER: Well, there are hidden problems perhaps, I don't know.

NÆSS: Too fast, you're too fast.

AYER: Yes, but I say a lot of things twice, that's all right, I catch it on the second time round.

I don't know; why should integrity demand consistency? One thinks that it does, but why shouldn't one judge things differently when the circumstances are always different? Why shouldn't one have the same flexibility in one's moral and political judgments as one wants for one's theoretical ones? I suppose one thinks that people are insincere if they don't maintain similar opinions in similar cases; but then the question of even what cases are similar is theoretically difficult.

I don't know: I dislike what you have just said—I think it's really the first thing that you have said at all, that I have disliked. This seems to me to be really a conception of, well, I don't mind if it's called philosophy or not, and I don't mean that someone's trying in all honesty to solve problems that he thinks important, theoretically important or even practically important, but that somehow this represents a kind of deep narcissism, a digging down into oneself, contemplating: I'm not concerned with this. All right, it is possible that if I spent a year meditating I should perhaps dig up some very pleasant things; I don't know, I don't care. I've got better things to do in a way. I've got this problem, that problem, the other problem, I've got a certain intelligence, I'm going to use it for as long as it lasts. And perhaps, when I'm gaga I'll start contemplating in your sense.

NÆSS: Too late!

AYER: And of what interest will that be to anybody?

ELDERS: I'll ask the same question, but not on a personal level. Would you say, Mr. Næss, that in your total philosophy intellectuals have a special responsibility at this moment?

NÆSS: Yes, because they are highly articulate. They are trained at universities in situations where they have at least three quarters of an hour to think what could be argued against this, what could be argued against that; they get to be narrow and clever, too clever. I think that intellectuals might consider their intellects in a more Spinozistic way, as *intellectus* in the Spinoza way, and cultivate *amor intellectualis*.

ELDERS: Can you translate it?

NÆSS: *Amor intellectualis* would be a kind of loving attitude towards what you have insight into, while considering it in an extremely wide perspective. And intellectuals might do this without making the terrible mistake of becoming sentimental or fanatical. They would be able to say things to people in a more direct way and to articulate evaluations, their attitudes—*Enstellungen* or total attitudes—in a very forceful way while at the same time using some of the, in a narrow sense, intellectual training they have acquired in the universities.
They should be able to make us feel that to elaborate total views that are not expressive of something like "I am more clever than you are" is neither portentous nor necessarily favors some kind of fanaticism. When I say that you are, perhaps, deficient in articulation, it is because I feel you jump too fast to particular opinions on so-called facts, instead of taking a broad view and letting yourself say things which sound portentous and which might make you sound like a rhetorician or a politician, or even a prophet.
In this way I think that the intellectual of today, and especially the philosophically educated one, has a larger and wider function than that of being analytically minded. I'm sorry I use that catchphrase.

AYER: Well, I don't disagree with you on the question he asked. I do think that intellectuals obviously have a responsibility to do their job as they see it, and as well as they can do it; and also, I think, a social responsibility. I'm not a believer in the ivory tower at all; I think that anyone who has the capacity to think and to reason and perhaps believes, rightly or wrongly, that he can see things clearly, should try to contribute to social and even to political questions, so I don't in the least dissent from you there. I don't think that we quarrel at all about what we should be doing. What I think we may quarrel about is perhaps how we should do our job, and you might think that I do it in the wrong way.

NÆSS: Well, couldn't you send me a copy of a speech made by you about a political situation?

AYER: Indeed, I could send many. I mean, I'm constantly doing this; I've even stood for office, but I lost. I've stood on soapboxes on street-corners. . . .

NÆSS: And there you use descriptions and norms.

AYER: Ah, mainly normative, my language is then pretty emotive.

NÆSS: May I ask, for instance, could you act as if you were now on a political platform? Say something real, "Bang!" like this.

AYER: Well, I think that you can't. Political speeches are not made in the abstract. But if I knew local politics, I dare say I could make quite an effective political speech. I would point out how one side was acting in its own interest, more than the other, and how such and such a measure was perhaps an attempt to preserve privileges, or was associated with corruption, and all this would be highly charged emotionally.
Of course, we have to have facts behind it; it's no good saying so-and-so is corrupt, unless you produce some evidence. But these two elements are mixed, obviously; and political speech has got to be factual, but with emotive overtones.

ELDERS: What's your attitude towards the Common Market?

AYER: This I regard as a factual and technical question. I'm emotionally in favor of it, in the sense that I'm in favor certainly of larger units, against nationalism.
But economically I simply don't know; whether from the point of view of the ordinary English man in the street the economic price will become too high or not. And the economists are totally in disagreement. So, as a rational man, I suspend judgment. But I myself, if you like, feel European. I am by origin not purely English, I have some French blood, even on my mother's side Dutch, and therefore I'm emotionally in favor of a larger unit.
But I think this is partly a question of fact where I acknowledge ignorance. Whereas Næss, with his total philosophy, brings in different little facts. If he doesn't believe in facts, then why should he joke about them in this issue?

NÆSS: This is rhetoric, isn't it? (Laughter.)

AYER: Of course it was, yes.

NÆSS: You shouldn't immediately give up so quickly in this way. Behind the rhetoric there are sets of value judgments.

I'm in a fight against Norway joining the Common Market. And one of the main things I'm against is putting larger units in place of smaller ones. I think that the larger units achieve greater technological advances and larger units of production, instead of getting together with other people in a nice personal way. We will get bigger markets, more standardized products, and we will take over some clever ideas from British universities instead of using our own less clever ideas about the university.

AYER: I would think that some ideas from Norwegian universities might even be more clever than the ones I get at Oxford.

NÆSS: I doubt it, really. On the whole we are not clever, but we are provincial in the good sense of living in our own way undisturbed by pressures from the great centers.

Notes

This dialogue is reprinted with minor revisions from *Reflexive Water: The Basic Concerns of Mankind*, ed. Fons Elders (London: Souvenir Book, 1974), 13–68.

Chapter 4

Ayer on Metaphysics: A Critical Commentary by a Kind of Metaphysician

Arne Næss

What Sir Alfred Ayer has found worthwhile to publish about metaphysics is, as one could expect, carefully formulated. He may have an integrated, highly consistent view about metaphysics in one or two senses of the vague and ambiguous term such as metaphysics, but I shall not offer a condensed exposition of it. I do not think I am able to. I shall offer some comments, which mainly refer to central quotations from his article "Metaphysics and Common Sense."[1]

The way I shall organize my comments is to concentrate on a fairly small number of quotes.

Quotation 1

If we go by appearances, it can hardly be disputed that metaphysics is nearly always in conflict with common sense. This is most obvious in the sense of the metaphysician who professes to find a logical flaw, a contradiction or a vicious infinite regress, in one or other of the ways in which we commonly describe the world, and so comes to such startling conclusions as that time and space are unreal, or that nothing really moves, or that there are not many things in the Universe but only one, or that nothing which we perceive through our senses is real or wholly real. [2]

The slogans or key sentences of most metaphysicians are, and are presumably meant to be, shocking, to most people.

But read in context I think the somewhat shaky statistical hypothesis breaks down. Most people get bored or frustrated feeling they don't understand and perhaps ought to understand. From the context they presumably understand that a sentence like "nothing really moves" is not to be interpreted as synonymous to "nothing moves." People who read a little history of philosophy understand that "exist" in Gorgias's slogan "nothing exists" is not used in quite the same way as in "some rhinoceroses still exist." The shock is milder or disappears.

"Nothing exists" in the phraseology of Gorgias is a formulation taken out of context that elucidates what is referred to through the shocking slogan. It is a question of that branch of empirical communication research to approach an understanding of the context and its relation to the slogan. We probably agree that it has to do with conception and perception of timelessness, unchangingness, permanence. I suspect that there are ways, W1–W10, of experiencing and conceptualizing the world or "everything" that make it tempting to say something like "what is real is unchanging." As analytical, academic philosophers we may, and personally I think we must, try to find ways of expressing at least one of the Ws in a way more understandable and connectable (von Mises) with our scientific ways of talking. The crucial point for me in the case of Gorgias, and hundreds of other metaphysical key slogans is that always something remains unexpressed and often the analyses of the key slogans are felt by their constructors to be inadequate. The metaphysical key slogans are not to be eliminated; there is no complete substitutability.

Suppose non-academic people hear this uttered: "matter tells space how to curve, and space tells matter how to move." Nonsense? Shocking misuse of terms? Literally false? Or perhaps something profound? Told that it is a quotation from a physicist (J. A. Wheeler) and inspired by Einstein, people may dismiss it as un-understandable, and sometimes with a feeling of awe. There is an interpretation of the quotation making it an elegant popularization of acceptable physical theory, and nothing else. Nothing remains. What I hint at is that many metaphysical sentences may be precised in various ways, some of them scientific, but not restless, like the quotation from Wheeler. For me questions of common sense do not enter.

It is tempting to use Neurath's term *Ballungen* about metaphysical key slogans. They are slimy in the sense that you cannot neatly separate individual components of their meanings or uses, and some of them are deep—using a very different metaphor. That is, they touch basic attitudes, value-priorities, concepts.

Let us return to the key sentence attributed to the sophist Gorgias: "Nothing exists." Diogenes' strategy as a listener would be to say, for instance, "What about you, Gorgias? Are you there? Did I hear you say something?" Another way of tackling the situation—in the absence of any existing writings of Gorgias—is to guess what he intended to convey by uttering what he did. One guess is that he opposed a view attributed to Parmenides that only the unchangeable can be counted as really existing. Neglecting the difficult adverb "really," Gorgias might have meant, among other things, to convey that if the absolutely unchangeable deserves the predicate "existing," then nothing exists, because nothing is absolutely unchangeable. A Parmenidian then asks for proofs that tackle the paradoxes of Achilles and the Tortoise, in part through a kind of mathematics Gorgias could not know. But there seems still to be an open question whether change is ever adequately conceptualized. Maybe it is, I ought not to wonder. Anyhow, I appreciate the Diogenes strategy, but not in a discussion of adequate conceptual frameworks. I assume Ayer would agree "the victory [over metaphysics] has been won on the wrong terrain."[3] Metaphysicians treat external questions; Moore's "technique"[4] presumes they are internal. More about that later.

Quotation 2

G. E. Moore "looked at metaphysics with the devastating simplicity and candor of the child in the Andersen story of the Emperor's Clothes. His technique was to take metaphysical assertions at their face value and show how extraordinary their implications were."[5]

One may fully appreciate Moore's uproar against the domination of the Hegelians and their way of metaphysical communication. The way the strategy of Moore is described in the quotation presents, however, a generalization of that of Zeno. He cannot be said to take in a non-selective way "metaphysical assertions at their face value." He picked out some, and isolated them from contexts. A slogan like "time is unreal!" he treated as synonymous with "time does not exist." But even if this very implausible interpretation is valid, one may from a rigorous point of view question the validity of the consequences. Birth may be constructed to precede death without letting any definite concept of time enter our conceptual frame of reference. This is not important, however. What is important is the issue, but which certainly must be discussed in order to get nearer to the intended message of the sender of the dark utterance. What was a valuable "new departure in the history of philosophy" in the first year of our century is not a new departure now. And I think Ayer does not really (?) think that Moore offered a philosophically acceptable way of handling the metaphysical discussions.

Discussions about the nature of time are as lively today as in the time of Bradley, and if a participant only says "time is unreal" within a prolonged discussion it may only provoke laughter. But not as a title of a book, or as a slogan. Like "the will is free," "existence precedes essence," "God is but does not exist."

The use of the word "real" is of course often frustrating in metaphysicians, including Spinoza, but nonacademic people use it in senses very near, or even identical with those of metaphysicians. Example A: To me Mr. B does not appear real. C: Yes, there is something lacking in him; to me he is less real than any other I know. They do not talk of the existence of Mr. B. It has to do to a certain person with genuineness, authenticity as a personality. On the whole I find so-called ordinary people rather often talking metaphysics. This is one of my obstacles when trying to get a clear conception of what Ayer means by common sense. It seems to have little to do with how people ignorant of academic philosophy talk and reason. It seems to relate to what I might consider a rather implicit metaphysical frame of reference; I shall refer to it as the common sense of science.

Quotation 3

The important question for the plain man is whether the statements that are made within his conceptual framework are true: the same applies to the scientist at his level of discourse. The important questions for the philosopher are how these different sorts of statement are related, and what are the criteria by which their truth or falsehood is determined. Once these questions are satisfactorily answered, it does not very greatly matter how the ontological medals are bestowed.[6]

The task of the philosopher as depicted above seems to me more like that of a low-level administrator. Not the philosopher, but unspecifiable others create conceptual systems and erect conceptual frameworks. These others find themselves having visions of the world, pictures of the world, ways of looking at the world. (Ayer uses such expressions.) And others struggle to verbalize and clarify these ways of looking at the world. They struggle to get from vague and ambiguous, perhaps "dark" spontaneous utterances to more clear and precise ones, even utilize scientific conceptualizing. They struggle to investigate possibilities of testing rival views—and they freely wonder.

Very late in the show the philosopher arrives on the scene inspecting already formulated conceptual frameworks and making clear how different sorts of statements have related. Inspiring?

The study of Spinoza makes me conclude that his system in a way colors the conception of the whole existence, the conception of everything, not only every thing. The hundreds of conceptual interrelations postulated through his definitions and propositions contribute to the impression of a metaphysics that affects every aspect of our existence. I take the written exposition of Spinoza's system in his *Ethics*—whether it is intended to be conceptual or nominalistic—to present a verbalization of what Ayer calls a vision of the world. This vision concerns me as an existential and academic philosopher because his power of thinking and intensity of vision is greater than mine.

How would the Spinozist vision most effectively be verbalized today? This is a grave question. Very few sentences of the *Ethics* might be retained. The question is philosophical and empirical. The kind of theory of communication needed concerns empirically given texts of his and our century. But there is no science of communication of much use for us as philosophers. Philosophical inquiry is as much empirical as logical; to concentrate on logic is a blind alley.

The use of the term "real" in metaphysics, I agree with Ayer, is largely a dismal story. I am glad to say that it plays a minor role in the *Ethics*. It does not occur a single time in propositions, proofs, or definitions. But "reality" and "to have realness (reality)" occur a few times, seven in all. "To have realness" is a term capable of degrees, as it is capable of degrees in the Latin and English vernacular. In a contemporary exposition of the *Ethics* one may without great mistake eliminate the term "reality" through the use of conceptual near-synonyms, equivalencies, for instance through definition 6 in Part 2: "By reality (*realitas*) and perfectedness (*perfecto*) I understand the same." In turn the Spinozist "perfectedness," the Latin *per-facere* may here approach the meaning of "carry through," may be elucidated by referring to other equivalencies.

This is necessary in order to understand a definition close to my vision of the world, "Gladness is man's transition from a smaller to a greater perfectedness" (second definition of affections, Part 3). Here again we must patiently try to find out what definition and gladness stand for in the system. (Berkeley's complaint about Spinoza is well founded!) Equivalencies are helpful in these matters of interpretation, and I have an easily available list of 243.

In short, in order to understand what a metaphysician tries more or less imperfectly to convey, and to verbalize this understanding with some interpersonal preciseness, requires a lot of patience. For good reasons some philosophers do not find it rewarding. But Spinoza is to me always rewarding.

Visions of the world and their conceptualization are a central task of philosophers. On the other hand, lifelong study of philosophy on the highest academic level contributes to philosophical culture whether the participants feel they are philosophers in the sense I use the term, or not. Today I feel we need more philosophers, but not less academic philosophy. It is my suspicion that Ayer is more of a philosopher than one might think reading his *Metaphysics and Common Sense*.

Quotation 4

As we have seen, it is not an arbitrary judgment. One can give reasons for going one way or the other. But they are not compelling reasons. Whether we opt for naive realism, or physical realism, or phenomenalism, or whatever, there is going to be some consequences, which make us, feel intellectually uncomfortable. If most of us feel least uncomfortable with naive realism, it is mainly, I suppose, because it is the picture of the world with which we are most familiar, having lived with it since our childhood, and also because it occupies a safe, or comparatively safe, middle position, the phenomenalist picture being too fragmentary and the physical realist one too abstract.

My second point is that the question whether or how this decision is taken does not seem to me to be of any great importance.[7]

After this fragment of the text, quotation 3 follows, presenting the last lines of Ayer's article "What Must There Be?" It is, I think, pertinent to distinguish pictures of, or ways of looking at, the world from conceptual frameworks. The three "pictures" referred to by Ayer I would class as three kinds of ontological fragments of a total conceptual framework tentatively adapted to present in words fragments of a way of looking at the world (or, more in my terminology, a total view).

Speaking of consequences, I agree that more or less logically derived consequences of basic ontological conceptualizations may make us in various ways uncomfortable. We may try to change some of the links in our derivation, in ways suggested by Quine, or we may radically change parts of the basic ontological conceptualization, or even get to experience the world differently. The philosopher with a systemic bent finds himself or herself in the middle of questions and queries which engage all human capacities. Feelings, passions, attitudes, inclinations, logic.

Quotations 5 and 6

Thus if a philosopher is to succeed not merely in involving us in logical or semantic or epistemological puzzles but in altering or sharpening our vision of the world, he cannot leave common sense too far behind him.[8]

In philosophy, nothing should be absolutely sacrosanct: not even common sense.[9]

In quotation 5 it seems that Ayer agrees with my view that a philosopher may involve us in altering our vision. And in the context of quotation 6, and others, it seems that a philosopher may legitimately as a philosopher, engage in creating, discussing, and changing not only conceptual frameworks, but also refer them to visions of the world, including his own. To me it seems that it is not easy to make these quotations legitimizing and defending what I would call metaphysical undertakings together with quotation 3. Possibility: I have misinterpreted that quotation.

In attempts to explicate a total view, the expression felt to be the most adequate at least at the first stages of the work are likely to be heavily metaphysical and formed in short sentences. At later stages some but scarcely all these expressions are eliminated. I see no general reason to eliminate them, but strong reasons to comment upon them and their function. Intuition is here a central slogan. Unhappily, there has been a tendency to stress the kind of methodical features of a vision of the world. That is perhaps one of the reasons why at graduate philosophical seminars (at some universities) expressions of such kinds are frowned upon. Without methodical tolerance, efforts to explicate total views soon grind to a halt.

To catch the attention metaphysicians have often to leave common sense, as the expression is used by Ayer, far behind. Thus, in the metaphysical mass communication of Gandhi he would say such things as "God is the hungry millions." Short sentences with great power. Sometimes he engaged in conceptual clarifications, but from a statistical point of view, very rarely.

After years of intense interest in the so-called common sense view of truth I don't think there is anything deserving that name. There is not much to be found, I think, to contrast a conceptual framework of "the plain man" (see quotation 3 with those of metaphysics. Very prolonged interviews with bright schoolchildren who never have read a line of professional philosophy tend to make them approach professional status! They exhibit embryonic systems and they are able to criticize, not totally incompetently, quotations from philosophers. And if one does not by "common sense" refer to so-called ordinary people but to my ideally reasonable worldview, I cannot see much difference from calling it *"my* view."

Quotation 7

The recognition of the autonomy of morals on the one hand, and on the other the continued adherence to a well-established set of moral values, have led to a certain narrowing of the scope of moral philosophy. It concerns itself less with the question what our duties are and more with the question what our talk about our duties means. The promulgation of moral judgments has given way to their analysis. [10]

Statistically Ayer may be right. From the point of view of articulation of total views this tendency is to be regretted. In trying to set up priorities of action, consideration of priorities of duties and articulation of sets of duties and their logical relations are important undertakings. And philosophical training may be of help. Terminology is secondary; like many others I do not often use the term duty, but rather expressions like "what we ought to do."

When students raise questions on morals, the shift from substance to meaning is pernicious if done in a way that suggests philosophy is more about meaning than direct answers to questions of ethics. But I would join Ayer in holding that the direct propaganda for particular moral opinions or systems cannot be a function of academic teachers.

The "question what our talk about duties means" is understood by Ayer in accordance with his own demand for a frame of reference as a question within what he takes to be common sense. This is the nearest I come to a conclusion about how to suggest a frame. Suppose a student accepts what Ayer considers "what our talk about duties means," is this a considerable plus, or a minus for him and for us as fellow citizens? A pragmatic question, I admit. If the student has metaphysical views, like I have, I answer negatively, but of course a tentative, open answer.

Let me mention a field of metaphysical thinking among nonphilosophers. About 125 people were interviewed about the rights of animals and plants, and the acceptability of exterminating dangerous and poisonous ones. A very frequent argument among these people for rejecting extinction is that they all have a place to fill and that they are part of the whole. Discussion of such sayings reveals that they function often as ultimate normative points of view.

As superbly stated already by Aristotle, one cannot prove every assertion or norm. There are some which always, however deep we are digging, are taken as ultimates. This is one of the reasons that I do not find grounds for rejecting the validity of the above ultimates. Another reason is that I essentially share them myself.

As philosophers we may find it necessary to try to interpret the statements, for instance, trying to transform them into psychological statements, or otherwise making them testable. Very good! But so far there are no good analyses, and even if there were, I doubt they would be restlessly brought out of metaphysical realms.

Among my own statements within ecophilosophy there are hundreds which need further clarification, but this does not imply that I ought to stop accepting them before I (five hundred years old?) have found analyses satisfactory to myself. I cannot see any good reasons for giving analytic work generally higher priority than synthetic. For instance why stop using the term intrinsic value because of lack of satisfactory analyses? Or truth? To fight confusion is one thing, to invariably search for clarification of certain particular kinds quite another.

Quotation 8

For Heidegger there remains one metaphysical question: Why is there anything at all and not rather nothing? Perhaps this should be treated in Collingwood's way as the senseless querying of an absolute presupposition. At least, if it is treated as a question, there is no way of answering it. If the "Why" is construed as a request for a cause, then even if an answer is forthcoming, it merely relates one existent item to all the others, or leaves us with a theory for which we have no more general explanation. If it is construed as a request for a reason, then not only are we making the unwarranted assumption that the totality of what there is has been designed, but we are still committed to the being of the designer. [11]

Heidegger's sentence ending with a question mark is today spontaneously experienced as a genuine question by many people, including myself. I am ready, but not eager, to incorporate it in my (somewhat fictional) system as a philosophical question. More often, but not always! I wonder *that* there is something rather than nothing, and sometimes perhaps not less often, I wonder that I wonder that there is something. But I do not, for instance, wonder that I wonder that I wonder that there is something, because I take this wondering as natural for some philosophers like me.

The way Ayer treats the strange question strikes me as impatient. Too fast! It is as if we ought to be in a haste to find a piece of analysis, which can stop our wonder, if, there was any. What I wonder about is, for instance, why so little in our publications as academic philosophers reflects the frequent state of wonder, which I suspect (and hope) my colleagues experience. To publish a book favorable to epistemological skepticism, as I have done, is not of much help here. It is too argumentative. It scarcely reflects pervasive wondering. I shall end my comments with a sentence put forth in wonder as well as in regret:

It is a weakness of our situation as academic teachers of philosophy that it intensively favors learning arguments and learning conclusions at the expense of relaxed wondering.

Quotations 9 and 10

But why put things in a portentous way when they can be put in a simple way? Why not say that as you grow older you come to comprehend more things; your knowledge perhaps increases, and then after a certain point, I'm afraid, diminishes again. But up to a point it increases. Perhaps your range of sympathy is greater; perhaps you *identify* with more things and sometimes again with less.[12]

When one has a fairly precise method, a precise way of describing all these facts, why does one have to make such portentous statements about one's self expanding and including everything. It sounds romantic, but it's quite superfluous.[13]

The written account of the television debate in 1974 between Ayer and myself carries the excellent subtitle "an empiricist versus a total view." As a philosopher I find it inevitable to pretend in a mild way to have a total view. Not only a vision, but a practice more or less logically connected with a verbalization of the vision. One of the crucial points in the discussion is the following remark: "I think I believe in the ultimate unity of all living beings." This is a very vague and ambiguous phrase, but I have to rely on it. It is a task for analytical philosophy to suggest more precise formulations. Because I have such principles, I also have a program of action, the main outline of which is part of my philosophy.[14] One of Ayer's reactions to this, the only one I find inadequate, is to say that I am "simply false," "in any literal sense just false," "not only I and a mosquito, but even you and I are not one."[15] This is to me playing the Diogenes card. Obviously to me, and also to Ayer, "ultimate unity" must be interpreted differently from "identity" in a certain trivial sense. And he soon in a constructive way proposes a substitute for my metaphysical phraseology— quotation 9!

My use of "identification" is related to the one we can meet in description of employees who strongly identify with their big corporations. The essential point is not that they consciously plan their vacations and place of living in accordance with the requirements of the corporation, but that their tastes, choice of friends, emotional stability, sense of achievement are such as are good for the corporation. This has all to do with what William James terms their social self, as something wider than their ego.

The main thing is that I do not find any single less "portentous" set of sentences which completely covers what I intend by the metaphysical sentences. I try out psychological, or more general, social science terminology, and try out many for what I call "precizations" (analyses of a certain kind), but it always turns out that something might still be lacking. Therefore I do not easily discard a metaphysical sentence which clearly has deep relations to basic attitudes towards reality as I conceive it. I do not use the "unity of life" formulation any more, but retain metaphysical use of the terms identification and self-realization. It is easier to trace practical applications this way.

In asking for a less portentous, simpler way of expressing a philosophical point, Ayer exhibits a characteristic British trait from which European philosophers have profited immeasurably through the centuries. And Ayer in his writings contributed significantly to this tradition which may be as important in the future as it is today. But whereas a metaphysical terminology like mine may tend towards the portentous and romantic, Ayer's way of expression may occasionally trivialize or amputate. There may be too fast transitions from the vague and ambiguous but deeply spontaneous and inspiring, to the particular and rational in a narrow sense. And to wonder is not to be confused. Contemplating and using certain carefully selected metaphysical key terms and sentences need not confuse us. Not if we retain or wonder when employing them. Exactly what does the expression "living beings" cover? The vision or intuition does not cover viruses. Mosquitoes, yes. Obviously the depth of intention from the point of view of zoology and botany is small. But this is not confusing. It exemplifies a kind of unavoidable limitation.

One of the most repulsive characteristics of the metaphysical style of writing is the seemingly utter neglect of the distinction between descriptive and ascriptive or normative. A description of the authentic life has clearly a normative function, "You ought to live like that!" The sentence "ultimately all life is one" is obviously intended to have a normative function. Why not transform it into a kind of moral precept about treating nonhuman life forms decently? Because moral precepts are weak, whereas a changed way of conceiving reality is potentially very strong in its motivational force. If you tend to see yourself in all living beings, decent treatment is quite natural (provided your relation to yourself is good).

In trying to untangle normative and nonnormative ingredients one has to be patient, otherwise too much potential insight is lost. The metaphysical primordial soup of normative and descriptive ingredients does not imply confusion. In everyday life we function well with some of this soup. Perhaps some of us shall have to search for expressions of our vision of reality, which do not immediately and basically introduce that distinction. As Ayer puts it, common sense is not sacrosanct, and the same holds of any distinction introduced by philosophers.

Summing up, what I try to convey is that philosophy, even as a field of inquiry at the university level gains by accepting metaphysical ways of expressing visions or intuitions of reality as genuine sources of insight. Efforts to try to find equivalent nonmetaphysical expressions are central, but need not pretend to exhaust the potential insights. And the metaphysical versions may, even after partly successful analytical work, turn out to be the simplest way of expressing a vision or intuition. I think Ayer might agree with this, but continue rejecting the dogmatism and the obscure and portentous style of much metaphysics. And perhaps more than anything else, fight the tendency to rest content with abstract metaphysical pronouncements without clarifying their relations to concrete problems we all understand or to problems of scientific research.

Notes

This chapter is reprinted with minor revisions from *The Philosophy of A. J. Ayer*, ed. Lewis Edwin Hahn (Chicago: Open Court, 1992), 329–340. Shortened here.

[1] "Metaphysics and Common Sense" in *Metaphysics and Common Sense* (San Francisco: Freeman, Cooper & Company, 1970), 64–81.

[2] Ayer, *Metaphysics and Common Sense*, 64.

[3] Ayer, *Metaphysics and Common Sense*, 71.

[4] Ayer, *Metaphysics and Common Sense*, 71.

[5] Ayer, *Metaphysics and Common Sense*, 64.

[6] Ayer, *Metaphysics and Common Sense*, 63.

[7] Ayer, *Metaphysics and Common Sense*, 63.

[8] Ayer, *Metaphysics and Common Sense*, 81.

[9] Ayer, *Metaphysics and Common Sense*, 81.

[10] Ayer, *Metaphysics and Common Sense*, 7.

[11] Ayer, "Phenomenology and Existentialism," in *Philosophy in the Twentieth Century* (New York: Random House, 1982), 229.

[12] Ayer, in *Reflexive Water: The Basic Concerns of Mankind*, ed. Fons Elders, (London: Souvenir Press, 1974), 35.

[13] Ayer, in *Reflexive Water*, 36.

[14] Arne Næss, in *Reflexive Water*, 29

[15] Ayer, in *Reflexive Water*, 32.

Chapter 5

A Reply to Arne Næss

Alfred J. Ayer

I am happy to be reminded by Professor Næss of the debate in which we engaged on Dutch Television in 1971. We had both moved a considerable distance from the positions that we had occupied under the influence of the Vienna Circle in the 1930s. If I remember rightly, he did not even then embrace their views so whole-heartedly as I did. I doubt if he ever committed himself to the "elimination of metaphysics" on which I embarked in *Language, Truth and Logic*. Nevertheless I remember being surprised by our failure to find more common ground in the course of our debate. Looking back on it I now think that this failure was in some degree artificial. Appearing on this occasion officially as antagonists, we tended, or at any rate I tended, to exaggerate the differences between us rather than explore the possibilities of a common understanding.

This is brought out in his quotation from *Reflexive Water*, the published version of the set of debates, which included ours, of my reaction to one of his expressions of his "total view." It must have been obvious to me that when he said that he was inclined to believe in the ultimate unity of all living beings he was not owning to a disposition to regard two different human beings, let alone a man and a mosquito, as literally identical. To pretend that he was committed to this absurdity was indeed to make a cheap debating point. I made some amends in another passage that Næss quotes from our discussion by speaking of the possibility of one's acquiring "a greater range of sympathy," of one's coming to "identify with more things," and Næss says that he now uses the terms "identification" and "self-realization" metaphysically in preference to talking about "the unity of life."

But what is it to use such terms metaphysically and what is to be gained by it? Towards the end of his essay Næss provides a clue to the way in which he would answer these questions when he says that "the sentence: 'Ultimately all life is one,' is obviously intended to have a normative function," and then asks, "Why not transform it into a kind of moral precept about treating nonhuman life forms decently?" His answer is that moral precepts lack the requisite strength. People will be more apt to treat all living beings decently if they can be induced to see themselves in them. This may well be true; at any rate let us assume that it is. What still puzzles me is why Næss supposes that the best way to induce people to see themselves in other living beings is to secure their assent to the metaphysical pronouncement that they are identical with them. There is indeed, the suggestion that they obtain more from this metaphysical pronouncement, than a reinforcement of the moral precept.

We are not, however, told in what this "more" consists. I suspect that whatever it may be, its function is to associate the moral precept with what Næss would call an insight into the nature of things. Again we are not given even any hint as to what this insight amounts to, but I should not now say that this was a sufficient reason for denying its existence. For instance it might be analogous to the insight we are said to obtain from works of art, which also defy translation into plain narrative terms.

In this connection I was interested in Næss's example of what he calls "a field of metaphysical thinking among nonphilosophers." He does not say what proportion of the 125 or so people interviewed were against exterminating dangerous and poisonous animals and plants on the ground that "they all have a place to fill and that they are part of the whole," but I assume that he would not have used the example unless the proportion was quite high. I have to say that I find this astonishing. It is possible of course that the people in question had been influenced by stories such as that of the ecological damage caused by the overabundant use of certain insecticides and that they rashly drew the conclusion that any interference with natural processes would do more harm than good. But can they really have been so ignorant of, or indifferent to the progress of medicine? In any case Næss characterizes them not as misguided biologists but as metaphysicians. It looks therefore as if they had succumbed to a version of Leibniz's proposition that this is the best of all possible worlds. If I had been the interviewer. I should have advised them to read Voltaire's *Candide*.

In fairness to Næss, I should say at once that his reason for introducing this example was to show that the distinction between metaphysics and common sense was not nearly so sharp as my essay with that title, on which he was chiefly commenting, originally made it out to be. And here I confess that he was right. In composing that essay I failed to make it clear that it was closely related to G. E. Moore's celebrated "Defense of Common Sense" and Moore's account of what he called the commonsense view of the world was not the outcome of any sociological research into what the man in the street actually believed. For instance it is likely that in the 1920s when Moore's article was written, most Englishmen, let alone Americans or Spaniards, held some form of religious belief but Moore refused to include religious belief in his summation of common sense, effectively though not explicitly because the principal theme of his essay was that he knew the commonsense view of the world to be wholly true, and he himself held there to be no good reason to believe in the existence of a God.

Moore's need to uphold the commonsense view led him to restrict it to four propositions: the existence of physical objects, the existence of acts of consciousness, the reality of space and that of time. As Næss has noticed, Moore was declaring war on the neo-Hegelians who threatened to dominate British philosophy at the start of his career and he took it for granted both that the man in the street shared his knowledge of the truth of the propositions in question, and that his metaphysical adversaries denied it. What else the man in the street believed, how far he had been infected with what Næss would count as metaphysics were questions which Moore ignored. Even if he had been provided with evidence that neo-Hegelian slogans were frequently employed in the conversation of persons who were not philosophers, he would still have insisted that these persons knew the truth of such propositions as that they possessed hands and feet, that they had memories and feelings, that a bookcase stood a short distance to the right of the table at which they were seated, that the events of today were later than those of yesterday and earlier than those of tomorrow.

On this last point, I am on Moore's side, though I continue to hold that his defense of common sense, even on his own terms, is very much weakened by his extreme openmindedness with regard to the analysis of the propositions of which he claims that we all know the truth. I shall not, however, pursue the issue here. What I wish to discuss is Moore's other assumption that his metaphysical adversaries seriously denied the reality of matter, space, and time in such a way as to fall victims to his assumption of the role of the child in Hans Andersen's story of the Emperor's clothes.

There is some evidence that they did. Thus, in a conversation with John Wisdom, Moore was able to cite a passage in McTaggart's works where McTaggart claims to have proved matter to be as mythical as Gorgons. Moreover the conclusions which those philosophers reached were, in my judgment, not at all illuminating. I frankly have no idea what Bradley thought he meant by the absolute. McTaggart's theory that what we misperceive as chairs surrounding a table were really selves standing in emotional relations to one another strikes me as simply ridiculous.

Nevertheless I think it unlikely that when McTaggart denied the reality of time what he had in mind could be refuted by such commonplaces as that Moore had his breakfast before he had his lunch. Suppose that McTaggart had been content to deny the passage of time. In that case he would have had the support of many scientists and philosophers who represent the universe as a four-dimensional continuum. Time enters into it only as an enduring relation which makes the whole picture static; for the fact that one event precedes or succeeds or is simultaneous with another is not itself subject to change.

In fact McTaggart did not take this view. He opted for the passage of time taking the concepts of past, present, and future as primordial and attempting to show that their use was incoherent. His attempt did not succeed, because it depended on his misconstruing demonstratives as descriptions. Nevertheless it did illuminate the concept of time just as the paradoxes of Zeno, who would surely not have betted against Achilles in any actual race, illuminated the concepts of time and space and motion and infinity. I am sorry that Næss did not pay more attention to my view that to appreciate metaphysicians one should look primarily, if not exclusively, at their arguments.

I think that Næss may have been slightly unfair to me in the passage in which he says that I depict the task of the philosopher as being like that of a low level administrator. His quotation on which he delivers this verdict occurs in the book to which my essay "Metaphysics and Common Sense" lends its title, but it is not part of that essay. It is the conclusion of an essay entitled "What Must There Be?" which ends with the questions whether we should give preference to what I called the plain man's conception of physical objects, one that endows them with properties corresponding to Locke's ideas of secondary as well as primary qualities, or to the electrons, neutrons, and so forth which embody what I called physical realism. It was the relation between these views that I left it to the philosopher to elucidate, with the rider if he was able to make the relation clear it did not much matter how he cast his vote. My remark was tailored to this context and I was not implying that philosophy had no other function to fulfill.

At the same time I do maintain, perhaps in opposition to Næss, that in terms of C. D. Broad's serviceable distinction between speculative and critical philosophy, a philosophical inquiry into what there is should only be critical. It still seems to me that metaphysicians go astray when they try to usurp the scientists' practice of devising theories and testing them by observation. How in the end can one tell what the world contains except by examining it?

Here Spinoza, whom Næss so greatly prizes, provides a good example. He is a philosopher to whom I admit that I have paid much less attention than he surely deserves, but I am able to recognize that he does throw light on particular philosophical problems such as that of determinism and that a sympathetic study of him can deeply affect one's attitude to life. Nevertheless I draw the line at what anyhow appears to be his attempt to incorporate the world in a deductive system. The system appears to be based on his definition of substance as something that contains in itself the reason for its own existence, where what he means by a reason is a logical ground. But then he encounters the fatal objection that his definition cannot be satisfied. Nothing that exists concretely is such that its existence can be deduced merely from a description of its character. I repeat that this does not imply a rejection of everything that Spinoza then goes on to assert.

Concerning Heidegger, however, I am unrepentant. I do think that there is nothing more of interest to be said about his metaphysical question than is contained in the eighth of Næss's quotations. If a question is posed to which it is so easily shown that there can be no answer, I cannot admit that a lengthy answer is called for. Næss values the question as the expression of wonder at the existence of the universe but here it seems to me that someone like Wordsworth achieves more with his poetry. Perhaps I should end with the admission that I am not temperamentally a pantheist. I do not know whether it has been more of an advantage or a handicap to me as a philosopher that I am entirely devoid of any religious feeling.

Chapter 6

Arne Næss, a Philosopher and a Mystic: A Commentary on the Dialogue between Alfred Ayer and Arne Næss

Fons Elders

This famous dialogue between Næss and Ayer took place on television at a late Sunday evening in 1971 in the International School for Philosophy in the Netherlands. The title "The Glass Is on the Table, an Empiricist versus a Total View" shows the core of the difference between both thinkers and their respective philosophies. It was a lively discussion with an empiricist surface-structure, presented and defended brilliantly by Freddy Ayer, and an ontological depth-structure, presented and defended equally brilliantly by Arne Næss. I use the words surface-structure and depth-structure in a metaphorical, non-Chomskian sense.

The dialogue was beautiful for more than one reason. Both philosophers understand every single statement of each other and are able to express themselves as precisely as language permits them. They are also able to argue extensively in favor of their own ideas, while willing to listen to each other's arguments. There is honesty in both parts, and the common desire to unveil what the two philosophers consider as truth or as the impossibility to reach truth. I hardly know any dialogue in twentieth century philosophy, which combines the sheer intensity of an exchange with such profoundness in the search for meaning and truth.

The discussion made a deep impression on the audience. A seventeen-year-old student *saw*, for the first time in his life, people thinking. Twenty years later he still remembered this television event. For all participants philosophy came to life—without tricks or special visual effects, through the mastery of Næss and

45

Ayer, who were able to use and demonstrate the inherent qualities of the dialogue form as an imaginative, literary, and hermeneutic model of the search for truth.

In "Dialogue and Meaning"[1] I describe the dialogue as a mental electromagnetic field that in its form shows some resemblance with the polar forces of all organic matter, viz. the simultaneity of centrifugal and centripetal movements. It is like our heartbeat or the rhythm of music, poetry, and dance, an ongoing movement balancing around an invisible center or axis.

I asked both philosophers about their philosophical views and their tasks as philosophers. Ayer answered that these are today very much the same questions that have been asked since the Greeks, mainly about what can be known, how it can be known, what kind of things there are, how they relate to each other, "and I hope, in a sense, to finding the truth." Næss responded by saying that he saw it a little differently because philosophy included the most profound, the deepest, the most fundamental problems. These problems have not changed much over the last two thousand years. But Næss agreed with Ayer that the epistemological and ontological questions belong to philosophy, and are among the most profound questions we can ask.

Ayer immediately retorted with: How does Næss measure the profundity of a problem? Næss threw the question back at him by asking rhetorically: "How do we measure? Well, that's one of the most profound questions of all."

The two gentlemen did not lose one minute trying to take the lead, each using their own language game with a different kind of semantics and logic to gain some ground.

The words "profound" and "deep" played an important role for Næss in this dialogue, as they do in Næss' s philosophy in general. He uses these terms both with regard to epistemological as well as to ontological questions. The epistemological and ontological questions are for Arne Næss so deeply interrelated that they form a Möbius string.

Let me quote some statements of Næss, which capture the intimate connections between his philosophy and his particular form of mysticism. Næss continues the philosophic-mystical tradition of Spinoza and combines his world of nature-experiences with an effort to change the Western, dualistic paradigm into a green worldview, not so different perhaps from the earth-bound worldview in Europe before the Indo-European invasion in the middle of the fourth millennium before our Christian era.[2]

1. "In moments of high concentration and integration, not at the times when I am merely functioning, I have this feeling—and it is not just a feeling—that we don't have any decisive arguments for any conclusions whatsoever."
2. "The mysteries that we 'know' include those of 'I know' and the link between the knower and the known."
3. "I can be shaken and I wish others to be able to be shaken!"
4. "I think I believe in the ultimate unity of all living beings."

5. "But the ecological movement may change the European tradition. The formulation 'all living beings are ultimately one,' is neither a norm nor a description. . . . It is the kind of utterance you make in support of something I would call an intuition, by which I do not mean that it is necessarily true. . . . My self is not my ego, but something capable of immense development."

6. "Yes, biologically we are just centers of interactions in one great field."

7. "More central is the fact that, as a philosopher, I think I have a kind of total view, which would include logic, epistemology, and ontology, but also evaluations, and that I do not escape from the relevance of them at any moment."

8. "It's not the great Self, it is the small self that needs limitation: it is when I'm functioning in tough practical situations, but not when I'm deciding what it is worthwhile doing in life, when the very widest perspectives are involved and when one is concentrating and meditating."

9. "I do not think we need a concept of fact, and we do not even need a concept of knowledge, in what I would call fundamental philosophical discussion."

10. "It is only true *if* it *is* so."

11. "Let me formulate it thus: I hope I would prefer to be killed by someone else rather than to kill, and I *ought* to prefer it."

12. "With my Spinozist leanings towards integrity—being an integrated person as the most important thing—I'm now trying to close down on all these vagaries. I am inviting you [Alfred Ayer] to do the same."

I have left out the questions or answers of Ayer's, not because they are not interesting. On the contrary, I am convinced that the usual tactics of Freddy Ayer to use his language and mind as a razor blade to cut through the metaphysical utterances of his opponents, forced Arne to be equally sharp, if not sharper, in presenting and protecting his deeper aspirations and intuitive notions. I want to use these statements in order to clarify the intimate relationship between Arne's philosophical and mystical endeavors.

A common denominator in most of the quotations is Næss's realization of boundlessness with regard to knowledge and identity (see 1, 2, 4, 5, 6, 8, 9, 10), while his total view consists of the interrelationship between all the domains or disciplines of philosophy, including normative questions such as the "right" to kill (see 7, 11). The experience of boundlessness which leads to the formulation "all living beings are ultimately one" forces or, at least, seduces Arne to argue *ad profundum* for a commitment of the whole person (see 3, 12).

The mystical experience of boundlessness and unity is at the heart of the philosophy of Arne Næss. From this existential experience, the development of his philosophical oeuvre becomes self-evident, leading from sympathy for empiricism and pragmatism to skepticism, and from there to a philosophy of the diversity of lifestyles and the diversity of life conceptions, and to the realization that there shouldn't or couldn't be a scientific worldview but that we do need a total view. During decades, Arne Næss had to argue systematically and coherently to create enough space for his inner experiences, which have become the source of his green philosophy.

"I got the impression that Næss approaches everyone, from the beginning, on the assumption that they are going to be both right and wrong." I wrote this sentence many years ago, trying to understand Næss's inclination never fully to identify with whatever position or statement. Both as a person and as a philosopher, Arne wanted to be so all-encompassing that he was forcing himself to escape any fixed position, both on the philosophical as well as on the emotional level. However, this impression or observation was formed at the beginning of the seventies. It doesn't hold anymore today. Arne Næss's philosophical need and duty to analyze, to decondition, to generalize, and to develop a coherent total view have merged into one desire. This is to clarify and to manifest as convincingly as possible his deeper intuitions about the real values of life and nature.

Arne's intuitions derive their strength and their "truth" from his mystical experiences. He uses all his philosophical talents to create as much space as possible for the songlines of our ancestors and for the songlines of the grand-children of our grandchildren. If I write "these intuitions derive their strength and their 'truth' from his mystical experiences," I am putting the word "truth" in quotes, solely to indicate that using the word is improper with regard to an in-tuitive statement as "the ultimate unity of all living beings." In doing so, I fol-low Næss's own advice not to use the word "truth" too easily. If we consider Næss's analysis of the notion of fact and truth, it may become clear that he has to defend this seemingly impossible position (see 9, 10). He has to do so be-cause of the fact that his most authentic experiences do not allow him to accept a less all-encompassing design (see 7, 8). Why is this so? Not only because mystic experiences are by their very nature authentic, but also due to the inner nature of such experiences, i.e., the dissolution of the "I" and "You" or "It" into a unity (see 2). Sentences like "I consider myself a philosopher when I'm trying to convince people of nonviolence, consistent nonviolence whatever happens," or "Philosophy is just this: that you develop something that I've started and gradually you introduce preciseness from different directions. Then you breathe three times, reinforce your intuition, and go a little further towards precision" become understandable, if we realize a deeper aspect of Arne's message.

This precision of Næss means also abolishing a distinction between des-cription and norm, fact and non-fact: "I do not think we need a concept of fact, and we do not even need a concept of knowledge, in what I would call funda-mental philosophical discussion," to end with the statement: "I hope I would prefer to be killed by someone else rather than to kill, and I *ought* to prefer it."

The combination of these four statements shows how Arne Næss stretches his commitment as a philosopher to the utmost limit, in defending the necessity of a total view with all its normative and emotional implications. The source of his philosophical commitment is the mystic experience of the unity of all living beings.

The aim of his philosophical commitment is action, viz. the transformation of our lifestyle through the application of the Eight Points.

"I can be shaken and I wish others to be able to be shaken!" (see 3). This is not a statement of an armchair philosopher but rather of a prophet or philosopher who feels responsible for "a kind of total view, which would include logic, epistemology, and ontology, but also evaluations, and *that I do not escape from the relevance of them at any moment*" (see 7, my emphasis). This is not a nonpersonal, academic statement but the commitment of a warrior or mystic philosopher for whom nothing any more belongs to the domain of indifferent or unimportant issues. Rudolf Carnap told me in 1970, three months before he died, that he couldn't understand that such an intelligent man as Arne Næss could write in one and the same book about him and Heidegger. The book *Four Modern Philosophers* (1968) dealt with Carnap, Heidegger, Wittgenstein and Sartre. It was nice to see in "The Glass Is on the Table," how also Freddy Ayer reacted in a similar way when Næss mentioned the name of Heidegger: "Let's keep him out of this. . . . We ought to maintain certain standards." Næss wouldn't be Næss to let pass such a chance. So he continued by saying "Well, a man whose name begins with H and ends with R thinks. . . ."

Næss's capacity for joking makes the seriousness of his philosophy acceptable. He maintains a balance between the extremes by balancing on a tightrope with a priest on his left side, and a jester on his right, as the authors of the Preface suggest.

Notes

[1] Fons Elders, "Dialogue and Meaning," in *Dialogue and Universalism* (Warsaw: Polish Academy of Sciences, 1990), 28.

[2] See Marija Gimbutes, *The Language of the Goddess* (San Francisco: Harper and Collins, 1989).

Chapter 7

Remarks on *Interpretation and Preciseness*

Paul Feyerabend

During the discussions in this circle [a philosophy of science conference at Us-taoset in Norway, 1955], the requirement was often voiced that high-flown analysis should be replaced by empirical investigations. This requirement was in itself of a very high-flown type, since it had not been decided what the word "empirical" was really supposed to mean.

We are indebted to Professor Næss for making this requirement concerning empirical investigations more precise by outlining a concrete procedure. The basis for this procedure and its area of application must now be investigated. First of all: countless assertions made in philosophical debates really presuppose a foundational analysis of this kind. Philosophically motivated critiques of the quantum theory often contain passages like: "It is true that quantum physicists now claim that it is meaningless to talk about causality. But in support of this claim they take for granted, all the same, that there is a causal connection be-tween certain events." Frege criticizes, in part II of his *Foundations of Arithme-tic,* the formalistic conception of mathematics, especially as it was formulated in the nineteenth century by Heine and Thomae. He demonstrates that even though these mathematicians claim that mathematics is to be formalistic in a certain meaning of this word, they contradict this by the way they do mathematics. Frege's account is not difficult to transform into an occurrence analysis. It dif-fers from such an analysis only by having the form of a discourse, while occur-rence analysis sticks to a fixed scheme. The entire literature of philosophy and the theory of science are saturated with claims of this kind. The strict form, which Næss has given to, the discourse he investigates helps to facilitate the analysis of the meaning of the sentences one finds there. This demonstrates the importance of discussing his contribution.

Here we will emphasize two kinds of analysis: analysis of the occurrence of certain expressions in texts and analysis of the comportment of the respondent in certain situations. Analyses of the first kind lead to a list of descriptive definitions, like "'democracy' means in text A to author B the same as C" (1). Analyses of the second kind lead to lists of sentences, like "a uses '. . . .' in situation S synonymously with '____' in situation T" (2). And now we can account for the following claims:

(a) Sentences of the first kind (1) state nothing about the occurrence of specific letters or characters in particular places in a specific text; sentences of the second kind (2) state nothing about the comportment of the actual individuals in a way that can be accounted for in space-time coordinates.

(b) Sentences of the first kind (1) state nothing about the psychological condition which the author of the text was in by the time he wrote his text. The relevant concepts ("means," "synonymous," etc.), then, have neither physicalistically nor psychologically relevant connotations.

Regarding (a): The analysis of the meaning of "democracy" in Vishinski's *The Soviet Democracy* serves as an example. S is a sentence of the form (1), which describes the result of the analysis in this case. We now assume that because of specific political conditions all the copies of the book are burnt. All the same, we continue to maintain S, and I believe that even Professor Næss does not make the truth of S dependent upon how many copies exist of *The Soviet Democracy* or even if any copies of this book are to be found at all.

Regarding (b): Let us consider the following case: Ten years after S has been put forward, it becomes known that Vishinski at the time of the writing of the book suffered from a severe mental disorder. It is probable that he wrote the book under irresistible pressure and did so more or less automatically. We can imagine that he has written each page in order to please the powers that be. We can even find out that the man "Vishinski" never existed. Often enough we find ourselves in such situations, when we discover that we erroneously held A to be the author of the work W and that B is the real author. A and B can be totally different characters, and the transition from one to the other need not be less than that between mental health and mental disorder. And yet in such cases we do not say that the work has become another, different work. On the contrary, the result of an analysis of W will have some illuminating things to say about the mental state of B. And we certainly learn something about the character and mental state of a person from his works, and not about the nature of the work from the character of the person. But this presupposes that we can perform an analysis of a work by means of concepts, which have no psychological connotations. A sentence like "W can only have been written by an intelligent person" does not mean, then, that "W is of such-and-such a character" has psychological connotations, but that "X is intelligent" follows from "X has written W."

Finally, it is not necessary that there is an X who has written W. We could imagine that an army of spiders has fallen into an ink stand, and thereafter performs a dance on some pieces of paper, and that the text has come about in this way. When Næss now investigates the text, makes the claim S, and publishes the results of the investigation, and when one afterwards discovers how the text has come about, then the publication acquires a somewhat strange character. This is not because S is false, but because it is of little interest to write treatises on texts, which have come about in this haphazard way. If, however, such a text contains an important new discovery, then we have a different story altogether: We will consider the text valuable, even if it has come about in a totally unintelligent way. And this shows that our demand for an intelligent individual behind the text rests upon a prejudice. (See Ryle, *The Concept of Mind.*)

An objection which one could raise against the previous account is the following: How is it in the end possible to understand how a group of people makes use of certain expressions, without somehow relying upon how they behave and how they respond to things? Bronislaw Malinowski visited primitive tribes, lived amongst them, investigated their behavior, and finally came to understand their language. This understanding is based upon the fact that he took note of regularities in behavior, etc., and drew his conclusions from these.

Suppose that the members of the tribe T in the proximity of the place S emit a characteristic sound or that they prostrate themselves in front of a deity. What conclusion can we draw from this? Carnap (and perhaps also Næss) would be prone to assume that the sound or the gesture somehow makes up a name of the object, which is in place S, but here he could be completely wrong. Suppose there is a tree at S. The sound can then be a sign referring to the religious ceremony. In Catholic countries one makes a certain gesture (crossing oneself) when one passes a church, and this sign cannot be interpreted as "here is a church."

The sound can also be a sign of fear, or a gesture of rejection. It is also possible that the members of the tribe have decided to play a game that goes on for several years, and where these gestures play an important role.

We can easily multiply such examples. What is important here is this: It is not possible to replace the relation "x means X" by a number of relations, like "x is regularly performed in the vicinity of X," "after X, the members of T go to x!" "where the T utter x, they always point to X," etc. The expression "x means X" has no connotations that allow you to draw a conclusion of this kind. All the same, the behavior of the T stands in a certain relation to what is meaningful to them and to the language they speak. The following example will help to make this clear: Suppose the respondents still do not know the meaning of the word "red." We will use an ostensive definition in order to explain "red" to them. The respondents can misunderstand this definition. Suppose we have at first only pointed out large objects to them. Then they can construct a small theory of the kind "'Red' means the same as 'large'." Further examples will demonstrate that they are wrong. Of importance now is that an ultimate understanding of "red" has no connection with the truth of a sentence like "'red' is such-and-such," where such-and-such is a compound of expressions which does not include "red." What is peculiar about words like "red" is, of course, that every sentence which includes it already presupposes that we know how to use the word. The ostensive definition is an approach (not a deduction) which us suited to change the dispositions of the respondents in certain ways. It is important that through this procedure large objects are also included (otherwise the opinion might arise that only small objects are necessarily red). But it is not the case, that "large" appears as one of the connotations of "red." An approach might be suggested by an ingenious surgeon, which forsakes ostensive definitions as totally superfluous: He has discovered which part of the brain one has to influence in order to attain the right use of the word "red" by the respondents. He invites the respondents to his clinic, brings out his surgical instruments, administers an anesthetic to them, removes part of the skull, and operates. In this case one has to include "skull" in the connotations of "red," if one wants to proceed in a way similar to the ostensive definitions. Nobody in his or her right mind would hold this claim to be true. More likely people will mean that one can replace "x means X to the T in S" by "x is always used by the T in S whenever X is present." Thereby one will forget that there are cases in which words, which on the other hand can be meaningfully employed in debates, often play the same role as the instruments of a surgeon.

From all this we can deduce that the observation of the behavior of certain individuals creates phenomena, on the basis of which hypotheses on meaning can be tested, but that this behavior itself cannot be the object of a semantic description. And the same will be the case with investigations that in the end lead to sentences of the form (1) and (2). Here we have first and foremost an apparent difference between the criteria which are used by the respondents in order to pass their judgments, and the criteria which are used by the investigator in order to test his hypotheses. In the tests, in which the synonymy of two expressions has been settled, the respondents make an immediate, intuitive decision. The investigator, on the other hand, makes a series of observations and brings forward his experimental instruments. What counts as verification also seems to be radically different from that of the respondents.

But let us find out what is presupposed by this analysis. Let us assume that the respondents hold this task to be very difficult. They get up and walk about the room. They have second thoughts and their cheeks flush. They are annoyed and emit quiet curses. The investigator must have the opportunity to distinguish relevant from nonrelevant movements and expressions. Or, in the case of analyzing texts: He must be certain that a particular sign has a meaning and that it has not come about through periodical cramps. He must, then, have been through the particular stage which Malinowski is in the middle of when he wants to investigate the language of the natives: He must already know the language of the respondents.

On the other hand he will suggest a descriptive definition which covers all relevant occurrences and is perhaps capable of predicting future occurrences. He must, then, when he writes "democracy," have all those connections present which Vishinski had present when he was writing his book. And this goes to show that he must use those very same criteria which Vishinski used, as he attempted to give clear expression to his thoughts. And if that was not possible from the start, then this is again a reference to the role that occurrence analysis really plays: It is not the case that it collects empirical material which will support scientific hypotheses. It is more correct to say that it creates this material. The analysis is not to be tested against isolated occurrences, but against certain phenomena, which appear along with the reading of the parts quoted. And the final result is carried through in the same way as a mathematical investigation, similar to the ways in which the often-vilified armchair philosophers have reached their results.

Even though the investigator uses the same criteria as the respondent, he does not investigate the same object. Vishinski investigates democracy, Næss investigates democracy-according-to-Vishinski. Up to now we have tried to point out what meaning the result of such investigations have, in what way they can be verified, and how they relate to the observation of the molar behavior of the respondent. It seemed necessary to take a stand against a psychological interpretation, especially since such an interpretation comes easily to mind when one reads *Interpretation and Preciseness* and because it has been suggested by the author himself in other publications (*Erkenntnis und wissenschaftliches Verhalten, Notes on the Foundation of Psychology as a Science*).

We have now to look into the relationship between this newly created discipline and other disciplines. And it is, from a historical point of view, a remarkable coincidence that again there is a tendency to resurrect investigations from other disciplines, investigations which have long since been concluded, and expose them to fresh criticism. This is the case when Næss begins to talk about mathematics.

In part III of *Interpretation and Preciseness* we find a very significant investigation of the function of definitions, which deserves careful scrutiny by mathematicians and theoreticians of science. We have here a number of explanations of mathematical theorems, which can be brought under the form: "Mathematical theorems are analytical, and analytical theorems are theorems, which derive from definitions alone." (See E. Kaila, *Den menskliga kunnskapen.* See also Carnap, *The Logical Syntax of Language.*) The point is now, that a mathematical theorem should always be true. In what way is its truth dependent on the definitions from which it is supposed to follow? Surely it is possible that A can suggest a definition, then forget that he has done so and go on to use the definiendum in other ways. We must therefore distinguish between two things in a definition: (a) the request to use an expression in a particular way and (b) the theorem which is true, in case the request is complied with. A definition has the general form of "R is per definition the same as S." "Per definition," then, this says nothing more than the connotation of "R" and "S." Rather it is first and foremost a request to change one's usage in particular ways, secondly a tool that is supposed to further this change, and thirdly a historical record which indicates how we should understand that "R" is eventually used synonymously with "S." When we now infer that "From P (S) is deduced P (R)," then this inference is not supported by the condition that such a request was given or that an operation was performed, but is based on the true theorem "S is R." It is not obvious that such a theorem is true, not even when we know that a definition has been suggested, which clearly aims at this. We must have an independent investigation of S and R themselves.

From all this some light should fall on some of the work done in modern philosophical logic. One is there confronted by the ways in which in everyday language one moves in an immediate way from one sentence to the next, and also by the necessity of explicitly mentioning, through rules and definitions, the ways of inference which are permitted and the synonymities that are used. The analysis referred to above demonstrate, however, that the construction of such a hierarchy of rules cannot replace a renewed investigation of the immediate relations within a natural language. Here the methodology of Næss seems to be relevant. We have to check if this is indeed the case.

Let us assume that Næss analyzes an investigation in which an object A is mentioned. He discovers that A is used in different meanings. He puts forward a number of sentences of type (1), in which the particular meanings have been more closely identified. And he blames the author for not having conclusively terminated his investigation, and that he therefore cannot claim to have solved a particular problem. To this, the author can respond: "You blame me for not using my concepts unambiguously. But from this I can see that you really haven't understood what I mean by these concepts. You are in the same position as a person who is color blind, who reproaches those that are not that they don't use the word 'red' unambiguously, since they sometimes refer to big, sometimes to small, and then sometimes to heavy, sometimes to light objects by this word. Your discourse can perhaps have the effect that I have to talk to you in a different way in order to be understood by you. But I will not recognize it as an argument."

Let's compare this with the situation in mathematics. Let's assume that Næss attempts to take a stand and find out if the mathematicians really stick to their definitions. He writes a thesis on *The Foundations of Mathematics* in which he concludes that 14 out of 18 definitions are not observed. What can be inferred from such a result?

First of all we must ask the authors of *Foundations*. And it is possible that they will answer, "You wish to dictate to us what we should do, or better, serve as an example to us. But you have not at all understood what we mean by 'sticking to a definition.'"

The possibility of such an answer is of significance. It demonstrates that the result of an occurrence analysis cannot be used as an argument against the substance of an account from which the analysis has taken its material. And that Næss is not in a position above the sciences, being able to dictate to the sciences, but is placed on the same footing as them. But his investigations have a specific role.

Let us assume that the contact between American and European science one day is broken off. Assume that in both continents they use the same language, but that new ways of inferring appear irregularly, new proofstructures are developed, etc., so that there is an ever greater difference between the respective scientific infrastructures. Some decades after the separation, there is an exchange of scientists. They discover that they have difficulties understanding one another and resort to occurrence analysis. And then it might be possible that they will have a dialogue like the one we have described. But this dialogue may have as a result an adjustment of languages. It may have as a result that one party finally sees a connection where there previously seemed to be none, or that the other party gives up its ways of inference and thinks out other procedures. The result of the analysis, then, is an instrument, which leads to new uses of language and thereby to improved communication, but it does not have the form of an argument, which can decide that a particular use is contradictory or meaningless. And when Næss publishes his accounts he hopes to influence, but not to prove something. It is above all of importance that we have effective means of improving the possibility of communication.

A final remark: The analysis of the role of definitions demonstrates that we cannot once and for all create certainty within mathematics. Definitions are not piles driven into the ground, on which we can erect a solid and unchallenged building. But what does it mean that mathematics has become uncertain? This does not mean that mathematics has come closer to the state of the empirical sciences. From what was said above it seems more reasonable to infer that a structure which today counts as evidence cannot be sure to keep this role in future times. But in that case something else has not become true, neither has the same theorem become false. Rather the proof structure and the proven theorem have completely disappeared.

To sum up: The account we have given here is not some kind of "disproof." It is not intended as such at all. What has been done and investigated cannot be easily refuted. It was more a case of giving a clear presentation of the substance of the theory and its relationship to other disciplines. And here we found out that even by the suggested, nonpsychological interpretation, a prominent position for this discipline was not justified. It is not necessary to throw out every investigation of an analyst but because he does not have the ability to do anything else but turn the investigation in another direction in a purely active (political) way.

Chapter 8

Paul Feyerabend: A Green Hero?

Arne Næss

I. Mild and Green?

It is not without a certain feeling of guilt that some of us admit to always finding great pleasure in reading Feyerabend, including his many digressions and footnotes. Speaking of footnotes, who else has managed to place a footnote on his title page, which refers to yet other footnotes? (See the title page of *Against Method: Outline of an Anarchistic Theory of Knowledge*).

The feeling of guilt occurs when reading the serious criticism of Feyerabend's manners, his "offensive and wounding comments," his limited "respect for truth," and his relentless attacks on the reading abilities of his colleagues.

Feyerabend sees himself as mild and considerate. But in the very footnote in which he defends his innocence he says that he wants "to remove the ideological and financial exploitation of common citizens by a small gang of power- and money-hungry intellectuals."[1] The reader may easily interpret this as an even harsher attack upon his colleagues than that concerning their lamentable literacy. Without going into further analysis of a personal nature, my conclusion is that the mildness of Feyerabend is genuine and that even his monumental stylistic arrogance is nonviolent.

This unexpected conclusion makes me wonder to what extent the arrogant style of Renaissance scientists was combined with smiling mockery. Luigi Ferrari expresses his pleasure in the belief that his writings against Tartaglia have broken the back of the latter and made him scarcely able to move his tail, etc. Perhaps scientists at that time enjoyed themselves immensely, not only talking to each other in this way, but also making scathing personal criticisms as widely known as possible by means of the new invention, the printing press.

At any rate Feyerabend's exuberance has elicited many rhetorical jewels. Ernest Gellner's "Beyond Truth and Falsity" is a case in point. Perhaps we shall witness the rise of a tradition of scientific rhetoric in the near future. There are illustrious precedents. Pascal expressed *rhetorically* the theorem that "the arc length of an arch of the generalized cycloid" is equal to "the semicircumference of the ellipse."[2]

But those of us whose rhetorical talents are rather modest should, I think, stick to our old pedantic ways. That at least is what I shall do in the following.

What I would like to do is to suggest a qualified positive answer to the questions, "May we, who are proponents of green philosophy and politics, count Feyerabend as one of our heroes?" and "Does he support the idea of a green policy of science?"[3]

II. Traditions and Rationality

From a rather narrow point of view green policies are characterized only in terms of pollution, resources, and population control. As far as I know Feyerabend has at least not published anything contrary to green policies in these fields. Pointing to his new car (his first) he remarked: "I have joined the eco-criminals!" I leave it to the readers to find the most plausible interpretation.

The philosophical central green issues concern human ecology, which today covers much of social and cultural anthropology. The term "tradition" belongs to the central ones. Feyerabend says something about the function of rationality in relation to traditions, which deserves further development:

> There are therefore at least two different ways of collectively deciding an issue, which I shall call a guided and open exchange respectively. In the first case some or all participants adopt a well-specified tradition and accept only those responses that correspond to its standards. If one party has not yet become a participant of the chosen tradition he will be badgered, persuaded, "educated" until he does—and then the exchange begins. A *rational debate* is a special case of a guided exchange. If the participants are rationalists then all is well and the debate can start right away. If only some participants are rationalists and they have power (an important consideration!), then they will not take their collaborators seriously until they have also become rationalists: a society based on rationality is not entirely free; one has to play the game of the intellectuals.
>
> An open exchange, on the other hand, is guided by a pragmatic philosophy. The tradition adopted by the parties is unspecified in the beginning and develops as the exchange goes along. The participants get immersed into each other's ways of thinking, feeling, perceiving to such an extent that their ideas, perceptions, worldviews may be entirely changed—they become different people participating in a new and different tradition. An open exchange respects the partner whether he is an individual, or an entire culture while a rational exchange promises respect only within the framework of a rational debate.

The outcome of seemingly friendly interactions between nonindustrial and industrial traditions or cultures is largely determined by the superior power of the latter. The kind of rational debate and decision making characteristic of the powerful prevail. The Lapps of northern Scandinavia could not be expected to be able to fight effectively for their rights when invited to play the decision-making game of the powerful opponents. The same holds well in the hopeless fight of the Buddhist Sherpas to maintain their cultural integrity in a land ruled by Hindu bureaucracy. In both cases the decision-making processes of the weaker side are different from those of the stronger. If more or less forced to adopt the ways of the stronger, the weaker side is doomed to be dominated by the strong. Today there is scarcely any intention to dominate or exploit the Lapps, or to weaken what remains of their culture, but the interaction or exchange is a "guided" one in Feyerabend's terminology, and the stronger party wins. That is, it wins in the short run, but loses in the long run, according to green philosophy; the absence of contact with a genuinely different culture makes the winner poorer.

The terminology of Feyerabend does not seem to me very wise, however. The decision-making process in nonindustrial traditions may not be less rational than in our traditions, if the term rational is taken in a wide sense adapted to general cultural anthropology. When the Sherpas say that Tseringma (Gauri Shankar) is a mountain, a princess, and a kind of mother, of course all at the same time, this is only irrational when integrated in a rather superficial way with our thinking and in our language. Rationality in a wider sense does not imply that one has to "play the game of the intellectuals." In short, I think it unwise to restrict the terms rational and even rationalism in such a way that industrial societies acquire a monopoly.

This terminological remark does not oppose the view that when two (widely different) cultures or traditions interact, the resulting changes cannot be adequately understood as a rational interchange even in a wide sense.

III. Maximum Diversity

One of the fundamental key terms of green philosophy and politics is diversity. Diversity of life forms, diversity of functions, environments, niches, traditions, practices, is basic to change, and particularly to evolution of new life forms and cultures.

Respect and tolerance of diversity on a more and more crowded planet therefore get to be politically increasingly urgent. The view is gaining credence, that the cultural diversity seemingly manifest in great industrial cities is only a superficial variation. Basic attitudes are increasingly standardized, in part due to the centralization of technologies and communication.

Cognitive diversity is an integral part of cultural diversity. If, therefore, education is increasingly stereotyped through the adoption of worldwide criteria of learning, the path towards monoculture is made smoother. That is, the con-

temporary stereotyped institutions of learning undermine the possibility of escape from cultural stagnation on this planet.

These are pessimistic, but rather common, views. Nevertheless in order to
change the schools and universities, political changes are necessary which today
seem unlikely. The chances of change increase somewhat, if more and more
teachers boldly introduce changes based on an epistemological pluralism (Feyerabend proposes anarchism, I refer to possibilism[4] which cannot easily be refuted, if at all). Great impact cannot be expected, but the work in favor of a deep
change must itself be of a diverse kind. Education is one field of struggle.

IV. Minimum Interference

A cubic foot of good soil contains hundreds of species of organisms; each represented through hundreds, millions, or even billions of specimens. They interact with nonorganic ingredients in a more complex way than can be grasped in
detail. But details or specialized complex functions are often decisive for the
function of the whole as "good soil." Field ecologists hired to effect this or that
change in a natural environment, or asked about which short-range and long-
range effect an interference will show, often are brought to the limits of desperation: neither technical experts nor politicians seem to appreciate the basic
ignorance of today and tomorrow about practically any concrete processes in
nature. I say "concrete" because abstract knowledge of "laws" may increase
exponentially without much influence on our ignorance in matters of field ecology. Therefore *docta ignorantia* is a new key term of green philosophy.

Field ecologists, when asked about a new plan to interfere in nature, tend to
answer "rather not interfere" because of ignorance of effects, not because of
proclaimed insight into negative effects.

What holds good about interference in nature holds also about nonindustrial
cultures. Many of the benevolent interference's in these cultures, offering them
help in the form of food, dams, or books, have had deplorable effects. Often
noninterference seems to be the most responsible policy. The theme is complicated and the state of affairs is rather depressing, cultures dying at an alarming
rate.

A principle of minimal interference applies to subcultures within industrial
societies. Paul Feyerabend says provoking things about this:

> The possibilities of Mill's liberalism can be seen from the fact that it provides
> room for any human desire, and for any human vice. There are no general
> principles apart from the principle of minimal interference with the lives of in-
> dividuals, or groups of individuals who have decided to pursue a common aim.
> For example, *There is no attempt to make the sanctity of human life a principle*
> *that would be binding for all.* Those among us who can realize themselves only
> by killing their fellow human beings and who feel fully alive only when in
> mortal danger are permitted to form a subsociety of their own where human
> targets are selected for the hunt. . . . (*SFS*, p. 132.)

In any crowded society a subculture with a lot of killings going on interferes too heavily with outsiders. In the Valhalla of the Vikings, those who did not relish fighting and killing stayed home having a good time. The enthusiastic fighters never intentionally or accidentally molested them. In the evenings they got as much beer as the heroes did.

Unfortunately there are today geographical limitations which make the practical application of very broad tolerance of cultural diversity difficult. The Valhalla model is inapplicable.

In green politics the protection of animal societies, not only protection of individual humans against undue interference, is a key issue. The matter is complex, however, and the maxim of "maximizing life potentials" clearly sometimes makes it a justifiable policy of humans to interfere in the animal world, protecting one animal society against another. I do not see why we should not gently assist golden trout (*Salmo aguabonita*) if it is threatened with complete extinction through weakness in its competition with the brown trout.

Since Descartes and Bacon, fortified by the labor theory of value, interference has become somewhat of a criterion of efficiency. What proceeds naturally tends to be classed as valueless or indifferent. It is characteristic of green policies to minimize interference, and we find the same point expressed by Feyerabend:

> As far as science is concerned, I am as fit as a fiddle. Not being restricted by an undying loyalty to science I started looking for other kinds of healers and I found there are lots of them. Herbalists. Faith healers. Acupuncturists. Masseurs. Hypnotists. All quacks, according to the established medical opinion. The first thing that caught my attention was their method of diagnosis. No painful interference with the organism. Many of these people had developed efficient methods of diagnosing from pulse, color of eye, of tongue, from gait, and so on. (Later on, when reading the *Nei Ching* which develops the philosophy behind acupuncture, I found that in China this was intentional: the human body must be treated with respect which means one has to find methods of diagnosis that do not violate its dignity). (*SFS*, p. 137.)

The use of the term "dignity" is instructive. Green politics is concerned about dignity as much as about material standard of living. Dignity is essential to life quality. And it is extended to animals. Animal factories interfere with the dignity of pigs.

On the whole, the green philosophy of nature is inspired by an appreciation of life forms that is broader than the usual. One would agree with Paul: "As far as I am concerned, a world in which a louse can live happily is a better world, a more mature world than a world in which a louse must be wiped out." (*SFS*, p. 133.)

V. Fundamental Philosophies, Ecophilosophy T

In general, I think, a basic norm of "live and let live" is characteristic of green philosophy. In terms of traditional western philosophy it corresponds to a norm of maximum fulfillment of life potentials. This norm implies norms of diversity, complexity (of structure and function), and of maximum symbiosis, that is, arrangement of life forms and life styles with minimum negative interference with each other. An interaction counts as negative if it decreases the potentialities of life fulfillment of the participants.

Being fond of neat systematizations, I have worked out several versions of a particular kind of green philosophy and politics, which I call "ecosophy T."[5] One version of its key slogans is formulated in the following diagram, with lines of derivation pointing downwards from the top of the normative pyramid. Only the "highest" norms and hypotheses are given in the diagram. Serious normative argumentation presupposes that the formulations are made more precise in different directions.

The system ecosophy T is in Paul's terminology a *Gedankenelaborat*[6] and should not be forced upon anybody, including green philosophers with different philosophical tastes or convictions. Because philosophies as I see them concern fundamentals, no philosopher can refute any other. Basically there is room for several, and efforts even to describe the differences may founder because of specific presuppositions necessary in descriptions. (Rational incomparability of fundamental systems.) To be rational, if it is something desirable, seems to require the realization of an essential philosophical pluralism that cannot be rationally verified.

What does Feyerabend write on this matter?

> *Philosophical relativism* is the doctrine that all traditions, theories, ideas are equally true or equally false or, in an even more radical formulation, that any distribution of truth values in traditions is acceptable. This form of relativism is nowhere defended in the present book. It is not asserted, for example, that Aristotle is as good as Einstein, it is asserted and argued that "Aristotle is true" is a judgment that presupposes a certain tradition, it is a relational judgment that *may* change when the underlying tradition is changed. (*SFS*, p. 83.)

This is completely compatible with ecosophy T. His "political relativism" is compatible, but I find the term "relativism" misleading. The more authentic our search for truth the more firm is our membership of a particular philosophy or kind of "practice" or kind of "tradition." In so far as there is any meaning or validity attached to announcements of the kind "x is a right," it is not relative, but relational, i.e., basically related to a philosophy or practice. This relationalism, rather than relativity, is implied in Feyerabend's own unqualified, nonrelativist affirmation of equal rights:

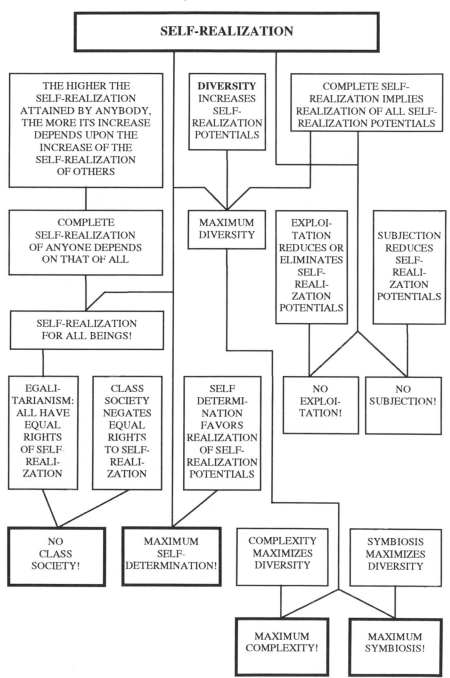

Figure 8.1. First Levels of Ecosophy T.

Political relativism affirms that all traditions have equal *rights*: the mere fact that some people have arranged their lives in accordance with a certain tradition suffices to provide this tradition with all the basic rights of the society in which it occurs. (*SFS*, p. 82.)

As an example of something, which is not a philosophy in the above sense, anarchism, in the terminology of Feyerabend, may be mentioned. "Even here I don't defend anarchism as an 'eternal philosophy' but as a 'medicine' that may have to be withdrawn when conditions change." (*Against Method*, p. 22.) But on the basis of which norms and hypotheses will it be withdrawn? Their formulation will reveal deeper issues and take us a step in the direction of articulation of a philosophy. But I do not see why anybody like Feyerabend who is inspired by Kierkegaard's *Concluding Unscientific Postscript* should formulate any systematic philosophy. Kierkegaard did not, and we are thankful that he didn't.

VI. The Web of Communities and its Administration

It is common in green politics to conceive local communities as the basic political unit. In big urban areas the term "local" has to be taken in a rather wide sense so that moving groups with a common lifestyle and high degree of cohesion are included.

Every more comprehensive unit of people is conceived as basically administrational, even if termed societies or nations. There are many reasons for this stress on small units. In political theory, its history is joined with that of the distinction between *Gemeinschaft* (community) and *Gesellschaft* (society)—between fairly autonomous groups with genuine personal bonds, strong sense of belonging, and locally manageable technology, and the vast structures of states and nations.

Feyerabend announces that a "free society is a society in which all traditions are given equal rights, equal access to education and other positions of power." (*SFS*, p. 30.)

Let us take an example. In arctic Norway there is among the Lapps a nomadic tradition, very different from those of the now sedate Germanic tribes of other parts of Norway. The latter think it is important to have a lot of big roads and they love making extensive dams in order to increase the production of electricity. This "progress" is incompatible with the lifestyles of reindeer and their owners. Those Lapps who deeply want to maintain and further develop their culture cannot in any genuine way live together with urbanized people. What is needed for coexistence is a common administration, the state structure called Norway. I think the use of the term "society" in Feyerabend's utterances about "free society" might be a little misleading. Norway as an administration for two cultures is not a society. If deeply different traditions are to be defended, this requires of us that we do not take the bigger units of humanity too seriously as societies. They are rather administrational structures.

Some will feel that this goes against world solidarity. But one green policy towards developing nations is that of mutual aid (Kropotkin) from community to community. Communities within industrial states (not "societies") try, for instance, to cooperate with communities in Africa and other places without too much interference from higher administrational levels.

What Feyerabend primarily has in mind is probably the varieties of traditions, or lifestyles, of groups *within* a state or federation. Here I suppose that differences in ways of living (technologies, language, and willingness to pay taxes) are in some aspects rather limited. Feyerabend mentions equal access to education. This suggests a similarity in appreciation of (formal?) education. Some traditions, such as those of the culturally conscious Lapps, go contrary to this. They might ask for the right not to be educated. They prefer communities without formal education (schools, etc.), but of course where a lot of teaching goes on, the older teaching the younger. Hopefully, in the future (at least before the year 3000) it will be practicable to maintain and develop deeply different traditions even within fairly small areas. This evidently implies that the interchange between the traditions, the dealings between members of deeply different groups, functions without undue interference from those who monopolize scientific or expert reason. "The exchange between traditions is an open exchange, not a rational exchange." (*SFS*, p. 85.) But there must be a kind of top level administration, I am inclined to think, in order to avoid exploitation by groups which resemble certain well known ones in our own century.

How does Feyerabend propose to solve these problems? Strange question. Did Kierkegaard propose to solve *anything*?

Self-determination is a key word in green philosophy, and it includes finding out things for oneself and by oneself: cognitive self-determination. Feyerabend has said things about expertise that fit in very well here and he asks to let "people" solve problems. (*Unter dem Pflaster*, p. 138.) A scientist or technician placed in the so-called center may have the solution of a problem, but mostly problem solving is part of greater units or gestalts of action. The expert may help by offering fragments, but this often spoils the development of the greater wholes of action and living. Ivan Illich has said things worth considering in this area. Main point: science undermines the capacity of people to think for themselves.

VII. There are no Scientific Worldviews

Freedom is regained, old traditions are rediscovered, both among the minorities in Western countries and among large populations in non-Western continents. But science still reigns supreme. It reigns supreme because its practitioners are unable to understand, and unwilling to condone, different ideologies because they have the power to enforce their wishes, and because they use this power just as their ancestors used their power to force Christianity on the people they encountered during their conquests. Thus, while an American can now choose the religion he likes, he is still not permitted to demand that his children learn magic rather than science at school. (*Against Method*, p. 299.)

Some pedantic comments:

Science means basically something different from what it means to Feyerabend when one has lived with science as a naturalist. The "soft" sciences, like geography of plants, taxonomy of butterflies, invite us to join a practice and style of life very different from that of a particle physicist at Geneva or a mathematician at Princeton. The soft scientist need not play the game of intellectuals.

The discoverer of the "pecking order law," Schjelderup-Ebbe, the only world famous Norwegian psychologist and ethnologist, was early in life inordinately fond of watching the sexual and general social behavior of hens. He could of course have avoided discovering or inventing the law, but it did not require anything like intellectual games or games of intellectuals. In debate his arguments were often of a kind that made the occasion more charming than brainy. Sample: "But what you say only shows that you do not really know the hen Marie." His insect poems are less well known than his law, but closer to his heart. Nobody would insinuate that he ever considered joining a so-called scientific worldview. As a researcher, why bother? Philosophy and religion offer worldviews.

For the naturalist, there is no reason to reject magic if one is raised with it. Most kinds of genuine research do not interfere violently with traditions in nonindustrial cultures. In some of them western medicine is adopted in a way that does not imply rejection of myths.

Superficially, hard science and a so-called scientific worldview dominate the minds, but careful scrutiny often reveals nonconformity. The beauty and immense diversity of form of extinct animals struck early researchers. They regarded such animals as divine creatures. But it was at that time difficult to make enough money to continue such research indefinitely. Then came the discovery of the close connection between certain genera of fossil forms and the presence of oil. Suddenly there was plenty of money around. The soft researchers continued approximately as before, sometimes doing a little bit of hard science, but only enough to placate the boss. Their minds were unruffled, not dominated by (hard) science.

In short, I think children could learn both magic and science. There is no necessary conflict. It all depends upon how things are introduced. Or more generally: research can be explained and exemplified without interfering with basic beliefs of nonindustrial cultures. This holds good even of theoretical physics. A physicist who today is an adherent of beliefs that are generally classed as "mythological," and who is firmly convinced of the superiority of mythological thinking, translates the crucial parts of the language of contemporary physics into his own language. It is not easy, one of them told me, but it works.

Because of the considerable freedom in choice of theoretical constructs, and also because of the intimate link between the scientific vocabulary and empirical procedures (i.e., actions, practices), to force science on people is rather different from forcing a definite dogmatic religious worldview upon people.

What is happening today in schools and universities may be understood in part as a forceful adaptation of science to suit the basic goals of centralized industrial societies. Science may thus function as an ideology, but not eternally and out of any historical or other kind of necessity.

In short, I would like to modify one of the formulations of Feyerabend; whereas an American can now choose the religion he likes, he is unfortunately not permitted to choose the kind of science he likes. If he likes science along the lines of green science and teaching policy, his offspring should be treated as children naturalists, enjoying backyard zoology and other marvelous experiences.

VIII. Conclusion

Both regarding rationality and its special expression, science, I differ at least in terminology from Feyerabend. But some eminent green philosophers, Ivan Illich among others, favor a view closely similar to Feyerabend's.

Feyerabend has not, as far as I know, taken up certain central green issues such as self-reliance and decentralization. They have important implications in policy of science. Where he does take up central issues, they belong, broadly speaking, within the sphere of green philosophy and politics.

Hero worship or advocacy of the dichotomy hero/nonhero is not characteristic of green philosophy. It suggests a kind of competition and subservience that limits self-realization. If Feyerabend rejects the thought of being a green hero, or finds it contradictory, it is a good sign.

The ultimate conclusion might be thus formulated: Feyerabend writes as if he maintains many views, which are characteristic of, green philosophy and politics, and applies them to science, education, and rationality in an original way.

Notes

This chapter is reprinted with minor revisions from G. Munevar (ed.) *Beyond Reason* (Dordrech: Kluwer, 1991), 403–416.

[1] P. Feyerabend, *Science in a Free Society* ("*SFS*"), 131.

[2] C. B. Boyer, *A History of Mathematics* (New York, 1968), 400.

[3] The use of the term "green" in the above sentences certainly needs some clarification. It refers to general views and attitudes in the main part inspired by the international environmental ecological movement. Some well-known authors: Gregory Bateson, Kenneth Boulding, Rachel Carson, William O. Douglas, René Dubos, Jaques Ellul, Johan Galtung, Clarence Glacken, Edward Goldsmith, Ivan Illich, Sigmund Kvaløy, Aldo Leopold, Ian McHarg, Joseph Meeker, E. J. Mishan, John Rodman, Roderick Nash, Theodore Roszak, Marshall Sahlins, E. F. Schumacher, Paul Shepard, Lynn White. These authors do not agree, and they have different styles. But there are important overlappings, which manifest themselves in similar political and cultural stances in some of their publications. We may treat it as a case of Wittgensteinian "family resemblance."

⁴ Feyerabend's characterization of Imre Lakatos as a "fellow anarchist" caused some indignation and protest. But his views were basically rather close to those labeled "anarchist" by Feyerabend (and perhaps by nobody else). As an argument in favor of this interpretation I shall quote his conclusion in reference to the pluralist and possibilist views in my work referred to above: "I did not previously realise how far our philosophical views coincided and it was a great pleasure for me that we are close allies." (Letter of 4 November 1968). The possibilist approach I take to be a little more "anarchist" in Feyerabend's terminology than his own.

⁵ Arne Næss, "Notes on the Methodology of Normative Systems," *Methodology and Science* 10 (1977): 64–79.

⁶ P. Feyerabend, *Unter dem Pflaster liegt der Strand*, 5, 135.

Chapter 9

Comment: Næss and Feyerabend on Science

Bill Devall

Næss and Feyerabend engaged in discussions on the "external relations" of science, that is, the social institutions and ideology that support science in most Western nations. Feyerabend's main concern seems to be that there is no "pure" science, that is, science for science's sake. Scientific enterprises are connected with the political decisions of the political elites. Scientists have too much status and too much power in contemporary societies.

Feyerabend takes a social libertarian approach to education. If parents want their children to learn magic as well as science in school, then the schools should teach magic as well as science.

As a sociologist, I find myself accepting many of Feyerabend's assertions and find that some of his hopes for reforming society are occurring.

Feyerabend hopes that "financial support for sciences, however, will be drastically reduced (here the rules are exactly the same as in the case of religions)." In the United States there has been a reduction in support of "big" science. NASA, the linear accelerator, funds for basic research of all sorts have been greatly reduced by the U.S. Congress.

Modern medicine has seen some reduction in support and public approval because of its inability to "solve" such riddles as AIDS. Some insurance companies are paying for acupuncture and other "nonconventional" medical treatments for AIDS patients. Some medical doctors suggest that such non-conventional treatments will probably help their patients just as much as any drugs they prescribe.

Feyerabend is concerned with the monopoly of science as the only way to truth, as taught in universities. In U.S. universities, a kind of radical subjectivity and postmodernism seems to have swept into favor. Social constructionism abounds. Knowledge systems of Native Americans and other non-Western cultures are taught as equally truthful as Western, modern science. Post-modernists suggest that everything is perception, that men and women have different systems of truth, and that different ethnic groups have different systems of truth.

There is extensive literature comparing ancient systems of knowledge and modern science. Fritjof Capra's *The Tao of Physics* illustrates the parallels between ancient eastern wisdom and twentieth century physics. Millions of people read and appreciate his book. Joanna Macy in *World as Lover, World as Self* shows parallels between classical Buddhist thought and modern systems theory. Her books are read as texts in university courses.

The status and financial rewards given to scientists seem to be decreasing. With the end of the Cold War, atomic physicists are unemployed.

And science is seen as an adventure, in some instances. For example, an AIDS patient has doctors design and obtain approval from the government to conduct an experiment whereby bone marrow from a baboon is injected into his body in an attempt to build another immune system that will protect him from infections as his own immune system fails.

Desperate adventure? Perhaps, but an example of the power of citizen pressure groups to influence medical experts.

Is Feyerabend a "green hero" as Næss asserts? Perhaps. He certainly finds favor among those who support multiculturalism. Bioregional communities could develop their own "sense of place" and out of careful observations of natural processes in their bioregion, develop a kind of regional science. Science could be in the service of the search for ecosophy. Ecosophy is the search for wisdom of place. Careful observation, inductive generalizations, intuitive awareness, even rituals focused on seasonal changes in the bioregion, could be woven into cultural expressions.

Some fear, however, that pluralist expressions of science will be subverted not by central governments but by multinational corporations. Corporate scientists serve the interests of corporations. Corporations want us to believe that what is good for the corporation is good for the people and good for nature. With the globalization of the economy, multinational corporations are centers of power and propaganda. The development of alternative institutions is a central concern of green economists.

For supporters of the deep, long-range ecology movement, maximum cultural diversity is desirable. Thus, many supporters oppose centralized power of corporations. They support cognitive diversity.

Chapter 10

Reply to Bill Devall

Arne Næss

In the 1950s Feyerabend wrote a (critical but favorable) analysis of my *Interpretation and Preciseness*. When we later had a discussion he pretended to agree with me on all essential philosophical questions, whereas I thought that he did not separate heuristic methodology and methodology of testing hypotheses. "Anything goes!" is an excellent slogan in heuristics, but not in questions of testing. The Indian mathematical genius Ramanujan did not take proofs seriously, and when pressed by Westerners, he said that what a certain goddess told him in dreams certified his conclusions. Magic is fairly weak with regard to requirements of intersubjective, intercultural ways of testing. But I found Feyerabend's idea of freedom to choose magic instead of science in schools—and leaving out science if parents and pupils (mainly teenagers) agreed—very stimulating. And of course we agreed to talk about the scientific enterprise as a social undertaking. Industrial societies support science primarily for the sake of economic growth. The scientific enterprise of a Spinozistic society would focus on life quality, freedom, and strength of positive emotions.

Feyerabend was one of the very few colleagues who immediately endorsed my possibilism. I don't quite understand that we did not engage in public debates after the 1950s, and he did not mention our discussions in his autobiography. I certainly did not provoke him in any way. Perhaps that is the reason?

Bill Devall is right when he points to a certain mellowing of the cult of science at universities since the 1960s. Cultural and social anthropology and the Vietnam War have largely contributed to the decline of the cult of Western knowledge. Feyerabend with his *Feuer* and *Feier* has been one of the relevant forces. As to "social constructivism" and the so-called postmodern philosophy,

71

he would have detested these tendencies. He was after all a passionate seeker, not an advocate of petty, cozy cultural narratives.

Chapter 11

Spinoza's Environmental Ethics

Genevieve Lloyd

Some contemporary philosophers concerned with ethical issues related to the environment are looking to Spinoza in the hope of finding a firm metaphysical basis for environmental ethics.[1] Such a hope is by no means entirely misplaced. Spinoza, perhaps more than any other modern philosopher, is concerned with the integration of metaphysics and ethics, with the metaphysical bases of ethical positions. A very dominant theme in his thought, moreover, is the cultivation of what can only be described as an attitude of reverence for nature. Spinoza extends to the world as "Deus sive Natura" the attitude of reverence, love, and humility which religious orthodoxy had given to a transcendent God. He himself calls this attitude the "intellectual love of God." Related to this theme is Spinoza's constant insistence that man has no privileged position in nature. The cultivation of reason involves coming to grasp one's own status as part of a whole, subject to the same necessities that govern the rest of nature. This persistent theme of man as part of nature does, on the face of it, readily lend itself to the development of an environmental ethic. And it is reinforced by his treatment of individuality as essentially demanding integration between the individual and its surrounding totality of being.[2] Spinoza lays constant stress on the wider systems that comprise the sustaining framework for individual existence. His metaphysics of individuality, if it can be extricated from the assumptions of seventeenth-century dynamics, may well seem to flow naturally into an ethic of concern for the nonhuman constituents of reality. Finally, there is, of course, a certain ironic appeal in the prospect of being able to enlist a seventeenth-century arch-rationalist into the ranks of the environmental movement.

Despite all this, it would, I think, be quite misplaced to claim Spinoza as patron philosopher of the environmental movement. This is partly for obvious reasons. Spinoza's system is an extremely complex network of interconnected theses. And the whole is too abstruse and, in some crucial respects, too alien to modern thought for us to seriously envisage environmental education for the future fruitfully including a solid dose of Spinoza's repudiation of individual substance. But there is, in any case, another cluster of themes in Spinoza's thought which seems in fact to be strongly inimical to the possibility of an environmental ethic. Spinoza claims that morality is entirely circumscribed by the human species; that it is inextricably grounded in drives for human self-preservation; that other species can be ruthlessly exploited for human ends. And these are not, I think, themes that can be readily removed from Spinoza's system while leaving intact the theses that cluster around the theme of man as part of nature. Both spring from the same metaphysical presuppositions, and Spinoza himself certainly saw them as interconnected. It is precisely because Spinoza recognizes no privileged position for man with respect to nature that he is, in the contemporary phrase, a speciesist.[3] The very recognition of man as part of nature that looks, at first sight, so promising as a basis for an environmental ethic, for Spinoza goes hand in hand with a reasoned acquiescence in the exploitation of other species. Anyone who looks to the *Ethics* for a viable, coherent metaphysical system to ground a belief in the rights of the nonhuman will look in vain.

Is the relevance of Spinoza for environmental ethics then restricted to the possibility of extracting a few purple passages stimulating to the perception of man as part of nature? I think not. From our perspective, there is an extraordinary tension in Spinoza's juxtaposition of the theme of man, as part of nature, with a strongly anthropocentric morality. And this is itself of considerable philosophical interest. Spinoza sets himself firmly against a man-centered perception of the universe; against the view that man has a privileged place in the universe. But from this very insight he derives a moral position that seems unequivocally speciesist. The apparent strangeness of this juxtaposition throws into relief some major differences between the kinds of view that can be plausibly combined in seventeenth-century thought and in our own. Such contrasts serve, at the very least, to illuminate the structures of our own thought. But the apparent tension in Spinoza's thought also throws light, I think, on some confusing aspects of current debates on environmental ethics. Spinoza manages to combine a strong rejection of anthropocentric perception with an equally strong affirmation of a man-centered morality. That he manages to do so throws into question, I think, the assumption of many contemporary thinkers on environmental ethics that condemning man's exploitation of his environment involves extending the moral community to include the nonhuman.

To bring out the apparent tension in Spinoza's thought on man's relationship to his environment I will begin from a passage in the *Ethics* where he speaks on the rights of animals, and try to explicate some of the background assumptions of the stand he takes there. I will then look at some possible responses to Spinoza's rejection of animal rights from a contemporary standpoint.

Figure 11.1. *Ethica* is read in the cabin.

Finally, I will suggest that this tension becomes more intelligible in the light of Spinoza's treatment of the importance of truth to human beings; and that this throws into relief a puzzling tension in at least some contemporary formulations of the theme of man as part of nature.

The Rights of Animals

Spinoza addresses himself to the question of animal rights in the following passage:

> It is plain that the law against the slaughtering of animals is founded rather on vain superstition and womanish pity than on sound reason. The rational quest of what is useful to us further teaches us the necessity of associating ourselves with our fellowmen, but not with beasts, or things, whose nature is different

from our own; we have the same rights in respect to them as they have in respect to us. Nay, as everyone's right is defined by his virtue, or power, men
have far greater rights over beasts than beasts have over men. Still I do not
deny that beasts feel: what I deny is, that we may not consult our own advantage and use them as we please, treating them in the way which best suits us;
for their nature is not like ours, and their emotions are naturally different from
human emotions.[4]

Spinoza thinks, contrary to Descartes, that animals are sentient beings. This
follows from his account of minds as ideas of bodies. Any idea of a body with a
requisite degree of complexity will be for him a sentient mind. But being of a
different nature from ourselves—being, that is, ideas of bodies of a different
structure—their emotions are different from ours:

Horse and man are alike carried away by the desire of procreation, but the desire of the former is equine, the desire of the latter is human. So also the lusts
and appetites of insects, fishes, and birds must needs vary according to the several natures.[5]

Other species have their own joys, their own lusts. And this being so, they
cannot enter into collaboration with us in the shared pursuit of self-preservation,
of the enhancement of our own activity, which is the sole basis of morality.

No individual thing, which is entirely different from our own nature, can help
or check our power of activity, and absolutely nothing can do us good or harm,
unless it has something in common with our nature.[6]
. . . that which is entirely different from our nature can neither be to us good
nor bad.[7]

Everything that is incapable of entering into collaboration with us, Spinoza
sees as morally indifferent. This is a consequence of his grounding morality in a
Hobbesian drive towards self-preservation.

To act absolutely an obedience to virtue is in us the same thing as to act, to
live, or to preserve one's being (these three terms are identical in meaning) in
accordance with the dictates of reason on the basis of seeking what is useful to
one's self.[8]

This end is served by collaboration with other men. The rational pursuit of
intraspecies collaboration rests, for Spinoza, not on any Aristotelian conception of
man as by nature a social animal. He sees it rather as a natural extension of the
Hobbesian drive towards individual self-preservation. The Hobbesian principle
that every man is bound to seek what is useful to himself Spinoza sees not, as did
some of his contemporaries, as the foundation of impiety but rather that of piety
and virtue.[9] Man's self-preservation is fostered by collaboration with others of the

same species. An active fostering of the good of other men is a natural outcome of the rational man's pursuit of his own individuality.

> As every man seeks most that which is useful to him, so are men most useful one to another. For the more a man seeks what is useful to him and endeavors to preserve himself, the more is he endowed with virtue (IV. xx.), or, what is the same thing (IV Def. viii), the more is he endowed with power to act according to the laws of his own nature, that is, to live in obedience to reason. But men are most in natural harmony when they live in obedience to reason . . . therefore . . . men will be most useful one to another, when each seeks most that which is useful to him.[10]

> Let satirists then laugh their fill at human affairs, let theologians rail, and let misanthropes praise to their utmost the life of untutored rusticity, let them heap contempt on men and praises on beasts; when all is said, they will find that men can provide for their wants much more easily by mutual help, and that only by uniting their forces can they escape from the dangers that on every side beset them.[11]

The pursuit of self-preservation, which for Spinoza is what the life of reason really amounts to, would naturally issue, if left to itself, in willing collaboration without any need for external restraints. It is the passions that are the source of conflict and division in the pursuit of self-interest. The shared cultivation of reason draws men together, enhancing their own powers, their own activity, their own perfection. But men for the most part do not live in accordance with reason. And, given this, the Hobbesian picture of man emerging from the state of nature through recognition of the necessity of external restraints is an accurate one. Men come to avoid inflicting injury through fear of incurring a greater injury themselves.[12] The harmful, destructive passions are inhibited by the stronger emotion, fear. In an ideal situation this role of curbing the harmful passions would be played by reason. The knowledge of good and evil—the understanding of the passions—would be at all times a stronger emotion curbing the destructive impulse to harm others. But in the lack of reason's dominance it must be replaced by fear.

The contrast between the state of nature and the moral community which replaces it when men contract to accept a common authority is crucial to the understanding of Spinoza's position on animal rights and its relationship with the theme of man as part of nature. This contrast is reflected in a distinction between two kinds of rights. There are, first, the rights that apply to men in the state of nature along will everything else. And, secondly, there are rights that apply to men as citizens who have contracted into a state, agreeing to collaborate for the sake of thereby avoiding greater evil.

Animals have rights only in the first sense. And, for Spinoza, unlike Locke, natural right has no moral connotation. That animals have rights in this sense does not make them in any way members of a moral community. It is, for Spinoza, trivially true that the stronger—those who can do more, those with more power—have greater rights than the weaker. And it is in this sense that he says we have more rights in respect of animals than they have in respect of us. This is just because human bodies are superior to animal bodies; they are capable of a greater range of activity. We have more rights with respect to animals just in virtue of the fact that we have more power than them; that is to say, just in virtue of the fact that we can do more.

In the *Tractatus Theologico-Politicus*, Spinoza is more explicit about the amorality of the state of nature. Like Hobbes, he rejects any conception of natural law or natural rights as a basis of morality. Moral laws and rights are consequent on the emergence from the state of nature.

> By the right and ordinance of nature, I merely mean those natural laws wherewith we conceive every individual to be conditioned by nature, so as to live and act in a given way. For instance, fishes are naturally conditioned for swimming, and the greater for devouring the less; therefore fishes enjoy the water, and the greater devour the less by sovereign natural right.[13]

> In the state of nature every individual has sovereign right to do all that he can; in other words, the rights of an individual extend to the utmost limits of his power as it has been conditioned. Now it is the sovereign law and right of nature that each individual should endeavor to preserve itself as it is, without regard to anything but itself; therefore this sovereign law and right belongs to every individual, namely, to exist and act according to its natural conditions.[14]

This emphasis on the amorality of the state of nature is associated with Spinoza's rejection of a prevalent conception of reason. Like Hobbes he refuses to see the laws of reason as governing the whole of nature, or man as separated out from the rest of nature by having an innate grasp of those laws. Men in the state of nature are "no more bound to live by the dictates of an enlightened mind than a cat is bound to live by the laws of the nature of a lion."[15]

> The right and ordinance of nature, under which all men are born, and under which they mostly live, only prohibits such things as no one desires, and no one can attain: it does not forbid strife, nor hatred, nor anger, nor deceit, nor, indeed, any of the means suggested by desire.
> This we need not wonder at, for nature is not bounded by the laws of human reason which aims only at man's true benefit and preservation; her limits are infinitely wider and have reference to the eternal order of nature, wherein man is but a speck. . . . [16]

Here we see the interconnection between Spinoza's anthropocentric morality and his view of man as part of nature. It is a fundamental illusion, Spinoza thinks, to think of everything being arranged according to the dictates of human reason. Reason is a means for achieving what is good for us. It has no bearing on what is good for the rest of reality. It is of importance only for that small speck of reality which consists in human life. But, having thus put reason in its place, Spinoza goes on to insist on the crucial importance of the dictates of reason for human good.

> Nevertheless, no one can doubt that it is much better for us to live according to the laws and assured dictates of reason, for they have men's true good for their object. . . .
>
> When we reflect that men without mutual help, or the aid of reason, must needs live most miserably . . . we shall plainly see that men must necessarily come to an agreement to live together as securely and well as possible if they are to enjoy as a whole the rights which naturally belong to them as individuals, and their life should be no more conditioned by the force and desire of individuals, but by the power and will of the whole body.[17]

Spinoza comes back to the theme of the irrelevance of the dictates of reason to the rest of reality in the Appendix to Part One of the *Ethics*, in a virulent attack on those "prejudices and superstitions" which have taken root in the human mind around the theme of final causes:

> As they find in themselves and outside themselves many means which assist them not a little in their search for what is useful, for instance, eyes for seeing, teeth for chewing, herbs and animals for yielding food, the sun for giving light, the sea for breeding fish, etc., they come to look on the whole of nature as a means for obtaining such conveniences. Now as they are aware, that they think they have found these conveniences and did not make them, they think they have cause for believing, that some other being has made them for their use.[18]

They come then to believe in some "ruler or rulers of the universe endowed with human freedom, who have arranged and adapted everything for human use," who direct the whole course of nature for the satisfaction of men's "blind cupidity and insatiable avarice."[19]

> Thus the prejudice developed into superstition, and took deep root in the human mind; and for this reason everyone strove most zealously to understand and explain the final causes of things; but in their endeavor to show that nature does nothing in vain, i.e., nothing which is useless to man, they only seem to have demonstrated that nature, the gods and men are all mad together.[20]
>
> Such persons firmly believe that there is an *order* in things, being really ignorant both of things and their own nature.[21]

The basic form of these superstitions is mistaking man's position in nature, in thinking that it is in reference to him that things are to be judged more or less perfect. But such reasoners, Spinoza says in concluding the Appendix, are:

> easily confuted, for the perfection of things is to be reckoned only from their own nature and power; things are not more or less perfect, according as they delight or offend human senses, or according as they are serviceable or repugnant to mankind.[22]

The doctrine of man's privileged place in the universe was of course prevalent in the Judaeo-Christian tradition. It was, no doubt, part of popular consciousness in the seventeenth century. The targets of Spinoza's attack here were probably some fairly crude theological statements of the doctrine. But there is no lack of evidence of the same idea occurring in sober philosophical treatises in the seventeenth century. Thus Locke, in his discussion of man in the state of nature in the early sections of the Second Treatise says

> there cannot be supposed any such subordination among us that may authorize us to destroy one another, as if we were made for one another's uses, as the inferior ranks of creatures are for ours.[23]

The doctrine occurs, in a rather more sophisticated form, also in Leibniz. "If we think that God has made the world only for us, it is a great blunder," he says in the *Discourse on Metaphysics*.[24] But he does think nonetheless that all the other creatures should serve intelligent souls, the "citizens of the republic of the universe whose monarch is God."[25]

> The difference between intelligent substances and those which are not intelligent is quite as great as between a mirror and one who sees.[26]
> The spirits with which (God) can, so to speak, enter into conversation and even into social relations by communicating to them in particular ways his feelings and his will so that they are able to know and love their benefactor, must be much nearer to him than the rest of created things which may be regarded as the instruments of spirits.[27]

But for Leibniz the role of other creatures as "instruments of spirits" is not confined to such mundane purposes as providing food:

> A single spirit is worth a whole world, because it not only expresses the whole world, but it also knows it and governs itself as does God. In this way we may say that though every substance expresses the whole universe, yet the other substances express the world rather than God, while spirits express God rather than the world. This nature of spirits so noble that it enables them to approach divinity as much as is possible for created things, has as a result that God derives infinitely more glory from them than from the other beings, or rather the other beings furnish to spirits the material for glorifying him.[28]

Spinoza's acquiescence in the exploitation of other species has, we have seen, a very different basis from this anthropocentric perception of the world, which he categorically condemns. But this rejection of anthropocentric perception, we have also seen, is linked with a thoroughly anthropocentric morality. We are more perfect than the animals: that is, we are capable of a wider range of activities. It is not that he sees this as a reason or a justification for our having "more rights over them than they should have over us." To be more perfect is just to be more active, to have more power. And virtue is just doing what enhances our activity.[29]

The Requirements of an Environmental Ethic

Animals, then, have rights only in the sense of natural right. And for Spinoza—like Hobbes, and unlike Locke—natural right is not a moral matter. Moral rights arise only within the framework of a moral community and this is species-relative. It depends on a shared nature. What is good for us is not at all commensurable with the goods of other species. There is, I think, no way for Spinoza to even express the view that our goods ought to be curtailed for the sake of the goods of other animals. The "ought" will not straddle the gap between our moral community and the state of nature where the other animals reside. To use Passmore's distinction, man is not a "despot of nature" in the way suggested by the perception of other species as existing for human good; but nor is he a "steward of nature," responsible for the good of other species less perfect than himself.[30]

It seems, then, that we cannot extract from Spinoza's thought even a basis for the responsible concern for the environment which Passmore expresses in the picture of man as steward of nature; an approach which many contemporary writers find too conservative to provide a viable basis for a genuine environmental ethic.

Spinoza's system does, of course, provide a basis for so-called instrumental arguments, grounded in human interest, for responsibility towards nature, for concern with man's habitat. But this, of course, is not what many environmental philosophers are looking for. The demand is for an ethic, which will give other species a claim on human concern in cases where this seems not to be demanded by what is good for human beings. "Human interests and preferences," Richard Routley claims, "are far too parochial to provide a satisfactory basis for deciding on what is environmentally desirable."[31] And Rolston, in an article dissecting what requirements would have to be met by an ethic that was "genuinely ecological," says:

> If Leopold's preserving the ecosystem is merely ancillary to human interests, the veiled antecedent ought is still that we ought to maximize human good. Were we so to maximize the ecosystem we should have a corporate anthropological egoism, "human chauvinism," not a planetary altruism. The optimum ecosystem would be but a prudential means to human welfare, and our antecedent ought would no longer be primarily ecological, but as before, simply a familiar one, incidentally ecological in its prudence.[32]

It is not clear that such an "incidentally ecological" ethic stands to gain much from the provision of a metaphysical basis. We do not, after all, need metaphysical arguments to get men to pursue what can be shown to be in their own self-interest. Spinoza himself has a very strong statement of the overridingness of self-interest:

Everyone will, of two goods, choose that which he thinks the greatest, and of
two evils that which he thinks the least. . . . This law is so deeply implanted in
the human mind that it ought to be counted among eternal truths and axioms.[33]

What environmental philosophers seem to be looking for, in contrast, is a
basis for the judgment that some activities that are regarded as good for human
beings should be curtailed *because* they are bad for other parts of nature. And
we seem to have drawn a blank in looking for this in Spinoza's thought.

Can we patch up Spinoza's thought to make its central insights more amenable to reconstruction as a genuinely ecological ethic? Much of what Spinoza
says, we might think, reflects the circumstances and knowledge of the time
rather than what we might claim as the timeless truth of the ethical system itself.
Can it be brought into line with the contemporary scene in ways that would
enable us to salvage it as a basis for an environmental ethic? For a start, we
might try to break down the rigidity of Spinoza's conception of what does and
does not "share a common nature with us." Is there not something arbitrary
about the setting of boundaries between natures? Can we perhaps recognize, as
he could not, a common nature between ourselves and at any rate some other
species? But in so far as it rests on scientific knowledge, Spinoza's insistence on
a difference in nature between us and other animal species rests ultimately on
difference in bodily structure. The availability of more information about bodily
structure might uncover unsuspected continuities. But it could also be expected
to reinforce Spinoza's perception of the differences between human beings and
other animals. The concept of sharing a nature is too imprecise here to allow of
any confidence that advances in scientific knowledge would allow for an extension of the privilege of "sharing our nature" to other kinds of animals.

There is, in any case, another aspect of Spinoza's talk of common natures
which seems to go against any attempt to extend his notion of sharing our nature
to nonhumans. There is a nominalist strand in his thought which does not readily lend itself to the abstracting of common natures. Men's common nature that
underlies their creation of a moral community is not something statically present
to be discerned by reason. The morally significant common nature between men
seems rather to be something that is *achieved* through the cultivation of reason.
There seems little prospect of extending the relevant kind of nature-sharing to
the nonhuman without departing completely from Spinoza's thought.

Stanley Benn has suggested that the range of "right-bearer" might be extended to include animals capable of engaging in projects.[34] But on Spinoza's
concept of a moral right the mere capacity to engage in projects would not suffice for membership of the moral community. The moral significance of the
shared nature of human beings derives from their being able to collaborate in the
pursuit of reason. Those who share our nature in the relevant way have to be not
merely capable of engaging in projects; they have to be capable of realizing the
advantages to them of accepting a common authority. Thus even the current
generation of apes who have been taught sign language would not be moral right

bearers for Spinoza unless they were able, for example, to realize the advantages to them of being brought up like human children. The mere fact that they can talk to humans would not, I think, shake Spinoza's speciesism.

It is not clear that we can salvage Spinoza's thought here by pointing to advances in knowledge. We might, alternatively, try to reconstruct it by extricating it from its surrounding social circumstances. Spinoza in a contemporary setting, we might say, would surely see man's well-being as more bound up with that of other species than it was possible to foresee in the seventeenth century. It was at that stage possible to see the well-being of animals as quite independent of that of man. And it was plausible, therefore, to see concern for their well-being as anti-human, as expressing a preference for beasts; or else as expressing an exaggerated sense of our own importance in the universe. But the impact of human beings on the environment has of course accelerated since then. The capacity of animals to get on with "enjoying their own lusts" depends to a greater extent than Spinoza would have thought possible on our decisions. And this, we might say, *makes* valid the perception of human beings as responsible for the rest of nature. Man's activity in the world has made it true. It is no longer, then, a matter of how we *ought* to perceive our position in the universe but of acknowledging what we have done.

Whatever the intrinsic merits of these points I do not think they can be utilized in a reconstruction of Spinoza's thought. The suggestion amounts to an adaptation of Spinoza's insights to take account of the humanization of the world. I do not think it can withstand the intrusion of that perception. Spinoza would in fact, I think, reject this way of describing what has happened to man's relationship to the rest of nature. The supposed humanization of the world he would see as an illusion, as a product of the very anthropocentric perception that he castigates in the *Ethics*. What has happened, he would say, is a falsification of reality. And, whatever the remedy, it does not lie in treating as a fact the humanization of the world. To pursue this approach to the problem would, I think, amount not to an extension of Spinoza's system but to abandoning it.

There is, however, another way of approaching the challenge to reconcile Spinoza's thought with contemporary ethical insights about the environment. Spinoza's ethical system is centered in self-preservation, in the survival of human beings. He sees the pursuit of human activities as an extension and enrichment of this basic pursuit of self-preservation—the maintenance and enrichment of human existence. But he has a very definite conception of the kind of behavior that in fact enhances human activity and hence human perfection. It is, basically, the cultivation of reason, the pursuit of truth. And the ultimate expression of this human endeavor is the intellectual love of God, a detached, selfless perception of things as parts of wholes and as modes of substance. These are the ends Spinoza sees as the achievement of human good, in relation to which concern with the goods of other species is an irrelevant, anthropomorphic distraction. But the contemporary human activities and ends that prompt the concern of the environmentalists are, of course, very far removed from these rationalist ideals.

We can, Spinoza says, use animals in any way useful to us. But his conception of what is useful to human beings would certainly exclude many of the projects taken in the contemporary scene to justify the use of animals. Some current goals which involve as means the exploitation of other species are very far removed from Spinoza's conception of the intellectual love of God. Many of them could readily be brought under his criticism of men's distracted preoccupation with short-term goals pursued in the blindness of passion against their long-term interests.[35] Using animals in ways that are useful for us means, for him, using them in ways that enhance *our* activity, *our* perfection. But this human perfection characteristically issues in an attitude of reverence for the whole of nature. Spinoza's remark that we can use animals in any way we see fit has to be taken in the context of a much more limited range of exploitative acts than that since made possible by advanced technology. It may be that we could extract from a Spinozistic ethic a condemnation of some forms of human exploitation of other species. But again, this would be based on assessment of the activities involved from the point of view of human well-being—on the irrelevance, or, in some cases, the inconsistency of the end with Spinoza's paradigm of virtuous activity—the detached appreciation of oneself as part of nature, the "intellectual love of God." All that this yields is some restriction on what use of other species a contemporary Spinoza would recognize as enhancing human good.

We are here still within the limits of an ethic grounded in human interests. What has emerged is that, given Spinoza's conception of what are ultimate human goods, his claim that we can use animals in any way useful to us is less exploitative than might at first appear. But, it might be replied, all this presupposes that we are prepared to accept Spinoza's valuation of the contemplative life. And this, after all, is, in our contemporary scene, a restricted taste. Intellectual contemplation is not a basic human interest of a kind we could expect to impress on all those individuals and institutions whose current laying waste of the environment is a cause for concern.

It now seems, at best, that we can salvage for Spinoza some basis for that condemnation of the use of other species in pursuing trivial human ends, or ends that can be shown to be in conflict with the acquisition of what he calls the intellectual love of God. We can perhaps reconcile some of his heavier remarks about the use of animals with contemporary sensitivity to the exploitation of other species. But this is a far cry from being able to find in the *Ethics* a basis for concern with the well-being of the rest of nature.

Can we extract more than this from Spinoza? Can we utilize his thought in articulating what Rolston calls a genuinely ecological ethic, which treats the nonhuman as in themselves proper objects of human moral concern?[36] Or are we to say that Spinoza's thought cannot be reconciled with the most important moral insights of the environmental movement? Environmental ethics wants to be able to express the moral judgment that human goods should in some circumstances be curtailed for the sake of what is good for the rest of the world; that the goods of other things should be taken into account in our moral judgments.

If Spinoza's ethical system, making morality entirely species-relative, makes it impossible to say such things, then does not that in itself show that system to be defective as a vehicle for the articulation of contemporary moral consciousness? But what exactly is it that Spinoza cannot express? And how crucial is it to a viable environmental ethic? Spinoza's system does make it impossible to extend the moral community to include other animals. And it also makes it impossible to conceive of ourselves as stewards of nature, as morally answerable for its well-being. These ways of construing the claims of the nonhuman on our moral concern seem to be ruled out by Spinoza's rejection of the view of reason as relevant to the whole of reality and of man's rationality as conferring on him a privileged position in the scheme of things. He would regard them as unacceptably anthropocentric in their perception of man's position in the universe. But this emphasis on the point of view, as it were, of the nonhuman should perhaps itself be seen as a rather dubious element in contemporary debate on environmental ethics.

It is common for contemporary writers on environmental ethics to run together being an object of moral concern and being included in a moral community. The proper locus of moral questions, we are told, should shift from the interests of the human individual or even the species to the ecosystem. As Aldo Leopold puts it:

> The land ethic simply enlarges the boundaries of the community to include soils, waters, plants, and animals, or collectively, the land.[37]

> A thing is right when it tends to preserve the integrity, stability, and beauty of the biotic community. It is wrong when it tends otherwise.[38]

Studying Spinoza's version of the theme that man is part of nature is of value here in casting doubt on the assumption that we need to extend the moral community, to treat the nonhuman as bearers of rights, etc., in order to treat the nonhuman as morally relevant. The nonhuman for Spinoza have no rights in any moral sense. What is not human is not part of our moral community. It is quite wrong to suggest, as George Sessions has done, that Leopold and Spinoza share the view that the total system of nature should be seen as ethically fundamental.[39] Nonhuman things can be objects of moral concern. But this does not involve, as Leopold suggests, their goods entering into our moral judgments.

Let us look again at what is involved in Spinoza's repudiation of man's supposed privileged position in nature. This involves seeing reason as a speck in the universe. But that speck is nonetheless absolutely crucial for the good of man. What this means is that truth becomes for Spinoza an absolute good, an intrinsic value, although this value of course remains circumscribed as what is good *for man*. In the concern for truth, which plays so central a role in Spinoza's system, we have a "human interest" with a difference. Spinoza's thought here straddles the gap that is assumed in much current debate on environmental ethics between instrumental, man-centered values and intrinsic values. Spinoza cannot say: "Things (such as butterflies, whales, rain forests) are good, or have value, or have rights, independently of man." But he can say: "It is *good for man* to perceive things as independent of himself. It is good for man, that is, to perceive things as they really are. It is good for man to perceive things truly."

Conclusion

We began with the apparent strangeness of Spinoza's juxtaposition of a morality circumscribed by human interests and repudiation of an anthropocentric perception of the world. By now, I hope, this juxtaposition should appear less strange. And, at the same time, the juxtaposition of stances characteristic of much current debate on environmental ethics can be seen as itself containing some tensions. A rejection of anthropocentricity in morals is quite often juxtaposed with what seems nonetheless a thoroughly anthropocentric way of perceiving the nonhuman. And this seems strange. We are, it seems, supposed to render morality less anthropocentric by humanizing the nonhuman. We are recommended to extend to animals the status of "preference-havers" or "project-initiators" and, on the basis of this, to regard them as "right-bearers". Again, we are urged to regard nonhuman things as bearers of intrinsic value, as things whose existence and preservation we ought to see as somehow good in themselves, independently of us, demanding that our own good be curtailed accordingly.

Consideration of Spinoza's *Ethics* casts light on what seems incoherent about this talk of nonhuman intrinsic values, and, at the same time, on what it is about this notion that captures something we very much want to be able to say. According to Spinoza, we cannot recognize any nonhuman intrinsic values. But we do not have to think that there are such values in order to be able to see it as a *human* good to perceive things as independent of ourselves: the contrast here is the one I adverted to earlier between (1) things are good, are of value, independently of human beings; and (2) it is good for human beings to perceive things as independent of them, that is, to perceive them as they really are.

Spinoza's approach captures also, I think, something of what is attractive in the suggestion that concern for the ecosystem should replace concern for the self construed as set over against and competing with its environment. Rolston makes the point in a picturesque way:

> Ecology does not know an encapsulated ego over against his environment . . .
> The self metabolically, if metaphorically, interpenetrates the ecosystem. The
> world is my body.[40]

Spinoza's system gives metaphysical content to this fanciful sounding idea of perceiving the world as my body. But it is a matter of transcending a distorted perception of our true position in nature; not of treating the nonhuman as bearers of rights or values in relation to which human rights and values should be curtailed. In a letter, Spinoza compares our fragmented, distorted perception of the world to that of a worm in the blood, perceiving parts without grasping their relation to wider wholes:

> Let us now, if you please, imagine that a small worm lives in the blood, whose sight is keen enough to distinguish the particles of blood, lymph, etc., and his reason to observe how each part on collision with another either rebounds, or communicates a part of its own motion, etc. That worm would live in this blood as we live in this part of the universe, and he would consider each particle of blood to be a whole, and not a part. And he could not know how all the parts are controlled by the universal nature of blood, and are forced, as the universal nature of blood demands, to adapt themselves to one another, so as to harmonize with one another in a certain way.[41]

Human individuals, for Spinoza, are located in wider systems to which they stand in the same kind of relationship as that in which, in his example, the particles of the blood stand to the blood. And the cultivation of reason involves the mind's coming to grasp the body of which it is the idea, and hence itself, as parts of a whole.

The concern for truth is here not without moral relevance. Such a change in perception can be expected to have some influence on behavior. Children educated to regard themselves as "but a part of nature" would, for the most part, surely, orientate themselves differently towards other species from those who are explicitly taught that man holds a privileged position in the universe. At least some of our exploitative responses to the nonhuman rest on the implicit belief that the rest of nature exists for us and can be expected to wither away if this implicit belief is brought into the open and rejected.

Spinoza, I have argued, would endorse the condemnation of any exploitation of the rest of nature, that rests on an implicit belief in man as the center of the universe. But what would concern him about it is precisely that it does express a false belief about man's place in nature; that it expresses an ignorant, distorted attitude. As Stuart Hampshire puts it, such behavior manifests a false philosophy of dominance, "as if men were situated in the world as in their own garden."[42]

Morality, on the Spinozistic approach, remains circumscribed by what is good for the human species. But it is good for human beings to perceive themselves as parts of wider systems, as parts of wholes; to perceive themselves as they really are.

Such an ethic remains man-centered. Spinoza would not endorse Sessions's condemnation of the failure of what he sees as the "humanistic approach to Nature" to put the stability and well-being of the total system before the survival and well-being of human beings:

> An ostensibly humanitarian rationale, untempered by a knowledge of population dynamics, provided the impetus for the technological assistance which led to the dramatic declines in death rates in the "underdeveloped" countries after WWII, thus contributing significantly to their unparalleled population explo-

sions. And now when this added population is starving in great numbers, a humanistic attitude dictates trying to feed all of these people together with their exponentially increasing progeny, again blissfully ignoring the ecological consequences of this course of action. . . .[43]

A Spinozistic ethic, in contrast, would treat the survival and well-being of human beings as the proper locus of morality, regarding any attempt to shift the locus of morality beyond human concerns to the well-being of the total system as itself expressing an anthropocentric perception of man's place in the universe.

We may still feel that Spinoza's ethical system can be judged as deficient from the standpoint of contemporary concern with man as part of his environment. Spinoza sees human beings as parts of wider systems. But his rationalism precludes not only anthropocentric perception of man as the center of the universe, but also the recognition of any bonds of sympathy between ourselves and the rest of nature. Again, without his account of the emergence of the state, his dichotomy between the human and the nonhuman parts of the total system of nature may well strike us as altogether too sharp. But, from the other direction, we can also see, I think, from the standpoint of Spinoza's version of the theme of man as part of nature, some gaps in contemporary argumentation for extending the moral horizons to take account of the nonhuman. Rejecting any privileged position for man in the universe does not commit us to regarding the nonhuman as having moral rights; or to introducing any new, epistemologically puzzling, nonhuman intrinsic values. It can be seen as just a reaffirmation of a pretty old intrinsic value—the concern for truth. Whether Spinoza's own explanation of exactly why truth is good for human beings can be salvaged in a form that would be relevant to contemporary moral consciousness is, of course, another matter.

Notes

This chapter is reprinted with minor revisions from *Inquiry* 23 (1980): 293-311.

[1] See especially George Sessions, "Anthropocentrism and the Environmental Crisis," *Humboldt Journal of Social Relations* 2 (Fall/Winter, 1974); "Panpsychism versus Modern Materialism: Some Implications for an Ecological Ethics," expanded version of paper delivered at the conference on "The Rights of Nonhuman Nature" held at Pitzer College, Claremont, California, April 1974; and "Spinoza and Jeffers on Man in Nature," *Inquiry* 20 (1977). The implications of Spinozism for ecology are also discussed by Arne Næss in "The Shallow and the Deep, Long-Range Ecology Movement: A Summary," *Inquiry* 16 (1973) and "Spinoza and Ecology," *Philosophia* 7 (1977).

[2] See especially the treatment of individual bodies in the digression after Prop. XIII of Pt. II of the *Ethics*.

[3] Sessions notes the existence of this opposed theme in Spinoza's thought in his informal newsletter "Ecophilosophy," No. 1, April 1976; and in "Spinoza and Jeffers on Man in Nature," 507. But he does not recognise its interconnection with the theme of man as part of nature.

[4] Note I to Prop. XXXVII, Pt. IV of the *Ethics*; in R. H. M. Elwes (trans.), *The Chief Works of Benedict de Spinoza* (New York: Dover, 1955) 11: 213.

[5] Note to Prop. LVII, Pt. III; Elwes, 170.

[6] Prop. XXIX, Pt. IV; Elwes, 206.

[7] Proof to Prop. XXIX, Pt. IV; Elwes, 206.

[8] Prop. XXIV, Pt. IV; Elwes, 204.

[9] Note to Prop. XVIII, Pt. IV; Elwes, 202.

[10] Corollary 2 to Prop. XXXV, Pt. IV; Elwes, 210. Note to Prop. XXXV, Pt. IV; Elwes, 210.

[11] Note to Prop. XXXV, Pt. IV; Elwes, 210.

[12] Note 2 to Prop. XXXVII, Pt. IV; Elwes, 214.

[13] *A Theologico-Political Treatise*, in R. H. M. Elwes (trans.), *The Chief Works of Benedict de Spinoza* (New York: Dover, 1951) 1: 200.

[14] *A Theologico-Political Treatise*, 200–1.

[15] *A Theologico-Political Treatise*, 201.

[16] *A Theologico-Political Treatise*, 202.

[17] *A Theologico-Political Treatise*, 202–3.

[18] *Ethics,* App. to Pt.1; Elwes, 11: 75–76.

[19] *Ethics*, 76.

[20] *Ethics*, 76.

[21] *Ethics*, 79.

[22] *Ethics*, 81.

[23] Locke, *An Essay Concerning the True Original, Extent and End of Civil Government* (London: Everyman, 1924), chap. 11, p. 120.

[24] Leibniz, *Discourse on Metaphysics*, chap. 19; in G. R. Montgomery (trans.) *Leibniz: Basic Writings* (La Salle: Open Court, 1962), 34.

[25] *Discourse on Metaphysics*, chap. 12, p. 19.

[26] *Discourse on Metaphysics*, chap. 35, p. 59.

[27] *Discourse on Metaphysics*, chap. 35, p. 60.

[28] *Discourse on Metaphysics*, chap. 36, p. 61.

[29] *Ethics*, Prop. XXIV, Pt. IV; Elwes, 11: 204.

[30] Passmore, *Man's Responsibility for Nature* (London: Duckworth, 1974).

[31] Routley, "Is There a Need for a New, an Environmental Ethic?" *Proceedings of the XVth World Congress of Philosophy* (Varna 1973), 210.

[32] Holmes Rolston III, "Is There an Ecological Ethic?", *Ethics* 85 (1975): 103.

[33] *A Theologico-Political Treatise*, chap. XVI, Elwes, 1: 203.

[34] Benn, "Personal Freedom and Environmental Ethics: the Moral Inequality of Species," paper at the World Congress on Philosophy of Law and Social Philosophy, St. Louis, Missouri, Aug. 1975.

[35] *Ethics*, Prop. LXVI, Pt. IV; Elwes, 11: 231.

[36] Rolston, "Is There an Ecological Ethic?"

[37] Leopold, "The Land Ethic," in *A Sand County Almanac* (Oxford: Oxford University Press, 1949), 219.

[38] *A Sand County Almanac*, 240.

[39] George Sessions, "Panpsychism versus Modern Materialism," 24; "Anthropocentrism and the Environmental Crisis," 10.

[40] Rolston, "Is There an Ecological Ethic?" 104.

[41] Spinoza, Letter to Oldenburg (XXXII); in A.Wolf (ed.), *The Correspondence of Spinoza* (London: Cass, 1966), 210–11.

[42] Hampshire, *Two Theories of Morality* (Oxford: Oxford University Press, 1977), 91. George Sessions, "Anthropocentrism and the Environmental Crisis," 10.

[43] George Sessions, "Anthropocentrism and the Environmental Crisis," 10.

Chapter 12

Environmental Ethics and Spinoza's Ethics: Comments on Genevieve Lloyd's Article

Arne Næss

1. Spinoza is unsuitable as a patron philosopher of any contemporary movement, including the environmental and ecological. His system and his thinking in general are overwhelmingly complicated, and his terminology in central areas utterly foreign to contemporary jargons.

But this does not exclude the possibility that he is an inexhaustible source of inspiration for those who look for a philosophy explicating deep attitudes and assumptions within certain parts of the international ecological and environmental movement.

Admirers of Spinoza quite naturally tend to interpret him so as to minimize the conflicts between his and their thought. The result is a variety of representations of Spinoza. But if the intention is to provide more or less free reconstructions, well and good. And this is what is relevant, as I see it, in relation to what is sometimes called the "deep ecological movement" and the "green philosophy and ecopolitics."[1]

2. Genevieve Lloyd rightly points to some aspects of Spinoza's philosophy which seem severely to limit its possibilities as a kind of metaphysics of environmental movements. Of the many points worth commenting upon in her article, I shall pick out some on which I disagree. Roughly, my conclusion here is that Lloyd makes Spinoza too much like Hobbes, that she makes "intellectualis" in the formula "intellectualis amor Dei" too intellectual, and *amor Dei* a love that is aloof in relation to particular beings, as if one could love this *Deus sive*

Natura otherwise than through particulars—all of them more or less animated (IIP13S).[2] Thirdly, Lloyd seems to think that an active life, like that of Jan de Witt or Rachel Carson, could not be a life of somebody who intensively cultivates the third, the intuitive, way of understanding.

3. Harry Austyn Wolfson, the historian and interpreter of Spinoza, asserted, and even confirmed to a remarkable degree, that there are practically no ideas in the *Ethics* which are not borrowed from or at least inspired by others. But he also maintained that every part is built into a whole that is distinctively and uniquely Spinoza's. The more than one hundred terms with important functions within the structure of Spinoza's system are intimately and explicitly connected, not only through definitions, but also through various expressions of kinds of equivalence. (Examples: "x is the same thing as y," "x is nothing else than y," "x signifies the same as y," "by x I mean the same as y," "by x and y I understand the same.")[3] It is therefore unlikely that Spinoza should have any crucial concept (if as a nominalist he has any) such as "self-preservation" in common with another philosopher, for instance Hobbes.

Spinoza's *Ethics* is an unhomogeneous work with parts probably stemming from somewhat different periods and written under different influences. Some parts are rather rigorously constructed: the propositions, axioms, definitions. The structure of the system is revealed at its purest in these parts. Then come the demonstrations, often quite as rigorous, but occasionally conversational and in the manner of notes. Some of the latter contain points of importance for the structure of the system, e.g. IIP40S2, but on the whole they reflect opinions more loosely connected and presented with less systematic import. In them, Spinoza talks more directly and personally to us; the same holds good of the Appendices. In what follows I attach more weight to the propositions than to the notes, and more weight to the interrelations of terms (for instance, between virtue, power, perfection, joy, rationality) than to isolated terms.

4. Central to Lloyd's conception of a metaphysics of environmentalism is the moral badness of exploiting animals for the sake of humans, and in general, of not treating the nonhuman realm as an end or value in itself. The term "moral" is used throughout her argumentation. But isn't Spinoza's philosophy one of generosity, fortitude, and love rather than of morals? Do we need to shift to moralizing in order to find a satisfactory metaphysics of environmentalism? If so Spinoza cannot be of much help. Let us elaborate this point a little.

Spinoza does not use the terms "morale," "moralis" in his *Ethics*. The term "mos" he uses sometimes, as in "more geometrico," but not in senses we would nowadays translate as "moral" or "morals." The nearest term for what we call morals is "pietas." This term is often translated as "moral". But its relation to reason is much closer than that of our term "moral": "the desire . . . to do good, that stems from this, that we live led by reason I call piety" (IVP37S1). It follows: When we are not led by reason we cannot experience the desire Spinoza terms "pietas." Anyhow, "pietas" like "religio" does not belong to the basic structure of the system.

It is doubtful whether the translation "moral" is adequate anywhere in the *Ethics* where Spinoza rigorously exhibits his system. The opinion that he is one of the greatest opponents of moralism that ever lived seems not altogether unreasonable.

In any case, to talk of "Spinoza's concept of a moral right" is misleading. The same holds of the concepts "the moral community," "moral right bearers," "moral laws," "morality" and "immorality." Such concepts are not part of his system.

Lloyd is right to insist that the human communities, according to Spinoza, cannot have other members than humans. But these communities are hardly moral communities. I suspect that Lloyd goes wrong when she makes a distinction between moral and natural right, which is foreign to Spinoza. Spinoza may be said to have a concept of natural right (different from that of Hobbes), but not a concept of moral right. (She thinks this makes Spinoza unsuitable for some or all environmental ethicists, but I think the opposite is the case. More about this below.)

Furthermore, in the *Ethics* Spinoza uses the term *jus civitatis* to cover rights upheld by force, not by morality. The members of society, that is, those protected by its laws are the citizens (IVP37S2). Laws nowadays protect animals in many ways, and there is a tendency to say that certain animals have certain rights under these laws. Presumably such a terminology would be unacceptable to Spinoza, but not because only humans have moral rights.

5. Let us then inspect the natural right of animals according to Spinoza. "The same right (*jus*) that they [the beasts] have in relation to us, we have in relation to them" (IVP37S1). But humans "have much more right in relation to animals (*bruta*) than they have in relation to humans" (IVP37S1). It seems that Spinoza derives this pronouncement from an equivalence of virtue and power. Or rather, at least in this context, a reduction of relations of the kind "x has a right in relation to y" to relations of the kind "x has power in relation to y."

Clearly this kind of right is universal and operates among people. It is not superseded by *jus civitatis*, rights of the citizen. Because "each one's right is defined by his virtue or power" (ibid.), and people have virtues and powers when living in societies, the natural right is present under every circumstance. Power and virtue being unequally distributed among men, some men will have more natural right than others. What we can do to other people we have the natural right to do, whatever the circumstances.

This sounds rather crude, but only when we forget the peculiar position of the term "power" within the system.

It is natural today to think of power as power *over* rather than power *to*. But in Spinoza *potentia* is a mere substantivation of the verb *posse*, to be able to. There is an intimate connection between "to be able to" and to act, rather than to be acted upon. The second definition of Part Three is crucial here:

We say that we act (*agere*), when something in us or outside us happens, of which we are adequate cause, that is (by the previous definition), when something in us or outside us follows from our nature, which can be clearly and distinctively understood by it [our nature] alone.

Our power is proportional to the extent to which we are the adequate cause of something, which again, according to the above definition, is proportional to the extent to which what is done follows from our nature or essence alone, and not from any pressure upon us. When we act in the sense introduced, we persevere (*perseverare*) in our being or essence.

The power or essence of a particular human being is a genuine part of God's or nature's power or essence: "Man's power, in so far as it explicates his actual essence, is part of god's or Nature's infinite power, that is (*per Prop. 34, Part 1*), essence" (IVP4Dem).

People who are powerful in the sense of being able to crush others need not be powerful in Spinoza's sense. They may be slaves under passive affects, rarely being able to act, and mostly being acted upon (*pati*).

Let us consider two hunters, one is shooting a fox for fun, the other as part of a plan to exterminate rabies. They both have power *over* the animal. What Spinoza asks the hunters is whether their reactions are proper acts, that is, whether their behavior can be understood on the basis of their nature and essence alone. If so, the behavior suggests powerfulness, if not, powerlessness (slavery).

Whereas Spinoza's system makes use of the term "power" to express ability to act from one's nature or essence alone, Spinoza may of course, in notes or letters, use the term in ways which are not consistent with this use.

Adopting the terminology of the system, "to have the right to do anything that is in our power" is not menacing. The more powerful the agents the less chance of reactions due to hatred, jealousy, and the other passive affects. The menace stems from those who have much power over us, but are largely powerless in Spinoza's sense.

6. According to IVP29 things with a completely different nature from ourselves cannot help or hinder our power to act (and therefore our self-preservation and level of perfection). If we use the harsh Notes IVP37S1 (quoted by Lloyd) and IVP57S to establish the strange thesis that human and nonhuman beings are completely different, the latter cannot either help or hinder our power to act. They are on a par with stones.

But Spinoza's use of the term "entirely" or "completely" (*prorsus*) lends itself to an overestimation of the difference according to what he himself maintains, namely that animals, like humans, feel and have drives and ideas.

The examples offered by Spinoza in IVP37S show that he admits of identical or similar traits in beasts and men. "Horses and men are filled with the desire of procreation." Men and insects have "lusts and appetites" in common. Men and all living beings have in common that they rejoice in the specific nature (or essence) they possess: "The joy of one only differs in nature from the joy of another in so far as the essence of one differs from the essence of another." They all have joys (*laetitia*) and sorrows (*tristitia*).

On the basis of Definitions 2 and 3 of the emotions in Part Three, this may imply that animals may increase or decrease in perfection. If one points out that the definitions are of human joy and human sorrow, this is not a decisive objection. Spinoza certainly allows animals to have desire (*cupiditas*), but he nevertheless confines himself to a definition of human desire. The narrowness of the definition does not imply that the term cannot be applied to a wider area.

Spinoza also stresses that there are great differences of nature or essence among individual humans: "There is a considerable difference between the joy of, for instance, a drunkard and that which possesses a philosopher" (IVP57S).

From all this I conclude that there is no abyss between men and beasts such as would make it always unprofitable for humans "to associate (*jungere*) with beasts," provided "associate" is not taken in a narrow sense of "associate as fellow citizen."

Thus I plainly reject Spinoza's formulations in his famous Note. I do this convinced that the structure of his system admits a considerable softening of the harsh words in that personal note.

What I do, in contrast to Lloyd, is dissociate IVP29 and IVP30 from IVP37S and IVP57S. I take it that in these Notes Spinoza is elaborating on the broad theme that it is good for humans to form societies and states, with the rule of law, and that the solid foundation of these structures is the identity of certain traits of the nature and essence of all humans and no animals.

Admitting that humans have traits in common with animals, the system does not exclude that we can do things for the sake of nonhumans. Humans may enjoy doing good things for animals, thereby increasing their level of self-preservation. We may do things, which are useful to animals, treating them as valuable in themselves. On the other hand, the less the animals appear to have things in common with us, the less we feel motivated to be helpful; just as with humans who seem "different." And, of course, in the case of conflict of interests, we mostly give ourselves and our friends substantial priority over animals.[4]

Actually, IVP29 on "complete difference in nature" may not be intended to cover the relation of humans to animals.[5] The system implies that the nature of animals does not *agree* (*convenire*) with that of humans, but perhaps not that their natures are completely different.

Perhaps we should see Spinoza's eagerness to reject animal companionship as partly motivated by his insistence that humans are capable of living together without conflict of interest, because their natures fit together *in a unique way*.

Spinoza seems at least occasionally to imply that there are unavoidable conflicts between man and brutes, but no unavoidable ones between humans. If there is too little food, friends living according to reason quite naturally divide it among themselves, whereas rats try to get it all for themselves. The term he uses in these cases is mostly "cum nostra natura convenire" (to agree with or fit our nature) (IVP31, IVP31Dem., IVP31C, IVP32, etc.). With men there is a possibility of coming to a complete understanding through appeal to reason. With animals this is impossible. It is a point that does not touch the question to what extent animals and men have traits in common in their natures. Nor does it support the sharp distinction concerning the question what kind of conflict can be avoided and what kind cannot.

Against the possibility of there being traits of nature common to humans and nonhumans, Lloyd maintains that "the morally significant common nature between men seems rather to be something that is *achieved* through the cultivation of reason. There seems little prospect of extending the relevant kind of nature-sharing to the nonhuman without departing completely from Spinoza's thought." This I completely accept, but only if the term "morally" is omitted in favor of reference to citizenship. Animals cannot be citizens. But animals may, as far as I can understand, be members of *life communities* on a par with babies, lunatics, and others who do not cooperate as citizens but are cared for in part for their own sake.[6]

7. "To preserve one's being" is the same as "to persevere in one's essence" and not to persevere in someone else's essence, says Spinoza (IVP25Dem.). Altruism in the sense of doing things for the sake of others does not imply shedding one's essence and jumping into the essence of something else.

A being is the more free the more it acts out, or is caused by, its own nature alone. It is a question of maintaining identity, not of strengthening ego or egocentricity.

Thus if we keep to Spinoza's own terminology, there is nothing egocentric in each single particular thing's striving to persevere in its essence, or in a more sloppy language, to preserve its being. Nor is there anything egocentric in striving for an increase of one's own perfection, in so far as perfection is related to individual essences.

Acts of generosity, things we do among friends for the sake of others, do not require us to give up our essence. On the contrary, according to Spinoza. The more we act from our essence alone, the more we act out of love and generosity. Perseverance through acts motivated by genuine emotions, not through some kind of trivial fight for mere survival. And there is no indication in the system that love is only possible, or realized, in relation to a tiny subset of particular beings, namely humans. All things are animated expressions of God. (But how large is the realm of individual things? What characterizes a thing? This is a great problem in Spinoza research. Perhaps gestalt thinking can help better than thinking in terms of some kinds of atoms.)

The intimate relation of self-preservation (essence-preservation) to the immanent God is already made clear in Part Two: the essence of each human being is part of the essence of God, its mind is part of God's infinite intellect. (The system implies, so far as I can see, that without these essences, there would be no God.)

The proof of the thesis (IIIP6) that each thing, insofar as it is in itself, strives to persevere in its being, is of central significance in this connection. Its basic premises Spinoza formulates as follows:

> Individual things are . . . modes through which the attributes of God are expressed in a certain determined way . . . that is, they are things which express in a certain determined way the power of God whereby he is and acts. . . . A thing cannot in itself have anything whereby it can be destroyed. . . .

As a unique expression of the power of God or nature, the singular thing does not strive to become something else. The absence of this striving does not imply that humans cannot do things for the sake of others.

The above is intended to make it clear that the term self-preservation acquires its function from its position within a structure that is unique to Spinoza's system and profoundly different from the function of the term in that of Hobbes.

For the dedicated field ecologist each living thing has an essence and a value in itself, and the bird or human mother that risks life in order to protect the children persevere in their essence through this very act.

What is good and useful is what strengthens perseverance in one's essence. The essence is not something static, but a set of strivings, specific for each individual and pointing towards greater power or perfection or freedom.[7] Thus the terms "preservation" and "essence" are today somewhat misleading, suggesting that what is to be preserved is a *status quo* and not a trend or a vector. What is called good and useful depends on how far one has developed.

With an increasing level of perfection (etc.), the substitution of active affects for the passive ones (etc.), the individual increasingly seeks what Spinoza considers to be the really good and useful: to live and act in accordance with the dictates of reason. Reason points to the importance of understanding: the free man preserves his being through increase of the extent and depth of his acts of understanding.

Hobbes has been lost on the way from Part Three to Part Five of the *Ethics*.

While for Hobbes there is a main distinction between the state of nature and the state of being a citizen, there is for Spinoza, in his *Ethics*, a main distinction between the slaves and the free. The self-preservation of the slaves is similar to Hobbesian self-preservation in the natural state, but the self-preservation of the free does not correspond to that of citizens, neither in Hobbesian dictatorships nor in Spinozist democracies. The former are not communities of free men, but structures based on force.

Spinoza's philosophy is one of emancipation from slavery, not a philosophy of becoming civilized, nor one of becoming morally less guilty.

Spinoza makes it difficult for the reader because the third part contains many propositions intended to be valid only about individuals low on the scale of freedom and hard pressed through passive affects, but formulated as if valid in full generality. In the later sections of Part Four and, of course, in Part Five, propositions refer to individuals who have reached higher levels and are called "free."

Lloyd seems to stick too much to the first sections of Part Three where the influence of Hobbes is fairly obvious. The requirement of consistency demands an interpretation of the term "to persevere in one's being" which takes into account the universally valid dictates of reason and the supreme good of understanding love (*intellectualis amor*).

Lloyd says:

> Everything that is incapable of entering into collaboration with us, Spinoza
> sees as morally indifferent. This is a consequence of his grounding morality in
> a Hobbesian drive towards self-preservation.

Nothing is indifferent to Spinoza, because everything is a necessary expression of God or nature. I would add: and therefore all things acquire value in themselves. But this cannot be expressed in the system. Nor can Spinoza's position concerning collaboration be described adequately in terms of morality.

"Self-preservation"[8] is part of the structure of the system and acquires a content very different from any egocentric Hobbesian drive. Along with the increase of active (positive) emotions, perfection, capacity to act from one's own nature alone, increased area and depth of loving understanding, the drive to persevere in one's essence changes. It is not a blind drive to survive or to dominate others.[9]

8. Environmentalism is a form of activism, passionately concerned not only with life conditions today, but with the state of the planet several generations from now. Lloyd suggests that concentration of the mind on understanding and perception, especially through the third kind of understanding, is not conducive to, perhaps not even compatible with, environmentalism. For this reason Spinoza cannot be a patron of activist movements. But perhaps a very special image of Spinoza's system is involved here.

Spinoza led a less externally active life than did his friend Jan de Witt, but his system does not entail any passivism in the face of ecological crisis. He considered his work to have pedagogical value, helping his fellow humans to emancipate themselves and join in communities of friends. Destruction of nature is bad for such communities! In spite of his handicaps, Spinoza tried to influence politics, and it would be strange if his system somehow entailed passivism in the face of deep ecological questions.

Nevertheless, it is customary to interpret the third kind of understanding as a kind of contemplative *Schauen*, detached from the world. This ruins the basic principle of immanence of God in the world. It ruins the central terminological distinction between *Deus quatenus infinitus* (God as infinite) and *Deus quatenus finitus et modificatus* (God as finite and as mode).[10]

The third kind of understanding covers particular things, therefore God as modes cannot be neglected. "The more we understand the singular things, the more we understand God" (VP24).

Lloyd conceives what she calls "intellectual" love (and I call "understanding love") as detached. In relation to ultimate ends, "concern with the goods of other species is an irrelevant, anthropomorphic distraction." This agrees well with the other-worldly image of Spinoza, the mystic turned away from all except the experience of union with a God that is not fully expressed and only expressed through particular beings. But nothing in Spinoza's system suggests what God might be if abstracted from the expressions. Just as *natura naturans* and *natura naturata* are ultimately one, *Deus infinitus* and *Deus modificatus* are one. Thus adherence to Spinoza's system is consistent with being a *karma-yogi*, an externally active person on all levels of existence, but highly integrated through salvation from passive affects.

Concluding Remarks

1. We need not say that today man's relation to the nonhuman world is immoral. It is enough to say that it lacks generosity, fortitude, and love. That is, it also decreases man's own level of self-preservation, freedom, and joyfulness.

2. If we accept (1) we are within or near the system and structure of Spinoza's *Ethics*.

3. If we insist on a moralism that implies giving ourselves away, giving up things that are good for us (in the sense of our nature and essence) in favor of the nonhuman world, then we recede from the system and structure of the *Ethics*.

4. What might a Spinozist say about contemporary human policy towards nature? He would use fairly strong words:

5. It is acting from ignorance, not from knowledge of the intimate bonds between all living and nonliving beings. Further, it is not genuinely acting, it is succumbing to passive affects. (These are, among others: hope and fear, despair, pity, humility [from weakness], cowardice, indignation, contempt, disparagement, aversion, hatred, envy, cruelty, dejection, pride, luxury, avarice.)

6. Today's ecopolitics is an expression of ignorance, of the individual human being's low level of freedom, and of the choice of leaders who conform to that level.

7. In order to persevere in their essence, people sometimes do things for the sake of others, even for the sake of valleys and landscapes. The terminology of Supreme Court Judge Douglas is well understood.[11] It reveals that the nature or essence of humans may comprise and encompass more than their present policies towards nature attest to. Spinoza's view of the closeness of each to all is, incidentally, stressed in a new way by Genevieve Lloyd when she refers to Spinoza's "physics." (The digression after IIP13.) The treatment here of individuality demands essentially "an integration between the individual and its surrounding totality of being."

8. Spinoza was personally what we today call a speciesist, but his system is not speciesist.

Notes

This chapter is reprinted with minor revisions from Arne Næss, "Environmental Ethics and Spinoza's Ethics: Comments on Genevieve Lloyd's Article," *Inquiry* 23 (1980): 313–325.

[1] Arne Næss, "The Shallow and the Deep, Long-Range Ecology Movement," *Inquiry* 16 (1973): 95–100. Arne Næss *Økologi, samfunn og livsstil*, 5th ed. (Oslo: Universitetsforlaget, 1976). George Sessions, *Ecophilosophy*, No. 2. (California: Mimeo, Philosophy Department, 1979). See also George Sessions, "Spinoza and Jeffers on Man in Nature," *Inquiry* 20 (1977): 481–528.

[2] In abbreviated references to the *Ethics* the first (roman) numeral refers to the Part, the subsequent combination of "P" and Arabic numeral to the proposition, and "C," "Def.," "Dem.," and "S" refer respectively to Corollary, Definition, Demonstration, and Scholium.

[3] For more on this subject see Arne Næss, *Freedom, Emotion and Self-Subsistence. The Structure of a Central Part of Spinoza's Ethics*, preliminary ed. (Oslo: Universitetsforlaget, 1976). See also Jon Wetlesen, *The Sage and the Way. Studies in Spinoza's Ethics of Freedom* (Oslo: Institute of Philosophy, 1978), and M. Gueroult, *Spinoza, I Dieu, II L'Ame* (Paris: 1968, 1974).

[4] Statistically, this is well founded. But during the war many people working with animals gave them liberally of their rations, sometimes to the detriment of their own health and antagonizing their families and friends.

[5] See, e.g., Wolfson's very different interpretation in Harry A. Wolfson, *The Philosophy of Spinoza* (New York: Meridlian Books, 1958), 2: 242.

[6] See Arne Næss, "Self-realisation in Mixed Communities of Humans, Bears, Sheep and Wolves," *Inquiry*, Vol. 22, No. 1–2, 231–41. See also Arne Næss, "Spinoza and Ecology," in S. Hessing (ed.), *Speculum Spinozanum 1677–1977* (London: Routledge & Kegan Paul, 1977); see also *Philosophia* 7 (1977): 45–54.

[7] The "or's" remind one of the great system of equivalencies of terms in the *Ethics* (see Arne Næss, *Equivalent Terms and Notions in Spinoza's Ethics, Inquiry* (Oslo: Institute of Philosophy, University of Oslo, 1976). An equivalence between terms x and y does not imply substitutability everywhere in the text, but various forms of intimate closeness of function.

[8] The Latin perseverare carries the dictionary meanings abide, adhere strictly, continue steadfastly, persist, persevere. In his dictionary, C. T. Lewis does not mention the usual translation "preserve" and "preservation." (The Everyman's Library translation has "persist in its being," while Elwes's has "preserve one's being.")

[9] In a reconstruction of parts of the *Ethics* (Arne Næss, *Freedom*, 1975) I have found it justifiable to adopt the following theorems (among others): An increase in level of self-preservation implies an increase in perfection, and conversely. An increase in level of self-preservation implies a state of joy, and conversely. Something is useful if and only if it increases the level of self-preservation in some relation. An increase in level of virtue implies an increase in level of self-preservation, and conversely. To behave rationally, act virtuously, and preserve one's being in relation to something mutually imply each other.

[10] Occurrences of God as finite: IP28Dem, IIP9Dem, IIP11C, IIP12Dem, etc.

[11] Christopher D. Stone, *Should Trees Have Standing? Towards Legal Rights for Natural Objects*, rev. ed. (New York: Avon Books, 1975).

Chapter 13

Comment: Lloyd and Næss on Spinoza as Ecophilosopher

John Clark

Genevieve Lloyd and Arne Næss take widely divergent approaches to the problem of assessing Spinoza's contribution to ecological thought. For Lloyd, it is a matter of weighing the ecological against the nonecological aspects of the philosopher's position. After putting both on the scales, she finds too much weight on the nonecological side to make Spinoza a suitable "patron" for ecologists. Næss adopts, I would argue, a more reasonable methodology. He examines Spinoza's system as a whole, in order to determine its contribution to the development of ecological thought. While he wisely dismisses the suggestion that the great heretic be named anyone's patron, he finds the philosopher's system to be an abundant source of inspiration for ecological thinking.

The case for Spinoza's relevance to ecology is, I think, at least as strong as Næss claims it to be. If we consider Spinoza in the context of the history of Western philosophies of nature, this becomes quite apparent. The dominant tendencies in modern European thought have pointed in directions that are far from hospitable to an ecological perspective. On the one hand, a pervasive dualism has prevailed, separating humanity from nature, spirit from matter, mind from body, and fact from value. On the other hand, there have been diverse attempts to overcome this dualism by privileging one or the other side of these oppositions, resulting in reductionist forms of materialism and idealism. Spinoza is one of the foremost exponents in modern thought of a long tradition of holistic ontology, which seeks to avoid such dualisms and reductionisms, and which forms the philosophical heritage of much of contemporary ecological thought.

In Spinoza's holistic metaphysics, nature (and perhaps we should say nature/spirit) is seen as a dynamic, all-inclusive, self-creating system—*Natura Naturans*. This conception clearly has many affinities with important trends in contemporary ecological thinking. In his concept of the universe as a system of "motion-and-rest," Spinoza anticipates the post-Newtonian physics that has influenced ecological thought so profoundly through its conception of all things as configurations in a universal field of energy. There are also rather clear links between Spinoza's thought and systems philosophy, another important influence on contemporary ecological thinking. Spinoza's rejection of individual substances and his idea of the Divine Substance as a self-creative, self-manifesting power ties him to contemporary process philosophy, another important tendency in recent ecological thought. It is not difficult to find echoes in contemporary ecological discourse of Spinoza's discussion of a "coherence of parts" in which "the laws or nature of one part adapts itself to the laws or nature of another part in such wise that there is the least possible opposition between them," and his description of things constituting "parts of a whole to the extent that their natures adapt themselves to one another so that they are in the closest possible agreement."[1] In view of his many affinities with contemporary holistic ecological thought, it should not be surprising that many ecophilosophers look back to Spinoza, if not as a patron, certainly as an honored forebear.

In her assessment of Spinoza, Lloyd concedes that certain aspects of Spinoza's thought have such ecological implications. She mentions, in particular, his attitude of reverence for nature, his anti-anthropocentrism, and his situating of humanity metaphysically within a larger system of nature. Yet she sees other aspects—which she seems to grant equal significance in his system—as fundamentally anti-ecological. She includes in this category his supposedly anthropocentric ethics, his speciesism, and his purported refusal to grant intrinsic value to beings other than humans. She concludes that Spinoza's thought lacks the basis even for an ecologically-backward "stewardship" conception of humanity's relationship to nature, much less for an authentically ecological one. In view of her method of comparing Spinoza's individual statements to those of contemporary ecophilosophers, such a conclusion follows, one is tempted to say, by necessity.

But despite this negative judgment on Spinoza as an ecophilosopher, Lloyd in fact summarizes his relevance to ecological thought quite accurately. Spinoza's contribution, she says, consists "of transcending a distorted perception of our true position in nature; not of treating the nonhumans as bearers of rights or values in relation to which human rights and values should be curtailed." To use Næss's terminology, Spinoza's contribution to ecological thought is therefore on the "deep" level of a fundamental questioning of our concepts of humanity and nature, rather than on the "shallow" level of specific conclusions about humanity and nature as understood in existing environmental discourse. Spinoza's ecological significance lies in his depth of questioning, not in every detail of his system—unless one confuses taking inspiration from Spinoza with establishing a Spinozistic orthodoxy (which neither Næss nor any other admirer of Spinoza wishes to do today).

As Næss points out, much of Lloyd's evidence for the nonecological quality of Spinoza's thought depends on his failure to express himself in terms of contemporary problematics that are fundamentally alien to his own. Certainly, one will not find in Spinoza a defense of the "rights of the nonhuman," an inclusion of "the nonhuman" in the "moral community," or an attempt at "extension" of "the range of right-bearer." In fact, some of these concepts whose absence in Spinoza's thought is taken as evidence of his inadequately ecological outlook are themselves far from ecological ones. For example, there is rather wide agreement among ecophilosophers today that the sort of "moral extensionism" that Lloyd often takes as an ecological standard by which to measure Spinoza is a fundamentally nonecological approach to ethics. While it might be argued (correctly, I think, as does Næss) that Spinoza should have given more attention to animal welfare, nevertheless, granting "moral consideration" or "rights" to individual animals is in no way indicative of an ecological outlook (though a failure to give adequate ontological and ethical consideration to their place in nature would conflict with an ecological outlook).

Lloyd claims that "environmental philosophers" are "looking for . . a basis for the judgment that some activities that are regarded as good for human beings should be curtailed because they are bad for other parts of nature." (Næss correctly rejects the view that such a quest is essential to ecological ethics or ecophilosophy, for their principles can be expressed quite adequately in terms of the attainment of certain cardinal virtues or of an ideal way of life (as has been done since ancient times in various Buddhist and Taoist traditions, for example). Lloyd's formulation seems narrowly tied to the view—perhaps most notably associated with Kant—that morality is essentially a constraint on the moral agent, a concept with roots in a dualistic, and ultimately repressive, view of human nature. Such a view is certainly not a necessary element in an ecological philosophy. Indeed, we might consider whether the anti-dualistic intent of a fully ecological outlook is even compatible with such a conception.

Such an idea of constraint might make sense if Spinoza's ethics were really centered in self-preservation, in the survival of human beings, as Lloyd contends. But it would be difficult for even the most naive ethical system, much less Spinoza's quite sophisticated one, to be focused on mere "survival." Næss corrects Lloyd's one-sided reading of Hobbesian, egoistic implications into many of Spinoza's statements. As Næss points out, this interpretation overlooks the psychological subtlety of Spinoza's ethics, with its goal of self-realization through philosophic wisdom and the development of the emotions. Spinoza's idea of self-preservation must be understood within the context of an overall non-dominating sensibility in which "persevering in one's essence" implies— far from any "war of all against all" in which one seeks to assert one's will against other beings—a reconciliation with all of nature. It is this outlook that Spinoza calls "blessedness" at the end of the *Ethics*.

Ironically, Lloyd seems to give Spinoza more credit in areas in which he is less deserving, while underestimating some of his most distinctive contributions to ecological thought. While the critique of teleology and final causes that she cites is certainly non-anthropocentric, the rejection of a privileged place in the cosmos for humanity does not in itself make a view ecological. For example, a mechanistic materialism or an ethical nihilism could adhere to such non-anthropocentrism while having no ecophilosophical implications at all. It is not this dimension of Spinoza's thought, but another, rather obvious one, that is most crucial ecologically.

The central concept in Spinoza's ideal for humanity, far from being any kind of domination of nature or exploitation of other beings in nature, is rather the "intellectual love of God." By this he means a love arising out of wisdom, and directed toward nature itself, and in particular, nature seen as the dynamic, self-creating whole *(Natura Naturans)*. In Part V, Proposition 35 of the *Ethics* he describes "the mind's intellectual love towards God" as "part of the infinite love wherewith God loves himself."[2] While he deduces from this principle the idea that we should equate our own intellectual love of God, with "the love of God towards men," we may also validly deduce from his principles that it is equivalent to God's "infinite love" of "himself." Stated otherwise, it is equivalent to the love of nature. This is the conclusion that Næss draws when he states that it is implied in Spinoza's system that "all things acquire value in themselves," since we may reasonably presume that what is loved is perceived as having great value.

Lloyd in fact recognizes that the "ultimate expression" of human perfection is for Spinoza the intellectual love of God, and that this goal has practical consequences with distinctly ecological implications (though she typically specifies these in terms of treatment of animals, rather than of a general sensibility toward nature). Næss draws out these implications by considering the centrality to Spinoza's ethics of such virtues as "generosity, fortitude, and love." In envisioning a life in which these ideals are realized, Spinoza's ethics not only transcends anthropocentrism, but, more concretely, constitutes a determinate practice aimed at dissolving a kind of egoism that is fundamental to the human project of control and domination of nature.

In considering this context, Næss makes a good case for the view that Spinoza's harsh statements about animals are at odds with the most fundamental aspects of his system. As Næss states it, "Nothing is indifferent to Spinoza, because everything is a necessary expression of God or nature." The inescapable implication of Spinoza's metaphysics is that our deepest concern must extend outward toward the whole of nature. Spinoza forms part of a long tradition that asks us to see ourselves as part of a cosmic process in which the whole, conceived of as the larger self, as the divine, or as active nature, knows itself, enjoys itself, realizes itself, or, in Spinoza's words, "loves itself."

Like Arne Næss, I cannot imagine any view with more profound implications for ecological thinking and for the development of an ecological ethos.

Notes

[1] From Letter 32 in Spinoza, *The Ethics and Selected Letters,* trans. Samuel Shirley (Indianapolis: Hackett Publ. Co., 1982), 244–45.

[2] Spinoza, *The Ethics and Selected Letters,* 221.

Part II

Deep Ecology: Norms, Premises, and Intuitions

Figure 2. The Tree of Life (livets tre).

Chapter 14

A Critique of Anti-Anthropocentric Bio-centrism

Richard A. Watson

I

Anthropocentric is defined specifically as the position "that considers man as the central fact, or final aim, of the universe" and generally "conceive[s] of everything in the universe in terms of human values."[1] In the literature of environmental ethics, anti-anthropocentric biocentrism is the position that human needs, goals, and desires should not be taken as privileged or overriding in considering the needs, desires, interests, and goals of all members of all biological species taken together, and in general that the earth as a whole should not be interpreted or managed from a human standpoint. According to this position, birds, trees, and the land itself considered as the biosphere have a right to be and to live out their individual and species' potentials, and that members of the human species have no right to disturb, perturb, or destroy the ecological balance of the planet.

An often quoted statement of this right of natural objects to continue to be as they are found to be occurs in John Rodman's "The Liberation of Nature?":

> To affirm that "natural objects" have "rights" is symbolically to affirm that ALL NATURAL ENTITIES (INCLUDING HUMANS) HAVE INTRINSIC WORTH SIMPLY BY VIRTUE OF BEING AND BEING WHAT THEY ARE.[2]

In "On the Nature and Possibility of an Environmental Ethic," Tom Regan follows an implication of this view by presenting a "preservation principle":

> By the "preservation principle" I mean a principle of nondestruction, non-inter-
> ference, and, generally, nonmeddling. By characterizing this term as a princi-
> ple, moreover, I am emphasizing that preservation (letting-be) be regarded as a
> moral imperative.[3]

Support of this hands-off-nature approach is provided by George Sessions in his "Spinoza, Perennial Philosophy, and Deep Ecology, " where, among other things, he describes how Aldo Leopold moved from a position considering humans as stewards or managers of nature to one considering humans as "plain members" of the total biotic community.[4] As Leopold himself puts it:

> A thing is right when it tends to preserve the integrity, stability, and beauty of
> the biotic community. It is wrong when it tends otherwise.[5]

According to Sessions, Leopold reached this position in part as a result of his dawning realization that ecological communities are internally integrated and highly complex. He saw how human activities have disrupted many eco-logical communities and was himself involved in some unsuccessful attempts to manage communities of animals in the wild. These failures led Leopold to con-clude that; "the biotic mechanism is so complex, that its workings may never be fully understood."[6]

Like many other environmentalists, Sessions associates Leopold's position with Barry Commoner's first law of ecology: "Everything is connected to eve-rything else,"[7] according to which "any major man-made change in a natural system is likely to be *detrimental* to that system."[8] This view, which considers all environmental managers who try to alter the environment to be suffering from scientific hubris, leads to an almost biblical statement of nascence. In this connection, Sessions quotes the ecologist Frank Egler as saying that "Nature is not only more complex than we think, but it is more complex than we can ever think."[9] The attitude of humble acquiescence to the ways of nature which fol-lows from this view, Sessions says, is summed up in Commoner's third law, "Nature knows best."[10]

The position is presented at length by G. Tyler Miller, in another quotation cited by Sessions:

> One of the purposes of this book [*Replenish the Earth*] is to show the bank-
> ruptcy of the term "spaceship earth." . . . This is an upside-down view of real-
> ity and is yet another manifestation of our arrogance toward nature. . . . Our
> task is not to learn how to pilot spaceship earth. It is not to learn how—as Teil-
> hard de Chardin would have it—"to seize the tiller of the world." Our task is to
> give up our fantasies of omnipotence. In other words, *we must stop trying to
> steer* [my italics]. The solution to our present dilemma does not lie in attempt-
> ing to extend our technical and managerial skills into every sphere of exis-
> tence. Thus, *from a human standpoint our environmental crisis is the result of*

our arrogance towards nature [Miller's italics]. Somehow we must tune our senses again to the beat of existence, sensing in nature fundamental rhythms we can trust even though we may never fully understand them. We must learn anew that it is we who belong to earth and not the earth to us. Thus rediscovery of our finitude is fundamental to any genuinely human future.[11]

Sessions, at least, is not naive about some of the problems that arise from these pronouncements. He says that if an environmental ethic is to be derived from ecological principles and concepts, this raises

> the old problem of attempting to derive moral principles and imperatives from supposedly empirical fact (the "is-ought problem"). The attempt to justify ecosystem ethics on conventional utilitarian or "rights and obligations" grounds presents formidable obstacles. And, so far, little headway has been made in finding other acceptable grounds for an ecosystem ethics other than a growing intuitive ecological awareness that it is right.[12]

The anti-anthropocentric biocentrists have sought a metaphysical foundation for a holistic environmental ethic in Spinoza. The clearest statement of this appears in Arne Næss's "Spinoza and Ecology." Næss expands from Spinoza in sixteen points, several of which are crucial to my discussion of anti-anthropocentric biocentrism:

> 1. The nature conceived by field ecologists is not the passive, dead, value neutral nature of mechanistic science, but akin to the *Deus sive Natura* of Spinoza. All-inclusive, creative (as *natura naturans*), infinitely diverse, and alive in the broad sense of panpsychism, but also manifesting a structure, the so-called laws of nature. There are always causes to be found, but extremely complex and difficult to unearth. Nature with a capital N is intuitively conceived as perfect in a sense that Spinoza and outdoor ecologists have more or less in common: it is not narrowly moral, utilitarian, or aesthetic perfection. Nature is perfect "in itself." *Perfection* can only mean completeness of some sort when applied in general, and not to specifically human achievements. . . .
> 2. The two aspects of Nature, those of extension and thought (better: non-extension), are both complete aspects of one single reality, and *perfection characterizes both*. . . .
> 3. As an absolutely all-embracing reality, Nature has no purpose, aim, or goal. . . .
> 4. There is no established moral world-order. Human justice is not a law of nature. There are, on the other hand, no natural laws limiting the endeavor to extend the realm of justice as conceived in a society of free human beings. . . .
> 5. Good and evil must be defined in relation to beings for which something is good or evil, useful or detrimental. The terms are meaningless when not thus related. . . .
> 6. Every thing is connected with every other. . . . Intimate interconnectedness in the sense of internal rather than external relations characterize ecological ontology. . . .
> 9. If one insists upon using the term "rights," every being may be said to have the right to do what is in its power. It is "right" to express its own nature as

clearly and extensively as natural conditions permit. That right which they [the animals] have in relation to us, we have in relation to them (*Ethics*, Part IV, first scholium to proposition 37). That rights are a part of a separate moral world order is fiction. Field ecologists tend to accept a general "right to live and blossom. Humans have no special right to kill and injure, Nature does not belong to them."[13]

Spinoza has also been cited for the general position that the ultimate goal, good and joy of human beings, is understanding, which amounts to contemplation of nature. In "Spinoza and Jeffers on Man in Nature," Sessions says:

> Spinoza's purpose in philosophizing, then, is to break free from the bonds of desire and ignorance which captivate and frustrate most men, thus standing in the way of what real happiness is available to them, and to attain a higher Self which is aligned with a *correct* [my italics] understanding of God/Nature.[14]

The position, however, is not restricted to Spinoza, for, as Sessions notes elsewhere, the best-known statement of this view is probably found in Aldous Huxley's *Perennial Philosophy*:

> Happiness and moral progress depend, it is [mistakenly] thought [today], on bigger and better gadgets and a higher standard of living. . . . In all the historic formulations of the Perennial Philosophy it is axiomatic that the end of human life is contemplation, or the direct and intuitive awareness of God, that action is the means to that end; that a society is good to the extent that it renders contemplation possible for its members."[15]

A difficult question that arises for advocates of this position is whether or not humans can be activists. For example, near-total passivism seems to be suggested by Michael Zimmerman in his approving summation of what he takes to be Heidegger's admonition to the Western world:

> Only Western man's thinking has ended up by viewing the world as a store-house of raw material for the enhancement of man's power. [A] new kind of thinking must pass beyond the subjectivist thinking of philosophy-science-technology. Heidegger indicates that the new way must "let beings be," i.e., it must let them manifest themselves in their own presence and worth, and not merely as objects for the all-powerful Subject.[16]

On the other hand, Næss is an activist; he and others think that civil disobedience is appropriate to thwart human misuse of the environment. And although Næss stresses what he calls the "biospherical egalitarianism" of all biological species on earth,[17] he says in "Environmental Ethics and Spinoza":

> Animals cannot be citizens [i.e., members of a human moral community]. But animals may, as far as I can understand, be members of *life communities* on a par

with babies, lunatics, and others who do not cooperate as citizens but are cared for in part for their own good.[18]

This is consistent with Næss's Spinozistic approach, but the more general implication of the species-egalitarian approach seems to be inactivism. In summary, advocates of anti-anthropocentric biocentrism such as Sessions speak of the Judeo-Christian-Platonic-Aristotelian tradition as leading to

> an extreme subjectivist anthropocentrism in which the whole of nonhuman nature is viewed as a resource for man. By way of a long and convoluted intellectual history, we have managed to subvert completely the organic ecological worldview of the hunter and gatherer.[19]

Sessions goes on to deplore "the demise of pantheism and the desacralization of Nature."[20] He then makes a statement highly typical of anti-anthropomorphic biocentrists:

> Part of the genius of Bacon and Descartes was to realize contrary to the conservatism of the Church authorities, that a new science was needed to consummate the goal of Judeo-Christian-Platonic-Aristotelian domination of nature. The Enlightenment retained the Christian idea of man's perpetual progress (now defined as increasing scientific-technological control and mastery over nature), thus setting the stage for, and passing its unbridled optimism on to, its twentieth-century successors, Marxism and American pragmatism. The floodgates had been opened. The Pythagorean theory of the cosmos and the whole idea of a meaningful perennial philosophy were swept away in a deluge of secularism, the fragmentation of knowledge, pronouncements that God was dead and the universe and life of man meaningless, industrialization, the quest for material happiness, and the consequent destruction of the environment. The emphasis was no longer upon either *God* or *Nature* but *Man*.[21]

Sessions by no means advocates or thinks possible a simple return to pre-Socratic religion or pantheism. But what, on the basis of ecological principles and concepts, is the underlying motif or guiding ideal today for "a correct understanding of God/Nature?"[22] According to Næss, the proper position is an *ecosophy* defined as "a philosophy of ecological harmony or equilibrium."[23] Thus, while deploring the Greek contribution to the present desacralization of nature, these ecosophers do acknowledge the Stoic and Epicurean contributions to the philosophy of balance, harmony, and equilibrium. They present a holistic vision of the earth circling in dynamic ecological equilibrium as the preferred and proper contemplative object of right-thinking environmental man.

In pursuing a statement of anti-anthropomorphic biocentrism, then, I have exposed five principles of the movement:

1. The needs, desires, interests, and goals of humans are not privileged.
2. The human species should not change the ecology of the planet.

3. The world ecological system is too complex for human beings ever to understand.
4. The ultimate goal, good, and joy of humankind is contemplative understanding of nature.
5. Nature is a holistic system of parts (of which man is merely one among many equals) all of which are internally interrelated in dynamic, harmonious, ecological equilibrium.

The moral imperative derived from this ecosophy is that human beings do not have the right to, and should not, alter the equilibrium.

II

I do not intend to challenge the controversial naturalistic assumption that some such environmental ethic can be derived from ecological principles and concepts. Whatever the logical problems of deriving value from fact, it is not (and probably never has been) a practical problem for large numbers of people who base their moral convictions on factual premises.

Nevertheless, it must be obvious to most careful readers that the general position characterized in section I suffers from serious interplay contradictions. I think they are so serious that the position must be abandoned. In what follows I detail the problems that arise in the system, and then offer an alternative to the call for developing a new ecosophic ethics.

To go immediately to the heart of the matter, I take anti-anthropocentrism more seriously than do any of the ecosophers I have quoted or read. If man is a part of nature, if he is a "plain citizen," if he is just one nonprivileged member of a "biospherical egalitarianism," then the human species should be treated in no way different from any other species. However, the entire tone of the position outlined in section I, is to set man apart from nature and above all other living species. Næss says that nonhuman animals should be "cared for in part for their own good."[24] Sessions says that humans should curb their technological enthusiasms to preserve ecological equilibrium.[25] Rodman says flatly that man should let nature be.[26]

Now, the posing of man against nature in any way is anthropocentric. Man is a part of nature.[27] Human ways—human culture—and human actions are as natural as are the ways in which any other species of animals behaves. But if we view the state of nature or Nature as being natural, undisturbed, and unperturbed only when human beings are *not present*, or only when human beings are curbing their natural behavior, then we are assuming that human beings are apart from, separate from, different from, removed from, or above nature. It is obvious that the ecosophy described above is based on this position of setting man apart from or above nature. (Do I mean even "sordid" and "perverted" human behavior? Yes, that is natural, too.)

To avoid this separation of man from nature, this special treatment of human beings as other than nature, we must stress that man's works (yes, including H-bombs and gas chambers) are as natural as those of bower birds and beavers.

But civilized man wreaks such havoc on the environment. We disrupt the ecology of the planet, cause the extinction of myriad other species of living things, and even alter the climate of the earth. Should we not attempt to curb our behavior to avoid these results? Indeed we should as a matter of prudence if we want to preserve our habitat and guarantee the survival of our species. But this is anthropocentric thinking.

Only if we are thinking anthropocentrically will we set the human species apart as *the* species that is to be thwarted in its natural behavior. Anti-anthropocentric bio-centrists suggest that other species are to be allowed to manifest themselves naturally. They are to be allowed to live out their evolutionary potential in interaction with one another. But man is different. Man is too powerful, too destructive of the environment and other species, too successful in reproducing, and so on. What a phenomenon is man! Man is so wonderfully bad that he is not to be allowed to live out his evolutionary potential in egalitarian interaction with all other species.

Why not? The only reason is anthropocentric. We are not treating man as a plain member of the biotic community. We are not treating the human species as an equal among other species. We think of man as being better than other animals, or worse, as the case may be, because man is so powerful.

One reason we think this is that we think in terms of an anthropocentric moral community. All other species are viewed as morally neutral; their behavior is neither good nor bad. But we evaluate human behavior morally. And this sets man apart. If we are to treat man as a part of nature on egalitarian terms with other species, then man's behavior must be treated as morally neutral, too. It is absurd, of course, to suggest the opposite alternative, that we evaluate the behavior of nonhuman animals morally.

Bluntly, if we think there is nothing morally wrong with one species taking over the habitat of another and eventually causing the extinction of the dispossessed species—as has happened millions of times in the history of the earth—then we should not think that there is anything morally or ecosophically wrong with the human species dispossessing and causing the extinction of other species.

Man's nature, his role, his forte, his glory and ambition has been to propagate and thrive at the expense of many other species and to the disruption—or, neutrally, to the change—of the planet's ecology. I do not want to engage in speculation about the religion of preliterate peoples, or in debates about the interpretation of documented non-Judeo-Christian-Platonic-Aristotelian religions. I am skeptical, however, of the panegyrics about pantheism and harmonious integration with sacred nature. But these speculations do not matter. The fact is that for about 50,000 years human beings (*Homo sapiens*) have been advancing like wildfire (to use an inflammatory metaphor) to occupy more and more of the planet. A peak of low-energy technology was reached about 35,000 years ago at which time man wiped out many species of large animals. About 10,000 years ago man domesticated plants and animals and started changing the face of the earth with grazing, farming, deforestation, and desertification. About 200 years ago man started burning fossil fuels with results that will probably change the climate of the planet (at last temporarily) and that have already resulted in the extinction of many species of living things that perhaps might otherwise have survived. In 1945 man entered an atomic age and we now have the ability to desertify large portions of the earth and perhaps to cause the extinction of most of the higher forms of life.[28]

Human beings do alter things. They cause the extinction of many species, and they change the earth's ecology. This is what humans do. This is their destiny. If they destroy many other species and themselves in the process, they do no more than has been done by many another species. The human species should be allowed—if any species can be said to have a right—to live out its evolutionary potential, to its own destruction if that is the end result. It is nature's way.

This is not a popular view. But most alternative anti-anthropocentric biocentric arguments for preserving nature are self-contradictory. Man is a part of nature. The only way man will survive is if he uses his brains to save himself. One reason why we should curb human behavior that is destructive of other species and the environment is because in the end it is destructive of the human species as well.[29]

I hope it is human nature to survive because we are smart. But those who appeal for a new ethic or religion or ecosophy based on an intuitive belief that they know what is right not only for other people, but also for the planet as a whole, exhibit the hubris that they themselves say got us in such a mess in the first place.[30] If the ecosphere is so complicated that we may never understand its workings, how is it that so many ecosophers are so sure that they know what is right for us to do now? Beyond the issue of man's right to do whatever he can according to the power-makes-right ecosophic ethic outlined by Næss, we may simply be wrong about what is "good" for the planet. Large numbers of species have been wiped out before, e.g., at the time the dinosaurs became extinct. Perhaps wiping out and renewal is just the way things go. Of course, a lot of genetic material is lost, but presumably all the species that ever existed came out of the same primordial soup, and could again. In situations where genetic material was limited, as in the Galapagos Islands or Australia, evolutionary radiation filled the niches. Even on the basis of our present knowledge about evolution and ecology, we have little ground to worry about the proliferation of life on earth even if man manages to wipe out most of the species now living. Such a clearing out might be just the thing to allow for variety and diversity. And why is it that we harp about genetic banks today anyway? For one thing, we are worried that disease might wipe out our domesticated grain crops. Then where would man be?

Another obvious anthropocentric element in ecosophic thinking is the predilection for ecological communities of great internal variety and complexity. But the barren limestone plateaus that surround the Mediterranean now are just as much in ecological balance as were the forests that grew there before man cut them down. And "dead" Lake Erie is just as much in ecological balance with the life on the land that surrounds it as it was in pre-Columbian times. The notion of a climax situation in ecology is a human invention, based on anthropocentric ideas of variety, completion, wholeness, and balance. A preference for equilibrium rather than change, for forests over deserts, for complexity and variety over simplicity and monoculture, all of these are matters of human economics and aesthetics. What *would* it be, after all, to think like a mountain as Aldo Leopold is said to have recommended?[31] It would be anthropocentric because mountains do not think, but also because mountains are imagined to be thinking about which human interests in their preservation or development they prefer.[32] The anthropocentrism of ecosophers is most obvious in their pronouncements about what is normal and natural. Perhaps it is not natural to remain in equilibrium, to be in ecological balance.

As far as that goes, most of the universe is apparently dead—or at least inanimate—anyway. And as far as we know, the movement of things is toward entropy. By simplifying things, man is on the side of the universe.

And as for making a mess of things, destroying things, disrupting and breaking down things, the best information we have about the origin of the universe is that it is the result of an explosion. If we are going to derive an ethic from our knowledge of nature, is it wrong to suggest that high-technology man might be doing the right thing? Næss does try to meet this objection with his tenth principle:

There is nothing in human nature or essence according to Spinoza, which can *only* manifest or express itself through injury to others. That is, the striving for expression of one's nature does not inevitably imply an attitude of hostile domination over other beings, human or nonhuman. Violence, in the sense of violent activity, is not the same as violence as injury to others.[33]

But "injury" is a human moral concept. There is no injury to others in neutral nature. Næss and Spinoza are still bound by Judeo-Christian-Platonic-Aristotelian notions of human goodness. But to call for curbing man is like trying to make vegetarians of pet cats.

I have often been puzzled about why so many environmental philosophers insist on harking to Spinoza as a ground for environmental ethics. It is perfectly plain as Curley[34] and Lloyd[35] point out that Spinoza's moral views are humanistic. They show how difficult it is to reconcile Spinoza's sense of freedom as the recognition of necessity with any notion of autonomy of self that is required to make moral imperatives or morality itself meaningful. That is, to recognize and accept what one is determined to do—even if this recognition and acceptance were not itself determined—is not the same as choosing between two equally possible (undetermined) courses of action. Moral action depends on free choice among undetermined alternatives.

III

There are anthropocentric foundations in most environmental and ecosophical literature. In particular, most ecosophers say outright or openly imply that human individuals and the human species would be better off if we were required to live in ecological balance with nature. Few ecosophers really think that man is just one part of nature among others. Man is privileged—or cursed—at least by having a moral sensibility that as far as we can tell no other entities have. But it is pretty clear (as I argue in "Self-Consciousness and the Rights of Nonhuman Animals and Nature"[36]) that on this planet at least only human beings are (so far) full members of a moral community. We ought to be kinder to nonhuman animals, but I do not think that this is because they have any intrinsic rights. As far as that goes, human beings have no intrinsic rights either (as Næss and Spinoza agree). We have to earn our rights as cooperating citizens in a moral community.

Because, unlike many ecosophers, I do not believe that we can return to religion, or that given what we know about the world today we can believe in pantheism or panpsychism. I think it is a mistake to strive for a new environmental ethic based on religious or mystical grounds. And I trust that I have demonstrated both how difficult it is to be fully biocentric, and also how the results of anti-anthropocentric biocentrism go far beyond the limits that ecosophers have drawn. Ecosophers obviously want to avoid the direct implications of treating the human species in the egalitarian and hands-off way they say other species should be treated. It is nice that human survival is compatible with the preservation of a rich planetary ecology, but I think it is a mistake to try to cover up the fact that human survival and the good life for man is some part of what we are interested in. There is very good reason for thinking ecologically, and for encouraging human beings to act in such a way as to preserve a rich and balanced planetary ecology: human survival depends on it.

Notes

This chapter is reprinted with minor revisions from Richard Watson, "A Critique of Anti-Anthropocentric Biocentrism," *Environmental Ethics* 5 (Fall, 1983): 245–256.

As the endnotes indicate, the author has depended greatly on the published and unpublished work of George Sessions, whose generous help he very much appreciates. J. Baird Callicott and an anonymous referee also provided substantive discussion of an earlier draft.

[1] *Webster's New World Dictionary*, 2nd ed. (Cleveland, Ohio: William Collins and World Publishing Co., 1976), 59.

[2] John Rodman, "The Liberation of Nature?" *Inquiry* 20 (1977): 108 (quoted with emphasis in capitals by George Sessions in *Ecophilosophy III*, 5a.

[3] Tom Regan, "The Nature and Possibility of an Environmental Ethic," *Environmental Ethics* 3 (1981): 31–32.

[4] George Sessions, "Spinoza, Perennial Philosophy, and Deep Ecology," unpublished paper, 15.

[5] Aldo Leopold, *A Sand County Almanac* (Oxford: Oxford University Press, 1966), 240 (quoted by George Sessions in "Spinoza, Perennial Philosophy, and Deep Ecology," 15).

[6] Leopold, *A Sand County Almanac*, 240.

[7] Barry Commoner, *The Closing Circle: Nature, Man and Technology* (New York: Alfred A. Knopf, 1971), 33 (quoted by George Sessions in "Panpsychism versus Modern Materialism: Some Implications for an Ecological Ethics," unpublished paper, 35).

[8] Commoner, *Closing Circle*, 41.

[9] Frank Egler, No reference given; quoted in Sessions's "Shallow and Deep Ecology. A Review of the Philosophical Literature," unpublished paper, 44. What Egler says about nature, of course, is what has been said about God, and perhaps explains why so many people in the environmental movement capitalize Nature.

[10] Commoner, *Closing Circle*, 41.

[11] G. Tyler Miller, *Replenish the Earth* (Belmont, Calif.: Wadsworth, 1972), 53 (quoted by George Sessions in "Shallow and Deep Ecology: A Review of the Philosophical Literature," unpublished, 44–45).

[12] George Sessions, "Shallow and Deep Ecology," 16.

[13] Arne Næss, "Spinoza and Ecology" in Sigfried Hessing, ed., *Speculum Spinozanum 1677–1977* (London: Routledge & Kegan Paul, 1977), 419–21.

[14] George Sessions, "Spinoza and Jeffers on Man and Nature, *Inquiry* 20 (1977): 494–95.

[15] Aldous Huxley, *Perennial Philosophy* (New York: Harper's, 1945), 159–60, 294 (quoted by Sessions in "Shallow and Deep Ecology," 47).

[16] Michael Zimmerman, "Technological Change and the End of Philosophy," unpublished paper, no page given (quoted by Sessions in "Spinoza and Jeffers on Man and Nature," 489).

[17] Arne Næss, "The Shallow and the Deep, Long-Range Ecology Movement. A Summary," *Inquiry* 16 (1973): 95.

[18] Arne Næss, "Environmental Ethics and Spinoza's Ethics. Comments on Genevieve Lloyd's Article," *Inquiry* 23 (1980): 319.

[19] Sessions, "Spinoza and Jeffers on Man and Nature," 482.

[20] Sessions, "Spinoza and Jeffers on Man and Nature."

[21] Sessions, "Spinoza and Jeffers on Man and Nature," 487.

[22] Sessions, "Spinoza and Jeffers on Man and Nature," 494–95.

[23] Næss, "The Shallow and the Deep, Long-Range Ecology Movement. A Summary," 99.

[24] Næss, "Environmental Ethics and Spinoza's Ethics. Comments on Genevieve Lloyd's Article," 319.

[25] Sessions, "Spinoza and Jeffers on Man and Nature," 482.

[26] John Rodman, "The Liberation of Nature?" *Inquiry* 20 (1977): 108.

[27] Richard A. Watson and Patty Jo Watson, *Man and Nature: An Anthropological Essay in Human Ecology* (New York: Harcourt Brace and World, 1969).

[28] Watson and Watson, *Man and Nature*.

[29] Biocentrism does not imply radical anti-anthropocentrism, for what is best for man may also be best for the whole biological community. See, e.g., J. Baird Callicott, "Elements of an Environmental Ethic: Moral Considerability and the Biotic Community," *Environmental Ethics* 1 (1979): 71–81. See also R. and V. Routley, "Against the Inevitability of Human Chauvinism," in K. E. Goodpaster and K. M. Sayre, eds. *Ethics and Problems of the 21st Century* (Notre Dame: University of Notre Dame Press, 1979). Sophisticated arguments in diverse fields support the view that cooperation leading to ecological balance is best for the whole biologic community. See, e.g., Robert Axelrod and William D. Hamilton, "The Evolution of Cooperation," *Science* 211 (1981): 1390–96.

[30] Sessions, "Shallow and Deep Ecology," 16.

[31] Susan Flader, *Thinking Like a Mountain: Aldo Leopold and the Evolution of an Ecological Attitude toward Deer, Wolves, and Forests* (Columbia: University of Missouri Press, 1974).

[32] Christopher D. Stone, *Should Trees Have Standing? Toward Legal Rights for Natural Objects* (Los Altos, California: William Kaufmann, 1974).

[33] Arne Næss, "Spinoza and Ecology," 421.

[34] E. M. Curley, "Man and Nature in Spinoza," in Jon Wetlesen, ed., *Spinoza's Philosophy of Man* (Oslo: Universitetsforlaget, 1978), 19–26.

[35] Genevieve Lloyd, "Spinoza's Environmental Ethics," *Inquiry* 23 (1980): 293–311. See also the reply by Næss, "Environmental Ethics and Spinoza's Ethics. Comments on Genevieve Lloyd's Article," 313–25.

[36] Richard A. Watson, "Self-Consciousness and the Rights of Nonhuman Animals and Nature," *Environmental Ethics* 1 (1979): 95–129. See also "Self-Conscious Rights," *Ethics and Animals* 2 (1981): 90–92, and "Interests, Rights, and Self-Consciousness," *Environmental Ethics* 4 (1982): 285–87.

Chapter 15

A Defense of the Deep Ecology Movement

Arne Næss

I

In his article Richard A. Watson criticizes a position he calls "anti-anthropocentric biocentrism."[1] He also attacks what he considers to be misplaced mysticism and religion. According to Watson, man should learn to behave in an ecologically sound manner simply because this is necessary for human survival. To touch deeper issues is unwarranted. The value of human survival he (implicitly) takes to be an intrinsic value—and I agree. But those who have dedicated, and wish to dedicate, much of their life and energy to protecting nature against destruction have had this planet with all its life forms in mind. In order to be heard they have had to argue almost exclusively in terms of *human* health and well-being, even though their motivation has been both broader and deeper.

Very few, and probably none, of the pioneers in the fight against the destructive activity of human beings on our planet in this century have envisaged that this activity would or could lead to the extinction of the human species. The possibility that there would be *no* areas where a sufficient number of humans could survive, is one that has not concerned them.

Consider a recent example. A handful of wolves in southern Norway kill sheep and frighten parents who imagine that the wolves will attack their children on their way to school. Parents should be able to feel that their children are safe, all agree, but it costs a lot of money to hire "shepherds" for the children. Conclusion: kill the wolves. Professional hunters try hard to do this, but Norwegian wolves know too much about hunters and how to avoid them.

Those who might argue that man should not try to kill the wolves, since they are good for human survival, are unlikely to stop the hunters. Human sur-

121

vival is a weak argument not only from the point of view of parents, sheep owners, and hunters, but also from that of politicians.

The strong opposition to killing the wolves stems from people who:

(1) consider these animals to have intrinsic value, every one of them, and maintain that in principle each of them has the same right to live and blossom as we and our children have, and

(2) those who consider it the duty of a rich industrial nation to safeguard both sheep and wolves.

We cannot send sheep, who are rendered helpless through thousands of years of human manipulation, into wolf territory without a shepherd, if at all. The opponents also dig into cultural history explaining how wolves came to have a worse public image than bears, for instance, and how this bad public image has been exploited by great authors, like the brothers Grimm, resulting in baseless fears, that children may be attacked on their way to school. Last but not least they work out proposals on how to solve the economic problems involved, for instance, the payment of shepherds.

Abstract reasons about living in harmony with the natural order, about the possible medical and scientific value of every species, are important, but man has a heart, not only a brain. Strong philosophical or religious views are required. Among nonacademics they are mostly unarticulated, but are influential if they are appealed to.

Watson argues against the views of those he calls the "ecosophers." From the names he mentions it is more appropriate to consider his argument to be against the members of the deep ecology movement.

The absence of anti-anthropocentric biocentrists in the sense of Watson does not, in my mind, make the article of Watson uninteresting or unimportant. Let me try to substantiate this, but at the same time try to eliminate some misunderstandings.

The term *ecosopher*, which he uses, usually refers to a philosopher whose total view is inspired by ecology and the deep ecology movement. Both Sessions and myself are supporters of the movement and we are also ecosophers, but the great majority of the supporters have not articulated any ecosophy. Moreover, the important groups of Christian supporters tend to repudiate the term because they find their total view is primarily inspired by the Bible. In what follows I write as if Watson had used the term "supporter of the deep ecology movement" rather than the term ecosopher.

II

Watson is right if he is of the opinion that supporters of the deep ecology movement sometimes write or talk as if human needs, goals, or desires should under no circumstances "be taken as privileged or overriding" in considering "the needs, desires, interests, and goals" of a nonhuman living being. Such a norm if followed uncritically, would, of course, make humans into a strange kind of proletarian and would result in their extinction. Rather, what engages the supporters of the deep ecological movement is the question "under *what* circumstances . . . ?" This question is not capable of any precise, general answer.[2] A short formula runs as follows: "A vital need of the nonhuman living being A overrides a peripheral interest of the human being B." There is substantial support of this vague sentence among large groups of people as long as the set of As is restricted to the set of those mammals and birds which are not used for food. Supporters of the deep ecology movement are in favor of a much wider set of beings under a wider set of circumstances, but there are of course large individual and cultural differences. It is undesirable to try to establish complete conformity.

III

The sentence expressing Watson's definition of anti-anthropocentric biocentrism might conceivably be interpreted in such a way that some supporters of the movement might find it suitable as an expression of their position. The same holds true of many other sentences in his article, but rarely have I found semantical clarifications as relevant as when I try to understand a colleague in environmental debates!

For example, the second of five alleged principles of the "movement"—and here Watson uses the term *movement*—runs as follows: "The human species should not change the ecology of the planet." Inevitably, humans change and will change the ecology of the earth, if ecology here implies "at least one of the ecosystems." This holds even if the human population mercifully is reduced to one-tenth of the present population, and even if the "ecological consciousness" (Sessions) deepens considerably.

But Watson may interpret his sentence differently. Anyway, many of us subscribe to the maxim of Barry Commoner: "any major man-made change in a natural system is likely to be detrimental to that system." This is a typical maxim of a movement, not a proposition in an ecosophy, a systematic philosophy. It has a comparable rhetorical function to Commoner's fourth "law," "There is no such thing as a free lunch," and to the maxim "Nature knows best." Confusion increases when the rhetoric of a movement is treated like seminar exercises in university philosophy.

IV

According to Watson, he has exposed "five principles" of anti-anthropocentric biocentrism. I have already commented on number two. Number one is similar to a part of Watson's proposed definition: "The needs, desires, interests, and goals of humans are not privileged." For some interpretations ("not" = "not in every case") the formulation of the "principle" is acceptable. However, if "not privileged" is interpreted in the direction of "never privileged," it is obviously unacceptable, whatever the plausible interpretation of *privileged*.

The third principle runs as follows: "The world ecological system is too complex for human beings ever to understand." It seems that this formulation is an absolutist modification of Aldo Leopold's expression: ". . . may never be fully understood." If there is a question of understanding fully what goes on in one gram of soil when a thousandth part of a milligram of a certain poison is administered, we must answer, I think, in the negative. We would have to understand countless millions of living beings in their close interaction. But if only general notions about what happens on our planet are implied, some humans, including Watson, already understand quite a lot. Again vagueness and ambiguity render it difficult to be for or against the "position."

The fourth principle, according to Watson, is that "the ultimate goal, good, and joy of humankind is contemplative understanding of nature." This principle apparently has something to do with a misunderstood interpretation of Spinoza and has little to do with the deep ecology movement. Activeness is a basic concept in Spinoza and active life in nature is a goal of most participants in the movement.

The more complex fifth principle may sound adequate to many deep ecologists, but some of the terms such as *harmonious* and *equilibrium*, which were highly valued as key terms in the sixties, are, I think, less adequate today. Every species in the long run alters ecosystems and mankind cannot be an exception. It is the kind of alteration that matters. Humans have special responsibilities because of their capacity at least to pose the problem of long-term consequences of their behavior.

V

Watson does contribute effectively to the fight against superficial views about diversity, complexity, and ecological balance:

> Another obvious anthropocentric element in ecosophic thinking is the predilection for ecological communities of great internal variety and complexity. But the barren limestone plateaus that surround the Mediterranean now are just as much in ecological balance as were the forests that grew there before man cut them down. And "dead" Lake Erie is just as much in ecological balance with the life on the land that surrounds it as it was in pre-Columbian times.

The "maximum diversity and complexity" *norms* of ecosophy cannot be derived from the *science* of ecology. Often supporters of the movement write as if they believed in such a derivation. In part it is due to broad, normative usages of the term ecology, including much that cannot be part of a science. But the term ecosophy—eco-wisdom—was introduced in order to contrast normative, philosophical views from facts and theories within the science of ecology. It was also introduced to stress the necessity of clarifying the relation between abstract principles and concrete decisions. Wisdom, not science, implies such a relation.

Neither giraffes nor crocodiles have developed any ecosophical norms or theories of gravitational waves. These are specific human products. I do not see, however, why ecosophy or theory of gravitational waves should therefore be classed as "anthropocentric." Human "predilections" are human. Thus far I agree with Watson.

VI

Watson mentions a "hands-off-nature" position and shows convincingly that it implies "setting man apart." Excellent. The supporters of the movement are, in my view, intensively active in their relation to nature, but not in the sense of large-scale digging, cutting, and altering ecosystems. However, are they mainly meditating? Life in and with nature may or may not involve contemplation.[3]

Nils Faarlund has introduced the potent slogan "traceless *ferd* [movement and conduct] in nature" as a main slogan for his international school of outdoor life. Cross-country skiing? Yes. Vast machinery of slalom centers? No. As other valuable slogans of the movement, they are useless or false when interpreted in an absolutist way. (Traceless? Impossible!) As objects of analysis they are in my view indispensable in philosophical seminars at universities, but not as concepts and propositions. Wilderness experience often includes meditation in certain senses, but it also includes the active use of natural resources. Heidegger, I suppose, does not contrast use of tools, for instance, the use of an ax, with "letting beings be." Zimmerman says only that Heidegger is against treating beings "merely as objects for the all-powerful Subject." We may be active in relation to a flower almost every step. That is not a sufficient reason not to live in deserts after rain falls. There is no general norm in ecosophy against our full life in nature, and this implies acceptance of hurting and killing. Ecosophy, as I conceive it, says yes to the fullest self-realization of man.

Tom Regan's "preservation principle" is a slogan that lends itself to passivist, utopian interpretations, especially out of context, but it is also capable of reasonable applications in everyday life, for instance, in the offices of regional planners: when interfering with this river, are we just meddling, or are we doing something necessary in order to satisfy basic needs of humans? Are we destroying this forest or are we merely changing it in a nondestructive way?

In conclusion, I think it may be appropriate to note that in Protagoras' statement about *homo mensura* nothing is said about what is measured. Man may be the measure of all things in the sense that only a human being has a measuring rod, but what he measures he may find to be greater than himself and his survival.

Notes

This chapter is reprinted with minor revisions from Arne Næss, "A Defense of the Deep Ecology Movement," *Environmental Ethics* 6 (Fall, 1984): 265–270.

[1] Richard A. Watson, "A Critique of Anti-Anthropocentric Biocentrism," *Environmental Ethics* 5 (1983): 245–56.

[2] A particular answer is given tentatively in an article by Ivar Mysterud and Arne Næss; "Philosophy of Wolf Policies (I) General Principles and Preliminary Exploration of Selected Norms," in *Conservation Biology* 1 (May 1987). [Reprinted in this volume.]

[3] This reference of Sessions to perennial philosophy, quoted by Watson on page 246, is misleading. I do not think that Sessions insists that meditation is a central feature of man/nature relations. Nor does he think that this is so for Spinoza.

Chapter 16

Against Biospherical Egalitarianism

William C. French

Introduction

In an effort to overcome anthropocentric traditions of ethics, some in the various ecology movements have come to espouse a "biospherical egalitarian" position.[1] In its strict version, proponents of this view hold, first, that all life forms—trees, microorganisms, humans, wolves—have inherent value, and, second, that this inherent value is held equally, such that the members of one species cannot be considered superior (in terms of moral value) to any other. This biospherical egalitarian principle calls for a wide expansion of direct moral consideration, concern, and respect for the value of all life.

This expansion of what counts as the moral community far beyond the borders of the human community is, I believe, correct. What I find problematic, however, is the egalitarian view that not only do all living entities have inherent moral value, but that they all have *equal* inherent moral value. Biospherical egalitarian claims, as I show, tend to be developed inconsistently and often do not in fact govern the concrete moral reasoning of even the theorists who most strongly espouse such beliefs. Many biospherical egalitarians are not, on close examination, the radical egalitarians that they first appear to be. Rather they continue to allow certain species-ranking procedures to control their moral casuistry when they grapple with concrete cases of conflict between and among the interests of humans and members of other species.

In what follows, I first provide a close analysis of the claims about the moral equality of species made by Arne Næss and others of the deep ecology movement as well as those made by Paul Taylor in his book, *Respect for Nature*.[2] In the deep ecology literature, species equality is stressed "in principle," while sotto voce it is acknowledged that vital human interests may legitimately override vital interests of nonhumans. Taylor develops a more consistent and indeed strident emphasis on species equality; yet, at the end of his book, when he addresses concrete cases of conflict between the interests of humans and nonhumans, he too argues that there are many occasions when it is morally proper for humans to kill or injure nonhuman life forms. While never backing off from his insistence on the equality of inherent moral value of all life forms, he too supports ranking procedures that in many cases permit human interests, even nonbasic ones, to override the basic interests of nonhumans.

Both deep ecologists and Taylor appear to toss species ranking out the front door of their arguments only to have it sneak around and into the house from the back. They attempt to preserve consistency by holding that our decisions to kill and injure plants and animals are performed under the aegis of necessity, not under the authority of some appeal to any superior inherent value of humans. Ranking procedures based on necessity and self-defense are permitted, but great efforts are taken to try to show that these in no way imply any rejection of species equality. This strategy, however, oddly suggests that ethical principles ought to be consigned solely to some ideal sphere of pure theory, while our concrete decisions about human action ought to be made outside the sphere of moral review and governed strictly by concerns of power and raw necessity. Biospherical egalitarian claims are secured, but at the cost of transforming them into utopian abstractions that exert no decisive normative weight in our moral decision and practice. By so separating moral principle from practice, this strategy prevents one from providing a clear account of why the necessity of human interests should be morally privileged over the necessity recognized to exist in the survival interests of nonhuman forms of life.

After exploring the claims of deep ecology and Taylor about species equality, in the next section I turn to an examination of a critical, species-ranking position developed in detail in Lawrence Johnson's recent book, *A Morally Deep World*.[3]

In the concluding section, I argue that the biospherical egalitarian ethic is utopian and, even in the hands of its proponents, fails to provide normative guidance in decision and action. If biospherical egalitarianism is promulgated as a moral principle, but is not actually employed as a controlling, normative principle, then ecologists would do well to drop claims of species equality. The growth of a broad-based, ecological movement is ill-served by "deeper than *Thou*" postures and by conceptual and moral confusion.

Deep Ecology and Biospherical Egalitarianism

As anyone familiar with this journal knows, deep ecology refers to the views of a particular school of theorists—Arne Næss, Bill Devall, George Sessions, Warwick Fox, and others—who have articulated a broad ethical, political, economic, and ontological vision pertaining to ecology. Deep ecology poses a sharp and well-aimed critique against anthropocentric traditions of ethics, views of the good life that are bound up with high-consumption lifestyles, and notions of progress that stress industrial expansion and an ever-growing GNP. Deep ecology is not some "finished philosophical system," but rather a dynamic movement whose development is still open to the input of others, especially "artists and writers."[4] According to Næss, what is characteristically "deep" in deep ecology is its level of questioning. As he puts it:

> The decisive difference [between shallow and deep ecology approaches] concerns [the] willingness to question and to appreciate the importance of questioning every economic and political policy in public. . . . The deep ecology movement is therefore the ecology movement which questions deeper.[5]

Two distinctive and central affirmations of deep ecology are the principle of "self-realization" and the principle of "biospherical egalitarianism." The former calls for an empathetic broadening of intimate identification with the entire earth community and all of its members. It requires a process of consciousness raising whereby we overcome being dominated by narrow, egoistic interests and expand to identify our individual selves with the greater self and our interests with those of the entire earth community.[6]

The latter principle—biospherical egalitarianism at first appears to signal a commitment to the remarkably radical proposition that there are no relevant moral differences in value between and among humans and the various animal and plant species. Næss in his first delineation of deep ecology holds that it is committed to *"biospherical egalitarianism*—in principle." But he qualifies this commitment quickly, noting that realistically in concrete practice "some killing, exploitation, and suppression" of nonhuman life forms must occur. However, he immediately stresses species equality by asserting that we need to recognize "the equal right" of all living things "to live and blossom."[7] This strong ambivalence runs throughout Næss's writings.

Devall and Sessions summarize deep ecology's "basic intuition" as rooted in its holistic view: "All organisms and entities in the ecosphere, as parts of the interrelated whole, are equal in intrinsic worth." They continue:

> There are no boundaries and everything is interrelated. But insofar as we perceive things as individual organisms or entities the insight draws us to respect all human and nonhuman individuals in their own right as parts of the whole without feeling the need to set up hierarchies of species with humans at the top.[8]

In 1973 Næss noted that "any realistic praxis necessitates some killing, exploitation, and suppression," but quickly passed on to other concerns of an ecologically holistic outlook. By the mid-1980s, however, he regularly stressed that humans "have no right to reduce this richness and diversity [of life forms] except to satisfy vital needs."[9] As he elaborates, "If their [human] nonvital needs conflict with the vital needs of nonhumans, humans might yield." He notes, moreover, that confusion often arises over the deep ecologists' affirmation of egalitarianism. Some interpret such affirmation to mean a denial of the claim "that humans have any 'extraordinary' traits, or that in situations involving vital interests, humans have no overriding obligations towards their own kind." Næss, however, rejects this interpretation and holds that humans do have overriding obligations to defend and serve human life when "vital" human interests are at stake.[10]

In responding to Richard Watson, a critic of deep ecology, Næss admits that it is true that some advocates of deep ecology "sometimes write or talk *as if* human needs, goals, or desires should *under no circumstances* 'be taken as privileged or overriding.' " Nevertheless, Næss quickly states that such "a norm, if followed uncritically, would, of course, make humans into a strange kind of proletarian and would result in their extinction. Rather, what engages the supporters of the deep ecological movement is the question 'under what circumstances.' " He concludes with an affirmation of a general formula, namely, "A vital need of the nonhuman living being A overrides a peripheral interest of the human being B." Most people, he thinks, already agree to this point with regard to our treatment of wild mammals and birds, but he argues that deep ecology wants to extend this position to a much broader class of nonhumans (presumably including those we have domesticated as providers of food).[11] Næss rejects the view that the "needs, desires, interests, and goals of humans" must never be privileged over those of nonhuman living beings. Rather, he holds that human well-being must not "in every case" be privileged.[12]

In *Ecology, Community and Lifestyle*, the 1990 English-language version of his book originally published in 1976, Næss develops what is, I believe, his fullest clarification of deep ecology's emphasis on "the universal right [of all life forms] to live and blossom." He argues that "no single species"—including the human species—has more of this right than others.[13] Again, he makes a distinction between the articulation of an ethical principle and the application of that principle in concrete practice. He concludes that the "principle of equal rights of all fellow beings" is one norm among a cluster of others, all of which bear on our decision about where our actual moral duty lies. This principle, as Næss puts it, suggests

> a guideline for our behavior, but it does not tell anything about behavior. . . . It is not some kind of unconditional *isolatable* norm to treat everything the same way. It is only a fragment of a total view apprehension of the actual conditions under which we live our own lives . . . makes it crystal clear that we have to injure and kill, in other words actively hinder the self-unfolding of other living beings. Equal right to unfold potentials as a principle is not a practical norm about equal conduct towards all life forms. It suggests a guideline limiting killing, and more generally limiting obstruction of the unfolding of potentialities in others.[14]

He rejects the view that "living beings can be ranked according to their relative intrinsic value." Instead of such a ranking, which could justify a "right to kill or injure the less valuable" species, Næss believes that it is better to elaborate "under which circumstances it is justifiable to hunt or kill other living beings." He holds that we "might agree upon rules such as will imply different behavior towards different kinds of living beings" and still consistently holds that "there is a value inherent in living beings which *is* equal for all." His "intuition" of the unity of all life commits him, he believes, to holding that it is wrong to say: "I can kill you because I am more valuable." However, he finds it acceptable to say: "I will kill you because I am hungry." Næss believes that a key difference between the two is that in the second formulation there arises an "implicit regret"—a sorrow for the killing. Yet, he confesses that his analysis leads to some remaining, normative confusion. "In short, I find obviously right, but often difficult to justify, different sorts of behavior with different sorts of living beings." [15]

Later he rejects any interpretation of "biospheric egalitarianism" which suggests that "human needs should never have priority over nonhuman needs." "In practice, we have . . . greater obligation to that which is nearer to us" and this obligation "implies duties which sometimes involve killing or injuring non-humans." [16] Næss stresses that "each living being" is "in principle on an equal footing with one's own ego." Yet, he quickly notes:

> This does not imply that one acts, wishes to act, or consistently *can* act in harmony with the principle of equality. The statements about biospheric equality must be merely taken as guidelines. Even under conditions of intense identification, killing occurs. The Indians in California, with their animistic mythology, were an example of equality in principle, combined with realistic admissions of their own vital needs. When hunger arrives, brother rabbit winds up in the pot. [17]

Næss elaborates finally how our acts must be morally guided by a "realistic egalitarian attitude." For an example of this attitude, he points to how animist cultures allow the killing of animals for food and clothing, but only if the killing is conducted with reverence for the animal and regret for the act. This realistic attitude is followed when a hunter "has a long discussion with the spirit of the bear, and explains apologetically that the larder is bare and that he must now kill the bear to nourish his family." [18]

Critique of Deep Ecology

Næss's deep ecology appears to be normatively inconsistent. First, it is not helpful in ethics to separate as definitively as Næss does moral principles from moral practice. If Næss's species egalitarianism can only be promulgated "in principle" and must be consistently reshaped into a qualified "realistic egalitarianism" that allows humans to kill or injure animals and plants and damage ecosystems in practice, then the latter formulation is the genuine normative position that governs decision and action. As Næss elaborates, "strict egalitarianism" remains "an abstract ideal," and even he accepts that if one were to follow it in the sphere of concrete action, one would act wrongly.

Second, Næss rejects ranking schemes based on claims that certain life forms have greater inherent value than others in part, it seems, because he feels that such claims necessarily lead to a loss of regret when we find that we must kill or injure animals or plants to protect vital human interests. Nevertheless, this conclusion does not necessarily follow. Such a ranking system entails no necessary undercutting of the grounds for a deep sense of regret for the tragic dimension of our acts when they involve killing or injuring other life forms. To hold that a wolf or a worm has less inherent moral value than a child does not imply at all that to kill a wolf or a worm entails no grave loss or taking of a being with significant inherent value.

Third, Næss's transformation of the equality principle, under the pressure of necessity, into a "realistic egalitarianism," which permits the killing or injuring of animals and plants to protect vital human interests, seems to take these decisions out of the sphere of morality altogether and turns them into assertions of raw power. By insisting that there are no gradations of inherent value between and among the various species, Næss seems to give us no moral foundation for making the decision to kill or injure nonhumans except on the basis of raw need. He accepts that in some cases vital human needs are privileged, but he gives us no moral basis to justify this privileging.

Næss appeals to the principle that we have "greater obligation to that which is nearer to us" (and notes that other humans are "closer" to us than animals).[19] What he cannot show, however, is how this principle has any moral grounding, for to do so requires, Næss seems to believe, some scheme of species ranking. Without a moral ranking of the various vital interests in conflict, we simply have a ranking of assertions of power. We or the Indians simply explain our vital need, and that is it. This approach, however, fails to provide a moral reason for why our vital need deserves to override an animal's, a plant's, or an ecosystem's vital need. If "strict egalitarianism" is truly the moral ideal, then should not cases involving conflicts between the vital needs of humans and nonhumans be concluded by flipping a coin to give each side a fifty-percent chance? Would not such a system be a more direct application of the moral ideal of justice and equity?

A great tension is produced by Næss's commitment to "biospherical egalitarianism," and his equal commitment to account realistically for the tragic, conflictual conditions of life. I do not think that he can have it both ways. It is no wonder that he must finally admit that he finds it "right, but difficult to justify, different sorts of behavior with different sorts of living beings." My view is that without some notion of species ranking—critically formulated and compassionately and contextually applied—it may well be impossible to provide the moral justification that Næss admits his position seems to lack.

Fourth, commitment to a belief in "a value inherent in living beings which is *the same value* for all" need not exclude the possibility that different species might have additional claims to respect and protection generated by their additional capacities, interests, and needs. Our assessments of moral significance must take seriously both the commonalities that all life forms share and the significant differences that distinguish the various species from one another. Later I examine Lawrence Johnson's species-ranking scheme, which develops this approach.

Paul Taylor's Position

In his book *Respect for Nature*, Paul Taylor develops an endorsement of the radical equality of the inherent value of all life forms that is even more thoroughly sustained than that of the deep ecologists. Taylor holds that a "biocentric outlook on nature" entails a rejection of any hierarchical "idea of human superiority over other living things."[20] It requires that one commit oneself to "the principle of species-impartiality," according to which

> every species counts as having the same value in the sense that, regardless of what species a living thing belongs to, it is deemed to be prima facie deserving of equal concern and consideration on the part of moral agents. . . . Species-impartiality . . . means regarding every entity that has a good of its own [humans, animals, and plants] as possessing inherent worth—the *same* inherent worth, since none is superior to another.[21]

While Næss regularly qualifies his commitment to a strict species-equality view, Taylor seems at first to allow no qualifications whatsoever. Taylor holds that animals and plants

> possess a degree or amount of inherent worth equal to that of humans. To say that they possess worth equal to ours means that we owe duties to them that are prima facie as stringent as those we owe to our fellow humans.[22]

Yet Taylor, too, at the end of his book, is forced to grapple with the inevitable conflict of interest cases that occur so often between humans and nonhumans. Those committed to both a respect for persons and a respect for nature must, according to Taylor, give equal consideration to moral claims that arise from both "systems of ethics."[23] The fact that conflict cannot be avoided leads him to elaborate and apply priority principles that provide a means for adjudicating these cases. Taylor articulates five such principles: self-defense, proportionality, minimum wrong, distributive justice, and restitutive justice. Methodologically, he is committed to developing and applying these principles so as to avoid any anthropocentric bias in order to respect species impartiality. While granting that humans "alone are full-fledged bearers of moral rights," Taylor insists that those who "adopt the attitude of respect for nature" will "consider morally irrelevant the fact that wild animals and plants, unlike human persons, are not bearers of moral rights."[24]

The principle of self-defense holds that "it is permissible for moral agents to protect themselves against dangerous or harmful organisms by destroying them." This measure may only be taken as a "last resort" after all other means to avoid the danger have been exhausted.[25] Taylor notes that, at first, this requirement seems biased in favor of humans, but he insists that "humans are not given an advantage simply on the basis of their humanity." His formulation of the principle, he insists, is "species-blind."

> The fact that (most) humans are moral agents and (most) nonhumans are not is a contingent truth which the principle does not take to be morally relevant. Moral agents are permitted to defend themselves against harmful or dangerous organisms that are not moral agents. This is all the principle of self-defense allows.[26]

In elaborating his priority principles Taylor draws a distinction between basic and nonbasic interests. He also distinguishes between practices harmful to nonhuman nature that are intrinsically incompatible with the attitude of respect for nature and those practices that, while harmful to nonhuman nature are not intrinsically incompatible with a stance of respect for nature. He restricts the scope of the principle of proportionality "to situations of conflict between the basic interests of wild animals and plants and those nonbasic human interests that are intrinsically incompatible with respect for nature."[27] Among the practices prohibited by this principle, Taylor lists:

a.   the slaughtering of elephants for ivory to make tourist novelties,
b.   picking rare wildflowers for private collections,
c.   capturing tropical birds for sale as pets,
d.   hunting rare wild mammals for the luxury fur trade, and
e.   all sport hunting and recreational fishing.[28]

The principle of minimum wrong, likewise, is limited by Taylor to cases involving a clash between "basic interests of wild animals and plants" and nonbasic interests of humans. Additionally, this principle only covers cases in which the nonbasic human interests are "not intrinsically incompatible with respect for nature."[29] Interestingly, Taylor holds that there is a class of human values and preferences which, though they themselves are not basic human interests, are still "so highly valued" that they often warrant the overriding of the basic interests of nonhumans. He cites among other practices the construction of museums, libraries, public parks, airports, harbors, highways, and hydroelectric dams, all of which disturb or destroy natural habitats. Such activities do not, Taylor believes, "express a purely exploitative attitude toward nature." This set of nonbasic, yet "highly valued," human interests, Taylor states, may properly "outweigh the undesirable consequences" of harming wild animals and plants. Such practices are only justified, of course, if all less ecologically damaging ways of reaching these human goals have been exhausted.[30]

Though nonbasic, this set of human interests are still, for Taylor, "so important that rational and factually informed people who have genuine respect for nature" would not be "willing to relinquish the pursuit of those interests even when they take into account the undesirable consequences for wildlife."[31] Such valued interests, Taylor believes, are "essential to a whole society's maintaining a high level of culture," "carry great weight," and, indeed, may legitimately override even the basic interests of the "earth's nonhuman inhabitants."[32] The principle of minimal wrong holds that when rational and informed persons "who have adopted the attitude of respect for nature are nevertheless unwilling to forgo" intrinsically valued social ends "shared by a whole society as the focus of its way of life," then it is "permissible for them to pursue those values" so long as they have opted for the policy that does the least harm to nonhuman living entities.[33]

The principle of distributive justice, for Taylor, covers cases in which the competing human and nonhuman interests are all basic ones and in which the nonhumans are not harmful to us. Given that all the interests are basic, they all must be accorded equal "moral weight." This principle requires that when "there exists a natural source of good that can be used for the benefit of any of the parties, each party must be allotted an equal share."[34] Yet, Taylor allows that if human survival requires the killing and eating of animals, fish, or plants, then it is morally permissible for humans to do so. Even here, however, he does not back off from his insistence that, animals, plants, and humans have equal inherent worth. He sees no contradiction because he holds that humans have no obligation to sacrifice themselves "for the sake of animals" or plants. As he puts it: "Animals are not of greater worth, so there is no obligation to further their interests at the cost of the basic interests of humans." Similarly, for Taylor, plants are humans' "equals in inherent worth," but "we have no duty to sacrifice ourselves to them."[35]

Critique of Taylor's Account

If I understand Taylor's arguments correctly, then I find his system bizarre. Næss at least makes clear that his formulation of biospherical egalitarianism still accepts that vital human interests outweigh nonhuman interests. Taylor, while insisting throughout that all species have equal inherent value, sees no contradiction in allowing that even various nonbasic, human interests morally outweigh the basic interests of nonhumans. For Taylor, humans may kill animals and plants out of necessity. Humans may use animals and plants in many ways and may continue actively to develop the earth to support our important cultural and societal values. How does this position square with his sustained, strict acceptance of species equality? If I follow his arguments correctly, only methodological contortion permits their reconciliation. In my critique, I focus on five points.

First, Taylor holds that the principle of proportionality requires that in conflict cases "greater weight is to be given to basic than to nonbasic interests, no matter what species, human or other, the competing claims arise from."[36] Yet, when he delineates the principle of minimum wrong, he holds the contradictory position, that in a wide range of cases it is proper for humans' "highly valued," but nonbasic, interests to be given greater moral weight than the basic interests of animals and plants. In an ethical system that is supposed to provide substantive guidance for decision and action, should the normative bite of different moral principles clash so directly? Taylor seems to believe that there is no normative contradiction because each principle covers a different set of cases. I, however, do not believe that moral principles are best viewed as strictly separate from one another and only narrowly applicable to this, but not that, range of cases. There are significant continuities of value across the whole set of cases that Taylor's approach obscures.

Second, recall Taylor's attempt to defend the principle of self-defense as "species-blind." Although this principle privileges the interests of "moral agents" over beings who aren't agents, Taylor argues that it does not necessarily entail that only humans can possibly count as moral agents. Taylor dismisses as merely a "contingent truth" the fact that in the only world in which we live and act, almost all humans become moral agents and almost all nonhumans don't. He uses an analytical razor to cut remarkably formal distinctions. If ethics is primarily an exercise in practical reason, then the data of our common world should be treated not as a "contingent," but rather as a central truth of our moral experience. In the realm of decision and action Taylor's formulation provides wide-ranging justification for acts by humans that harm animals, micro-organisms, and plants. Analytical sleight of hand should not be allowed to hide this fact. Clarity would be promoted, I believe, by acknowledging directly that Taylor's normative privileging of moral agents over non-agents constitutes a general privileging (under normal conditions) of human over nonhuman life.

Third, Taylor's gravest contradiction seems to lie in his appeal to a shadowy set of human interests that while dubbed "nonbasic," are still of such "special importance" that they morally outweigh the basic interests of nonhumans. If nonbasic interests can outweigh basic interests, then the distinction between basic and nonbasic is rendered deeply problematic. If such human interests are so special, then why are they not classed as basic? More importantly, if such societal interests in maintaining a "high level of civilized life"[37] are normatively weighty, what is the moral basis of that weight? Even though high levels of human culture play a governing role in Taylor's ethical theory, his insistence upon species equality requires him simultaneously to refuse to grant any distinctive moral weight to the inherent value of human individuals—the beings who create and sustain that high culture. Taylor's strict commitment to species equality thus contorts his theory, pushing him to hold that human culture has especially weighty normative value, but human life does not.

Fourth, when Taylor analyses the requirements of distributive justice, he first holds that all concerned parties must be accorded an equal share of some good—food, water, air, land. Yet, he concludes, it is permissible to kill animals and plants because they do not have greater value than humans, and because we have no obligation to sacrifice ourselves for them. But if a just distribution is an equal share, why not hold to that position in concrete decision and action? Why not prescribe a random method for deciding who or what should get the food or habitat space? Or perhaps the moral agent could work out a schedule whereby each privileging of the agent's own claims to the resources would next time be followed by an explicit privileging of the non-agent's claims. Taylor stresses normative equality; yet, he regularly formulates his principles so as to justify all sorts of cases in which humans may kill or injure animals and plants.

Fifth, these concerns taken together make it unclear just what scope Taylor wants the principle of species equality to play in his ethical system. He states that the adjudication between respect for nature and respect for human cultural and civilizational interests depends on "people's total systems of value."[38] However, by not delineating just how principles derived from our "respect for persons" are to be joined with principles derived from our "respect for nature" to form a coherent total system, Taylor leaves us unclear about the moral grounding of our final, concrete, normative weightings.

Especially vague is Taylor's use of the terms equal concern and consideration. Recall Taylor' s view that species equality means that plants and animals "possess a worth equal to ours" and we thus "owe duties to them that are prima facie as stringent as those we owe to our fellow humans." Cases of conflict between the interests of humans and those of wild animals and plants are cases in which "validly binding prima facie duties of equal stringency . . . are in conflict."[39]

Nevertheless, almost immediately gaps appear in his argument. Taylor acknowledges that species equality does not rule out how the "duty not to destroy or harm animals and plants in natural ecosystems" may be legitimately overridden by "duties that moral agents owe to humans."[40] Far from cashing out his view at the normative level as a strict species-egalitarian position, Taylor holds, to the contrary, that various human practices harmful to nature may be justified on moral grounds when they are required for human survival. He backs this claim with an appeal to ethical principles rooted in "a system of human ethics" and "a priority principle that makes the duty to provide for human survival outweigh those duties of nonmaleficence, noninterference, and fidelity that are owed to nonhumans."[41]

Taylor can defend his position against the charge of contradiction in two ways. First, he seems to believe that there are two sharply distinct spheres of ethics—human ethics and environmental ethics. Perhaps he means that his claim of strict species equality only applies in the sphere of environmental ethics, and thus does not govern the "total system." This position would save his claim of species equality, but at the cost of radically qualifying its range of relevance and application. A concrete decision regarding what one's actual moral duty is in a given case would thus not be controlled by the principle of species equality, but by whether one's total ethical system allows human survival and cultural interests to override one's prima facie duties to animals and plants. If so, then, although Taylor may stress species equality, he still subscribes to an ethical view which, in fact, normatively gives a privileged position to the interests of moral agents—namely, most humans.

Second, Taylor may argue that his principle of species equality is only meant to hold for our prima facie duties but not for our judgment of our concrete duty at the point of decision and action, what W. D. Ross calls our "actual duty."[42] This position would allow Taylor to say that our prima facie duties to humans, animals, and plants are all equally stringent and yet hold that our actual duties—as he puts it, the "all-things-considered judgment that a certain action ought or ought not be done"[43]—at times rightly give priority to human survival and cultural interests. If so, then Taylor appears to want to have his cake and to eat it too. He loudly endorses what on first blush appears to be a radical species-equality position, but quietly constructs many methodological walls to hem in that position and to restrict sharply its authority at the point of a moral agent's final determination of his or her actual moral duty. If this reading of Taylor's position is correct, then he restricts his species-equality principle to a claim about *prima facie* duties, while allowing certain undeveloped species-ranking judgments and weightings to control the actual—the "all-things-considered"—normative judgment.

Lawrence Johnson's Species-Ranking Scheme

Biospherical egalitarianism, as I believe the preceding analysis of Næss's and Taylor's ethical theories shows, seems unable to guide concrete normative judgments without reintroducing some normative ranking of species. If, finally, even the proponents of species equality must accept a normative privileging of human interests and worth, then, I believe, concerns for ethical consistency and clarity suggest that it is better to articulate our value hierarchy plainly, rather than having it remain cloaked and unarticulated. In what follows, I provide a brief sketch of such a critical, anti-anthropocentric, species-ranking position.

Lawrence Johnson in his recent book, *A Morally Deep World*, has given a sustained and well-nuanced account of a critical species-ranking ecological ethic. In opposition to anthropocentric traditions, which exclude all nonhumans from direct moral consideration, and hedonist utilitarian schemes, which exclude plants and microorganisms from such moral consideration, Johnson argues that *all* living beings and entities have morally significant interests in their own well-being that we humans must respect. Against Taylor and others who hold that only individual living beings have inherent moral worth, Johnson holds that both living individuals and living "holistic entities"—for example, species, discrete ecosystems, and the entire biosphere itself—have significant inherent moral worth.

Johnson tries to chart a mid-course between atoms and ethical holism and between anthropocentrism and biospherical egalitarianism. For Johnson, although all the relevant interests of all living individuals and holistic entities potentially impacted by our decision must be considered, not all of these interests need be weighted equally in our normative consideration of our actual moral duty or duties. While stressing that *"all* genuine interests must be recognized as having some moral weight," Johnson holds that

> some interests have more weight than others. It is a matter of degrees. In arguing that the interests of a mouse are morally considerable, I am not claiming that setting a mousetrap is on a par with the premeditated murder of a human being. Normally, a human being has more interests than does a mouse.[44]

As he puts it later: "Although we ought to revere life . . . some life is more valuable than other life. This is not because only some interests count while some do not—all interests count—but because not all interests are equivalent."[45] To illustrate his position concretely, he ranks a chimpanzee as having a morally more significant interest in life than an amoeba (under normal conditions). Likewise, he holds that the interests of individual plants are, under normal conditions, usually quite slight, certainly less than the interests of humans who eat them. However, the interests of a whole plant species threatened by extinction normally are morally privileged, thereby thwarting human interests in consuming the last few of that species in a salad for lunch.[46]

The key normative principle, for Johnson, is: "Give due respect to all the interests of all beings that have interests, in proportion to their interests."[47] He believes the "bad news" is that no moral theory can generate a complete set of principles to cover all possible ecological cases of conflict of interests.[48] Still, the "good news" is that we generally do well morally when we adopt a stance of genuine respect for the "well-being interests" of all. When doing so, we may well make mistakes, but at least we avoid utter callousness toward nature and thus avoid acting as sheer exploiters and vandals. If people ever came to view every animal, plant, species, and ecosystem as a valuable and morally significant "end in itself," they would have to develop terribly significant changes in moral perception, sensitivity, and habits of action, but still would not solve all dilemmas.[49]

Johnson sees inherent value running deeply throughout the full range of living beings and entities, and hence holds that the world is a "morally deep" one. Unlike the deep ecologists and Taylor, however, Johnson believes that we must adopt "a multilevel approach to multilevel problems in a multilevel world."[50] Individuals of different species have different types of well-being interests, and, while all of these interests are morally significant, their significance is a "matter of degree."[51]

Johnson avoids Taylor's confusion over what it means to give different individuals of different species "equal moral consideration" by distinguishing clearly between giving something or someone moral consideration and holding that something or someone is morally significant. A being or entity either deserves or doesn't deserve moral consideration. Moral consideration tends not to be a scalar term mapping degrees or levels, but rather is used to register a claim about admission into, or denial from, the circle of beings or entities to which inherent value is ascribed. When a being or an entity is evaluated as being morally considerable, the level of its moral significance vis-à-vis other morally considerable beings and entities remains to be established. In Johnson's view, all interests are morally significant and thus should be taken into account in our moral decision making. However, some individuals, species, and ecosystems have greater moral significance than others.

What then for Johnson are the criteria of moral significance? He employs the notion of "interest packages" to chart how individuals of one species may share a particular well-being interest with individuals of another species and yet also have an additional, distinctive well-being interest that is not shared by the individuals of that other species.[52] As he puts it:

> Certainly rational beings have interests involving their rationality, interests that nonrational beings lack, and these interests are morally significant. . . . Sentient beings have interests involving their sentience, interests that nonsentient beings lack and these interests are morally significant. As these interests of different sorts are all morally significant, we must try to give them all their due weight—whatever that is.[53]

For Johnson, although humans, dogs, and trees all have "intrinsic moral importance," "they have very different interests" and thus "very different [moral] importance."[54]

Johnson holds that "any even moderately viable means of morally assessing a life or a life system would, at the very least, have to take into consideration the degree of complexity of the life system in question and its degree of coherent, integrated, functional organic unity. Thus, a human by virtue of his or her greater "complexity" over a dandelion has a "greater interest in life and a higher moral status."[55] Elsewhere, he argues that certain "well-being configurations are better than others, in terms of having greater complexity, diversity, balance, organic unity or integrity. . . ."[56] He suggests that "more developed individuals [of different species] will have greater self identity" than less developed and less complex, so that amoebas have much less moral importance vis-à-vis their species than do individual humans vis-à-vis ours.[57]

Ranking as a Response to Needs and Vulnerability

Both Taylor and the deep ecologists seem to believe that when we acknowledge any superiority of capacities of certain species, we immediately find ourselves on the slippery slope to flat-out anthropocentrism. Hence they adopt the strategy of denying species ranking in principle, even if not in practice. Talk of certain species having inherent moral superiority over others seems to Taylor and the deep ecologists to violate the holistic ecological understanding of the interdependency of the community of life.

Johnson's approach is helpful because he suggests that the key issue in our ranking of species in conflict-of-interest cases is not some reward for merit based on some superiority of capacities, but rather is an appropriate response to protect, as best we can, individuals and species that have greater ranges of vulnerability than others. When Johnson claims that a human has a higher moral status than a dandelion, he is not granting some moral reward to the human for his or her superior capacities. Rather, Johnson's claim rightly flags the fact that the human not only has the well-being interests of a dandelion (for example, the need for air and water), but also has a whole range of additional well-being needs. The claim that certain individuals, species, and ecosystems have higher moral status than others is, I believe, at bottom, a comparative normative claim that is supposed to draw attention to the fact that certain individuals, species, and ecosystems have greater development and complexity, and thus a greater range of vulnerability and need.

Species ranking is not some prize awarded to those having superior capacities. Rather, it is an appropriate attempt under the conditions of finitude to give special protection to *some* when we are not able to give equal protection to *all*. In a perfect world we would not need to make forced choices, and thus would not need to allow a harm to occur to one in order to protect another from harm. In our world, however, we often must make such choices.

Part of our problem arises from the use of the term *inherent value*. When using this term, we are usually trying to assert that some being or entity is a moral "end in itself"—that is, that it has its own worth independent of its instrumental worth for us. Unfortunately, some seem to hear in the term *inherent* some suggestion of a type of essential metaphysics according to which different levels of being have different levels of value wired into them. Species ranking from this point of view understandably appears methodologically crude and morally arrogant.

If ethics is understood, however, as a relational discipline centered on assessments of responsibility to diverse beings and entities in relation to each other and in relation to us, then species ranking is simply a necessary part of our moral practice of setting priorities. Rankings should not be thought of as static assessments of some mysterious and fixed levels of ontological value. Rather, rankings are relational assessments about where—in particular cases and under distinct conditions—our moral priority lies to defend those who have the greatest range of potential vulnerability. I think it best not to think of rankings as an assessment of some "inherent" superiority, but rather as a considered moral recognition of the fact that greater ranges of vulnerability are generated by broader ranges of complexity and capacities.[58] As Johnson suggests, species and ecosystem rankings are really based on a recognition that more developed, more complex individuals, species, and ecosystems are more vulnerable in the sense that they have more to lose. As Johnson puts it, both a dead mouse with bacterial growth and a mature rain forest constitute distinctive ecosystems. Yet, the growth in the "dead-mouse ecosystem" is in no way unique or complex and almost nothing "would be lost were that tiny ecosystem disrupted."[59] In contrast

to Taylor, who fears ascribing greater inherent worth to species with wider
ranges of capacities, Johnson rightly accepts normative priorities grounded in
duties to protect vulnerability and to minimize loss. Species ranking is not, at
bottom, based on human hubris, but rather on a commitment to responsible
choice and action under the constraints imposed by conditions of finite resources, time, and energy.

Conclusion

Biospherical egalitarianism, even in the hands of its most consistent proponents,
breaks down when dealing with the necessary choices that must be made under
the conditions of life. In my analysis, I have tried to chart a pattern of argument,
common to many egalitarians, in which they initially enunciate a broad principle
of species equality, but later back away from it as they struggle to account for
our moral responsibilities in conflict-of-interest cases. When those who most
consistently reject notions of human superiority over nonhumans later reach for
the functional equivalent of species-ranking procedures, one must conclude that
no ecological ethic that attempts to be comprehensive can dispense with some
sort of hierarchical ranking of moral priorities based, at least in part, on critical
evaluations of the different capacities, needs, and vulnerabilities of different
individuals, species, and ecosystems. An ecological ethical scheme that makes
this point clear from the start avoids much methodological confusion.

Some, I suspect, are attracted to the species-egalitarian position because of
the sheer force and sweep of its indictment of anthropocentric traditions of ethics. Its absolutism provides a strong platform for radical prophetic indictment.
Nevertheless, we must be mindful of the costs of this moral strategy. Those who
wave the banner of biospherical egalitarianism may well score points with an
already converted, radical few; yet, they may also be leading a broad segment of
the general public to conclude that the radical wing of the ecology movement is,
at best, unrealistic, of worse, anti-human.

Næss and other deep ecologists have made many important and timely
points that deserve a broad hearing, particularly, their emphasis on the need for
a radical identification with nature, their advocacy of appropriate technologies
and sustainability, and their potent critiques of consumerism, high-growth economics, and population expansion. Taylor, too, makes important contributions
with his analysis of what the attitude of "respect for nature" entails. However,
the insistence of Taylor and the deep ecologists on biospherical egalitarianism, I
fear, draws attention away from their other more solid and serviceable contributions. Their insistence on a principle that does not finally seem intended to govern moral judgment about concrete duty and practice purchases little normative
work at high cost in conceptual contortion.

If, as I have tried to show, both Næss and Taylor—two of the strongest advocates of biospherical egalitarianism—move away from that principle when
adjudicating conflict-of-interest cases, then both the coherency and usefulness

of that principle are called sharply into question. It would be a shame if the stress on biospherical egalitarianism led people to dismiss deep ecology as deeply confused, for many of deep ecologys other affirmations are significant and deserve a broad hearing. Until more consistent and stronger defenses of biospherical egalitarianism can be marshaled, I believe, deep ecologists and other ecological theorists would do well to drop this principle from their portfolio of affirmations.

Notes

This chapter is reprinted with minor revisions from William C. French, "Against Biospherical Egalitarianism," *Environmental Ethics* 17 (spring, 1995): 39–57.

[1] This term and *ecological egalitarianism* are used interchangeably by Arne Næss in his now classic essay, "The Shallow and the Deep, Long-Range Ecology Movement: A Summary," *Inquiry* 16 (1973): 95–100. This position is also endorsed by some eco-feminists who are understandably suspicious of appeal to hierarchical models as a means of understanding either social or natural relationships.

[2] Paul W. Taylor, *Respect for Nature: A Theory of Environmental Ethics* (Princeton: Princeton University Press, 1986).

[3] Lawrence E. Johnson, *A Morally Deep World: An Essay on Moral Significance and Environmental Ethics* (Cambridge: Cambridge University Press, 1991).

[4] Arne Næss, "The Deep Ecological Movement: Some Philosophical Aspects," *Philosophical Inquiry* 8 (1986): 22, 18.

[5] Næss, "The Deep Ecological Movement: Some Philosophical Aspects," 21–22.

[6] See Bill Devall and George Sessions, *Deep Ecology: Living as if Nature Mattered* (Salt Lake City: Peregrine Smith Books, 1985), 66–67, 76. Also see Arne Næss, *Ecology, Community and Lifestyle: Outline of an Ecosophy*, trans. David Rothenberg (Cambridge: Cambridge University Press, 1989), 8–11, 84–92, 164–66, 171–76.

[7] Næss, "Shallow and the Deep Movement," 95–96.

[8] Devall and Sessions, *Deep Ecology,* 67–68.

[9] Næss, "Deep Ecological Movement," 14.

[10] Næss, "Deep Ecological Movement," 20, 22.

[11] Arne Næss, "A Defence of the Deep Ecology Movement," *Environmental Ethics* 6 (1984): 267.

[12] "A Defence of the Deep Ecology Movement," 268 (emphasis added).

[13] Næss, *Ecology, Community and Lifestyle*, 166.

[14] Næss, *Ecology, Community and Lifestyle*, 167.

[15] Næss, *Ecology, Community and Lifestyle*, 167–68.

[16] Næss, *Ecology, Community and Lifestyle*, 170.

[17] Næss, *Ecology, Community and Lifestyle*, 174.

[18] Næss, *Ecology, Community and Lifestyle*, 176.

[19] Næss, *Ecology, Community and Lifestyle*, 170–71.

[20] Taylor, *Respect for Nature*, 44–45.

[21] Taylor, *Respect for Nature*, 155.

[22] Taylor, *Respect for Nature*, 151–52.

[23] Taylor, *Respect for Nature*, 259.

[24] Taylor, *Respect for Nature*, 261–62. For Taylor's argument that humans have "rights" and animals and plants do not, see 150–52, 219–55, 262.

[25] Taylor, *Respect for Nature*, 264–65.

[26] Taylor, *Respect for Nature*, 266–67.

[27] Taylor, *Respect for Nature*, 277–78.

[28] Taylor, *Respect for Nature*, 274.

[29] Taylor, *Respect for Nature*, 278, 280.

[30] Taylor, *Respect for Nature*, 276–77.

[31] Taylor, *Respect for Nature*, 280.

[32] Taylor, *Respect for Nature*, 281.

[33] Taylor, *Respect for Nature*, 282–83.

[34] Taylor, *Respect for Nature*, 292.

[35] Taylor, *Respect for Nature*, 294–95.

[36] Taylor, *Respect for Nature*, 278.

[37] Taylor, *Respect for Nature*, 281.

[38] Taylor, *Respect for Nature*, 277.

[39] Taylor, *Respect for Nature*, 152.

[40] Taylor, *Respect for Nature*, 171.

[41] Taylor, *Respect for Nature*, 183.

[42] See W. D. Ross, *The Right and the Good* (1930; rpt., Oxford: Clarendon Press, 1973), 19–20.

[43] Ross, *Right and the Good*, 192.

[44] Johnson, *Morally Deep World*, 7. For an important articulation of a position similar to Johnson's, see Louis G. Lombardi, "Inherent Worth, Respect, and Rights," *Environmental Ethics* 5 (1983): 257–70. See also Taylor's responses to Lombardi, "Are Humans Superior to Animals and Plants?" *Environmental Ethics* 6 (1984): 149–60 and *Respect for Nature*, 147–52.

[45] Johnson, *Morally Deep World*, 135–36.

[46] Johnson, *Morally Deep World*, 136, 172.

[47] Johnson, *Morally Deep World*, 118, 185, 198.

[48] Johnson, *Morally Deep World*, 185, 189.

[49] Johnson, *Morally Deep World*, 189–200.

[50] Johnson, *Morally Deep World*, 247.

[51] Johnson, *Morally Deep World*, 243, 278.

[52] Johnson, *Morally Deep World*, 279.

[53] Johnson, *Morally Deep World*, 198.

[54] Johnson, *Morally Deep World*, 267.

[55] Johnson, *Morally Deep World*, 188.

[56] Johnson, *Morally Deep World*, 227.

[57] Johnson, *Morally Deep World*, 243.

[58] For an excellent account of how more advanced organisms pay for their increased capacities and vitalities by increased habitat and energy needs, see Hans Jonas, *The Phenomenon of Life: Towards a Philosophical Biology* (Chicago and London: University of Chicago Press, 1966, Phoenix edition, 1982), 99–107, 183–87. Also see Robert E. Goodin, *Protecting the Vulnerable* (Chicago and London: University of Chicago Press, 1985) for an explicit attempt to analyze ethics as centered in our responsibilities for the vulnerable. See especially pp. 179–88, where Goodin turns his attention to ecological issues.

[59] Johnson, *Morally Deep World*, 278.

Chapter 17

An Answer to W. C. French: Ranking, Yes, But the Inherent Value is the Same

Arne Næss

In the spring issue of 1995 of *Environmental Ethics* William C. French published an excellent article "Against Biospherical Egalitarianism." French asks for moderation: "The expansion of what counts as the moral community far beyond the borders of the human community is, I believe, correct. What I find problematic, however, is the egalitarian view that not only do all living entities have inherent moral value, but that they all have *equal* inherent value."

It is, unfortunately, as late as in the 1990s that I changed "equal" into "the same," avoiding as well as I could the question of grading. My position may be formulated as follows: "Living beings have in common a same sort of value, namely inherent value." It makes sense to do something strictly for their own sake. I don't like the grading of this value, but some supporters of the deep ecology movement introduce grading and I do not see any reason to try to make them feel about this in the same way as I do. Deep ecology is not a sect.

Very few supporters use the term "biospherical egalitarianism," and this is good because it is natural to interpret the word "egalitarianism" in an absolutist sense, like absolute equality, or value in every respect, a sense which I never had in mind, and which must make everybody inconsistent sinners. The sense I tried to give the expression refers to point 1 and point 2 of the 8 points. It relates to the (for me) fundamental question: "inherent or merely instrumental value?" Inherence does not (logically) imply absence of ranking, for instance species ranking of different sorts. I use a kind of ranking with a level of consistency compatible with a moderate (ethical) latitudinarian attitude as opposed to a rigorist one. (These terms I borrow from the history of theology.) In short, I don't know of any very helpful general ranking, but together with an ecologist we have tried to systematize norms of ranking which are highly controversial but of vital concern for the continual existence of certain communities: the "mixed" communities of sheep, (small) sheep-owners, bears, and wolves. The small scale sheep-owners are at the same time agriculturists, foresters, hunters and gatherers. Ecological aristocrats!

To systematize a set of prescriptions and descriptions closely adapted to the situation in these areas of Norway is a Herculean task. A contribution worked out together with the ecologist Ivar Mysterud (who has worked more than ten years on the relevant questions) stresses, among other things, the special responsibility of sheep-owners in relation to *their* sheep.[1] When Norway was poor the owners nevertheless hired shepherds; when Norway now is very rich, it costs too much for sheep-owners to hire shepherds. My proposal is that for the next ten years the district authorities and the sheep-owners pay for shepherds. It is a clear obligation to protect our sheep against wolves. Within ten years Norway is likely to be part of a gigantic free market (the European Union) and the small culturally and ecologically high level communities are scarcely able to compete. There may be no small sheep-owners left. The point I am trying to make here is to refer to the complexity and the local character of the problems involved, when saying yes to sheep and to wolves and bears.

Ranking is a complex affair: how do I, for instance, rank insects? Should they all have the same rank? Where I have lived many years, the climate is so tough that some species appear there only because the wind has carried them upwards too high for them to live more than a short time. It feels natural for me to take special care of certain species of butterflies. I see them on the snow patches more or less weakened. Attempts—which I ought to make—to revive them are successful in less than 50 percent of the cases, using my own methods. But I don't find that I (ethically speaking) *ought to* use more refined, time consuming, methods. Ranking is not wholly an ethical affair.

Specimens of other families of insects do not get careful treatment; they are mostly ignored. In some cases I find my behavior ethically not quite as it should be, in other cases I don't feel that in spite of the obvious practical possibility of being helpful, I do nothing. I let them slowly die on the snow. I use the term "feel" extensively in discussing these matters because the ethical analysis of the many situations would be much too complex to handle for me if I referred only to thinking.

Those who find they are able to introduce a sophisticated grading of inherent value perhaps use the term as a technical expression capable of being made fairly precise. As I define it, it is the expression of something largely intuitive. The moment I perceive something as alive, it is apperceived as something with a *kind of* value or standing which I have myself. Ranking does not quite have the same sort of intuitive evidence because it has to do with an act of comparing. Ranking for me has primarily to do with differences of obligation. In wintertime my cottage receives "mice and men" as guests, but my obligations are enormously greater towards the humans than towards the mice. The latter are absolutely forbidden to enter more than one outer room, but considering the terrific climate, their braveness calls for *some* recognition. They are acceptable in one of the rooms. It *feels absurd* for me to think: "You are mere mice, I have higher inherent value because:

a)   I am much more intelligent,
b)   I am much more complex,
c)   I am much higher on the evolutionary ladder,
d)   I am capable of profound sorts of spiritual suffering,
e)   I am self-reflecting, you don't even know yourself, and
f)   . . .

I cannot see that the principle of sameness of inherent value of all living beings makes it difficult to introduce rank consideration in mixed communities. The members of the communities feel obligations of various kinds and intensities, but it is hazardous to integrate them into a system with a set of basic norms, and more so to extend the intended field of validity in favor of a global environmental ethics. A sheep-owner cried out to his children "Come and see through the window!" A big brown bear was coming straight up to the farm, but the sheep were out of reach of the bear. Marvelous sight! Full respect for the bear—its inherent value, its right to eat the sheep. But also the right of the sheep-owner to chase the bear away if it, against expectation, tried to break down the door protecting the sheep. He furthermore accepted fully the rule that he was not supposed to kill the bear if he met it in the woods, except when it attacked. Extremely complex moral and non-moral questions for people whom it concerns!

"My view is that without some notion of species ranking—critically— formulated and compassionately and contextually applied—it may well be impossible to provide the moral justification that Næss admits his position seems to lack." Very well formulated and I completely agree. But ranking does not imply quantification of inherent value.

Suppose French proposes a definite ranking system and applies it compassionately and contextually. Has he given me and the sheep-owners a moral basis? A fundament? I don't know. A system may seem to be too much to ask for as an ultimate basis.

French finds Lawrence Johnson's species-ranking scheme helpful. "A human, by virtue of his or her greater 'complexity' over a dandelion, has a greater interest in life and a higher moral status." French uses "range of vulnerability and need" as a basic criterion. "Our moral priority lies to defend those [species?] who have the greatest range of potential vulnerability," "generated by broader ranges of complexity and capacities."

The proposal of French I feel to be very considerate. Even the tremendous expansion, domination, and vitality of the human species is, I grant, not a sign that it is *not* the most vulnerable. But if I act according to his ranking, I am not sure it furnishes me a general moral *basis*. I shall be on the outlook for something that to me is more intuitively convincing, and perhaps I am not sure how important morally it is in practice to find a *general* ranking scheme.

Notes

[1] Arne Næss, Iver Mysterud, "Philosophy of Wolf Policies I: General Principles and Preliminary Exploration of Selected Norms," in *Conservation Biology* 1 (May 1987).

Chapter 18

Comment: On Næss versus French

Baird Callicott

The philosophical genius expresses itself in two dialectically related modes—the creation of ideas and the criticism of them. Pythagoras is the archetypal incarnation of the former; Socrates, the gadfly, the midwife, is the archetypal incarnation of the latter. Without creative thinkers, critics would have nothing with which to cavil. Without critics, creative thinkers would be unbridled. It seems to me that Arne Næss belongs to the line of philosophers going back to Pythagoras, and that Richard Watson and William French belong to the line of philosophers going back to Socrates. That ecology might be "deep" as well as broad, "biospherical egalitarianism—in principle," and "the equal right of all things to live and blossom"—these are wonderful new ideas, the progeny of a fertile philosophical mind. But are they wind eggs? Yes, say the dour midwives, Watson and French, abandon them on the mountainside as deformed and unwanted children. But wait, they show some promise, let them grow up and gain strength, says their parent. Can they withstand critical philosophical scrutiny? No, say the gadflies. Oh yes, says Arne, they can, with a little modification. . . . And so another chapter to a long, old book is begun.

I'm not sure that the parents of new ideas are their best guardians, however. To the critic's cold question, "Just what is deep ecology?" Næss, who gave birth to the idea, answers, weakly, that it is the ecology that asks deeper questions. This tepid response may have been nobly motivated. In sharp contrast to some of his exponents—Warwick Fox, for example—Næss has always avoided the temptation to insist upon doctrinal orthodoxy as a litmus test for membership in the movement. Asking profound questions presupposes no particular answers. In Næss's view, one may arrive at the deep ecology platform from a wide variety of starting

150

points. Thus a Christian who believes that the God of Abraham made the creation and imbued each of His creatures and the creation as a whole with intrinsic value is no less entitled to be called a deep ecologist than someone who arrives at a functionally similar conclusion from a Buddhist point of departure. But then why call it deep *ecology*, as opposed to the less arresting but more descriptive rubric, "biocentrism?" Better to have answered the question, "What is deep ecology?" by saying that ecology, like the theory of evolution, has deep conceptual ramifications. That doesn't presuppose any particular doctrines either, but it does narrow the inquiry and directly relates deep ecology to the ecological sciences.

What deep ecology ought to be is the exploration of the metaphysical and moral implications of the science of ecology. Foundational to Næss's biocentrism is not deep ecology, in this sense, at all, but two species of monism. At first, Næss founded biocentrism on Spinoza's monism. Then, having been also influenced by Mahatma Gandhi, he founded it on Advaita Vedanta. From either perspective reality is one. There is one substance, God, with two known attributes and infinitely many modes, according to Spinoza. Each human being is a mode of the one substance. But so is every other organism. And as such, all are equal. There is one reality, Atman/Brahman, according to Vedanta, which is the self-same in all its manifestations in the domain of maya. From this perspective too, all are equal. The connection that these two species of monism have with scientific ecology, however, is superficial at best. From the perspective of mid-twentieth-century ecology terrestrial nature is also one. Soils and waters, plants and animals are unified by internal ecological relationships. But they remain distinct realities; they are not absorbed by the oceanic oneness of some transcendent absolute. Thus the way things are one, the sense in which things are one, in ecology (at the zenith of its holistic phase) is very different from the way things are one either in Spinozaland or in Vedantaland. (Making matters worse, the ecological paradigm has shifted toward biotic atomism and reductionism over the last twenty-five years.)

Had Næss been more of a deep ecologist—that is, had he striven to explore the metaphysical and moral implications of ecology, rather than to draw (implausible) analogies between Spinoza's metaphysics and ecology and Vedanta metaphysics and ecology—he might not have made himself so vulnerable to the criticisms of Watson and French. To assert the moral equality of all living beings ("biocentric egalitarianism") and then to try to hedge that assertion ("in principle") is bound to fail, as French persuasively argues. But the corrective to Næss's "biospheric egalitarianism—in principle" that French finds in the work of Lawrence Johnson drifts even further away from ecology. A preferential system of ethics based on interests disregards two distinctions that are fundamental to *ecological* ethics: the distinction between wild and domestic organisms and the distinction between indigenous and exotic organisms. All beings with equal interests are equal in the environmental ethics recommended by French. That means that holsteins are equal to rhinoceroses, that domestic sheep are equal to wild wolves, and that rabbits have as much right to live and blossom in Australia as wallabies.

Just what would a true deep ecology exchange for biocentric egalitarianism in principle? The first deep ecologist (although he never called himself that), Aldo Leopold, suggested not biocentric egalitarianism in principle, but community-sensitive respect. The theory of evolution has undercut any pretense that we human beings transcend nature. We, *Homini sapiensi,* are fellow voyagers with other creatures (evolvents, rather) in the odyssey of evolution. Deep evolution, as Watson delights in pointing out, would imply, however, that human beings have no more obligation to other creatures than they have to us or to one another. But that's not the whole story. Ecology tempers epic evolutionary competition with a counter-plot of cooperation and symbiosis. The whole story is one of biotic community—of competition *and* cooperation. What do we owe members of the biotic community? Respect. And how do we respect them? We treat them in a way that befits their role in the community.

Let's get more specific. How should we treat wolves? As our peers, our colleagues; that is, as fellow social predators. How should we treat deer? As our prey; we hunt them, kill them, and eat them. But we should also leave plenty of deer for the wolves and for next year's hunt. In treating wolves as colleagues and deer as prey, we respect both, but in very different ways—in ways that are appropriate to their different roles in the biotic community, their different professions in the economy of nature. The beauty of communitarianism is that it is pluralistic and nuanced. We are members of multiple communities. And properly respectful behavior is derived from community relationship. Proper behavior toward neighbors is not the same as proper behavior toward family members. Proper behavior toward anonymous fellow citizens is not the same as proper behavior toward neighbors. And proper behavior toward fellow members of the biotic community is radically different from proper behavior toward fellow members of the human global village.

The community concept can even be of help in resolving the wolf–domestic sheep conflict with which Arne has struggled for decades. Domestic animals, as Mary Midgley has pointed out, are members of a "mixed community." We have bred them as chattel and we have an obligation to them as such. Arne's solution is the right one. The sheep that we have bred to dependency should be protected from the wild wolves, not by eradicating the wolves, but by hiring shepherds to ward off the wolves. But we are guided to that solution less by the blunt instrument of biospheric egalitarianism in principle than by sensitive and intelligent attention to balancing the various obligations and etiquettes imposed upon us by our multiple community memberships—in this case, obligations to the sheep owners (fellow Norwegians), to the sheep themselves (fellow members of the mixed community), and to the wolves (fellow members of the biotic community).

Chapter 19

Deep Ecology: A New Philosophy of Our Time?

Warwick Fox

The distinction between "shallow" and "deep" ecology was made in 1972 (and published the following year) by the distinguished Norwegian philosopher Arne Næss, and has subsequently been developed by a number of thinkers (most notably Bill Devall and George Sessions) to the point where we may now reasonably refer to an intellectual deep ecology movement.[1] The shallow/deep ecology distinction has generated so much discussion that it has become difficult to distill to any simple essence but, for the sake of brevity, it could be characterized by the following three points.

First, shallow ecology views humans as separate from their environment. Figure/ground boundaries are sharply drawn such that humans are perceived as the significant figures against a ground that only assumes significance in so far as it enhances humans' images of themselves qua important figures. Shallow ecology thus views humans as the source of all value and ascribes only instrumental (or use) value to the nonhuman world.[2] It is, in short, anthropocentric, representing that attitude to conservation that says: "We ought to preserve the environment (i.e., what lies outside the boundary) not for its own sake but because of its value to us (i.e., what lies inside the boundary)." Deep ecology, on the other hand, rejects "the (human)-in-environment image in favor of the relational, total-field image."[3] Organisms are then viewed rather "as knots in the biospherical net or field of intrinsic relations."[4] Figure/ground boundaries are replaced by a holistic or gestalt view where, in Devall's words, "the person is not above or outside of nature . . . (but) . . . is part of creation on-going."[5] This

153

total-field conception dissolves not only the notion of humans as separate from their environment but the very notion of the world as composed of discrete, compact, separate things. When we do talk about the world as if it were a collection of discrete, isolable things we are, in Næss's view, "talking at a superficial or preliminary level of communication."[6] Deep ecology thus strives to be non-anthropocentric by viewing humans as just one constituency among others in the biotic community, just one particular strand in the web of life, just one kind of knot in the biospherical net. The intrinsic value of the nonhuman members of the biotic community is recognized and the right of these members to pursue their own evolutionary destinies is taken as "an intuitively clear and obvious value axiom."[7] In contrast, the idea that humans are the source or ground of all value ("the measure of all things") is viewed as the arrogant conceit of those who dwell in the moral equivalent of a Ptolemaic universe. Deep ecologists are concerned to move heaven and earth in this universe in order to effect a "paradigm shift"[8] of comparable significance to that associated with Copernicus.

Second (and directly related to the above), in its acceptance of what Sessions refers to as "discrete entity metaphysics"[9] shallow ecology accepts by default or positively endorses the dominant metaphysics of mechanistic materialism. Viewing knowledge, too, as amenable to discrete compartmentalization, the shallow approach considers ethics in isolation from metaphysics with the consequence that the dominant metaphysics is usually implicitly assumed. Deep ecology, however, is concerned to criticize mechanistic materialism and to replace it with a better "code for reading nature."[10] This code can be generally described as one of "unity in processes."[11] By this is indicated both the idea that all things are fundamentally (i.e., internally) related and the idea that these interrelationships are in constant flux (i.e., they are characterized by process, dynamism, instability, novelty, creativity, etc.). This conception of the world lends itself far more readily to organismic rather than mechanical metaphors, and thus to panpsychic or pantheistic rather than inert, dead-matter conceptions of the nonhuman world. Among Western philosophers, Spinoza, Whitehead, and Heidegger are most often invoked for the purposes of articulating this vision of the world or, particularly in the case of Heidegger, for the purposes of articulating the "letting be" mode of being most appropriate to such a deep ecological understanding of the world.[12] Deep ecology also has an enormous respect for many non-Western views since unity in process and panpsychic conceptions of the world have received sophisticated elaboration in Eastern spiritual traditions and in the mythological systems of other non-Western peoples. This respect also extends to the entire sensibility or mode of being-in-the-world of some of these traditions since this often accords with the non-power-seeking sensibility of deep ecology.[13] In stressing the interconnection between ethics and metaphysics, deep ecology recognizes that an ecologically effective ethics can only arise within the context of a more persuasive and more enchanting cosmology than that of mechanistic materialism.[14]

Third, in terms of its social, political, and economic project, shallow ecology tends to accept by default or positively endorse the ideology of economic growth which characterizes industrial and developing societies of all political complexions. It is thus often referred to as the "resource management" or "resource conservation and development" approach. As such, it is content to operate in a reformist fashion within the "dominant social paradigm"[15] and, often, to accept the economic reduction (i.e., the reduction of all values to economic terms) for the purposes of decision making. Deep ecology on the other hand, is concerned to address existing social, political, and economic arrangements and to replace the ideology of economic growth with the ideology of ecological sustainability. It is insisted that economics (etymologically: "management of the household") must be seen as subsidiary to ecology ("study of the household"), and the economic reduction of values is thus firmly resisted.[16] Key ideas in deep ecology's social, political, and economic project include those of a just and sustainable society, carrying capacity, frugality (or voluntary simplicity), dwelling in place, cultural and biological diversity, local autonomy and decentralization, soft energy paths, appropriate technology, reinhabitation, and bioregionalism. These last two perhaps require some elaboration. Reinhabitation refers to the process of relearning how to live in place, how to establish a sense of place, how to dwell in and care for a place. Some people are attempting to cultivate consciously this sense, under the most difficult of circumstances, by moving into areas that have been degraded by industrial development and participating in the reestablishment of a rich and diverse ecosystem. Bioregions refer to areas possessing common characteristics of soils, watersheds, plants and animals (e.g., the Amazon jungle). It is argued that bioregions should replace nation-states as the fundamental geographical unit in terms of which humans think and live. The human carrying capacity for each bioregion should be determined in terms of the number of humans that can be supported living at a level of resource use that is adequate for their needs but minimally intrusive on their environment. Here, of course, lie a multitude of difficult questions for the political agenda of deep ecology. However, these questions have, in various forms, been addressed by numerous societies in the past (including a minority tradition in Western society) and are now being taken up by increasing numbers of thinkers in highly industrialized societies.

It should be clear from this summary that many writers whose work falls within the ambit of deep ecology do not necessarily describe themselves as deep ecologists. A good example is Theodore Roszak who, in his 1972 book *Where the Wasteland Ends*, pointed to the same kind of distinction as Næss:

> Ecology stands at a critical cross-road. Is it, too, to become another anthropocentric technique of efficient manipulation, a matter of enlightened self-interest and expert, long-range resource budgeting? Or will it meet the nature mystics on their own terms and so recognize that we are to embrace nature as if indeed it were a beloved person in whom, as in ourselves, something sacred dwells? . . .
> The question remains open: which will ecology be, the last of the old sciences or the first of the new?[17]

However, despite this and other attempts by philosophers, historians, and sociologists to distinguish between various streams of environmentalism, Næss's twelve-year-old shallow/deep ecology terminology seems to have stuck as the most economical and striking way of referring to the major division within contemporary environmental thought. The conceptualization of this division clearly constitutes a powerful organizing idea in terms of providing a focal point from which to view the relationships between a number of otherwise very diffuse strands of ecologically oriented thought.

The Intuition of Deep Ecology

It should be clear from my brief outline of the shallow/deep ecology distinction that many of the views held by deep ecologists go well beyond the data of ecology conceived as an empirical-analytic science. As Arne Næss said when introducing the shallow/deep ecology distinction: "the norms and tendencies of the Deep Ecology movement are not derived from ecology by logic or induction. Ecological knowledge and the life-style of the ecological field-worker have *suggested, inspired, and fortified* the perspectives of the Deep Ecology movement."[18] Deep ecologists have, therefore, taken the point made by Donald Worster in his study of the history of ecological ideas from the eighteenth century to the early 1970s:

> In the case of the ecological ethic . . . one might say that its proponents picked out their values first and only afterward came to science for its stamp of approval. It might have been the better part of honesty if they had come out and announced that, for some reason or by some personal standard of value, they were constrained to promote a deeper sense of integration between humans and nature, a more-than-economic relatedness—and to let all the appended scientific arguments go. "Ought" might then be its own justification, its own defense, its own persuasion, regardless of what "is."
>
> That more straightforward stance has now and again been adopted by a few intuitionists, mystics, and transcendentalists. Most people, however, have not been so willing to trust their inner voices, perhaps due to lack of self-confidence or out of fear that such wholly individual exercise of choice will lead to the general disintegration of the moral community. [19]

Deep ecologists *are* "willing to trust their inner voices" in the hope that the dominant social paradigm (within which the moral community is situated) *will* disintegrate—although in a creative rather than a destructive manner. Again, Arne Næss is quite explicit on these points in a recent interview in *The Ten Directions*, a magazine published by the Zen Center of Los Angeles:

> *Ten Directions*: This brings us back to the question of information versus intuition. Your feeling is that we can't expect to have an ideal amount of information but must somehow act on what we know?
> *Næss*: Yes. It's easier for deep ecologists than for others because we have certain fundamental values, a fundamental view of what's meaningful in life, what's worth maintaining, which makes it completely clear that we are opposed to further development for the sake of increased domination and an increased standard of living. The material standard of living should be drastically reduced and the quality of life, in the sense of basic satisfaction in the depths

of one's heart or soul, should be maintained or increased. This view is intuitive, as are all important views, in the sense that it can't be proven. As Aristotle said, it shows a lack of education to try to prove everything because you have to have a starting point. You can't prove the methodology of science, you can't prove logic, because logic presupposes fundamental premises.[20]

However, the *central* intuition of deep ecology, the one from which Næss's views on practice flow, is the first point I made in my summary of the shallow/deep ecology distinction. This is the idea that there is no firm ontological divide in the field of existence. In other words, the world simply is not divided up into independently existing subjects and objects, nor is there any bifurcation in reality between the human and nonhuman realms. Rather all entities are constituted by their relationships. To the extent that we perceive boundaries, we fall short of a deep ecological consciousness. In Devall's words: "Deep ecology begins with unity rather than dualism which has been the dominant theme of Western philosophy."[21]

The Intuition of Deep Ecology and Cross-Disciplinary Parallels

The central intuition of deep ecology finds a profound resonance in both the mystical traditions and the "new physics." For example, the perennial philosophy tells us, and the meditative process is claimed to reveal, that "*Thou* art That."[22] In other words, it is claimed that by subtracting your own self-centered and self-serving thoughts from the world you come to realize that "the other is none other than yourself: that the fundamental delusion of humanity is to suppose I am here and you are out there."[23] This understanding permeates the mystical traditions and is exemplified in the Taoist advice to "identify yourself with non-distinction."[24] Likewise, the Zen teacher Chü-chih would answer any question he was asked by holding up one finger, while the contemporary Zen roshi Robert Aitken says that "we save all beings by including them."[25] The mystical traditions are simply full of differing illustrations of this same point.[26] Ken Wilber, editor of the journal *Revision* and perhaps the most significant recent integrator of Eastern and Western worldviews, expresses the mystical understanding in these terms: "We fall from Heaven in this moment and this moment and—this, every time we embrace boundaries and live as a separate self sense."[27] Just so, adds the deep ecologist, do we fall short of a *deep* ecological consciousness.

It is now becoming commonplace to point to the fundamentally similar cosmologies embodied in the mystical traditions on the one hand and the new physics on the other.[28] What is structurally similar about these cosmologies is that they reveal a "seamless web" view of the universe. As David Bohm, the distinguished professor of theoretical physics at Birbeck College, University of London, has said in an interview with the philosopher Renée Weber:

Bohm: . . . the present state of theoretical physics implies that empty space has all this energy and matter is a slight increase of the energy, and therefore matter is like a small ripple on this tremendous ocean of energy, having some relative stability, and being manifest. (Thus, my suggestion of an 'implicate order') implies a reality immensely beyond what we call matter. Matter itself is merely a ripple in this background . . . in this ocean of energy. . . .

Weber: This view is of course very beautiful, breathtaking in fact, but would a physicist who pressed you on this . . . find some kind of basis in physics for allowing such a vision to be postulated?

Bohm: Well, I should think it's what physics directly implies.[29]

Both the mystical traditions and the new physics serve to generate, inter alia, what we might now call ecological awareness, that is, awareness of the fundamental interrelatedness of all things or, more accurately, all events.[30] The theoretical physicist Fritjof Capra has been quite explicit about this: "I think what physics can do is help to generate ecological awareness. You see, in my view now the Western version of mystical awareness, our version of Buddhism or Taoism, will be ecological awareness."[31] Where the physicist, the mystic, and the deep ecologist (as philosopher) differ is in their means of arriving at an ecological awareness. In terms of Wilber's typology of modes of inquiry, we could say that the physicist (like the scientific ecologist) emphasizes empirical-analytic inquiry (i.e., analysis of measurements), the mystic emphasizes transcendental inquiry (i.e., contemplations), and the deep ecologist (as philosopher) emphasizes mental-phenomenological inquiry (i.e., analysis of meaning; here we include such things as reflection on personal experience, the analysis of valuational arguments, and the meaning of knowledge furnished by the other two modes of inquiry).[32] However, all three modes of inquiry lead to a similar conception of the underlying structure of reality. Like the mystic and the new physicist, the deep ecologist is drawn to a cosmology of (in David Bohm's words) "unbroken wholeness which denies the classical idea of the analyzability of the world into separately and independently existing parts."[33]

A New Cosmology

While I refer to this view as the central intuition of deep ecology, I do not in any way mean that it is irrational or ungrounded. The deep ecologist who is pressed to say whether there is a basis in ecology for "allowing such a vision to be postulated" can reply, in the manner of David Bohm, that this cosmology is what ecology directly implies. Moreover, the deep ecologist can argue that if there is substance to the "hypothesis of emerging cross-disciplinary parallels" advocated by the neurophysiologist Roger Walsh, then the parallels between the structures of reality advanced by deep ecology, the mystical traditions, and the "new physics" are enormously significant rather than trivial coincidences or accidents of language. Briefly, Walsh's hypothesis is that we can enhance our perceptual sensitivity by the augmentation of normal sensory perception (as in science), by intellectual conceptual analysis (as in philosophy), or by direct perceptual training (as in meditation), and that:

> no matter how it is obtained, (perceptual) enhancement of sufficient degree may reveal a different order or reality from that to which we are accustomed. Furthermore, the properties so revealed will be essentially more fundamental and veridical than the visual, and will display a greater degree of commonality across disciplines. Thus as empirical disciplines evolve and become more sensitive, they might be expected to uncover phenomena and properties which point toward underlying commonalities, and parallels between disciplines and across levels.[34]

On the basis of emerging cross-disciplinary parallels such as those I discuss above, Walsh proceeds to argue that the classical Greek and, later, Cartesian concept of the universe as "essentially atomistic, divisible, isolable, static, nonrelativistic, and comprehensible by reductionism, is in the process of replacement, not just for physics where evidence for such a shift was first obtained, but for all sciences."[35] Deep ecology throws its full weight behind this shift, and is in accord with Walsh that the fundamental ontology now being revealed can be described as "largely dynamic, fluid, impermanent, holistic, interconnected, interdependent, foundationless, self-consistent, empty, paradoxical, probabilistic, infinitely over-determined, and inextricably linked to the consciousness of the observer."[36]

But beyond what the data of ecology—or of science generally—seem to imply, and beyond the significance or otherwise of emerging cross-disciplinary parallels, the central vision of deep ecologists *is* a matter of intuition in Worster's and Næss's sense. That is, it is a matter of trusting one's inner voice in the adoption of a value stance or a view that can not itself be proven or disconfirmed. There is nothing alarming or even unusual in the use of intuition understood in this sense. Philosophers of science generally accept that scientific theories, let alone metaphysical systems (or "ontic theories" as Quine calls them), are constrained by facts but are underdetermined by them. In other words, the same data can always be theorized or interpreted in a number of ways that are nevertheless consistent with the data. How then are we to decide between competing theories and worldviews? An evaluative stance must ultimately be adopted and, for the deep ecologists, this means the promotion of, in Worster's words, "a deeper sense of integration between [humans] and nature."[37]

Ecological Justice and "Procrustean Ethics"

In their zeal to effect this integration, deep ecologists have firmly coupled their central intuition of no boundaries in the biospherical field to the notion of "biospherical egalitarianism—in principle."[38] As a result, these notions tend to go everywhere together, almost as if they implied each other (although I shall argue they do not). These two ideas constituted the first two points in Næss's original seven-point outline of deep ecology, while Devall commented in his

1980 overview of the deep ecology movement that "in deep ecology, the whole-ness and integrity of person/planet together with the principle of what Arne Næss calls 'biological equalitarianism' are the most important ideas."[39]

Biospherical egalitarianism effectively refers to the equal intrinsic worth of all members of the biosphere: "the equal right to live and blossom is (taken as) an intuitively clear and obvious value axiom."[40] The "in principle" clause is added to this value axiom because it is recognized that "any realistic praxis necessitates some killing, exploitation and suppression."[41]

The idea that, in principle, no organism possesses greater intrinsic value than any other means that two major classes of value-theory have been condemned by deep ecologists as anthropocentric. First are those theories of value whose practi-cal application implies that the nonhuman world possesses only instrumental (or use) value. Traditional, mainstream Christian ethics, secular Western ethics such as utilitarianism and Kantian ethics, and modern economic theory are typically included in this class. In the second class are those recent attempts to develop a practical ecological ethics which recognizes the intrinsic value of the nonhuman world but which ascribes differential intrinsic value to organisms depending on their complexity and, hence, capacity for richness of experience.

Now those theories of value which fall into the first class are clearly anthro-pocentric in the most obvious sense—they embody that essential "arrogance of humanism"[42] which views the nonhuman world purely as a means to human ends. But to the extent that we can describe those theories of value in the second class as anthropocentric, we are using that term in a very different sense. The second class of value-theory (often inspired by Whitehead's thought) can be considered as philosophy catching up with the biological news. Humans are not posited as the source of all value, nor is it denied that organisms possessing nervous systems of comparable complexity to that of humans (such as whales and dolphins) also possess comparable intrinsic value. Moreover, and most importantly, it is not assumed or implied that organisms possessing greater intrinsic value have any right to exploit those possessing lesser intrinsic value. Quite the contrary. For example, in Birch and Cobb's recent elaboration of this second kind of value theory, their central ethic is that we have an obligation to act so as to maximize richness of experience in general—which includes the richness of experience of the nonhuman world.[43]

Yet deep ecologists dismiss this second class of value-theory, along with the first, as anthropocentric. For example, with respect to the second class, Sessions refers to the "pecking order in this moral barnyard" and argues that:

> The point is not whether humans do in fact have the greatest degree of sen-tience on this planet . . . (but that, for deep ecologists) . . . the degree of sen-tience is irrelevant in terms of how humans relate to the rest of Nature. And so, contemporary Whiteheadian ecological ethics does not meet the deep ecology insistence on "ecological egalitarianism in principle."[44]

I think deep ecologists tend to conflate principle and practice when they make judgments such as this. As Birch and Cobb's ethic makes clear, the second class of value theorists need have no argument with the axiom that all organisms have an "equal right to live and blossom" when genuine conflicts of value are absent. And this, I think, does satisfy the deep ecologist's insistence on ecological egalitarianism in principle. But, as Næss points out, value conflicts can never be completely avoided in practice; the process of living entails some forms of "killing, exploitation, and suppression." To this extent, then, the degree of sentience becomes extremely relevant in terms of how humans relate to the rest of nature *if* they are to resolve genuine conflicts of value in anything other than a capricious or expedient manner.

The deep ecologist who is thoroughgoing in confusing ecological egalitarianism in principle with ecological egalitarianism in practice is forced into the position that they might as well eat meat as vegetables since all organisms possess equal intrinsic value. In stark contrast to this position is the comment by Alan Watts that he was a vegetarian "because cows scream louder than carrots,"[45] and this is, in essence, the argument of the second class of value theorists—and the view, I am sure, that deep ecologists tend to adopt in practice. Deep ecology thus does itself a disservice by employing a definition of anthropocentrism which is so overly exclusive that it condemns more or less any theory of value that attempts to guide realistic praxis. This observation explains why deep ecological theorizing has shied away from considering situations of genuine value conflict and why it has not come forth with ethical guidelines for those situations where some form of killing, exploitation, or suppression is necessitated. Unless deep ecologists take up this challenge and employ a workable definition of anthropocentrism, they may well become known as the advocates of "Procrustean Ethics" as they attempt to fit all organisms to the same dimensions of intrinsic value. Again, diversity is the key.

Cross-disciplinary analogies may add emphasis to the above. When the new physicist considers matter as a ripple on a tremendous ocean of energy, this conception of unity in process does not then imply that, at any given moment, all ripples are of equal magnitude. In terms of cosmic time, these ripples are continuously rising and falling, but at any given moment real differences exist. Likewise, the mystic's conception of unity in process does not deny that, at any given moment, some forms are more significant expressions of pure consciousness than others—notwithstanding the knowledge that, from the aspect of eternity, all forms are fleeting. In fact, the notion of a hierarchy of states of mind/being, with greater value being ascribed to the higher states, is central to all mystical traditions. Similarly, the deep ecologist's conception of unity in process need not imply that, at any given moment, all "knots" (i.e., organisms) in the biospherical net are constituted of equally complex relations. To the extent that value inheres in complexity of relations, and to the extent that complexity of relations is evidenced in the degree of an organism's central organization (and therefore capacity for richness of experience), then organisms are entitled to moral consideration commensurate with their degree of central organization (or capacity for richness of experience) for the duration of their existence—as transient as that may be in terms of evolutionary time.

In pursuing their central intuition of unity (i.e., of no boundaries in the biospherical field), deep ecologists have possibly lost sight of the significance of the "in process" aspect of their unity in process metaphysics. Attention to this latter aspect suggests that any process continuously produces impermanent, uneven distributions (i.e., different values) of various attributes (and in the process of the world these attributes may be money, information, complexity of relations, and so on). If this were not so then we would have no process but a perfectly uniform, homogenous and, therefore, lifeless field. The only universe where value is spread evenly across the field is a dead universe.[46] Recognizing this, we should be clear that the central intuition of deep ecology does not entail the view that intrinsic value is spread evenly across the membership of the biotic community. Moreover, in situations of genuine value conflict, justice is better served by *not* subscribing to the view of ecological egalitarianism. Cows do scream louder than carrots. As Charles Birch and John Cobb have remarked: "Justice does not require equality. It does require that we share one another's fate."[47]

There is, however, a shallow and a deep sense of sharing one another's fate. The shallow sense is simply that of being subject to the same forces. It does not involve caring. The deep sense, intended by Birch and Cobb, involves love and compassion. It involves the enlargement of one's sphere of identification. The lesson of ecology is that we do share one another's fate in the shallow sense since we all share the fate of the earth. The message of deep ecology is that we ought to care as deeply and as compassionately as possible about that fate—not because it *affects* us but because it *is* us.

Notes

This chapter is reprinted with minor revisions from Warwick Fox, "Deep Ecology: A New Philosophy of Our Time?" *The Ecologist* 14 (1984): 194–200. It is a revised version of a paper delivered to the "Environment, Ethics and Ecology Conference," Australian National University, 26–28 August, 1983. A considerable number of people have read this paper in its original version and offered detailed criticisms, comments, and/or encouragement. In particular, I am grateful to Robin Attfield, Baird Callicott, John Cobb, Bill Devall, Brian Easlea, Jeremy Evans, Patsy Hallen, Judy Lockhart, Arne Næss, John Seed, George Sessions, Swami Shankarananda, Michael Zimmerman, and especially Charles Birch.

[1] See Bill Devall, and George Sessions, *Deep Ecology* (Layton, Utah: Peregrine Smith Books, 1984). Devall, "Reform Environmentalism," *Humboldt Journal of Social Relations* 6 (1979): 129–158. Devall, "Ecological Consciousness and Ecological Resisting: Guidelines for Comprehension and Research," *Humboldt Journal of Social Relations* 9 (1982). Devall, "Ecological Realism," in *Deep Ecology*, ed. M. Tobias (San Diego: Avant Books, 1984). Devall, "New Age and Deep Ecology: Contrasting Paradigms," manuscript. Devall, and

George Sessions, "The Development of Natural Resources and the Integrity of Nature: Contrasting Views of Management," *Environmental Ethics* 6 (1984). Arne Næss, "The Shallow and the Deep, Long–range Ecology Movement. A Summary," *Inquiry* 16 (1973): 95–100. Næss, "Notes on the Methodology of Normative Systems," *Methodology and Science* 10 (1977): 64–79. Næss, "Spinoza and Ecology," *Philosophia* 7 (1977): 45–54. Næss, "Validity of Norms—but which Norms? Self-realisation? Reply to Harald Afstad," in *In Sceptical Wonder: Inquiry into the Philosophy of Arne Næss on the Occasion of his 70th Birthday* ed. I. Gullvåg and J. Wetlesen. (Oslo: Universitetsforlaget, 1982), 257–269. Næss, "A Defence of the Deep Ecology Movement," *Environmental Ethics* 6 (1984). Næss, "Simple in Means, Rich in Ends: a Conversation with Arne Næss," *Directions* 3 (1982): 7, 10–12. George Sessions, "Ecophilosophy T," April 1976, "Ecophilosophy 2," May 1979, "Ecophilosophy 3," April 1981, "Ecophilosophy 4," May 1982, "Ecophilosophy 5," May 1983, Philosophy Dept., Sierra College, Rocklin, California. Sessions, "Anthropocentrism and the Environmental Crisis," *Humboldt Journal of Social Relations* 2 (1974): 1–12. Sessions, "Panpsychism versus Modern Materialism: Some Implications for an Ecological Ethics." Revised and extended version of a paper delivered at the conference on The Rights on Nonhuman Nature, Pitzer College, Claremont, California, April 18–20, 1974. Sessions, "Spinoza and Jeffers on Man in Nature," *Inquiry* 20 (1977): 481–528. Sessions, "Spinoza, Perennial Philosophy and Deep Ecology," paper presented to first national *Reminding* conference ("Philosophy, Where are You?"), Dominican College, San Raphael, California, June 29–July 4, 1979. Sessions, "Shallow and Deep Ecology: a Review of the Philosophical Literature, in *Ecological Consciousness: Essays for the Earthday Colloquium,* ed. R. Schultz, and J. Hughes (Washington, D.C.: University Press of America, 1981). Sessions, "Ecophilosophy, Utopias, and Education," *Journal of Environmental Education,* 15 (1983): 27–42. Sessions, "Ecological Consciousness and Paradigm Change," in *Deep Ecology,* ed. M. Tobias (San Diego: Avant Books, 1984).

[2] For an illuminating characterization of various classes of instrumental value, see: W. Godfrey-Smith, "The Value of Wilderness," *Environmental Ethics* 1 (1979): 309–319.

[3] Næss, "The Shallow and the Deep, Long-Range Ecology Movement. A Summary," 95.

[4] Næss, "The Shallow and the Deep, Long-Range Ecology Movement. A Summary."

[5] Devall, 1980, 303.

[6] Næss, "The Shallow and the Deep, Long-Range Ecology Movement. A Summary," 95.

[7] Næss, "The Shallow and the Deep, Long-Range Ecology Movement. A Summary," 96.

[8] Kuhn, T. *The Structure of Scientific Revolutions* (Chicago: University of Chicago Press, 1970).

[9] Sessions, 1983, 29.

[10] H. Skolimowski, *Ecophilosophy: Designing New Tactics for Living* (London: Marion Boyars, 1981).

[11] T, Roszak, *Where the Wasteland Ends: Politics and Transcendence in Post-industrial Society* (London: Faber, 1973), 400.

[12] For more internal relations, process metaphysics, organismic metaphors, and Whitehead, see my review of Birch and Cobb entitled "Liberating Life" in *The Ecologist,* no. 4 (1984). (Birch and Cobb's book cited as note 30 below.)

[13] Roszak describes the sensibility of ecology in its "subversive," or deeper, aspect as: "holistic, receptive, trustful, largely non-tampering, deeply grounded in aesthetic intuition" (*Where the Wasteland Ends*).

[14] The German sociologist Max Weber believed that with the "rationalization" of the world by scientific techniques (i.e., the rendering of all aspects of the world as potentially controllable and calculable) we have lost our sense of the sacred and the world has become "disenchanted." See G. Baum, "Does the World Remain Disenchanted?" *Social Research* 37 (1970): 153–203: Chapter 1 in J. Freund, *The Sociology of Max Weber* (London: Penguin, 1968); Max Weber's essay "Science as a Vocation" in *From Max Weber: Essays in Sociology,* ed. H. Gerth. and C. Mills, (London: Routledge and Kegan Paul, 1948).

[15] "Reformist environmentalism" and the "dominant social paradigm" are characterized by Devall, 1979. On the "dominant social paradigm" see also Devall, 1980.

[16] On the commensurability and incommensurability of economic and other values, see Godfrey-Smith, 1979.

[17] Roszak, 1973, 403–404.

[18] Næss, 1973, 98.

[19] D. Worster, *Nature's Economy: The Roots of Ecology* (San Francisco: Sierra Club Books, 1977), 336–337.

[20] Næss, 1982, 11–12.

[21] Devall, 1980, 309. The ecologist Paul Shepard speaks eloquently to this point: "Ecological thinking . . . requires a kind of vision across boundaries. The epidermis of the skin is ecologically like a pond surface or a forest soil, not a shell so much as a delicate interpretation". (Sessions, 1979, 8.)

[22] The phrase derives from the Sanskrit formulation "tat tvam asi" and is rendered "That art *Thou*" by Huxley and *"Thou* art That" in Juan Mascaro's translation of *The Upanishads* (Harmondsworth: Penguin 1965).

[23] R. Aitken, *Taking the Path of Zen* (San Francisco: North Point Press, 1982), 33 and 77 respectively.

[24] *Sacred Texts of the World: A Universal Anthology,* ed. N. Smart, and R. Hecht (London: Macmillan, 1982), 298.

[25] Aitken, 1982, 26 and 73 respectively.

[26] For a brief but illuminating demonstration of this claim see chapter 9 ("The One in World Scriptures") in J. Cooper, *Yin and Yang: the Taoist Harmony of Opposites* (Wellingborough: The Aquarian Press, 1982).

[27] K. Wilber, "Odyssey: A Personal Inquiry into Humanistic and Transpersonal Psychology," *Journal of Humanistic Psychology* 22 (1982): 57–90, 71.

[28] Some books either on, or which embody, this theme include David Bohm, *Wholeness and the Implicate Order* (London: Routledge and Kegan Paul, 1980); Fritjof Capra, *The Tao of Physics* (Glasgow: Fontana, 1976); Michael Talbot, *Mysticism and the New Physics* (New York: Bantam Books, 1981); and Gary Zukov, *The Dancing Li Masters: An Overview of the New Physics* (Bungay, Suffolk: Fontana, 1981). Despite this recent spate of books, it would be a mistake to assume that reference to the parallels between the cosmologies of physics and the mystical traditions is a "New Age" phenomenon. Oppenheimer explicitly pointed to such parallels in 1954: *Science and the Common Understanding* (London: Oxford University Press), as did Bohr in 1958, *Atomic Physics and Human Knowledge* (New York: John Wily). That being said, for an erudite critique of the dangers involved in drawing such parallels see Wilber's essay titled "Physics, Mysticism and the New Holographic Paradigm" in *The Holographic Paradigm and Other Paradoxes,* (Boulder: Shambhala, 1982), reprinted in *Eye to Eye: The Quest for the New Paradigm,* ed. K. Wilber (New York: Anchor Books, 1983). Against Wil-

ber's criticisms, however, one should balance Walsh's observations on the significance of these "emerging cross-disciplinary parallels" (see Walsh, 1979 and 1981).

[29] D. Bohm and R. Weber, "The Unfolding-unfolding universe: A conversation with David Bohm conducted by Renée Weber, in Wilber (ed.), 1982, 56–7.

[30] For an introduction to a "process" conception of life (via Whitehead) whereby "things," so-called, are viewed as *enduring societies of events*, see Charles Birch and John Cobb, *The Liberation of Life: From the Cell to the Community* (Cambridge: Cambridge University Press, 1981).

[31] F. Capra and R. Weber, "The Tao of Physics" revisited: A conversation with Fritjof Capra conducted by Renée Weber," in Wilber (ed.), 1982, 229.

[32] Wilber, 1983. See chapter 2: "The Problem of Proof."

[33] In Capra, 1976, 141–2.

[34] Walsh, 1979, 175.

[35] Walsh, 1979, 176.

[36] Walsh, 1979, 180.

[37] Worster, 1977, 337. Mary Hesse argues that "we can observe by hindsight that in the early stages of a science, value judgements (such as the centrality of (humans) in the universe provide some reasons for choice among competing underdetermined theories." See *Revolutions and Reconstructions in the Philosophy of Science* (Brighton, Sussex: Harvester, 1980, 190). For deep ecologists the situation is just the opposite: value judgments such as the *lack* of centrality of humans in the universe provide some of the reasons for choice among competing underdetermined theories (and here I include metaphysical views or "ontic theories").

[38] Næss, 1973, 95.

[39] Devall, 1980, 310.

[40] Næss, 1973, 96.

[41] Næss, 1973, 95.

[42] D. Ehrenfeld, *The Arrogance of Humanism* (Oxford: Oxford University Press, 1981).

[43] Birch and Cobb, 1981.

[44] Sessions, 1979, 18. The phrase "a pecking order in this moral barnyard" comes from John Rodman who used it in his insightful critique of Peter Singer's "Animal Liberation" and Christopher Stone's "Should Trees Have Standing?" See John Rodman, "The Liberation of Nature?" *Inquiry* 20 (1977): 85–145, 93.

[45] Aitken, 1982, 81.

[46] In a slightly different context, Wilber (1983, 295) argues that statements like "all is one" or "all is Brahman" typically give rise to a false picture of the universe that reduces all diversity and multiplicity to "uniform, homogenous, and unchanging mush" or to "uniform, all-pervading, featureless but divine goo."

[47] Birch and Cobb, 1981, 165.

Chapter 20

Intuition, Intrinsic Value, and Deep Ecology

Arne Næss

Which are the basic intuitions of deep ecology? How are we to verbalize them? How can we use them as guiding stars when formulating our policies? How can we avoid pseudo-agreements and pseudo-disagreements caused by incompatible verbal idiosyncrasies?

These are questions on the metalevel with the deep ecology movement on the object-level. The movement is not mainly one of professional philosophers and other academic specialists, but of a large public in many countries and cultures. As an academic philosopher, I find the questions important, but as a supporter of the movement I do not consider them central. We may discuss them in a relaxed way, noting richness of somewhat divergent and even incompatible answers with equanimity.

The following are some reflections elicited by the excellent article of Warwick Fox dealing with some of those questions.[1] I coined the terms "deep" and "shallow" ecology movement, but I do not of course try to monopolize those terms. And I only welcome some diversity of verbalization of basic attitudes and intuitions. I hope the following does not sound dogmatic.

Fox quotes Godfrey-Smith who says that "deep ecology . . . has an unfortunate tendency to discuss everything at once. Thus a social critique of deep ecology may be backed by such disparate authorities as Ginsberg, Castenada, Thoreau, Spinoza, Buddhist visionaries, and Taoist physics. With a cast of prima donnas like this on stage it gets very hard to follow the script."

In order to facilitate discussion it may be helpful to distinguish a common platform of deep ecology from the fundamental features of philosophies and religions from which that platform is derived, if the platform is formulated as a set of norms and hypotheses (factual assumptions).[2] The fundamentals, if verbalized, are Buddhist, Taoist, Christian, or of other religious colors, or philosophic with affinities to basic views of Spinoza, Whitehead, Heidegger, or others. The fundamentals are mutually more or less incompatible or at least difficult to compare in terms of cognitive contents. The incompatibility does not affect the deep ecology platform adversely.

The common platform within the deep ecology movement is grounded in religion or philosophy. In a loose sense it may be said to be derived from the fundamentals. Because these are different the situation only reminds us that a set of very similar or even identical conclusions may be drawn from divergent premises. The platform is the same, the fundamental premises differ.

In order to clarify the discussion one must avoid looking for one definite philosophy or religion among the supporters of the deep ecology movement. Fortunately, there is a rich manifold of fundamental views compatible with the deep ecology platform. Furthermore, there is a manifold of kinds of consequences derived from that platform.

The discussion has four levels to take into account: verbalized fundamental philosophical and religious ideas and intuitions, the deep ecological platform, the more or less general consequences derived from the platform—lifestyles and general policies of every kind. Lastly, descriptions of concrete situations and decisions made in them.

It is a characteristic feature of deep ecology literature that it contains positive reference to a formidable number of authors belonging to different traditions and cultures.[3] These references are not made in order to trace complete agreements but primarily to make tentative suggestions of deep similarities of views. Spinoza, only to mention one single great author, obviously entertained some opinions far removed from those of deep ecology. And his terminology is practically impenetrable for us today. Nevertheless, his texts are inexhaustible sources of inspiration for some deep ecologists.

Some may find it strange that I include Christian fundamental views. But Christian supporters of deep ecology belong to the most active groups, for instance, in Scandinavia. I do not think one can speak of any definite value theory common to contemporary Christian thinkers.[4]

From the point of view of derivation one may use the following diagram, the direction of derivation as shown by the Apron Diagram.

In this figure, B, P, and C are not made largely overlapping chiefly because of the difficulties of formulating agreements and disagreements in relation to texts written in religious language.

The Apron Diagram: 1, 2, 3 and 4 are levels in the direction of derivation. B, P, C are examples of kinds of philosophical or religious fundamental premises; B= "Buddhist," C= "Christian," P= "Philosophical." Level 2 is the Deep Ecology platform. Level 3 has more or less general consequences, with the platform and sets of hypotheses as premises. Level 4 deals with concrete decisions in practical situations.

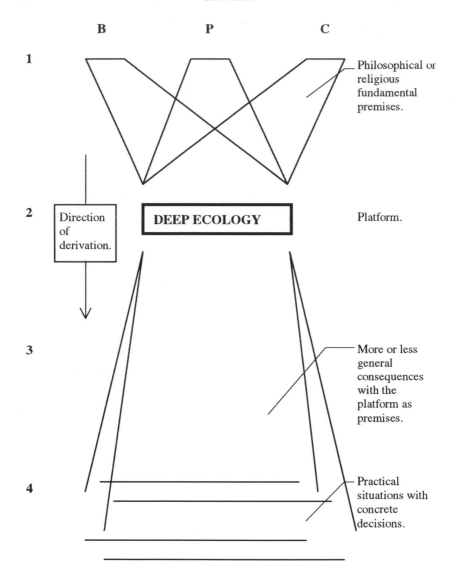

Figure 20.1. The Apron Diagram.

Warwick Fox seems to think that different behavior towards different kinds of living beings is difficult to justify without acknowledging different degrees of intrinsic value to different kinds of "organisms." But I accept certain established ways of justifying different norms dealing with different kinds of living beings. They do not necessitate grading a particular intrinsic value that living beings have simply as living beings. There is an attitude I cannot avoid, perhaps an intuition of some sort, which makes me proclaim that value to be ungraded. But to proclaim the existence of that value does not logically or otherwise necessitate a norm of equal behavior towards all living beings. There is room for vast differences. There is no pressure to introduce grading of the particular intrinsic value I am speaking about. Such grading does not fit the attitude and intention at hand.

Some intrinsic values may be graded. The value Warwick Fox speaks about may be graded. We probably do not speak about the same intrinsic value. A personal testimony:

I have injured thousands of the little arctic plant *salix herbacea* during nine years of accumulative stay in the mountains, and I shall continue to step on them as long as I live. But I have never felt the need to justify such behavior by thinking that they have less right to live and blossom, or less intrinsic value as living beings, than certain other living beings, including myself. It is simply not possible to live in certain mountains without stepping on these plants, and I maintain that it *is* justifiable to live there. When I behave as I do I can at the same time admire these plants, acknowledge their equal right to live and blossom with my right. At least not less and not more. Perhaps it is a better formulation to say that living beings have a right, or an intrinsic or inherent value, or value in themselves, that is *the same* for all of them. In so far as we speak of differences in value we do not speak of the value I have in mind.

What I now have done is to try to verbalize one rather deep intuition. But any such verbalization may mislead the verbalizer, and they certainly very often mislead the listeners or readers. There are other intuitions and there are thousands of differences of attitude reflecting differences of valuation. If there is a question whether to place my foot on a *salix herbacea* rather than on the small, overwhelmingly beautiful, and somewhat less common *gentiana nivalis*, I certainly, obviously, and deliberately place it on the former.

The abstract term "biospherical egalitarianism in principle" and certain similar terms, which I have used, do perhaps more harm than good. They suggest a positive *doctrine*, and that is too much. The importance of the intuition is rather its capacity to counteract, the perhaps only momentary, but consequential self-congratulatory and lordly attitude towards what seems less developed, less complex, less miraculous.

There is a rich variety of acceptable motives for being more reluctant to injure or kill a living being of kind A than a being of kind B. The cultural setting is different for each being in each culture and there are few general norms, only vague guidelines.[5] One factor: *felt nearness*. It determines largely our capacity to identify ourselves with a sort of being, to suffer when they suffer. One cannot put forth ethical rules of conduct without taking such feelings and our limited capacities seriously. If it is difficult to avoid killing A because of its smallness, whereas killing B is easily avoided, we tend to protect B rather than A. There is an obvious diversity of obligations. We have special obligations towards our children in most cultures—any animal may be killed in order to feed one's starving child. Obligations towards species that have been members of our life community for long periods are greater than toward accidental visitors. Furthermore, we have the relevance of suffering: is the suffering of A less than that of B? Has A the capacity of suffering?

The simple thing I try to convey here is that an ethics concerning differences between nonhuman living beings is of a comparable level of complexity of ethics concerning different people and groups with whom we have to do.

I prefer the term "living being" to the term "organism." The intuitive concepts of life sometimes cover a stream, a landscape, a wilderness, a mountain, an arctic "waste." The intuition has not much to do with biology or neurophysiology as sciences. Intrinsic value as posited by the intuition is influenced, but not decisively so, by "biological news," for instance news about whales' "comparable nervous system complexity to humans."

The kind of intuition I speak about I take as being common to supporters of the deep ecology movement. It is not easy to verify this, however, because of terminological or even conceptual divergences.

Notes

This chapter is reprinted with minor revisions from Arne Næss, "Intuition, Intrinsic Value, and Deep Ecology," *The Ecologist* 14 (1984): 201–203.

[1] I refer to the mimeographed version of Warwick Fox, "The Intuition of Deep Ecology".

[2] See example Arne Næss "Notes on the Methodology of Normative Systems," *Methodology and Science* 19 (1977): 64–79.

[3] See the review by George Sessions in *Ecological Consciousness*, ed. R. C. Schultz and I. D. Hughes (Lanham, Md.: University Press of America, 1981).

[4] The kind of trend in value theory I feel at home with when speaking about intrinsic values and intuitions is that of Max Scheler and Nicholai Hartmann. See Max Scheler, *Der Formalismus in der Ethik und dei materiale Wertethik* (1913–1916), and *The Nature of Sympathy*, translated in 1954. See also Nicolai Hartmann, *Ethik* (1926). Christian theologians within the deep ecology movement include: Ole Jensen, *Caught in the Violence of Economic Growth* (Copenhagen, 1976), and Gunnar Breivik, "Society in Equilibrium—a Theological Valuation," in *Toward a Society in Equilibrium*, ed. H. Olsen (1978), a work sponsored by Nordic Protestant Churches. (Titles are translated into English.)

[5] The relevance of tradition and culture is discussed in my "Self-realization in Mixed Communities of Humans, Bears, Sheep and Wolves," *Inquiry* 22 (1979): 231–241.

Chapter 21

On Guiding Stars of Deep Ecology

Warwick Fox
(Fox's Response to Næss's Response to Fox)

In his comments on "The Intuition on Deep Ecology," Arne Næss asks: "Which are the basic intuitions of deep ecology? How are we to verbalize them?" How can we use them as guiding stars when formulating our policies? "I dealt with some of these questions in my article, as Arne Næss notes. However, my concern there was primarily with the first two questions, which relate to the *content* of deep ecology. Here, it seems appropriate to take up an aspect of the third question. I want to consider how these basic intuitions are (and should be) used as guiding stars in advancing a distinctly deep ecological variety of environmental philosophy. That is, I am concerned with the differences between the structure of deep ecological thought and that of "normal" environmental philosophy. These differences are brought out by a consideration of the valuable four-leveled model of the structure of deep ecological philosophy outlined in Arne Næss's comments. But, first, it is necessary to clarify the way in which I believe Næss's systematization of deep ecological philosophy should be understood.

Arne Næss's systematization illustrates the relationship of deep ecology's basic principles or its "platform" (level 2), to various possible philosophical and religious "fundamental premises" on the one hand (level 1) and various possible theoretical and practical "consequences" on the other (levels 3 and 4). Although this systematization is presented in terms of "fundamental premises," "consequences," and a direction of "derivation" from levels (1) to (4), this should not be taken to mean that a sentence at one level is held to follow by virtue of necessity or probability from sentences at a previous level; i.e., Næss is not proposing a deductive or an inductive system. As he comments himself, it is only in a "loose

sense" that the deep ecology platform "may be said to be derived from fundamentals." Just as, in Næss's earlier words, "the norms and tendencies of the Deep
Ecology movement are not derived from ecology by logic or induction,"[1] neither
are they derived by (deductive) logic or induction from fundamental philosophical
or religious premises.

Næss's previous work suggests that, in the kind of very general worldview
systematization that he has in mind, the notion of "derivation" simply means
"making more precise."[2] (An instance of making a sentence more precise is referred to as a "precization.") One sentence is more derived than another in this
sense (i.e., more precise) if the range of interpretations it can admit is a subset of
the range of interpretations that the other sentence can admit. In other words,
derivation or preciseness is a matter of delimiting a range of possible interpretations. For example, we might proceed from a fundamental (i.e., level 1) religious
or philosophical premise such as "All is One" or the Spinozist idea that "there is
only one 'substance' " and, in the sense described, "derive" the (more precise)
central "plank" in the deep ecology platform that "there are no boundaries in the
biospherical field," or that "all entities are constituted by their relationships" (level
2). Further precization might express the realization that "the sense of oneself as a
skin encapsulated ego is not in accord with this 'seamless web' ontology" (level
3). This process of self-realization might then lead to a much greater degree of
personal identification with one's "surroundings" and, thus, an extension to
"others" of the same care and concern previously reserved for one's egoist self.

None of the steps in the above example is held to follow by necessity (deductive inference) or probability (inductive inference) from sentences at a previous
level. All we have (in logical terms) is a chain of precizations flowing in one or
many possible directions of interpretation. We could have easily started from the
same vague, general fundamental premises and proceeded to develop a chain of
precizations in a very different direction of interpretation. Thus, the "direction of
derivation" shown in the diagrammatic illustration of Næss's systematization
should be understood as referring to both the level of precization and the direction
of interpretation. The greater the level of precization the more evident the direction of interpretation (or what Næss has previously referred to as the "definiteness
of intention").

What is the value of trying to provide a systematization of deep ecology (or
any other fairly comprehensive view) when the connecting links between fundamental premises (level 1) and practical consequences (level 4) are as weak as that
of "possible interpretation?" An important answer must be that such a systematization emphasizes the continually-being-forgotten fact that our most sophisticated
and precise, non-trivial (i.e., non-tautological) reasoning are always embedded or
grounded in a very general "underlying perception of *the way things are*."[3] This
emphasis, this continual reminding, constitutes the most significant and distinctive
structural feature of deep ecological thought.[4]

In contrast to the deep ecologists, the vast majority of environmental philosophers pursue environmental philosophical discussion almost entirely at the level of
environmental ethics. Although the extent of this "ethical reductionism" can

hardly be overemphasized, it is, in fact, rarely even commented upon since this seems the "natural" way to conduct environmental philosophy. If environmental philosophy were a science then environmental ethical discussion constitutes what Kuhnian philosophers of science would call "normal science."[5] Janna Thompson, one of the few commentators to draw attention to what I have termed the ethical reductionism of normal environmental philosophy, argues correctly, I believe, that "the self-imposed limitations of ethical discourse" prevent most environmental philosophers from asking "the crucial question, namely, where do these new ethical attitudes come from?"[6] Deep ecologists, on the other hand, are characterized by their concern with this crucial question of the underlying or deeper bases of our ethical attitudes and theories. Næss's systematization is a clear illustration of this concern. But, again, we could ask: What is the point in being so concerned about the underlying bases (level 1) of our ethical theories (level 3) and practices (level 4) if the logical relationship between these bases, theories, and practices is no stronger than that of "possible interpretation?" The answer lies in the realm of psychology rather than logic. While a fundamental premise does not logically determine the direction of interpretation into which it is pressed, it will nevertheless be more conducive (in psychological terms) to some directions of interpretation rather than others. The "All is One" example, above, is a case in point. There are obvious and compelling psychological rather than logical reasons as to why a person is likely to theorize and behave quite differently depending on whether their "underlying perception of the way things are" is of the world as coextensive with themselves versus radically separate, a mother versus an enemy, inspirited versus inert matter-in-motion, and so on.

Deep ecologists agree with Birch and Cobb's insight that "human beings are more deeply moved by the way they experience their world than by the claims ethics makes on them."[7] Thus, where contemporary environmental philosophy is dominated by the question "How do we construct an adequate environmental ethic?," deep ecology asks the question "How do we cultivate a deep ecological consciousness?" The former question looks to conceptual answers, the latter to experiential answers. In seeking to change the way in which we experience the world, deep ecologists place their primary emphasis upon changing our "underlying perception of the way things are" (i.e., changing our ontology) rather than upon what we might term the "conceptual fix" approach of "bigger and better" ethics. This attempt to shift the primary focus in environmental philosophical concern from ethics to ontology clearly constitutes a fundamental or revolutionary challenge to normal environmental philosophy.[8] It is (and should be) deep ecology's guiding star.

Notes

This chapter is reprinted with minor revisions from Arne Næss, "'On Guiding Stars of Deep Ecology': Warwick Fox's Response to Næss's Response to Fox," *The Ecologist* 16 (1984): 203–204.

[1] A. Næss, "The Shallow and the Deep, Long-Range Ecology Movement. A Summary," *Inquiry* 16 (1973): 95–100.

[2] This paragraph and the following one draw on Arne Næss's *Interpretation and Preciseness* (1953), *Communication and Argument: Elements of Applied Semantics* (1966), *The Pluralist and Possibilist Aspect of the Scientific Enterprise* (1972), and "Notes on the Methodology of Normative Systems," *Methodology and Science* 10 (1977): 64–79. (The three books are published by the University Press, Oslo.)

[3] This phrase is used by Seymour Feldman in his introduction to Spinoza's *Ethics* (Baruch Spinoza, *The Ethics and Selected Letters*, trans. S. Shirley and ed. S. Feldman (Indianapolis: Hackett, 1982), 9. Pertinent to the present discussion of Næss's systematization of deep ecology, Feldman writes: "Some of the great systematic philosophers of the past proceeded to philosophise from an underlying perception of *the way things are*—an intuition, to use one of Spinoza's key terms, of the way everything hangs together. This fundamental insight gives birth to a system, which represents the unfolding of the ramifications and consequences of that intuition." In the present context, I use the word "ontology" as equivalent to Feldman's "underlying perception of the way things are." A metaphysical system would refer to the detailed working out or "unfolding" of the "ramifications and consequences" of an ontology.

[4] The most important feature of deep ecology's *content* being, to adopt Feldman's language (see note above), the fundamental intuition or the underlying perception that everything does, indeed, hang together.

[5] T. Kuhn, *The Structure of Scientific Revolutions* (Chicago: University of Chicago Press, 1970). On this point it is noteworthy that the only journal exclusively "dedicated to the philosophical aspects of environmental problems" is called *Environmental Ethics*. Excellent as they often are in their own right, the journal's contents nevertheless reflect the ethical reductionism implied in the tension between its avowed concerns and its title.

[6] J. Thompson, "Preservation of Wilderness and the Good Life," in *Environmental Philosophy,* eds. R. Elliot and A. Gare (St Lucia, Queensland: University of Queensland Press, 1983), 89.

[7] C. Birch and J. Cobb, *The Liberation of Life: From the Cell to the Community* (Cambridge: Cambridge University Press, 1981), 177.

[8] The primacy of ontological over ethical concerns in deep ecology suggests that the notion of "biospherical egalitarianism in principle" can be understood as follows. Certain "underlying perceptions of the way things are" (or ontologies) are more conducive than others to a general attitude or orientation of "letting be, living and letting live," or "sparing and preserving" (in Heidegger's phrase). However, such a general attitude or orientation is just that—a general attitude or orientation. It is not an ethical system. It does not offer specific guidance in those situations where "sparing and preserving" is difficult or impossible. It operates at a lower level of definiteness than an ethic. Arne Næss (see note 1) seems to agree when he comments that "biospherical egalitarianism . . . suggest(s) a positive *doctrine*, and that is too much." Biospherical egalitarianism rather refers to the attitude underlying specific ethical decisions and practices. Perhaps Aldo Leopold was getting at the same idea when he defined conservation as what a person thinks about while chopping wood or deciding what to chop. See Aldo Leopold, *A Sand County Almanac* (Oxford: Oxford University Press, 1949).

Chapter 22

Comment: Pluralism and Deep Ecology

Andrew Brennan

I. Trading Principles

From small beginnings in London, Marks and Spencer grew to become a major high street retailer. When I was young, the stores sold only clothing. But now Marks and Spencer have diversified into a wide range of goods including supermarket foods, confectionery, bathroom accessories, and bed linen. Despite these changes in the goods on offer, the company continued to trade under its original name, maintaining a high degree of brand loyalty among consumers.

Much the same is true for deep ecology. I wonder whether in 1972 Arne Næss had any expectation that the "deep ecology" brand goods he was then offering, would within a few years, be replaced by a new range. The interesting exchange between him and Fox reprinted here gives a significant insight into part of the process of diversification. In particular, we witness the discontinuation of two lines with limited sales appeal in favor of an option aimed at attracting a clutch of new customers.

In the 1973 paper, which launched the deep ecology movement, Næss provided a series of important propositions. Some of these did not pick out particularly "deep" or original commitments. For example, there was mention of the struggle for cleaner air and water, the need to reject class divisions, and the need to foster local autonomy and decentralized government. These already had widespread support. But there were three principles, which seemed to give the deep ecology movement its distinctive character:

a. adoption of a holistic, relational, total-field image in place of the "man-in-the-environment" concept;

b. commitment, in principle, to biospheric egalitarianism;
c. the moral requirement to protect symbiosis by maintaining natural diversity.

The relational, total-field holism amounted to the claim that boundaries between individuals were fuzzy and elastic; each living thing is a knot in a larger biospheric web. This is the view that Fox here defends by reference to physics, but which Næss is silent on. Biospheric egalitarianism meant that we should recognize that all living things have the same right to live and flourish. At first sight, it seems Næss is going to stick to the egalitarian principle despite Fox's concerns with it. Instead, it is weakened before our eyes.

The third ideal raises an interesting matter on which ecologists' opinions are split—the importance and naturalness of diversity. Some natural communities, such as forests, have a tendency to exclude diversity, which is only maintained by accident (for example, fires) or by human management.[1] There is wide agreement, however, that reduction in diversity can, in some cases, lead to ecological instability and undermine the interrelationships on which the flourishing of life depends.

In the discussion with Fox, the first two ideals come under challenge. Here is a critical moment in the evolution of the deep ecology position. Dependence on a specific doctrine—deep ecology—is to be replaced by adoption of a platform. In this new platform, the diversity of life will be celebrated as being of value in itself. The third principle survives the process of change. The second does not do so well. The ideal of biospheric egalitarianism is weakened to a general recognition that the flourishing of both human and nonhuman life have value in themselves. Finally, the first principle is to be entirely abandoned. To support the broad platform it will no longer be necessary to understand or accept the field concept. These transformations pose a problem. Will only the brand name survive through them? I would argue not. Despite changes to the product line, the trade name itself retains its significance.

II. Moral Pluralism

Næss points out that Christian supporters of deep ecology belong to some of the most active groups in Scandinavia. There seems to be no reason why they should not support the new platform without accepting anything more ontologically drastic than standard Christian metaphysics. Adoption of a process philosophy, the Copenhagen interpretation of quantum theory, or Taoism, are simply options, not the necessities implied in Fox's paper. In some of his later writings, Næss waggishly points out that "the ultimate premises of environmental philosophy are themselves rich and diverse." In this way, one of the main underpinnings of the newly-emerging platform is mirrored within the deep ecology movement itself.

Many people may worry, however, that Næss seems to support a moral and cultural pluralism, which lacks determinate structure. This anxiety is particularly urgent for those who think of our moral life as governed by determinate principles with their own internal harmony. Suppose I break my promise to meet you for lunch in order to help fight a small bush fire. We can give a moral justification for such behavior by appeals to principles. First, there is the principle to honor our promises. Second, there is the principle to protect property and species endangered by fire. When these collide, we may expect to be able to justify following one in preference to the other. For example, a promise to testify in court may override the requirement to fight a trivial fire; the obligation to fight a fire which threatens human life may override even the most solemn of promises.

For those who regard the moral economy as a well organized set of principles including within it prioritizing criteria, pluralism threatens disorder and opportunism. If there is no universal rational way to decide which rule has priority on a particular occasion, then principles become devices for rationalizing our action. Pluralists can apparently justify one action in one situation as the right thing to do; in a new, but similar, situation they may provide an equally moral justification for quite different behavior. If Næss is a pluralist, does his position in this exchange with Fox fall foul of these criticisms?

In fact, the new position cleverly disarms such objections. Of course Næss recognizes the diversity among ultimate premises. But this is combined with unity, not plurality, at the level of the platform itself. So here is one form of constraint on how far pluralism can extend. Any underlying philosophy which is inconsistent with the platform, will not be acceptable as a workable ecosophy. And there are other constraints too. At the basic level, each underlying philosophy may be monistic, rigorous, and systematic in its development of ethical principles. So there may be no scope for pluralism within particular philosophies. What the platform will celebrate, however, is the possibility of diversity among ultimate positions—a diversity that is just as much to be celebrated as the biological diversity which supporters of the platform seek to protect.

My own commitment to pluralism is probably more radical than anything that Næss would accept. For there are many pluralisms. The brands I support go well beyond the constraints just mentioned. It seems to me that rules and principles only have transparent application when they relate to a single domain of processes or entities characterized by unambiguous properties. This is why there are clear principles of Euclidean geometry, statistical mechanics, and chemistry. For such fields, we can define the items under study by unambiguous classification schemes and draw up strict laws governing their behavior. By contrast, there are only relatively vague rules and principles in the science of toxicology. As is well known, a dose of a substance that will kill or intoxicate one animal will have no apparent effect on another. The idiosyncrasy of toxicological response indicates that there is no classification scheme and identification of entities which permits the establishment of definitive laws.

Philosophy, it seems to me, is more like toxicology than chemistry. In fact, it deals with entities and systems that are far less well defined than the molecules, cells, tissues, and biochemical processes of interest to the toxicologist. Ethical theory inherits all the complication and equivocation that is the general lot of philosophy. Moral situations are typically complex, contested, and full of ambiguity. The idea that we can devise any single system of principles and priority measures to apply to such cases is pure fantasy. Næss need not share my general view on this nor my commitment to radical pluralism. None the less, I would argue that his move to introduce a platform, and his recognition of a plurality of underlying principles, is itself philosophically perceptive.

III. Brand Loyalty

Deep ecology is like a company that keeps its trademark while changing the lines on which its business is based. But there is one way in which the changes over the years are not well captured by the analogy. The restricted range of deep goods originally on offer in the 1973 manifesto have given way by 1984 to a platform which embraces plurality. My concluding thought—which may surprise some critics—is that the platform retains philosophical depth. The "deep" label has remained appropriate by trading on the different meanings of the word "deep." I do not mean that Næss has been deep in the sense of being a wily trickster who continually shifts the target at which his opponents have to aim. He has, of course, been exceptionally clever at confounding his critics, but this is not the kind of depth I have in mind. Rather, I would argue that recognizing pluralism of underlying premises is deep in the sense that it encourages us to think about our environmental and ethical situation from a number of perspectives. Those who agree on the need for specific action may arrive at that agreement by different routes. These routes, however, are not necessarily exclusive of each other. It is attentiveness to this point that distinguishes Næss's profound pluralism from a more pragmatic approach, which simply accepts the need to live with difference. By recognizing the inherent complexity and ambiguity of moral and political situations, Næss has moved beyond acceptance of the existence of cultural divergence and competing worldviews. He provides an alternative to competition by means of the ideal of reconciliation.

In some earlier work, I distinguished pluralism as an ethical or political idea from pluralism as a philosophical position.[2] As a moral ideal, pluralism accepts that we may all operate with different conceptions of the good. So long as my pursuit of the good does not interfere too much with yours, an ethically pluralist society should, in theory, make room for both of us. This kind of view allows that our separate ideas of what is good may compete with each other. A different kind of pluralism, however, sees that at least sometimes different ideas do not compete with, but instead complement, each other. They may do so because of the ambiguity and complexity of the situations we find ourselves in.

This reconciliationist view is one aspect of philosophical pluralism. For example, you may be concerned over the loss of a bluebell wood to development because you would like your children to enjoy it. Your friend may be concerned over the loss of the same wood because of the rarity of bluebells in the area. Another person may, in turn, be concerned because the wood is a place of inherent value. The local farmer may worry not about the bluebells, or the value of the wood in itself, but because of the loss of a windbreak. Although we might think that these different concerns compete with each other, closer inspection will show that each misgiving is compatible with the others: the wood may be valuable in itself, while also being a resource for future generations, a home to endangered species, and of use to the farmer. Each concern is just as real as the other and there will be many more that we can easily add to the list.

Real situations are much, much more complex than this. They provide also the prospect of conflict, as when we introduce a developer for whom the woods are an "under-utilized" area in need of a golf course and executive housing. In environmental arguments, there are often interesting alignments of parties, testifying to the plurality of views that can range over the different sides of a contested issue. A shallow analysis deems that a situation can best be described in terms of just one worldview. The language of economics, for example, with its tally of costs and benefits, may be put forward as providing a privileged description of all that matters. Such simplistic reductionism is resisted by a deeper analysis. There are many different perspectives on the same situation, some of which can be reconciled in some respects. Each particular view represents no more than part of a complex whole.

A central myth of recent ethical theory is that moral situations are unambiguously describable and that we can state precise and relatively simple reasons for action. Moral pluralists regard such an approach to ethics as intensely uncritical and depthless. It is a scandal in analytic philosophy that the project of theorizing about ethics has been carried out in such a shallow fashion. When we try to form an account of cultural divergence and reconciliation the problem becomes much more intense. To judge the reasons that someone from a culturally different background has for their decisions requires a depth of knowledge and experience that is far greater than that needed where there is a common cultural background.

Næss is one of the few thinkers in environmental philosophy who has been aware of these issues. The deep ecology platform surrenders the specificity of the original position in favor of breadth. This move recognizes the implications of pluralism in ethical and political life. Far from a betrayal of the original label it represents a new and profoundly insightful reinterpretation of it. To be aware that the same broad principles are mandated by a number of different philosophies is to deepen our grasp of the situations in which these maxims apply.

Notes

[1] Andrew Brennan, "Ecological Theory and Value in Nature," in *Environmental Ethics,* ed. R. Elliot (Oxford: Oxford University Press, 1995).

[2] Andrew Brennan, "Moral Pluralism and the Environment," *Environmental Values* 1 (1992): 15–33.

Chapter 23

Man Apart: An Alternative to the Self-Realization Approach

Peter Reed

One night in times long since vanished, man awoke and saw himself. He saw that he was naked under the cosmos, homeless in his own body. Everything opened up before his searching thoughts, wonder upon wonder, terror upon terror, all blossomed in his mind.

Then woman awoke, too, and told him that it was time to go out and kill something. And man took up his bow, fruit of the union between the soul and the hand, and went out under the stars. But when the animals came to their waterhole, where he waited for them, he no longer knew the spring of the tiger in his blood; but a grasped psalm to the brotherhood of suffering shared by all that lives.

That day he came home with empty hands, and when they found him again by the rising of the new moon, he sat dead by the waterhole.[1]

I

Peter Wessel Zapffe's retelling of the Fall of Man confronts us with one of the central problems in environmental philosophy: what is the human relationship with nature? In its normative voice, the question is: what *should* that relationship be? The question is an urgent one: we are a powerful species, and we hold the world hostage to whatever it is we think we are destined for. It must be hard to live with such a terrorist, and there is every indication that the earth is getting fed up with us.

Environmental philosophers have assumed a role as a sort of counselor, analyzing ways of improving our relationship with *Eros*. They do this in a number of ways, but two approaches crop up frequently in their analyses. Briefly, one approach sees humans as part of nature; the other sees nature as part of humans.

An example of the first approach is E. O. Wilson's sociobiology. "The urge to affiliate with other forms of life," writes Wilson, "is to some degree innate," and is part of the "program" of the brain.[2] Iltis, Loucks, and Andrews also see the ties that bind us to the earth as biopsychological. "It is likely," they write,

> That we are as genetically programmed to a natural habitat of clean air and a varied green landscape as any other mammal. To be relaxed and to feel healthy usually means simply allowing our bodies to react as evolution equipped them to for 100 million years. [3]

In the strongest form of this approach, moral thinking itself is a kind of evolutionary outgrowth.[4] Here the supposed gap between facts and values disappears, and a value becomes as much a fact as a tree, a rock, or a cloud.

The basic idea is simple: we need to think of ourselves as biological beings, in close kinship with the beasts of the field. "Men are not *like* animals," writes Joseph Meeker, "they *are* animals. . . . [We] need to find ethical principles and practices which will agree better with the biological requirements of the human species."[5]

The second approach, which I am most concerned with, goes at the problem from the other direction. The problem is still that humans and nature become estranged, but the solution is to expand our concept of self to include nature. Arne Næss, for example, argues that the mature human being achieves a "self-realization" by identifying with all of nature, something Warwick Fox calls "a state of being which sustains the widest possible identification."[6] For convenience I call this the "Self-realization approach."

What does Self-realization mean? What is the relation between the Self and the individual human being? For Arne Næss, *Self* (with a capital S) is the Hindu Atman, which "corresponds to the notion of the Absolute in Western philosophy—something completely beyond ordinary description but somehow basic to both God and the World."[7] The human individual is a self (with a small *s*), and of course part of the Self. The problem is that the small self does not see that it is a part of the *Atman* because the small self is too busy with its narrow self-interests—egotism. To get around this problem and "realize" itself, the small self is not expanded to encompass everything, but rather diminished. When it has reduced its egotism to zero (though this is unlikely to happen), it is realized, that is, it experiences a "oneness in diversity."[8] Self-realization has so little to do with the individual ego, in fact, that the true Self-realization of one individual is impossible without the Self-realization of all individuals.

Næss's formulation of Self-realization differs in particulars from other wider identification approaches. Nevertheless, the general idea seems to be that Self-realization is not egoism, a psychological projection of ourselves onto the world. Instead it is really the losing of the individual self in an "experientially incorporated world."[9] We substitute a narrow sense of the individual with a broader sense of self, which includes the whole universe.

Distinguishing the two approaches may seem like splitting hairs, because the end result is the same. That is, we try to break down the distinction between the human (subject) and the natural (object). We try to bridge the gap between ourselves, and the world, emphasizing how we are the same instead of how we are different.

No matter which side of the gap we start from, the moral assumption behind this bridge building is also the same: that once we understand how closely we are related to nature, we will lose interest in destroying it. In many ways both approaches are arguments from self-interest, even though the meaning of *self* is revised: "If it is rational for me to act in my own best interest and I and nature are one, then it is rational for me to act in the best interests of nature."[10]

I sympathize with this assumption, but I think the two approaches sketched above ignore another possibility: it is our very *separateness* from the earth, the gulf between the human and the natural, that makes us want to do right by the earth. According to this approach, nature is a stranger. It seems to me that recognizing the moral distance between ourselves and the world helps us recognize the values in nature that are totally independent of what we humans think is beautiful, right, and good. Moreover, recognizing these values, some strong conclusions for how we ought to behave suggest themselves. If we turn our attention from our petty hubris, insignificance, and appalling ignorance to a universe vast beyond our ability to comprehend, we might treat the earth a little less arrogantly.

II

In drawing a picture of nature as something separate from us, as a stranger, I draw on the work of Martin Buber and Rudolf Otto. As theologians, their work is primarily about God, not nature. Still, they give us some very suggestive analyses of the way we relate ourselves to other beings. These analyses are useful when we are thinking about our relationship with the environment.

Buber's seminal *I and Thou* builds on the intuition that we are apart from something before we are related to something. Before we become part of a socioecological organism, we are a single cell—alone. This isolation, however, leads neither to loneliness nor to solipsism. There is separation, but not a desolate or aggressive alienation. We can think, "I am not lonely in the Universe, but comforted. For when I look at nature, I know that I am not it. There is something else out there, with me." Buber's work is a call back to a commonsense idea that there is something that is not just part of us, a solid something we can kick in refutation of Berkeley's *esse es percipi*. It is a reminder of the power and being that exists independently of the human mind.

"To man," writes Buber, "the world is twofold, in accordance with his two-fold attitude."[11] Two "primary words" characterize these attitudes and express the two ways we relate ourselves to our surroundings. "The one primary word is the combination '*I-Thou.*' The other primary word is the combination '*I-It.*' "[12] Most commonly we relate to the world as I-It: the world is filled with tools or hindrances, dependable, even beautiful objects—*for us.* But, says Buber, when we do so, we are really relating to our own selves, without regard to the integrity of what it is we experience.

"Experience," in Buber's usage, is very self-centered. "The man who experiences has no part in the world," he writes:

> For it is "in him" and not between him and the world that the experience arises. The world has no part in the experience. It permits itself to be experienced, but has no concern in the matter.[13]

When you "experience" the world, it becomes "your object, remains it as long as you wish, and remains a total stranger, within and without."[14]

Nonetheless, our relation to nature need not be a relation to ourselves. It can happen that we meet nature itself. Here we confront it as a *Thou*, a self-sufficient being of whom we have an inkling, a relationship with something *else* which we cannot pass off as a figment of our imagination. Nature as a *Thou* is

> No impression, no play of my imagination, no value depending upon my mood; but it is bodied over and against me and has to do with me, and I with it. . . .[15]

We participate in a relation with something outside of ourselves, which commands our attention as long as the relationship lasts.

Two questions come to mind here: how can we tell if we actually are in a genuine relation with a *Thou* and how can we enter into such a relationship? Both of these questions are questions of a mind examining itself, and doubting what it sees. The essence of the *I-Thou* relationship is that there is no room, no time, for reflection. We are seized by the relationship; we cannot think about it as we would an object. It is here, now, and while it lasts, there is only now. Since we have no time to ourselves to think about the relationship, there is never any question of doubting its reality. This is akin to the clear and distinct ideas of Cartesian introspection, but with an important difference—what is clearly apprehended is *outside* the thinker, not inside her or his own consciousness. This perception "has more certitude for you than the perceptions of your senses"; "No deception penetrates here; here is the cradle of Real Life."[16] Asking "Is this a real *I-Thou* relationship?" makes about as much sense as asking "Am I having fun yet?"

As for how we can have this relationship with a *Thou*, Buber reminds us that it is not something that we "have." It is something that, in part, is given to us. "The *Thou* meets me through grace," Buber writes, "it is not found by seeking."[17] There is an undeniable mutuality to the *I-Thou* relation—while we step toward it, it must also step toward us. Buber believes there are no sure-fire techniques for taking these steps:

> Everything that has ever been devised and contrived . . . as precept, alleged preparation, practice, or meditation, has nothing whatsoever to do with the primal, simple fact of the meeting. . . . Going out into the relation cannot be taught in the sense of precepts being given.[18]

The *Thou* comes like a gift, or a thief in the night.

Rudolf Otto and the Idea of the Holy

Rudolf Otto's idea of "the Holy" is parallel in many respects to Buber's *Thou*. The "Holy" is, like the *Thou*, something that stands radically apart from us. It is the "Wholly Other," the "mysterium tremendum et fascinans."[19] When we meet the "Other," we are not devoured by it, as powerful as that meeting can be. We know that it is *we* who are faced with the Holy, the *Numen*, precisely because it is the Holy who confronts us.

Otto most neatly complements Buber when he tries to describe "by hint and suggestion" what it is we meet when we meet the Holy *Thou*. He uses words like *majestic, fascinating, awful*, but stresses that in the end none of these descriptions are really adequate. We lack the adjectives to describe the Holy in its manifest glory; we stand dumb, overcome by an encounter with something that is so obviously beyond our ability to capture in words. Not even value terms like *good* or *evil* will do: "this 'extra' in the meaning of 'holy' [is] beyond the meaning of goodness."[20] It is only in the wake of such a meeting that we can creep trembling back into the familiar structure of our language and try to describe what it was we saw.

The adjectives Otto sometimes uses give the impression that the *Numen* is something overwhelmingly large and mighty:

> whatever among natural occurrences or events in the human, animal, or vegetable kingdoms has set him [humans] a-stare in wonder and astonishment—such things have ever aroused in man, and become endued with . . . numinous feeling.[21]

But we should not let our scanty language bewitch us even so much, for Otto also writes that the numinous is represented in things as small as paintings or songs. Likewise, Buber makes it clear that we can enter into an *I-Thou* relation with any part of physical nature. In all natural objects there is the potential to fascinate us, to turn our minds away from ourselves in wondrous contemplation of natural complexity: in a tree, a leaf, a gram of soil, even Lewis Thomas's "lives of a cell."

Nature as the Thou or the Numen

My point here is that we can think of nature as a sort of *Thou* or *Numen*, something wholly other and awe inspiring. Put this way, the point sounds rather weak. Of course, someone might object, nature is something other than us—on the surface—but as proponents of the new physics, Buddhist thought, and the central intuitions of deep ecology have shown, this sense of separateness stems from a mistaken ontology. The truth is actually somewhere in between: we are interwoven into the fabric of nature; it is a part of us and we are a part of it.

What I am arguing here is that the view that "everything hangs together" is only one truth of the matter, one way of seeing the relation between humans and the cosmos. Otto and Buber see it in another way. The physical connections, the interchange of atoms and molecules between creatures and through time is an insubstantial link, merely physical. Certainly we are parts of food chains; certainly we have fellow feelings for nature; nevertheless, there is an existential gulf of awesome depth between ourselves and the Other, a gulf which no amount of "identification in otherness" can span. The Other is really other.

It is easy to see why we slide so readily into the "we are the world" mentality. We have lost, in our daily lives at least, a precious sense of our own insignificance. There are few enclaves of nature which have not been smudged obviously and unreasonably with human fingerprints. We are mesmerized by our own cleverness, whether it be the building of physical bridges across a canyon or philosophical bridges across the canyon between ourselves and nature.

Nature, we know, sometimes takes it upon herself to remind us of our insignificance. Human-caused "natural" disasters and the boomerang effects of our ecological malpractice are creeping into our public agendas. We are learning, slowly, a healthy contempt for our stinking cities, shrieking aircraft, and petty works of art, which are, of course, of more interest to *Homo sapiens* than to anyone else.

III

Who else is there? Are there things which matter apart from humans wanting them to matter? Or is value a gift from man to nature, which can be granted or rescinded on our whim? I want to argue that there is value apart from man, value that is intrinsic to nature, wholly independent of whether we perceive it or not.

What sort of value is this? In "Values in Nature," Holmes Rolston, III, has listed ten kinds of values nature has. These range from the evident economic values of natural resources to the intangible "sacramental values" that "generate poetry, philosophy, and religion, no less than science."[22] Some are values that are only "good for" something else; others are also inherently good experiences: the awe we feel observing the thundering surf is, so to speak, its own reward. All of these values are, nevertheless, values for humans. Realizing that such a list is incomplete, Rolston has supplemented it in a later article by adding "intrinsic values in nature."[23] Here, like some utilitarians, Rolston argues that an animal or plant has needs and desires, interests which make the creature a locus of value, an end in itself. Although this addition is quite a leap, it falls short of the idea of intrinsic value suggested by Buber and Otto. For Rolston, intrinsic value is very closely tied to a subject having interests, specifically, self-interests. Without a subject, there are no interests, and no loci of intrinsic value. True, Rolston (and others) stretch the notion of the interest-having subject very far to include even a mineral crystal,[24] but the feat of imagination required to see a crystal as having interests produces an overstrained metaphor. A better approach, in my view, is to uncouple "having interests" from "being of intrinsic value."

Intrinsic Value as the Other

Without the self-interest argument, what criteria are left for deciding what things have an intrinsic value? For Otto, the answer is none—at least none that can be described unambiguously. Recall Otto's argument that our ethical vocabulary is inadequate to meet the demands the Holy puts on it. Faced by the power of nature, its potential *Thou-ness*, there is very little that we can say about it. We end up trying to describe the indescribable. We try to speak of what we encountered, and then what was valuable about it, but we cannot really distinguish between the thing and its value, because they are too tightly entangled. The value is essential in, not an attribute of, the thing. When we try to express what we mean, we wind up saying with Rodman that "all natural entities have intrinsic worth simply by virtue of being what they are,"[25] or with McHarg, "That which is, is justified by being; it is unique, it needs no other justification."[26]

Of course, the experience of the Holy can be very enlightening, and this enlightenment has an inherent value—for humans—but the enlightening experience is not the whole value:

> There will, in fact, be two values to distinguish in the *Numen*; its "fascination" (*fascinans*) will be that element in it whereby it is of subjective value (*beatitude*) to man; but it is "august" (*augustum*) in so far as it is recognized as possessing in itself *objective* value that claims our homage.[27]

It is this sense of objective value that I call *intrinsic value*. So defined, intrinsic value is a value for no one, and there are some quirks to this kind of value that have to be admitted. First, there is no such thing as "greater" or "lesser" intrinsic value, at least not for humans to judge. If we made such gradations, we would be back at the idea that intrinsic value is the value that an experiencing subject compares with other values. What I am suggesting is that an "objective" intrinsic value is independent of being valued by something or a value for something.

The second quirk is that intrinsic value is not additive. That is, we cannot say, "such-and-such has various instrumental values, and in addition to these it has an intrinsic value, which brings its total value up to so-and-so much." It may be tempting for environmentalists to say this, but we are really talking about two distinct kinds of value here. We can certainly use intrinsic value in an argument for environmental preservation, but intrinsic values cannot be an entry in utilitarian ledgers.

So What?

At this point there are some objections that this theory of intrinsic value has to address. I am claiming that anything which we can relate to as a *Thou*, anything that can suggest the *Numen*, has an objective value. Because I have argued that we can relate to anything as a *Thou*, this means that everything has this intrinsic value. With this admission, a number of questions arise. Is everything equally good? If we are to care for good things, how are we supposed to care for everything simultaneously? Is there anything that has intrinsic disvalue? If not, isn't this an empty ethical theory? How could it possibly be a guide for action?

A few answers can be proposed. First, I am dealing here with only one special kind of value, and I admit that there are others. Even if all objects in the world were in the present sense good objects, that would not mean the end of ethics: there would still be questions about rights and duties, how to treat objects with both instrumental and intrinsic value, and so on.

More importantly, though, I want to argue that the intrinsic values that we are able to recognize not only can, but *do* suggest right actions to us. Again, the crux is the meeting with the *Thou* or the revelation of the Holy, as Buber describes it. Buber claims, echoing Otto, that there is very little we can say about what we get out of a meeting with a *Thou*. "As no prescriptions lead us to the meeting, so none leads from it."[28] Nonetheless:

> Man receives, and he receives not a specific "content" but a Presence, a Presence as Power . . . [and] the inexpressible confirmation of meaning. . . . What does the revealed and the concealed meaning purpose with us, desire from us? It does not wish to be explained (nor are we able to do that) but only to be done by us. . . . [T]his meaning is not that of "another life," but that of this life of ours, not of a world "yonder," but that of this world of ours, and it desires its confirmation in this life and in relation to this world. . . . But just as the meaning itself does not permit itself to be transmitted and made into knowledge generally current and admissible so confirmation of it cannot be transmitted as a valid Ought; it is not prescribed, it is not specified on any tablet to be raised above all men's heads. The meaning that has been received can only be proved true by each man only in the singleness of his life.[29]

What Buber is trying to say is that having met a *Thou*, we cannot be indifferent. We have to go out and do something about it. What we do will vary from person to person, but a meeting with the intrinsically valuable is not prescriptively empty.

Both Buber and Otto insist that the *Thou*, the Holy, is beyond our moral categories. Thus our subjective experience of the *Numen* is not like our experiences of other moral urges: "We cannot approach others," writes Buber, "and say, 'You must know this, you must do this.' We can only go, and confirm its truth. And this, too is no 'ought,' but we can, we *must*."[30] Nonetheless, it is clear that the feeling of moral obligation is something we carry away from the meeting, and not something that is valid only so long as we are in the meeting. The encounter with the *Thou* is not mystical in the sense of having nothing to do with our everyday life. On this reading, the problem of what moral prescriptions we get from meeting a *Thou*, is not really a problem—though to describe the voice of the *Thou* in conventional ethical language is.

Focusing more on the subjective side of the relationship with the Holy, Otto is a little more specific about what the content of the prescription is likely to be. When we meet the *mysterium tremendum*, he says, our natural reaction is to feel impressed, and small:

> There is a feeling of one's own submergence, of being but "dust and ashes" and nothingness. And this forms the numinous raw material for the feeling of religious humility.[31]

According to Otto, the Wholly Other contains in itself the "further element" of majesty. This majesty inspires respect, and a corresponding sense of "moral delinquency,"[32] a fear of affronting the *Numen*.

Here, then, is the backdrop for acting morally. "Inhuman nature in its towering reality"[33] inevitably arouses a feeling of obligation to it. As we play out this obligation in the ways each of us thinks is most appropriate, we use "things in accordance with the priorities established by the things themselves."[34] Although the outlines of this play are sketchy, I hope to have established that there is value we can recognize, that it is "there" whether we recognize it or not, and that recognition of it being there brings with it an indubitable obligation to respect that value. In the next section I flesh out what an appropriate response to the recognition of independent intrinsic value might be.

IV

I have argued that nature's intrinsic value is beyond humanity, that nature matters even if it doesn't matter to us. But do we matter to it? Can we destroy this distant, nonhuman good? Experientially, I think the answer has to be yes, that nature's values are not impervious to us. As humans we are different from nature, but we are related to it. When we create a work of culture, we usually destroy a thing in nature, and what is lost is often greater than what we gain. The continued existence of things as they were before the advent of man is not a matter of indifference; it is a matter of value. I want to suggest below how this is so.

When we modify or destroy natural systems or objects, we destroy something that did not take shape under our hands or spring from our brow. We destroy something that is essentially other. What we lose here are the "subjective values" (in Otto's sense) of nature, the value *to us* of a relationship with them.

This does not mean that we cannot lay hands on nature without killing it. It is a question of dominance or appropriateness. Although what is appropriate depends partly on culturally conditioned perceptions, we are entitled to criticize our culture's way of seeing nature on the basis of our encounter with it as a *Thou*. When the human elements of a landscape dominate, its wonder can die for us. We then know the landscape all too well, and we slip into thinking of the landscape as an *It* instead of a *Thou*.

The danger is not only in physical interferences with nature. Nature's wonder also recoils under the onslaught of our mental models and our sciences. The awe of the *Numen* cannot coexist with the drabness of the known:

> No one says, strictly and in earnest, of a piece of clockwork that is beyond his grasp or of a science he cannot understand; That is "mysterious" to me.[35]

There is peril in becoming too knowledgeable. When we can conquer a wilderness either by main strength or by ingenuity, its dying face appears as a reflection of our own. The myth of progress is the myth of Narcissus: it merely brings us back to ourselves.

As it happens, models are invented and discarded, and research programs usually raise more questions than they answer. Although the danger that we will "really" come to know the cosmos is negligible, the danger that we will come to think we *do* know it may not be. What is at stake for us is the potential for richness of experience that would be lost if we destroy the "holy" in the world.

Clearly, the reason we as humans want to preserve nature has a lot to do with nature's value for us, the potential for rich relationships with the nature/*Thou*. But if we can meet all things as *Thous*, what is so special about the intrinsic value of the nature/*Thou* as opposed to the intrinsic value of the human/*Thou*? Suppose our manifest obligations to one conflict with those to the other. Is there a hierarchy of more or less "valuable" *Thous*? Buber clearly thinks there is such a hierarchy. The *Thou* of true "fulfilment" is the "*Thou* that, by its nature, cannot become an *It*," in other words, God.[36] Ignoring for the moment this special case what are we to do with all the other *Thous*?

While we are in a relation with one *Thou*, of course, there is no question of comparing it with another. Comparisons are only a problem afterwards, when we have transformed the *Thou* into an *It* and can shuffle it around as an object of consciousness. Nevertheless, the problem of comparisons between these objects may be more theoretical than practical. While it is possible to see the whole world and all its parts as *Thou*, we are unlikely to be able to keep up an *I-Thou* relationship with all of them. We will seek an *I-Thou* relation to some things, and depending on whether bonds are established (remembering that it is not only we as individuals who decide this), those things will give us a "call and a sending"; attentiveness to them will take a natural priority over attentiveness to others.

The problem of ranking *Its* is not thereby solved, though, any more than moral choice can be reduced to rote rules by any ethical system. There will always be hard cases which challenge our intuitions as free actors. Recognizing the intrinsic value of a *Thou* is an incomplete guide for action. Nevertheless, because nonhuman nature is in some sense "more Other" than people, it is in our human interest to place a high priority on preserving the potential for meeting it.

In short, I argue that we can only experience the mysterious otherness of nature through meetings with a dominant nature. Although this is a familiar argument, it is nonetheless one that goes beyond human interests, for the crux of my argument is that there are values in nature that matter even if they do nothing for us. It is in this sense that the *Numen* demands our respect even when we do not experience the inherent benefits of meeting it. In other words, there are more important things than humanity, things that awe and stupefy us with their longevity, their imperturbability, and their indifference to us. Encountering them as *Thous*, we recognize that they have vast, nonhuman greatness and value, value that we do wrong to threaten. The gossamer Milky Way and the unmoving stars are still beyond us and above us, and they teach us of the Other that is not man. This Other, however, is also the curve of a petal, the delicate lattice of a diatom's shell, things we can easily crush. Faced with such values, the appropriate human virtues are self-restraint, hesitation, a respect for the mystery of the world, and a willingness to leave it at that.

But in practice we aren't willing to: our populations swell, as does our desire for an abundance of *Its* (instead of an abundance of *Thous*). *Terra incognita* shrinks; wonder flees. Do we really love ourselves enough that we are willing to lose the Other? Has our humanism puffed itself up until we cannot imagine that we are neither necessary nor sufficient for value to exist in the world? Who do we think we are?

What I suggest here is that we take self-restraint seriously, even if it is in our power to do without nature. Technological advances may make us independent of our natural life support system; we may learn to live on a barren planet or even to pour our essence into the durable shell of a robot. Faced with such a clash between human interests and the survival of the planet's nature, I think it is humans who must give way.

While this is certainly an inhuman suggestion, it is important to make clear just how inhuman it is. Consider Garret Hardin's well-known lifeboat ethic, i.e., that resourceful nations should work to ensure their own survival in the coming ecoholocaust.[37] If poorer or stupider nations drown under a tide of their own humanity, that is their own fault. Rich "lifeboat" nations should not jeopardize their own survival by helping the suffering. Compassion for the victims means catastrophe for the race.

As inhuman as this sounds, Hardin insists that he is arguing for the sake of future humanity. To serve that end, questions of distributional justice are irrelevant. In a way, my modest proposal is even more ghastly than Hardin's: I am suggesting that for the sake of the austere mystery of nature as *Thou*, we have to ask ourselves whether the preservation of humanity is of overriding importance.

The misanthropy of my argument runs parallel with the misanthropy in the writings of Peter Wessel Zapffe. Zapffe sees humanity as a sort of evolutionary monster, one that is outfitted with an overgrown brain that tries to figure out the meaning of the universe in human terms. The attempt is tragically doomed to failure because nature in itself is quite beyond our attempts to find meaning in it.

According to Zapffe, nature gives us special inspirations and joys; it makes possible human values that cannot be found except in relation to that which is not human. We find these values, and hints of values beyond them, in situations in which nature is terribly dominant. Encounters with these values are vital, providing challenges for the development of our peculiar talents as a species. It is for this reason, Zapffe says, that we are reluctant to lose the chance to meet free nature. Still there is no reason for us to think of ourselves as being the alpha and the omega of the universe. The universe can get on quite well without us, diminished, perhaps, but not greatly so. "For me," writes Zapffe, "a desert island is no tragedy, and neither is a deserted planet."[38] Or, as one of Zapffe's alter egos admonishes the throng, "The life on many worlds is like a rushing river, but life on this world is like a stagnant puddle and a backwater. . . . Know thyselves; be unfruitful and let there be peace on Earth after thy passing."[39]

Zapffe is *not* arguing for collective suicide. What Zapffe (and I) want to do is put a question mark—only a question mark—on the whole of human existence. When we question the right of other species to exist on the planet, it is only fair that we pose the same question with regard to ourselves: do we need, or deserve, to survive? When it is clear that there is value and beauty and wonder and greatness that is wholly independent of us, we cannot conclude that the universe would be a whole lot worse off without us.

V

What I have offered here is a picture of the world and our part in it that departs from the identification or Self-realization approach in ecophilosophical discussions. There is room for a plurality of approaches in environmental philosophy, and my proposal is only an alternative. In the main, I think its emphasis on human restraint is in line with other approaches even though the reasoning is a little different.

The present approach, though, may be more useful than Self-realization in some respects. As a practical matter, it seems to me that when we try to operationalize Self-realization we are put in an uncertain position. We are supposed to retain a sense of our individuality as we work to save the big Self from destruction—but at the same time we are supposed to *lose* interest in our individuality as we cultivate our identification with the big Self. True, Self-realization is not absolute holism, in which the individual is identical with the big Self. Nor is it absolute separatism, in which the individual is completely apart from the Self.

However, those practicing Self-realization seem to want it both ways: we are, somehow, both the big and the small self. How do we set to work with this ambiguous notion of self?

On the face of it, Buber's *I-Thou* model can seem a lot like the Self-realization approach. Both emphasize the virtues of humility, and both report that very little can be said about the *Thou* or the Self. But the two approaches are not the same. Fox points out that Self-realization depends on the "relative autonomy" of beings in nature.[40] For Buber, however, the autonomy is absolute: the *I* and the *Thou* do not depend on one another. They meet, but only as two ships which pass in the night. There is contact, perhaps a yearning to merge into one identity, but *Thou* remains separate from *I*. The *Thou* is not the *Atman*, because we are not a part of the *Thou*.

The "apartness" of my proposal is able to skirt a few questions that Self-realization raises: what is the position of humans in the Self? How important is it that *Homo sapiens* continue? Can a person who has "realized him or herself" agree to the extinction of the human race, believing that it would still exist in the *Atman*-Self? What about the sense of awe, on which Otto bases religious ethics? We, as small selves, can certainly feel awe toward the enormity of the Self—but at what price? How far must we depart from the path of Self-realization in order to retain this picture? How much must a "realized" person avoid "experientially incorporating" the world in order to feel awe for it? Can we feel an awe for nature when what we think we are looking at is a part of ourselves?

It is possible that Self-realization does not rule out an awe for nature. Yet the ethical argument of the Self-realization approach seems to be based not on awe but rather a kind of self-interest: "We ought to care about all entities/beings/things in the world because they are a part of our Self; their diminishment is our diminishment."[41] The idea of self has become so important that Callicott writes that environmentalists have "hopelessly supposed" that "objective intrinsic value could be persuasively established independently of self."[42]

It is clear that proponents of Self-realization are not talking about egoistic self-interests. Still, I hope we have not been so mesmerized by the concept of self that we think it is the only possible basis for an ethic. What I have tried to do here is suggest how values can exist in nature independently of self.

The ethic I have argued for here is intuitionist; it rests on a kind of revelation of value to the individual. This does not mean that other people, or groups of people, cannot share relations with a *Thou* that seem (in retrospect) very similar. What it does is base the ethic on the reality of an *I-Thou* relation.

The weakness of an intuitionist ethic, of course, is that there is no guarantee that everyone will have the same intuition. Nor can we be sure that everyone will act on their intuitions in compatible ways. Encountering the Other might be a revelation of terror and alienation for some, which would lead them to attack the Other in fear.

Despite these weaknesses, I believe an environmental ethic must at some level be connected with an intuition or a feeling for nature. While moral philosophy may involve detached reasoning, moral action must involve caring, committed, nonrational attitudes. As one philosopher puts it, "one cannot prove the beauty of Mozart's composition in a way that separates it from personal experience."[43] The likelihood that an encounter with the nature/*Thou* would lead to aggression toward nature seems small; Buber tells us that an *I-Thou* relationship is one of awe and compassion, not terror and alienation.

Whatever the verdict on ethical intuitionism, we should remember that Self-realization is also a kind of intuitionism. Some argue that the intuition it describes is superior because it "gets much closer to what many naturalists and environmentalists feel and *want* to say."[44] It may in some cases be true that the Self-realization approach meshes with the worldview of ecoactivists; nevertheless, some environmentalists seem to feel more *responsibility for* than *identification with* their natural surroundings.[45] Some surveys of visitors to wilderness areas, moreover, suggest that people set a high value on the ways that wilderness seizes their attention and on a sense of nature awe at least as much as on a sense of identification.[46]

VI

In any case, the idea that ecophilosophy should mesh with the intuitions of environmentalists is absolutely essential. If environmental philosophy is going to be useful in the environmental movement, it has to make sense to activists; it must give them conceptual tools and arguments with which to fight ecological degradation. It has to be common-sensical enough that it is easily graspable, and at the same time revolutionary enough that it points to reasons for changing our behavior.

What I have been trying to do is make awe for nature sensible to the inquiring intellect or environmental philosophers. In fact, there is nothing especially new about the concept of nature awe, and I think it fits quite nicely with what many environmentalists think about nature. Still, conceptual consistency and a handful of supporters is only part of an effective environmental ethic. So far (as often happens in environmental ethics) I have said something like, "If all of us had this feeling about ecological problems, we could solve them." This may be true, but it is not much help. There are steps missing. What about those who do not (basically) have the feeling? In the face of power struggles and inert political institutions, how do we implement an ethic based on awe for nature?

Even if (as is doubtful) people do wrong only because they don't understand nature's values, how is everyone going to be persuaded to understand those values the way environmentalists do? Academic philosophy can and should be a start at persuasion, but it cannot do the job without help. One place to look for help might be art and poetry, which can speak directly to our intuitions of nature's value:

> When the whole human race
> Has been like me rubbed out, they will still be here:

storms, moon, and ocean,
Dawn and the birds. And I say this: their beauty has
more meaning
Than the whole human race and the race of birds.[47]

Notes

This chapter is reprinted with minor revisions from Peter Reed, "Man Apart: An Alternative to the Self-Realization Approach," *Environmental Ethics* 11 (Spring, 1989): 53–69. Reed worked at the Council of Environmental Studies in Oslo, Norway from Fall 1986 until his death in March 1987, when he was killed in an avalanche in the Jotunheimen mountain area. After finishing research on Norwegian ecophilosophy and ecopolitics as a Fulbright Fellow (1985–86), he received funding from the Norwegian Ministry of Environment to examine environmental attitudes of bureaucrats at the county level of Norwegian environmental management. Reed worked on this project until his death. He also edited an anthology with David Rothenberg, *Wisdom and the Open Air: The Norwegian Roots of Deep Ecology* (Minneapolis: University of Minnesota Press, 1993).

[1] Peter Wessel Zapffe, "Den siste Messias" [1933], *Essays* (Oslo: Aventura, 1992), 15, translated by Peter Reed, Sigmund Kvaløy Sætereng, and David Rothenberg in *Wisdom in the Open Air*, 40.

[2] E. O. Wilson, *Biophilia: The Human Bond with Other Species* (Cambridge: Harvard University Press, 1984), 85.

[3] Hugh H. Iltis, Orie L. Loucks, and Peter Andrews, "Criteria for Optimum Human Environments," *Bulletin of the Atomic Scientists* 26, no.1 (January 1970): 2.

[4] See May Leavenworth, "On Bridging the Gap between Fact and Value," in *Human Values and Natural Sciences*, ed. E. Laszlo and J. B. Wilbur (New York: Gordon and Breach Science Publishers, 1970), 133–43.

[5] Joseph Meeker, *The Comedy of Survival: Studies in Literary Ecology* (New York: Charles Scribner's Sons, 1972), 52.

[6] Warwick Fox, *Approaching Deep Ecology: A Response to Richard Sylvan's Critique of Deep Ecology*, Environmental Studies Occasional Paper no. 20 (Hobart: Center for Environmental Studies, University of Tasmania, 1986), 67.

[7] Arne Næss, *Gandhi and Group Conflict: An Exploration of Satyagraha Theoretical Background* (Oslo: Universitetsforlaget, 1974), 41.

[8] Arne Næss, "Identification as a Source of Deep Ecological Attitudes," in *Deep Ecology*, ed. Michael Tobias (San Diego: Avant Books, 1985), 261.

[9] Fox, *Approaching Deep Ecology*, 67.

[10] J. Baird Callicott, "Intrinsic Value, Quantum Theory, and Environmental Ethics," *Environmental Ethics* 7 (1985): 275.

[11] Martin Buber, *I and Thou*, trans. Ronald Gregor Smith (Edinburgh: T. & T. Clark, 1944), 3.

[12] Buber, *I and Thou*.

[13] Buber, *I and Thou*, 6.

[14] Buber, *I and Thou*, 32.

[15] Buber, *I and Thou*, 8.

[16] Buber, *I and Thou*, 110, 9.

[17] Buber, *I and Thou*, 11.

[18] Buber, *I and Thou*, 77.

[19] Rudolf Otto, *The Idea of the Holy* (Middlesex: Penguin Books, 1959), 39.

[20] Otto, *The Idea of the Holy*, 20.

[21] Otto, *The Idea of the Holy*, 79.

[22] Holmes Rolston, III, "Values in Nature," *Environmental Ethics* 3 (1981):127.

[23] Holmes Rolston, III, "Beyond Recreational Value: The Greater Outdoors," in *A Literature Review: President's Commission on American Outdoors* (Washington: U.S. Government Printing Office, 1986), 103–13.

[24] Holmes Rolston, III "Are Values in Nature Subjective or Objective?" *Environmental Ethics* 4 (1982): 146.

[25] John Rodman, "The Liberation of Nature?" *Inquiry* 20 (1977): 108.

[26] Ian McHarg, *Design with Nature* (Garden City: Doubleday/Natural History Press, 1971): 125.

[27] Otto, *The Idea of the Holy*, 67.

[28] Buber, *I and Thou*, 111.

[29] Buber, *I and Thou*, 110–11. Buber is speaking here of the "ultimate" *Thou*, God. Without wanting to identify God with nature, I think we can use these ideas as models for our relationship with nature.

[30] Buber, *I and Thou*, 111.

[31] Otto, *The Idea of the Holy*, 34.

[32] Otto, *The Idea of the Holy*, 67.

[33] Robinson Jeffers, from "The Beauty of Things," in *Robinson Jeffers: Selected Poems* (New York: Vintage Books, 1963), 94.

[34] William Leiss, "A Value Basis for Conservation Policy," *Policy Studies Journal* 9 (1980): 613–22.

[35] Otto, *The Idea of the Holy*, 42.

[36] Buber, *I and Thou*, 75.

[37] Garrett Hardin, "Living on a Lifeboat," *Bioscience* 24 (1974): 561–68.

[38] Peter Wessel Zapffe, *Jeg velger sannheten* (A dialogue between Peter Wessel Zapffe and Herman Tønnessen), trans. Peter Reed (Oslo: Universitetsforlaget, 1983), 60.

[39] Zapffe, "Den siste Messias" [1933], *Essays* (1992), 28, translated by Reed and Rothenberg in *Wisdom of the Open Air*, 52.

[40] Fox, *Approaching Deep Ecology*, 84.

[41] Fox, *Approaching Deep Ecology*, 76.

[42] Callicott, "Intrinsic Value, Quantum Theory, and Environmental Ethics," 275.

[43] Richard Cartwright Austin, "Beauty: A Foundation for Environmental Ethics," *Environmental Ethics* 7 (1985): 201.

[44] Fox, *Approaching Deep Ecology*, 78.

[45] Peter Reed, "Verdier i miljøpolitikken" (Values in Environmental Decision Making), unpublished manuscript. Because this survey is narrow in scope and unfinished, this conclusion is tentative. It *is* the case that many writers on environmental is-

sues, especially those with a philosophical bent, make a point of identifying themselves with nature. Whether this holds true for a wider environmental public is an empirical question. I am unaware of comprehensive surveys that have collected information on precisely this attitude of identification with nature.

[46] For a treatment of the "awe-values" in nature, see David Douglas, "The Spirit of Wilderness and the Religious Community," *Sierra* 68, no.3 (1983): 56–57; Linda H. Graber, *Wilderness as Sacred Space* (Washington, D.C.: Association of American Geographers, 1976); W. E. Hammit, "Cognitive Dimensions of Wilderness Solitude," *Environment and Behavior* 14, no. 4 (1982): 478–93.

[47] Robinson Jeffers, "Their Beauty Has More Meaning," in *Selected Poems* (New York: Vintage Books, 1963), 77.

Chapter 24

"Man Apart" and Deep Ecology: A Reply to Reed

Arne Næss

I. Man Apart. A Tragic Being

Among the strong, lifelong critics of man's domination and exploitation of the earth, we find philosophers who would rather use the slogan "man apart" than "not man apart." Two exponents of the former trend are the outstanding Scandinavian existentialist philosopher Peter Wessel Zapffe and the young deep ecology theorist Peter Reed.[1]

Reed begins his paper with a quote from Zapffe in which he beautifully summarizes some of the main points of his early writings concerning the essential suffering of all beings capable of joy or suffering, and the terror upon terror in nature. Zapffe seems to conclude with a "no!" to *human* life in this universe of death and annihilation. At the same time, however, Zapffe expresses his awe in contemplating the serenity and majesty of wild nature: the mountains, the ocean, the stars. . . . Since the 1930s, Zapffe has written passionate and witty criticisms of man's destruction of nature. Nevertheless, his philosophy has another side.

According to Zapffe, humans, when not distracted by all sorts of ultimately meaningless activities, understand through their metaphysical attitudes (e.g., the requirement of justice and the rejection of death and utter annihilation) that they are utterly different from the other living beings that evolution has so far produced. The human brain makes us capable of seeing our own death and our essentially tragic position in nature. Thus, humans are truly and radically apart, man is homeless in nature, and since his body is a part of nature, man is even "homeless in his own body."

Later in life, Zapffe at times did not directly advise humanity to stop begetting children, but he expected that with increasing maturity people would refrain from producing children in such a world. Peter Reed also takes this more moderate position. The significance of Reed's article is, therefore, largely independent of the question of whether humans should disappear from the face of the earth or not.

II. Alternative Sets of Premises

On the metalevel, Peter Reed admirably emphasizes the positive aspect of a plurality of ultimate philosophical commitments among those who wish to contribute to the lessening of human destructiveness on earth. He proposes an alternative to my version of philosophical deep ecology, which I call Ecosophy T (Ecosophy T has as its logically ultimate norm the one word sentence "Self-Realization!" together with the hypothesis that identification functions "as a source of deep ecological attitudes").[2]

Reed is of the opinion, and I am sure that he is right, that some supporters of the deep ecology movement feel more at home with an overall worldview more in the direction of his alternative, than with Ecosophy T. They might, for example, agree with Reed that "it is our very *separateness* from the earth, the gulf between the human and the natural, that makes us want to do right by the earth . . . [where we see] nature as a stranger . . . [and where we respect] values in nature that are totally independent of what we humans think is beautiful, right and good." Reed holds that an appreciation of wilderness and wildness, overwhelming complexity, the enormity of the mountains and the oceans, and the efficiency and ferocity of the splendid great white shark, are values of this kind.

According to Reed, an acceptance of this kind of absolute philosophical nature makes it unwarranted to use Self-realization as an ultimate philosophical norm. As Reed puts it, "I hope we have not been so mesmerized by the concept of self that we think it is the only possible basis for an ethics." I am sure "we" have not been so mesmerized! Self-realization is an ultimate norm in only one kind of ecosophy exemplified by Ecosophy T. Ecosophy T is not to be identified as *"the* philosophy of deep ecology." There is no one single philosophy if, as I use the term, a verbally articulated philosophy contains the articulation of *ultimate* premises. The "eight points" of the "basic principles of deep ecology" (or better, the "deep ecology platform"), are, at best, penultimate.[3]

Why should we even wish to have conformity at the ultimate philosophical or religious level? We are on the way from we know not where to we know not where. Ecosophy T is only one of the several ecosophies inspired by ecology and by the deep ecology movement. Everyone need not accept it. Those around the world who feel that there must be deep changes in human lifestyles and policies can be members of the deep ecology movement without having to accept ecosophical positions which they find confusing, don't understand, or don't feel at home with, or simply dislike. I now do not feel at home with Reed's ultimate views, but I am glad that they exist and their proponents are strong supporters of the deep ecology movement.[4]

III. Interpretations of the Term *Identification*

Reed's primary concern in his paper is not the philosophy of Self-realization, but rather the notion of *identification*. The term *identification* as used in Ecosophy T "is rather technical, but there is scarcely any alternative."[5] There are several roots for this kind of use of the term.

The Social Science Context. In social science terminology one may say, "A identifies with his corporation more strongly than with his nation or with his family." Clearly, to make sense of this example one must rid oneself of the association of identification with resemblance. Furthermore, if A identifies with B, this does not weaken A's state of individuality. A does not fuse with B. Consider another example: "We must restore that high level of solidarity different groups of workers exhibited thirty years ago. But what can we do when workers today identify more closely with the middle class than with the working class?" The personal identities of these workers are not lost whether they identify with the working class or the middle class.

Nevertheless, acts of solidarity presuppose the process of identification and the same holds true for acts motivated by responsibility. In order to feel responsible for wilderness and for the penguins of Antarctica, a process of identification is a necessary but not a sufficient requirement. In this sense, "a process of identification" can be defined as "a process through which the supposed interests of another being are *spontaneously* reacted to as our own interests." This definition is of course intended to cover only beings which meaningfully, but not necessarily factually, can be said to have interests. The term *spontaneously* is stressed for reasons that might be clear from another example. If A strongly identifies with his organization (or his wife), the question as to how and where to spend his vacation will be answered in a way that spontaneously and implicitly takes care of the interests of his organization (or his wife), for he is not aware of his own interests as being potentially different from those of his organization (or his wife).

Insofar as my terminology parallels that of the social sciences, it is conceptually odd for anyone to hold, as Reed claims, that "some environmentalists seem to feel more *responsibility for* than *identification with* their natural surroundings." Reed is right, I think, as long as identification implies some kind of likeness or resemblance as it tends perhaps to do when used in ordinary conversation.

Alienation. The term *alienation* is extensively used in the social sciences and in philosophy. For example, if it is said that A suffers from alienation in relation to some group of people (B), or to a certain environment, a negative feeling or attitude on the part of A, may, or may not, be implied. As I use the term alienation in Ecosophy T, negative feelings or attitudes are not implied.

Rather, I am referring to indifference and "distance," together, implicitly, with some premises concerning what is a normal relationship between A and B. The alienation under discussion is usually partial, however, in the sense that the indifference does not cover every aspect of A's relation to B. For example, A may be alienated from his neighbors in every respect except his interest in the amount of their income. A young person may be alienated from his society except for several very narrow personal concerns. As far as he is concerned, society may "go to hell" as long as these narrow personal interests are served.

The term *alienation* as used tentatively in Ecosophy T is an antonym for *identification*. This terminology is not very far from that of Spinoza (and others) when using *in se* (in self) and *in alio* (in other) as an ultimate ontological distinction that is more basic and deeper than, for instance, the ontological distinction between substance/mode or God/mode.

Social Self and Ecological Self. Just as *social self* is an important term in William James's great work, *The Principles of Psychology*, *ecological self* is destined to be an important term in ecosophy,[6] for the process of identification, as interpreted above, is closely connected with the process of the development of the ecological self. It remains to be ascertained however, just how closely identification and ecological self are connected. The small child who identifies strongly with its mother, father, and other humans also identifies just as early with nonpersons (animals and other parts or aspects of its environment). Gestalts are formed which bridge the alleged fundamental gulf between humans and nonhumans.

Up to this point, the concept of a "process of identification" has been defined only for beings that meaningfully can be said to have interests. If there is a need to bring an essentially equivalent process under the same heading for those beings whom we normally would not say have interests, what can we do to satisfy this need? Two ways suggest themselves. First, we might introduce an *or* saying that the term covers beings with *interests or x*, introducing the appropriate term for x. Alternatively, we could extend the denotation of *interests* to include *x*. I choose the latter alternative. If we were to see ugly buildings or installations on the very summit of Mount Fujiyama, we would be spontaneously repelled by them, finding that the dignity, majesty, aloofness, etc., of the mountain had been violated. In this context, it would be in the interest of the mountain, as spontaneously experienced by us, to retain those characteristics on which its dignity, etc. rest. We would experience the same reaction if we saw people training an old polar bear to dance or saw the Pope advertising for Coca-Cola.

So much for the term "process of identification." An empirical study to determine whether people become environmental activists largely through a sense of awe *or* through the process of identification could scarcely, as Reed suggests, rely on direct questions in terms of identification, for they would inevitably think in terms of resemblance or likeness, etc., rather than in terms of identification in the technical senses discussed above.

One of the things I most deplore is the predominance of the utilitarian attitude towards nature. This attitude encourages people to identify with nature narrowly in terms of its usefulness to humans and it promotes alienation from the nonhumans—alienation not only from those aspects of nature that elicit awe, but also those that elicit compassion for the decent treatment of nonhuman nature. A pig in a factory farm is not treated as well as a dog who is "a member of our family." The difference is immense. The fulfillment of potentials (of self-realization, I would say) is taken care of to a large extent in the latter case, but not in the former. The dignity of pigs, great waterfalls, or mountains is not considered when narrow economic considerations (bacon, electricity, and tourism) are dominant.

IV. Awe and Separateness

If A identifies with B, the nontechnical use of *identification* may lead to the assumption that A is familiar with B and, at least sometimes, familiarity may breed contempt. Reed points strongly to intrinsic value of "things that awe and stupefy us," things that are dramatically different, *solidly apart*, from us:

> It is our very *separateness* from the earth, the gulf between the human and the natural that makes us want to do right by the earth. It seems to me that recognizing the moral distance between ourselves and the world helps us recognize the values in nature that are totally independent of what we humans think is beautiful, right, and good.

Reed proposes an environmental ethic based on "awe for nature." Although this is a possibility that certainly deserves further study, here I limit myself to the relation of such an ethical possibility to conceptualizations such as identification and self-realization.

In the traditional Sherpa culture of the Himalayas, the holy mountain they call Tseringma (commonly known as Gaurishankar) is viewed with holy awe. This feeling well suits the descriptions by Rudolph Otto and Martin Buber of this kind of attitude. Nevertheless, the process of identification is also strong in the Sherpa tradition: the very name of the mountain means "the mother of the long (good) life." Although vast snowstorms and deadly avalanches proceed from its flanks, there is till a positive, intimate relationship between the people and the mountain. Traditionally, people throw a little beer in the direction of the "inhuman" mountain before drinking any themselves. The recent "conquest" of the "mother of the long good life" by climbers, the Sherpas believe, was disliked by her and resulted in a bad harvest. Using *is* in a way we are not acquainted with in industrial societies, Tseringma *is* also a beautiful princess and, of course, a mother. A community of about one hundred and fifty people live just under the wild immense precipices of Tseringma. For these people, or at least the older generation, it is sacrilegious to "attack" and "conquer" Tseringma. Thus, when the community leader asked the heads of the forty-seven families whether they should try to protect the mountain against Western (and Japanese) climbing expeditions, they unanimously voted for protection, despite the vast amounts of money and goods (measured in their terms) to be gained from such expeditions.[7] In short, for the Sherpas, there was a relationship both of awe and identification with the mountain—humans identifying with the nonhuman. It sounds strange and points to the limitations of the fruitful use of the technical term in ordinary communication. Nevertheless, in the articulation of ecosophies like Ecosophy T, it may sometimes be of help.

Here is another example of the combination of awe and identification. A boy about ten years old, after some years of acquaintance from afar, starts to conceive a big mountain H as a kind of higher being, perhaps something like a godfather. Some years later, he begins to conceive of H as being serene, equa-nimous, unruffled, strong, and great (not only big) in contrast to his own char-acter, which he thinks of as being temperamental, shifting, listless, unbalanced, weak, and small. Clearly, the boy sees the mountain as having these characteris-tics in sharp contrast with himself. These characterizations of a thing that is not "really" a person are usually called personifications or anthropomorphisms. They are said to be "projections" from the inner life of the boy and attached by him (like a stamp?) to the object. Yet, in spite of its unreachableness and lack of human or animal features, the boy conceives of the mountain as friendly and as somehow communicating this. He would certainly, if he had the strength, de-fend the mountain against any kind of destruction by fellow humans. Along the alienation/identification axis, the boy may be said to have identified so strongly with the mountain that the term *identification* in this case requires a broader definition than the one used in previous examples above.

What surpasses human levels may elicit awe. It need not, however, be big. Even a leaf, an atomic structure, the smallest part of the human body, may elicit awe. (Curiously enough, the Japanese tradition of gardening, which concentrates on small natural "miracles," may actually work against the efforts of a minority to save large areas of "free nature".) If something is vast, inhuman, and utterly different from anything familiar, this does not in itself elicit awe. Nor do I see that we are led to protect it, or even to feel an obligation to protect it, contrary to Reed's claims. Rather, it tends to be meaningless. For example, "friends of big numbers," such as octillions, complain that most of their human friends find big numbers to be meaningless. They do not elicit awe.

The feeling of one's own nothingness and insignificance may occur consis-tently with feelings of nature awe, but in this case a real difference of attitude may be important. To me, the feeling of insignificance is transitory. The starry heavens may elicit this combination of insignificance and awe, but during long medita-tions, or several nights under the stars, an experience of expansion of the self may be had. To block out the sight of the heavens through artificial lights is felt by millions of people to be one of the saddest things that have happened to industrial societies. One of the sources of integration, of concentration on essentials, and of living at deeper levels, is lost.

The reduction of alienation and the increase of identification are obviously related to the process of increasing meaningfulness. If we look for an alternative to the technical term *identification,* the word *meaning* is worth considering.

V. A Gulf between Nature and Its Evolutionary Monstrosity: Man?

The separateness Reed experienced is unbridgeable: "there is an existential gulf of awesome depth between ourselves and the Other, a gulf which no amount of 'identification in otherness' can span." Zapffe experienced this separateness in a terrifying way: he felt even his own body to be a genuine part of nature and as such, unbridgeably separate from him-*self.* He felt himself to be an evolutionary monstrosity with metaphysical needs which nature could not possibly fulfill. In nature, the individual human life is meaningless.

Nevertheless, Zapffe has always been a fierce opponent of the destruction of free nature. Whatever his ultimate views, his identification with the animal, plant, and mineral worlds has been unusually strong and varied.[8] The essential and highly original existentialist point of view of Zapffe may be summed up as follows: evolution misfired when it created the human brain. The brain allows us to contemplate life as a whole, and we necessarily ask: to what purpose? What purpose does life serves? The valid answer "Nothing" is not good enough. We cannot accept the meaninglessness of life as a whole. "But what if there were no tragedies?" Not decisive. "What if there were no excruciating pain?" Not decisive. "What if we all loved each other?" Not decisive. The hypertrophy of our brain has made us outgrow life. Leave the earth to beings who cannot contemplate life as a whole!

Although the idea that there is an absolute gulf between humans and nature has not been a clearly recognizable force in the deep ecology movement, there could be a place for it. There is, for example, nothing in the eight points of the deep ecology platform that implies a denial of this absolute gulf as formulated by Peter Reed or Zapffe. If it were included, it would probably belong to "level 1" (the very ultimate norms and hypotheses) from which the eight points may possibly follow. Nevertheless, the particular ecosophy, which has Self-realization as the ultimate norm, is incompatible with the absolute unbridgeable gulf hypothesis (on level 1). If this hypothesis, together with a norm supporting "awe for nature," is taken to imply a subordinate norm of "extinction of mankind," then there is a clash with point one of the eight points: the intrinsic value of the diversity of human cultures.

The idea that an absolute existential difference and apartness is, as such, a source of awe and of norms of radical protection of nature is, to me and to many other supporters of the deep ecology movement, largely incomprehensible, but so are many of the ideas on the ultimate level. Differences of opinion at this level, does not mean that we cannot continue to work together, as we have worked for a long time, at the other levels. What has the practical level to do with environmental *philosophy*? In philosophy conceived of as a total view, the verbal articulations of derived decisions in concrete situations are no less characteristic of that philosophy than articulations of a more abstract and general character.

We look into the eyes of a living being in intense and deep suffering, and we ask: "What can I do, what can I do?" We feel nearness. This feeling has serious consequences for many of us. The infinite equanimity of a mountain makes me and others develop the lasting process of identification with the mountain, a process that is necessary in order to attribute equanimity to it. To others, like Peter Reed, a process of identification is required to feel the majesty, awe, and fear of a mountain.[9]

Notes

This chapter is reprinted with minor revisions from Arne Næss, "'Man Apart' and Deep Ecology: A Reply to Reed," *Environmental Ethics* 12 (Summer, 1989): 185–192.

[1] See Peter Reed, "Man Apart: An Alternative to the Self-Realization Approach," *Environmental Ethics* 11 (1989): 53–69.

[2] Arne Næss, "Identification as a Source of Deep Ecological Attitudes," in Michael Tobias, ed., *Deep Ecology: An Anthology* (San Diego: Avant Books, 1985), 256–70.

[3] The deep ecology platform appears in Arne Næss, "The Deep Ecology Movement: Some Philosophical Aspects," *Philosophical Inquiry* 8 (1986): 10–31; Bill Devall and George Sessions, *Deep Ecology: Living as if Nature Mattered* (Salt Lake City: Gibbs Smith, 1985), 69–73.

[4] All of this underlines the usefulness of distinguishing the four separate levels or components of ecosophies: the ultimate principles or norms level, the common platform (as a penultimate "philosophy of nature" position), the consequences of more or less general kinds, and the level of decisions in concrete situations (the "choice points," in the terminology of E. C. Tolman in his "Behavior Choice Point"). For a diagram of the four levels, see Devall and Sessions, *Deep Ecology*, 225–26.

[5] Næss, "Identification as a Source of Deep Ecological Attitudes," 261.

[6] The concept of *ecological self* is introduced in Arne Næss, "Self-Realization: An Ecological Approach to Being in the World," Roby Memorial Lecture, Murdoch University, Western Australia, March, 1986. (Reprinted in *The Trumpeter* 4, No. 3 [1987]: 35–42.)

[7] The petition to save Tseringma from assault was not even answered by the Nepalese bureaucracy and the Alpine Clubs of the world showed little interest.

[8] In his great work *On the Tragic (Om Det Tragiske)* Zapffe discusses animals and other natural beings in a way that exhibits a high level of empathy and positive identification in the technical sense.

[9] This last paragraph was added in 1997.

Chapter 25

Comment: Self-Realization or Man Apart? The Reed–Næss Debate

Val Plumwood

The Arne Næss–Peter Reed debate is one of the most remarkable exchanges in modern environmental philosophy. Reed and Næss had much in common: both were people of deep practical environmental commitment, and both sought a philosophical basis for that commitment and for developing an historic shift in consciousness away from the dominant instrumental relationship to nature towards one based on respect. Both argued for plural approaches, and conceived their own as only one among a number of possibilities. Lovers of mountains, they converged on appropriately montane virtues — humility and openness to the other, for example. Reed writes about nature in terms of majesty, awe, and fear. His death in an avalanche among the mountains of Jotunheimen dramatizes and lends great poignancy to this extraordinary conversation.

Despite their commonalities, Reed and Næss differed profoundly (so profoundly that we seem to need more in the way of resolution than an appeal to principles of tolerance or plurality) over the question of whether the abstract foundation for the desired new relationship will be found in human continuity with and embeddedness within the natural order, or in our "existential gulf," our discontinuity and difference from nature. Næss proposed foundations formulated in terms of identity: Reed's counter-advocacy, in a powerful essay published posthumously, of basing respect not on sameness but on difference, could hardly have presented a stronger contrast. I argue here that the criticisms both disputants make of each other are valid, which points to resolution via a third position which will allow us to combine elements of both continuity and difference, self and other.

How is this disagreement between Reed and Næss situated in terms of the previous debate? One of the most important historical achievements of Arne Næss's monumental contribution to environmental philosophy was to begin to push its questions beyond the overcontested, rather sterile and limited, academic argument over whether ethical principles could be extended to nonhumans. He did this in two ways, by directing attention first towards activist issues and, second, towards the more basic and philosophically productive questions of the analysis of human identity, alienation, and difference from nature. This does not mean, as Næss recognized himself, that his answers to these questions are the best possible, and that we should not pursue others. Næss's work opens up instead the big questions of how we have misconceived the reality, and how these misconceptions have foreclosed our options for responsible and ethical relationship, and, as he would put it, for mutual self-realization. In this reconception of the problem area, the balance of identity and difference in the conception of human/nature relationship is revealed as a crucial, underdetermined and highly sensitive matter.

Næss, focusing on human alienation from nature, elects for identification with nature and the realization of the Self based on the totality of these identifications as the foundation for respect for and defense of nature. That this position created a useful alliance with those forms of Buddhist thought which cast the sense of personal separateness as the ultimate illusion, contributed in no small measure to the political success of Næss's version of deep ecology. In spite of careful qualifications Næss's vision still ultimately draws on sameness and identity as the basis of respect. As Reed saw it, by contrast, respect could only be based on the very existential gulf Næss's work sought to remove. It is, he argued, "our very separateness from the Earth, the gulf between the human and the natural, that makes us want to do right by the earth."[1] There was an alternative to Næss's account, Reed argued, based on taking the other, nature, and not the human self to be basic: "one approach sees humans as part of nature, the other sees nature as part of humans."[2]

Relying on Martin Buber's theory of "I-*Thou*" relationship (but with some significant departures), Reed declares the other that is nature to be not part of the self but "a self-sufficient being of whom we have an inkling." It is "the Wholly Other," "a total stranger," "radically apart."[3] In the right spirit, we can meet this other, but only as "two ships that pass in the night," since the "I" and the "*Thou*" do not depend on each other. (It may be doubted that Reed follows Buber here, since in Buber's theory of mutuality the other is thought of as giving itself in what amounts to an act of self-revelation). Næss is certainly right to criticize Reed's dualism and failure to address the problem of alienation. Reed does not merely stress difference, he retains the existential gulf of the dominant dualistic tradition in its full form. This gulf yawns between humans and nature, according to Reed, because all we humans have in common with it, our merely physical nature, is an inessential and accidental element of our identities. Reed's absence from the present debate seems to me to do something to undermine this view of the physical as an unimportant element in human identity. Reed's reaffirmation of the existential gulf, a key and especially problematic part of the Western tradition, leads him to treat physical nature in a deeply ambivalent way: physical nature is both "mere" (in the human case) and the object of what amounts almost to worship (in the case of the other). We are left wondering why the supposed radical difference of the other should be a basis for awe and wonder in the one case and something like disdain or indifference in the other.

Reed's account is strongly oriented to wilderness. In contrast to Næss, who often focuses on mixed communities, Reed is plainly one of those who believe that it is only the "pure" landscape of human absence that represents nature. It is not only the otherness but the huge scale and indifference of wilderness landscapes that evokes awe, and leads to revelations of intrinsic value in nature. When nature is terribly dominant, says Reed, we have a sense of fear and of wonder which is missing in contexts too familiar and humanized. Nature is both related to us and other, but it is difference alone, it seems, which is the basis of the intuition of value.

It is hard to see how this kind of orientation to "the Wholly Other" can provide a basis for consideration of nature in the large number of situations where it is less impressive and more vulnerable—precisely the kind of context, one would have thought, where we especially need a respect ethic. In contrast to Næss's position and its politically useful alliances with the perennial philosophy and with Buddhist thought, the austerity, almost self-revulsion, of Reed's account, with its stress on human insignificance and final, frankly misanthropic, suggestion that the world might be a better place without human beings, seems unlikely to claim widespread appeal.

Nevertheless, Reed's critique of Næss points up some important problems and tensions in the use of identity as the foundation for an environmental ethic. On first glance, Næss's account does not appear to appeal to either fusion or to egoism—since we are supposed to defend not the self but the big Self as "the totality of our identifications." But, says Reed, there seem to be inconsistent requirements hidden here: we are supposed to retain a sense of our individuality as we work to save the big Self from destruction—but at the same time we are supposed to lose interest in our individuality as we cultivate our identification with the big Self.[4] We are required to be egoists and also not egoists, to retain the intensity and defense drive of egoism, but abandon certain key differentiations between ourselves and others. For Næss's position, on closer inspection, ultimately is based on a kind of self-interest and upon a form of fusion or expulsion of difference—taking the form, as Næss explains in his reply, of identity of interests. "Identification," writes Næss, is a process "through which the supposed interests of another being are spontaneously reacted to as our own interests."[5] Selves may not be fused, but interests are.

But analysis in terms of interest identity won't enable us to dispense with difference. When we identify in solidarity with an animal, say a wombat, we do not acquire identical specific interests, in grass eating, for example. Although we may (as relational selves) assume the overarching interest of the other's general well-being and react to that as bound up with our own, it is crucial to our being able to defend that well-being that we retain a clear sense of them as separate beings with different interests from ours.

If we must somehow "identify" with the other in their difference, identification and respect cannot be understood as processes of overcoming or eliminating otherness, and neither ethics nor motivation can be derived from extending egoism to a wider class of big Selves. Even if Reed goes on to develop his account of otherness in ways that turn out to be rather problematic, he is, I think, importantly right on what I take to be his main point, that an account based entirely on identity, continuity, and identification with Self provides an inadequate basis for respect for the nonhuman world, and one particularly inadequate for those issues, such as wilderness, where the otherness of nature is particularly salient.

It is tempting to conclude that both Næss and Reed remain within the "solipsistic omnipotence of the single psyche."[6] Reed's pure other-based account is a reversal of Næss's pure self-based one, but both seem to miss the importance of relational dynamics, the precarious balance of sameness and difference, of self and other involved in experiencing sameness without obliterating difference. Reed's positing of self and other as utterly disconnected, as "ships that pass in the night," misses the conceptual (and often material) dependence of self on other: if the other plays an active part in the creation of self, there is no pure other and no pure self. Reed reaffirms the Western tradition of denying nature and the radical distancing between humans and nature an environmental ethic must aim to counter. Næss is right to reject this picture as reproducing a key part of the problem. However, the pure self/pure other framework of choice presented by Næss and Reed is a false dichotomy: both continuity with and difference from self can be sources of value or disvalue, and both usually play a role.

The problems in each other's work, Næss's and Reed's mutual critiques point up, can be resolved using resources from feminist and post-colonial theory. To deal with the problems of identity the modern form of human colonization of nature generates, an adequate environmental ethic needs to provide a (usually sequenced) affirmation of both continuity and difference between humans and nature, as appropriate to the context. In the Western tradition especially, there is a need to stress continuity between self and other, human and nature, in response to the existential gulf created by the hyperseparated (radically distanced) and alienated models of nature and of human identity that remain dominant. These models define the truly human as (normatively) outside of nature and in opposition to the body and the material world, and conceive nature itself in alienated and mechanistic terms as having no elements of mind. The drive to hyperseparation is part of the colonizing conceptual dynamic which places the colonizer radically apart from, and above, those he conceives as part of the subordinated realm of nature.

But we also need to stress the difference and divergent agency of the other in order to defeat that further part of the colonizing dynamic that seeks to assimilate and instrumentalize the other, recognizing and valuing them only as a part of self, alike to self, or as means to self's ends. What makes it possible to combine this joint affirmation of continuity and difference consistently is the distinction between hyperseparation and difference, and the corresponding distinction between continuity and identity.[7] Neither Reed nor Næss distinguishes sufficiently between difference and normative hyperseparation, so that Reed treats difference, on his account the basis of the other's value and of their ethical recognition, as implying the denial of likeness and the maintenance of the existential gulf, while Næss treats removing the existential gulf as meaning the expulsion of difference and the basing of value on forms of identity. We need a concept of the other as interconnected with self, but as a separate being in their own right, accepting the "uncontrollable, tenaciousness otherness"[8] of the world as a condition of freedom and identity for both self and other.

Notes

[1] Peter Reed "Man Apart: an Alternative to the Self-Realisation Approach," *Environmental Ethics* 11 (1989): 56.

[2] Reed, 1989, 54.

[3] Reed, 1989, 57.

[4] Reed, 1989, 67.

[5] Arne Næss, "'Man Apart' and Deep Ecology: A Reply to Reed," *Environmental Ethics* 12 (1990): 187.

[6] Jessica Benjamin, *The Bonds of Love: Psychoanalysis, Feminism and the Problem of Domination* (London: Virago, 1990), 46.

[7] Val Plumwood, *Feminism and the Mastery of Nature* (London: Routledge, 1993).

[8] Benjamin, 1990, 48.

Part III

Schisms: Mountains or Molehills?

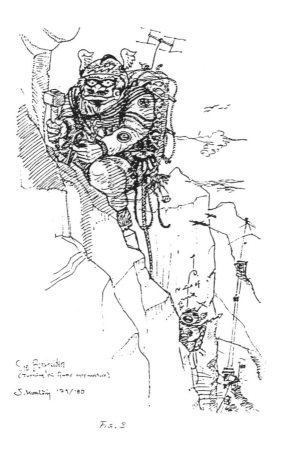

Figure 3. Climb Mountains Rather than Molehills!

Chapter 26

Deep Ecology and Its Critics

Kirkpatrick Sale

For me, the first indication that there was a concerted campaign afoot came at the Socialist Scholars Conference a year ago, where I appeared on a panel with Murray Bookchin, the author and co-founder of the Institute for Social Ecology, to discuss "The Politics of Ecology." Bookchin gave one of his elegant, impassioned, learned presentations, but I was surprised that it had a harsh edge to it of sourness and rancor—directed, it became clear, against those who might hold to any of the tenets of deep ecology, particularly the ideas embraced in the term "biocentrism." Deep ecology, it seemed, was a part of the broad ecological movement in America that was wrongheaded and dangerous, diverting attention from the serious tasks of eliminating capitalism and restructuring class society, and was in some way a threat to the reasonable, right-minded form of ecological truth—whose name was, so I gathered, social ecology.

Until that moment, I sincerely and naively thought that Bookchin and I were on the same wavelength (indeed, friends), that there was really only one great big ecology movement and that we shared an essentially similar position on the environmental destruction of the earth. But I suddenly realized that, in Bookchin's mind anyway, there was a battle going on within this movement and that the social ecologists were determined to distance themselves from—and argue their work superior to—all other sorts of ecologists. Not only that, but from the tone of his remarks (which was echoed by a colleague he had installed on the panel, Ynestra King, also from the Institute for Social Ecology) it seemed clear that they were actually out to destroy the influence of those thinkers and activists they found distasteful: the deep ecologists, in particular, but also members of the *Earth First!* and bioregional movements, who might have similar

ideas, and those they regarded as in the "spiritual" wing of the American Green
and ecofeminist movements. The awful, acrid smell of righteous factionalism
was in the air.

Next came a broadside presented by Bookchin to the national Green gathering in Amherst, Massachusetts, last July, a paper starkly and forthrightly
called "Social Ecology versus Deep Ecology." In extraordinary language that
was, I understand, shocking to and totally unexpected by most of the participants, Bookchin laid into those who fell short of the social ecology ideal, attacking the deep ecologists in particular with a vengeance—literally—that I
don't think has been equaled in political disputes since the 1930s. "They are
barely disguised racists, survivalists, macho Daniel Boones, and outright social
reactionaries," Bookchin said, who offer "a vague, formless, often self-contradictory and invertebrate [sic] thing called 'deep ecology'" and a "kind of crude
eco-brutalism" similar to Hitler's. Deep ecologists "feed on human disasters,
suffering and misery, preferably to Third World countries"; their ideas are "a
bottomless pit . . . an ideological toxic dump"; they are guilty of "a sinister
function [that] legitimates extremely regressive, primitivistic and even highly
reactionary notions." And so on, and on, twenty-three pages of it.

Thereafter, the arrows from the social ecology quiver fairly flew. A special
issue of the *Fifth Estate*, a Detroit-based alternative newspaper, featured a
twenty-eight-page article, "How Deep Is Deep Ecology?"; a widely circulated,
photocopied manuscript purporting to discredit *Earth First!*, the radical environmental group whose members have largely identified with deep ecology in
the last few years, arrived in the mail; the December 1987 *Utne Reader* gave
somewhat scandalized prominence to an *Earth First!* article that spoke favorably of AIDS as, in effect, a welcome and necessary control on human global
population; a lengthy, heated letter from Ynestra King was printed in *The Nation* [December 12, 1987], attacking deep ecology as "a philosophy utterly bereft of compassion for human beings, with no analysis of U.S. imperialism" (she
followed that with a column in *Zeta* saying that "the sooner the [American]
greens are rid of deep ecology the better"); and the winter issue of *Kick It Over*,
a Toronto quarterly, carried a special double-barreled section attacking deep
ecology, one salvo from a Bookchinite ecofeminist, who charged that it requires
"that women remain egoless, unformed, and supine," the other a reprint of
Bookchin's July blast.

Quite a parade. And, however much light, obviously a lot of heat.

So, now let us ask: What is this deep ecology, and why does it arouse so
much passion?

Deep ecology is a perspective—a "philosophy," some call it, others prefer
simply movement—that stems from the work of Arne Næss, a Norwegian academic philosopher, done in the early 1970s. He used the term "deep" to distinguish his sense of a probing, questioning, challenging kind of ecology from the
more conventional, apolitical kind, drawing a line between the biocentric vision
of deep ecology (which regards the human strictly as an equal participant in the

biosphere) and the anthropocentric stance of most professional ecologists and environmentalists (by which the human species, regarding itself as superior, deems all other species and resources as there for its use and enhancement). Shallow ecology, Næss said, the kind found in the universities, "does not ask what kind of a society would be the best for maintaining a particular ecosystem—that is considered a question for value theory, for politics, for ethics." In short, for deep ecologists.

After nearly a decade of writing, Næss joined with George Sessions, professor of philosophy at California's Sierra College, to develop a set of fundamental propositions for deep ecology. These basic principles, first published in 1984, contain what there is of a platform for the movement. In summary, they stress three points:

> *First*, all life, human and nonhuman, has value in itself, independent of human purposes, and humans have no right to reduce its richness and diversity except for vital needs.
>
> *Second*, humans at present are far too numerous and intrusive with respect to other life forms and the living earth, with disastrous consequences for all, and must achieve a "substantial decrease" in population to permit the flourishing of both human and nonhuman life.
>
> *Third*, to achieve this requisite balance, significant changes in human economic, technical and ideological structures must be made, stressing not bigness, growth, and higher standards of living but sustainable societies emphasizing the (nonmaterial) quality of life.

From these original basic ideas, deep ecologists have articulated a series of other key concepts in the last few years, around which general agreement seems to have developed:

The primacy of wilderness. Wilderness has a special value of its own, not only as a place where humans may understand "the intuitions of organic wholeness" (as Sessions and his colleague Bill Devall have put it), an essential and long-neglected need for true psychological health, but also where the intricate panoply of other species may "live and blossom for themselves," unhindered and apart. In the words of *Earth First!* editor Dave Foreman, "Wilderness is the real world [and] preservation of wildness and native diversity is the most important issue."

A sense of place. Basic to human well-being is rootedness, a sense of knowing a particular stretch of earth, experiencing a home. One seeks to find, and learn to live in, a particular place and to let it be, as ecologist Paul Shepard has said of the Australian aborigine, "the archive where the individual moves simultaneously through his personal and tribal past, renewing contact with crucial points, a journey into time and space refreshing the meaning of his own being."

Opposition to industrial society. The very basis of industrial civilization, in both its state-capitalist and corporate-capitalist forms, is the separation from and exploitation of the natural world. Deep ecology therefore opposes the industrial system and the myths of progress and technological dominance that drive it, and offers itself, as scholar and *Earth First!* member Christopher Manes says, "as an alternative to the whole of Technological Culture, exposing its irrationality within the larger context of Earth's natural cycles."

Opposition to stewardship. The trouble with the supposedly benign idea of the "wise stewardship" of nature is that it implies human decision-making, human intervention, human use and control—as in the root sense of the word, sty-warden, the master of the pigsty. As Sessions has said, "It still views the world as a collection of natural resources primarily for human use."

Identification with primal peoples. In general, it is in the traditions of the nature-based peoples of the world—the "primal" peoples such as the American Indians and other representatives of the Paleolithic tradition—that teachings and models for ecological consciousness are to be found. As historian J. Donald Hughes puts it, "The American Indians' cultural patterns, based on careful hunting and agriculture carried on according to spiritual perceptions of nature, actually preserved the earth and life on the earth."

Spirituality. Rationality has its place, but part of one's understanding of nature may also come from intuition, emotion, experience, and a spiritual connection with the nonhuman world. Arne Næss has written: "Most people in deep ecology have had the feeling—usually, but not always, in nature—that they are connected with something greater than their ego. . . . Insofar as these deep feelings are religious, deep ecology has a religious component . . . fundamental intuitions that everyone must cultivate if he or she is to have a life based on values and not function like a computer."

Self-realization. The true realization of the individual self is in a close and unfolding identification, spiritual and intellectual, with the larger biotic "self"; the more diverse and complex the larger one, the richer and more developed the smaller one. As Næss has put it, "The self-realization we experience when we identify with the universe is heightened by an increase in the number of ways in which individuals, societies and even species and life forms realize themselves."

Now those hardly sound like the elements of fascism, do they?

By listing such a set of general concepts, I don't mean to suggest that there is any absolute agreement among people who call themselves deep ecologists, or that all of them formulate their beliefs exactly this way. There is no oath-taking, no litmus-testing, in this any more than in any other such movement—people differ, as do interpretations and emphases and slogans. Nevertheless, after a decade of fairly extensive work, I think one can determine at least the outlines of a deep ecology perspective and see the beginnings of a real movement.

Now, it is easy enough to see why all of this might be upsetting to those in the political mainstream and to traditional socialists as much as die-hard capitalists. Taken in the broad, it represents a fundamental challenge not only to the typical American technological way of life, but too much of what constitutes Western civilization itself.

It does seem surprising, though, that these positions would have so alarmed other parts of the ecological world that there should suddenly be an outpouring against it. I must say I am at a loss to explain it adequately. It can't really be a battle over turf, since there's obviously plenty of room for all kinds of viewpoints here, or over power, since so far there is none. And of course, there is a great danger that this sort of a frontal attack is far more likely to lead to enervating and fractious bickering and backbiting of the kinds that destroy social movements than it is to a thoughtful, accommodative synthesis and a restrengthened movement. To me it is not only all very sad but bewildering. But, in the spirit of accommodation rather than confrontation, and in the hope that the fissures can be bridged rather than broadened, let me discuss what I see as the three major issues the critics of deep ecology have raised.

The first and probably most fundamental charge is that deep ecology has no explicit "social" analysis—that is, it does not adequately talk about matters of class, race, injustice, capitalism, imperialism, and the like, and instead tends to regard humans collectively and hence tar the whole species for environmental degradations with a brush that would be more appropriately aimed at specific social institutions and systems. Bookchin sees it as preaching "a gospel of a kind of 'original sin' that accurses a vague species called 'Humanity'—as though people of color are equatable with whites, women with men, the Third World with the First, the poor with the rich, the exploited with their exploiters."

I think it is true that most deep ecologists *have* tended to see humans as a species, since that is, after all, the ecological way to regard this particular large mammal of *Homo* genus, and I think that this has largely been useful: useful to help see, in planetary terms, overriding nation and culture and ideology, the large consequences of a triumphant, exploitative species enjoying a population boom and technological prowess. From this larger perspective, it does not really matter what the petty political and social arrangements are that have led to our ecological crisis, or even what dire consequences those arrangements have had for certain individuals, types, nations, or races. What matters is to understand the total effect of this crisis on the living earth and our fellow species, and the peril we have brought to them. This perspective does not deny the awful character of industrial society or its inherent destructiveness (to humans as well as nature). It says, rather, that the path to fundamental restructuring best comes about through the development of a new and profound ecological consciousness, which itself can only come about through, in philosopher Thomas Berry's words, "the reinvention of the human at the species level," and the understanding, that "we must reapply for admission to the biosphere."

It is not that the social dimension or an analysis of capitalism or a perception of racial injustice is absent from the deep ecology philosophy. In fact, Devall and Sessions, among others, are quite explicit about the evils of what they call the "dominant worldview" and the need for direct action to challenge it, and most of the deep ecology activists I have met, have quite a clear idea of the nature of repression, and subjugation in this society, and have often put their bodies on the line in resistance to it. But it is probably accurate to say that deep ecologists think primarily in biotic rather than social terms. They regard the fundamental issue to be the destruction of nature and the suffering of the rapidly dying species and ecosystems as distinct from those who regard the basic issue as the absence of justice and the suffering of human populations.

That, as I see it, is a clear difference in emphasis, in concern, in dedication—but not, God knows, such an extreme difference that it should prompt invective and opposition and outrage. There is no need, I would have thought, for pistols-at-dawn rhetoric.

The second and related issue is that of population size, specifically the deep ecologists' contention that a significant reduction in human numbers is essential for the proper balance and functioning of the biosphere. This, it is said, is Malthusian, holding, as *Fifth Estate* claimed, that "there are too many people and not enough resources to keep them alive" and that "scarcity and famine are thus explained as natural phenomena." This, it is said, is callous and crude, akin to genocide, since it must have in mind targeting the poorest, the darkest, and the sickest, designing their demise, according to Bookchin, "by measures that are virtually eco-fascist."

It is always difficult to deal with the population question, but for starters it should be noted that those deep ecologists who have confronted it do not begin with Malthusian assumptions and certainly do not arrive at Malthusian conclusions. Their argument is not—repeat not—that population reduction is necessary because of inadequate food in the world, since it is fairly evident (and the work of Frances Moore Lappe tends to confirm) that present populations could be adequately fed if political and economic arrangements were different, although long-term food stability would certainly depend on both intra- and interregional population distribution. The argument is, rather, that sustaining human population at present (not to mention predicted) levels puts too great a strain on all the resources, life forms, and systems of the earth. This affects most particularly our fellow species, whom we are killing at the estimated rate of one an hour to maintain ourselves at these numbers, but also the world's fertile soil, its waters, its air, its climatic and hydrologic systems—in short, the ability of the biosphere to survive.

Such a position does not argue that capitalism is not egregiously at fault for much of this assault, although it is patently clear that industrialized socialist systems are every bit as guilty in kind if not degree, as are many of the colonized states in the orbit of either empire. Indeed, the logic holds, as Devall and Sessions say explicitly, that it is the industrialized societies—particularly the most rapacious, exploitative, wasteful, and polluting one of all, found in this country—that are overpopulated the most, if I may put it that way. *Their* numbers (especially their wealthier numbers) are sustained at far higher living standards and do far greater ultimate damage to the biosphere. Nowhere here is there the idea that it's desirable or inevitable—or even useful, in biospheric terms—for poor people to die off; quite the contrary.

There is even less of a basis for the charges of genocide and fascism. In the deep ecology literature a good deal of attention has been given to the levels at which it might be desirable for the human population to stabilize—the figures I've seen range between 100 million (Næss's suggestion) and 1 billion—but very little to the means for doing this, except Næss's without revolution or dictatorship. The only other references I've found are to such vague ideas as Foreman's "over the long run," Næss's "through mild but tenacious political and economic measures," and Devall and Sessions's "the longer we wait, the more drastic will be the measures needed." There is nowhere any hint of a suggestion that people should be gassed, forced into starvation, or sterilized against their will, that one type or race or nation is to be preferred, that there is to be some agency or government or ruler to achieve this—all that is born, unfortunately, in the minds of deep ecology's detractors.

The third substantial charge, following from this, has to do with the issue of biocentric egalitarianism, or the place of the human in the natural world. Deep ecology, it is said, is essentially misanthropic, emphasizing as it does a reduction in human numbers and a relegation of the welfare of the human to a status secondary to that of the biosphere as a whole. "Deep ecologists have inverted the relationship of domination of people over nature," Ynestra King has written, "into one of nature over people." *Fifth Estate* charges that, "taking pains to defend every form of life from whales down to even the . . . smallpox virus," deep ecologists want "only human beings . . . banished from creation for their depredations."

Deep ecologists would hardly deny the specialness of the human animal, I feel sure—Næss himself emphasizes that humans have "extraordinary" and particular traits—but they would probably argue, that this specialness has tended to separate the human from nature in such a way as to allow the species' destructive characteristics to dominate, for which human societies since the Neolithic have been particularly notable. Now that these characteristics, embodied and empowered in industrial society as never before, threaten the globe with nothing less than ecocide, it is hard not to feel a certain antipathy to them, and a certain fear, and suspicion of the species that has been endowed with them.

Misanthropy, in my dictionary, is defined as "a hatred or distrust of mankind," but it seems useful to distinguish between the two. It is probably true that most deep ecologists are distrustful, or fearful, of the human role in the biosphere, but very doubtful that they hate the human species and wish its extinction. I am sure there are in the movement those who are led to despair of the human condition and those who would say that the ongoing survival of the living earth and its biosphere is more important than the survival of the human species. Indeed, it is plausibly argued that the survival of arboreal (especially tropical) species is far more important to the health of the biosphere as a whole than the survival of any mammalian primate, inasmuch as it is the former that are chiefly responsible for the processing of carbon dioxide and oxygen necessary for most of life. I do not see how that position, however, could be regarded as equivalent to the hatred of humans or the desire for their banishment.

Now it is true that, in trying to put its quite radical message across, both Dave Foreman and *Earth First!* have printed careless things that have, generally out of context, upset some people and led to charges of misanthropy of the "hatred" kind. Foreman once asserted, when asked in an interview about starvation in Ethiopia, that he thought "the best thing would be to just let nature seek its own balance, to let the people there just starve there," certainly an unnecessarily heartless way of putting it, although the point he was trying to make is that the Ethiopian population has overshot the capacity of its devastated environment to produce food, and that outside aid might alleviate that for the moment but wouldn't do anything to achieve the population reduction that is necessary for ecological balance there. Similarly, the *Earth First!* article on AIDS argued that, in spite of the suffering involved, it was a "welcome development" in the necessary reduction of human population, especially since (unlike war or environmental catastrophe) it appears to affect only humanity and not other species. Call it callous, if you will, but it is meant to be descriptive, not prescriptive—to suggest that the earth as a living ecosystem might have its own defense mechanisms, including viruses that strike at species that overstress it, to protect it in times of crisis. Agree or disagree, that is not misanthropy or fascism.

Other criticisms of deep ecology have been raised over the past year, mostly of the same order and too elaborate and arduous to rehash here. I suspect more will emerge in coming years, as the tenets of the biocentric point of view become more developed and widespread and the need for some such ecological consciousness in the face of ecocide becomes increasingly obvious to the population at large. There is every reason to suppose that some of those criticisms, the ones given to civil discourse and respectful language, will lead to rethinking and reformulation of elements of the philosophy, which after all is still quite new and still has much homework to do.

But there can hardly be any alteration of the basic deep ecology principles or the worldview, may I say the paradigm, in which those are embedded. As I have tried to elucidate them here, they represent not only a new (and to their adherents, necessary) way to reevaluate the world and the place of the human in it but also the core of the ecological vision that is leading people to reorder their lives and renew their actions. The tenets may not be perfectly formulated yet, and may admit of emendation as the struggle continues, but they certainly seem informed by exactly the kind of ecological consciousness that will permit us, if anything will, to save the biosphere before it is too late.

I cannot see why those principles should evoke anger and calumny, even among those whose analyses may differ and whose interests may lie elsewhere. Some participants in the debate may of course disagree, but I do think the questions here are ones of emphasis and priority, not of fundamental incompatibility. Social ecologists may want to say that ecological exploitation stems from social exploitation and concentrate their critique on what they see as hierarchy and patriarchy; deep ecologists will probably say that social exploitation stems from ecological exploitation and prefer to concentrate on biocentrism and wilderness. These both seem like sensible paths, and I don't see the point of either school trying to trash the other, working toward some imagined dominant theoretical purity, particularly since the ranks of ecologists of any kind are not at all that numerous to begin with, and the job we have to do in reversing the trend of five centuries of Western civilization is enormous.

Perhaps there is a basic natural principle we all ought to take to heart—that of cooperation with diversity, much as the rain forest works, or a coral reef, or an oak tree. As usual, I would suggest, nature has the answer.

Notes

This chapter is reprinted with minor revisions from Kirkpatrick Sale, "Deep Ecology and Its Critics," *The Nation* (May 14, 1998): 670–674.

Chapter 27

A European Looks at North American Branches of the Deep Ecology Movement

Arne Næss

At least three overlapping social movements are today deeply critical of the industrial societies: The peace movement, the radical movement against social ills, and the deep ecology movement. How do they live together? How do they compete for attention? The first and the last cooperate amicably. Supporters of the second sometimes severely chastise the third.

In the late 1960s some Marxist and anarchist opinion leaders in Europe formed phrases like "the European left has nothing to learn from the environmental movement," but soon a left movement, the "red-greens," were highly successful. In Norway they captured the main student organization. Their party name: "Green Grass!" Most of the politically active students were at this time socialists or anarchists, at least according to North American terminology.

Some members of the small communist party gave up their Marxist terminology and polemical excesses, and joined, large scale, environmental actions. As could have been foreseen, they have shown a quite exceptional willingness to live for what they chose to support, and also a laudable restraint facing angry local opponents during direct actions. ("Offer coffee *immediately*, listen patiently to their invectives, offer help to mend their fences or doing other odd jobs—without any other reward than the opportunity to explain the motives of direct action!")

In an excellent article, Kirkpatrick Sale ("Deep Ecology and its Critics," *The Nation*, May 14, 1988) says that he is sad because of the critical attacks on deep ecology by Murray Bookchin, Ynestra King, and others. With my Euro-

222

pean background I am astonished! Why be sad? A movement asking for deep changes in the established order should and must expect wild critical attacks, including blasts from people who disagree only on priorities. From what Ynestra King says (*The Nation*, Dec. 12, 1987), I see her as a supporter of the deep ecology movement. She dislikes its terminology and the lack of political protests in the (admirable) Californian branch of the movement. That is all.

It is suspicious that we who are vocal supporters of the deep ecological movement are so rarely the objects of vicious attacks. Are we weaklings? At least not the Earth Firsters! At least not Dave Foreman! But is he (in the words of Ynestra King) "bereft of compassion for human beings"? Does he advocate letting Ethiopian children starve to death? He emphatically denies that he does. I am glad that he does deny this, because his positive use of the deep ecology terminology would be embarrassing if he were against help to the starving. What he says that he means is that it is irresponsible to concentrate *only* on hunger, and not on the immense important ecological and other *causes* of hunger. The term "only" is crucial. Does he propose stopping research on AIDS? No, he says. But *only* concentrating on measures against the illness, neglecting the social and ecological causes which make AIDS such a formidable threat, is plainly irresponsible. Such neglect tends to make more likely what environmental "doomsday prophets" have repeated over and over since the 1960s: If we do not act with vigor, *Nature takes over*, that is, natural processes will stop human excessive interference in a way "utterly bereft of compassion for human beings."

One of the most characteristic differences between the shallow and the deep ecology movements is, that the former concentrates on population and pollution problems in the poor countries, whereas the deep acknowledges that the increase of one single citizen of a rich country may do more ecological damage, than 100 new citizens in a poor one. In Europe free nature has already been largely destroyed. Tree plantations have been substituted for forests. The rich will probably try to pressure the poor to stop the annihilation of rainforests, the immense scale of erosion, and other forms of destruction. It is important to combat ecological colonialism, and to admit that from the point of view of ecology a gradual decrease of population in the rich countries is a valuable goal. But how do people react to this idea?

There is near consensus, by people who have thought about it, that stabilization of a human population significantly smaller than at present would not threaten, but rather would help the realization of the ultimate aims of humankind, including the aim to maintain deep cultural diversity. At least this is the highly tentative conclusion I draw from preliminary studies in Norway. But in order to provoke more thinking I formed questions like the following: "Which arguments do you have against the thesis that 100 million people on earth would be enough to realize the ultimate aims of human life?" Very few arguments were proposed, but the question was by many conceived to be merely "academic." Some respondents reacted with anger or indignation, as if inhumane sorts of population policies were implied. Personally I have never, as suggested by Kirkpatrick Sale and others, asserted that 100 million, as an ideal human population of the planet would suffice, nor have I postulated any other definite number.

A desirable, significant population reduction—without recourse to inhumane policies—might take 500 years or more. This does not diminish the practical importance of discussing local reductions, not only stabilization, especially in the rich countries.

In Europe many supporters of the deep ecological movement prefer the name "political ecology." They are of the opinion that the political tasks are strategically the most important, or they tend to say that the spiritual, philosophical, or religious component should always be expressed in a way that does not lead people away from political engagement. It is lucky that the Californian trio of George Sessions, Bill Devall, and Gary Snyder, in their highly significant contribution to the deep ecology movement in the United States, do not underrate the political obstacles, nor the need for political engagement by all who are able to stand the kind of work it implies.

The backbone of the deep ecology movement is its "silent majority," who all over the world fight mindless destruction of free nature, with a passion derived from deep philosophical or religious, mostly unarticulated, attitudes. Often isolated, such people are helped by knowing that there are thousands, if not millions, from Australia to Canada, from Japan to South America, who feel very much the same way—desperation, sorrow and anguish. There is a tiny minority who eagerly, but more or less imperfectly, try to systematically articulate what these people stand for. It is a significant job, and different articulations are needed. The prospect of reformulation and revision is always to be greeted with gratefulness. But I do not think that any reformulation would do in which the deepest interests of human beings are thought to be in conflict with the maintenance of richness and diversity of life on earth. "Anti-anthropocentric biocentrism," or "the higher estimation of animals than of humans," are dead expressions. What do they mean?

In many countries today politicians *say* highly positive things, but when it comes to concrete decisions they support ecologically outrageous policies. The new slogan "sustainable development" implies in Norway and North America a giant step towards reducing the average material standard of living. Not necessarily our quality of life! We must live at a level that we seriously can wish others to attain, not at a level that requires the bulk of humanity *not* to reach.

Notes

This chapter is reprinted with minor revisions from Arne Næss, "A European Looks at North American Branches of the Deep Ecology Movement," *The Trumpeter* 5:2 (Spring, 1988): 75–76.

Chapter 28

Letter to the Editor of *Zeta Magazine,* 1988

Arne Næss

A friend sent me a copy of Ynestra King's recent article "Coming of Age with the Greens." From my point of view it was a competent article within the deep ecology movement, but strangely enough there was an inserted paragraph about a confused and obnoxious point of view given the name "deep ecology." The terms "deep" and "shallow" ecology movement were coined by me referring to social movements in United States and Europe in the 1960s. By the deep, long range, movement I have since 1971 referred to a many sided movement, also called political ecology, because in Europe the necessity of political "green" action was emphasized against the rather apolitical idealistic, and elitist classical nature protection movement. The deep movement implied fundamental changes in ideology, technology, economics, and had philosophical undertones. The term "deep" referred to the fundamental character of the premises of the participants of the movement. The majority of activists were in Europe people from within left political circles "turned green." Some liked to call themselves red-greens (Johan Galtung and others). Bookchin belonged to the authors we read—one of his books was translated into Norwegian.

From time to time I have tried tentatively to summarize what the supporters of the deep ecological movement have in common. It is a difficult task because contemporary diversity of philosophical fundamentals is of great value for the movement. In a summary in 8 points formulated together with George Sessions, the first point reads as follows: "The welfare and flourishing of human and non-human living beings has value in itself. The value of the nonhuman beings is independent of their usefulness to humans."

The concern for richness and diversity of human cultures makes it an urgent task for counteracting contemporary cultural destruction. The strange concept of the biosphere "as everything other than human beings" imputed by Ynestra King to "Arne Næss" refers perhaps to some other Arne Næss than myself. This other Næss assumes, I think unduly pessimistically, that full human self-realization is incompatible with an earth as rich in large scale organic and inorganic splendor as our planet was a few hundred years ago.

It has been a cause of joy and optimism within the deep ecological movement that supporters with partly incompatible opinions have been less unfriendly in their way of interpreting each other than within the great number of European Marxist groupings. I do not refer to Ynestra King's interpretations as unfriendly, but I have the feeling that somewhere along the line there must have been some misplaced negative (Spinoza: "passive") emotions.

Chapter 29

Letter to Dave Foreman, 23 June 1988

Arne Næss

Dear Dave,

Here are some reflections on *Ecodefense*. They have gradually turned into something more than a letter. Probably I will use some of it in an article. I have made five copies so please do not hesitate to make comments, e.g., written on the pages if that is convenient for you.

1. The norms of Ecodefense are non-violent but not nonviolent. "Nonviolence" is now a customary technical term for the Gandhian sort of non-violence. On the strict nonviolence see my *Gandhi and Group Conflict*. Non-violence I judge to be a wider term: not doing harm to humans or (certain kinds of) animals. You mostly use this term in Ecodefense. Good.

2. I am for limiting the way conflicts are to be carried out in Scandinavia to nonviolence. The state, the bureaucracy, the establishment is of an orderly, approachable, moderate kind, and not of vast dimension. In addition there is quite a strong nonviolent minority tradition. There is among the majority a fierce reaction against "sabotage" and "vandalism." Among politicians the term "terrorism" is often used even in relation to purely nonviolent direct actions, e.g., in defense of rivers.

I have the feeling that in the United States there is more mistrust of politicians and bureaucracy. There are also much less possibilities for "plain people" to communicate face to face with people in power. And fierce conflicts are thought of as more normal. This—among other factors—makes me see a justification for using various mild forms of sabotage in the United States.

3. When a Sami (Lapp) in Arctic Norway, a member of a very different culture from the Norwegian, tried to blow up a bridge made by "invading" Norwegians, he defended a place *where he belonged.* He said it was *part of himself.* A defense of "where one belongs" is mostly made in great distress and anger. Non-violent means of defense is obviously ethically justifiable. If violence is used I would in many cases refrain from any negative judgments.

In the United States very few people live near the still largely "untouched," big areas of wilderness. This makes the above-mentioned justification of non-violence or even violence not directly applicable. But I do not doubt that many people far from the wilderness have a personal vital need to protect what is left over of great wild places.

Here two factors seem relevant:

4. Many national forests in the United States have trees several hundred years old and have never been destructively interfered with by humans. These forests are irreplaceable, their loss must be considered definitive. Every forest in Europe (except in the Soviet Union and a tiny wood on the border between Poland and the Soviet Union) is man-made, and has on the whole the character of standardized tree-plantations.

That the immensely rich United States continues to decrease the area of its great forests is such a shame that the world will in the not very remote future look upon it as a serious blot on U.S. history.

Spiking of trees belongs to the obviously justifiable direct method to defend the fabulous U.S. forests. Of course: the actions should follow strict rules set down in the book *Ecodefense.* Sabotage to fight the abominable practice in trapping is clearly justifiable, especially if the police are soft on trapping. The animal defense chapter of *Ecodefense* I find very convincing.

Every year it gets clearer that all main ecological problems are global, not national. The U.S. wilderness does not belong more to Americans than to Norwegians or to any group of concerned people. A global insult to destroy still more!

5. Ecosabotage in the United States is fraught with great personal risks. Physical attack with serious injuries is a practical possibility. Prison, big fines, and harassment. The risks will perhaps increase dramatically in the years to come, eventually leading many people to come to the defense of the wilderness defenders. Two of the main features of Gandhi's teaching were an appeal not to avoid personal risks, and a trust that opponents mostly look for sacrifice as a convincing sign of seriousness and honesty.

So much about non-violence/nonviolence. But there are other comments I wish to make.

6. An old North American ecosopher prayed: "Great Spirit grant that I may not criticize my neighbor until I have walked a mile in his moccasins."

The process of identification with all life forms, which only humans are capable of naturally covers their own fellow humans. Differences in background have contributed substantially to different behaviors: some are trappers and wilderness degraders, others are wilderness defenders. *Ecodefense* makes innocent fun of snowmobiles in wilderness areas: they "are often driven by overweight, out-of-shape, poorly-prepared wimps. . . . Be conscious of the situation you may create and be concerned for the safety of the snowmobile." (p. 108) But other places people are called "evil," "rapers," "lazy bastards." It suffices to call their act evil.

Suffering caused by trappers is immense. In Colorado 1982–1983, 2,505 bobcats, 7,516 beavers, and 4,800 raccoons were cruelly trapped. But it is unnecessary to call the trappers "sub-humans" or "warped mental midgets" (p. 180).

I ask myself: how can people in the United States tolerate a policy, which makes trapping legal? Why don't they "raise hell?" But for the sake of *communication*, for instance with law enforcement agencies, it is unnecessary to talk about "the greedheads ravishing earth for a few greasy bucks" (p. 248).

The worldwide deep ecology movement has supporters who act out of despair, indignation, and white-hot anger. If the term "criminal" is at all to be used, people in power are acting criminally who let the destruction of wilderness proceed as it proceeds today. But the question of how to communicate this is a complex one for the editors of *Ecodefense* and *The Earth First! Journal*.

7. *Earth First!* wisely neither officially defends nor condemns ecosabotage. Members may be for or against. And it cooperates with environmental organizations which condemn ecosabotage. It sees the urgent need for moderate organizations rejecting ecosabotage.

This is one thing not to be forgotten when considering the ethical justification and the effectiveness of "ecotage" when carried out under the banners of *Earth First!* and of the deep ecology movement.

What should be done with "overgrazers" "who operate in particularly sensitive areas (Wilderness Areas, National Parks & Monuments, National Wildlife Refuges, etc.)?" Here is ecocriminality and it weakens the position of the rich industrial countries in their increasing efforts to pressure poor countries to stop their detrimental overgrazing. This and consequent erosion on a gigantic scale degrade life conditions on earth. The rich countries have no excuse whatsoever: sheer vandalism! What should be done?

Ecotage is accepted in *Ecodefense* (p. 83) and includes cutting fences, damaging water developments, moving salt blocks, spiking roads. That is to say: accepted when less drastic efforts to stop such overgrazing has proven ineffective.

Given the traditional level of trust between people in power and the populace in Scandinavia, ecotage against serious overgrazing is not justifiable, neither from the point of view of social ethics, nor from that of efficiency. It is, however, difficult for me to form an opinion when conditions are very different, as it seems to be in the United States.

And what about the relation to the deep ecology movement?

8. The editors of *The Earth First! Journal,* conceive themselves as supporters of the global deep ecology movement. Who should have the authority to
judge whether they really are supporters? Of course nobody. But George Sessions and myself formulated what have been called basic principles of Deep
Ecology. I look upon the formulation as tentatively expressing the most general
and basic views, which almost all supporters of the movement *have in common.*
They may differ in their ultimate beliefs of religious or philosophical kinds, for
instance their answers to the question *"Why Earth First!?"* Some are Buddhists,
others are not, or do not pretend to understand Buddhism, or are not interested
in philosophy at all.

The Næss–Sessions set of formulations does not face the question of justifiable means, but it could easily have done so. The direct actions within the deep
ecology movement have to an overwhelming degree been non-violent. They
have been a natural extension of the high level of identification with living beings, including opponents. The main thing has been to make people aware of the
outrageous things going on. In short: communication. Point 8 of the 8 point
characterization of the movement might have been widened: those who subscribe to the foregoing points have an obligation directly or indirectly to try—
within the limits of non-violence—to implement the necessary changes.

Here I write "non-violence" instead of "nonviolence" in order to leave it
open to what extent Gandhian norms should be followed strictly. With continued destruction of the life conditions of the planet, more and irreparable damage
is done, such as damage to primeval forests. On the other hand, the efforts at
communication with opponents might be radically increased. It is important that
Earth First! declares that *Earth First!*ers *"also* use confrontation, guerrilla
action, and civil disobedience" (my emphasis), that is, *in addition to* what
environmental groups with more limited strategies are doing.

9. Some supporters of the deep ecology movement are of the opinion that
Murray Bookchin has heavily criticized it. This is, as far as I can understand, not
the case. None of the 8 points have been criticized. He has emphasized and
reshaped point 6—the central idea, that deep social changes are required, to arrive at an ecopolitics in harmony with the foregoing points. Obviously he has
been upset by the opinions *or alleged opinions* expressed by some supporters of
the movement, in particular you—Dave Foreman. But that is not the same as
criticizing *Earth First!* as a group and very far from criticizing the deep ecology
movement. Murray Bookchin supported the deep ecology movement from its
start in the early 1960s.

10. We agree that biocentrism does not imply any devaluation of humans. It
is a broadening of the perspective. We reject the doctrine about the superiority
of the white "race," the inferiority of the mentally handicapped, etc. We focus
on life and life-conditions, globally. "Anthropocentrism" as I use the term is the
tendency to look at nonhumans and the ecosphere in general from the point of

view of narrow utilitarianism, a devaluation of anything but humans and a focus on their narrow, shallow interests, not their deep ones.

The term "narrow" is essential here because, as far as I can see, the human brain and capacities of identification are such that "all round" human maturity implies taking the life of the planet seriously. Many academic supporters of the deep ecology movement feel that ultimately we try to save the planet because we as humans estimate the planet highly. *We* proclaim that every living being has intrinsic value. It is in our interest as humans to respect living beings and their intrinsic value. In short many supporters with a philosophical bent help to emphasize that it is only through the narrowness of interest and partial immaturity that nature is destroyed. I would say (in Ecosophy T): high degree of human self-realization implies that we respect the planet with its full life.

These remarks I make because a too heavy use of the ambiguous terms biocentrism and anthropocentrism invites opponents to choose unfavorable interpretations, steering discussions away from the essential task: to go straight ahead with equanimity, not staring left or right.

11. The population question is emotionally loaded and long range perspectives are rare. But when people understand that we as supporters of the deep ecology movement combine "act now!" with norms with long perspectives, there is an astonishing unanimity: no basic human goal in life depends upon the existence of 5 billion of us. It is both instructive and amusing to see how little is put forth when we ask questions like: "Which are your arguments against the thesis that 100 million is enough to reach the basic goals of mankind?" (I have never *asserted* that any definite number is enough.) There is no basis for the suspicion that deep ecology supporters are in favor of harsh, inhuman measures against population increases. One of the important aims in debating population is to eliminate the instinctive aversions against reduction. Also: to point to economists (Tore Tronstad, etc.) who show that a slow decline may take place without economic stagnation and fall of standard of living.

Good Luck, greetings to John Davis,
Arne Næss

Chapter 30

Comment: Human Population Reduction and Wild Habitat Protection

Michael E. Zimmerman

Ever since Malthus published his (in)famous tract two centuries ago, disputes about human population growth have been acrimonious. Conservatives like Malthus argued that hunger resulted from the fact that agricultural output could not keep up with unchecked population growth, primarily among the poor. Solution: dramatically reduce the number of the poor, in part by letting nature "run its course," i.e., by letting them starve to death. Condemning Malthus's views as callous and overly pessimistic, many modern thinkers insist that his analysis overlooks the roles played by distorted politico-economic arrangements in generating material scarcity. Modernists assert that humans, unlike animals, are not subject to natural constraints and thus cannot "overshoot" their food supply. Instead, humanity is an historical species that can alter politico-economic practices and introduce technological innovations to increase productivity. Food shortages result not from some implacable "law of nature," but instead either from artificial impediments to the market's productive capacity (so say the liberals), or from private ownership that deprives people of the means needed to produce sufficient crops (so say the socialists).

For many years, the population debate focused on how a larger population would affect human well-being, but starting in the late 1960s environmentalists began warning that rapid population increases would not only outstrip growth in food supply, but would also eradicate most of the remaining habitat of wild plants and animals. In suggesting that there are natural limits to a sustainable human population, environmentalists challenged modernist assumptions about humankind's capacity for unlimited growth. A founding figure in the deep ecology movement, Arne Næss, agrees with those environmentalists calling for population reduction. Although maintaining that a profoundly fulfilling human life is not only compatible with, but perhaps even requires significantly fewer people, Næss is no Malthusian. He acknowledges that humankind is a very unusual species, not subject to all the constraints faced by most other species. Of course, humans depend on a functioning biosphere, but we create many of the conditions needed for our own survival. Agreeing with modernists that greater efficiencies in agriculture may enable more than ten billion people to live on earth, Næss concedes that most of the planet has become our niche. But such population "success" is helping to cause the most rapid loss of species in millions of years, as hungry people turn wild habitat into farmland and rain forests into timber. Far from blaming habitat loss solely on the poor, Næss emphasizes that Western consumerism is even more responsible for destroying wild habitat.

Even if more than ten billion people could survive while consuming vast quantities of products, Næss asks, what would the quality of life be like without large mammals such as elephants and tigers, rhinos and bears, not to mention countless other forms of life that are even more important for sustaining ecosystem vitality and that are no less extraordinary for being small or un-cuddly? He shares with many people the sentiment that human life without wild animals and plants would be lesser and lonely. Hence, he asks people to reflect critically on the deep assumptions of modern culture, including an anthropocentrism that regards other life forms primarily as instruments for human ends. By gradually reducing human population, by encouraging cultural diversity, by eschewing consumerism, and by promoting ecologically appropriate economic practices, he maintains, humankind would achieve a higher quality of life, not least because the marvelous variety of life on planet earth would be preserved.[1]

Despite attempting thoughtfully to discuss the population question, Næss has been criticized not only by modernists (as one might expect), but also by those environmentalists who fear that he is a neo-Malthusian, willing to accept draconian methods to reduce human numbers for the sake of protecting wildlife.[2] Understandably sensitive after so many centuries in which women's reproductive activities were largely controlled by males, some ecofeminists suggest that patriarchalism leads Næss and other deep ecologists to argue that controlling the birth rate is the key to solving ecological problems. For many ecofeminists and for members of the worldwide Green Movement, "overpopulation" is a shorthand expression for misery resulting from corrupt political regimes, exploitative economic systems, patriarchalism, and militarism. If social justice inequities are redressed, they argue, the problems associated with human population growth—including ecological problems—will dramatically decline. Social ecologists have most vociferously condemned what they claim to be Næss's views on population growth. Associating Næss with some irresponsible remarks made by a few *Earth First!*ers, some social ecologists accuse him of likening humans to a cancerous growth that must be checked at any cost. Supposedly, Næss promotes a kind of ecofascism in which the good of individuals must be sacrificed for the well-being of the ecological "whole."

Anyone familiar with Næss's personal history, which includes years spent under Nazi occupation in Norway, and with his Ecosophy T, which encourages cultural diversity while rejecting conformism and authoritarianism, knows that he is no ecofascist. Further, he criticizes the class structure, political oppression, authoritarianism, patriarchy and militarism that lead to human suffering and ecological destruction. Moreover, by affirming that humankind is an inventive species that is less subject to natural constraints (i.e., given conditions) than are other species, Næss seeks to avoid Kirkpatrick Sale's tendency to portray deep ecology as an "anti-anthropocentric biocentrism," according to which humans are just one species among many others. Nevertheless, Næss affirms the need to reduce human population in order to preserve wild habitat. Such preservation is worthwhile not only because it improves human life (e.g., by helping to prevent biospheric degradation), but also because "The well-being and flourishing of human and nonhuman life have value in themselves (synonyms: intrinsic value, inherent worth). These values are independent of the usefulness of the nonhuman world for human purposes" (first principle of the Deep Ecology Platform). Ending human hunger is a noble goal, Næss believes, but so is preserving the planet's rich biodiversity. These goals need not be mutually exclusive, although conflicts cannot be avoided.

Even though the Deep Ecology Platform encourages a non-anthropocentric, nonutilitarian affirmation of the inherent worth of all life, Næss's own Ecosophy T addresses the crucial *motivational* issue: Why should we care about wild plants and animals? The basic intuitions of Ecosophy T, inspired in part by Spinoza, Gandhi, Advaita Vedanta, and Mahayana Buddhism, are that self-realization is the highest good for all beings, and that human self-realization cannot be achieved apart from the self-realization of all beings.

Humans flourish only when they transcend their atomistic self-understanding in a way that discloses their profound affiliation with all other beings. As humans recognize that their own flourishing is integrally related to the flourishing of other forms of life, they will gradually alter their consumerist lifestyles and reduce population growth so as to conserve the habitat needed by those forms of life. Wider identification with other beings leads one spontaneously to care for them, just as one spontaneously takes care of oneself. No moral "guilt" is needed to motivate one to promote the well-being of all beings with which one identifies. In becoming ever more deeply aware of their kinship with all life, including humankind itself, people would develop humane ways to reduce human population, while also expanding wild habitat, over the course of four or five centuries. Ecosophy T's basic intuition of self-realization will not appeal to everyone, so Næss encourages people to discover their own deepest spiritual and moral intuitions. He is confident that most ecosophies derived from such intuitions will be compatible with the principle that it is worthwhile for all life to flourish.

By raising the population issue, Næss is promoting neither neo-Malthusianism, nor patriarchalism, nor ecofascism. Instead, he stresses that if biodiversity is worth protecting (and I agree with him that it is), special attention must be paid first, to understanding the decisive role played by large human populations in destroying such biodiversity, and second, to finding culturally and politically acceptable ways of decreasing the absolute numbers of humans. Recognizing the inherent worth of other forms of life takes nothing away from the special gifts with which our species has been endowed, including self-awareness. Such gifts, however, bring with them opportunities that an acquisitive mentality overlooks, namely, the opportunity of bearing conscious witness to and encouraging the well-being of all life on this planet.

In view of ecological damage associated with the doubling of human population in the past half-century, I am sympathetic with Næss's call for a long-term, humanely accomplished, significant reduction in human population. Given humanity's creative potential, however, ways may yet be found to sustain a large human population while protecting significant wild habitat. Næss's reflections on human population growth reveal neither a naively naturalistic interpretation of humankind, nor ruthless recommendations for halting population growth, nor any particular optimism that such growth can be stopped before grave damage is done to all terrestrial life. Næss himself is no ecofascist, but radical environmentalists must inform themselves of the dangers posed by ecofascism, an ideology that compels individuals to conform to the "laws of nature" in order to promote the good of the "whole." In these difficult times Næss reminds us to cultivate the two highest virtues of the great spiritual traditions: wisdom and compassion.

Notes

[1] Arne Næss, "A European Looks at North American Branches of the Deep Ecology Movement," *The Trumpeter*, vol. 5, no. 2 (Spring, 1988), 75–76.

[2] Kirkpatrick Sale, "Deep Ecology and its Critics," *The Nation* (May 14, 1988), 670–675.

Chapter 31

Class, Race, and Gender Discourse in the Ecofeminism/Deep Ecology Debate

Ariel Salleh

1. Liberal Patriarchalism and the Serviced Society

The separation of humanity and nature is the linchpin of patriarchal ideology, and both deep ecology and ecofeminism share a desire to dislodge that pin. For deep ecologists, overcoming the division between humanity and nature promises a release from alienation. For ecofeminists, it promises release from a complex set of exploitations based on patriarchal identification of femaleness with the order of nature. Perhaps because most deep ecologists happen to have been men, and middle class, their environmental ethic has had difficulty in moving beyond psychological and metaphysical concerns to a political analysis of the "materiality" of women's oppression. Building on earlier exchanges between ecofeminism and deep ecology, in particular, "The Ecofeminism/Deep Ecology Debate: A Reply to Patriarchal Reason," I amplify the claim that deep ecology is held back from maturation as a Green philosophy by its lack of a fully rounded political critique.[1] To this end, I urge adherents of deep ecology to become more reflexively aware of the sociohistorical grounding of their discourse.

Although there are different emphases among women's groupings internationally, a growing number of ecofeminists now address capitalist patriarchy as an oppressive system of global power relations.[2] They situate both environmentalism and women's struggle against the instrumental rationality and dehumanizing commodity culture that comes with industrial production. Accordingly ecofeminists of a socialist persuasion are disturbed to hear the father of deep ecology,

Arne Næss, claim that "total egalitarianism is impossible," that some human exploitation will always be "necessary."[3] Women's complex treatment as a sexual, reproductive, and labor "resource" is glossed over in the deep ecological agenda. Yet there are, and have always been, people who cultivate and prepare food, build shelter, carry loads, labor to give birth, wash and tend the young, maintain dwellings, feed workers, and mend their clothes. Whether in the First World or the Third World (which is two-thirds of the global population), women's labor "mediation of nature" serves as the infrastructure to what is identified as men's "productive economic" role. This subsumption of women's energies, most often by means of the institution of the family, is homologous to exploitative class relations under the capitalist system. The family is integrally connected with, and makes industrial production possible by "reproducing" the labor force, in the several senses of that word. However, as productivism intensifies with new technologies and the promise of ever-greater profits, labor becomes increasingly removed from the satisfaction of basic needs. As a result, under the guise of "development," a new dimension is added to the women's role constellation—that of conspicuous consumer. Moreover, as the economic fetish penetrates personal culture, even sexual relations between men and women come to resemble relations between things, thereby deepening women's exploitation even further.[4]

Deep ecologists do not recognize that women have not been consulted about their interests in this system of social relations. Just as the environment is damaged by "development," women's lives are vitiated by men's systematic appropriation of their energies and time. Writing by Brinda Rao in India, Berit Ås in Norway, and Barbara Ehrenreich in the United States provides ample documentation of this appropriation.[5] The work of Third World peasant women is fairly obviously tied to "natural" functions and material labor. These women grow most of the world's food and care for their families with a minimum of disruption to the environment and with minimum reliance on a cash economy. They labor with independence, dignity, and grace—and those of us looking for sustainable models may soon want to take advice from such women. In contrast, in supposedly advanced industrial nations, women's maintenance work as housewives or imported guest workers is made dependent on and largely mystified by "labor-saving devices," such as dishwashing machines, blenders, and the like. Nevertheless, cultural assumptions concerning women's apparently universal role of mediating nature still hold. It is for this reason that reproductive rights remain contentious in the United States. Ecofeminists join Dave Foreman's cry to "free shackled rivers," but more than rivers remain shackled!

Deep ecologist Warwick Fox, who has wondered why ecofeminists have not discussed the class basis of deep ecology, has failed to note that my early ecofeminist criticism in "Deeper than Deep Ecology" refers repeatedly to women's labor as validation of their perspectives.[6] As the sociology of knowledge teaches us, peoples' perception is shaped by their place in the system of productive relations. Nevertheless, the gulf between manual or sustaining productive labor and mental or conceptualizing work is especially profound in industrialized societies. A whole gamut of questions surrounding labor relations is ideologically suppressed, and in the United States it is clouded by the question of race as well. In late capitalism, the middle class, including academics, are "serviced" in their daily needs by hidden workers. Not surprisingly, deep ecology reflects the idealism and individualism of such a privileged group, its preoccupation being "cultural issues" such as meaning, the psychological, and "rights." However, even more invisible as labor, and not even recognized by a wage, are the domestic services of women. Michael Zimmerman's typically middle-class and white articulation of women's lot—he sees them enjoying "the advantages" of a consumer society—illustrates this standard oversight, though the fault is not entirely his, since it largely reflects the liberal feminist attitude he relies on to make his case against ecofeminism.[7] It is not only women's socialization, the various belief systems which shape "the feminine role," but also the very practical nature of the labor which most women do that gives them a different orientation to the world around them and, therefore, different insights into its problems. In both North and South, this labor may include the physicality of birthing, suckling, and subsequent household chores, but is not restricted to such activities. Even in the public work force, women's employment is more often than not found in maintenance jobs—reflecting cultural attitudes to women as "carers."[8]

Radical feminist analyses of the psychodynamic underlying patriarchal social relations, again and again, return to the symbolic killing of mother/nature/woman as the root cause of the "masculine" will to objectify and control other forms of being. Zimmerman's writing is fairly symptomatic in this respect. Although ten or more pages of his "Feminism, Deep Ecology, and Environmental Ethics" are generously given to exposition of the feminist literature, and a concluding paragraph endorses its findings, his article is still querulous. The same observation applies to Fox's response to ecofeminist criticisms of deep ecology. While both Zimmerman and Fox cast doubt on the reality of patriarchal power, Zimmerman's ambivalent article also contains information about how ideology works to protect men from seeing the actual nature of social relations under patriarchy. He quotes the following remark of Naomi Scheman: "Men have been free to imagine themselves as self-defining only because women held the intimate social world together by their caring labors."[9] Similarly, we know that the capitalist entrepreneur sees himself as a man of high achievement, blind to the fact that the wage laborer is responsible for the generation of his surplus. In the patriarchal perspective, self appears to be independent; yet, to quote Jim Cheney, "The atomistically defined self acts as a sponge, absorbing the gift of the other, turning it into capital." Cheney goes on: "This is one way of understanding the frequent feminist claim that males in patriarchy feed on female energy."[10] Capital can be psychological and sexual as much as economic. On the positive side, the actuality of caring for the concrete needs of others gives rise to a morality of relatedness among ordinary women, and this sense of kinship seems to extend to the natural world as well. Consider the reasoning of an Indian peasant woman whose drinking water has been spoiled by village men moving across to a pumped supply for status reasons, or the sensibility of a woman who watches a tree grow over the grave of a child she has suckled. These understandings engraved in suffering make sharp contrast to the abstract philosophical formulations of deep ecology. For ecofeminism, the body is indeed an instrument of our knowledge of the world.[11]

Professional versus Grassroots Base

As I put it in an earlier critique," what is the organic basis of [the deep ecological] paradigm shift? . . . Is deep ecology a sociologically coherent position?"[12] One of the most distressing things about the field of environmental ethics is the extent to which it has been taken over by paid professional specialists. What gives authenticity, validity, and "depth" to ecofeminism, in contrast, is that it is implicitly tied to a praxis rooted in life needs and the survival of habitat. Deep ecology is primarily concerned with identification, or rather, re-identification of the so-called "human" ego with nature. For deep ecologists, however, the recommended route for recovering this connected sensuous self is meditation or leisure activities, such as backpacking. How does such activity compare as an integrating biocentric experience with the hands-on involvement of the African subsistence farmer who tends her field with an astonishing knowledge of seeds, water habits, and insect catalysts—and whose land is the continuing staff of the children she has born out of her body? There is surely a large portion of illusion and self-indulgence in the North's comfortable middle-class pursuit of the cosmic "transpersonal Self." Despite Næss's careful reformulations, in an age of "me now," the deep ecologists' striving for "Self-realization" demands close scrutiny.

Many deep ecological difficulties in coming to terms with ecofeminism can be traced to the sociopolitical grounding of the deep ecology movement in bourgeois liberalism. Hence, it is probably no surprise that even as deep ecologists put forward their key concept of "ecocentrism" as "the way out" of our environmental holocaust, an implicit endorsement of the Enlightenment rationalist notion of ever upward progress threatens to collide with the principle. For instance, some deep ecologists believe that "anthropocentric" political critiques, such as socialism and feminism, can, in principle, be taken care of by the wider framework of ecocentrism. Fox writes, "Supporters of deep ecology hold that their concerns well and truly *subsume* the concerns of those movements that have restricted their focus to a more egalitarian human society."[13] Not only is Fox's ambitious totalizing program spoiled by the serious gaps in deep ecology's theorization, it is also out of sync with his pluralist claim to respect the unfolding of "other voices" in the universe: the words of women, among others. Fox's attraction to "transpersonal psychology" hangs on the self-actualizing logic of middle-class individualism. Similarly, his assertion that self-interest is fused with that of Gaia as a whole, strikingly resembles the guiding hand behind Adam Smith's libertarian political economy, or Rawls's theory of justice. Despite a will to transcendence, there is an implicit positivism or naive realism in these formulations.[14] Deep ecology has no sense of itself as spoken by a particular group lodged in history. Oblivious to its own cultural context, the deep ecological voice rings out as a disembodied absolute.

Abstract Essences versus Reflexivity

According to Rosemary Ruether, women throughout history have not been particularly concerned to create transcendent, overarching, all-powerful entities, or like classical Greek Platonism and its leisured misogynist mood, with projecting a pristine world of abstract essences.[15] Women's spirituality has focused on the immanent and intricate ties among nature, body, and personal intuition. The revival of the goddess, for example, is a celebration of these material bonds. Ecofeminist pleas that men, formed under patriarchal relations, look inside themselves first before constructing new cosmologies have been dismissed, for example, by Fox, in "The Deep Ecology: Ecofeminism Debate and its Parallels," as a recipe for inward-looking possessive parochialism and, hence, ultimately war![16] But that would surely only be the case if deep ecologists failed to shrug off their conditioning as white-Anglo-Saxon-Protestant-professional property holders, which they assure us, they are very keen to do. Interestingly, the universalizing, cosmopolitan stance of this particular protest by Fox is somewhat at loggerheads with the deep ecologists' own professed commitment to bioregionalism.

In the name of "theoretical adequacy," Fox's article disregards history. Consequently, his prose blurs who has done what to whom, over the centuries and on into the present. To quote:

> [Certain] classes of social actors have . . . habitually assumed themselves to be *more fully human* than others, such as women ("the weaker vessel"), the "lower" classes, blacks, and non-Westerners ("savages," "primitives," "heathens" . . .)
>
> That anthropocentrism has served as the most fundamental kind of legitimation employed by whatever powerful class of social actors one wishes to focus on can also be seen by considering the fundamental kind of legitimation that has habitually been employed with regard to large-scale or high-cost social enterprises such as war, scientific and technological development, or environmental exploitation. Such enterprises have habitually been undertaken not simply in the name of men, capitalists, whites or Westerners, for example, but in the name of God (and thus our essential humanity . . .) . . . (This applies, notwithstanding the often sexist expression of these sentiments in terms of "man," "mankind," and so on, and not withstanding the fact that certain classes of social actors benefit disproportionately from these enterprises.)[17]

This passage is a sample of liberal-pluralist mystification in its most blatant form. Its author next goes on to mention Bacon and the rise of science, but without touching on the corresponding elimination of one class of social actors, namely, the six million women who perished as witches for their scientific wisdom. Fox believes that all modern liberation movements have had recourse to the same legitimating device—"humanity." Apparently, a belief that this label is available for the use of everyone is the reason why deep ecologists still use the term man so persistently.

Zimmerman, in turn, entirely misses the point of ecofeminism by portraying it as an argument about women being "better than men."[18] Ecofeminism does not set up a static ontological prioritization of "woman." Instead, it is a strategy for social action. Equally, men in the Green and the eco-socialist movements, by examining the parallel exploitation of nature and women, are entering into a process of praxis, the results of which will unfold over time. Fox, in his own way, shelves the question of our political responsibility as historical agents by insisting that all people need to understand is that "evolutionary outcomes" simply represent "the way things happen to have turned out," nothing more. For someone concerned with "simplistic" and "facile" political theorization, his familiar charge against ecofeminism beats the lot. Notwithstanding earlier posturing about the "errors of essentialism" in ecofeminist thought, Fox soon emerges as a kind of Spencerian sociobiologist. In fact, the deep ecologists, for all their anxieties about "genetic doctrines" in feminism, seem to be strongly inclined this way. George Sessions too speaks favorably about "the recent studies in ethology and genetics which posit a basic human and primate nature."[19] Is this the old double standard again?

Technology—Productive and Reproductive Relations

When it comes to the question of technology, Zimmerman's text becomes as rudderless as the modern industrial apparatus itself. He notes that some feminists—"essentialists" he calls them, though they remain unnamed—are critical of science and technology, while other feminists, also unspecified, argue that it is not "intrinsically evil."[20] There are, indeed, differences among feminists on technology. Liberal feminists, like their brothers, the reform environmentalists, imagine that solutions to social and ecological problems can be found within "the advanced industrial technostructure." Liberal feminism should not be grouped with ecofeminism, however, any more than resource environmentalism should be grouped with deep ecology. Ecofeminists go further than both liberal feminists, who see technology as emancipatory, and Marxist feminists who argue that technology is neutral and that it is all a matter of who controls it. Ecofeminists observe that the instrumental-rational mode of production inevitably trickles over into the sphere of consciousness and social relations. As a Heideggerian, Zimmerman should know that there are ample reasons for dismantling the technomonster, given its far-reaching impact into human phenomenology. Yet, he still seems to hold a neutralist thesis, claiming that "Modern science and technology are potentially liberating. . . ." Further, he asks: "While benefiting from the material well-being and technological progress made possible by masculinist science and industry, do women rid themselves of responsibility . . . ?"[21] It is hard to believe that this "growth"-oriented statement should be made in defense of deep ecology. Perhaps Zimmerman genuinely does believe that societies accrue benefit from "advanced" technologies. Perhaps they do for the middle-class men who designed and sold them; nevertheless, the young Korean microchip worker steadily going blind at her bench and the California aerospace worker coming down with immune deficiencies have not experienced such well-being. The problem is, and this is a point well made in Don Davis's article, that deep ecology as a movement has no systematic analysis of multinational-corporate industrial society and its effects.[22]

Equally innocent of the force of contemporary instrumentalism, Wittbecker writes that "human populations are plastic and could probably be decreased without fascism, by economic, religious, or cultural means." Deep ecologist Bill Devall's tone is similarly managerial, preoccupied as he is with population control.[23] The phenomenon of "overpopulation" does need to be seriously examined. However, given the ethical issues of eugenics-genocide and of a woman's right over her own body, the targeting of "population control" by white male environmentalists in the North has both racist and sexist dimensions. Observe how many Americans opposed to abortion in the United States endorse population control programs in Asia and South America. Even as a matter of social equity, where children provide supplementary farm labor for overworked mothers in the South, it is inappropriate for gray-suited international policy advisers to demand population control. Such programs originated in a post-World War II middle-class urban desire to protect the quality of life—that is, high levels of consumerism. These days the argument for population control is formulated more prudently in terms of protecting the earth's "scarce" resources. Even this injunction, however, as it is applied to the Third World exclusively, is patently hypocritical. Each infant born into the so-called advanced societies uses about fifteen times more global resources during his or her lifetime than a person born in the Third World. Population restraint may well be called for in the North, hopefully complemented by a scaling back of high technology excess. On the other hand, subsistence dwellers in the South are producers as much as consumers: as "presumers" they are practical examples of human autonomy in a nonexploitative relation to the land. What much of this talk about population control may express is a projection and displacement of guilt experienced by those who continue to live comfortably off the invisible backs of working women in the Third World. Even deeper, the constant focus on population control may reflect some profound psychosexual fear of that "different" voice.[24]

With regard to biotechnology, Fox agrees with the ecofeminist position that deep ecologists should oppose it; nevertheless, given deep ecology's lack of attention to industrialism and technological rationality, it is not consistently opposed by most deep ecologists. Sessions has said that he believes there "might be a point one day down the road when we can handle genetic engineering." Næss has also defended its use. For example, he has proposed that a genetically engineered microorganism be released in order to counter a mite infecting the eyes of African children.[25] This proposal is a very anthropocentric focus for an ecocentric theory, and it matches oddly with earlier claims by Næss and Sessions that it is better not to approach the nonhuman world reductionistically in terms of its usefulness to humans. Devall's fine tenet that "there is wisdom in the stability of natural processes" is violated here, as is Devall's and Sessions's "refusal to acknowledge that some life forms have greater or better intrinsic value than others." Concern about the unintended consequences of human "hubris" is one level of argument. Feminist critiques of patriarchal science are another. It might be also added, following the logic of Frances Moore Lappe, that if the standard of living—the "vital needs"—of African villages were not decimated by pressures, from a predatory white-male dominated international economic order, such children might not succumb to malnutrition and disease in the first place. Given this line of reasoning, genetic engineering can scarcely be justified as a "vital need." In fact, there can be no emergence from this exploitative system as long as humans pursue expensive technological-fix panaceas, such as genetic engineering. Even so, according to Devall and Sessions, "cultural diversity today requires advanced technology, that is, techniques that advance the goals of each culture."[26] Is this why John Seed from the Council of All Beings can be seen traveling with a laptop computer? What some deep ecologists seem to forget when it comes to the question of technology is that there is no such thing as a free lunch. While Devall condemns "false consciousness" in New Age advocates of genetic engineering and computer technology, one looks in vain for a clear deep ecological praxis on these matters. His discussion of genetic engineering remains descriptive and agnostic in tone, eventually sliding off into renewed denunciation of human overpopulation as the most important "agent of extinction." In other words, women workers in the South can pick up the tab for ecological crisis.

2. Patriarchal Postures and Discursive Strategies

Another metalevel of the debate between ecofeminism and deep ecology is the psychosexual dynamic that runs through it. As with the class and ethnic grounding of deep ecology, gender politics also shapes the context in which philosophical judgments are made. Without an awareness of this fact, the Green, deep ecological, and socialist movements lose reflexivity and run the risk of being partial, single issue, and reformist in focus. Sadly, the deep ecologists' reception of ecofeminist views has been marked by resistance. Perhaps this resistance should be no surprise, since their spokespeople have been men, and the psychological literature suggests that masculine identity is defined by separation rather than closeness. There is certainly nothing uniquely deep ecological in their responses; the strategies used to shore up their standpoints are quite familiar to the experience of women working in male-dominated institutions. As Karen Warren reminds us, "Ecofeminists take as their central project the unpacking of connections between the twin oppressions of women and nature. Central to this project is a critique of the sort of thinking which sanctions that oppression."[27] Elizabeth Dodson Gray and many others have exposed the pervasiveness of the androcentric conceptual frame. Yet, it is not only the epistemol-

ogy itself that women must attend to, but to an armory of discursive techniques
that back up and protect the bastion of masculine meaning. Among these, the
index to Dale Spender's bibliographic history of feminism names the following
common patriarchal procedures for dealing with intellectual and political challenges by women: ageism, appropriation, burial (of contribution), contempt
(sexual), character assassination, the double bind, the double standard, harassment, isolation, charges of man hating, masculine mind, misrepresentation,
namelessness, scapegoating, and witch hunting.[28] Note that while these postures
have no substantive value, they are readily insinuated into the context of
evaluation. As late twentieth-century politics moves toward a holistic agenda, it
becomes crucial for activist men to be able to identify when they are falling
back on these time honored discursive practices.

Denial and Omission

Spender's catalogue is not exhaustive, as we shall see. Fox, a deep ecologist
who wants to dissolve "ontological divisions," adds to Spender's list by creating
a disposable hierarchy of ecofeminisms. What makes for a "better" ecofeminism? Apparently, it is the work of women building on the theoretical foundations of Buddhism, Taoism, Spinoza, Heidegger, and systems theory![29] Fox's
androcentrism is so strong that he remains unembarrassed by the implications of
this legitimation device. Because the entire history of patriarchy is an exercise in
suppressing the wisdom of women's experiences, deep ecologists would do well
to bear this ancient agenda in mind. A related example occurs in the book by
Devall and Sessions, whose text echoes snippets of my ecofeminist "Deeper
than Deep Ecology" critique, while denying its existence by omitting documentation. Published two years after that unacknowledged essay, the authors respond to the prod with a three-page acknowledgment of women's contributions
to ecology. Yet, there is no sign of any effort to integrate ecofeminism within
the book's conceptualization as a whole. Chapter one, which reviews environmentalist scenarios—reformist, New Age, libertarian—fails to mention the ecofeminist approach. Chapter two, which reviews "the minority tradition," including nameless native Americans and "primal peoples," gives eight lines to
the "Women's Movement." These remarks mislead because of their brevity,
moreover, and risk confusing not only sex and gender stereotypes, but also
paradigmatic differences within feminism itself. There is also a short
"appendix" on ecology and domestic organization by Carolyn Merchant, whose
other published work on patriarchal reason, would have resounding epistemological implications for deep ecologists, if they absorbed it.[30] Concerning Devall's later book, Greta Gaard has observed that it "gives the section on Eros,
Gender and Ecological Self less than five pages. . . . He devotes an entire paragraph [to] citing a series of feminist analyses, but does not even paraphrase or
address their objections to deep ecology. . . ."[31]

   In addition to the documentation of ecofeminist literature being flimsy, the deep
ecologists' preparation for debate and grasp of feminist thought is also lacking in

respect. Devall and Sessions cite Dorothy Dinnerstein, Susan Griffin, and Jessie Bernard purportedly on how "our culture inhibits the development of psychological maturity in women." In fact, each of these feminist authors discusses the inhibition of "masculine" psychic maturity under patriarchy. Only Griffin is referenced, however, and Bernard's name is given the masculine spelling "Jesse." This lack of respect strongly suggests that the material has been consulted very indifferently, if at all, by the deep ecologists.[32] Failing to recognize that women's perspectives are materially grounded in their working lives as carers, Fox and Zimmerman lean heavily on arguments about *essentialism.* No one who responded to "Deeper than Deep Ecology" follows up footnote citations offering a dialectical refutation of the essentialism question. Again, although Fox cites Janet Biehl's critique of deep ecology, he never grapples with it.[33] Given that they are happy enough to set up a normative taxonomy of women's writing, it is remarkable that defenders of deep ecology have read so little ecofeminist literature. Their discussions focus on the writings of a handful of North American authors and myself. No European or Third World material is acknowledged, let alone examined. Perhaps the most damaging instance of denial used by deep ecologists is their disregard of my original ecofeminist endorsement of their ideals. To repeat, *"The appropriateness of attitudes expressed in Næss and Devall's seminal papers is indisputable."*[34] This lapse has deflected the focus of subsequent exchanges between ecofeminism and deep ecology away from constructive mutuality.

Projection and Personalization

Bolstered by adjectives like "simplistic" and "facile"—three or four times on one page in connection with social ecology and what are to him the less acceptable species of ecofeminism—Fox says that the ecofeminisms simplistic analyses are overinclusive and that they target all men, capitalists, whites, indiscriminately as "scapegoats" for what is wrong with the world.[35] His personalization here mirrors the form of those arguments that produce the example of Margaret Thatcher as proof that feminism is wrong. Individual women can be powerful, wealthy, or racist, but their circumstances have no bearing on the structural oppression of the female sex. Conversely, while a class of men may be preserved by entrenched structural privilege, specific individuals may still commit themselves against their class interest. In my discussion of Australian politics in "A Green Party: Can the Boys Do without One?" I talk, for example, about men working together with women in dismantling patriarchy, and about the potential of conservative churchgoers and corporate wives as catalysts in social change.[36] Fox's tactic of personalization is one to guard against, for it is invariably resorted to by those, whose class has a vested interest in ignoring what a structural analysis tells them.

On the same page, Fox claims that "simplistic" ecofeminist analyses are "inauthentic" because they lead to "a complete denial of responsibility" on the part of those who theorize. Because the ecofeminist literature presents an interdisciplinary synthesis of epistemological, political, economic, cultural, psychodynamic and ecological insights, it can scarcely wear the label "oversimplified." The term essentialism is also plainly misapplied for the same reason. As for avoiding responsibility, most ecofeminist writers, North and South have practical experience of movement activism, and that is what stimulates their insights. Women in the thousands have taken up campaigns over toxics, wilderness, and peace, not only in autonomous separatist groupings, but also in mainstream environment organizations where they make up two-thirds of the labor force. Women are certainly embracing ecological responsibility, so much so that it has even been remarked that it looks like they are being used all over again in their traditional housekeeping role as unpaid keepers of *oikos* at large.[37] Since women actually receive less than ten percent of the world's wage, why should they want to maintain this destructive global economy? As women around the world make the connection between sustainability and equality, they are doing just what Fox's either/or logic claims they cannot do. They are becoming "a class in themselves."

When will men lay down their arms? Zimmerman takes up the offensive on behalf of deep ecology with a proposition that perhaps women really accrue benefit from patriarchy:

> Feminists try to temper [their] portrayal by saying that individual men are not to blame, since they have been socialized. . . . What traits, then, are women projecting on to men? And what benefits accrue to women through projecting such traits? Do women split off from themselves and project onto men violence, aggressiveness, selfishness, greed, anger, hostility, death hating, nature fearing, individuality, and responsibility? And as a result of bearing the projected traits, do men behave much more violently, selfishly, etc., than they would if women withdrew these traits?[38]

I have commented in relation to Fox's work that personalization is invariably used by those who have difficulty thinking about people in groups or classes. Here it is Zimmerman who loses grasp of the structural level of analysis. If women do simply "project characteristics" onto men, that is, if they are ideas only in women's heads, then why do patriarchal statistics corroborate that men commit ninety percent of violent crimes? Indeed, are men "responsible" at all for their behavior? What of the wholesale abandonment of 150,000 women and children in the United States each year? What about responsibility in the nuclear industry? What has gone wrong with women's self-fulfilling projection there? According to Zimmerman's "critique of feminism," feminists must realize that men, too, are victims of patriarchy. Of course, I made this point myself in "Deeper than Deep Ecology" with the allusion to masculine self-estrangement. Hilkka Pietila also picks up on it when she writes: "A long process of male liberation is needed . . . in order to meet feminine culture without prejudice. . . . Salleh still anticipates a new ally within the personality of men, and it is . . . the feminine aspects of men's own constitution. . . ."[39] Nevertheless, women have all but given up trying to get their brothers into self-discovery through mutually supportive consciousness-raising groups as pioneered by radical feminism in the 1970s. Zimmerman, in contrast, is confident that it is feminism itself, which must engage in searching self-criticism. Surely, the emergence of five or six feminist paradigms in the space of two decades already demonstrates the women's movements' vitality and openness to renewal. Where is the men's movement and its political, as opposed to psychological, analysis?

Women were early to point out how the personal and political intermesh, and hence how nineteenth-century moralizers like "blame" and "accuse" are not apt in a postmodern reflexive culture where people strive to understand their own class implications in repressive social structures. Instead, Zimmerman ponders whether patricentric attitudes become more or less entrenched with "education." As we can see from the present exchange, education as such is no panacea. Unless people learn how to recognize the social/personal infrastructure of labor that sustains them daily, a paradigm shift is not likely. Zimmerman is almost there when he remarks that "we are making use of norms and following cultural practices that threaten the future of life on earth." But who is this "we?" Women's and men's "roles" and values are not everywhere the same. He knows this. After all, he takes hope from the "global awakening of the quest for the feminine voice that can temper the one-sidedness of the masculine voice."[40] Although ecofeminists share this hope, they also want it known that as far as any "quest" goes, a majority of the world's population, North and South, are already "speaking the feminine." The problem is: do they have standing? What is called for now is a move beyond tokenism, an admission of all women into the ranks of humanity.[41]

Caricature and Trivialization

The quest for the "feminine voice" is a recurrent theme in late twentieth-century philosophy, as recent French poststructuralist writing reveals. Alice Jardine's extensive research into this trend suggests, however, that gynesis, or speaking like a woman, is somewhat suspect when it is fashionably pursued by affluent Parisian homosexual *litterateurs*.[42] It deteriorates into parody, and beyond that into an upmarket semi-academic export commodity. A revolution in gender relations cannot go anywhere at the level of ideas, language, or ritual alone; it needs an objective "material base." Such professional philosophers as Zimmerman, however, are far removed from this perception. His class-based idealism brings him to conclude that it is "epistemology, metaphysics, and ethics" that have "led to the present exploitation."[43] From an ecofeminist perspective, change demands that relationships of production and reproduction be equally rearranged between men and women and nature—in such a way that freedom and necessity are identically experienced. Equality and sustainability are closely interlinked.

The philosophy of "difference," so poorly served by the deep ecologists' cheap paraphrase of ecofeminism—"that women are better than men"—has been widely debated over the past decade among liberal, Marxist, poststructuralist, and ecofeminists. The exploration of this theme marks an important phase in women's political consciousness. It converges both with men's personal efforts to escape the strictures of patriarchy and with new epistemological directions in science.[44] It is true that some men may still "think the feminine" in an unreconstructed way. Look at Wittbecker's attempt to dispose of my own critique in the traditional manner: "Hysterical hyperbolism is a perilous path to consciousness. . . ."[45] Consider, too, the uncritical use of woman/nature imagery by some early *Earth First!* deep ecologists, whose lurid metaphors of familial rape are meant to highlight their manly self-sacrifice in protecting "Mother Earth" and her "virgin forests." The thought style of monkey-wrench politics has tended to reinforce the intrinsic psychosexual dynamic lying beneath the exploitation of nature, women, and less privileged peoples. Other men defensively subvert any notion of "difference" by using it to set up a double bind, affirming "what they knew all along about women." Zimmerman himself professes concern that arguments based on gender types "run the risk of simply reaffirming traditional views that women are 'feelers,' while men are 'thinkers.'"[46] If nothing else, the ecofeminism/deep ecology debate should put an end to this assumption.

Fox is especially given to caricature of those he wants to debate, even when he is not fully cognizant of his terms. While no doubt endorsing wolves' rights to be wolves, he takes my rhetorical line about women being allowed to "love themselves" entirely out of its context in cultural politics. His next gambit relies on Wittbecker's poorly reasoned charge that I treat "the sexes as if they were two species." This alleged dualism is cobbled together with the playful Irigarayan title "A Green Party: Can the Boys Do without One?" in order to illustrate an "oppositional" approach.[47] As Adorno would say, a totalitarian culture knows no irony. In a related vein, Fox has claimed that "The extent to which people in general are ready to equate opposition to human centeredness with opposition to humans per se can be viewed as a function of the dominance of the anthropocentric frame of reference in our society."[48] Fox does not see that the extent to which deep ecologists equate opposition to patriarchy with opposition to men per se can be viewed as a function of the dominance of their own androcentric frame of reference.

Discredit and Invalidation

It is easier to think through an issue if there is a clear distinction between "them and us," self and other; hence, Fox "weighs up" the "relative merits" of deep ecology and ecofeminism. Having polarized the two, he casts doubt over the value of ecofeminist "anthropocentrics" by means of a footnote reference to racism at Greenham Common in 1987.[49] In fact, the racism in question was felt to be displayed by socialist women from the Campaign for Nuclear Disarmament toward Wilmette Brown, an Afro-American legal aid adviser to ecofeminist activists and a well-known advocate in the wages-for-housework campaign. As those familiar with ideological crosscurrents within feminism know, many leftists are antagonistic to the wages-for-housework campaign, which cuts right across their ideal of socialized domestic production. The confrontation was thus an ideological one, but exacerbated in that a black activist stood at the center of it. Greenham ecofeminists, sensitive to the interconnectedness of all forms of domination—classism, racism, sexism, and speciesism—took all facets of the problem in hand and tried to work them out. Carrying this "inclusiveness" further, an April 1989 meeting of the Woman Earth Peace Institute in San Francisco pioneered an effective model for ensuring racial parity at ecofeminist gatherings.[50] Fox's divisive approach is a dubious one for a radical thinking man in the late twentieth century to engage in. Which brings up another question: where are the Afro-American or Third World "spokespeople" for the deep ecology movement?

Zimmerman writes that "Critics of feminism"—though, since these are not referenced, one must infer it is the author himself speaking—"regard as disingenuous the claim that the real motive of feminism is to liberate all people. Such critics contend that feminists have their own power agenda."[51] Obviously, feminists have a power agenda; they are involved in a political struggle designed to redress an inequitable system. Or, if Zimmerman means that individual feminist women are on a "power trip," then there is a margin of truth in that as well, in as much as women attempting to achieve equality alongside male peers have to compete harder to arrive at the same result because of structural discrimination and harassment along the way. However, if he is implying that women only want power, then that is silly. The personal costs of being a feminist in both career and domestic terms are enormous. Nobody would bother with the struggle unless she was committed to the vision of a just society. It may be at least several generations before the community at large even begins to digest what feminists are talking about. Current statistics, for example, indicate that twenty-five percent of Australian men still believe that it is all right for a man to hit "his" wife. In the United States, a woman is battered every eighteen seconds. In the meantime, there are few benefits for feminists or even their daughters in the foreseeable future. Ecofeminism is directed toward a long-term transvaluation of values. Women working to this end certainly glean no rewards from the system that they are trying to deconstruct. In a way, deep ecology's "critique of feminism" itself reflects why the ecofeminist sensibility came forward in the first place. In Charlene Spretnak's words, "Ecofeminism addresses the terror of nature and of female power, and the ways out of this mesmerizing condition."[52]

Ambivalence and Appropriation

While Zimmerman and Cheney, each from their different viewpoints, have observed that convergences between ecofeminism and deep ecology exist only "at first glance" or "on the face of it," a fraction of the deep ecological mindset still hopes for some sort of I/thou accommodation between the movements. Fox talks about a synthesis and, astonishingly, turns to Cheney's critique and Zimmerman's "evenhanded" examination in defense of his own claim that there is "no real incompatibility."[53] The logic of Fox's turn is incredible, first, in light of Zimmerman's highly ambivalent attitude toward feminism, and second, given

Cheney's skeptical thesis that deep ecology may be symptomatic of an inability to identify realistically with others, a manifestation of the patriarchal vacillation between "selfish appetite" and "oceanic fusion."[54] Ecofeminists certainly resist a patronizing subsumption of women's thoughtful labors under the deep ecological umbrella, just as much as they find it offensive to see men raiding and colonizing feminist ideas in order to modernize male dominance. Nevertheless, ignoring our disquiet over the deep ecologists' lack of regard for the environmental consequences of technology, economics, race, and gender relations, Fox recommends that in as much as ecofeminists "extend" their concerns to the ecological, then there is no "significant difference." He calls for an alliance with Patsy Hallen, in terms of her paper, subtitled "Why Ecology Needs Feminism," and with Marti Kheel, despite the latter's uncompromising exposé of patriarchal thinking in environmental ethics. On the next page, and relaxing back into the authoritative white, male, academic register, he announces "major problems associated with Kheel's critique."[55] In one important concession, he writes, "Deep ecologists completely agree with ecofeminists that men have been far more implicated in the history of environmental destruction than women."[56] This assertion more or less unhinges Fox's efforts to generate a coherent stand, providing a good example of what liberal pluralism looks like in practice.[57]

Zimmerman also arrives at a point where he is keen "to unite" and finds "no real disagreement on basics," etc., and he adopts the ecofeminist analysis that

> So long as patriarchally raised men fear and hate women, and so long as men conceive of nature as female, men will continue in their attempts to deny what they consider to be the feminine/natural within themselves and to control what they regard as the feminine/natural outside themselves.[58]

Does he really believe this statement? It seems doubtful, for with the next breath, he writes, "Salleh's critique is, in my opinion, only partly accurate. . . ."[59] This opinion, however, is never demonstrated, for he does not say which "part" he has in mind, or whether the "parts" represent a reader divided within his intellectual/emotional growth. Although intellectual capacities recognize what is true in ecofeminism, emotionally the reader is unsettled by the feminine voice. After all, Zimmerman reads the "Deeper than Deep Ecology" critique as "accusatory," rather than, say, "challenging" or "confronting."[60] Thus, the question is: since ultimately he endorses ecofeminist conclusions, what is Zimmerman defending at such length?

Ambivalence also marks Devall's work. He is happy to take on board the odd ecofeminist insight—for example, Starhawk's revisioning of power, the heroic example of India's Chipko women, or Sarah Ebenreck's farm ethic. He has even come to agree with the ecofeminist premise that "the ecological crisis has complex psychosexual roots." Yet, like other deep ecologists, Devall is anxious to move quickly beyond that messy problem "to explore the ecological self." The emphasis on gender difference runs the risk of "divisiveness," he claims, and "distracts us from the real work." This "after the Revolution" line is a familiar one to feminists who took their first steps hand in hand with brother Marxists. The language is identical, in fact, for what speaks here is the voice of patriarchy. Of course, many men want to avoid doing their personal/political homework; doing so could well upset their comfortable status quo. Nevertheless, humans cannot simply pass over their psychosexual conditioning in this way, as the present textual analysis demonstrates. In Devall's own words, "Healing requires bringing forth that which is suppressed in culture" and leveling with it, however painful and confusing this experience may be. As every deep ecologist knows, band-aid solutions do not work.[61]

Conclusion

Richard Ohmann is not himself a deep ecologist, but a man sensitive to the terrain of gender politics that now underlies both daily routine and theoretical work. He approaches our dilemma in this way:

> Progressive male intellectuals and professionals have arrived at feminism by an inexorable development and by a moral logic that flows from our strongest allegiances. . . . If we are "in" feminism at all, we are dragged into it kicking and screaming, and now that we're there, we should think of ourselves as on extended probation, still learning. What we do there with our experience, our competence, and our gender and class confidence, is a matter to be negotiated with caution, flexibility, improvisation, listening, and often doubtless through a strategic fade into the wallpaper. But I don't see drawing back from the knowledge that feminism is our fight, too.[62]

Clearly there is a long way yet to go. In terms of a Green or eco-socialist political practice, the new politics will demand of men and women more than just rational understanding of their respective positions as bearers of class, race, and gender domination, if they are to recover their shared human complementarity. Men, moreover, whose history has taken them on such a destructive path, will need to open up to a deep therapeutic acceptance of the process of mother/nature/woman killing in the making of their own identities. Although the personal and the transpersonal are intermeshed, as far as deep ecology goes, this inner movement has been lacking. Constructed by a class of men that is serviced by both patriarchal and capitalist institutions, deep ecology with its valuable move to "ecocentrism" remains out of touch with the material source of its continuing existence. Significantly, its theorization ignores the place of labor in the creation and sustenance of human life and its pivotal role in our human exchanges with nature. In short, as it is presently formulated, deep ecology reflects the disembodied conditions of its own production. This situation is, and should be, a matter for concern, if not despair, among committed environmental radicals, eco-socialists, and ecofeminists.

Notes

This chapter is reprinted with minor revisions from Ariel Salleh, "Class, Race, and Gender Discourse in the Ecofeminism/Deep Ecology Debate," *Environmental Ethics* 15 (Fall, 1993): 225–244.

[1] Ariel Salleh, "The Ecofeminism/Deep Ecology Debate: A Reply to Patriarchal Reason," *Environmental Ethics* 14 (1992): 195–216.

[2] For discussion of the international status of ecofeminism and its regional variations, see Ariel Salleh, "From Centre to Margin," *Hypatia* 6 (1991): 206–14.

[3] Arne Næss, "The Shallow and the Deep, Long Range Ecology Movement," *Inquiry* 16 (1973): 95–100. A qualification of Næss's view appears in *Ecology, Community and Lifestyle: Outline of an Ecosophy*, trans. David Rothenberg (New York: Cambridge University Press, 1989). Here, the impact of culture and personal experience on ethical intuition is acknowledged in a way that could serve as a model for other deep ecologists.

[4] Ariel Salleh, "Epistemology and the Metaphors of Production," *Studies in the Humanities* 15 (1988): 136.

[5] Brinda Rao, "Gender and Ecology and India," *Capitalism, Nature, Socialism* 2 (1989): 65–82; Berit As, "A Five Dimensional Model for Change," *Women's Studies International Quarterly* 4 (1980); Barbara Ehrenreich, *The Hearts of Men* (New York: Anchor, 1983).

[6] Warwick Fox, "The Deep Ecology–Ecofeminism Debate and its Parallels," *Environmental Ethics* 11 (1989): 14. Compare Ariel Salleh, "Deeper than Deep Ecology: The Ecofeminist Connection," *Environmental Ethics* 6 (1984): 335–41, especially points 3 and 4.

[7] Michael Zimmerman, "Feminism, Deep Ecology, and Environmental Ethics," *Environmental Ethics* 9 (1987): 21–44.

[8] For an early ecofeminist ethic based on "caring," see Marti Kheel, "The Liberation of Nature: A Circular Affair," *Environmental Ethics* 7 (1985): 135–49. The analysis of caring has since become a veritable growth area for professional philosophers, thus, neutralizing the radical feminist impulse which originally politicized it.

[9] Zimmerman, "Feminism, Deep Ecology, and Environmental Ethics," 31. The reference is to Naomi Scheman, "Individualism and the Objects of Psychology," in *Discovering Reality*, ed. S. Harding and M. Hintikka (Boston: Reidel, 1983), 234.

[10] Jim Cheney, "Ecofeminism and Deep Ecology," *Environmental Ethics* 9 (1987): 124.

[11] Vandana Shiva, *Staying Alive* (London: Zed, 1989) conveys the voice of Indian women farmers to a Western educated readership. Alternatively, an academic feminist argument connecting pain with political insight is made in Ariel Salleh, "On the Dialectics of Signifying Practice," *Thesis Eleven* 5/6 (1982): 72–84.

[12] Salleh, "Deeper than Deep Ecology," 339.

[13] Fox, "Deep Ecology–Ecofeminism Debate," 9 (emphasis added). Since writing this piece, I have discovered that Jim Cheney explicates the totalizing implications of Fox's stand powerfully and eloquently in "The Neo-Stoicism of Radical Environmentalism," *Environmental Ethics* 11 (1989): 293–325.

[14] Unfortunately, Robyn Eckersley's recent book *Environmentalism and Political Theory: Towards an Ecocentric Approach* (New York University at Stonybrook Press, 1992) perpetuates Fox's naive realism.

[15] Rosemary Ruether, *New Women, New Earth* (New York: Seabury, 1975).

[16] Fox, "Deep Ecology–Ecofeminism Debate," 12.

[17] Fox, "Deep Ecology–Ecofeminism Debate," 22–23.

[18] Zimmerman, "Feminism, Deep Ecology, and Environmental Ethics," 34.

[19] Bill Devall and George Sessions, *Deep Ecology: Living as if Nature Mattered* (Salt Lake City: Peregrine Smith, 1985), 225. On *essentialism* as red herring, see Salleh, "The Ecofeminism/Deep Ecology Debate," and "Essentialism and Ecofeminism," *Arena* 94 (1991): 167–73.

[20] Zimmerman, "Feminism, Deep Ecology, and Environmental Ethics," 40.

[21] Zimmerman, "Feminism, Deep Ecology, and Environmental Ethics," 40, 41–42.

[22] Don Davis, "The Seduction of Sophia," *Environmental Ethics* 8 (1986): 151–62.

[23] Alan Wittbecker, "Deep Anthropology, Ecology and Human Order," *Environmental Ethics* 8 (1986): 269; and Bill Devall, *Simple in Means, Rich in Ends* (Salt Lake City: Peregrine Smith, 1988).

[24] This paragraph is adapted from Ariel Salleh, "Living with Nature: Reciprocity or Control," in *Ethics of Environment and Development* ed. R. and J. Engel, (London: Pinter/University of Arizona Press, 1990), 251.

[25] George Sessions, personal communication, Los Angeles, March 1987; Arne Næss, personal communication, Oslo, August 1987.

[26] See Bill Devall and George Sessions, *Deep Ecology*, 71–73.

[27] Karen Warren, "Feminism and Ecology: Making Connections," *Environmental Ethics* 9 (1987): 6

[28] Dale Spender, *Women of Ideas and What Men Have Done to Them* (London: Routledge, 1982). See also Margo Adair and Sharon Howell, *The Subjective Side of Politics* (San Francisco: Tools for Change, 1988).

[29] Fox, "The Deep Ecology–Ecofeminism Debate," 13, n.20.

[30] Bill Devall and George Sessions, *Deep Ecology*; compare Carolyn Merchant, *The Death of Nature* (San Francisco: Harper and Row, 1980).

[31] Greta Gaard, "Feminists, Animals, and the Environment," paper presented at the annual convention of the National Women's Studies Association, Baltimore, 1989, 10.

[32] Devall and Sessions, *Deep Ecology*, 180; 221, n.2. The missing references are Dorothy Dinnerstein, *The Mermaid and the Minotaur* (New York: Harper and Row, 1976) and Jessie Bernard, *The Future of Marriage* (New York: World Publications, 1972).

[33] Janet Biehl's article "It's Deep but Is It Broad?" appeared in *Kick It Over* (winter 1987), p.2A–4A, at a time when she identified herself with social ecofeminism.

[34] Salleh, "Deeper than Deep Ecology," 339 (emphasis added).

[35] Fox, "The Deep Ecology–Ecofeminism Debate," 16.

[36] Ariel Salleh, "A Green Party: Can the Boys Do without One?" in Drew Hutton, ed., *Green Politics in Australia* (Sydney: Angus and Robertson, 1987), 88.

[37] See the special women's issue of *Environmental Review* 8 (1984); and Ariel Salleh, "The Growth of Ecofeminism," *Chain Reaction* 36 (1984): 26–28.

[38] Zimmerman, "Feminism, Ecology, and Environmental Ethics," 41.

[39] Hilkka Pietila, "Daughters of Mother Earth," in Engel and Engel, *Ethics of Environment and Development*, 243 (emphasis added).

[40] Zimmerman, "Feminism, Ecology, and Environmental Ethics," 41.

[41] The participation of women from all continents in the 1992 United Nations Conference on Environment and Development is a case in point. Even so, at one point, Third World government negotiators were prepared to "trade off" women's rights, if the United States would concede its high level of resource depletion by leaving references to "overconsumption" in Agenda 21 texts.

[42] Alice Jardine, *Gynesis* (Cambridge, Mass.: Harvard University Press, 1985).

[43] Zimmerman, "Feminism, Ecology, and Environmental Ethics," 44. The same tendency is manifest in his book *Heidegger's Confrontation with Modernity* (Indiana University Press, 1990), even while a "feminist perspective" is incorporated into the last five pages of text.

[44] See Benjamin Lichtenstien, "Feminist Epistemology," *Thesis Eleven* 21 (1988).

[45] Wittbecker, "Deep Anthropology and Human Order," p. 265, n.18.

[46] Zimmerman, "Feminism, Ecology and Environmental Ethics," 34.

[47] Fox, "Deep Ecology–Ecofeminism Debate," 17–18. As well as being poorly informed, notes 33 and 41 of this article are classic examples of misrepresentation by trivialization.

[48] Fox, "Deep Ecology–Ecofeminism Debate," 20.

[49] Fox, "Deep Ecology–Ecofeminism Debate," 14, n.24.

[50] Jacinta McCoy, personal communication: Eugene, Oregon, June 1989.

[51] Zimmerman, "Feminism, Ecology, and Environmental Ethics," 41.

[52] Charlene Spretnak: Address to the First International Ecofeminist Conference, University of Southern California, Los Angeles, March 1987.

[53] Fox, "Deep Ecology–Ecofeminism Debate," 9, n.7.

[54] Cheney follows Carol Gilligan, *In a Different Voice* (Cambridge, Mass.: Harvard University Press, 1982).

[55] Fox, "Deep Ecology–Ecofeminism Debate," 9, n.7; 10, n.11. Patsy Hallen, "Making Peace with Nature: Why Ecology Needs Feminism," *The Trumpeter* 4, no.3 (1987): 3–14; Marti Kheel, "The Liberation of Nature."

[56] Fox, "Deep Ecology–Ecofeminism Debate," 14.

[57] In tandem with Fox, Eckersley, in *Environmentalism and Political Theory*, also tries to appropriate ecofeminism for deep ecology. In quite uncritical language, she describes ecofeminist theory as "nesting within" ecocentrism and as an "essential tributary." Moreover, focusing exclusively on the world of ideas, Eckersley sees ecocentrism as waiting to be "fleshed out in a political and economic direction." Women's ongoing political/economic resistance, North and South, remains invisible to her.

[58] Zimmerman, "Feminism, Ecology, and Environmental Ethics," 24.

[59] Zimmerman, "Feminism, Ecology, and Environmental Ethics," 39.

[60] Zimmerman, "Feminism, Ecology, and Environmental Ethics."

[61] Devall, *Simple in Means, Rich in Ends*, 56–57.

[62] Richard Ohmann, "In, With," in *Men in Feminism* ed. A. Jardine and P. Smith, (New York: Methuen, 1987), 187.

Chapter 32

Ecofeminist Philosophy and Deep Ecology

Karen Warren

Introduction

Deep Ecology is perhaps the most widely known philosophical position in environmental ethics. The deep ecology movement is of singular importance to ecofeminist philosophers not only because of its obvious presence in environmental politics, but also because it seems to have answered the ecofeminist call for a nondominating attitude toward nature. Indeed, it is often praised for its alleged feminist sensibility.

Often it is assumed that the term "deep ecology" refers to a single philosophy, with its various advocates differing only on minor points with one another. Such is not the case, however, and the differences are exceedingly important for ecofeminist philosophy and practice. In this essay I will disentangle two (of several) widely differing directions in deep ecology thought, that of Næss, on the one hand, and that of Fox, Sessions, and Devall on the other,[1] and offer an ecofeminist philosophical perspective on each. I will suggest that Næss's deep ecology position is or could be compatible with ecofeminism, while the positions of Fox, Sessions, and Devall, in large part, are not.

Deep Ecology: Common Ground

The central tenets of deep ecology, as outlined in Næss's 1973 article on the subject—tenets to which all philosophical deep ecologists subscribe—are as follows.[2] First, "deep ecology" is contrasted with "shallow ecology," that is, such environmental issues as resource conservation and pollution. These forms of environmentalism are faulted to the extent that they are anthropocentric in motivation, i.e., to the extent that they advocate resource conservation and pollution control solely or primarily in the interests of human well-being. In so doing, of course, nonhuman nature is treated as a mere means to human well-being; shallow or reform environmentalism is thereby rejected for seeing nonhuman nature in instrumental terms only and for failing to recognize a second tenet of deep ecology, namely, the "intrinsic value" or "inherent worth" of nonhuman nature. According to all deep ecologists, *biocentric egalitarianism,* i.e., the "equal right to live and blossom" of all living things, is basic to deep ecology.

Third, deep ecologists are critical of the animal liberation movement in both its rights and utilitarian forms. This movement prides itself on extending that series of liberation movements, which includes the liberation of women, people of color, and the underclass to the liberation of nonhuman animals. Deep ecologists have noted, however, that animal liberationism is inherently problematic on three counts. First, it is not a true liberation of nature, but only of the sentient forms of life within nature. Second, the criteria for determining which entities have moral standing, employed in the animal liberation movement, ensure the continuance of a worrisome, hierarchical moral pecking-order with humans at the apex and, say, shrimp at the bottom. In fact, the way of determining a being's ability to suffer— namely, a central nervous system—is a human-centered rather than bio-centered criterion. Third, environmentally speaking, those crucial aspects of nature so important to deep ecologists, e.g., wild animals, plants, species, and ecosystems, simply aren't included in the realm of the morally considerable. So, environmentally speaking, animal liberationism fails to be a bona fide *environmental* ethic at all.

Fourth, and most importantly perhaps, the linchpin which holds the tenets of deep ecology together, the guiding insight, is Næss's original "Rejection of the man-in-environment image in favor of the relational, total-field image." In other words, humans are *not* discontinuous with nature, above (or superior) and essentially different from nature, but part of an interconnected web of relationships. This is often expressed by the principle of *self-realization,* i.e., that the human self (small "s") is only fully realized when it *identifies* with the larger cosmos, nature, the Self (capital "S").

The Deep Ecology–Ecofeminist Debate

Many ecofeminists, however, find the positions of deep ecology problematic. The so-called "deep ecology–ecofeminism debate"[3] focuses on at least five main issues:

1. Anthropocentrism versus androcentrism: Does ecofeminism commit itself to the view that the root cause of the domination of nature is androcentrism? If so, deep ecologists such as Warwick Fox insist that ecofeminists are mistaken: anthropocentrism is the root cause, and ecofeminists ought to

    acknowledge that they really are deep ecologists or ecofeminism ought to be abandoned.[4]

2. Is deep ecological practice, especially the activities of monkey-wrenching, tree-spiking and other acts of "eco-sabotage," expressions of male-gender, white-race, middle-class, and Western privilege? If so, then ecofeminists ought to reject deep ecology in practice.

3. Does deep ecology presuppose a masculinist psychology and sensibility? Is it just a position glommed on to an otherwise masculinist conceptual framework? If it is, then ecofeminists ought to reject it.[5]

4. Is the "deep ecology platform" male-gender biased? and

5. Are the principles of bioegalitarianism and self-realization problematic from an ecofeminist philosophical point of view? If so, then in both cases, deep ecology ought to be rejected in principle.

    With regard to question (1), some ecofeminists (e.g., Ariel Salleh, Vandana Shiva) do (or do sometimes) speak as if *androcentrism*—male-centeredness—is the root cause of the exploitation of women and the earth, not, as deep ecologists claim, *anthropocentrism*—human centeredness. To the extent that they do, I disagree with them: There is no single root cause of oppression, domination, or exploitation; indeed, one could argue that it is typical of patriarchal thinking that one looks for single, unitary causal explanations for phenomena. Rather, it is a set of interlocking "isms of domination," "united" by a *logic of domination*, viz., the moral premise that superiority justifies subordination, that is needed to explain unjustified domination. So my response to deep ecologists like Warwick Fox[6] who claim that patriarchy could end while the exploitation of the earth continues, is that he is mistaken about what ecofeminist philosophers like myself claim. My claim is that, at least in Western societies, *anthropocentrism* has *historically functioned* as *androcentrism*, such that no accurate historical account of anthropocentric attitudes towards nature can be explicated without reference to patriarchy or androcentrism. Furthermore, if patriarchy would be eliminated, then, by my account, at least conceptually, so would all the other "isms of domination" (including "naturism," or the unjustified domination of nonhuman nature by humans), *because* patriarchy is conceptually tied with all these other "isms of domination" through the logic of domination. If patriarchy is eliminated, so is the logic of domination, which conceptually and morally glues the various systems of domination together. By extension, conceptually, naturism (which presupposes a logic of domination) also would be eliminated. Thus, for ecofeminist philosophers like myself, it really is the logic of domination that is explanatorily basic in any description of "causes" of oppression and domination.

    In fact, I would even challenge the very "anthropocentrism versus androcentrism" dualism which must be presupposed in order for the question, "Is anthropocentrism or androcentrism the root cause of environmental exploitation?" to be raised at all. As an ecofeminist philosopher, I challenge such dualistic thinking. The very formulation of the question rests on two sorts of conceptual mistakes, viz., that of supposing that anthropocentrism is oppositionally and exclusively opposed to androcentrism in such a way that no third option is possible *and* that of supposing that one can meaningfully raise the question in the first place. Rather, I claim that the question is conceptually flawed and, quite literally, cannot meaningfully be raised without failing to understand the ecofeminist philosophical position about dualisms mediated by a logic of domination—dualisms which have functioned historically *within* the contexts of oppression and domination. To meaningfully raise the question at all, one must presuppose the very sort of oppositional and mutually exclusive dualism, which (other ecofeminists), and I are anxious to deny.

With regard to question (2), those activities most often associated with *Earth First!* in the United States, such as tree-spiking, *are* indeed the expressions of male-gender, middle- or upper-class, typically white and Western privilege.[7] As an ecofeminist philosopher I ask, "Who can afford to engage in such activities? Can poor women, working women, Hindu women or Third World women responsible for domestic households afford to spend their 'free' time practicing such acts of civil disobedience, especially in areas where maintenance of the indigenous forest is essential to the livelihood of these women and their families?" When women of the Chipko movement initiated the "tree-hugging movement," this was not an act of civil disobedience motivated by deep ecological concerns; it was a nonviolent, grassroots act of women protecting the forests in which they lived and on which they depended for their very survival. It is that women-gender-identified connection with trees which ecofeminist philosophy is inspired to capture and explain. These women are not in any social or economic position of power and privilege to engage in acts of ecosabotage as conceived, defended, and practiced by First World *Earth First!*-ers.

Question (3), (4), and (5) are interrelated and cannot be answered quite so quickly or easily. In what follows, I answer questions (4) and (5) in the affirmative: Yes, at least a certain version of deep ecology (viz., that of Fox, Sessions, and Devall) is "masculinist" and does presuppose some of the patriarchal assumptions (e.g., the erasure of difference and individuality), the merging of self-with-Self) ecofeminist philosophy is bent on exposing and dismantling. But that this involves any psychological thesis about innate differences between the sexes, I deny; gender differences are socially constructed, economically fashioned, historically molded differences. There is no such thing as "pure (i.e., unsocially constructed) biology" and, hence, (pure) biology cannot be destiny. Whatever psychological differences there may be between men and women—if, indeed there are any—are, at worst, *both* socially constructed *and* biologically predisposed ones and, at best, simply socially constructed ones.

Having said that, consider now a more elaborate defense of my answer to question (3), (4), and (5). That defense constitutes the remainder of this essay and builds largely on the work of ecofeminist philosopher Val Plumwood.

Val Plumwood's Critique of Deep Ecology

Australian ecofeminist philosopher Val Plumwood offers a discussion of the notion of the self in her critique of deep ecology. I offer Plumwood's view here because I think she is correct in her criticisms of much of deep ecology, and because her account explicitly draws on salient features of my own account of ecofeminism, as expressed through my earlier writings. But I also suggest that Plumwood's account clearly fits the ecosophies of Fox, Sessions, and Devall, and is less compelling regarding the ecosophy of Næss.

According to Plumwood, there are three accounts of the self which emerge in deep ecological writing, each of which is unsatisfactory and all of which fail to recognize that the "problem of discontinuity" is created by the mind/body dualism—a recognition familiar to ecofeminist philosophical critiques of both rationalism and nonfeminist environmental philosophies. The first deep ecological account of the self is *the indistinguishability or holistic self.* This self rests on what we call an *identity thesis*: humans are identified with nature as just another strand in one large biotic web. There are no clear boundaries between the self and nature since the human-in-environment image is replaced with a gestalt or holistic view of humans as identical with nature. This is the sense of self, John Seed presupposes when he says, "I am protecting the rain forest is the same as I am part of the rain forest protecting myself. I am that part of the rain forest recently emerged into thinking." [8]

Plumwood's correct ecofeminist philosophical critique of the indistinguishability self is that it mistakenly solves the discontinuity problem by obliterating *all* distinctions between humans and nonhuman nature. This is simply too powerful a solution. It fails to distinguish the correct concept of the self, the *relational self* I, (and others) have defended, from the incorrect indistinguishability metaphysics which is presupposed as the basis of the self. The truth is that humans are *both* continuous with and distinct from the natural world.

The second account of the self sometimes assumed by deep ecologists is what Plumwood calls *the expanded self.* It rests on what I call an *empathy thesis*. The self's identification with other beings leads to a larger self which is detached from the particular concerns of the individual self. According to Plumwood, this is the sense of self, Fox assumes when he quotes with approval John Livingstone's statement: "When I say that the fate of the sea turtle or the tiger or the gibbon is mine, I mean it. All that is in my universe is not merely mine; it is *me*. And I shall defend myself. I shall defend myself not only against overt aggression, but also against gratuitous insult." [9]

According to Plumwood, an ecofeminist philosophical critique of the expanded self is that it is an extension of rational egoism, rather than a rejection of it. It mistakenly assumes that human nature is individualistically egoistic and that the alternative to such egoism is self-sacrifice. As I have argued elsewhere, [10] others are recognized only to the extent that they are incorporated into one's own self and their difference denied. This denial of the importance of difference is unacceptable: an ecology and politics of difference is central to ecofeminist philosophy.

The third and last account of the self sometimes presupposed by deep ecology is what Plumwood calls *the transcended or transpersonal self.* This assumes what I call a *triumph-over thesis.* Humans are to strive for impartial identification with all particulars by overcoming or triumphing over the personal or individual self, its attachments with particular concerns, personal emotions, and sensuality. Plumwood cites Fox again here as presenting the deep ecology version of universalization in the notion of the transcended self, with its emphasis on the personal and particular as corrupting and self-interested—"the cause of possessiveness, war and ecological destruction."[11]

The ecofeminist philosophical critique of the transcended self, Plumwood offers is, again, compelling. Deep ecology's treatment of particularity and the personal here reflects a rationalist preoccupation with the universal and the ethical as *opposed to* the particular and personal. Of course, reformulating a position with which I agree—Plumwood's critique of three notions of the self (the identity, empathy, and triumph-over theses), and the underlying metaphysics, which supports them in deep ecology—does not constitute arguing for it. In what follows, I suggest an alternative way of critiquing deep ecology, one which differs from Plumwood's account in that it provides a way of interpreting what Arne Næss says about the self and deep ecology, which *does* or *may* escape Plumwood's criticism of what Fox, Sessions, and Devall say about the self and deep ecology.

American and Australian Deep Ecology: Ecosophy S

Like all deep ecologists, including Arne Næss, the deep ecologists Warwick Fox, George Sessions, and Bill Devall make a distinction between what they call the *deep ecology platform* (or, alternatively, the eight *basic principles* of deep ecology) and "the fundamental features of philosophies and religions from which that platform (basic principles) is derived"[12]—i.e., the various "ecosophies" from which the platform can be derived. Unlike Næss, however, who keeps his own ecosophy, what he calls Ecosophy T, distinctly separate from the deep ecology platform, the philosophers I consider here identify deep ecology itself with their own particular ecosophy which, borrowing from Jim Cheney's work, I will call Ecosophy S (*S* for *Self-realization,* a central concept in their ecosophy). As I will show, in this way they tend to undercut Næss's hope for a broad-based deep ecology movement, i.e., one not based on any particular ecosophy. Worse, Ecosophy S is deeply problematic from an ecofeminist philosophical perspective in a way in which Arne Næss's version of deep ecology, Ecosophy T, is or may not be.

As Plumwood has argued, the concept of identification, which plays such a crucial role in Ecosophy S, is intimately tied to the three notions of the identity, expansion, and transcendence of the self. One of the basic hypotheses included in Fox's version of Ecosophy S is that "The self is as comprehensive as the totality of our identifications." Or, more succinctly: "Our Self is that with which we identify." The norm of Ecosophy S, on Fox's reading, is a state of being in which one "sustains the widest (and deepest) possible *identification* and, hence, sense of meanings of self-in-Self, of identification Self." The "slipperiness" (Plumwood) of what is meant by *identification* of the self-in-Self is also a suggestion of what Jim Cheney calls "the neoStoicism of Ecosophy S."[13]

According to Cheney, the literature of American and Australian deep ecology is remarkably similar to the literature of the ancient Stoic sensibility:

> The veneration of the cosmos is the veneration of the whole of which man himself is a part. The recognition of and compliance with his position as a part is one aspect of man's proper relation to the universe in the conduct of his life. It is based on the interpretation of his existence in terms of the larger whole, whose very perfection consists in the integration of all its parts. In this sense man's cosmic piety *submits* his being to the requirements of what is better than himself and the source of all that is good. But at the same time man is not just a part like other parts making up the universe, but through the possession of a mind a part that enjoys *identity* with the *ruling principle* of the whole. Thus the other aspect of man's proper relation to the universe is that of *adequating* his own existence, confined as it is as a mere part, to the essence of the whole, of reproducing the latter in his own being through understanding and action. . . . In achieving this knowing relation, human reason assimilates itself to the kindred reason of the whole, thereby transcending the position of a mere part.[14]

Something very close to this constitutes the dominant image governing Ecosophy S. Yet this passage suggests endorsement of all three notions of the self which Plumwood correctly identifies and critiques: the indistinguishability self ("that enjoys *identity* with the *ruling principle* of the whole"), the expanded self (human existence is seen in "terms of the larger whole"), and the transcendental or transpersonal self ("human reason assimilates itself to the kindred reason of the whole, thereby transcending the position of a mere part"). Thus, these deep ecologists are asking us to submit to the modern equivalent of the divine *logos*—traditional transcendental, objective, impartial detached reason— to discern that logos at work in the ecosystem, and to identify with it.

Thus, on Cheney's account (with which I agree), Ecosophy S seems to be placed in that Stoic tradition which conceives of correct environmental practice as involving, in some fundamental way, an understanding of the cosmos and humanity's place in the wider scheme of things. The central concept of this approach is what is called by deep ecologists *ecological consciousness*. This is the notion that "the ideal state of being is one that sustains the widest (and deepest) possible *identification* and, hence, sense of Self."[15] Once again, the thought here is that the self (small s) expands to Self (capital S) as it incorporates more and more of nature through self-identification—understood minimally as transpersonal or transcendent self. To the extent that the notion of the genuine self as the transcendent self ought to be rejected, so too should versions of deep ecology associated with it.

Second, ecological consciousness figures into an understanding of "correct behavior" in the world by an empathetic or "expanded self" (to use Plumwood's terminology). As stated by Fox, supporters of Ecosophy S

> See correct behavior as a natural consequence of aligning ourselves with "the nature of reality and our place . . . in the larger scheme of things." And by "aligning" is not meant the following of certain rationally constructed rules so much as an "empathizing" of this vision of reality, i.e., an incorporation of it that goes beyond (as distinct from substituting for) intellectual assent. . . .[16]

Since, according to ecofeminist philosophy as I've construed it, the notion of the expanded self ought to be rejected, so should Fox's version of Ecosophy S.

A third problematic aspect of deep "ecological consciousness" is that it is closely connected to the totalizing vision of reality of Ecosophy S. Knowledge of the other at the "highest level of knowledge" is experienced as the "union that the mind has with the whole of Nature"[17] (on any of the three notions of the self explored by Plumwood). Ethics is the antinomian behavioral correlate of this epistemic union, what one naturally does once this "union" is experienced. There is no genuine ethics, metaphysics, or politics of *difference* here; the other is there, certainly, but colonized.

Ecofeminist Philosophy and Relational Selves

There is a superficial similarity between the deep ecological notion of selves achieved through identification and the notion of selves as constituted by relationships—relational selves. In this sense of "self," relationships are not something extrinsic to whom we are, not an "add-on" feature of human nature; they play an essential role in shaping what it is to be human. As Plumwood states, "that people's interests are relational does not imply a holistic view of them— that they are merged or indistinguishable."[18] The *self-in-relationships* or *relational self* avoids egoism and enables a recognition of interdependence without "falling into the problems of indistinguishability; it acknowledges both continuity [with nature] and difference; it breaks the culturally imposed false dichotomy of egoism and altruism of interests."[19] It provides an appropriate notion of self that can serve as a foundation for an ethic of connectedness, appropriate reciprocity, or justice-with-care for which I argue elsewhere.[20] It is an ethic where ego boundaries are important for a respect for the "otherness" of others, including nature. It is an ethic where, though I am a co-member of the ecological community shared by rocks, trees, and bison, I am, quite literally, not a rock, tree, or bison. I am, to use Næss's language, "an ecological self" but distinguishable from other particulars and species (e.g., bison) of ecological selves.

Arne Næss and Ecosophy T

Næss's hope in articulating the deep ecology platform is both to foster a solidarity movement based on a core set of more or less shared beliefs *and* to promote diversity among environmentalists. That is, his aim is to produce a "solidarity" movement rather than a "unity in sameness" movement in which adherence to a shared ecophilosophy (or, ecosophy) is required, or even desired. This is laudatory from an ecofeminist philosophical perspective. It also suggests, quite correctly, that there are significant differences between Næss, on the one hand, and his leading American and Australian followers, on the other. It has been an unfortunate feature of the literature to date that both proponents and critics tend to think of deep ecology as though it were a philosophically unified movement. I hope to help rectify this misperception here, since I applaud much of what I find in Næss's ecosophical position while remaining troubled by much of what we find in the ecosophical views of Fox, Sessions, and Devall, the deep ecology philosophers most visible to English-speaking philosophers.

Næss defines an *ecosophy* as "one's own personal code of values and a view of the world which guides one's own decisions" as "applied to questions involving ourselves and nature"[21]—*earth household wisdom.* An ecosophy "serve[s] as an individual's philosophical grounding for an acceptance of the principles or platform of deep ecology."[22] The importance of constructing for oneself a total view (ecosophy) looms large in Næss's book. However, Næss is equally insistent upon the partial arbitrariness concerning the choice of ultimate norms in one's system and prefers a vague or ambiguous articulation of norms and hypotheses allowing variant readings. Næss calls his own ecosophy Ecosophy T. His view is that there are many roads and differing sets of intuitions leading to advocacy of roughly the same deep ecological *platform.* Næss's concept of a total view is therefore as distant as may be from an absolutist position while still remaining non-subjectivist.

It is the empiricist bent of decision- and policy-makers which requires the articulation of total views in which value priorities are explicitly articulated within wider frameworks and not left dangling as subjective responses to the "facts." This is the respect in which those views must be and be seen as *contextual.* Næss insists on the close interconnection between norms and factual hypotheses and the importance for rational debate of articulating these. Such an articulation involves uncovering the "roots of valuations and total systems," including "deep psychological and social motivations as well as logically basic norms and hypotheses."[23] The justification of choices leads to "the elaboration of a philosophical system, a representation of the contextual associations between all aspects of our existence."[24] This is a striking position, for it brings together the notion of a *system* with Cheney's, Plumwood's, and my notion of *contextualism,* the notion that ethical decisions and evaluations emerge from the context or texture of one's life and the thought that is contextually embedded within that life ("contextual and systems thinking is to be emphasized throughout this work"[25]). This juxtaposition indicates why Næss does not aim for *one* system and why subtextual analysis, in addition to logical analysis, is important in understanding total systems. In this sense, Næss is an ecosophical pluralist.

Næss's advocacy of ecosophical pluralism is based on his view that "the value-laden, spontaneous and emotional realm of experience [is] as genuine a source of knowledge of reality as mathematical physics."[26] As such, his view is not prone to the sort of critique of deep ecology as presupposing traditional rationalism, which Plumwood correctly identifies with the deep ecology of Fox, Sessions, and Devall. Næss's emphasis on total views is not an attempt to forge a single descriptive/normative view to which any informed, rational person would adhere; rather, it is a result of his conviction that "the limitation of the shallow movement is . . . due to a lack of explicit concern with ultimate aims, goals, and norms."[27] His concern is not with the "correct" total view, but with the personal and political importance of *having*, and negotiating from, ecologically acceptable (because in accordance with the deep ecology platform) total views. Næss does offer us his personal ecosophy (Ecosophy T) but claims no more than coherence or consistency for it, and stresses that his "main goal . . . is to emphasize the responsibility of any integrated person to work out his or her reaction to contemporary environmental problems *on the basis of a total view.*"[28]

This could, of course, be understood as saying that a rational person is not simply to take an ecosophy on authority but to think it through for herself or himself, but this would be a mistake. Næss is a *pluralist* with respect to total views and holds that they are to be understood as tools, as syntheses of one's norms and hypotheses for the purpose of practical engagement with others on environmental issues. We might understand them as conceptual and practical *lenses* through which to see, describe, analyze, and act in the world.

Næss is aware of the importance of such an understanding of total views for solidarity movements involving people who would not agree upon particular details of total views, but who can nonetheless come together with respect to a common political platform. The total system which one articulates functions both to articulate one's personal worldview *and* as the personal medium for interpersonal exchange and discussion. Deep ecology platform statements function as mid-level statements where the total views of many *intersect*. It is not *sameness* achieved by identical intuitions and ecosophies which is critical, but the *solidarity* achieved by agreement to the values and beliefs expressed through the (deep ecological) platform.

Such a position makes good sense. The women's movement, for example, was severely criticized by black, Third World, and other women to the extent that it advertised itself as a movement based on experiences common to all women *as* women, or on a single analysis of the nature of women's oppression. Feminist pluralism, a solidarity movement based on shared opposition to sexism in all its forms, is much more promising, not only because it makes more political sense, but because it also makes more ethical and epistemological sense. The same can be said for Næss's advocacy of ecosophical pluralism—multiple ecosophies deriving from a wide diversity of cultural and experiential backgrounds, in relationship to the deep ecology *movement* based on the set of shared beliefs stated in the deep ecology platform. By validating the norms of others in this way, Næss opens the door to concerns of the Third World and others much more so than deep ecology in the United States has been perceived to do.

The acceptance and encouragement of ecosophical plurality, along with the stress on systematization of one's own view, is laudable. Nonetheless, what I find lacking in Næss's position is an explicit acknowledgment and fostering of the plurality of voices *within* (as well as *among*) individuals. Just as systematic clear thinking and discussion is possible between people with various ecosophies, so something analogous is possible within the (plural) individual—and desirable for very much of the same reasons as it is culturally desirable. It is very likely that Næss would agree: in personal communication to Rothenberg, Næss has said that "Actually there is a lot to say about too tightly integrated characters. Not enough room for inconsistencies, spontaneity, play. . . ."[29] For Næss, the task of ecophilosophy becomes the task of thinking through what one "actually wants, not simply as a personal matter, but in a social and ecospherical perspective. The question here is . . . one of clarification of attitudes, of "finding oneself," not in isolation, but in deep connection to all that surrounds."[30]

It is certainly consistent with Næss's Ecosophy T, that the concept of self-realization be understood not as involving the *identity, expansion,* or *transcendence* of the self, but rather as the notion, that the construction of an ethic is the construction of one's world, a world in relationship to which one *defines* one's self; or perhaps as the view that we define ourselves by means of the ethical orientations we take to the world and that our various self-realizations are a function of these defining relations to the world. Either way, this is what the notion of a *relational self* in ecofeminist philosophy attempts to get at.

This view is also clear if one looks at the starting point of Næss's development of Ecosophy T in the notion of *ecospheric belonging*[31] as developed in the view that "the identity of the individual . . . is developed through interaction with a broad manifold, both organic and inorganic."[32] This theme can be developed in a number of different directions, but Næss is clear that he wants a reading which does not abrogate individuality, although he acknowledges that "here is a difficult ridge to walk: To the left we have the ocean of organic and mystic views, to the right the abyss of atomic individualism."[33] He chooses to understand claims such as that "All living creatures are fundamentally one" and that plants and animals have a right to unfolding and self-realization as having *mythic* components, "associated . . . with the more or less mythic conception of a just or unjust order in the world."[34] He chooses that these notions not be analyzed in less mythic directions. At this point he leaves it at the thought that we participate in something greater than our individual and social careers. *Ecological consciousness* is understood here simply as "understanding and appreciating [one's] relations with all other life forms and to the earth as a whole."[35] It does not come attached with the identity, empathy or triumph-over theses identified above with Fox, Sessions, and Devall's deep ecology.

Næss's response to the difficulty that an equal right to live and blossom for all ways and forms of life provides no guideline in cases of conflict is to point out that this right is not an "unconditional isolatable norm to treat everything the same way," but, rather, that its behavioral implications can be derived only from the system of norms and hypotheses of which this right is but one component. "We might agree," he says, "upon rules such as will imply different behavior towards different kinds of living beings without negating that there is a value inherent in living beings which is *the same value* for all," that is, without implying that some things are "intrinsically more valuable than others."[36] He adopts, for example, a priority principle according to which "we have . . . greater obligation to that which is nearer to us"[37] and holds that "human beings are closer to us than animals."[38]

What should an ecofeminist philosopher say about the deep ecologist's commitment to the principle of "biocentric [or, biospheric] egalitarianism"—a mainstay of the deep ecology platform? On the one hand, many believe that the principle of biospherical egalitarianism is untenable within a theory, which hopes to resolve conflict. On the other hand, many believe that the principle is true. I suggest that we go between the horns of the dilemma and claim that Næss's addition of the qualifying phrase "in principle" is an important amendment to the principle. Suggesting that it is a prima facie principle both implies a respectful attitude toward all ways and forms of life and acknowledges the need to provide a way of ordering those ways and forms of life in cases of conflict. It's just that, from an ecofeminist philosophical point of view, that ordering may, in a given context, require that considerations of care or appropriate reciprocity or ecosystem "diversity, integrity, and beauty" (Leopold's land ethic) trump considerations of rights.

The concepts of *equality* and *rights* without the qualifying principle are indeed problematic. But the way to an ethical understanding of human–nonhuman natural relationships is *not* by holding the line with the notion of biospherical egalitarianism, but by recognizing the need to locate the proper realm of rights, e.g., when nonlitigous, nonmediated, nonconsensual decision-making is not the appropriate avenue for conflict resolution. An ecofeminist ethic is *contextual* partly because it recognizes that the nature of the *relationship,* and not just the nature of the *relator,* is important; rights attach primarily to relators, whereas *care* and *justice-through-care* and *appropriate reciprocity* and *friendship* attach primarily to relationships.

Conclusion

Utilizing the work of Val Plumwood and Jim Cheney, I have argued that there is a superficial similarity between the notions of an indistinguishable, expanded, or transpersonal self achieved through identification and the notion of defining relationships which, while acknowledging dependencies and bonds of care and responsibility, leave selves intact. However, the former notion leaves in place a fundamentally dualistic notion of the self, which is absent in the latter. Consequently, Ecosophy S defines itself in relation to a false dichotomy: we are either egoistically defined selves who are strangers to one another, or each self (in any of the three senses of "self") is (potentially, ideally) a gigantic Self inclusive of all the rest. Rightly rejecting the first alternative, Ecosophy S opts for a position which, in effect, tries (impossibly) to combine the notion of defining relations with a "safe" but alienating atomism. The concept of an indistinguishable, expanded, or transpersonal Self is what mediates the two (in fact, incompatible) notions. What makes the notion of an indistinguishable, expanded, or transpersonal Self ultimately alienating is the fact that the identification, which makes such a self is achieved by the empathic incorporation of a totalizing vision—true to the rationalist tradition. It is even questionable whether it is even possible to empathize in the required way.

A patriarchal conceptual framework makes otherness or difference a problem to be overcome, rather than a value to be celebrated and centralized in one's philosophy and politics. I think deep ecology, at least in the versions given by Fox, Sessions, and Devall, does this, and it does it largely because of its neostoicism (Cheney) and its umbilical attachment to the Western rationalist tradition of superior and dichotomous reason, separated from all that is bodily, matter, particular, personal, partial, connected, and interested (Plumwood). The failure of such deep ecological stances, then, is that ultimately they do not form a critique of Western rationalism (as they purport) or a sympathetic springboard for feminism (a feminism from which they initially purported to draw inspiration). This represents its own kind of "tragedy of the West."

Notes

[1] Fox, Sessions, and Devall would argue that there are important differences, philosophical in nature, between their own positions. For my purposes, however, the similarities I discuss do not rule out those differences. As such, I treat Fox, Sessions, and Devall as offering one type of position, which contrasts with that of Næss (despite and in addition to whatever internal differences there are among the particular versions offered by Fox, Sessions, and Devall).

[2] Næss, "The Shallow and the Deep Ecology Movement." Quotations in this and the next three paragraphs are from pages 95–98.

[3] See, e.g., Jim Cheney, "Eco-feminism and Deep Ecology," *Environmental Ethics* 9, 2 (1987): 115–145; Warwick Fox, "The Deep Ecology–Ecofeminism Debate and Its Parallels," *Environmental Ethics* 11, 1 (1989): 5–25; Ariel Kay Salleh, "Deeper than Deep Ecology: The Eco-Feminist Connection," *Environmental Ethics* 6, 4 (1984): 340–345; Robert Sessions, "Deep Ecology versus Ecofeminism: Healthy Differences or Incompatible Philosophies?" *Hypatia* 6, 1 (Spring 1991): 90–107; Deborah Slicer, "Your Daughter or Your Dog?" *Hypatia* 6, 1 (1991): 108–124; Michael Zimmerman, "Feminism, Deep Ecology and Environmental Ethics," *Environmental Ethics* 9, 1 (1987): 22–44.

[4] See Fox, "The Deep Ecology–Ecofeminism Debate."

[5] See Cheney, "Eco-Feminism;" Val Plumwood, "Nature, Self, and Gender: Feminism, Environmental Philosophy and the Critique of Rationalism," *Hypatia* 6, 1 (1991): 3–27; and Salleh, "Deeper than Deep."

[6] Fox, "The Deep Ecology–Ecofeminist Debate," in *Environmental Philosophy: From Animal Rights to Radical Ecology*, ed. Michael Zimmerman et al. (New York: Prentice Hall, 1993): 213–232.

[7] As Australian environmental philosopher Patsy Hallen commented on an earlier version of this chapter, we should not therefore dismiss the actions of *Earth First!* as unworthy or frivolous: They reflect the historical position of privilege of the actors, but an exercise of power and privilege which has, for instance in the case of *Earth First!*er Dave Foreman, contributed to habitat preservation and other important environmental causes.

[8] John Seed, Joanna Macy, Pat Fleming, and Arne Næss, *Thinking Like a Mountain: Towards a Council of All Beings* (Philadelphia and Santa Cruz: New Society Publishers, 1988): 36.

[9] Warwick Fox, "Approaching Deep Ecology: A Response to Richard Sylvan's Critique of Deep Ecology," *Environmental Studies Occasional Paper 20* (Hobart: University of Tasmania Center for Environmental Studies, 1986), 60; cited in Plumwood, "Nature, Self."

[10] Karen J. Warren, "The Power and the Promise of Ecological Feminism," *Environmental Ethics* 12, 2 (Summer 1990): 125–146.

[11] Warwick Fox, *Towards a Transpersonal Ecology: Developing New Foundations for Environmentalism* (Boston: Shambhala, 1990): 12; cited in Plumwood, "Nature, Self."

[12] Devall and Sessions, *Deep Ecology: Living as if Nature Mattered (Salt Lake City, 1985):* 225. See also Arne Næss, "Intuition, Intrinsic Value and Deep Ecology," *The Ecologist* 14 (1984): 201–202; Warwick Fox, "On Guiding Stars in Deep Ecology," *The Ecologist* 14 (1984): 203–204.

[13] Jim Cheney, "The Neo-Stoicism of Radical Environmentalism," *Environmental Ethics* 11, 4 (Winter 1989): 293–325.

[14] Cheney, "The Neo-Stoicism," 293-294, quoting from Hans Jonas, *The Gnostic Religion: The Message of the Alien God and the Beginnings of Christianity* (Boston: Beacon Press, 1963): 246–247.

[15] Fox, "Approaching Deep Ecology," 87.

[16] Fox, "Approaching Deep Ecology," 34; the internal quote is from Devall and Sessions, *Deep Ecology*, 69.

[17] George Sessions on Spinoza, in Devall and Sessions, *Deep Ecology*, 239.

[18] Plumwood, "Nature, Self," 20.

[19] Plumwood, "Nature, Self."

[20] Karen J. Warren, *Ecofeminism: A Philosophical Perspective on What it is and Why it Matters*, forthcoming).

[21] Warren, *Ecofeminism: A Philosophical Perspective*, 36.

[22] Warren, *Ecofeminism: A Philosophical Perspective*, 38.

[23] Næss, *Ecology, Community*, 44.

[24] Næss, *Ecology, Community*, 45.

[25] Næss, *Ecology, Community*, 38.

[26] Næss, *Ecology, Community*, 32.

[27] Næss, *Ecology, Community*, 33.

[28] Næss, *Ecology, Community*, 163.

[29] Næss, *Ecology, Community*, 14.

[30] Næss, *Ecology, Community*, 80.

[31] Næss, *Ecology, Community*, 168.

[32] Næss, *Ecology, Community*, 164.

[33] Næss, *Ecology, Community*, 165.

[34] Næss, *Ecology, Community*.

[35] Næss, *Ecology, Community*, 166.

[36] Næss, *Ecology, Community*, 168.

[37] Næss, *Ecology, Community*, 170.

[38] Næss, *Ecology, Community*, 171.

Chapter 33

The Ecofeminism versus Deep Ecology Debate

Arne Næss

1.

What follows is a set of comments by one ecofeminist about the articles by two others. Ariel Salleh argues in her article that "deep ecology is held back from maturation as a Green philosophy by its lack of a fully rounded political critique. To this end, I urge adherents of deep ecology to become more reflexively aware of the sociohistorical grounding of their discourse." And further: "Deep ecologists do not recognize that women have not been consulted about their interests in this system of social relations. Just as the environment is damaged by 'development,' women's lives are vitiated by men's systematic appropriation of their energies and time. Writing by Brinda Rao in India, Berit Ås in Norway, and Barbara Ehrenreich in the United States provides ample documentation of this appropriation."

I shall not go into Ariel Salleh's criticism of some of the deep ecology theorists who write approvingly about ecofeminism: she misunderstands some of their points, I think.

There are today a variety of important social movements. The peace movement, the ecological movement, and a set of others which may roughly be called the social justice movement. One of them is the feminist movement. It is increasingly clear that their goals overlap: Certainly the objectives of the ecological movement cannot be reached without significant victories for the peace movements. The interdependence of them does not eliminate their differences: We cannot be activists in all of them. We must choose. Support all, but work mainly in one.

As far as I can see, there is no incompatibility between the goals of feminism and those of deep ecology. Of course, this kind of compatibility and even cooperation does not imply the agreement of every deep ecology supporter with every feminist. If we characterize the deep ecology movement by means of the 8 points, then there is no incompatibility. In my own ecosophy T, the notion of self-realization potential is central. Today, as one hundred years ago, the self-realization potential of women is restrained, sometimes even "crushed." Under patriarchal conditions, the potential of females has been largely defined by men. Today, to the consternation of many, both men and women invade areas of activity where they were generally supposed to have no potentials (i.e., competence). Nevertheless the exploitation of women as "sexual, reproductive and labor resource" remains a problem in most corners of the world. This state of affairs is, according to Salleh, "glossed over in the deep ecological agenda."

But, for instance, Ecosophy T reserves a prominent place for ecofeminism. It does not show on the diagram in this book, but ecofeminism is a direct consequence of the three norms marked in the diagram: "Maximize self-determination!," "No exploitation!," "No subjection!" The norms are derived from the basic norm and three hypotheses of the kind "Exploitation reduces self-realization potentialities." Men cannot determine which potentials the females have. They must try it out themselves. In short, feminism belongs within the deep ecology movement, but formal ecofeminists are expected to develop the theme properly. As a supporter of the enterprise I reckon myself as an ecofeminist.

In direct ecological actions, where hundreds of men and women cooperate, it is still mainly the women who clearly display caring attitudes. An unforgettable scene: a Sami girl chained with others to a rock, remarked when a small army of police approached the protesters: "They (the police) are not wearing proper gloves!" It disturbed her that the authorities had not furnished the policemen with gloves sufficiently warm to cope with the arctic temperature.

It is difficult to imagine a man having such a spontaneous reaction. Not only did she note the inappropriate gloves; she expressed her concern in front of others!

I am glad to say that, at least on one point, Salleh's mind can be put at rest. She says that "ecofeminists of a socialist persuasion are disturbed to hear the father of deep ecology, Arne Næss, claim that 'total egalitarianism is impossible,' that some human exploitation will always be 'necessary.'" Firstly, I regret having used the term "egalitarianism." Secondly, I regret that I did not make it sufficiently clear that I meant the relation of humans to nonhumans. I do not see the elimination of human exploitation as an impossible task. But clearly (and here Salleh will probably agree), there is a long way to go.

Nothing whatever hinders supporters of the deep ecology movement from joining "women's struggle against the instrumental rationality and dehumanizing commodity culture that comes with industrial production." Though it is unacceptable to envision a future green society as "industrial," I suppose every, or nearly every, kind of green society will have some industrial production.

It is lamentable that among deep ecology theorists there are so few who are able to write extensively from within the areas of social and political theory. Such a state of affairs is neither motivated by chance nor by necessity. But Green political theorists (note the capital G!) and Green economists are doing an excellent job.

Some have socialist leanings, others do not—but none have very much good to say about past socialist or capitalist ecological policies.

2.

To respond to Karen Warren is a pleasant undertaking because she interprets me with great care and on the basis of close study. Let me first mention some small differences between my and Warren's characterization of the deep ecology movement.

Supporters of the deep ecology movement reject what I presume she means by an "atomistic" view of nature. Their views are compatible with many kinds and degrees of holism. But these views, however, are incompatible with the kind of holism which obliterates individuality, particularly that of persons and single specimens of any species. There can be no room for "triumphing over [the] personal or individual self." With extended and deepened care, some kinds of ecocentric carelessness can be overcome, but I would not want to think in terms of a triumph. To widen and deepen does not mean to destroy. And emotions are always personal, derived from sensitivity and attached to particular concerns. When Warwick Fox professes to feel as a leaf on the tree of life, he embraces a stronger or more radical form of holism than I do. I assume that, as long as the intrinsic value of each living being is respected, such radical kinds of holism may be compatible with support for the deep ecology movement.

I am in favor of letting point 1 of the 8 points refer only to individuals: "Every living being has intrinsic value." Point 2 will then concern richness and diversity. My strong emphasis on individuals is inherent in the distinction between *importance* and intrinsic value. Ecosystemic features may be of overwhelming importance for individuals without thereby acquiring inherent value. Water is of overwhelming importance to humans—and to fish—but I do not do anything strictly for water's own sake. What Warren calls "naturism" is, I assume an extreme point of view incompatible with the deep ecology movement. Some supporters of the deep ecology movement tend to talk *as if* everything "natural" was good, or argue that humans should always let "nature" guide their behavior. But surely they do not consider that humans should never interfere with an ecosystem, such as "brutally" changing it in order to satisfy vital needs (e.g., by letting a pond dry up, or by destroying a nest of ants in a kitchen). "Nature knows best" is an excellent slogan, but not a thesis. Supporters feel they neither dominate, nor are dominated by nature. They look forward to a future society which will make it easier to avoid behavior which involves domination in complete generality.

When the police in the course of a confrontation asked a Sami who was trying to protect a river from hydroelectric developments why he was there, he answered: "The river is part of myself." He did not say: "I am part of the river." There are many utterances of a similar kind, which reveal what I consider to be deep ecology attitudes. They do not imply domination.

I agree with Warren that a widening and deepening of the self does not imply domination, but rather a widening and deepening of the web of relational entities. According to people who are engaged, or have been engaged, in the highly admirable Chipko movement in India, it has had and still has (activist) supporters who are pragmatically motivated and supporters who are motivated by a philosophy of life, very much like the supporters of the deep ecology movement.

It was not difficult for Gandhi to make very poor people respect living beings in general, including even those poisonous snakes which sometimes entered the rooms of the "ashrams." This regard for all living beings in some places in India may, or may not, be consistent with what Warren writes about the Chipko movement: "When women of the Chipko movement initiated the 'tree-hugging movement,' this was not an act of civil disobedience motivated by deep ecological concerns; it was a nonviolent, grassroots act of women protecting the forests in which they lived and on which they depended for their very survival. It is that women-gender-identified connection with trees which ecofeminist philosophy is inspired to capture and explain. And such activities are not done from 'save the pristine wilderness' motivations." In India, as elsewhere, we find mixed pragmatic and religious motivations.

Warren believes that "If patriarchy would be eliminated, then, by my account . . . so would all the other 'isms of domination' (including 'naturism') *because* patriarchy must be reconceived as connected with all these other 'isms of domination' through the logic of domination. If patriarchy is eliminated, so is the logic of domination."

For me, it is difficult to believe that the elimination of patriarchy would have such heterogeneous consequences, but I certainly do *wish* such elimination. And such a wish leads me and others to support every attempt to get rid of patriarchy. Since Warren acknowledges the plurality of forms of ecofeminist philosophy, I imagine my doubt about the elimination of *all* "isms of domination" will not exclude me.

"At least a certain version of deep ecology is 'masculinist' and does presuppose some of the very patriarchal assumptions ecofeminist philosophy is bent on exposing and dismantling," Warren writes. It is likely that among the views of the 15–20 theorists of deep ecology, many are in undeniable conflict with some aspects of Warren's ecofeminist philosophy. It may also be the case that her own interpretation of their views (especially those of the three theorists of the deep ecology movement: Sessions, Fox, and Devall) makes the conflict more pronounced than it needs to be. This does not prevent me from endorsing and encouraging her activism.

In short, male supporters of the deep ecology movement should be grateful to Warren since she sees "masculinist" ways of thinking or talking, to which they may themselves be blind. In no way, however, do I think that any supporter would wish to perpetuate male privileges and ways of domination. The deep ecological message is simple. More care is needed: extended care for nonhumans and deepened care for humans.

Chapter 34

The Ecofeminism–Deep Ecology Dialogue: A Short Commentary on the Exchange between Karen Warren and Arne Næss

Patsy Hallen

Beginning with the Personal

On my desk is a postcard of a woman in local national costume playing the lure (a type of horn) atop a boulder in the mountains of Norway. It looks as if she is trumpeting a vital message to the world. Arne Næss sent it to me when my first article on ecofeminism appeared in *The Trumpeter*.[1] On the front of the card Arne has written me in as the horn-blower with himself as an affirming listener on a mountain peak across the valley and my message as: "Come, Feminist Science!" On the reverse side of the post card, Arne scrawled these words: "Dear Patsy, at last I see your monumental article in print! My heart gets rid of a heavy burden. I hope the article will be reprinted in many [more] majestic journals. (Today a day of big words, but I mean them.) Arne."

I have kept that postcard these ten years because I was touched by it. In 1986 Arne had visited Australia to give a guest lecture at Murdoch University where I teach. I had helped to arrange his visit and so Arne had stayed at our home, for several weeks, as it turned out. He was excellent company and I learned many important things from living with him. One day he asked to read my writing. He told me he liked what I wrote. He said it had passion. He encouraged me to publish (until then I had only written for my students). When I explained why I wasn't keen (too much noise, not enough silence; the often stultifying format of academic publications; the dominance of careerism, combativeness, and ego; and did I have anything original to say?), he gently told me that people could learn from my articles.

I open with this story because it demonstrates Arne Næss' support for eco-feminism. His lifelong commitment to skepticism prohibits any dogmatic position (such as claiming that Deep Ecology is the definitive posture) and his intellectual style is playful and iconoclastic. For this good reason (among others, such as his keen encouragement of diversity), Arne escapes the ire of many ecofeminist commentators who critique deep ecology,[2] while other theorists of deep ecology such as the transpersonal ecologist, Warwick Fox, cop much more flak.[3]

In 1995, Karen Warren was invited to be the ecofeminist visiting scholar at Murdoch University (for which I had obtained a grant) and she spent six months in Australia, teaching a very successful course in ecofeminism, running seminars for staff on critical thinking, presenting papers and videos regarding her work on philosophy for children, and giving electrifying public lectures. As the contribution by Karen testifies, her knowledge of deep ecology is scholarly, her evaluation is informed and her goal is to encourage dialogue.

Checklist against Possible Blind Spots

I would like to introduce the illuminating exchange between Karen Warren and Arne Næss by attempting to summarize the various criticism theorists of each position have made of the other.[4] This may help us to face up to some of the disagreement between ecofeminists and deep ecologists and thus may serve to strengthen each movement. It is my view that deep ecology and ecofeminism can complement each other. So we should seek to discover what they could learn from each other.

Both deep ecology and ecofeminism are complex philosophies with a significant number of contributors, each of whom has their own, often developing, position. Each movement has a malleable identity. Thus many of the criticisms which I list may not apply to the majority of the proponents. In addition, each movement has altered and improved as a consequence of such discussions, so a comforting number of the flaws which I mention no longer apply. Nonetheless, I hope to have provided a checklist of past and potential blind spots.

Ecofeminist Criticisms of Deep Ecology Theorists

First of all, I should like to clearly distinguish between the supporters of deep ecology and the theorists of deep ecology. Thus, for the purpose of this article, when I use the term deep ecology, I mean the *theorists* of deep ecology (who are relatively few) and not the *supporters* of deep ecology movement (who are numerous and varied, from indigenous nomads to sedentary city dwellers).

I summarize ecofeminists' critique of deep ecology thus:

1. Deep ecology theorists do not recognize, value, or connect in significant ways with feminism, even though the two areas have many insights and aspirations in common. They have tended to overlook the contribution feminist theory can make to radical green theory. Even when they have addressed ecofeminism, they have had a propensity to focus on the male commentators, such as Zimmerman, and to overlook the primary ecofeminist sources. (Versions of this criticism are voiced by Slicer, Salleh, Warren, Plumwood, and Mathews among others). They also tend to conflate one version of ecofeminism with the whole movement.

2. Deep ecology does not explicitly undertake a gender analysis and, because of the ruling ideology, to be "gender neutral" is, in fact, to be gender biased. (Warren, Hallen, Plumwood.)

3. Deep ecology does not sufficiently integrate theories of gender, race and class oppression with that of the domination of nature. (Salleh, Plumwood, Warren.)

4. Deep ecology tends to be foundationalist, to view anthropocentrism as the primary form of domination and to regard deep ecology as an umbrella for ecofeminism. It thus does not see clearly enough the links between the various forms of domination, such as the domination of woman and the domination of nature. (Warren, Slicer, et. al.)

5. Deep ecology focuses on the human/nature dualism whereas ecofeminists identify that as just one instance of a more pervasive dualistic pattern of thought. According to feminist analysis, dualism is the principal ideological strategy of patriarchy, yet deep ecologists do not refer to this. (Plumwood, Mathews, King, Griffin.)

6. Deep ecology's analysis of human population pressure does not pay adequate attention to women's lack of power to control their own reproductive processes. (Shiva, et. al.)

7. In its focus on identification, interconnectedness, and the overcoming of separation, it fails to adequately affirm difference and hence inadvertently participates in the colonizing self. (Plumwood, Warren, Cheney.)

8. Deep ecology does not critically analyze the self as it is given in patriarchal culture and so it smuggles in a masculine, white, middle class persona as the norm. (Warren, Plumwood, et. al.)

9. Deep ecology also tends to vacillate between different accounts of the self: indistinguishability, expansion of self, and transcendence of self. (Plumwood.)

10. Some theorists of deep ecology are not equipped with an adequate political understanding. Their notions of identification tend to emphasize personal transformation and to ignore social structures and political realities. (Plumwood.)

11. Deep ecology does not deconstruct reason and the rationalist tradition and so continues inadvertently to participate in a culture of denial and oppression, which is unable to acknowledge dependency on nature. (Plumwood.)

12. Some versions of deep ecology theory devalue particular ties and inferiorize specific attachments. It therefore tends to avoid the personal as a trap rather than an entry point (not relational but isolationist). (Mathews, Plumwood, Warren, et. al.)

13. Deep ecology tends to be stuck at an abstract and cognitive level; it is the product of an alienated consciousness and thus the self it seeks to identify with the rest of nature is disconnected. (Salleh, et. al.)

14. Deep ecology tends to be disembodied and not in touch with the labor required to produce, reproduce, and sustain life. (Salleh.)

15. Deep ecology tends to be too cosmic and to retreat to a neo-stoical ivory tower, beyond human tragedy. (Cheney.)

16. In its grand theory making and its sweeping metavision of cosmic self-realization, deep ecology leaves out the individual, compassion, and an ethic of kinship and care. (Mathews.)

17. Deep ecology theorists tend to flee to wild pristine places devoid of people and their painful entanglements. (Plumwood, Cheney, et. al.)

18. Deep ecology's concepts of wilderness might write out indigenous peoples whose lives and cultures are imprinted on the land. (Plumwood, et. al.)

Criticisms of Ecofeminism

Several criticisms of ecofeminism have been offered:

1. The term "woman" is not sufficiently deconstructed by some ecofeminists so that the experience of white, middle class feminists becomes the norm. (Zimmerman et. al.)

2. In its early forms, ecofeminism had a tendency to essentialism implying that women by nature are better nurturers. (Fox, Zimmerman, Warren, Hallen, et. al.)

3. In its preoccupation with social justice issues, ecofeminists can background the natural world. (Hallen.)

4. Some ecofeminists employ feminized images of the earth and they run the danger of reinforcing rather than challenging the patriarchal visions of the all-forgiving mother; such earth imagery must be consciously politicized (Garb, Curtin) and so must earth-based spiritualities. (Spretnak, Warren.)

5. Ecofeminists may not always problematize the sex–gender distinction. While such a distinction provides an irreplaceable tool of analysis, it is impossible to disentangle the nature-nurture nexus. (Hallen.)

6. Ecofeminism tends to privilege some women's accounts of the world. (Lahar, Mellor, Bagby, et. al.)

7. Some versions of ecofeminism are preoccupied with lifestyle issues while economic oppression and environmental vandalism continue. (Salleh.)

8. In searching for the causes of the ideology of domination, ecofeminism may posit oversimplified or idealized accounts of matrilineal and matrifocal societies. (Eckersley, Mies, et. al.)
9. It can tend to make patriarchy responsible for all the domineering and destructive agendas. (Zimmerman, Næss.)
10. It may not problematize sufficiently the twin dominations of woman and nature. (Eckersley, Plumwood, et. al.)
11. Ecofeminism can tend to dump at the door of deep ecology the ills of patriarchy. (Hallen.)

Why So Many?

In devising these lists, I realized that I had gathered more criticisms of deep ecology than of ecofeminism. Was I being unfair? This troubled me, as I believe both positions are necessary and complementary. So I looked for explanations other than my bias. Here goes:

Ecofeminism has developed partly in response to deep ecology and as a direct consequence of criticizing it, so it would make sense if it managed to avoid a few of the pitfalls of deep ecology. Furthermore, feminism, as a radical position, is keenly aware of the inbuilt and often concealed presuppositions of the dominant paradigm; so ecofeminism might be inherently more self-critical (e.g., some of the criticisms of ecofeminism are by ecofeminists). Ecofeminism also has strong links with "third-world" women and with postcolonial theory, so its range of opinions might be greater and it should be sensitized to the issues of oppression and colonization, homogenization and the denial of difference. Finally, deep ecology is more easily identified with patriarchy and its attendant disfunctionalities, because (at least superficially) its origins are white, male, middle class, and "first" world.

Responsive Revisioning

It is important to note two things: (1) that none of these criticisms affects the core concept of either deep ecology or ecofeminism; and (2) that if each philosophy avoids these potential pitfalls, each will be strengthened as a consequence.

The ecofeminist critique of the deep ecologist theorists does not undermine in any way the core concepts of the intrinsic value of life forms and the claim that humans have no right to reduce the richness and diversity of nature except to satisfy vital needs. Likewise, deep ecology does not fundamentally challenge the highest common factor uniting ecofeminists, namely the position that there are significant connections (historical, symbolic, empirical, conceptual, linguistic, literary, ethical, and experiential) between the domination of women (and other marginalized groups) and the unjustified domination of nature, and that failure to address these connections will contribute to worsening of social and environmental conditions.

Moreover, if the theorists of deep ecology do seriously take up the numerous challenges offered by ecofeminists (such as a gender analysis related to class, race, and culture and critical attention to notions of the self reproductive labor, reason, dualistic thinking, and wilderness), I am confident that the theory of deep ecology will be enriched. Likewise if ecofeminism, in response to its criticisms, views patriarchy as part of a larger and more complex structure, recognizes the links between women and other sub-dominant peoples, perpetually problematizes its standpoint and foregrounds wild nature, then it, too, will be theoretically stronger.

Wholesome Exchanges

"The true," declares Hegel, "is the whole."[5] This sounds like a tautology, as informative as "in the night, all crocodiles (whether salties and human-eating or freshies and fish-eating) are black." But, contrary to first impressions, it is illuminating. For it indicates that truth is alive and dynamic. Truth is organic, each aspect related to every other, each part false in isolation. This process view of truth ensures conceptual humility. It also means that everything must be mediated by difference if it is to have integrity. Truth, for Hegel, is the integration of "antagonistic claims grown mutually implicative."[6]

As a result of the exchange between Karen Warren and Arne Næss, we are closer to the view that truth depends for its coherent integrity upon a series of incomplete and initially incompatible claims. I believe we are closer to the truth.

Notes

[1] Patsy Hallen, "Making Peace With Nature: Why Ecology Needs Feminism," *The Trumpeter* 4 (1987).

[2] See, for example, Karen Warren, "Feminism and Ecology: Making Connections" *Environmental Ethics* 9 (1987): 3–20, in Val Plumwood, *Feminism and the Mastery of Nature* (London: Routledge, 1993): 180.

[3] See, for example Deborah Slicer's article "Is There an Ecofeminism–Deep Ecology Debate?" *Environmental Ethics* 17 (1995): 151–169, where she undertakes a six point critique of Warwick Fox's 1989 article.

[4] See Jim Cheney, "The Neo-Stoicism of Radical Environmentalism," *Environmental Ethics* 11 (1989): 293–325. Deane Curtin, "Toward an Ecological Ethic of Care," from *Hypatia* special issue: Ecological Feminism, 1991, Vol. 6, No. 1. pp. 60–74. Robin Eckersley, *Environmentalism and Political Theory: Toward an Ecocentric Approach* (New York: State University of New York Press, 1992). Warwick Fox, "The Deep Ecology–Ecofeminism Debate and its Parallels," *Environmental Ethics* 11 (1989): 5–25. Stephane Lahar, "Ecofeminist Theory and Grassroots Politics," *Hypatia* 6 (1991): 28–45. Freya Mathews," Relating to Nature," *The Trumpeter* 11 (1994): 159–166. Freya Mathews, *The Ecological Self* (London: Routledge, 1991). Maria Mies and Vandana Shiva, *Ecofeminism* (Melbourne: Spinifex, 1993). Val Plumwood, *Feminism and the Mastery of Nature* (London: Routledge, 1993). Ariel Kay Salleh, "Deeper than Deep

Ecology: The Ecofeminist Connection," from *Environmental Ethics* 6 (1984): 339–345. Salleh, "The Ecofeminism/Deep Ecology Debate: A Reply to Patriarchal Reason," *Environmental Ethics* 14 (1992): 195–216. Salleh, "Class, Race and Gender Discourse in the Ecofeminism/Deep Ecology Debate," *Environmental Ethics* 15 (1993): 225–244. Vandana Shiva, *Staying Alive: Women, Ecology and Development*, (London: Zed Books, 1989). Deborah Slicer, "Is There an Ecofeminism–Deep Ecology Debate?" *Environmental Ethics* 17 (1995): 151–169. Charline Spretnak, *States of Grace* (San Francisco: Harper Collins, 1991). Karen Warren, "Feminism and Ecology: Making Connections," *Environmental Ethics* 9 (1987): 3–20. Warren, "The Power and the Promise of Ecological Feminism," *Environmental Ethics* 12 (1990): 125–146. Warren, *Quilting Ecological Feminism*, Westview Press, forthcoming. Michael Zimmerman, "Feminism, Deep Ecology and Environmental Ethics," *Environmental Ethics* 9 (1987): 21–44.

[5] G. W. F. Hegel, *The Phenomenology of Mind*, Preface, translated by Walter Kaufmann (New York: Doubleday, 1966), 28.

[6] G. W. F. Hegel, *The Science of Logic*, translated by A. V. Miller (London: Allen and Unwin, Ltd., 1964), 159.

Chapter 35

Social Ecology versus Deep Ecology: A Challenge for the Ecology Movement

Murray Bookchin

The environmental movement has traveled a long way beyond those annual "Earth Day" festivals when millions of school kids were ritualistically mobilized to clean up streets and their parents were scolded by Arthur Godfrey, Barry Commoner, Paul Ehrlich, and a bouquet of manipulative legislators for littering the landscape with cans, newspapers, and bottles.

The movement has gone beyond a naive belief that patchwork reforms and solemn vows by EPA bureaucrats to act more resolutely will seriously arrest the insane pace at which we are tearing down the planet.

This shopworn "Earth Day" approach toward "engineering" nature so that we can ravage the earth with minimal effects on ourselves—an approach that I called "environmentalism" in the late 1960s in contrast to social ecology—has shown signs of giving way to a more searching and radical mentality. Today, the new word in vogue is "ecology"—be it "deep ecology," "human ecology," "biocentric ecology," "antihumanist ecology," or, to use a term that is uniquely rich in meaning, "*social* ecology."

Happily, the new relevance of the word "ecology" reveals a growing dissatisfaction among thinking people with attempts to use our vast ecological problems for cheaply spectacular and politically manipulative ends. As our forests disappear due to mindless cutting and increasing acid rain, as the ozone layer thins out because of the widespread use of fluorocarbons, as toxic dumps multiply all over the planet, as highly dangerous, often radioactive pollutants enter into our air, water, and food chains—all, and innumerable hazards that threaten the integrity of life itself, raise far more basic issues than any that can be resolved by "Earth Day" cleanups and faint-hearted changes in existing environmental laws.

For good reason, more and more people are trying to go beyond the vapid environmentalism of the early 1970s and develop a more fundamental, indeed, a more radical, approach to the ecological crises that beleaguer us. They are looking for an *ecological* approach: one that is rooted in an ecological philosophy, ethics, sensibility, image of nature, and, ultimately, an ecological movement that will transform our domineering market society into a non-hierarchical cooperative society—a society that will live in harmony with nature because its members live in harmony with each other.

They are beginning to sense that there is a tie-in between the way people deal with each other, the way they behave as social beings—men with women, old with young, rich with poor, white with people of color, First World with Third, elites with "masses"—and the way they deal with nature.

The question that now faces us is: what do we really mean by an *ecological* approach? What is a coherent ecological philosophy, ethics, and movement? How can the answers to these questions and many others fit together so that they form a meaningful and creative whole?

Just as the earlier environmental movement was filled with well-meaning people, riddled by "spokesmen" like Arthur Godfrey and his kind who sold detergents over television while driving "environmentally" sound electric cars, so today the newly emerging ecological movement is filled with well-meaning people who are riddled by a new brand of "spokesmen," individuals who are selling their own wares—usually academic and personal careers.

If we are not to repeat all the mistakes of the early 1970s with their hoopla about "population control," their latent anti-feminism, their elitism, their arrogance, and their ugly authoritarian tendencies, so we must honestly and seriously appraise the new tendencies that today go under the name of one or another form of "ecology."

Two Conflicting Tendencies

Let us agree from the outset that the word "ecology" is no magic term that unlocks the real secret of our abuse of nature. It is a word that can be as easily abused, distorted, and tainted as words like "democracy" and "freedom."

Nor does the word "ecology" put us all—whoever "we" may be—in the same boat against environmentalists who are simply trying to make a rotten society work by dressing it in green leaves and colorful flowers, while ignoring the deep-seated *roots* of our ecological problems. It is time to honestly face the fact that there are differences within the so-called "ecology movement" of the present time that are as serious as those between the "environmentalism" and "ecologism" of the early 1970s. There are barely disguised racists, survivalists, macho Daniel Boones, and outright social reactionaries who use the word "ecology" to express their views, just as there are deeply concerned naturalists, communitarians, social radicals, and feminists who use the word "ecology" to express their own views.

The differences between these two tendencies in the so-called "ecology movement" consist not only in quarrels with regard to theory, sensibility, and ethics. They have far-reaching *practical* and *political* consequences. They consist not only in the way we view nature, or that vague word "Humanity," or even what we mean by the word "ecology:" they also concern how we propose to *change* society and by what *means*.

The greatest differences that are emerging within the so-called "ecology movement" of our day are between a vague, formless, often self-contradictory and invertebrate thing called "deep ecology" and a long-developing, coherent, and socially oriented body of ideas that can best be called "social ecology." "Deep ecology" has parachuted into our midst quite recently from the Sunbelt's bizarre mix of Hollywood and Disneyland, spiced with homilies from Taoism, Buddhism, spiritualism, reborn Christianity, and, in some cases, eco-fascism, while "social ecology" draws its inspiration from such outstanding radical decentralist thinkers like Peter Kropotkin, William Morris, and Paul Goodman among many others who have advanced a serious challenge to the present society with its vast hierarchical, sexist, class-ruled, statist apparatus and militaristic history.

Let us face these differences bluntly: "Deep ecology," despite all its social rhetoric, has virtually no real sense that our ecological problems have their ultimate roots in society and in social problems. It preaches a gospel of a kind of "original sin" that accurses a vague species called "Humanity"—as though people of color are equatable with whites, women with men, the Third World with the First, the poor with the rich, the exploited with their exploiters.

This vague undifferentiated "Humanity" is essentially seen as an ugly "anthropocentric" thing—presumably, a malignant product of natural evolution—that is "overpopulating" the planet, "devouring" its resources, destroying its wildlife and the biosphere—this, as though some vague domain called "Nature" stands opposed to a constellation of nonnatural things called "Human Beings" with their "Technology," "Minds," "Society," etc. "Deep ecology," formulated largely by privileged male white academics, has managed to bring sincere naturalists like Paul Shepard into the same company with patently antihumanist and macho mountain-men like David Foreman of *"Earth First!"* who preach a gospel that "Humanity" is some kind of cancer in the world of life.

It is easy to forget that it was out of this kind of crude eco-brutalism that a Hitler, in the name of "population control," with a racial orientation, fashioned theories of blood and soil that led to the transport of millions of people to murder camps like Auschwitz. The same eco-brutalism now reappears a half-century later among self-professed "deep ecologists" who believe that Third World peoples should be permitted to starve to death and desperate Indian immigrants from Latin America should be excluded by the border cops from the United States lest they burden "our" ecological resources.

This eco-brutalism does not come out of Hitler's *Mein Kampf*. It appeared in *Simply Living*, an Australian periodical, as part of a laudatory interview of David Foreman by Professor Bill Devall, who co-authored *Deep Ecology* with Professor George Sessions, the authorized manifesto of the "deep ecology" movement. Foreman, who exuberantly expressed his commitment to "deep ecology," was to frankly inform Devall that "When I tell people how the worst thing we could do in Ethiopia is to give aid—the best thing would be to just let nature seek its own balance, to let the people there just starve—they think this is monstrous. . . . Likewise, letting the United States be an overflow valve for problems in Latin America is not solving a thing. It's just putting more pressure on the resources we have in the United States."

One can reasonably ask such compelling questions like what does it mean for "nature to seek its own balance" in a part of the world where agribusiness, colonialism, and exploitation have ravaged a once culturally and ecologically stable area like East Africa. Or who is this all-American "our" that owns the "resources we have in the United States?" Are they the ordinary people who are driven by sheer need to cut timber, mine ores, and operate nuclear power plants? Or are they the giant corporations that are wrecking not only the good old United States but have produced the main problems these days in Latin America that send largely Indian folk across the Rio Grande? As an ex-Washington lobbyist and political huckster, David Foreman need not be expected to answer these subtle questions in a radical way. But what is truly surprising is the reaction—more precisely, the *lack* of any reaction—which marked Professor Devall's behavior. Indeed, the interview was notable for the laudatory, almost reverential, introduction and description Devall prepared in his description of Foreman.

What is "Deep Ecology?"

"Deep ecology" is so much of a "black hole" of half-digested, ill-formed, and half-baked ideas that one can easily express utterly vicious notions like Foreman's and still sound like a fiery radical who challenges everything that is anti-ecological in the present realm of ideas.

The very words "deep ecology," in fact, clue us into the fact that we are not dealing with a body of clear ideas but with a bottomless pit in which vague notions and moods of all kinds can be sucked into the depths of an ideological toxic dump.

Does it make sense, for example, to counterpoise "deep ecology" with "superficial ecology" as though the word "ecology" were applicable to *everything* that involves environmental issues? Given this mindless use of "ecology" to describe anything of a biospheric nature, does it not completely degrade the rich meaning of the word "ecology" to append words like "shallow" and "deep" to it—adjectives that may be more applicable to gauging the "depth" of a cesspool rather than the "depth" of ideas? Arne Næss, the pontiff of "deep ecology," who inflicted this vocabulary upon us, together with George Sessions and Bill Devall who have been marketing it out of Ecotopia, have taken a pregnant word—ecology—and deprived it of any inner meaning and integrity by designating the most pedestrian environmentalists as "ecologists," albeit "shallow" ones, in contrast to their notion of "deep."

This is not an example of mere wordplay. It tells us something about the "mindset" that exists among these "deep" thinkers. To parody the word "shallow" and "deep ecology" is to show not only the absurdity of this vocabulary but to reveal the superficiality of its inventors. Is there perhaps a "deeper ecology" than "deep ecology?" What is the "deepest ecology" of all that gives "ecology" its full due as a philosophy, sensibility, ethics, and movement for social change?

This kind of absurdity tells us more than we realize about the confusion Næss–Sessions–Devall, not to speak of eco-brutalists like Foreman, have introduced into the current ecology movement as it began to grow beyond the earlier environmental movement of the 1970s. Indeed, the Næss–Sessions–Devall trio rely very heavily upon the ease with which people forget the history of the ecology movement. The way in which the same wheel is re-invented every few years by newly arrived individuals who, well-meaning as they may be, often accept a crude version of highly developed ideas that appeared earlier in time. At best, these crudities merely echo in very unfinished form a corpus of views, which were once presented in a richer context and within a different tradition. At worst, they shatter such contexts and traditions, picking out tasty pieces that become utterly distorted when they re-appear in an utterly alien framework. No regard is paid by such "deep thinkers" to the fact that the new context in which an idea is placed may utterly change the meaning of the idea itself. German "National Socialism," which came to power in the Third Reich in 1933, was militantly "anti-capitalist" and won many of its adherents from the German Social-Democratic and Communist parties because of its anti-capitalist denunciations. But its "anti-capitalism" was placed in a strongly racist, imperialist, and seemingly "naturalist" context which extolled wilderness, sociobiology (the word had yet to be invented) but its "morality of the gene," to use E. O. Wilson's delicious expression, and its emphasis on "racial memory" to resort to William Irwin Thompson's Jungian expression, and anti-rationalism—these are all features one finds in latent or explicit form in Sessions' and Devall's *Deep Ecology*.[1]

Note well that neither Næss, Sessions, nor Devall have written a single line about decentralization, a nonhierarchical society, democracy, small-scale communities, local autonomy, mutual aid, communalism, and tolerance that was not worked out in painstaking detail and brilliantly contextualized into a unified and coherent outlook by Peter Kropotkin a century ago and his admirers from the 1930s to the 1960s in our own time. Great movements in Europe and an immense literature followed from these writers' works. These were anarchist movements, I may add, like the Iberian Anarchist Federation in Spain, a tradition that is being unscrupulously "red-baited" by certain self-styled "Greens" as "leftist," or "eco-anarchist." The extent of misrepresentations is illustrated by George Sessions, who, at a recent eco-feminist conference, described the differences between "deep ecology" and social ecology as one between "spiritualism" and "Marxism," a particularly odious and conscious falsehood!

But what the boys from Ecotopia proceed to do is to totally recontexualize the framework of these ideas, bringing in personalities and notions that basically change their radical libertarian thrust. Deep Ecology mingles Woody Guthrie— a Communist Party centralist who no more believed in decentralization than Stalin (whom he greatly admired until his physical deterioration and death)—with Paul Goodman, an anarchist who would have been mortified to be placed in the same tradition with Guthrie. In philosophy, Spinoza, a Jew in spirit if not in religious commitment, is intermingled with Heidegger, a former member of the Nazi party in spirit as well as ideological affiliation—all in the name of a vague word called "process philosophy." Almost opportunistic in their use of catchwords and what Orwell called "double-speak," "process philosophy" makes it possible for Sessions–Devall to add Alfred North Whitehead to their list of ideological ancestors because he called his ideas "processual," although he would have differed profoundly from a Heidegger who earned his academic spurs in the Third Reich by repudiating his Jewish teacher, notably Edmund Husserl, in an ugly and shameful way.

One could go on indefinitely with this sloppy admixture of "ancestors," philosophical traditions, social pedigrees, and religions that often have nothing in common with each other and, properly conceived, are commonly in sharp opposition with each other. Thus a repellent reactionary like Thomas Malthus and the neo-Malthusian tradition he spawned is celebrated with the same enthusiasm in Deep Ecology as Henry Thoreau, a radical libertarian who fostered a highly humanistic tradition. "Eclecticism" would be too mild a word for this kind of hodgepodge, one that seems shrewdly calculated to embrace everyone under the rubric of "deep ecology" who is prepared to reduce ecology to a religion rather than a systematic and deeply critical body of ideas. However, behind all of this is a pattern. The kind of "ecological" thinking which enters into the book seems to surface in an appendix called "Ecosophy T" by Arne Næss, who regales us with flow diagrams and corporate-type tables of organization that have more in common with logical positivist forms of exposition (Næss, in fact, was an acolyte of this repellent school of thought for years) than anything that could be truly called organic philosophy.

If we look beyond the spiritual "Eco-la-la" (to use a word coined by a remarkable eco-feminist, Chiah Heller) and examine the *context* in which demands like decentralization, small-scale communities, local autonomy, mutual aid, communalism, and tolerance are placed, the blurred images that Sessions and Devall create come into clearer focus. Decentralism, small-scale communities, local autonomy, even mutual aid and communalism are not intrinsically ecological or emancipatory. Few societies were more decentralized than European feudalism, which, in fact, was structured around small-scale communities, mutual aid, and the communal use of land. Local autonomy was highly prized and autarchy formed the economic key to feudal communities. Yet few societies were more hierarchical. Looming over medieval serfs, who were tied to the land by an "ecological" network of rights and duties that placed them on a status only slightly above that of slaves, were status groups that extended from villeins to barons, counts, dukes, and rather feeble monarchies. The manorial economy of the Middle Ages placed a high premium on autarchy or "self-sufficiency" and spirituality. Yet oppression was often intolerable and the great mass of people who belonged to that society lived in utter subjugation of their "betters" and the nobility.

If "nature-worship" with its bouquet of woodspirits, animistic fetishes, fertility rites, and other such ceremonies—magicians, shamans and shamanesses, animal deities, gods and goddesses that presumably reflect nature and its forces—all, taken together, pave the way to an ecological sensibility and society, then it would be hard to understand how ancient Egypt managed to become and remain one of the most hierarchical and oppressive societies in the ancient world. The pantheon of ancient Egyptian deities is filled with animal and part animal, part human deities with all-presiding goddesses as well as gods. Indeed, the Nile River, which provided the "life-giving" waters of the valley, was used in a highly ecological manner. Yet the entire society was structured around the oppression of millions of serfs and opulent nobles, indeed, a caste system so fixed, exploitative, and deadening to the human spirit that one wonders how notions of spirituality can be given priority to the need for a critical evaluation of society and the need to restructure it.

That there were material beneficiaries of this spiritual "Eco-la-la" becomes clear enough in accounts of the priestly corporations which "communally" owned the largest tracts of land in Egyptian society. With a highly domesticated, "spiritually" passive, yielding, and witless population—schooled for centuries in "flowing with the Nile," to coin a phrase—the Egyptian ruling strata indulged themselves in an orgy of exploitation and power for centuries.

Even if one grants the need for a new sensibility and outlook—a point that has been made repeatedly in the literature of social ecology—one can look behind even this limited context of "deep ecology" to a still broader context: the love affair of "'deep ecology" with Malthusian doctrines, a spirituality that emphasizes self-effacement, a flirtation with a supernaturalism that stands in flat contradiction to the refreshing naturalism that ecology has introduced into social theory, eruptions of a crude positivism in the spirit of Næss that work against a truly organic dialectic so needed to understand development, not merely bumpers ticker slogans, and a regular tendency to become unfocused, replacing ideas by moods, when a Devall, for example, encounters a macho mountain-man like Foreman. We shall see that all the bumper sticker demands like decentralization, small-scale communities, local autonomy, mutual aid, communalism, tolerance, and even an avowed opposition to hierarchy go awry when we place them in the larger context of a Malthusian anti-humanism and orgies about "biocentrism" that mark the authentic ideological infrastructure of "deep ecology."

The Art of Evading Society

The seeming ideological "tolerance" which "deep ecology" celebrates has a sinister function of its own. It not only reduces richly nuanced ideas and conflicting traditions to their lowest common denominator; it legitimates extremely regressive, primitivistic, and even highly reactionary notions that gain respectability because they are buried in the company of authentically radical contexts and traditions. Consider, for example, the "broader definition of community (including animals, plants); intuition of organic wholeness" with which Devall and Sessions regale their menu of "Dominant and Minority" positions in their book (pp. 18–19). Nothing could seem more wholesome, more innocent of guile, than this "we-are-all-one" bumper sticker slogan. What the reader may not notice is that this all-encompassing definition of "community" erases all the rich and meaningful distinctions that exist between animal and plant communities, and above all between nonhuman and human communities. If community is to be broadly defined as a universal "whole," then a unique function which natural evolution has conferred on human society dissolves into a cosmic night which lacks differentiation, variety, and a wide array of functions. The fact is that human communities are consciously formed communities—that is to say, societies with an enormous variety of institutions, cultures that can be handed down from generation to generation, lifeways that can be radically changed for the better or the worse, technologies that be redesigned, innovated, or abandoned, and social, gender, ethnic, and hierarchical distinctions that can be vastly altered according to changes in consciousness and historical development. Unlike most so-called "animal societies" or, for that matter, communities, human societies are not instinctively formed or genetically programmed. Their destinies may be decided by factors—generally, economic and cultural—that are beyond human control at times, to be sure, but what is particularly unique about human societies is that they can be radically changed by their members—and in ways that can be made to benefit the natural world as well as the human species.

Human society, in fact, constitutes a "second nature," a *cultural* artifact, out of "first nature," or primeval, nonhuman nature. There is nothing wrong, "unnatural," or ecologically "alien" about this fact. Human society, like animal and plant communities, is in large part a product of natural evolution—no less so than beehives or anthills. It is a product, moreover, of the human species, a species that is no less a product of nature than whales, dolphins, California condors, or the prokaryotic cell. "Second nature" is also a product of *mind*—of a brain that can think in a richly conceptual manner and produce a highly symbolic form of communication. Taken together, "second nature," the human species which forms it, and the richly conceptual form of thinking and communication so distinctive to it, emerges out of natural evolution no less than any other life form and nonhuman community—and this "second nature" is uniquely different from first nature in that it can act thinkingly, purposefully, willfully, and, depending upon the society we examine, creatively in the best ecological sense or destructively in the worst ecological sense. Finally, this "second nature'" we call society has its own history:

its long process of grading out of "first nature," its long process of organizing or institutionalizing human relationships, its long process of human interactions, conflicts, distinctions, richly nuanced cultural formations, and its long process of actualizing its large number of potentialities—some eminently creative, others eminently destructive.

Finally, a cardinal feature of this product of natural evolution we call "society" is its capacity to intervene in "first nature" to alter it, again in ways that may be eminently creative or destructive. But the capacity of human beings to deal with "first nature" actively, purposefully, willfully, rationally, and, hopefully, ecologically is no less a product of evolution than the capacity of large herbivores to keep forests from eating away at grasslands or of earthworms to aerate the soil. Human beings and their societies alter "first nature" at best in a rational and ecological way—or at worst, in an irrational and anti-ecological way. But the fact that they are constituted to act upon nature, to intervene in natural processes, to alter them in one way or another is no less a product of natural evolution than the action of any lifeform on its environment.

In failing to emphasize the uniqueness, characteristics, and function of human societies or placing them in natural evolution as part of the development of life or giving full, indeed, unique due to human consciousness as a medium for the self-reflective role of human thought as nature rendered self-conscious, "deep ecologists" essentially evade the *social* roots of the ecological crisis—this, in marked distinction to writers like Kropotkin who outspokenly challenged the gross inequities in society that underpin the disequilibrium between society and nature. "Deep ecology" contains no history of the emergence of society out of nature, a crucial development that brings social theory into organic contact with ecological theory. It presents no explanation of—indeed, it reveals no interest in—the emergence of hierarchy out of society, of classes out of hierarchy, of the state out of classes—in short the highly graded social as well as ideological development which gets to the roots of the ecological problem in the social domination of women by men and men by men, ultimately giving rise to the notion of dominating nature in the first place.

Instead, what "deep ecology" gives us, apart from what it plagiarizes from radically different ideological contexts, is a deluge of "Eco-la-la." "Humanity" surfaces in a vague and unearthly form to embrace everyone in a realm of universal guilt. We are then massaged into sedation with Buddhist and Taoist homilies about self-abnegation, "biocentricity," and pop spiritualism that verges on the supernatural—this for a subject-matter, ecology, whose very essence is a return to an earthy naturalism. We not only lose sight of the social and the differences that fragment "Humanity" into a host of human beings—men and women, ethnic groups, oppressors and oppressed; we lose sight of the individual self in an unending flow of "Eco-la-la" that preaches the "realization of self-in-Self where the 'Self' stands for organic wholeness" (p. 67). That a cosmic "Self" is created that is capitalized should not deceive us into the belief that it has any more reality than an equally cosmic "Humanity." More of the same cosmic "Eco-la-la" appears when we are informed that the phrase "one includes not only men, an individual human, but all humans, grizzly bears, whole rain forest ecosystems, mountains and rivers, the tiniest microbes in the soil and so on."

A "Self" so cosmic that it has to be capitalized is no real "self" at all. It is an ideological category, as vague, faceless, and depersonalized as the very patriarchal image of "Man" that dissolves our uniqueness and rationality into a deadening abstraction.

On Selfhood and Viruses

Such flippant abstractions of human individuality are extremely dangerous. Historically, a "Self" that absorbs all real existential selves has been used from time immemorial to absorb individual uniqueness and freedom into a supreme "Individual" who heads the state, churches of various sorts, adoring congregations—be they Eastern or Western—and spellbound constituencies, however much such a "Self" is dressed up in ecological, naturalistic, and "biocentric" attributes. The paleolithic shaman, regaled in reindeer skins and horns, is the predecessor of the pharaoh, the institutionalized Buddha, and, in more recent times, a Hitler, Stalin, or Mussolini.

That the egotistical, greedy, and soloist bourgeois "self" has always been a repellent being goes without saying, and "deep ecology" as personified by Devall and Sessions make the most of it. This kind of "critical" stance is easy to adopt; it can even find a place in *People* magazine. But is there not a free, independently minded, ecologically concerned, indeed, idealistic self with a unique personality that can think of itself as different from "whales, grizzly bears, whole rain forest ecosystems (no less!), mountains and rivers, the tiniest microbes in the soil, and so on?" Is it not indispensable, in fact, for the individual self to disengage itself from a pharonic "Self," discover its own capacities and uniqueness, indeed, acquire a sense of personality, of self-control and self-direction—all traits indispensable for the achievement of *freedom*? Here, I may add, Heidegger and, yes, Nazism, begin to grimace with satisfaction behind this veil of self-effacement and a passive personality so yielding that it can easily be shaped, distorted, and manipulated by a new "ecological" state machinery with a supreme "SELF" embodied in a Leader, Guru, or Living God—all in the name of a "biocentric equality" that is slowly re-worked as it has been so often in history into a social hierarchy. From Silaman to Monarch, from Priest or Priestess to Dictator, our warped social development has been marked by "nature worshippers" and their ritual Supreme Ones who produced unfinished individuals at best or deindividuated the "self-in-Self" at worst, often in the name of the "Great Connected Whole" (to use exactly the language of the Chinese ruling classes who kept their peasantry in abject servitude, as Leon E. Stover points out in *The Cultural Ecology of Chinese Civilization*).

What makes this "Eco-la-la" especially sinister, today, is that we are already living in a period of massive deindividuation—not because "deep ecology" or Taoism is making any serious inroads in our own cultural ecology but because the mass media, the commodity culture, and a market society are "reconnecting" us into an increasingly depersonalized "whole" whose essence is passivity and a chronic vulnerability to economic and political manipulation. It is not an excess of "selfhood" from which we are suffering but selfishness—the surrender of personality to the security afforded by corporations, centralized government, and the military. If "selfhood" is identified with a grasping, "anthropocentric," and devouring personality, these traits are to be found not so much among the ordinary people, who basically sense they have no control over their destinies, but among the giant corporations and state leaders who are not only plundering the planet but also women, people of color, and the underprivileged. It is not deindividuation that the oppressed of the world require, much less passive personalities that readily surrender themselves to the cosmic forces—the "Self"—that buffet them around, but re-individuation that will render them active agents in remaking society and arrest the growing totalitarianism that threatens to homogenize us all as part of a Western version of the "Great Connected Whole."

We are also confronted with the delicious "and so on" that follows the "tiniest microbes in the soil" with which our "deep ecologists" identify the "Self." Here, we encounter another bit of intellectual manipulation that marks the Devall–Sessions anthology as a whole: the tendency to choose examples from God–Motherhood–and–Flag for one's own case and cast any other alternative visions in a demonic form. Why stop with the "tiniest microbes in the soil" and ignore the leprosy microbe, the yearning and striving viruses that give us smallpox, polio, and, more recently, AIDS? Are they too not part of "all organisms and entities in the exosphere . . . of the interrelated whole, equal in intrinsic worth . . . " as Devall and Sessions remind us in their effluvium of "Eco-la-la?" At which point, Næss, Devall, and Sessions immediately introduce a number of highly debatable qualifiers, i.e., "we should live with a minimum rather than a maximum impact on other species" (p. 75) or "we have no right to destroy other living beings without sufficient reason" (p. 75) or, finally, even more majestically: "The slogan of *non-interference* does not imply that humans should not modify (!) some (!) ecosystems as do other (!) species. Humans have modified the earth and will probably (!) continue to do so. At issue is the nature (!) and extent (!) of such interference (!)" (p. 72).

One does not leave the muck of "deep ecology" without having mud all over one's feet. Exactly who is to decide the "nature" of human "interference" in "first nature" and the "extent" to which it can be done? What are "some" of the ecosystems we can modify and what are not subject to human "interference?" Here, again, we encounter the key problem that "Eco-la-la," including "deep ecology," poses for serious, ecologically concerned people: the social bases of our ecological problems and the role of the human species in the evolutionary scheme of things.

Implicit in "deep ecology" is the notion that a "Humanity" exists that accurses the natural world; that individual selfhood must be transformed into a cosmic "Selfhood" that essentially transcends the person and his or her uniqueness. Even nature is not spared from a kind of static, prepositional logic that is cultivated by the logical positivists. "Nature" in "deep ecology" and David Foreman's interpretation of it becomes a kind of scenic view, a spectacle to be admired around the campfire (perhaps with some Budweiser beer to keep the boys happy or a Marlboro cigarette to keep them manly)—not an evolutionary development that is cumulative and includes the human species, its conceptual posers of thought, its highly symbolic forms of communication and, grading into "second nature," a social and cultural development that has its own history and metabolism with pristine "first nature." To see nature as a cumulative unfolding from "first" into "second nature" is likely to be condemned as "anthropocentric"—as though human self-consciousness at its best is not nature rendered self-conscious.

The problems "deep ecology" and "biocentricity" raise have not gone unnoticed in the more thoughtful press in England. During a discussion of "biocentric ethics" in *The New Scientist* 69 (1976), for example, Bernard Dixon observed that no "logical line can be drawn" between the conservation of whales, gentians, and flamingos on the one hand and the extinction of pathogenic microbes like the smallpox virus. At which point, God's gift to misanthropy, David Ehrenfeld, cutely observes that the smallpox virus is an "an endangered species" in his *Arrogance of Humanism*, a work that is so selective and tendentious in its use of quotations that should validly be renamed "The Arrogance of Ignorance." One wonders what to do about the AIDS virus if a vaccine or therapy should threaten its "survival?" Further, given the passion for perpetuating the "ecosystem" of every species, one wonder how smallpox and AIDS viruses should be preserved? In test tubes? Laboratory cultures? Or, to be truly "ecological," in their "native habitat," the human body? In which case, idealistic acolytes of "deep ecology" should be invited to offer their own bloodstreams in the interests of "biocentric equality." Certainly, "if nature should be permitted to take its course," as Foreman advises us for Ethiopians and Indian peasants, plagues, famines, suffering, wars, and perhaps even lethal asteroids of the kind that exterminated the great reptiles of the mesozoic should not be kept from defacing the purity of "first nature" by the intervention of "second nature." With so much absurdity to unscramble, one can indeed get heady, almost dizzy with a sense of polemical intoxication.

At root, the eclecticism which turns "deep ecology" into a goulash of notions and moods is insufferably reformist and surprisingly environmentalist—all its condemnations of "superficial ecology" aside. It has a Dunkin' Donut for everyone. Are you, perhaps, a mild-mannered liberal? Then do not fear: Devall and Sessions give a patronizing nod to "reform legislation," "coalitions," "protests," the "women's movement" (this earns all of ten lines in their "Minority Tradition and Direct Action" essay), "working in the Christian tradition," "questioning technology" (a hammering remark, if there ever was one), "working in Green politics" (which faction, the "fundies" or the "realos?")—in short, everything can be expected in so "cosmic" a philosophy. Anything seems to pass through "deep ecology's" Dunkin' Donut hole: anarchism at one extreme and eco-fascism at the other. Like the fast-food emporiums that make up our culture, "deep ecology" is the fast food of quasi-radical environmentalists.

Despite its pretense of "radicalism," deep ecology is more "New Age" and "Aquarian" than the environmentalist movements it denounces under these names. "If to study the self is to forget the self," to cite a Taoist passage with which Devall and Sessions regale us, then the "all" by which we are presumably "enlightened" is even more invertebrate than Teilhard de Chardin, whose Christian mysticism earns so much scorn from the authors of *Deep Ecology*. Indeed, the extent to which "deep ecology" accommodates itself to some of the worst features of the "dominant view" it professes to reject is seen with extraordinary clarity in one of its most fundamental and repeatedly asserted demands: namely, that the world's population must be drastically reduced, according to one of its acolytes, to 500 million. If "deep ecologists" have even the faintest knowledge of the "population theorists" Devall and Sessions invoke with admiration—notably, Thomas Malthus, William Vogt, and Paul Ehrlich—then they would be obliged to act by measures that are virtually eco-fascist. This specter clearly looms before us in Devall's and Sessions's sinister remark: "the longer we wait [with regard to population control] the more drastic will be the measures needed" (p. 72).

The "Deep" Malthusians

The "population issue" has a long and complex pedigree—one that occupies a central place in the crude biologism promoted by Devall and Sessions—and one that radically challenges "deep ecologists" very way of thinking about social problems, not to speak of their way of resolving them.

The woefully brief "history" Devall and Sessions give us of the population issue on page 46 of their book can only be considered embarrassing in its simplemindedness were it not so reactionary in its thrust.

Thomas Malthus (1766–1854) is hailed as a prophet whose warning "that human population growth would exponentially outstrip food production . . . was ignored by the rising tide of industrial/technological optimism." We shall see that this statement is pure hogwash and what Devall and Sessions call the "rising tide of industrial/technological optimism" were in fact the nineteenth century radicals who opposed the vicious abuses inflicted by industrial capitalism on the oppressed of the world, often in the name of Malthusianism. Devall and Sessions thereupon extol William Catton, Jr., for applying "the ecological concept of carrying capacity" for an ecosystem (I used this expression years before Catton in my mid-1960s writings on social ecology, albeit for very different purposes than Catton's) and George Perkins Marsh for warning "that modern man's impact on the environment could result in rising species extinction rates" (by no means a novel notion when the passenger pigeon and bison were facing extinction, as everyone knew at the time). Devall and Sessions finally land on all fours. "The environmental crisis," we are solemnly told, "was further articulated by ecologist William Vogt *(Road to Survival,* 1948), anticipating the work of radical (!) ecologist Paul Ehrlich in the 1960s."

Devall and Sessions often write with smug assurance on issues they know virtually nothing about. This is most notably the case in the so-called "population debate," a debate that has raged for over two hundred years and more—and one that involves explosive political and social issues that have pitted the most reactionary elements in English and American society (generally represented by Thomas Malthus, William Vogt, and Paul Ehrlich) against authentic radicals who have called for basic changes in the structure of society. In fact, the "Eco-la-la" which Devall and Sessions dump on us in only two paragraphs would require a full-sized volume of careful analysis to unravel.

First of all, Thomas Malthus was not a prophet; he was an apologist for the misery that the Industrial Revolution was inflicting on the English peasantry and working classes. His utterly fallacious argument that population increases exponentially while food supplies increase arithmetically was not ignored by England's ruling classes; it was taken to heart and even incorporated into social Darwinism as an explanation for why oppression was a necessary feature of society and the rich, the white imperialists, and the privileged were the "fittest" who were equipped to "survive"—needless to say, at the expense of the impoverished many. Written and directed in great part as an attack upon the liberatory vision of William Godwin, Malthus's mean-spirited *Essay on the Principle of Population* tried to demonstrate that hunger, poverty, disease, and premature death are *inevitable* precisely because population and food supply increase at different rates. Hence war, famines, and plagues (Malthus later added "moral restraint") were necessary to keep population down—needless to say, among the "lower orders of society"; whom he singles out as the chief offenders of his inexorable population "laws." (See Chapter 5 of his *Essay,* which, for all its "concern" over the misery of the "lower classes," inveighs against the poor laws and argues that the "pressures of distress on this part of the community is an evil so deeply seated that no human ingenuity can reach it.") Malthus, in effect, became the ideologue par excellence for the land-grabbing English nobility in its effort to dispossess the peasantry of their traditional common lands and for the English capitalists to work children, women, and men to death in the newly emerging "industrial/technological" factory system.

Malthusianism contributed in great part to that meanness of spirit that Charles Dickens captured in his famous novels, *Oliver Twist* and *Hard Times.* The doctrine, its author, and its overstuffed wealthy beneficiaries were bitterly fought by the great English anarchist, William Godwin, the pioneering socialist, Robert Owen, and the emerging Chartist movement of the English workers in the early nineteenth century. When the "rising tide of industrial/technological optimism" proved that Malthus was sucking his ideas out of his thumb and his mutton, indeed, when improved economic conditions revealed that population growth tends to diminish with improvements in the quality of life and the status of women, Malthusianism was naively picked up by Charles Darwin to explain his theory of "natural selection." It now became the bedrock theory for the new *social* Darwinism, so very much in vogue in the late nineteenth and early twentieth centuries that saw society as a "jungle" in which only the "fit" (usually, the rich and white) could "survive" at the expense of the "unfit" (usually, the poor and people of color). Malthus, in effect, had provided an ideology that justified class domination, racism, the degradation of women, and, ultimately the empire-building of

English imperialism, later to phase into German fascism, with its use of industrial techniques for mass murder.

All of this occurred long after the English ruling classes, overstuffed on a diet of Malthusian pap, deliberately permitted vast numbers of Irish peasants to starve to death in the potato "famines" of the 1840s on the strength of the Malthusian notion that "nature should be permitted to take its course."

Malthusianism was not only to flourish in Hitler's Third Reich; it was to be revived again in the late 1940s, following the discoveries of antibiotics to control infectious diseases. Riding on the tide of the new Pax Americana after World War II, William F. Vogt and a whole bouquet of neo-Malthusians were to challenge the use of the new antibiotic discoveries to control disease and prevent death—as usual, mainly in Asia, Africa, and Latin America. Again, a new "population debate" erupted with the Rockefeller interests and large corporate sharks aligning themselves with the neo-Malthusians and caring people of every sort aligning themselves with Third World theorists like Josua de Castro, who wrote highly informed critiques of this new version of misanthropy.

Paul Ehrlich and his rambunctious "Zero Population Growth" fanatics in the early 1970s literally polluted the environmental movement with demands for a government bureau (no less!) to "control" population, advancing the infamous "triage" ethic as a standard for aiding or refusing aid to so-called "undeveloped" countries. The extent to which this "ethic" became a formula for dispensing food to countries that aligned themselves with the United States in the Cold War and for refusing aid to those which were non-aligned would make an interesting story by itself. Ehrlich, in turn, began to backtrack on his attempts to peddle a 1970s version of neo-Malthusianism—perhaps until recently, when "deep ecology" has singled him out for a prophetic place in the pantheon of "radical" ecology. Rumor has it that black students in Ehrlich's own academic backyard viewed his *Population Bomb* as basically racist and neatly tailored to American imperialism.

In any case, it is a novelty to learn that Ehrlich is to be regarded as a "radical" and "anti-reformists" like Devall and Sessions are splashing around in the cesspool of Malthusianism—as do many people who innocently call themselves "deep ecologists." One wonders if they realize how reactionary a role this doctrine has played over the centuries?

In *Food First*, Francis Moore Lappe and Joseph Collins have done a superb job in showing how hunger has its origins not in "natural" shortages of food or population growth but in social and cultural dislocations. (It is notable that Devall and Sessions *do not* list this excellent book in their bibliography.) The book has to be widely read to understand the reactionary implications of "deep ecology's" demographic positions.

What is no less important: demography is a highly ambiguous and ideologically charged social discipline that cannot be reduced to a mere numbers game in biological reproduction. Human beings are not fruit flies (the species of choice, which the neo-Malthusians love to cite). Their reproductive behavior is profoundly conditioned by cultural values, standards of living, social traditions, the status of women, religious beliefs, socio-political conflicts, and various socio-political expectations. Smash up a stable, precapitalist culture and throw its people off the land into city slums and, due ironically to demoralization, population may soar rather than decline. As Gandhi told the British, imperialism left India's wretched poor and homeless with little more in life than the immediate gratification provided by sex and an understandably numbed sense of personal, much less social, responsibility. Reduce women to mere reproductive factories and population rates will explode.

Conversely, provide people with decent lives, education, a sense of creative meaning in life, and, above all, free women from their roles as mere bearers of children—and population growth begins to stabilize and population rates even reverse their direction. Indeed, population growth and attitudes toward population vary from society to society according to the way people live, the ideas they hold, and the socio-economic relationships they establish. Nothing more clearly reveals "deep ecology's" crude, often reactionary, and certainly superficial ideological framework—all its decentralist, antihierarchical, and "radical" rhetoric aside— than its suffocating "biological" treatment of the population issue and its inclusion of Malthus, Vogt, and Ehrlich in its firmament of prophets.

The close connection between social factors and demography is perhaps best illustrated by the fact that throughout most of the nineteenth and twentieth centuries in Europe, improved living conditions began to reduce rates of population increase, in some cases leading to negative population growth rates. During the inter-war period, such declines became so "serious" to countries readying themselves for World War II that women were granted awards for having sizable numbers of children (read: cannon fodder for the military). More recently in Japan, industrialists were so alarmed by the decline in the country's labor force due to the legalization of abortion that they demanded the abrogation of this legislation.

These examples can be generalized into a theory of demography in which the need for labor often plays a more important role historically in population fluctuations than biological behavior and sexual desire. If women are seen as female fruitflies and men as their mindless partners, guided more by instinct than the quality of life, then Devall and Sessions have an argument—and, almost certainly, a crude, patronizing, gender-conditioned outlook that requires careful scrutiny by feminists who profess to be "deep ecologists." If people are not fruitflies, then "deep ecology" reeks of the odor of crude biologism that is matched only by its naive reading of Malthus and Company.

Not surprisingly, *Earth First!*, whose editor professes to be an enthusiastic "deep ecologist," carried an article titled "Population and AIDS" which advanced the obscene argument that AIDS is desirable as a means of population control. This was no spoof. It was carefully worked out, fully reasoned in a paleolithic sort of way, and earnestly argued. Not only will AIDS claim large numbers of lives, asserts the author (who hides under the pseudonym of "Miss Ann Thropy," a form of black humor that could also pass as an example of macho-male arrogance), but it "may cause a breakdown in technology (read: human food supply) and its export, which could also decrease human population" (May 1, 1987). These people feed on human disasters, suffering, and misery, preferably in Third World countries where AIDS is by far a more monstrous problem than elsewhere.

Until we can smoke out "Miss Ann Thropy" (is it David Foreman again?), we have little reason to doubt that this mentality—or lack thereof—is perfectly consistent with the "more drastic . . . measures" Devall and Sessions believe we will have to explore. Nor is it inconsistent with a Malthus and Vogt, possibly even an Ehrlich, that we should make no effort to find a cure for this disease which may do so much to depopulate the world. "Biocentric democracy," I assume, should call for nothing less than a "hands-off" policy on the AIDS virus and perhaps equally lethal pathogens that appear in the human species.

What Is Social Ecology?

Social ecology is neither "deep," "tall," "fat," nor thick." It is social. It does not fall back on incantations, sutras, flow diagrams, or spiritual vagaries. It is avowedly rational. It does not try to regale metaphorical forms of spiritual mechanism and crude biologism with Taoist, Buddhist, Christian, or shamanistic "Eco-la-la." It is a coherent form of naturalism that looks to evolution and the biosphere, not to deities in the sky or under the earth for quasi-religious and supernaturalistic explanations of natural and social phenomena.

Philosophically, social ecology stems from a solid organismic tradition in Western philosophy, beginning with Heraclitus, the near-evolutionary dialectic of Aristotle and Hegel, and the superbly critical approach of the famous Frankfurt School—particularly its devastating critique of logical positivism (which surfaces in Næss repeatedly) and the primitivistic mysticism of Heidegger (which pops up all over the place in deep ecology literature).

Socially, it is revolutionary, not merely "radical." It critically unmasks the entire evolution of hierarchy in all its forms, including neo-Malthusian elitism, the eco-brutalism of a David Foreman, the anti-humanism of a David Ehrenfeld and a "Miss Ann Thropy," and the latent racism, First World arrogance and yuppie-nihilism of postmodernistic spiritualism. It is rooted in the profound eco-anarchistic analyses of a Peter Kropotkin, the radical economic insights of a Karl Marx, the emancipatory promise of the revolutionary Enlightenment as articulated by the great encyclopedist, Denis Diderot, the *Enrages* of the French Revolution, the revolutionary feminist ideals of a Louise Michel and Emma Goldman, the communitarian visions of Paul Goodman and E. A. Gutkind, and the various eco-revolutionary manifestos of the early 1960s.

Politically, it is Green—and radically Green. It takes its stand with the left-wing tendencies in the German Greens and extra-parliamentary street movements of European cities, with the American radical eco-feminist movement that is currently emerging, with the demands for a new politics based on citizens' initiatives, neighborhood assemblies, New England's tradition of town meetings, with unaligned anti-imperialist movements at home and abroad, with the struggle by people of color for complete freedom from the domination of privileged whites and from the superpowers of both sides of the Iron Curtain.

Morally, it is avowedly *humanistic* in the high Renaissance meaning of the term, not the degraded meaning of "humanism" that has been imparted to the word by David Foreman, David Ehrenfeld, a salad of academic "deep ecologists," and the like. Humanism from its inception has meant a shift in vision from the skies to the earth, from superstition to reason, from deities to people—who are no less products of natural evolution than grizzly bears and whales. Social ecology accepts neither a "biocentricity" that essentially denies or degrades the uniqueness of human beings, human subjectivity, rationality, aesthetic sensibility, and the ethical potentiality of this extraordinary species. By the same token, social ecology rejects an "anthropocentricity" that confers on the privileged few the right to plunder the world of life, including women, the young, the poor, and the underprivileged. Indeed, it opposes "centricity" of any kind as a new word for hierarchy and domination—be it that of nature by a mystical "Man" or the domination of people by an equally mystical "Nature." It firmly denies that "Nature" is a scenic view, which Mountain Men like a Foreman survey from a peak in Nevada or a picture window that spoiled yuppies place in their ticky-tacky country homes. To social ecology, nature is natural evolution, not a cosmic arrangement of beings frozen in a moment of eternity to be abjectly "revered," "adored," and "worshipped" like the gods and goddesses that priests and priestesses place above us in a realm of "Super-nature" that subverts the naturalistic integrity of an authentic ecology. Natural evolution is nature in the very real sense that it is composed of atoms, molecules that have evolved into amino acids, proteins, unicellular organisms, genetic codes, invertebrates and vertebrates, amphibia, reptiles, mammals, primates, and human beings—all, in a cumulative thrust toward ever greater complexity, ever greater subjectivity, and finally, ever greater mind with a capacity for conceptual thought, symbolic communication of the most sophisticated kind, and self-consciousness in which natural evolution knows itself purposively and willfully.

This marvel we call "Nature" has produced a marvel we call homo sapiens— "thinking man" and, more significantly for the development of society, "thinking woman" whose primeval domestic domain provided the arena for the origins of a caring society, human empathy, love, and idealistic commitment. The human species, in effect, is no less a product of natural evolution than blue-green algae. To degrade that species in the name of "anti-humanism," to deny the species its uniqueness as thinking beings with an unprecedented gift for conceptual thought, is to deny the rich fecundity of natural evolution itself. To separate human beings and society from nature is to dualize and truncate nature itself, to diminish the meaning and thrust of natural evolution in the name of a "biocentricity" that spends more time disporting itself with mantras, deities, and supernature than with the realities of the biosphere and the role of society in ecological problems. Accordingly, social ecology does not try to hide its critical and reconstructive thrust in metaphors. It calls "technological/industrial" society capitalism—a word which places the onus for our ecological problems on the living sources and social relationships that produce them, not on a gutsy "Third Wave" abstraction which buries these sources in technics, a technical "mentality," or perhaps the technicians who work on machines. It sees the domination of women not simply as a "spiritual" problem that can be resolved by rituals, incantations, and shamanesses, important as ritual may be in solidarizing women into a unique community of people, but in the long, highly graded, and subtly nuanced development of hierarchy, which long preceded the development of classes. Nor does it ignore class, ethnic differences, imperialism, and oppression by creating a grab-bag called "Humanity" that is placed in opposition to a mystified "Nature," divested of all development.

All of which brings us as social ecologists to an issue that seems to be totally alien to the crude concerns of "deep ecology:" natural evolution has conferred on human beings the capacity to form a "second" or cultural nature out of "first" or primeval nature. Natural evolution has not only provided humans with ability but also the necessity to be purposive interveners into "first nature," to consciously change "first nature" by means of a highly institutionalized form of community we call "society." It is not alien to natural evolution that a species called human has emerged over billions of years that is capable of thinking in a sophisticated way. Nor is it alien for that species to develop a highly sophisticated form of symbolic communication which a new kind of community—institutionalized, guided by thought rather than by instinct alone, and ever-changing—has emerged called "society."

Taken together, all of these human traits—intellectual, communicative, and social—have not only emerged from natural evolution and are inherently human; they can also be placed at the *service* of natural evolution to consciously increase biotic diversity, diminish suffering, foster the further evolution of new and ecologically valuable life-forms, reduce the impact of disastrous accidents or the harsh effects of mere change.

Whether this species, gifted by the creativity of natural evolution, can play the role of a nature rendered self-conscious or cut against the grain of natural evolution by simplifying the biosphere, polluting it, and undermining the cumulative results of organic evolution is above all a *social* problem. The primary question ecology faces today is whether an ecologically-oriented society can be created out of the present anti-ecological one.

"Deep ecology" provides us with no approach for responding to, much less acting upon, this key question. It not only rips out invaluable ideas like decentralization, a nonhierarchical society, local autonomy, mutual aid, and communalism from the liberatory anarchic tradition of the past where they have acquired a richly nuanced, anti-elitist, and egalitarian content—reinforced by passionate struggles by millions of men and women for freedom. It reduces them to bumper sticker slogans that can be recycled for use by a macho Mountain Man like Foreman at one extreme or flaky spiritualists at the other extreme. These bumper sticker slogans are then relocated in a particularly repulsive context whose contours are defined by Malthusian elitism, antihumanist misanthropy, and a seemingly benign "biocentricity" that dissolves humanity with all its unique natural traits for conceptual thought and self-consciousness into a "biocentric democracy" that is more properly the product of human consciousness than a natural reality. Carried to its logical absurdity, this "biocentric democracy"—one might also speak of a tree's morality or a leopard's "social contract" with its prey—can no more deny the "right" of pathogenic viruses to be placed on an "endangered species list" (and who places them there, in the first place?) than it can deny the same status to whales. The social roots of the ecological crisis are layered over by a hybridized, often self-contradictory form of spirituality in which the human "self," writ large, is projected into the environment or into the sky as a reified Deity or deities—a piece of anthropocentrism if there ever was one, like the shamans who are dressed in reindeer skins and horns—and abjectly "revered" as "Nature." Or as Arne Næss, the grand pontiff of this mess puts it: "The basic principles within the deep ecology movement are grounded in religion or philosophy" (p. 225)—as though the two words can be flippantly used interchangeably. Selfhood is dissolved, in turn, into a cosmic "Self" precisely at a time when de-individuation and passivity are being cultivated by the mass media, corporations, and the state to an appalling extent. Finally, "deep ecology," with its concern for the manipulation of nature, exhibits very little concern for the manipulation of human beings by each other, except perhaps when it comes to the "drastic" measures that may be "needed" for population control.

Unless there is a resolute attempt to fully anchor ecological dislocations in social dislocations, to challenge the vested corporate and political interests we should properly call capitalism—not some vague entity called "industrial/techno-logical" society, which even a Dwight D. Eisenhower attacked with a more acer-bic term—to analyze, explore, and attack hierarchy as a reality, not only as a sen-sibility, to recognize the material needs of the poor and of Third World people, to function politically, not simply as a religious cult, to give the human species and mind their due in natural evolution, not simply regard them as "cancers" in the biosphere, to examine economies as well as "souls" and freedom as well as im-merse ourselves in introspective or in Scholastic arguments about the "rights" of pathogenic viruses—unless, in short, North American Greens and the ecology movement shift their focus toward a social ecology and let "deep ecology" sink into the pit it has created for us, the ecology movement will become another ugly wart on the skin of society.

What we must do, today, is return to nature, conceived in all its fecundity, richness of potentialities, and subjectivity—not to supernature with its shamans, priests, priestesses, and fanciful deities that are merely anthropomorphic exten-sions and distortions of the "Human" as all-embracing divinities. And what we must "enchant" is not only an abstract "Nature" that often reflects our own sys-tems of power, hierarchy, and domination—but rather human beings, the human mind, and the human spirit that has taken such a beating these days from every source, particularly "deep ecology."

"Deep ecology" with its Malthusian thrust, its various "centricities," its mys-tifying "Eco-la-la," and its disorienting eclecticism degrades this enterprise into a crude biologism that deflects us from the social problems that underpin the ecological ones and the project of social reconstruction that alone can spare the biosphere from virtual destruction.

We must finally take a stand on these issues—free of all "Eco-la-la"—or acknowledge that the academy has made another conquest: namely that of the ecology movement itself.

June 25, 1987
Burlington, Vermont

Notes

This chapter is reprinted with minor revisions from Murray Bookchin, "Social Ecology versus Deep Ecology," *Green Perspectives, Newsletter of the Green Program Project* 4/5 (double issue), (Summer 1987): 1.

[1] Unless otherwise indicated, all future references and quotes come from this book, which has essentially become the bible of the "movement" that bears its name.

Chapter 36

Note Concerning Murray Bookchin's Article "Social Ecology versus Deep Ecology"

Arne Næss

The deep ecology movement as characterized by me since 1973 is a social movement, its participants being on the whole nonacademic people. The inspiration for the deep/shallow distinction came especially from participation in direct nonviolent actions where there is time to speak with many people who are emotionally strongly engaged, but who have little access to the means of mass communication. The deep ecology theorists make up a tiny minority. If Bookchin is right, I have, as a theorist, misunderstood the people I wish to serve.

Two great Norwegian internationally known direct actions might here be mentioned, the Mardøla and Alta actions, because of their social and political core. The sites of the actions were carefully chosen because they combined the protection of nature with that of local communities and in the Alta case with the protection of a First *and* Fourth world community. The Sami people in Alta were protesting against a hydroelectric power plant project, which would impede the free movement of their reindeer herds. This interference was experienced by them as self-destructive. In a lawsuit, the following dialogue was heard:

Prosecutor: "Why did you obstruct the work at that place along the river?" Reindeer nomad: "It is part of myself."

The combination of "spiritual" and "material" factors of the deep ecology movement is essential and manifests itself most convincingly in overt, nonviolent struggles. Terms such as "political ecology" and "social ecology" were used in Europe, but in spite of some weaknesses, the term "deep ecology movement" has prevailed.

As with every social movement, it is difficult or impossible to grasp its peculiarities in a few words. As long as it lives, it will also develop, reach maturity, get old, get "out of date" and die. The deep ecology movement is a response to a process, which I in 1973 have described in the following synoptic formula: "An exponentially increasing, and partially or totally irreversible environmental deterioration or devastation perpetuated through firmly established ways of production and consumption."

Thoroughgoing, nonviolent opposition to this kind of process links together all the followers of deep ecology. The movement has, using the expression of Murray Bookchin, "gone beyond a naive belief that patchwork reforms and solemn vows by EPA bureaucrats to act more resolutely will seriously arrest the insane pace at which we are tearing down the planet. . . . Innumerable hazards that threaten the integrity of life itself, raise far more basic issues than any that can be resolved by 'Earth Day' cleanups and faint-hearted changes in existing environmental laws."[1]

The term "basic issues" is important here. It is a vague term, but hints at something ultimate, which goes beyond what is mostly labeled, "social issues."

The synoptic formula applies to industrial societies with or without a dominant market economy. But it also applies to the Third World. In Kenya, for instance, neither the traditional nor the modern methods of agriculture are ecologically sustainable. The population is big and increasing. Even if it were slightly reduced, the application of modern ideas of nonsustainable development (i.e., production and consumption) would make the situation ecologically critical).

This brings us to the problems of population (of humans). Perhaps I maintain a rather eccentric view compared to the majority within the deep ecology movement. My original formulation was encapsulated by point 3 in the 18-point survey:

> 3. *Stabilization of the population.* This can be viewed as a special case of the second point. "Resource-policy, resource-distribution." *Optimization of population*: What size locally and globally serves in the best way human values and life in general? Possibly a reduction of the population of *homo sapiens* in the long run. Consideration of the population of animals and plants "is relevant." Today primarily a problem in the industrial countries because of their pollution and resource-consumption. In the long run a problem also for the Third World.

In the early 1970s the European red-green movement tended to see population problems as uniquely a problem for industrial states, but this has changed. The slogan "sustainable development!" has made population stabilization an ethically acceptable position among many policy makers in the Third World.

People dissatisfied with environmentalism of the early 1970s look for, according to Bookchin, "an *ecological* approach: one that is rooted in an ecological *philosophy*, *ethics*, *sensibility*, *image of nature*, and, ultimately, an ecological movement that will transform our domineering market into . . . a society that will live in harmony with nature, because its members live in harmony with each other."

This formulation might be gladly endorsed by people in the red-green European movement. Johan Galtung, to mention a prominent member, would presumably do so, and find it completely compatible, as also I would, with firm support of the deep ecology movement. The invocation of old Malthus is irrelevant.

The question to what extent members of a society where members live in harmony with each other tend also to live in harmony with nature is one of social and cultural anthropology which I wish would get more attention. This holds good also of the causal relation between the two aspects of society. I expect that decreased violence between people in a society on the whole will decrease violence against nonhumans.

It seems that, from about page 5 in his article, Bookchin loses connection with what he is denouncing. For instance "decentralization" has often been a central concept for the deep ecology movement. But since the early 1970s the term has gradually been less used in isolation because of great social and political problems that were not clear 15–20 years ago. In the early 1970s it was hoped that local communities on the whole would stand up against unecological forms of industrialization that gave short-term profits for the locals. But the wisdom of local communities was often counteracted by local administrations. And now it is clear that many sound ecological decisions must be made centrally in spite of strong local objections. This is for instance the case when trying to protect Sami reindeer interests and thereby their culture. The obvious importance of this can be derived from points 1 and 2 of the deep ecology platform concerning the richness and diversity of human and nonhuman life. One of the outstanding characteristics of Sami-land has been its extreme decentralization—unfortunately making it easily conquerable by centralized nation-states.

In the early 18-point characterization of the deep ecology movement, point 4 is totally concerned with the same theme and five other points have much to do with it: classlessness, self-rule, local community, development of districts (areas of small communities), self-reliance. I do not see any disagreement with these points in the valuable book of Devall and Sessions, *Deep Ecology*. But the book certainly centers more on the "spiritual" aspects of the movement than on the social and political.

One of the main applications of the principles of nonviolence as preached by Gandhi and others inevitably centers upon verbal communication. In our gigantic industrialized societies it is often not easy to get in personal touch with opponents. It is my feeling after reading six pages of Bookchin's article that his style prevents me from doing justice to his basic ideas in this note.

Notes

[1] *Green Perspectives, Newsletter of the Green Program Project* 4/5 (1987): 1.

Chapter 37

Unanswered Letter to Murray Bookchin, 1988

Arne Næss

Oslo, August 27, 1988

Dear Murray Bookchin

For some time I thought I should ask you what you propose we should do to avoid political forces which both of us oppose taking advantage of what they like (erroneously) to see as a "dispute so divisive and acrimonious that it could disrupt environmentalism as a cohesive force." (Quotation from an influential Australian Newspaper, *The Age*, 25 June.)

So far as I can understand you think it wise to give up the term "the deep ecology movement" as a positive term. But I do not think the best way to do this is to associate it with utterances such as "The human race could go extinct and I for one would not shed any tears . . ." or with any others in the article and quoted from your writing.

When the term "the deep ecology movement" was introduced we, as activists, had two alternative terms under consideration, "ecopolitics" and "political ecology." Some preferred the latter terms.

The difference in terminology reflected of course some difference in priorities, but we thought it imperative and not difficult to retain friendly cooperation. In the great direct actions it was clear that only a small minority of the strong supporters of the deep ecology or ecopolitical movement were academics eager to debate (important) theoretical points of view. Personally I have (nearly) consistently favored the term "the deep ecology movement." I still do that, and for

305

similar reasons I would not shift in favor of the term "social ecology." This in spite of my conviction that deep changes of "economic, technological, and ideological structures" of the rich countries are required to radically change policies towards nature.

Your work was known in Norway since the early 1970s, and one of your books was translated. My impression was that you participated in the deep ecological movement, but of course I did not expect you to use a similar terminology. The term "political" or "social" ecology would probably have suited you better.

The language you use when referring to the deep ecology movement has surprised me. You do not seem to attack the point of view characteristic of that movement, and I am glad you don't. But outsiders have reason to believe you are attacking the international movement that I, and many others, *call* the "deep ecology movement."

It is impossible for me to follow in detail the discussions going on between various groups of environmentalists in the United States. I would be grateful if you send me references to any "divisive" and "acrimonious" *exchange of views* between supporters and opponents of the deep ecology movement. So far I have not seen any. I just received a letter from Australia asking about what is going on.

At the moment there is a concern in Norway that there will be a (mild) decrease of population in that tiny extremely rich country. Some of the reasons for concern I guess you would call "barely disguised racism." Plans for Norwegian development from now to year 2020 (and further) are irresponsible and thoroughly unecological. From a green point of view all of them must be opposed, and I think it includes the population policy. If the government did not counteract a decrease of population by means of taxation, etc., but made decrease a point in their dealings with the poor countries, our credibility would increase.

Sorry that we have not met each other considering the many interests we have in common.

Yours sincerely
Arne Næss

Chapter 38

To the Editor of *Synthesis*

Arne Næss

Oslo, 1988

Dear Editor of Synthesis,

I have been made aware of your newsletter and journal through its issue no. 27. Very encouraging!

Unfortunately, the way of communication within the Green Movement in central Europe has often been colored by hostility and unfriendly interpretations. A result has been a divisiveness that has obscured the common ground and has complicated common action. It need not happen in the United States. The article by D. B. Perry on communication needs wide distribution.

Being revolutionary in a wide sense of the term the Green Movement must expect to be met with abuse, falsification, and persistent unfriendly interpretations. But within the movement we want passionate engagement combined with clarity, responsibility, and equanimity.

"Social ecology," "deep ecology," "the greens," "bioregionalism," and "ecofeminism," are designations which can only be defined very tentatively. It is and will continue to be an open question, exactly what they stand for and exactly how they are related to each other. What they stand for has much in common and this fact must be exploited for all it is worth. If that is done differences of opinion are an asset.

Among those who feel most at home with what they call the deep ecology movement there are at least three areas of interesting disagreeing, or ways of talking. Some talk as if they looked upon humans as intruders in wonderful nature. They do not talk much about green society but they nevertheless sincerely hope it will be a reality. Others, "the spirituals," concentrate on personal development without belittling political engagement (but start with yourself). The "socials" tend to talk and write about the ills of the present industrial society, exploring avenues of deep green change. The ecologically responsible way of relating to nature not only presupposes such change, but work for its realization must today have the highest priority. Proper relations to nature will largely come as a result of that work.

The above is of course only a loose description of our debates within the deep ecological movement. They do not seem to diminish our ability to cooperate in practice. Different ways and habits of talking are not a barrier of crucial importance.

The European deep ecology supporters often prefer the names "political ecology" and "ecopolitics" distinguishing their activity from "classical nature preservation." Opinions closely related to point 6 of the 8-point formulation of George Sessions and myself have expressed a central point: the way to proceed is political in a wide sense, but continued trends of irreversible environmental destructions require immediate action within the framework of present lamentable social conditions. Even if those destructions somehow illustrate, or even are caused by, these conditions, there should be a movement to act locally and globally to defend what is threatened but not yet destroyed. One of the versions of point 6 reads as follows:

Policies must therefore—because of what is said in points 1–5—be changed. The policies affect basic economic, technological, and ideological structures. The resulting state of affairs will be deeply different from the present.

An earlier (1973) characterization of the deep ecology movement has 18 points the majority of which were social and political, reflecting trends in Green politics in northern Europe. At that time the destruction of local and global life conditions was not as glaring as today. The social and political questions remain and must be of high priority—as suggested in point 6.

All short sets of formulations or characterizations of a social movement are highly tentative and reflect more or less unstable terminological idiosyncrasies. They are not worth fierce quarrels. But one may in a relaxed way compare points formulated within different movements. Point 1 of the Committees of Correspondence version of the "Ten Key Green Values" runs as follows: "How can we operate human societies with the understanding that we are *part* of nature, not on top it." As a firm supporter of the deep ecological movement I immediately feel that *for me* this understanding is not enough. That somehow respect for nature is important, not only cold understanding of being a part of it. Analogy: If U.S. industry contributes too much to the environmental degradation in Canada, it is not enough that the United States operates with the understanding that it is *part* of North America. Respect for other parts is relevant. And in my view, respect for life anywhere is relevant, and not only because it is good for our societies.

Do I write this as a critique of point 1 of the CC version of green values? Not at all! All 10 sentences permit interpretations such that they could be part of a deep ecology pronouncement. And even if some could not, this does not worry me too much. Absence of disagreement is not a good sign.

The Vermont Version of the Ten Green Values (p. 11 in Issue No. 27) is a valuable document. But again there is a feeling of being more at home among the articulations by colleagues using deep ecology terminological preferences. "We believe that the attempt to dominate nature stems from the domination of human by human." This is the first sentence of the first point of the Vermont Version. Perhaps "stems in part from" would be a better expression than "stems from." Both cultural anthropology and the history of Western hard technology reveal more intricate relationships. But only unfriendly interpretations would hold that "stems from" is to mean the same as "stems absolutely only from." Condensed statements like the Vermont Version and the 8 points of deep ecology are, of course, open to "absolutist" interpretations because of their essential shortness.

The second sentence of the first point is, of course, also open to misleading interpretations. "We are working to reharmonize humanity with nature by reharmonizing human with human." It is scarcely meant that "reharmonizing human with human" is undertaken to "reharmonize humanity with nature." The former goal is not meant to be a subordinate goal in relation to the latter.

In European debates some groups would immediately object to a positive use of the terms "harmony" and "harmonize." In the "conflict" and "confrontation" model of history such terms were to be avoided. Those using the former words tended to be excluded from the group.

In short, there is no limit to the opportunity within movements to misunderstand or get into quarrels without much substance.

One of the most encouraging aspects of the great wave of ecological and environmental engagement in the late 1960s and early 1970s was the similarity of ideas and plans cropping up all over the world. In continental Europe people often found the active U.S. groups lacking in political consciousness, "privatizing" the problems, whereas groups in the United States found the continental Europeans excessively eager to debate theory and underestimating lifestyle and practice. But basically there was a remarkable unanimity. This unanimity is not lost, as far as I can judge. The frontier of struggle is complex and long. It is understandable that those working on one sector tend to underestimate the importance of work on other sectors. We need more actions and campaigns where we work together.

Yours sincerely
Arne Næss

Chapter 39

Comment: Deep Ecology and Social Ecology

Andrew McLaughlin

Over the last decade Murray Bookchin has launched several invectives against deep ecology, creating an appearance of fundamental differences between social ecology and deep ecology. This appearance, however, is misleading. Although there are some divergences between deep ecology and social ecology, the convergences are substantial and significant.

Most importantly, as Arne Næss notes, supporters of the deep ecology movement agree that fundamental social and political transformation towards societies with harmonious relations with the rest of nature is urgent. Although concern about societies' relations with nonhuman nature has grown considerably in the last few decades, even a cursory survey of contemporary politics and social movements would show that creating ecologically sound societies is a relatively low priority for many. The convergence between social ecology and supporters of the deep ecology movement on the urgency of ecologically oriented social and political change is important and fundamental. Further, I find no reason to think that Bookchin disagrees with any part of the eight-point platform. So in the near term at least, the range of agreement is surely large enough for fruitful collaboration.

Nevertheless, some differences can be discerned, although they will only become important in the medium to long term future. In particular, the question of human population calls for further dialogue. Bookchin correctly notes the complexity of the problems of human demographics and points out that social change and the empowering of women is vital in achieving the stabilization of

310

population. Supporters of deep ecology may well agree with this; I certainly do, for the evidence is there. But there is an important absence in Bookchin's discussion of the human population, for he never discusses what he thinks is an optimum population level. Can we look with equanimity at the projected doubling of the human population in the next century? Or are we already too many? The question of the optimum human population is a key issue shaping our vision of the future we seek. Unless one seeks a gradual decline in human numbers, the rest of nature on earth will become at best a garden farmed to support more than ten billion humans.

This leads to a second area needing further discussion. Seeking an optimum human population well below present numbers facilitates the goal of the preservation and expansion of wilderness. Supporters of the deep ecology movement endorse wild spaces for a broad spectrum of reasons, ranging from the importance of wilderness for human well-being to the well-being of the rest of nature to the need for wild spaces where biological history can continue to unfold. Unless human populations scale themselves back over time, there will be no space left for the ongoing speciation of middle and large sized creatures. Many or all supporters of deep ecology feel strongly that some places should be left for the rest of nature to evolve outside of interference from industrial society.

This in turn raises a third issue: what is the proper relation between humans and the rest of evolving nature? Bookchin believes that humans, once organized into nonhierarchical societies living harmoniously with nature, can place themselves "at the service of natural evolution," diminishing suffering and fostering new forms of life. In fact, he has endorsed the transformation of the "Canadian barrens" to an "area supporting a rich variety of biota."[1] In that context he did not discuss what would happen to the indigenous peoples of these "barrens" when this transformation is effected. Many supporters of the deep ecology movement would reject this view of humans being in "service" to the course of evolution. Certainly some areas must be managed by humans to support human life, and we may yet become skillful in restoring areas already damaged. But, if possible, other areas should be freed from interference by industrial societies and allowed to flourish in their own terms. Many supporters of the deep ecology movement would agree with Thoreau's claim that "in Wildness is the preservation of the World."

These disagreements, important as they may be, do not justify rhetoric so heated as to preclude communication. The differences are relatively few and their importance will become central only after major social transformations have been achieved. I think no supporter of deep ecology would hesitate to agree with Bookchin's conclusion that our primary question today is "whether an ecologically oriented society can be created out of the present anti-ecological one." This urgent task provides ample space for cooperative and creative collaboration between social ecologists and supporters of deep ecology.

Notes

[1] See Murray Bookchin, "Recovering Evolution: A Reply to Eckersley and Fox," in *Environmental Ethics* 12 (Fall 1990): 272.

Chapter 40

Radical American Environmentalism and Wilderness Preservation: A Third World Critique

Ramachandra Guha

> Even God dare not appear to the poor man except in the form of bread.
> *Mahatma* Gandhi

Introduction

The respected radical journalist Kirkpatrick Sale recently celebrated "the passion of a new and growing movement that has become disenchanted with the environmental establishment and has in recent years mounted a serious and sweeping attack on it—style, substance, systems, sensibilities and all."[1] The vision of those whom Sale calls "New Ecologists"—and what I refer to in this article as deep ecology—is a compelling one. Decrying the narrowly economic goals of mainstream environmentalism, this new movement aims at nothing less than a philosophical and cultural revolution in human attitudes toward nature. In contrast to the conventional lobbying efforts of environmental professionals based in Washington, it proposes a militant defense of "Mother Earth," an unflinching opposition to human attacks on undisturbed wilderness. With their goals ranging from the spiritual to the political, the adherents of deep ecology span a wide spectrum of the American environmental movement. As Sale correctly notes, this emerging strand has in a matter of a few years made its presence felt in a number of fields: from academic philosophy (as in the journal *Environmental Ethics*) to popular environmentalism (for example, the group *Earth First!*).

In this article I develop a critique of deep ecology from the perspective of a sympathetic outsider. I critique deep ecology not as a general (or even a foot soldier) in the continuing struggle between the ghosts of Gifford Pinchot and John Muir over control of the U.S. environmental movement, but as an outsider to these battles. I speak admittedly as a partisan, but of the environmental movement in India, a country with an ecological diversity comparable to the United States, but with a radically dissimilar cultural and social history.

My treatment of deep ecology is primarily historical and sociological, rather than philosophical, in nature. Specifically, I examine the cultural rootedness of a philosophy that likes to present itself in universalistic terms. I make two main arguments: first, that deep ecology is uniquely American, and despite superficial similarities in rhetorical style, the social and political goals of radical environmentalism in other cultural contexts (e.g., West Germany and India) are quite different; second, that the social consequences of putting deep ecology into practice on a worldwide basis (what its practitioners are aiming for) are very grave indeed.

The Tenets of Deep Ecology

While I am aware that the term deep ecology was coined by the Norwegian philosopher Arne Næss, this article refers specifically to the American variant.[2] Adherents of the deep ecological perspective in this country, while arguing intensely among themselves over its political and philosophical implications, share some fundamental premises about human–nature interactions. As I see it, the defining characteristics of deep ecology are fourfold:

First, deep ecology argues that the environmental movement must shift from an "anthropocentric" to a "biocentric" perspective. In many respects, an acceptance of the primacy of this distinction constitutes the litmus test of deep ecology. A considerable effort is expended by deep ecologists in showing that the dominant motif in Western philosophy has been anthropocentric—i.e., the belief that man and his works are the center of the universe—and conversely, in identifying those lonely thinkers (Leopold, Thoreau, Muir, Aldous Huxley, Santayana, etc.) who, in assigning man a more humble place in the natural order, anticipated deep ecological thinking. In the political realm, meanwhile, establishment environmentalism (shallow ecology) is chided for casting its arguments in human-centered terms. Preserving nature, the deep ecologists say, has an intrinsic worth quite apart from any benefits preservation may convey to future human generations. The anthropocentric–biocentric distinction is accepted as axiomatic by deep ecologists, it structures their discourse, and much of the present discussion remains mired within it.

The second characteristic of deep ecology is its focus on the preservation of unspoiled wilderness—and the restoration of degraded areas to a more pristine condition—to the relative (and sometimes absolute) neglect of other issues on the environmental agenda. I later identify the cultural roots and portentous consequences of this obsession with wilderness. For the moment, let me indicate three distinct sources from which it springs. Historically, it represents a playing out of the preservationist (read radical) and utilitarian (read reformist) dichotomy that has plagued American environmentalism since the turn of the century. Morally, it is an imperative that follows from the biocentric perspective; other species of plants and animals, and nature itself, have an intrinsic right to exist. And finally, the preservation of wilderness also turns on a scientific argument—viz., the value of biological diversity in stabilizing ecological regimes and in retaining a gene pool for future generations. Truly radical policy proposals have been put forward by deep ecologists on the basis of these arguments. The influential poet Gary Snyder, for example, would like to see a 90 percent reduction in human populations to allow a restoration of pristine environments, while others have argued forcefully that a large portion of the globe must be immediately cordoned off from human beings.[3]

Third, there is a widespread invocation of Eastern spiritual traditions as forerunners of deep ecology. Deep ecology, it is suggested, was practiced both by major religious traditions and at a more popular level by "primal" peoples in non-Western settings. This complements the search for an authentic lineage in Western thought. At one level, the task is to recover those dissenting voices within the Judeo–Christian tradition; at another, to suggest that religious traditions in other cultures are, in contrast, dominantly if not exclusively "biocentric" in their orientation. This coupling of (ancient) Eastern and (modern) ecological wisdom seemingly helps consolidate the claim that deep ecology is a philosophy of universal significance.

Fourth, deep ecologists, whatever their internal differences, share the belief that they are the "leading edge" of the environmental movement. As the polarity of the shallow/deep and anthropocentric/biocentric distinctions makes clear, they see themselves as the spiritual, philosophical, and political vanguard of American and world environmentalism.

Toward a Critique

Although I analyze each of these tenets independently, it is important to recognize, as deep ecologists are fond of remarking in reference to nature, the interconnectedness and unity of these individual themes.

Insofar as it has begun to act as a check on man's arrogance and ecological hubris, the transition from an anthropocentric (human-centered) to a biocentric (humans as only one element in the ecosystem) view in both religious and scientific traditions is only to be welcomed.[4] What is unacceptable are the radical conclusions drawn by deep ecology, in particular, that intervention in nature should be guided primarily by the need to preserve biotic integrity rather than by the needs of humans. The latter for deep ecologists is anthropocentric, the former biocentric. This dichotomy is, however, of very little use in understanding the dynamics of environmental degradation. The two fundamental ecological problems facing the globe are (1) overconsumption by the industrialized world and by urban elites in the Third World and (2) growing militarization, both in a short-term sense (i.e., ongoing regional wars) and in a long-term sense (i.e., the arms race and the prospect of nuclear annihilation). Neither of these problems has any tangible connection to the anthropocentric–biocentric distinction. Indeed, the agents of these processes would barely comprehend this philosophical dichotomy. The proximate causes of the ecologically wasteful characteristics of industrial society and of militarization are far more mundane: at an aggregate level, the dialectic of economic and political structures, and at a micro-level, the lifestyle choices of individuals. These causes cannot be reduced, whatever the level of analysis, to a deeper anthropocentric attitude toward nature; on the contrary, by constituting a grave threat to human survival, the ecological degradation they cause does not even serve the best interests of human beings! If my identification of the major dangers to the integrity of the natural world is correct, invoking the bogey of anthropocentrism is at best irrelevant, and at worst a dangerous obfuscation.

If the above dichotomy is irrelevant, the emphasis on wilderness is positively harmful when applied to the Third World. If in the United States the preservationist/utilitarian division is seen as mirroring the conflict between "people" and "interests," in countries such as India the situation is very nearly the reverse. Because India is a long settled and densely populated country in which agrarian populations have a finely balanced relationship with nature, the setting aside of wilderness areas has resulted in a direct transfer of resources from the poor to the rich. Thus, Project Tiger, a network of parks hailed by the international conservation community as an outstanding success, sharply posits the interests of the tiger against those of poor peasants living in and around the reserve. The designation of tiger reserves was made possible only by the physical displacement of existing villages and their inhabitants; their management requires the continuing exclusion of peasants and livestock. The initial impetus for setting up parks for the tiger and other large mammals such as the rhinoceros and elephant came from two social groups, first, a class of ex-hunters turned conservationists belonging mostly to the declining Indian feudal elite and second, representatives of international agencies, such as the World Wildlife Fund (WWF) and the International Union for the Conservation of Nature and Natural Resources (IUCN), seeking to transplant the American system of national parks onto Indian soil. In no case have the needs of the local population been taken into account, and as in many parts of Africa, the designated wildlands are managed primarily for the benefit of rich tourists. Until very recently, wildlands preservation has been identified with environmentalism by the state and the conservation elite; in consequence environmental problems that impinge far more directly on the lives of the poor—e.g., fuel, fodder, water shortages, soil erosion, and air and water pollution—have not been adequately addressed.[5]

Deep ecology provides, perhaps unwittingly, a justification for the continuation of such narrow and inequitable conservation practices under a newly acquired radical guise. Increasingly, the international conservation elite is using the philosophical, moral, and scientific arguments used by deep ecologists in advancing their wilderness crusade. A striking but by no means atypical example is the recent plea by a prominent American biologist for the take-over of large portions of the globe by the author and his scientific colleagues. Writing in a prestigious scientific forum, *The Annual Review of Ecology and Systematics*, Daniel Janzen argues that only biologists have the competence to decide how the tropical landscape should be used. As "the representatives of the natural world," biologists are "in charge of the future of tropical ecology," and only they have the expertise and mandate to determine whether the tropical agroscape is to be populated only by humans, their mutualists, commensals, and parasites, or whether it will also contain some islands of the greater nature—the nature that spawned humans yet has been vanquished by them." Janzen exhorts his colleagues to advance their territorial claims on the tropical world more forcefully, warning that the very existence of these areas is at stake: "if biologists want a tropics in which to biologize, they are going to have to buy it with care, energy, effort, strategy, tactics, time, and cash."[6]

This frankly imperialist manifesto highlights the multiple dangers of the preoccupation with wilderness preservation that is characteristic of deep ecology. As I have suggested, it seriously compounds the neglect by the American movement of far more pressing environmental problems within the Third World. But perhaps more importantly, and in a more insidious fashion, it also provides an impetus to the imperialist yearning of Western biologists and their financial sponsors, organizations such as the WWF and IUCN. The wholesale transfer of a movement culturally rooted in American conservation history can only result in the social uprooting of human populations in other parts of the globe.

I come now to the persistent invocation of Eastern philosophies as antecedent in point of time but convergent in their structure with deep ecology. Complex and internally differentiated religious traditions—Hinduism, Buddhism, and Taoism—are lumped together as holding a view of nature believed to be quintessentially biocentric. Individual philosophers such as the Taoist Lao Tzu are identified as being forerunners of deep ecology. Even an intensely political, pragmatic, and Christian influenced thinker such as Gandhi has been accorded a wholly undeserved place in the deep ecological pantheon. Thus the Zen teacher Robert Aitken Roshi makes the strange claim that Gandhi's thought was not human-centered and that he practiced an embryonic form of deep ecology which is "traditionally Eastern and is found with differing emphasis in Hinduism, Taoism and in Theravada and Mahayana Buddhism."[7]

Moving away from the realm of high philosophy and scriptural religion, deep ecologists make the further claim that at the level of material and spiritual practice "primal" peoples subordinated themselves to the integrity of the biotic universe they inhabited.

I have indicated that this appropriation of Eastern traditions is in part dictated by the need to construct an authentic lineage and in part a desire to present deep ecology as a universalistic philosophy. Indeed, in his substantial and quixotic biography of John Muir, Michael Cohen goes so far as to suggest that Muir was the "Taoist of the [American] West."[8] This reading of Eastern traditions is selective and does not bother to differentiate between alternate (and changing) religious and cultural traditions; as it stands, it does considerable violence to the historical record. Throughout most recorded history the characteristic form of human activity in the "East" has been a finely tuned but nonetheless conscious and dynamic manipulation of nature. Although mystics such as Lao Tzu did reflect on the spiritual essence of human relations with nature, it must be recognized that such ascetics and their reflections were supported by a society of cultivators whose relationship with nature was a far more active one. Many agricultural communities do have a sophisticated knowledge of the natural environment that may equal (and sometimes surpass) codified "scientific" knowledge. Yet the elaboration of such traditional ecological knowledge (in both material and spiritual contexts) can hardly be said to rest on a mystical affinity with nature of a deep ecological kind. Nor is such knowledge infallible; as the archaeological record powerfully suggests, modern Western man has no monopoly on ecological disasters.

In a brilliant article, the Chicago historian Ronald Inden points out that this romantic and essentially positive view of the East is a mirror image of the scientific and essentially pejorative view normally upheld by Western scholars of the Orient. In either case, the East constitutes the Other, a body wholly separate and alien from the West; it is defined by a uniquely spiritual and nonrational "essence," even if this essence is valorized quite differently by the two schools. Eastern man exhibits a spiritual dependence with respect to nature—on the one hand, this is symptomatic of his prescientific and backward self, on the other, of his ecological wisdom and deep ecological consciousness. Both views are monolithic, simplistic, and have the characteristic effect—intended in one case, perhaps unintended in the other—of denying agency and reason to the East and making it the privileged orbit of Western thinkers.

The two apparently opposed perspectives have then a common underlying structure of discourse in which the East merely serves as a vehicle for Western projections. Varying images of the East are raw material for political and cultural battles being played out in the West; they tell us far more about the Western commentator and his desires than about the "East." Inden's remarks apply not merely to Western scholarship on India, but to Orientalist constructions of China and Japan as well:

> Although these two views appear to be strongly opposed, they often combine together. Both have similar interest in sustaining the Otherness of India. The holders of the dominant view, best exemplified in the past in imperial administrative discourse (and today probably by that of development economics), would place a traditional, superstition-ridden India in a position of perpetual tutelage to a modern, rational West. The adherents of the romantic view best exemplified academically in the discourses of Christian liberalism and analytic psychology concede the realm of the public and impersonal to the positivist. Taking their succor not from governments and big business, but from a plethora of religious foundations and self-help institutes, and from allies in the consciousness industry, not to

mention the important industry of tourism, the romantics insist that India embodies a private realm of the imagination and the religious which modern, western man lacks but needs. They, therefore, like the positivists, but for just the opposite reason, have a vested interest in seeing that the Orientalist view of India as
spiritual, mysterious, and exotic is perpetuated. [9]

How radical, finally, are the deep ecologists? Notwithstanding their self
image and strident rhetoric (in which the label "shallow ecology" has an oppro-
brium similar to that reserved for "social-democratic" by Marxist-Leninists),
even within the American context their radicalism is limited and it manifests
itself quite differently elsewhere.

To my mind, deep ecology is best viewed as a radical trend within the wilderness preservation movement. Although advancing philosophical rather than
aesthetic arguments and encouraging political militancy rather than negotiation,
its practical emphasis—viz., preservation of unspoiled nature—is virtually
identical. For the mainstream movement, the function of wilderness is to provide a temporary antidote to modern civilization. As a special institution within
an industrialized society, the national park "provides an opportunity for respite,
contrast, contemplation, and affirmation of values for those who live most of
their lives in the workaday world."[10] Indeed, the rapid increase in visitations to
the national parks in post-war America is a direct consequence of economic
expansion. The emergence of a popular interest in wilderness sites, the historian
Samuel Hays points out, was "not a throwback to the primitive, but an integral
part of the modern standard of living as people sought to add new 'amenity' and
'aesthetic' goals and desires to their earlier preoccupation with necessities and
conveniences."[11] Here, the enjoyment of nature is an integral part of the consumer society. The private automobile (and the lifestyle it has spawned) is in
many respects the ultimate ecological villain, and an untouched wilderness the
prototype of ecological harmony; yet, for most Americans it is perfectly consistent to drive a thousand miles to spend a holiday in a national park. They possess a vast, beautiful, and sparsely populated continent and are also able to draw
upon the natural resources of large portions of the globe by virtue of their economic and political dominance. In consequence, America can simultaneously
enjoy the material benefits of an expanding economy and the aesthetic benefits
of unspoiled nature. The two poles of "wilderness" and "civilization" mutually
coexist in an internally coherent whole, and philosophers of both poles are as-
signed a prominent place in this culture. Paradoxically as it may seem, it is no
accident that Star Wars technology and deep ecology both find their fullest
expression in that leading sector of Western civilization, California.

Deep ecology runs parallel to the consumer society without seriously questioning its ecological and socio-political basis. In its celebration of American
wilderness, it also displays an uncomfortable convergence with the prevailing
climate of nationalism in the American wilderness movement. For spokesmen
such as the historian Roderick Nash, the national park system is America's
distinctive cultural contribution to the world, reflective not merely of its eco-

nomic but of its philosophical and ecological maturity as well. In what Walter Lippmann called the American century, the "American invention of national parks" must be exported worldwide. Betraying an economic determinism that would make even a Marxist shudder, Nash believes that environmental preservation is a "full stomach" phenomenon that is confined to the rich, urban, and sophisticated. Nonetheless, he hopes that "the less developed nations may eventually evolve economically and intellectually to the point where nature preservation is more than a business."[12]

The error which Nash makes (and which deep ecology in some respects encourages) is to equate environmental protection with the protection of wilderness. This is a distinctively American notion, born out of a unique social and environmental history. The archetypal concerns of radical environmentalists in other cultural contexts are in fact quite different. The German Greens, for example, have elaborated a devastating critique of industrial society which turns on the acceptance of environmental limits to growth. Pointing to the intimate links between industrialization, militarization, and conquest, the Greens argue that economic growth in the West has historically rested on the economic and ecological exploitation of the Third World. Rudolf Bahro is characteristically blunt:

> The working class here [in the West] is the richest lower class in the world. And if I look at the problem from the point of view of the whole of humanity, not just from that of Europe, then I must say that the metropolitan working class is the worst exploiting class in history. . . . What made poverty bearable in eighteenth or nineteenth-century Europe was the prospect of escaping it through exploitation of the periphery. But this is no longer a possibility, and continued industrialism in the Third World will mean poverty for whole generations and hunger for millions.[13]

Here the roots of global ecological problems lie in the disproportionate share of resources consumed by the industrialized countries as a whole and the urban elite within the Third World. Since it is impossible to reproduce an industrial monoculture worldwide, the ecological movement in the West must begin by cleaning up its own act. The Greens advocate the creation of a "no growth" economy, to be achieved by scaling down current (and clearly unsustainable) consumption levels.[14] This radical shift in consumption and production patterns requires the creation of alternate economic and political structures — smaller in scale and more amenable to social participation—but it rests equally on a shift in cultural values. The expansionist character of modern Western man will have to give way to an ethic of renunciation and self-limitation, in which spiritual and communal values play an increasing role in sustaining social life. This revolution in cultural values, however, has as its point of departure an understanding of environmental processes quite different from deep ecology.

Many elements of the Green program find a strong resonance in countries such as India, where a history of Western colonialism and industrial development has benefited only a tiny elite while exacting tremendous social and environmental costs. The ecological battles presently being fought in India have as their epicenter the conflict over nature between the subsistence and largely rural sector and the vastly more powerful commercial-industrial sector. Perhaps the most celebrated of these battles concerns the Chipko (Hug the Tree) movement, a peasant movement against deforestation in the Himalayan foothills. Chipko is only one of several movements that have sharply questioned the nonsustainable demand being placed on the land and vegetative base by urban centers and industry. These include opposition to large dams by displaced peasants, the conflict between small artisan fishing and large-scale trawler fishing for export, the countrywide movements against commercial forest operations, and opposition to industrial pollution among downstream agricultural and fishing communities.[15]

Two features distinguish these environmental movements from their Western counterparts. First, for the sections of society most critically affected by environmental degradation—poor and landless peasants, women, and tribals—it is a question of sheer survival, not of enhancing the quality of life. Second, and as a consequence, the environmental solutions they articulate deeply involve questions of equity as well as economic and political redistribution. Highlighting these differences, a leading Indian environmentalist stresses that "environmental protection per se is of least concern to most of these groups. Their main concern is about the use of the environment and who should benefit from it."[16] They seek to wrest control of nature away from the state and the industrial sector and place it in the hands of rural communities who live within that environment but are increasingly denied access to it. These communities have far more basic needs, their demands on the environment are far less intense, and they can draw upon a reservoir of cooperative social institutions and local ecological knowledge in managing the "commons"—forests, grasslands, and the waters—on a sustainable basis. If colonial and capitalist expansion has both accentuated social inequalities and signalled a precipitous fall in ecological wisdom, an alternate ecology must rest on an alternate society and polity as well.

This brief overview of German and Indian environmentalism has some major implications for deep ecology. Both German and Indian environmental traditions allow for a greater integration of ecological concerns with livelihood and work. They also place a greater emphasis on equity and social justice (both within individual countries and on a global scale) on the grounds that in the absence of social regeneration environmental regeneration has very little chance of success. Finally, and perhaps most significantly, they have escaped the preoccupation with wilderness preservation so characteristic of American cultural and environmental history.[17]

A Homily

In 1958, the economist J. K. Galbraith referred to overconsumption as the un-asked question of the American conservation movement. There is a marked selectivity, he wrote, "in the conservationist's approach to materials consumption. If we are concerned about our great appetite for materials, it is plausible to seek to increase the supply, to decrease waste, to make better use of the stocks available, and to develop substitutes. But what of the appetite itself? Surely this is the ultimate source of the problem. If it continues its geometric course, will it not one day have to be restrained? Yet in the literature of the resource problem this is the forbidden question. Over it hangs a nearly total silence."[18]

The consumer economy and society have expanded tremendously in the three decades since Galbraith penned these words, yet his criticisms are nearly as valid today. I have said "nearly," for there are some hopeful signs. Within the environmental movement several dispersed groups are working to develop ecologically benign technologies and to encourage less wasteful lifestyles. Moreover, outside the self-defined boundaries of American environmentalism, opposition to the permanent war economy is being carried on by a peace movement that has a distinguished history and impeccable moral and political credentials.

It is precisely these (to my mind, most hopeful) components of the American social scene that are missing from deep ecology. In their widely noticed book, Bill Devall and George Sessions make no mention of militarization or the movements for peace, while activists whose practical focus is on developing ecologically responsible lifestyles (e.g., Wendell Berry) are derided as "falling short of deep ecological awareness."[19] A truly radical ecology in the American context ought to work toward a synthesis of the appropriate technology, alternate lifestyle, and peace movements.[20] By making the (largely spurious) anthropocentric–biocentric distinction central to the debate, deep ecologists may have appropriated the moral high ground, but they are at the same time doing a serious disservice to American and global environmentalism.[21]

Notes

This chapter is reprinted with minor revisions from *Environmental Ethics* 11 (1989): 71–83. This essay was written while the author was a visiting lecturer at the Yale School of Forestry and Environmental Studies. He is grateful to Mike Bell, Tom Birch, Bill Burch, Bill Cronon, Diane Mayerfeld, David Rothenberg, Kirkpatrick Sale, Joel Seton, Tim Weiskel, and Don Worster for helpful comments.

[1] Kirkpatrick Sale, "The Forest for the Trees: Can Today's Environmentalists Tell the Difference?" *Mother Jones* 11 no. 5 (November 1986): 26.

[2] One of the major criticisms I make in this essay concerns deep ecology's lack of concern with inequalities within human society. In the article in which he coined the term deep ecology, Næss himself expresses concerns about inequalities between and within nations. However, his concern with social cleavages and their impact on resource utiliza-

tion patterns and ecological destruction is not very visible in the later writings of deep ecologists. See Arne Næss, "The Shallow and the Deep, Long-Range Ecology Movement: A Summary," *Inquiry* 16 (1973): 96 (I am grateful to Tom Birch for this reference).

[3] Gary Snyder, quoted in Sale, "The Forest for the Trees," p. 32. See also Dave Foreman, "A Modest Proposal for a Wilderness System," *Whole Earth Review* 53 (Winter, 1987): 42–45.

[4] See, for example, Donald Worster, *Nature's Economy: The Roots of Ecology* (San Francisco: Sierra Club Books, 1977).

[5] See Centre for Science and Environment, India: *The State of the Environment 1982: A Citizens Report* (New Delhi: Centre for Science and Environment, 1982); R. Sukumar, "Elephant–Man Conflict in Karnataka," in *The State of Karnataka's Environment* ed. Cecil Saldanha, (Bangalore: Centre for Taxonomic Studies, 1985). For Africa, see the brilliant analysis by Hedge Kjekshus, *Ecology Control and Economic Development in East African History* (Berkeley: University of California Press, 1977).

[6] Daniel Janzen, "The Future of Tropical Ecology," *Annual Review of Ecology and Systematics* 17 (1986): 305–6, emphasis added.

[7] Robert Aitken Roshi, "Gandhi, Dogen, and Deep Ecology," reprinted as appendix C in Bill Devall and George Sessions, *Deep Ecology: Living as if Nature Mattered* (Salt Lake City: Peregrine Smith Books, 1985). For Gandhi's own views on social reconstruction, see the excellent three volume collection, edited by Raghavan Iyer, *The Moral and Political Writings of Mahatma Gandhi* (Oxford: Clarendon Press, 1986–87).

[8] Michael Cohen, *The Pathless Way* (Madison: University of Wisconsin Press, 1984): 120.

[9] Ronald Inden, "Orientalist Constructions of India," *Modern Asian Studies* 20 (1986): 442. Inden draws inspiration from Edward Said's forceful polemic *Orientalism* (New York: Basic Books, 1980). It must be noted, however, that there is a salient difference between Western perceptions of Middle Eastern and Far Eastern cultures respectively. Due perhaps to the long history of Christian conflict with Islam, Middle East cultures (as Said documents) are consistently presented in pejorative terms. The juxtaposition of hostile and worshipping attitudes that Inden talks of applies only to Western attitudes toward Buddhist and Hindu societies.

[10] Joseph Sax, *Mountains Without Handrails: Reflections on the National Parks* (Ann Arbor: University of Michigan Press, 1980), 42. See also Peter Schmitt, *Back to Nature: The Arcadian Myth in Urban America* (New York: Oxford University Press, 1969) and Alfred Runte, *National Parks: The American Experience* (Lincoln: University of Nebraska Press, 1979).

[11] Samuel Hays, "From Conservation to Environment: Environmental Politics in the United States Since World War Two," *Environmental Review* 6 (1982): 21. See also the same author's book entitled *Beauty, Health and Permanence: Environmental Politics in the United States, 1955–85* (New York: Cambridge University Press, 1987).

[12] Roderick Nash, *Wilderness and the American Mind*, 3rd ed. (New Haven: Yale University Press, 1982).

[13] Rudolf Bahro, *From Red to Green* (London: Verso Books, 1984).

[14] From time to time, American scholars have themselves criticized these imbalances in consumption patterns. In the 1950s, William Vogt made the charge that the United States, with one-sixteenth of the world's population, was utilizing one-third of the globe's resources. [Vogt, cited in E. F. Murphy, *Nature, Bureaucracy and the Rule of*

Property (Amsterdam: North Holland, 1977), 29]. More recently, Zero Population Growth has estimated that each American consumes thirty-nine times as many resources as an Indian. See *Christian Science Monitor*, 2 March 1987.

[15] For an excellent review, see Anil Agarwal and Sunita Narain, eds., *India: The State of the Environment 1984–85: A Citizens Report* (New Delhi: Centre for Science and Environment, 1985). See also Ramachandra Guha, *The Unquiet Woods: Ecological Change and Peasant Resistance in the Indian Himalaya* (Berkeley: University of California Press, forthcoming).

[16] Anil Agarwal, "Human–Nature Interactions in a Third World Country," *The Environmentalist* 6, no. 3 (1986): 167.

[17] One strand in radical American environmentalism, the bioregional movement, by emphasizing a greater involvement with the bioregion people inhabit, does indirectly challenge consumerism. However, as yet bioregionalism has hardly raised the questions of equity and social justice (international, intranational, and intergenerational) which, I argue, must be a central plank of radical environmentalism. Moreover, its stress on (individual) experience as the key to involvement with nature, is also somewhat at odds with the integration of nature with livelihood and work that I talk of in this paper. See Kirkpatrick Sale, *Dwellers in the Land: The Bioregional Vision* (San Francisco: Sierra Club Books, 1985).

[18] John Kenneth Galbraith, "How Much Should a Country Consume?" in *Perspectives on Conservation* ed. Henry Janett, (Baltimore: Johns Hopkins Press, 1958), 91–92.

[19] Devall and Sessions, *Deep Ecology*, 122. For Wendel Berry's own assessment of deep ecology, see his "Amplications: Preserving Wildness," *Wilderness* 50 (Spring 1987): 39–40, 50–54.

[20] See the interesting recent contribution by one of the most influential spokesmen of appropriate technology, Barry Commoner, "A Reporter at Large: the Environment," *New Yorker*, 15 June 1987. While Commoner makes a forceful plea for the convergence of the environmental movement (viewed by him primarily as the opposition to air and water pollution and to the institutions that generate such pollution), and the peace movement, he significantly does not mention consumption patterns, implying that "limits to growth" do not exist.

[21] In this sense, my critique of deep ecology, although that of an outsider, may facilitate the reassertion of those elements in the American environmental tradition for which there is a profound sympathy in other parts of the globe. A global perspective may also lead to a critical reassessment of figures such as Aldo Leopold and John Muir, the two patron saints of deep ecology. As Donald Woster has pointed out, the message of Muir (and, I would argue, of Leopold as well) makes sense only in an American context; he has very little to say to other cultures. See Worster's review of Stephen Fox's "John Muir and His Legacy," in *Environmental Ethics* 5 (1983): 277–81.

Chapter 41

Comments on Guha's "Radical American Environmentalism and Wilderness Preservation: A Third World Critique"

Arne Næss

I

Glorification of the ecological policies of nonindustrial peoples was fashionable in the 1960s, especially in the United States. But the valuable increase of literature on the subject forced a much more discerning attitude. Because of interest in the vast diversity of cultures among the American Indians, for example, theoreticians of the deep ecology movement in the United States have become significantly more aware of the variety of ecologically relevant attitudes among nonindustrial cultures, including some whose attitudes are narrowly utilitarian. In his critique of the deep ecology movement, Ramachandra Guha has chosen both to ignore this development and to distort the main features of deep ecology.

I do not know of any theoretician of deep ecology who would subscribe to the following sweeping generalization by Guha: "Deep ecology," it is suggested, "was practiced both by major religious traditions and at a more popular level by 'primal' peoples in non-Western settings." More to the point, I think, is the following statement: "The coupling of (ancient) Eastern and (modern) ecological wisdom seemingly helps to consolidate the claim that deep ecology is a philosophy of universal significance." But this is still much too sweeping. It is also misleading because one of the most important characteristics of supporters of the deep ecology movement is adherence to diverse philosophies and religions. Or, more accurately, their ultimate premises show great variations. Deep ecology is certainly transcultural in its aspirations. It may thus be said that the total views found among supporters of the deep ecology movement may occasionally correspond with (some ancient) Eastern and (some modern) ecological wisdom. But to cherish some of the ecosophic attitudes convincingly demonstrated by people from the East does not imply the doctrinal acceptance of any past definite philosophy or religion conventionally classified as Eastern. Supporters of the deep ecology movement tend to refrain from interference with each other's ultimate beliefs. Whether one derives inspiration from people or texts from the East or West, North or South of the Arctic Circle, is of no ultimate concern.

Speaking of influence: There are significant (sometimes unbridgeable) cultural differences between so called "Western" and "Eastern" attitudes to nature. Even when the "environmental concern" of poor Third World communities seems to Westerners to relate to "environment per se," matters can be much more complex. An example: The people of the Buddhist community of Beding (Peding) in the Ralwaling Himalaya live with the majestic holy mountain Gauri Shankar (Tseringwa) straight above their heads. It had long been an object of cult and some of us (mountaineers and deep ecology supporters) asked whether they wished to enjoy the profit they would get from expeditions by Westerners and Japanese trying to "conquer the mountain" or whether they would rather protect the mountain from being trodden upon by humans who had little knowledge or respect for its cultural status. The families came together and unanimously voted for protection. I had the honor to walk a week with the chief of the community, Gönden, to deliver at Katmandu a document addressed to the King of Nepal, asking for a prohibition on climbing Gauri Shankar.[1]

Was the Beding protest a case of environmental concern? For the villagers of Beding the cleavage between humans and their environment is certainly less pronounced than in the West. For them, however, Gauri Shankar has been both a mountain in our sense and a God, or better, a Deva, and also a Princess. In short, their cultural tradition includes a mythology of a specific kind, which makes it misleading to say that the protection of Gauri Shankar is an instance of "protecting the environment per se."

II

Ramachandra Guha writes: "In contrast to the conventional lobbying efforts of environmental professionals based in Washington, it [deep ecology] proposes a militant defense of 'Mother Earth,' an unflinching opposition to human attacks on undisturbed wilderness."

This kind of description fits some supporters of the deep ecology movement. But this is usually in connection with the destruction of wilderness in the United States. There is ample justification for activists in the United States to oppose the mindless, destructive activities that are still going on there. But to my knowledge, American environmentalists tend not to publish their proposals on how to treat apparently similar problems in the Third World. At least this is true of theoreticians of the deep ecology movement. To mention but one example: Paul Ehrlich says explicitly that even an additional square inch of old growth forest should not be destroyed—in the United States. Nobody has, as far as I know, "argued forcefully that a large portion of the globe must be immediately cordoned off from human beings."

Just as there were people who thought that what was good for General Motors was good for the United States, there today are people who think that what is good for the United States is good for the rest of the world, including the Third World. They infer that the rhetorics and tenets of American "radical" environmentalism may be verbatim fit for the Third World. The enormity of the claim is obvious. We should not and cannot deploy the same rhetorics, set of slogans and priorities of environmentalism in all cultures.

The distinction between a "radical" and a "reformist" American environmentalism is interesting. There is a potential total view, an ecosophy, which comprises a cult, or at least a metaphysic, of wilderness. Aldous Huxley, Paul Shepard, and Gary Snyder have published valuable contributions. But the deep ecology movement, as characterized roughly by the 8 points proposed by George Sessions and myself, does not imply the acceptance of any definite ecosophy. Ergo: contrary to Guha's argument, it does not imply any metaphysical cult of wilderness as a necessary component of the deep ecological stance.[2]

The term "wilderness" covers different levels of noninterference by the human enterprise on earth. It is an interesting experiment to try to keep some areas as free as possible from human interference. This implies, e.g., a prohibition of flying over them. Next, there are areas set apart except for fire protection or similar happenstance and/or scientific investigation. A third degree of interference is at hand when there is tourism of a limited kind. There are rules against camping, strolling outside definite areas or paths, as part of a more or less severe set of rules.

In Europe the term "free nature" is more important than "wilderness," and it is increasingly used when discussing very large parts of the Third World. The difference between the two terms is that "free nature" is compatible with human habitation, provided that this habitation is in no way dominant. Thus delimited, it is of course a rather vague and ambiguous term—but it is a term which implies a context-dependent compromise between the human and natural habitus.

III

Some deep ecology theorists like myself have "radical" views about population reduction. But this does not mean that I insist that all supporters of the deep ecology movement hold views about population, which are as "radical" as mine. It is my firm belief that supporters generally hold that it would be better for the life of humans, and very much better for nonhumans, if there were fewer homini sapiens around.

Today, the general reluctance to think or do anything about overpopulation is understandable: In Europe the despicable effort by people like Mussolini and Hitler to increase their populations and the equally abominable effort to decrease "undesirables" casts a shadow on any discussion of this issue.

I agree that the question of population must be worded very carefully. Unfortunately my proposal of a population paragraph, only reluctantly agreed to by George Sessions, suggests population reduction.[3] It is better to leave "reduction" out, and to refer instead to what is "better." This would more in line with the function of the 8 points as a description of a common view held by supporters of deep ecology. Most people think in time spans of say, four or thirty years, not of centuries. Personally I think an appropriate kind of reduction may not be forthcoming before the twenty-second century and it will take a long time. (Incidentally, a statistical average of about two children per family results fairly rapidly in a substantial decrease of population.)

IV

"The anthropocentric–biocentric distinction is accepted as axiomatic by deep ecologists, it structures their discourse, and much of the present discussion remains mired within it," argues Guha.

Clearly "anthropocentric" is a negative—and "biocentric" positive—word in all deep ecology literature. But one has to look for examples and elaborations to see what the words stand for. "Center" and "centering" have many senses. In at least one sense, the center of responsibility and concern of humans are humans themselves: We are all anthropocentric!

The "belief that man and his works are the center of the universe" is extreme. So are claims to the effect that "Man is only one species among millions of others." However, so far as I can judge, the human brain and human capacities are generally such that human development toward full maturity fosters a genuinely human need to live on a planet with a full richness and diversity of life forms. Therefore there is no necessary long-range conflict of interest between these life forms and humanity seen in the broad perspective (i.e., one, which takes into account the interest of other life forms). We do things for our children both for own sake and for the sake of the children. We water the flowers for their own sake as well as for our own. (In terms of ultimate philosophical questions the distinction is problematic—but not on the level needed here.)

V

I grant that if the term "deep ecology" is given the four defining characteristics Guha mentions, then "it is inappropriate when applied to the Third World." But, then, it may also be added that it is largely inappropriate to the First, Second, and Fourth Worlds. Very few supporters and theoreticians of deep ecology would, however, find Guha's characterization of the movement adequate. Perhaps there are trend-setting people who call themselves deep ecologists and who accept Guha's four tenets or some such set? If so, I may have to change the terminology. Perhaps I should think of another name for what I have so far referred to as the "deep ecology movement" and continue my efforts exactly as before. But I do not believe what some of my friends occasionally assert—that the terminology of deep ecology is in ruins. Several years ago *the Los Angeles Times* reported on some people who "liberated" zoo animals in the name of deep ecology. The *Los Angeles Times* is read by many people who certainly do not read small ecosophical journals. Murray Bookchin has used such strong terms ("fascism," etc.) against what he calls "deep ecology" that warnings appeared in newspapers all over the world. But any and every term (including "freedom," "truth" and such like) used as key indicators of big social movements is similarly abused. To create new ones every time this occurs would only increase rather than decrease confusion.

It may be relevant at this point to mention how the term "deep ecology" was introduced in the United States. In 1984 the term "deep ecology" was known to many people in the U.S., Australia, and Canada. Deep ecology literature in the English language consisted of articles, mostly in small periodicals or newsletters of limited distribution. Bill Devall and George Sessions worked on a book to introduce the deep ecology movement to a larger readership. It was far from completed when they got to know that a book with the title *Deep Ecology*, edited by Michael Tobias, was due for publication in 1985. This collection had many excellent articles, but it would certainly confuse those who thought that it was mainly concerned with the deep ecology movement. George Sessions was of the opinion that his and Devall's book needed at least one more year in order to be properly structured and more adequate in its treatment of social and political issues. Bill Devall and the publisher considered it fatal if the book edited by Tobias were to be the only introduction to deep ecology for at least a whole year before an adequate account reached the market. Devall and the publisher won—George Sessions protested vehemently.

Looking back, I do not know what to think. The book was published and the public understood that, whatever the qualities of Tobias's book, the work of Devall and Sessions was nearer to being an account of deep ecology.

The book has a short section: "Basic principles of deep ecology." Point 6 runs as follows: "Policies must therefore be changed. These policies affect basic economic, technological, and ideological structures. The resulting state of affairs will be deeply different from the present." There was no time to elaborate on the appropriate social and political policies. The book therefore is at its best when Devall, Sessions, and Gary Snyder introduce their special interests within the deep ecology context. The lack of an adequate discussion of the policy implications of deep ecology certainly does not mean that the authors underrated the social and political aspects of the international long-range deep ecology movement.

If we accept that the realization of the goals of the deep ecology movement implies wide sustainability, two questions immediately arise:

1. does the realization of wide sustainability presuppose or require acceptance of the views of the deep ecology movement? and
2. does the realization of wide sustainability require significant changes both in First and Third World societies?

If we answer "yes" to the first question, this might be interpreted as asserting that the realization of wide sustainability would require that most members of the relevant societies accept the views of the deep ecology movement. As I see it, this is not necessary (and it would imply a change of heart of an extremely unlikely kind!)

As to question 2, a "yes" answer seems warranted as far as I can judge. It should be clear that the realization of wide ecological sustainability will require deep changes in the rich societies of the world having to do, in part, with policies of growth and overconsumptive lifestyles. In Third World countries at present there is a general tendency to attempt to follow an "economic growth and development" path which emulates that of the rich countries. This must be avoided, and to avoid it requires significant changes in the orientation of these societies.

It is obviously pertinent to ask: "Exactly what changes need to be made?"

A short answer to this question seems much more difficult to provide in the 1990s than in the 1970s. Practically every major concrete change envisaged in 1970 today seems either more difficult to realize, or not unreservedly desirable in the form it was proposed in 1970. As an example one may mention various forms of decentralization. Today the global nature of all the major ecological problems is widely recognized, along with the stubborn resistance of most local, regional, and national groups to give global concerns priority over those which are less-than-global.

The Indian environmentalist Anil Agarwal is right when he says that "environmental protection per se is of the least concern to most of these groups. Their main concern is about the use of the environment and who should benefit from it."

In 1985, at the international conservation biology conference in Michigan, a representative of a Third World country stood up and asked, "What about our problems? What is going on here is not of great concern in my country." For this and other representatives of the tropical countries it must have been bizarre to hear, day after day, discussions on the future of their countries, debates that hardly touched their main problems.

If the conference had been organized by one of the international green movements, the agenda would surely have been different. Discussion of how to deal with the ecological crisis would have taken up only one third of the time, at the most. Two-thirds would concern the main problems of social justice and of peace. The representatives of the Third World would have introduced the two latter areas of concern and would have stressed that the efforts to protect what is left of the richness and diversity of life on earth must not interfere with efforts to solve their main problems today. Supporters of the deep ecology movement might have brought up the following question for discussion: How can the increasing interest in life on earth be used to further the cause of economic growth in the Third World?

Having said all this, it must be acknowledged that the Chipko movement in India is widely known and influential in counteracting the misconception that groups of poor people are doing nothing to protect their environment for economic reasons, or have an indifferent attitude towards "where they belong." The work of Vandana Shiva and others shows how women in rural India continue to try to promote an economy that is largely ecologically sustainable. But do they have the power to resist Western inspired unecological development?

VI

With increased education, combined with economic progress in the Third World, the goal is not only to halt the excessive rate of extinction of animals and plants but also to protect whole ecosystems and ensure the continuation of evolution. (The Bern Convention is a step towards protection, but of course very fragmentary and limited). The First World nations increase their effort to protect what is left of free (not man-dominated) nature. But they forget that this is asking the Third World to adopt policies that developed countries never pursued themselves and which they, even today, pursue only half-heartedly.

Let me refer to an example close to home. According to the Bern Convention ratified by Norway, wolves are to be completely protected. But according to old Norwegian tradition everybody is free to kill the wolves. Local communities depending in part upon sheep farming continue to kill wolves in spite of the prohibition. "Kill and dig!" clubs are formed. That is, people organize hunts, the dead wolves are buried, and the community protects the culprits. The government does not mobilize great resources to stop the killing.

How do supporters of the deep ecology movement react? Not all in the same way. One of them, the bear- and wolf-specialist of international standing, Ivar Mysterud, shows great understanding for the point of view of local communities. He is largely criticized by "radical" environmentalists who think his view is shameful and unworthy of an ecologist. I have even been warned not to collaborate with such a person. Nevertheless, we have written two articles together and we agree that, according to the platform of deep ecology we have to protect the culture of the communities in question which is otherwise of a high ecological level.[4] One promising solution would be somehow to incorporate the wolf into the economy of the community. (As in some places in Alaska.) To move the population is out of the question. To furnish housing and work outside the wolf-area, and invite them to move, is also considered too radical.

Why mention this? Because supporters of the deep ecology movement cannot propose, and have not proposed, more radical ways of protecting wild life in the Third World than in the First World. The "uprooting of human populations"—something going on, on a vast scale in the Third World—is a completely foreign thought to supporters of the deep ecology movement.

Large-scale destruction may have a long-range adverse effect on development in the Third World and prolong the dependence of the economy and survival of its populations upon the First World. Does this mean that the prospect for protecting a large part of what is left of free nature in the Third World looks dim? Not at all. The possibility is still open of combining ecologically sustainable development with such protection.

VII

Guha writes: "Deep ecology provides, perhaps unwittingly, a justification for the continuation of such narrow and inequitable conservation practices under a newly acquired radical guise. Increasingly, the international conservation elite is using the philosophical, moral, and scientific arguments used by deep ecologists in advancing their wilderness crusade."

Establishing nature reservations in the Third World is a complex matter: not just a whim of the First World biologists or an economic enterprise. It is a project to preserve what is left of free nature; it is a gift to the world. In the 1960s and 1970s shamefully small efforts were made towards the establishment of nature reserves in the Third World, which were consistent with the aims of economic development. In the 1980s and 1990s additional efforts were made in permitting the poor people in and around nature reservations to profit from tourism. These efforts must be kept up. But the use of coercion in this process is a kind of neo-colonialism. One of the main motives of people supporting the deep ecology movement is extended compassion, reaching out beyond the human species. But the concern for the exploited and dominated, including the concern for the less powerful nonindustrial cultures is equally important. It is absurd to think that deep ecology supporters would continue the old paternalistic or imperialistic trends compatible with the outlook of the rich power elites in the Third World.

There are many writers who, like Guha, look upon Radical environmentalism, including deep ecology, as a threat to the poverty-stricken people of the Third World. The opinion is not uncommon that people in the rich Western world tend to support wild animals and wilderness rather than poor people. The real question is, however: How can the poor be helped in a way that is sustainable in the long run?

In the last part of his article Guha expresses hope that there will be a "true, radical ecological movement in the United States which will look towards a synthesis of the appropriate technology, alternate life style and peace movements."

I agree. In my opinion cold calculation in terms of cost/benefit analysis will not improve human attitudes towards ecological systems or the earth as a whole. Neither will narrow utilitarian considerations solve the ecological crisis or satisfy human needs. There must be a widespread respect for the earth with all its life forms—for their own sake. There will be no green society worthy of human aspirations if it is incompatible with efforts to maintain the earth in its fullness of life.

Notes

[1] There was no answer. The Hindu government of Nepal is economically interested in big expeditions, and the opinion of the far away Buddhist community of very poor people carries no weight.

[2] In the work of Warwick Fox, for example, there is no such cult of wilderness.

[3] New version: "(4) The flourishing of human life and cultures is compatible with a substantially smaller human population. The flourishing of nonhuman life would gain from the presence of a substantially smaller one."

[4] Arne Næss and Ivar Mysterud, "Philosophy of Wolf Policies I: General Principles and Preliminary Exploration of Selected Norms," *Conservation Biology*, No.1, May 1987, 22–34.

Chapter 42

Comment: Næss and Guha

Stephan Harding

Ramachandra Guha has quite clearly gleaned a regrettably misleading impression of what deep ecology is about. In my experience as a biologist and teacher of deep ecology, Guha's misunderstanding of deep ecology is in fact relatively common even among people who would be supporters were they given a correct account of what Arne Næss, its founding voice, means by deep ecology. The misunderstanding probably comes from various sources. One is that the terms "deep" and "ecology" are open to imaginative interpretation without need to refer to written material. When combining these terms, one can make what one likes of them, easily coming to the conclusion that deep ecology is misanthropic and favoring nature over humans. Another possible source of the misunderstanding stems from eye-catching statements made by certain so-called "deep ecologists" that AIDS and famines are a good thing because they kill off people and thereby lead to fewer humans and to less disturbance of wild nature. Dave Foreman, cited by Guha in his article, has made such statements, although he has now accepted that humans must also be nurtured. The lamentable attacks on deep ecology by Murray Bookchin (whom Arne sees as a colleague working at a distinctive point on the "long frontier" of the movement for change) may also have played a role in perpetuating this perspective.

Nowhere in Arne's extensive writings on deep ecology does he adopt a misanthropic role. Indeed, in the deep ecology platform he developed with George Sessions it is stated that humans have the right to satisfy *vital* needs. Clearly in rural India this means that villagers and tribals have a right to graze their animals within areas set aside for nature with the proviso that the ecological integrity of those areas is not compromised by overgrazing. Most pristine ecosystems can tolerate a certain amount of human presence, and indeed in some cases low to intermediate human presence can actually increase biodiversity, particularly if settled agriculture is not involved.

If evidence is required of deep ecology's support of local peoples' vital needs, one can cite the case of the Sariska Tiger Sanctuary, part of Project Tiger, where the Indian government would like to expel the Meena tribal people who have lived for centuries in the area as livestock herders. Yet Aman Singh, an Indian deep ecology supporter who has met and studied with Arne, is involved in opposing their expulsion and in ensuring their right to live traditionally. Similarly, the international agencies such as WWF and IUCN now realize that wildlife areas cannot be preserved unless local people have a stake in their preservation. A good example is the CAMPFIRE project in Zimbabwe, which gives local people direct access to monies generated from small-scale safari hunting on tribal lands, based on wildlife surveys the local people have themselves have carried out. Even among the mainstream conservation organizations the days of conservation imperialism are over.

Perhaps Guha should reconsider his assertion that the anthropocentric–biocentric distinction is irrelevant to explaining overconsumption in the industrialized world and growing militarism. Both can be seen as stemming directly from anthropocentrism. Overconsumption arises directly from the perception that nature is a dead machine which has value only as a resource for humans, while militarism is often motivated by a need to access or protect these same resources, as was the case in the Gulf war.

As far as unspoiled wilderness is concerned, we could state that by "unspoiled" is meant not "in the absence of humans," but "in the absence of human-induced disruptions of essential ecosystem functions." Too much impairment of ecosystem physiology results in a deterioration in climate-regulating and other essential "services" at both local and global (Gaia'n) levels. Therefore, it is in humans' long-term interests to maintain the health of ecosystems, but, as outlined above, this does not mean no human presence.

Any culture is inspiring to deep ecology supporters in so far as it shows or showed a respect for and integration with human and nonhuman nature. What is important is not that deep ecology is a philosophy of universal significance (probably it can't be, since it has arisen specifically in the West), but that humans can reach a place of respect for nature, for whatever reasons.

Lastly, nowhere in Næss's writing can one detect a sense of deep ecology as the "leading edge" of a movement. In fact, his emphasis is specifically and intentionally pluralistic, stressing that there are many and diverse ways of operating on the "long frontier" of ecological activism and involvement. If there is anything leading at an edge, it must be the whole movement itself, which, on various fronts, strives to raise awareness and to bring about change peacefully and democratically.

In his reply, Næss follows his precept of nonviolence admirably— by not resorting to polemics in any shape or form. Instead, carefully, respectfully, and exhaustively he addresses Guha's concerns one by one. Guha has no doubt unwittingly fallen for a narrow, distorted view of deep ecology. It is important that Næss's intentionally un-sensational but profound and diverse statements about deep ecology be carefully studied before putting pen to paper on this subject. Not to embark on serious study of Næss's works when writing about deep ecology would be like ignoring Marx when writing about communism or ignoring Lovelock when writing about Gaia theory. Indeed, Guha's article points to an opportunity to contrast what he calls "American" deep ecology with Arne's own, evolving, formulations.

Had Guha been familiar with Næss's thought, he would have realized that the founder of deep ecology is a wonderfully subtle, sophisticated thinker who stresses tolerance and plurality, and who is concerned as much for the welfare of humans as nonhumans, since in the end the two are utterly intertwined.

Part IV

Deep Ecology and Environmental Policy

Figure 4. The Wolf in the Driver's Seat.

Chapter 43

Philosophy of Wolf Policies (I): General Principles and Preliminary Exploration of Selected Norms

Arne Næss and Ivar Mysterud

Introduction

Wolves (*Canis lupus*) and humans are carnivores, and domestic sheep (*Ovis aries*) are food for both of them. Depredation of sheep might therefore be interpreted as competition for food between wolves and humans. But the raising of sheep is also economics for the sheepholder, who in Norway has been part of a farming culture that has traditionally invested in bounties to get rid of wolves. Other groups of people identifying with trends in modern industrial culture invest money in the opposite, to experience and enjoy wolves. A collision of subcultures?

The wolf is today nominally protected by law in Norway and Sweden. Nevertheless, what man should and should not do to sheep and wolves is a grave question that illustrates well the problems of letting large predators live in sparsely populated areas. The problems are at present under intense debate.

The debate goes all the way down to the rock-bottom problems of philosophy and political ideology. The practical solutions to the so-called "wolf problem" reveal philosophical premises as much as they reflect concrete economic and other mundane interests. Philosophical research tries to codify our deepest and most comprehensive attitudes and beliefs. This philosophical aspect is essential when we try to codify our attitudes toward living beings other than humans. We recognize a "wolf problem" as well as a "man problem."

"Live and Let Live!" Inescapable Identification

The basic development of human behavior patterns seems to have provided us with an inescapable feeling of kinship with all living beings, but only if our culture, society, or group membership does not actively inhibit this feeling. From an early age we "identify" and perceive ourselves in something else.[1] The proposition that we only perceive *similarity* with other kinds of living beings is based on a misunderstanding. The spontaneous experience of relatedness is better expressed by the term "sameness"; that is, "identity." But it is, of course, an identity with awesome differences: we can change our attention and immediately be aware of profound differences. One's dog is vastly different from oneself, but as "a member of our family," we intuitively identify strongly with it.

One of the most compelling cases of identification is furnished by our awareness of suffering. Even if we do not think that plants suffer, plants have traits that we spontaneously perceive as symptomatic of imperfect conditions of well-being. We actually "see" them suffer from dryness, heat, cold, or lack of nutrition as we "see" the suffering of humans.

Identification need not result in love. We may see our own bad characteristics in an animal. Except in people who are well acquainted with them, rats elicit disgust for obvious social reasons. The cultural setting of wolves is similar but formidable in its complexity and variation. Naturalists and mammalogists have "lived with" wolves and followed up with extensive reports. Not surprisingly, the process of identification has been intense and positive in these cases. But so far, the general pull inside wolf localities has scarcely been influenced the rapidly increasing pro-wolf literature.

Even exquisitely "ugly" animals such as the Tasmanian devil (*Sarcophilus ursinus*), which seems to be unflinchingly aggressive toward humans and completely devoid of gratitude for whatever we do to satisfy its hunger and needs, elicit sympathy and respect not only when considered *sub specie aeternitatis* as a natural wonder, part of the richness and diversity of life on this planet, but also as a symbol of our own aggressiveness and lack of gratitude. The Tasmanian devil permits us to laugh at ourselves.

Identification motivates norms of at least partial protection: rules of how to respect the dignity and status of even an obnoxious animal are similar to our respect for the dignity of murderers in prison. Such norms are, of course, also established through the operation of other motives, but identification must be considered if we are to understand truly both the strength of protective efforts in favor of wolves and the passionate urge to exterminate them.

Mixed Communities with Wolves, Sheep, and Sheep Owners[2]

Sociology distinguishes Gemeinschaft (community) from Gesellschaft (society). The distinction is somewhat differently defined by different authors. In sociology, "community" is defined in such a way that only human beings are considered members. Concepts of human community are obviously needed, but today broader concepts are also needed. We need to break down some of the barriers commonly erected between humans and other forms of life within our common space. We need a concept of "mixed community" defined in such a way that humans and limited groups of animals that play a more or less well-known role in human affairs are included as members.

It is unfortunate that the organizational cleavage between social and natural sciences has made many students of the former seemingly incapable of conceiving mixed communities. Dogs and cats have long been considered sort of members of the family, not quite on a par with children and the mentally handicapped, but certainly the subject of privileges and status not accorded people or animals outside the family. The same holds true of sheep, cows, pigs, and others of the same category in traditional herder communities.

The concept of mixed community may be seen as a subconcept of a general "life community" embracing all kinds of life. Considering that humans know about only a microscopic part of the living beings to which they are hosts and even less of those living beings in their nearest environment, human relations to all other members of a life community are significantly different from those within mixed communities.

We do not favor the term "life community" because of the abstractness of its relations. We follow ways of thinking conceptualized in phenomenological philosophy. It is presumed that there are conscious relationships between members of a mixed community and an occasional awareness of each other even when there is no physical nearness. This concept of mixed community does not compete with concepts within biology. Plant ecology and animal ecology embrace the collection of species populations in a given space and treat them collectively in the field of community ecology.[3]

For thousands of years the wolf has been part of mixed communities in the Nordic countries. Until this century the fairly large number of wolves and the limitations of available weapons made wolves a threat. This has totally changed. Furthermore, the deep ecological movement, the recent extensive pro-wolf literature, and the material richness of Nordic countries have, as an inevitable consequence, influenced the willingness of people outside wolf localities to give wolves a new and better chance to survive.

Here are a few facts about our Norwegian mixed community. At present we are 4.1 million humans and 2.3 million sheep on 323,886 square kilometers of land (Spitsbergen and Jan Mayen excluded). Norway is part of the great Fenno-Scandinavian mountain range, and 50 percent of the land area of the country is bedrock. A mere 2.8 percent of the land is cultivated soil, 5 percent is lakes, 20 percent is productive forest, and less than 1 percent is populated. Norway is the country with the second lowest population density in Europe and the fifth largest in terms of area. The human population density is 13.1 inhabitants per square kilometer.

The wolf has been regarded as nearly extinct and is at present directly threatened in Norway. Wolf numbers have been estimated at 5–10 during the 1960s and 1970s and 14–20 during the early 1980s.[4] Today these "Norwegian" animals roam a limited area covering part of Sweden and parts of Finland. Probably 5–10 wolves share the Norwegian area with sheep and men; this corresponds to a wolf population of less than 0.0005 individuals square kilometer. They kill at present about 400 sheep per year, less than 0.2 per thousand of the country's total sheep stock.

It is paradoxical that this very small sheep loss compared to the total sheep loss and the minute population of wolves has elicited such vigorous debate and socially important plans of action at local and central levels of administration and management. The paradoxical situation can only be explained by searching much wider and deeper than the biology and economics of wolves. It leads us to consider the unique position of wolves within Norwegian and many other cultures.

It is irrelevant that the total number of sheep in Norway is vastly greater than the number of wolves. The same holds true when comparing the large number of sheep that die or disappear due to inadequate efforts to protect them with the number of those killed by wolves. What counts is the attitude in local communities in the wolf area. Here people live and support themselves through small-scale agriculture and husbandry. They wish and demand to continue with what they have done for generations. They are not willing to go into agribusiness or any other large-scale business in "safer" areas; they are not interested in living in cities, not eager to acquire power as members of the bureaucracy or by other kinds of "success." They consider the loss of thousands of sheep in traffic accidents, the sudden onset of winter, etc., as inevitable, but the loss of 20 sheep to wolves as easily avoidable. Just kill the wolf! But the comparison is not quite fair. If a sheep owner of 40 sheep lost 20 in traffic, he understandably would make a lot of fuss about it and ask for full compensation. The actual situation is that a small-scale sheep owner suddenly loses a considerable part of his total number of sheep by wolf attack and the *whole community* is outraged.

"So what?" officials in many countries would say. But Norway is a welfare state and supports a cultural philosophy stressing intense respect for old, local, nonurban communities. Communities that mobilize to fight any policies protecting wolves are ecologically long-term sustainable, *Homo sapiens* habitats. Northern and western Europe, which suffer increasing ecological destruction through unsustainable development, are examples. These communities exemplify subcultures in danger of being destroyed for reasons not very different from those which are bringing wolves to the verge of extinction: habitat deterioration and shrinkage. That is the awkward situation in the question of wolf policy: respect for wolves, but also respect for old, ecologically unobjectionable human communities.

Wolf Policies Reflect Philosophies as Total Views

A philosophy of the wolf–man relationship must be part of a more general philosophy. How general? *Philo-sofia* is love of wisdom, and wisdom must show up in wise action as implementation of wise decisions. Knowledge is not enough. Decisions, if they are to be wise must take everything relevant into account. Because knowledge of what will be the immediate, not to mention remote, consequences of an action is limited, the decision will be made on the basis of uncertain premises of very different kinds. Therefore in principle the premises of any decision are all embracing. In wolf–man philosophy we neglect astronomy and astrology, implicitly asserting the first irrelevant and the second perhaps a more complicated verdict. We cannot neglect politics, and politics is from a cognitive (knowledge and acquaintance-related) point of view based on a political philosophy. An example concerns the justification of a central government or a national majority decision to make illegal the shooting of wolves by locals. Hypotheses in sociology, psychology, and cultural anthropology are clearly relevant.[5] They concern our decisions, and are expressed here by sentences ending with a period. A philosophy is needed that connects the hypotheses with norms—sentences ending not with a period but an exclamation mark. We believe that the normative aspect of the basis of wolf policies needs more comprehensive and clear articulation. We shall therefore be somewhat pedantic in our use of exclamation marks.

It is a common notion that every animal, however fierce and destructive, has a place in the whole of nature.[6] The notion is especially forceful when we talk about the larger ones and not "animals" such as bacteria. The idea that each species of animal has a place in nature has a strong implicit normative aspect. We might reformulate and express this in many ways: "Every kind of animal rightfully possesses a place in the whole!" "Mankind cannot violate this right!" "But we may defend ourselves against attacks and hunt for purposes of food and clothing!"

Empirical studies suggest that such a normative view is prevalent in Norway, and we guess it is prevalent in many other countries as well. This should be taken into account when planning controversial conservation measures.

The view clearly applies to wolves, but it does not automatically apply to wolves in every particular region, say in Norway. People know that there are plenty of wolves in other countries, for instance, in the Soviet Union. There is no question of global extinction of the species. However, there is an awareness that wolves have, until this century, been common in Norway. They "belonged" there, but there were no norms discouraging killing, no limitation of the right to kill on sight. Today we think one may say that the prevalent, if unformulated, view is that the wolf is not only a genuine part of Norwegian nature but a genuine part of mixed communities.

No empirical studies have been conducted in this area, and unfortunately such studies of opinions about wolves in Norway have little chance of revealing genuine attitudes. Those for or against wolf protection seek principally to influence government policy one way or another. Opinions are "mobilized" as in wartime. The general philosophical and ethical attitude in favor of having a viable population of wolves in Norway is strong, but so is that of people concerned with protecting their livestock and economy. The resulting norm conflict is common in other countries,[7] but the long-range concern has, for simple reasons, not been clearly or repeatedly formulated in the conflict.

To what extent should prejudices, unreasonable fear, and cultural stereotypes of wolves be taken into account in policy decisions? A direct answer will properly end with an exclamation mark: "We *should* do so and so!" Are we really in a position to judge the threat to children, for instance, from immature wolves straying near settlements? A direct answer may end with a period: "No." This is a hypothesis in the form of a negation. But is the direct answer certain enough to justify our including it in a research report? Direct answer: "No!"

The decisions of wildlife managers have intricate, non-normative economic aspects.[8] But to what extent is it justifiable to "commercialize" wolves through safaris and placate local communities by opening ways of making wolves "profitable" as sheep are today? And what is the normative relevance of the pain inflicted on sheep? Should their owners or the Department of the Environment or some other institution or group finance protection of some sort? The ethical and legal problems are difficult and of a necessity involve a fundamental priority of values.[9]

For simplicity of discussion we need some kind of model to facilitate the complex pattern of argument. We propose an "ecosophic" model in the form of a "normative system." A normative system is not a psychological system showing how we actually think and how people or institutions actually arrive at decisions. It is not a causal or genetic system. It shows logical priority: a premise is logically prior to a conclusion. In it fundamental value priorities form ultimate premises. The term is used for a set of norms and hypotheses arranged to show what is derived from what—rarely by strict logical inference, but derived in a looser way from premises.[10]

In a normative system three levels may be distinguished. One contains ultimate or fundamental norms and hypotheses. A second consists of intermediate norms derived from the first level sentences plus further hypotheses. A third level contains sentences expressing concrete decisions in specific situations. The situations are described by factual assertions, or hypotheses in Figure 43.1.

A model of such a system is not constructed once and for all but articulated as we continue to debate the merits and demerits of alternative decisions, using what we already have articulated and adding what is needed to reach new decisions.

Two Norms about Suffering

A first example is of a norm of fairly high standing within a model of what we call "Ecosophy T":

A$_1$: Severe suffering endured by a living being x is of no less negative value than severe suffering endured by a living being y, whatever the species or population of x and y!

NORMATIVE SYSTEM

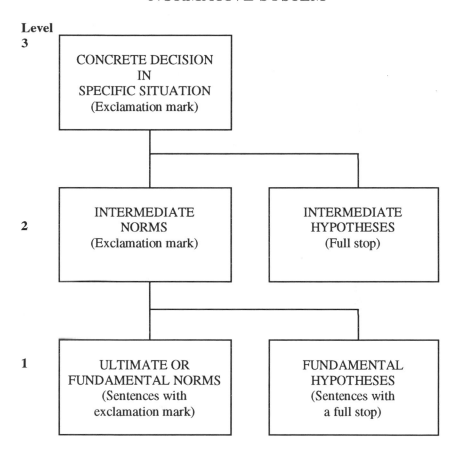

Level

3

CONCRETE DECISION
IN
SPECIFIC SITUATION
(Exclamation mark)

2

INTERMEDIATE
NORMS
(Exclamation mark)

INTERMEDIATE
HYPOTHESES
(Full stop)

1

ULTIMATE OR
FUNDAMENTAL NORMS
(Sentences with
exclamation mark)

FUNDAMENTAL
HYPOTHESES
(Sentences with
a full stop)

Figure 43.1. The normative system diagram showing logical priorities. This is not a diagram picturing the genesis of a decision; it only traces the logical derivation. It does not explain decisions on the basis of biology, sociology, or psychology, nor is it causal or motivational.

The term "living being" is ambiguous. It includes the human species, but, until further notice, we shall think mostly of nonhumans. The norm A$_1$ is highly relevant in discussing the severe pain of mauled sheep and of other domestic animals attacked but not killed by wolves or other large carnivores. We believe that, among certain groups of wolf enthusiasts, these pains are not taken seriously enough. Suffering comprises not only all sorts of extreme fear, panic, and terror, but also an increase in general nervousness.[11] It may affect a whole herd, even if only one sheep is physically attacked.

A second example of a norm in Ecosophy T:

> A$_2$: Humans have an obligation not to place their domestic animals in a situation where there is a significant risk of severe suffering!

Who is responsible for the suffering of sheep in a mixed community including wolves? Laws against killing the wolves may be thought to make the lawmaker to some extent responsible, therefore obliging him to help protect the sheep by, for instance, financing shepherds.

Scarcely covered by the norm A$_1$ is the general *decrease of life quality* of a group or herd of sheep that has suffered after a wolf attack. This decrease is, in part, reflected in a decrease of economic value of the affected sheep on the market.[12] But that is another matter. As for a definition of "life quality," we limit ourselves to referring to recent literature on the subject.[13]

Rational Policies Rest on Ultimate Norms

> A$_3$: Long-range global concern for the life conditions on our planet requires national announcement and acceptance of long-range global norms directing conservation strategies!

Standard cost/benefit analysis cannot do the whole job. Factual analysis presupposes norms in order to arrive at proposals for decisions. Benefit for which ethically acceptable goals? For which longrange global goals? Adequate wolf policies require consideration of ultimate or fundamental norms and their application to local and global strategies of action. The ultimate question is: Cost/benefit in relation to which ultimate norm?

The appropriate concerns correlate with levels of education. It is clearly the responsibility of the highly educated (in the limited sense of university education) to articulate the norms and hypotheses beyond standard cost/benefit analysis. But, unfortunately, experts and researchers have a tendency to avoid norms and values at a fundamental level.[14] One of their ways of justifying this is to proclaim that technology and science are based only on facts and hypotheses, not norms, not on sentences with unavoidable, irreducible exclamation marks. This claim of "objectivity" is an illusion well worth speaking to in some detail.

Given that chains of derivation cannot be infinite, they must start with definite statements.[15] One can justify A with B and B with C, but at a definite time in a definite situation one has to stop somewhere—taking certain norms as ultimate or fundamental. In methodology there are rules of procedure, in logic there are rules of inference. They can be derived from fundamental rules. A rule as a kind of norm is properly expressed with an exclamation mark, not a period. That a rule, if followed, has certain consequences, may be expressed by a sentence ending with a period, but a sentence saying that the rule or the consequence is good should properly end with an exclamation mark. Most rules assumed to be fundamental seem to be absolutely obvious, but sometimes derived rules seem more intuitively obvious, for instance in arithmetic. In normative systems, the fundamental norms, which constitute kinds of rules, normally appear to be obviously valid to those accepting the system. One may say that they tend to be accepted through intuition, like the basic rules of logical inference. In the philosophy of mathematics and metamathematics, controversies exist about competing systems (constructivist, logicist, formalist, intuitionist, etc.) in which intuitive acceptance plays an inescapable role.

The importance of the above stems from the widespread, insupportable view that if one is a scientist one starts and ends with factual statements/sentences ending with a period. But one never gets going without methodological and logical rules, and some of them cannot be validated within one's system. *Unvalidated rules are necessary to validate a claim that such and so is a fact.* To show that a fundamental rule (R_1) is useful, successful, or valid, one must include these properties in the conclusion one infers from premises, say observation sentences. But how, from those premises, does one reach a conclusion? Only by rules. So one either uses R_1, going in circles, or a new fundamental rule, R_2, whereby the same trouble as to how to "prove" the rule is encountered.

The appreciation of the necessity of taking some rules as fundamental in scientific work makes it easier to accept that we have to do the same in handling normative systems. Here the most important rules are of an ethical character. However, that should not make one call them "subjective" or "expressions of feeling." There is less agreement, it seems, and certainly less *clear* disagreement on fundamental ethical views than on methodology and logic. The statistics of agreement or disagreement do not, however, make them subjective or objective in any strict sense.

Some researchers think that by sticking to science and avoiding open, clear announcements of ethical views in questions of wolf management they can remain safely within the realm of what can be "shown" and "tested." But by definition, *if* rule R_1, is taken as fundamental it cannot be tested. It can be exchanged with R_2 and this change may be psychologically motivated, but there is no question of "showing" and "testing" in a methodological sense. Changes of paradigm in research furnish ample examples.[16]

Speaking as a scientist is not like speaking as a machine; the scientist cannot avoid speaking as a responsible person. He is not in a social and ethical vacuum. Researchers dealing with the "wolf problem" inevitably take part in discussions both locally in wolf territory and centrally among policy makers. They can, of course, avoid explicit announcements of norms artificially by always using an "if" sentence: If we accept the norms (and hypotheses) such and such then the decisions "D_1!" will lead to contradiction, but not "D_2!" But this use of conditional sentences in research reports will not and should not prevent one from revealing which norms one personally accepts as valid. To do this today is a social obligation. The deterioration of life conditions on this planet as seen by researchers necessitates activity at the social and political level. For some of us the fundamental basis of this obligation is provided by norms elicited inevitably through the process of identification: we cannot but subscribe to the motto "man not apart!" At least one sociobiologist has found it problematic as to how social obligations expressed by sentences with an exclamation mark can enter the system. Obligations belong to social philosophy and their normative premises are requirements announcing what is considered a good society and what must be done to keep it functioning.[17] In industrial societies there are obligations (and duties) related to all public offices. But even today many researchers and experts seem to think that they don't have social obligations related to the actual consequences of their activity of publication and expertise.

Members of the Ministry of Environment have, in Scandinavia and many other countries, obligations either to refrain from severe criticism of their government or resign. In their nature conservation policy they usually try to push their government in the right direction, but they are narrowly limited as to what they can do. Researchers and experts have no such obligations. On the contrary, we believe there is a valid obligation never to act "as a mere functionary." Their task in modern society depends upon their efforts to remain independent from government in their public views and, in general, from those who finance their activity. The public has a right to know where they stand as people. The more research and expertise contribute to public policies concerning wolves and other matters, the more important it is that the public be properly informed. The obligation is heavy but inevitable.

So much for the relationship of normative systems to science and of norms to the function of scientists. Let us return to the question of norms within the framework of wolf management.

Protection of Sheep against Suffering

If x and y are calamities and *more* people suffer in y than in x, then y is properly called a greater calamity. Applied to wolf depredation of sheep, we tentatively (as always in handling norm systematizations) accept the following:

> A_4: If, of two decisions, the first is likely to contribute to the probability that a greater number of animals will suffer than the second, then the second is to be taken *pari passu* (other things being equal)!

We should be careful when talking about *greater* suffering. Referring to consciously experienced suffering, including simple pain, we have to do with a *quality* admitting degrees of intensity, but in an important sense unquantifiable and nonadditive.

Strictly speaking, *experienced* suffering is not additive. If suffering could be measured and two geographically unrelated animals suffered with an intensity of degree 3, this would not result in a suffering of degree 6. Suffering in other places in the Milky Way does not add to our suffering as long as we do not have any relation to that suffering. Here is a very simple case of nonadditivity: If we experience the water in a tub as pleasantly warm, it does not get hotter if we add more water of the same warmth.

Suffering is a quality, so we must be careful or we get into a lot of philosophical trouble. But, of course, there are clear cases in which we can properly speak of more or less, mainly where it involves more or less *intense* suffering. Qualities admit of differences in intensity. In our decisions we are justified in making number relevant, and we ask: "Exactly how significant is number in judging suffering among animals?"

These reflections have to do with the crucial point that shooting or continually harassing one single wolf results in the suffering of only one, whereas the decision not to shoot a wolf sometimes has the suffering of a great number of sheep as a result. Exactly how relevant is number? We say very little in terms of *experienced* suffering. But if a wolf attacks a herd of 20 sheep, at least one of them is likely to suffer more than a hunted wolf. And, most important of all, we are responsible for not making sheep suffer unduly.

Let us look at yet another norm favorable to the defense of sheep. It is argued among people eager to support conservation of wildlife that, given that there are more than two million sheep in Norway but only a handful of wolves, the violent death or suffering of a sheep should not be taken as seriously as that of a wolf. A very doubtful norm. We would rather accept the following:

A$_5$: The negative value of the severe suffering of an animal belonging to a large population has a no less negative value than that of an animal of a small population!

This norm goes against the grain. It is human to treat animals more coldly when there are masses of them. In years when lemmings are abundant, people hiking with their dog are more likely to let it "have fun" with lemmings than in years when lemmings are interesting as a rarity. We also reject the view that the sheep is a less developed, "dumb" animal compared to the superbly intelligent and beautiful wolf, and that it therefore deserves less consideration. Beauty or intelligence are completely irrelevant in application of the norm. There are considerable differences in identification among people. Some tend, we are glad to say, to identify positively with the underdog or ugly duckling; others identify with the winner, the clever, the intelligent, the beautiful. This influences our attitudes toward spectacular predators. Some, not all, take into account the suffering itself and our responsibility.

Let us now introduce the third of the *dramatis personae*, the local sheep holders. When anger prompts the holders to go public, they tend to stress both the economic loss through wolf predation, the suffering of sheep, and the deep frustration and guilt feelings due to the entirely natural feeling of responsibility for the sheep. The extreme aggression against wolves and wolf conservationists by concerned sheep holders that is sometimes seen in newspaper articles may, in part, be explained by feelings of guilt. Some sheep holders even cry in hopelessness and become severely depressed when they witness the suffering of sheep but are physically and economically unable to protect them from repeated carnivore attacks. Repeated perception of the intensive suffering of sheep due to wolf attacks, plus the culturally formed aversion to wolves, bring some sheep holders into such a state of emotional agitation that they sometimes relinquish their sheep ownership and may work fanatically against any kind of protection of the wolf. One may safely say that letting domesticated sheep be exposed to wolves tends locally to brutalize and dehumanize the man–animal relationship.

Man has domesticated, modified, and pitifully degraded an animal once capable of taking care of itself on wolf ranges. The result is a pathetically helpless being—the modern, economically profitable sheep, "the meat and wool producer." When Norway was poor, sheep holders could afford to hire shepherds; today it is economically impossible. An ethical impasse has developed.

In recent years, organized use of grazing lands has expanded in many parts of Norway. Sheep holders in local areas are organized in groups, each selecting a board that develops common supervision with inspectors patrolling the grazing area and a common sheep-gathering operation during the fall. About 60 percent of the country's sheep stock is today organized in such units.[18] But because the sheep population is large and many parts of the country are so rugged or bushy, it is impossible to prevent carnivore attacks. Many sheep holders experience carnivore problems every year.

The above five norms and non-normative statements tend to favor sheep at the expense of wolves. Now let us look at some views favoring wolves.

Protection of Wolves as Members of Mixed Communities

The scarcity of wolves in many countries in Europe and the decrease in number of habitats—qualitatively and quantitatively in this century—is well known.[19] It may be of help, however, to note that protection of a species may mean vastly different things.

In the narrowest interpretation, the sentence "Protect the wolf!" is conceived as only protecting the wolf's structural biology. The survival of specimens in zoological gardens is considered enough. Then there is an interpretation asking for at least one area on this planet where the wolf is protected, completely or at least in such a way that its natural way of life, is not disastrously disturbed. Still wider interpretation asks for the protection of areas wherever there now are wolves.

What Soulé says about relative preciousness of different populations of the same species should be borne in mind:

> Returning to the population issue, we might ask if *all populations of a given species have equal value.* I think not. The value of a population, I believe, depends on its genetic uniqueness, its ecological position, and the number of extant populations. A large, genetically polymorphic population containing unique alleles or genetic combinations has greater value, for example, than a

small, genetically depauperate population of the same species. Also, the fewer the populations that remain, the greater the probability of the simultaneous extinction (random or not) of *all* populations, and thus of the species. Hence, how *precious* a population is a function of how many such populations exist. [20]

A still wider interpretation says that, where at all feasible, protection of wolves implies protection of existing ranges plus introduction into past habitats (e.g., those prior to 1850). Protection is sometimes proposed for traditional wolf ranges. Of course this poses considerable problems in Europe. There are vast traditional ranges in the Soviet Union, but what about stray wolves occasionally "invading" Norway and other countries where they obviously occupied areas with considerable populations 100 years ago? Are these areas still traditional ranges? How are we to understand tradition? Clearly, where, during the last 100 years, sheep have been foraging and local people have been active as sheep holders, one might as well label the area a traditional sheep range. But how do we delimit areas of some wolves, mainly strays, dispersing with no fixed home range? What is the wolf minimum viable population size for the maintenance of "fitness and adaptive potential?" According to Soulé:

A useful device for considering the relevance of population and evolutionary genetics to conservation is the "time scale of survival." Employing this scale one can see, somewhat arbitrarily three survival problems or issues:

1. the short-term issue is immediate fitness—the maintenance of vigor and fecundity during an interim holding operation, usually in an artificial environment;
2. the long-term issue is adaptation—the persistence of the vigor and evolutionary adaptation of a population in the face of a changing natural environment:
3. the third issue is evolution in the broadest sense—the continuing creation of evolutionary novelty during and by the process of speciation. [21]

A norm may here be tentatively formulated as:

A$_6$: If a traditional sheep area, by decree from central authorities, is to be considered an area where wolves are protected, it is up to the central authorities to arrange for fair and swift compensation for losses, and/or financial support for hiring shepherds!

The word "fair" here denotes compensation properly adjusted to the economic level at the time of the argument.

This norm presupposes a kind of political philosophy that favors local communities in their conflict with non-local authorities. As regards the idea of compensation by *central* institutions, it is important to add that the norms seem to imply both decentralization and centralization. This makes them controversial because local community philosophy in Scandinavia has been very strong on decentralization. "Decentralization" ought to remain one of the key terms. But it is becoming more and more clear that strong, central authorities are also needed in matters both of local and global conservation. Cases have occurred where local communities, not to mention local administrative units, have successfully opposed environmental points of view put forth by central authorities.[22]

It is difficult to impose wolf protection on people who give up traditional sources of income such as gathering berries and keep indoors for fear of wolves in their mixed community. People deriving income from pearl diving or other occupations in shark-infested waters acquire knowledge of the habits and signals of these fishes, and work out a kind of coexistence. But Norway has no income from wolves. Compare mixed communities with snakes. A market for snakes—e.g., Hong Kong—has eliminated fear, or at least significantly influenced tolerance, of poisonous snakes within the areas of profitable snake catching or hunting. Rules of coexistence have been established. A similar development could materialize in a human–wolf relations, yet it has not, so far.

If the coexistence of wolves and sheep farmers causes insoluble problems in the future, territorial changes must be considered: the removal of wolf or sheep or farmers. It now seems that moving sheep away is not enough because of the anxiety of the farmers, not least for the safety of their children. The farm families might accept moving with their sheep out of a territory if very substantial financial and other compensation were guaranteed. This solution is ethically debatable. The territorial question is not the only one, however. To "remove" farmers involuntarily is, in Norway, totally out of the question—least of all in favor of an animal! (Enforced removal because of motorways or other purposes of development is another question.) Sheep holders therefore must agree upon changing their resource regime from sheep raising to other forms if they are guaranteed economic activity securing reasonable income during an extensive period of transition.

In any case, *if* there is to be a protected wolf area in Norway, considerable sums of money must be set aside centrally for that purpose. This might be appropriate even if the local communities gradually gain economically from their own activity due to the presence of wolves.[23]

So much about the vague and ambiguous sentence "Protect the wolf!" We must remember to ask specifically: "Just what *degree* of protection?" and "Just *where?*" There are many pitfalls to avoid when discussing the means of protection.

Norms of protection do not follow from hypotheses about scarcity. Among many needed premises we require general norms concerning the protection of life forms on this planet. We can use the following three norms, which are derived directly from three still more general norms.[24] Their subject is living beings in general, but these norms have a particular kind of living being as the subject, *Canis lupus.*

A_7: The well-being of the species wolf as part of human and nonhuman life on earth has value in itself (intrinsic value, inherent value)! The value is independent of the narrow usefulness of the nonhuman world for human purposes!

A_8: Richness and diversity of wolf races and habitats as part of the general richness and diversity of life forms contribute to the realization of these values and are also values in themselves!

A_9: Humans have no right to reduce this richness and diversity including wolf habitats and races, except to satisfy vital needs!

These norms are meant to furnish important *guidelines*. When codifying norms, as in the case of laws, certain expressions with carefully calculated ambiguity are essential for the realization of wise applications.

We shall limit ourselves to commenting on norm A_9. The general aim of this norm is to remind us that humans are not alone on this planet and that solidarity with other forms of life requires that we consider their needs. Interference with each other's lives is, of course, unavoidable. But some things we do not consider ethically justifiable to do to others, and the simple expressions "You have no right to . . ." is well known from infancy to death. The same holds true for the expression "He (she) really needs so and so!" Instead of "real needs" we use in norm A_9 "vital needs."

The term "vital needs" permits considerable latitude in judgment. Differences in climate and related factors, together with differences in structures of societies as they now exist, must be considered.[25]

Many authors have tried to classify basic or vital needs and to clarify the philosophically important, but often elusive, distinction between vital needs and mere desires, wishes, and habitual inclinations. For some sheep holders, the need to protect their sheep from wolves or to be in some way compensated is today vital. It means protecting the basis of their economy and homes where they have lived for generations.[26]

The three norms are slight reformulations of the first points in an eight-point formulation of basic traits of the so-called "deep ecology movement"—a convenient name for a class of tendencies in contemporary environmentalism.[27] Are we going to give up a search for still more basic views justifying our intense concern for life on earth?

What is more or less basic or deep when applied to views? If an old lady falls into a ditch, our view is that we should do what we can to get her out. Why? We have norms of politeness, but more basic are norms saying we should help others survive. Why survive? Most of us have a notion that it is *good* to be alive and that suicide should be "explained away"—that attempts to quit life are not basically motivated by a clear rejection of being alive but are a kind of cry for help. These examples indicate a direction from less to more basic. In general, if a view, as expressed by a norm for instance, is justified by another norm that bestows validity on the first one, the latter is more basic. It belongs to a "deeper level" of a total view.

From the point of view of philosophy—especially that part of it which is sometimes called "metaphysics"—it is desirable to go as "deep" as possible. But this does not imply that we all should end up with the same metaphysics. Here only one possible position shall be mentioned briefly, namely the fundamental sentences of a version of Ecosophy T. Starting from "Self-realization!," clarifications explain that the "Self" here is a metaphysical entity—something perhaps being realized in the development of the cosmos. The process is one of realizing individual potentials, and this implies diversity of life forms including cultures. Diversity is gained by complexity, therefore development of complexity is implied. The self is of a kind that implies the process of identification. This means that a level of complexity that fosters sensibility as the conscious goal, inevitably takes place to protect the self-realization process of all living beings—a goal of "symbiosis," "live and let live!," in a philosophical sense.[28]

The main thing is to note that we need value strategies to guide our behavior, otherwise our thought has no home; we stroll around in a metaphysical nowhere on a meaningless, vast, flat plain. The articulation of these strategies of thought in the form of norms and of basic hypotheses about ecological systems can only be the job of a few. But the job is of increasing importance. It involves survival of humans and their environment.

In conflicts concerning conservation policies, the supporters of Ecosophy T (the authors included), and more generally, supporters of far-reaching, radical policies, meet practical, economic, and political objections but rarely philosophical or metaphysical ones. It seems that the conscious effort to bring in the most basic questions of a philosophy of life and of our relation to nature weakens the objections against far-reaching, radical policies. The practical, economic, and political objections are in a sense admitted to be inadequate for long-run planning and policy choice. This is one of the reasons we must support training of conservation specialists in argumentation on a philosophical level. We are not confronted with any well-articulated, anti-conservation philosophy, but myriad conflicts of interest. Without neglecting them, we are trying to bring wide, long-range perspectives into focus.

The *dignity* of wolves has, in modern literature, been persuasively conveyed to an increasing audience. This opens still other spheres of debate. Do paid safaris, for instance those centering around the wilderness experience of chorus howling,[29] commercialize the wolves and interfere with their dignity, degrading them to showpieces? Some certainly feel that way, and the corresponding norms are not difficult to formulate. But they are perhaps not so easily derived from the norms and hypotheses of Ecosophy. Wolves in our view are sufficiently aloof in their dignity not to be easily ruffled by tourists well hidden in bushes. Elsewhere we conclude that *if* Norway is to establish preserves and areas where wolves are protected, an attempt must be made to "market" wolves in the broad, modern sense of the word.[30] One way is to somehow make them economically interesting to people living inside wolf ranges. Income from safaris must be reserved for people traditionally living with the wolves.

Respect for International Agreements

Still another theme of high relevance is respect for international agreements. Considering the irrelevance of national borders in ecological matters, such agreements are of decisive importance for the future of life on earth. The Norwegian government has ethical and tactical reasons to obey.

A tactical reason concerns repercussions if we violate agreements. For example, if Norway insists that migratory birds on their way to Norway should not be hunted in Italy, Norway's voice is little heeded if it violates international conventions concerning whales and wolves. Suppose Norway nevertheless says "No!" to wolf protection for welfare and economic reasons. Would norms of international solidarity to some degree be satisfied if Norway contributed heavily to the maintenance of protected European (e.g., Swedish or Finnish) wolf areas that have a significantly less dense human population inside wolf ranges? Our tentative answer is "yes."

International opinion is probably not quite aware of the kind of scattered settlement typical of Norway and the high priority accorded to the indefinite continuation of that structure. It belongs to one of the most outstanding features of the Nordic lifestyle and does not resemble the pattern found elsewhere in Europe. Many farmers have no close neighbors; "neighborhood" does not exist. This sometimes causes a feeling of isolation and insecurity in forest areas. The mere thought of wolves frightens isolated families. However, the international community will not be overly impressed by the difficulties cited by Norway, because the implementation of international agreements has always gone against some interests. Thousands of people and large local communities were hurt in their vital interests when nations accepted the Convention on International Trade in Endangered Species of Wild Fauna and Flora (CITES).

If Norway or another of the world's richest nations decides to go, at least temporarily, against a wolf protection convention, it might be more easily condoned by the international public, provided that they instead contributed heavily to one of the many other goals of the "World Conservation Strategy"—such as point 12 in Section 15.

> Assistance should be made available to enable requesting nations to develop the capacity to carry out national conservation strategies, ecosystem evaluations and environmental assessments. . . .

In view of catastrophic deterioration outside Norway, millions might possibly be better spent elsewhere rather than in establishing and maintaining wolf protection areas in Norway. This possibility is mentioned here to emphasize the importance of always having both the local and the global point of view.[31]

In accordance with our basic philosophy (Ecosophy T), a long-range goal of mankind is to let evolution on earth continue and, to some extent, restore or at least save many wildlife habitats that are now suffering from human encroachment. Without the slightest doubt, we recommend wolves as members of the

Nordic life community. But this clear theoretical acceptance of wolves on the basis of our philosophy of nature does not imply any definite practical wolf policy.

Given the complicated philosophical, cultural, political, and economic situation, a realistic and vigorous pro-wolf police in Norway and Sweden may have to be accorded low priority compared with other major, central conservational efforts. Such efforts may, however, prove even more difficult to put into practice, and in that case we would recommend going ahead with the strong wolf policy. This is a tentative, preliminary conclusion based on the argumentation in this article.

There is no end to the areas of relevance of wolf policies. Here we have focused on the cultural and general philosophical aspect of wolf policies, neglecting the intricacies of wolf ecology and wolf conservation strategy and action programs in general. In other articles we shall consider these subjects.[32]

Notes

This chapter is reprinted with minor revisions from Arne Næss and Ivar Mysterud, "Philosophy of Wolf Policies (I): General Principles and Preliminary Exploration of Selected Norms," *Conservation Biology* 1 (1987): 23–34.

[1] Different cultures at different times have had significantly different attitudes toward nature, and within each culture, each nation, and each community there are differences of philosophic importance. On identification refer to Arne Næss, "Identification as a Source of Deep Ecological Attitudes," in *Deep Ecology*, ed. M. Tobias, (San Diego: Avant Books, 1985), 256–270. On the change of attitude toward nature as evidenced in the new environmental movements, refer to: R. E. Dunlap, "The Social Bases of Environmental Concern: A Review of Hypotheses, Explanations, and Empirical Evidence," *Public Opinion Quarterly* 44 (1980): 181–197. R. E. Dunlap and K. D. Van Liere, "Commitment to Dominant Social Paradigm and Concern for Environmental Quality," *Social Science Quarterly* 65 (December, 1984). For one of the best surveys about American Indian cultures refer to: J. D. Callicott, "Traditional American Indian and Traditional Western European Attitudes Toward Nature: an Overview," in eds., R. Elliot and A. Gare, *Environmental Philosophy* (University Park: Pennsylvania State University Press, 1983). Evidently different cultures have had different concepts of natures, and some have not had any concepts similar to the one we are talking about, the conservation of nature.

[2] Our concept of "mixed communities" was introduced in Arne Næss, "Self-realization in Mixed Communities of Humans, Bears, Sheep and Wolves," *Inquiry* 22 (1977): 231–251.

[3] For accounts of plant and animal community concepts refer to: M. L. Cody and J. M. Diamond, eds. *Ecology and Evolution of Communities* (Massachusetts and London: Belknap Press, 1975). See also D. R. Strong, D. Simberloff, L. G. Abele, and A. B. Thistle, eds. *Ecological Communities: Conceptual Issue and the Evidence* (Princeton: Princeton University Press, 1984).

[4] For population estimates refer to: T. Heggberget, and S. Myrberget, *Viltrapport* 9 (1979): 37–45. For the most recent survey refer to: O. J. Sørensen, P. Wabakken, T. Kvam, and A. Linda, *Viltrapport* 34 (1984): 54–59.

[5] The authors have written another paper exploring these matters: I. Mysterud and A. Næss, "Philosophy of Wolf Policies II: Selected aspects of wolf-human relationships." (Not published).

[6] A. Næss, "Holdninger til mennesker, dyr og planter" (Attitudes towards men, animals and plants), *Samtiden* 94 (1985): 68–76.

[7] Norm-conflicts very similar to the one seen in Norwegian wolf ranges are found wherever white people settled in North America with herds of husbandry animals. Even in areas with no husbandry, but where locals depend on cervid hunting, conflicts may arise, for instance in Alaska. Refer to: ed., L. N. Carbyn, "Wolves in Canada and Alaska," *Canadian Wildlife Service*, Rept. Ser. 45 (1983): 1–135.

[8] For preliminary discussions of economy enhancing animal survival refer to: I. Mysterud, "Economic and philosophical considerations on wolf survival," *CIC Symposium: Problems Concerning Predation on Game* (Lisbon: March, 1985).

[9] Properly expressed they form sentences with exclamation marks. Priorities behind "wise actions" in wildlife management should be ecologically correct, socially and politically acceptable, and economically profitable. In management procedures based on such diverse strategies, the landscape will profit most.

[10] For details about the concept of normative systems as conceived here refer to A. Næss, "Notes on the Methodology of Normative Systems," in *Methodology and Science* 10 (1979): 64–79.

[11] The term "suffering" is ambiguous, of course. Sometimes it is made to cover complex states of affairs, for instance the suffering of a thwarted ambition, but in A_1 we think of rather more narrow notions with simple pain as a core connotation.

[12] For discussions on how carnivore attacks affect sheep herds and sheepholder activity refer to: I. Mysterud, *Viltrapport* 9 (1979): 173–161. *Bear Biol. Ass Conf. Ser.* No. 3 (1980): 233–241.

[13] For a valuable bibliography of life quality research refer to: K. Chamberlain, "Value dimensions, cultural differences, and the prediction of perceived quality of life," *Social Indicators Research* 17 (1985): 345–401. The term "self-realization" is a somewhat more general and derivationally more basic term than "life quality."

[14] On the causes of researchers in conservation biology not announcing their value priorities refer to: A. Næss, "Intrinsic value: will the defenders of nature please rise?" ed., M. E. Soulé, *Conservation Biology: The Science of Scarcity and Diversity* (Sunderland: Sinauer Associates, 1986), 512–513.

[15] In what follows we do not consistently distinguish a sentence from its meaning. The term "statement" has a convenient degree of ambiguity, sometimes referring to meaning, sometimes being used as a near synonym for "sentence." This holds true for all sciences including mathematics and logic. Their sentences (expressing the statements) can, just as in the case of normative systems, be divided in two: sentences ending in a period and sentences, such as rules, ending with some sort of exclamation mark.

[16] Refer to: T. Kuhn, *The Structure of Scientific Revolutions* (Chicago: University of Chicago Press, 1970).

[17] Refer to: John Rawls, *A Theory of Justice* (Oxford: Oxford University Press, 1971), 108, 344–348.

[18] For survey of sheep-holding and its implications on carnivore management planning in Norway refer to: A. B. Vaag, A. Haga, and H. Granstuen, *Viltrapport* 39 (1986): 1–169.

[19] Refer to: D. M. Pimlott, *Wolves: Proceedings of the First Working Meeting of Wolf Specialists and First International Conference on Conservation of the Wolf* (Morges, Switzerland: IUCN, 1975).

[20] Michael Soulé, "What is Conservation Biology?" *BioScience* 35 (1985): 727–734.

[21] Michael Soulé, "Thresholds for Survival: Maintaining Fitness and Evolutionary Potential," in *Conservation Biology*, M. E. Soulé and B. A. Wilcox, eds. (Sunderland MA: Sinauer Associates, 1986), 151.

[22] The opposition to letting wolves live where they now are in Norway is for natural reasons fiercely fought in many local communities. There is a well-developed "No to wolf" campaign, being organized locally in Hedmark in southern Norway, and in adjacent Värmland, in southern Sweden. If local communities within parts of the present wolf range were given the right to decide, all wolves might be exterminated, provided there were enough able hunters.

[23] A basic problem in human environments is maintenance of animal and plant populations of species that now have low, no, or negative economic value such as pests and predators. We are therefore concerned about creating an economy of endangered species (conservation capitalism) to increase the probability of their survival, to be discussed in another paper: I. Mysterud and A. Næss, "Philosophy of Wolf Policies III: Emergent Wolf Management, Applications and Conclusions." (The paper has not yet been published.)

[24] Norms A_7 to A_9 are special applications of the first three general norms, a set of eight points. The eight points with comments were originally published in the newsletter *Ecophilosophy* IV, May 1984, but are now to be found also as "The Science of Scarcity and Diversity" in *Conservation Biology*, eds., M. E. Soulé and B. A. Wilcox, (Sunderland MA: Sinauer Associates, 1986).

[25] Refer to: A. H. Maslow, *Motivation and Personality* (New York: Harper & Row, 1970). A. S. Kaufman, "Wants, Needs and Liberalism," *Inquiry* 14 (1971): 191–206.

[26] People in the materially richest countries cannot be expected to reduce overnight their excessive interference with the nonhuman world to a moderate level. The stabilization and reduction of the human population will take time. Interim strategies must be developed. But this in no way excuses the present complacency—the extreme seriousness of our current situation must first be realized. The longer we wait the more drastic will be the measures needed.

[27] For more about Ecosophy T refer to the article cited in Section 5 and Appendix A in *Deep Ecology*, Bill Devall and George Sessions, eds., (Salt Lake City: Gibbs M. Smith, Inc., 1985).

[28] For more on self-realization as a fundamental norm refer to: Arne Næss, *Self-realization. An Ecological Approach to Being in the World* (Institute of Social Inquiry Murdoch University, 1986).

[29] In some Canadian national parks, field trips are being provided so people can listen to and see wolves in the wild. This is part of a management strategy to improve people's image of wolves. Refer to: R. R. Stardom, *Canadian Wildlife Service Report Series* 45 (1983): 30–34.

[30] Ivar Mysterud, "Economic and philosophical considerations on wolf survival," *CIC Symposium: Problems Concerning Predation on Game* (Lisbon: March, 1985).

[31] The philosophically interesting area of self-verifying and self-refuting hypotheses is also relevant. The local population that feels threatened by wolves knows that people with power to impose wolf protection entertain conflicting hypotheses about the seriousness of anti-wolf sentiments locally. It is, of course, in the interest of locals, to convince others that the hypothesis of a very high degree of seriousness in anti-wolf attitudes is verified. Pro-wolf people are therefore silenced. It is not difficult to see how this can influence the behavior of locals and result in verification of the hypothesis of universal, intense opposition to wolves. This state of affairs must be considered if and when central authorities plan to investigate public opinion in the affected regions.

[32] These articles have not yet been published, eds. note.

Chapter 44

Næss's Deep Ecology Approach and Environmental Policy

Harold Glasser

I. Introduction

The term "deep ecology" was introduced into the English literature by Arne Næss with his 1973 article, "The Shallow and the Deep, Long-Range Ecology Movement: A Summary."[1] Næss's paper distinguished two approaches for problematizing (Problematizierung) and responding to the environmental crisis. His work over the past several decades developed and extended this contrast into a conceptual system for helping individuals to consider decisions involving society and nature, what I refer to here as Næss's deep ecology approach to ecophilosophy. To draw a distinction between other interpretations of "deep ecology," which are not so closely coupled to Næss's earlier philosophical work and for the sake of brevity, I have coined the acronym DEA. The purpose of this paper is to relate some of Næss's earlier philosophical work to the DEA and to develop its implications for environmental policy.

The DEA represents a logical culmination and fusing of Næss's philosophical inquiry with his political activism and love of nature. It is Næss's general, philosophical approach for encouraging and assisting individuals to develop ecologically responsible lifestyles, policies, and concrete decisions.[2] The DEA is meant, primarily, to aid individuals in the process of weaving their own descriptive and prescriptive premises into a normative framework which melds a value system with an ontology. In developing the DEA Næss has been motivated by the belief that many regrettable environmental decisions are made in a "state of philosophical stupor," where people confuse narrow, superficial goals with broader, more fundamental goals that are reasoned, consistently and coherently, from ultimate premises.[3]

Rather than calling for a new environmental ethic or a change in our fundamental values, Næss's DEA focuses on transforming environmental policy by helping individuals to develop more thoroughly reasoned, well-informed, and consistent policy positions. Although some will certainly take issue with the core premise underlying this goal, namely that thoroughly reasoned and consistent policy positions do lead to better policies, they should also take care to consider the indirect procedural benefits that may result from pursuing such a decision strategy. Næss does not ignore social decision-making, rather, he emphasizes the potential to fortify it by strengthening the process individuals use to arrive at, and reason through, their policy positions. Developing these skills, Næss argues, better equips us to participate in fruitful dialogue and debate.

I take there to be six elements that are necessary for characterizing, but not necessarily sufficient for characterizing, the DEA.[4] First is Næss's concept of total views as broad, all-encompassing philosophical systems that incorporate an ontology, an epistemology, a logic, a semantics, an ethics, and a social philosophy. Our total views vary tremendously in explicitness and preciseness, but they nevertheless guide our individual decision-making. While it is inevitable that these total views will be fragmentary, we have the prospect of making them either more or less precise, although preciseness often comes at the cost of intercomparability.[5]

Second is Næss's methodology of normative-derivational systems as a generalized framework for exploring the consequences of collections of norms and hypotheses. This methodology, which is used to construct tentative and revisable normative systems, is employed to improve the consistency of decisions, to explore the logical implications of proposed decisions, and to help expose norm conflicts.[6]

Third is a philosophical device, "deep questioning," for highlighting norm and hypothesis conflicts by pointing to the possibly problematic character of what is generally taken for granted. Fourth is a complementary philosophical device, "loose derivation," for supporting the process of reasoning consistently from fundamentals.

Fifth is the adoption of particular ultimate premises that incorporate some form of "wide identification." This wide identification might be rather limited in scope, as in the extending of care and concern to nonhumans based upon broad instrumental concerns. For example, "God made the earth, and then made humans to steward it, with respect and empathy for all of creation" or "the earth is a living system, Gaia, in which our interests are coupled to the interests of all of the earth's other inhabitants and all of our actions have an effect upon the earth's system properties." In contrast, an expansion of identification might be motivated by non-instrumental considerations. For example, "all entities have intrinsic value and we have an obligation, in pursuing our interests, to not diminish their potential for flourishing" or "some nonhuman entities have intrinsic value because of sentience, the ability to feel pain, or the existence of autopoetic properties and we must accord rights and respect to these entities." Naturally, it is also possible for wider identification to be motivated by combinations of these and other instrumental and non-instrumental considerations, based upon a vast plurality of ontological perspectives.

Sixth is the eight points of the deep ecology platform, which Næss characterizes as representing a provisional statement of the basic and general views supporters of the deep ecology movement share in common.[7] To understand the provisional nature of the eight points, it may be helpful to point out, for instance, that some individuals may find it unnecessary to embrace even Næss's nontechnical notion of "intrinsic or inherent value" to embrace the subsequent seven points, providing they modify the second point to state that, "richness and diversity of life forms contribute to the well-being of humans."[8] In light of this nondogmatic interpretation of the eight points, I must add the caveat that my requirement of their necessity for characterizing the DEA be interpreted loosely.

The process of attempting to articulate one's total view places significant demands, in terms of accountability and responsibility, upon the individual. Næss argues, however, that we have no choice: "The essential idea is that, as humans, we are responsible in our actions as to motivations and premises relative to any question that can be asked of us."[9] Thus, it is this responsibility, the need to be prepared to participate actively in the process of social decision-making that enjoins us to articulate and make more explicit our total views. A central purpose of the DEA is to support individuals in carrying out this responsibility.

This focus upon praxis (responsibility and action) separates the DEA from more traditionally descriptive inquiries into ecophilosophy.[10] The importance of Næss's DEA rests on its manner of structuring and focusing our thinking about decision-making. The DEA's significance is in its procedural contributions rather than its clear ability to improve the substantive aspects of decision-making. Wendell Berry has said that while a farmer works good land, the land also has a way of working the farmer. The practice of forming a total view may work similarly, by inspiring accountability and encouraging systematic, methodical reasoning.

II. The "Depth" Metaphor

Næss's use of the terms, "deep" and "shallow," is drawn primarily from his empirical semantics and communication theory.[11] His technical semantic distinction refers, in part, to the different levels of intention that can be shown to characterize individuals' (and societies') interpretations of propositions. In relation to the DEA Næss enormously broadens his use of "depth" to include both the general level of argumentation one employs in seeking out the underlying, interlinked, and often systemic causes of a problem and one's willingness to consider a wide range of policy alternatives, even if they call for changes that represent a radical departure from the status quo. Næss's distinction, however, is still limited to argumentation patterns and to the diversity of policy changes that are given consideration; it was never intended to shed light on the character of people's values. While Næss cannot be completely exonerated of not foreseeing the unfortunate derogatory connotations of his terminology, we should pay heed to the sources of his distinction.

In Næss's semantics, the most general statements, T_0 statements (words or sentences), are phrased in ordinary language and are intended to be philosophically neutral. T_0 statements serve as points of departure for investigations of possible interpretations. When a new interpretation of an expression eliminates some of the ambiguity of the preceding interpretation, without adding any new ambiguity, it is said to be a precization. Thus, a sentence, T_1 is more precise than a sentence, T_0, when every plausible interpretation of T_1 is also a plausible interpretation of T_0, but at least one plausible interpretation of T_0 is not a plausible interpretation of T_1.[12]

Each successive order of precization following a particular path implies a greater definiteness of intention on the part of a particular interpreter. It is not possible in general however, to comment on the definiteness of intention of different interpretations of T_0 statements that have followed divergent paths of precization. This is because a particular T_1 interpretation of a T_0 statement may represent a far greater level of discrimination than a particular T_{211} interpretation of the same T_0-statement. Interpretations of T_0 statements on different levels of precization that have followed different paths of precization are not comparable in terms of their depth of intention. Thus, in general, it is only possible to comment on the level of intention of different interpretations of T_0 statements that can be viewed as following the same continuous path of precization and where the only difference between the two interpretations is determined by the point at which they terminate the precization process. For example, it is possible to say that a particular T_{1211} interpretation of a T_0 statement represents a greater depth of intention than a T_1 interpretation of the same T_0 statement.

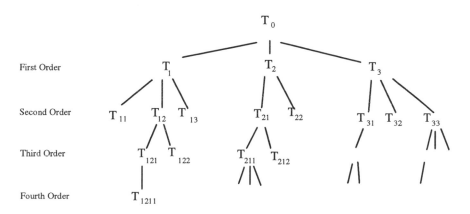

Figure 44.1. Precization Diagram.[13]

Næss, in his empirical semantics, is primarily concerned with developing a methodology for exploring the possible interpretations of particular point-of-departure sentences. In the context of environmental policy such an approach may be useful when particularly contentious interpretation issues arise, but its practical utility is rather limited because plausible precizations must not introduce new information. When interpretations of expressions introduce new information Næss defines them as either specifications or elaborations. A sentence "b" is a specification of a sentence "a" for a particular person, in a particular situation, if and only if the following two criteria are satisfied:

1. what is asserted by "a" is explicitly or implicitly asserted by "b" and "b" also asserts something more and
2. both "b" and "a" express assertions about the same subject.[14]

A sentence "b" is an elaboration of a sentence "a" for a particular person, in a particular situation, when it adds information or other attributes that appear to transcend the limits of precization and specification.[15] Elaborations add new information that is often independent from whatever was discussed before and they often delimit this information with the prepositions "and" and "but."

As an example, let us start with an initial sentence, "a" = "global warming is occurring." A sentence "b_1" = "an increase in average global temperature is occurring," is a precization of "a." A sentence "b_2" = "global warming is occurring as a result of an increase in greenhouse gas emissions," is a specification. A sentence "b_3" = "global warming is occurring as a result of an increase in greenhouse gas emissions, but its effects may be mitigated by reducing these emissions," is an elaboration. In order to make Næss's semantics relevant to the policy arena, an enormous expanding, from the realm of precization to the realm of specification and elaboration must occur. By introducing the coupling of norms and hypothesis in premise-conclusion chains, Næss's DEA bridges this gap by enabling us to vastly broaden the analysis from an exploration of interpretations of particular sentences to the general analysis of argumentation patterns.

The analytic origins of this broader depth reference are in Næss's concept of levels of premise-conclusion chains. A premise-conclusion chain, $p \supset q$ and $q \supset r$ and $r \supset s$, can be formed from a series of premise-conclusion statements, p, q, r, and s, where $x \supset y$ symbolizes, from premise x, or set of premises x, follows conclusion y. Næss characterizes an argumentation pattern starting with q as shallower than one starting from p. In the same sense, a problematization of s based upon p would be deeper than one based upon q.[16] For example, let us assume a policy for mitigating climate warming, s, is recommended on the basis of premises showing that it will have a positive impact upon economic growth, r. Now imagine that the conclusion, r, can be shown to rest on premises, q, that incorporate how people's consumption generates both the increased greenhouse gas emissions, which are responsible for climate warming, and economic growth. A policy, s, based upon q would then be taken as deeper than one based only on r.

Næss's more metaphorical characterization of "shallow" or reform approaches to the ecological crisis is based upon their tendency to constrict the realm of problematizing, to employ a narrow incrementalism that may create blinders. From this perspective, appropriate responses to the environmental crisis are limited to less resource intensive and energy efficient technologies, improved valuation, "compensating projects," and market-based incentives.[17] This effort to palliate human impacts results in a search for technical solutions to what are often ethical, social, and political problems. "Shallow" approaches, grounded in technological optimism and economic efficiency, tend to focus on treating the symptoms of environmental degradation rather than the causes. "Deep" approaches on the other hand, call for a broader, longer-term, more skeptical stance that emphasizes a vigilant search for the underlying, interlinked and often systemic, root causes of the impacts. Efforts to improve efficiency are in no way excluded by "deep" alternatives, but they are grounded in a healthy skepticism of technological optimism that calls for searching out and assessing any possible new side-effects. "Deep" approaches call for individuals, and society as a whole, to engage actively in the process of systematically questioning and challenging practices, goals, aspirations, and values. They assume the existence of, and seek to address, root causes.

Næss's concerns over the hazards of limiting the realm of problematizing have been taken up independently by Kristin Shrader-Frechette, who goes so far as to argue that society's characterization of environmental problems tends to be "epistemologically loaded."[18] Shrader-Frechette contends that we have prematurely, and perhaps erroneously, framed environmental problems as technical problems and thus, not surprisingly, arrived at technical solutions. She asserts that we have come up with reasonable responses to the technical questions; the issue, however, is that these technical questions are only weakly related to the underlying and systemic ethical, social, and political problems whose consequences motivated the original inquiry.

Næss offers the deep/shallow contrast to help bring attention to these two opposing approaches to policy.[19]

> The decisive difference [between "deep" and "shallow" approaches] concerns [a] willingness to question and to appreciate the importance of questioning every economic and political policy in public. . . . [The "deep" approach] asks "why" more insistently and consistently, taking nothing for granted.[20]

Næss emphasizes his practical, policy-oriented focus by asserting that "'deepness' must include not only systematic philosophical deepness, but the 'deepness' of proposed social changes."[21]

By juxtaposing these two, almost caricatured, perspectives, Næss employs a technique of Gandhian nonviolent communication designed to confront core disagreements.[22] The premise is that the ability to forge significant agreements and debate significant disagreements, by carefully assessing and weighing alternative arguments, rests upon maneuvering discussion to what are conjectured to be the root causes of the environmental crisis. One of the primary root causes, Næss asserts, is the general disjunction between people's core beliefs and actions. A crucial, underlying hypothesis of Næss's DEA is that drawing out the presumed inconsistencies between an individual's actions and their fundamental beliefs will help to effect constructive change. This hypothesis also rests on the assumption that individuals, on the level of their core beliefs, desire a socially and ecologically sustainable existence.

Advancing to this stage of discussion, however, is no simple matter. In Næss's theory of communication it first requires eliminating the misunderstandings that seem to plague effective communication.

III. Argumentation

The issue of eliminating misunderstandings, "pseudo-agreements" and "pseudo-disagreements," is one of the core elements of Næss's theory of communication.[23] It is also a prerequisite for progressing to the stage where core disagreements can be discussed, debated, assessed, and evaluated. Misunderstandings result from confusion over the interpretation of expressions, not disagreement over what was taken to be expressed (a concept, norm, assertion, etc.). A key element of Næss's approach to reducing misunderstandings and facilitating communication in policy debates is his emphasis upon non-dogmatism and suspension of judgment, drawn from Sextus Empiricus and the Pyrrhonic Skeptics.[24]

Owing to pseudo-agreements at the level of general policy statements, two individuals from opposing policy camps may choose to support a policy that they might not have otherwise supported if they had examined its implications more clearly. Similarly, because of pseudo-disagreements at the same level of general policy statements, the two individuals might choose to oppose policies, which upon more careful examination they might have otherwise supported. Næss argues that discussions of environmental policy issues are stymied, all too often, by our inability to communicate effectively. This failure to reach core issues, the content-laden statements that express areas of serious agreement and disagreement, often derails discussion before we can be offered the opportunity to address the issues that might enable us to mount a meaningful response to the environmental crises.

Næss's approach to eliminating misunderstandings relies on precization, his technique, mentioned earlier, for clarifying the plausible interpretation of statements. Because of the inherent vagueness of language, a given expression can normally be interpreted in many different ways.[25]

Suppose we hear uttered the expression,

T_0 = "biodiversity protection is necessary."

Three obvious directions for precization exist, clarifying what is meant by "biodiversity," clarifying what is meant by "protection," and clarifying what is meant by "necessary." Focusing on possible interpretations of "biodiversity," at least four first order precizations come to mind,

T_1 = "protection of charismatic megafauna is necessary,"
T_2 = "protection of endemic species is necessary,"
T_3 = "protection of endemic and non-endemic species is necessary,"
T_4 = "protection of all species and cultures is necessary."

A variety of possible interpretations of "protection" and "necessary" might be similarly explored. For instance does "protection" mean active management or "hands-off" management? Does "necessary" mean only in certain special situations or always, and what might "necessary" mean when there are conflicts between other "necessary" acts?

Næss adds two important caveats to the use of precization. First, precization is always context dependent. A statement T_1 is a precization of expression T_0 for person Y in context X. Second, precization, while restricting the set of possible interpretations and adding detail, always comes at a cost. Excessive precization adds extraneous details, which can, themselves, become the source of misunderstandings. The essential point is that precization should only take place when there is a need for it, when misunderstandings might arise as a consequence of the possibility of attributing different statements to the same expression.

Once misunderstandings have been eliminated it can be established that the agreements and disagreements are, in fact, real or significant. The way to resolve true conflicts, Næss suggests, is to weigh alternative views against each other.[26] The goal is to establish which viewpoint is the most acceptable. Assessing the relative acceptability of alternative viewpoints is performed by carefully evaluating the arguments for and the arguments against each viewpoint.

Næss recommends developing two types of surveys, *pro-et-contra* (for *and* against) and *pro-aut-contra* (for *or* against), to facilitate this assessment process. The *pro-et-contra* survey identifies the most important arguments both in favor and against a particular assertion. The *pro-et-contra* survey never contains a conclusion, the arguments are never weighed against each other; the purpose of this survey is to set out the strongest, most exhaustive cases, both for and against, the assertion under consideration. The *pro-aut-contra* survey, which represents a particular perspective, presents a case either for, or against, the given assertion. The goal of this survey is to weigh the arguments against one another so as to arrive at a conclusion. Næss suggests that it is often helpful to create a *pro-et-contra* survey in preparation for performing a *pro-aut-contra* survey on the same issue. The relevance of these surveys for environmental policy analysis will be considered in the final section of this paper.

Completeness is often impossible and, in any case, comes at significant cost of time and effort. Næss's point is not to strive for idealized completeness, but rather to improve the process of justifying our decisions by engaging in the exercise. In light of this overarching goal, he recommends focusing our attention on the counterarguments to the position we initially support, both because we might be surprised and because it will strengthen our understanding of our own position.

Again, we must remember that the concept of acceptability, like precization, is not an absolute, but rather a comparative concept. In attempting to resolve real disagreements over environmental policy issues, however, the goal is to arrive at collective decisions that will be collectively supported. In this case, where the goal is to convince others (and sometimes ourselves) via rational discussion, it becomes crucial to present carefully articulated arguments that can be scrutinized for their relevance and tenability. When weighing arguments, Næss contends, we must consider both their relevance (justifiability and proof potential) and their tenability (feasibility and plausibility).

The importance of deep problematizing and the deep/shallow contrast now take on new meaning. While the deep and reform policy approaches are themselves in-contest, it does not logically follow that particular policies advocated by the opposing approaches will always be in opposition. Different individuals who subscribe to different policy approaches and embrace different ultimate values may support the same policy for different reasons, at different times. What Næss is asserting, however, is that from the standpoint of tenability and justifiability the reasoning process counts. If we are attempting to justify a policy, or persuade others to support it, especially one that involves concessions or personal sacrifice, how we argue for the policy and the merits of the policy position itself become consequential. Upholding a policy and ensuring compliance with its rules and regulations is likely to be much more successful when an individual's support for the policy is based upon real agreement as opposed to pseudo-agreement.

The significance of Næss's deep/shallow distinction rests not so much on the character of particular "deep" solutions, as on the fact that fundamental questions are taken seriously and raised, that the underlying and interlinked causes are sought out, and that seemingly radical responses to surmounting the environmental crises are thoughtfully considered.

IV. Deep Ecology and Policy

The challenge of today is to save the planet from further devastation which violates both the enlightened self-interest of humans and nonhumans, and decreases the potential of joyful existence for all.[27]

Contributing to overcoming the ecological crisis through systematic and methodical exploration of perceptions, values, actions, and policies is the primary purpose of the DEA. An effort to tightly integrate philosophy-of-life with social policies and practice has been a concern throughout Næss's life. His work on policy matters includes: antiwar and antinuclear issues,[28] democracy,[29] protests against the construction of Norwegian hydroelectric facilities,[30] campaigns against Norway's bid to join the European Union,[31] clarifications of "sustainability" terminology,[32] mountaineering issues,[33] Norwegian whaling,[34] and bear, sheep, and wolf policy.[35]

Næss underscores the limitations of attempting to motivate response to the ecological crisis solely through ethical appeals, by arguing that we must first have an ontological foundation, a view of reality, that is capable of supporting a meaningful and lasting environmental ethic.[36] He also cautions against relying exclusively upon appeals through scientific description, omitting discussions of norms. Science describes and predicts, while calls for action require the existence of normative premises, of prescriptions.[37] "Objective" science cannot provide principles for ecologically responsible policies or guidelines for reaching ecological harmony.

> Ecology as a science does not ask what kind of a society would be the best for maintaining a particular ecosystem—that is considered a question for value theory, for politics, for ethics. As long as ecologists keep narrowly to their science they do not ask such questions.[38]

A key purpose of the DEA is to assist in the breakdown of this partitioning of the scientific enterprise from ethics and politics. In contrast, the dominant response to environmental deterioration, often referred to as "reform environmentalism," tends to foster this partitioning. It assumes that environmental problems are, in the main, amenable to scientific management. The primary issue is to work with the political process to see that responsible environmental policies, those which incorporate the necessary technical innovations, are promulgated.[39] No major shift in ethics or practice is called for because efficiency improvements and technological innovation will rescue the environment.

Calls for the Integration of Science, Ethics, and Politics: NEPA and the DEA

Although one might presume that shallow ecological argumentation undergirds all major environmental policy, this has not been the case.[40] The reform approach is inconsistent with the thrust of the paramount environmental policy legislation of the United States, the National Environmental Policy Act (NEPA), as reflected upon in the *Twentieth Annual Report of the President's Council on Environmental Quality*:

> In essence, NEPA was enacted to ensure that the federal government, when it planned any significant action, would consider *all* possible deleterious effects on environmental quality. Thus NEPA was intended to inculcate into the federal government, in all its policies, regulations, and laws, a practical environmental ethic [my emphasis].[41]

NEPA is such a profound example of thoughtful environmental policy legislation precisely because it symbolizes an effort to integrate deep problematizing with value-based considerations.

It may be helpful to ponder the text of NEPA, which is little known, to understand its architects' immense scope and vision.[42] They recognized both the human role in creating the ecological crisis and the interrelatedness of its causes, including "population growth, high-density urbanization, industrial expansion, resource exploitation, and new and expanding technological advances." NEPA's stated purpose is to "encourage productive and enjoyable harmony between man and his environment." It calls for: "efforts which will prevent or eliminate damage to the environment and biosphere," improving our understanding of ecological systems, considering "unquantified environmental amenities and values . . . along with economic and technical considerations," preservation of diversity, characterizing and studying alternatives when unresolved resource-use conflicts exist, and implementing a "systematic, interdisciplinary approach which will insure the integrated use of the natural and social sciences and the environmental design arts in planning and decision-making which may have an impact on man's environment." NEPA's goal of comprehensive impact assessment, commitment to public participation, concern for future generations, and willingness to question all aspects of the ecological crisis supports Næss's contention that significant improvement of environmental policy rests on problematizing the environmental crises with more depth of intention.

Besides "man's" implied ownership of the environment and the absence of explicitly nonanthropocentric language, which can scarcely be expected of national legislation in the late 1960s, the concerns and provisions of NEPA are laudable and momentous. When one recognizes that NEPA was passed four years before Næss's famous 1973 paper, its landmark nature becomes evident. Both the DEA and NEPA assume that to respond successfully to such problems as loss of species and indigenous cultures, climate change, encroachment upon wildlands, and persistent pollutants, a new approach to environmental policy is warranted.

The DEA, with its focus on semantic clarity, depth of argumentation, and responsibility, provides an underpinning and grounding for NEPA's vision. Concretizing the prescience of NEPA, the DEA asserts that individuals and society must be unmerciful in their realm of questioning (no sacred cows), undaunted in their pursuit of definiteness of intention, and broad-minded in their consideration of significant social, political, and lifestyle changes.

Twenty five years have passed since NEPA was enacted, yet the *practical environmental ethic* has still to emerge. One of NEPA's principal architects, Lynton K. Caldwell, argues that its ostensible ineffectiveness is, in large part, due to a dearth of executive and legislative support. He explains that "[l]egislation of such novelty or purpose and so contrary to strongly entrenched interests requires positive, unequivocal executive support to be fully effective."[43] Caldwell points to the critical importance of establishing clear value priorities for environmental protection and the significance of engendering a willingness to consider conflicting goals and alternative viewpoints.

Næss insists that individuals' perception of the world and their relationship to it need fundamental reevaluation before a practical environmental ethic can take hold and effectively respond to environmental problems with the comprehensive vision that NEPA demanded. This is because the creation of value priorities for environmental protection rests upon the existence of a compatible ontological or worldview foundation.[44] The failure to invoke and enforce the provisions of NEPA supports Næss's assertion that appeals to duty will likely be unsuccessful when the underlying value priorities, the reinforcing inclinations, are weak.

Calls for Broad Reevaluation of the Environmental Crisis: Gore and Næss

Today, however, from the highest halls of U.S. government, come pleas to re-evaluate our worldviews and calls to consider the systemic character of the environmental crisis. Despite his misguided criticism of deep ecology, largely based upon pseudo-disagreements, Vice President Gore, in his best-selling *Earth in the Balance*, seems to endorse many of its insights, particularly the importance of deep problematizing.

> [W]hatever its genesis, our willingness to ignore the consequences of our actions has combined with our belief that we are separate from nature to produce a genuine crisis in the way we relate to the world around us. . . . [A]ny solution to the problem will require a careful assessment of that relationship as well as the complex interrelationship among factors within civilization and between them and the natural components of the earth's ecological system. . . . The transformation of the way we relate to the earth will of course involve new technologies, but the key changes will involve new ways of thinking about the relationship itself.[45]

What distinguishes these statements by Gore from a more traditional reform environmentalism approach? Their acknowledgment of the inter-relatedness of causation. Their emphasis on addressing underlying causes. Their call for systemic changes. And their recognition that technology has only a limited role to play in overcoming the environmental crisis. Næss and Gore both assert that incremental improvements to the "technique" oriented, dominant "environmental paradigm" will leave us with an impoverished world. In Gore's words, "our relationship to the world may never be healed until we are willing to stop denying the destructive nature of the current pattern."[46] In short, Gore explains, while the intentions of many politicians and citizens are valiant, their efforts will tend to stymie effective response and drive ecological crises as long as their problematization of the environmental crises remains limited to a shallow response.

> The problem is not so much one of policy failures: much more worrisome are the failures of candor, evasions of responsibility, and timidity of vision that

characterize too many of us in government. . . . [O]ur current public discourse is focused on the shortest of short-term values and encourages the American people to join us politicians in avoiding the most important issues and postponing the really difficult choices.[47]

The DEA, as a framework for helping people to reconsider their relationship to the world, is meant to stimulate the renewal of candor, reinvigorate our sense of responsibility, expand our values, and broaden our vision. Gore's statements resonate with Næss's claim that the distinction between "deep" and "reform" approaches is significant. I suggest that there is a close compatibility between the policy approach advocated by Gore, legislated by NEPA, and outlined in careful philosophical detail by Næss. Furthermore, this general approach, as embodied in the DEA, is both theoretically and practically different from the "reform" approach. It calls for integrating 'spontaneous experience,'[48] our unmediated acquaintance with the world's contents, with evolving scientific understanding. Næss and Gore both emphasize how embracing this approach necessitates spawning significantly different value priorities, practices, institutions, and policies.

Norton's *Toward Unity Among Environmentalists*

Recently, however, Næss's assertion that there is a significant distinction between "deep" and "reform" approaches to environmentalism has been challenged by Bryan Norton. In his insightful and thought provoking *Toward Unity among Environmentalists*, Norton contends that while environmentalists do not share a single, common worldview they nevertheless do share common policy goals and objectives.[49] For instance, despite different ultimate premises and fundamental values, environmentalists are all interested in overcoming the ecological crises.[50] This premise of shared intentions as "unity" serves as Norton's organizing principle.

Norton argues that there are a wide variety of values that may be consistent with, and used to justify, particular policy objectives. This range of values, he believes, need not lead the environmental movement to divisiveness.

[A] diversity of value concerns need not debilitate the movement. Indeed, freedom to appeal to a variety of value systems may ultimately prove the greatest strength of the movement.[51]

Norton's analysis, much like Næss's contention that there exist a wide plurality of ultimate premises which are consistent with the DEA, demonstrates that individuals with conflicting worldviews (or technically speaking, total views) *may* rally behind the same sets of policies.[52]

Næss argues that the history of ideas offers us a diverse array of ultimate premises. Two individuals may find each other's ultimate premises incomparable and conflicting, yet still find these premises consonant with the DEA. If these individuals embrace ultimate premises from the subclass of ultimates that incorporate some form of wide identification and if they subscribe to the other five elements of the DEA that I outlined earlier, Næss contends that he cannot imagine a situation where they would, in general, choose clearly unecological policies over ecological ones. But even in this case where our two individuals embrace the DEA, the two sets of policies, or policy priorities, they arrive at could very well be substantially different or even conflicting.

Norton's analysis, however, goes well beyond Næss's modest contention to conclude that environmentalists' differing worldviews, in most instances, ought not give rise to significant discord on the level of concrete environmental policies. Norton puts forward two key claims: "there exist no important differences between deep and reform policy goals"[53] and there is an "emerging consensus regarding desirable environmental policies."[54] In Norton's argument the second claim follows from, and is logically dependent upon, the validity of the first claim. Because the different worldviews of seemingly opposed environmentalists do not yield significantly different policy goals, and because changing policy is taken to be a primary concern of environmentalists, Norton contends that there is every reason for environmentalists of all persuasions to forge an accord and rally behind the same policies.

There are, however, three important clarifications to be made. First, agreement on broad policy goals does not guarantee consensus on particular policies. Second, consensus on the general desirability of particular policies does not guarantee consensus on policy priorities in particular situations. Third, whatever consensus on particular policies that might arise need not be generated from a prior agreement on policy goals.

When evaluating a spectrum of competing policies for addressing a particular problem, individuals with congruent policy goals may have decidedly different views on the relative efficacy of the different policies. Different orderings of a constellation of agreed upon goals and objectives will very likely lead to different preference orderings of the "most suitable" policy for addressing a particular policy problem. Even in situations where agreement exists on the general desirability of particular policies, conflicting views on the relative efficacy of the different policies or different views on their relative ability to satisfy a range of policy objectives may generate divergent orderings of the policies, particularly in situations where there is stiff competition for scarce resources. Finally, given the nature of politics, individuals with decidedly different worldviews, even those whose worldviews incorporate conflicting policy perspectives, might, after carefully weighing a variety of social, political, scientific, ecological, and economic factors, still choose to forge a consensus and support the same policy in a particular situation. An emerging consensus on particular policies might in fact be developing, but it need not be based upon a preexisting confluence of goals.

Norton, however, does not address these possibilities. His argument seems to rest on a more brittle claim, namely that because of a presumed confluence of goals, the differing, and often conflicting, worldviews of environmentalists, in particular those who subscribe to Næss's DEA and those who subscribe to reform strategies, ought not give rise to incongruent concrete policy recommendations.

While Norton's contention regarding policy agreement may, in principle, be justifiable, his argument rests on denying the possibility of real and fundamental conflicts between the policy priorities of the deep and reform approaches. His assumption of policy consensus arising from a priori agreement on policy goals is inconsistent with the premises of the DEA, regarding depth of intention, and it is inconsistent with practical reason. Lacking an elaboration of the implications of a particular policy in relation to particular worldviews, including their associated ultimate values, it is simply impossible to make a priori claims regarding policy affinities without recourse to pseudo-agreements.

If there is an emerging consensus on beneficial environmental policies, and if this consensus is to prove meaningful, then it must be able to transcend the possibility that basic value conflicts might lead to significant policy differences. Parrying this potentiality can only yield a fragile and ephemeral consensus. Because Norton's first claim is far stronger, more restrictive, less tenable, and a prerequisite for his second claim, it will be the focus of my analysis. This claim regarding the affinity of deep and reform goals rests upon two key hypotheses: the convergence hypothesis and scientific naturalism.

Norton's convergence hypothesis postulates that "[e]nvironmentalists believe that policies serving the interests of the human species as a whole, and in the long run, will also serve the 'interests' of nature, and vice versa."[55] At least two difficulties exist with this hypothesis.

First, while it might be possible to demonstrate in some idealized sense that the long-term interests of humans and nature are perfectly coincident (entirely without conflict), such a "proof" would have little practical utility on the level of policy analysis. This is because human interests are neither monolithic nor homogeneous. Since environmentalists cannot be expected, in general, to agree on the "interests of the human species" or what constitutes the "long run," we certainly cannot anticipate their agreement on policies to serve these interests. Environmentalists do have very serious debates over: how to characterize "sustainability" and "ecosystem health," desirable population targets, how to define or even whether to accept long-term discount rates, the relative benefits of preservation and restoration, the appropriate scale of "active management," reintroducing species such as grizzly bears and wolves, the role of technological innovation, and the importance of roadless areas. Their disagreements on these issues can lead to contrasting policies, and these in turn can have widely varying effects upon the natural world.

Second, the "convergence hypothesis" is plagued by a critical asymmetry; it is not commutative.[56] Humans are ultimately dependent upon nature for their sustenance, even if we do not yet realize it, but nature is not dependent, at least not in quite the same way, upon humans. From a strict utilitarian standpoint, it is likely that the most expeditious way to promote the long-run flourishing of nature would be to extinguish *Homo sapiens*, but this would certainly be undesirable from the standpoint of humans. Similarly, depending upon how environmentalists characterize and prioritize human interests, policies that benefit these interests might easily result in the diminution of nature.

Environmentalists are humans first, and humans have diverse and competing interests as well as plural rationalities for assessing these interests.[57] Seemingly enlightened policies for flood control, water storage, fire suppression, and the creation of recreation areas have often, albeit inadvertently, reduced diversity and nature's potential to flourish. The critical point is that we cannot assume confluence of interests; we must carefully analyze the implications of our policies both from the perspective of human interests and from those of life on earth in general, which itself will express species- and location-dependent multiple interests.

Norton's convergence hypothesis is subject to significant validation difficulties. Because even the long-run interests of humans are diverse and contrasting, as well as sometimes conflicting, they can neither be assumed to be equivalent to the interests of nature nor can they be interchanged with the interests of nature.

Næss offers a much weaker version of Norton's convergence hypothesis, that while rectifying its critical asymmetry still necessitates several caveats, "[s]ince most policies serving the biosphere also serve humanity in the long run, they may, at least initially, be accepted on the basis of 'homocentric' arguments."[58] Norton's second argument for the affinity of deep and reform goals asserts that "[b]ecause of a shared commitment to scientific naturalism, environmentalists of differing value commitments gravitate toward similar policies. . . ."[59] This hypothesis also has two primary difficulties.

First, as long as Norton wishes to maintain a fact/value distinction, basing policy consensus exclusively upon an assumed scientific consensus seems to make committing the naturalistic fallacy unavoidable. While Norton acknowledges that some may view him to be flirting with the "naturalistic fallacy," he contends that our expanding understanding of ecological science both informs us and sets the context for discussion and debate, without demanding a consensus on values.[60] I certainly concur with this modest contention regarding the positive role of science in contributing to policy formation, as long as it is viewed as one of a host of interrelated considerations. But when discussing the basis for environmentalists' presumed consensus on wetlands policy, Norton asserts, "[s]cientific understanding of the ecological context affecting all of their diverse values *forces* them to adopt a common-denominator objective, wetlands preservation" (my emphasis). One can only infer that an appropriate course of action, a prescription, is being drawn from factual statements which describe the way the world *is*.[61]

Second, Norton's assumed scientific consensus does not, and will likely never, exist. Richard Norgaard argues in a recent paper, "Environmental Science as a Social Process," that the notion of scientific unity is outdated and indefensible; scientists do not agree upon a "single logical paradigm, set of assumptions, and data set from which conclusions can be deduced."[62] Norgaard adds that the "scientific" process of reaching consensus on understanding cannot be separated from the "political" process of choosing an appropriate action. Even if we were to assume that Norton is correct in asserting that science could "force" people to agree on general policy goals, such as wetlands preservation, science, alone, could not answer the critical questions of which wetlands should be preserved, how much total acreage should be preserved, and by what criteria such decisions should be made? Norgaard suggests that if "the public better understood the pluralistic conceptual basis of the sciences and environmental science as social process, a more productive discourse could begin to evolve."[63] The upshot for Norton is that even if environmentalists do share a commitment to scientific naturalism, it would be ill-founded and unable to provide consensus, as current scientific debate on global warming, biodiversity protection, and ecological restoration demonstrate. This criticism of scientific naturalism highlights the importance of building policy upon clear, deeply problematized arguments which are carefully evaluated, openly discussed, and debated in public.[64]

Having established that Norton's unity thesis rests on shaky ground, I can argue that his claim that the distinction between deep and reform approaches is not consequential rests on similarly unstable foundations. Norton offers a rhetorical query, "perhaps the whole idea that there are deep and shallow ecologists reduces to a distinction desperately seeking a difference."[65] He questions whether a "deep" analysis leads to different policy recommendations and he asks if its policy recommendations are arrived at, justified, or supported through dissimilar means and tactics.

Næss's argument is not that there are deep and shallow ecologists, but that individuals and decision-making bodies vary in the depth to which they problematize and in their willingness to consider profound social and political change. Norton's argument against the deep/shallow contrast is that it contributes to an inappropriate polarization of environmentalists, based upon the character of their values. While Norton may be correct about his assessment of the deep/shallow contrast leading to an inappropriate polarization of environmentalists, the basis of his criticism, however, rests on a pseudo-disagreement.[66] The character of environmentalists' values has never been at issue. The issue is with their patterns of argumentation and their depth of intention.

Norton introduces the "environmentalist's dilemma" by highlighting the quandary posed by embracing both economic rationality and the notion of intrinsic value as an inviolable moral principle.[67] He then associates "moral monism" with deep ecology by contending that it is based upon "biocentric moralism." But Næss's concept of "intrinsic" or "inherent" value is ontological, not ethical or epistemological.[68] The DEA does not rest on a single moral principle, quite the contrary. In fact, it eschews the two criteria Norton sets out as the basis for moral monism.[69]

First, the DEA is based on a belief that there cannot exist perfect sets of principles to guide us through all moral dilemmas. This realization inspires the requirement for developing and articulating our own total views. Second, the DEA is also based upon the premise that because each problem is context dependent and because a diverse array of viable alternatives usually exists, the existence of single "right" answers for every quandary is illusory. Næss's concept of "vital needs," his emphasis upon respecting diverse cultural perspectives, and his insistence that there will usually exist a wide plurality of concrete policy responses that are consistent with the DEA all confirm this perspective.

To demonstrate how by applying the DEA one arrives at and justifies policies differently, it is essential to recognize that Næss views ends and means and facts and values as internally related. For instance, Næss avoids the dreaded "naturalistic fallacy" by arguing that scientific information is, itself, value-laden. It is thus inappropriate to respond to Norton's dichotomization by attempting to decouple policy formation from policy justification. Although we may employ a host of pragmatic arguments to justify our policy choices, these arguments, explicitly or implicitly, represent a strategic implementation of our values. While the approach and tactics inspired by the DEA are clearly different from the reform approach, the recommended policies will not always lead to different policy recommendations.

Even if we do accept Norton's claim that individuals coming from both reform and deep ecology perspectives agree on some broad goals, such as the desirability of improved environmental quality, this agreement is not sufficient to guarantee that individual's value priorities in support of these broad goals will not lead to disparate concrete policies on particular issues. While Norton, no doubt, recognizes this issue he seems to argue for inverting causal explanation: "Muir and Pinchot, in the pursuit of their divergent policy goals came to emphasize quite different values."[70] Norton is certainly correct in asserting that Muir and Pinchot, in particular, and that individuals, in general, pragmatically employ a whole host of arguments to justify their policy positions. By focusing on pragmatic policy justification, however, Norton appears to position our choice to pursue particular policies ahead of the value constellations which support these policies.

My disagreement with Norton is with his implicit assertion that the basis for our policy justifications (or our policy choices) is somehow weakly related to our underlying values. I am asserting quite the opposite. I do not suggest that people need a coherent, articulated philosophy to deduce policies from their values.[71] Policies may follow implicitly or intuitively from our values and worldviews, but they *do* follow from them, regardless of what arguments we use to justify our policy choices. Muir and Pinchot's policy disagreements resulted from their underlying worldview differences. Norton's concern over whether or not we derive our policies from a sophisticated philosophical system or develop a complex ideology to support our intuitive policy preferences only obfuscates the critical interdependence between policies and values.

As Næss's discussion of total views makes clear, values are not an afterthought; they explicitly, or implicitly, motivate our policy preferences. Whether or not we attempt to make such structures explicit and regardless of our particular policy justifications, Næss argues that we act as if we have systematic conceptual structures (total views) for relating to the world and guiding our decisions regarding society and nature.[72] Muir and Pinchot did not pull their divergent policies out of thin air and then begin a search for values to justify them.

Muir accepted both use-value and intrinsic value.[73] Pinchot, focusing on use-value and growth, was more concerned with maximizing efficiency.[74] In this case, Muir's efforts to incorporate a broader range of values led to very significant policy differences; it resulted in the battle between preservation and conservation.

Næss asserts that fruitful debate and interchange, as well as the creation of policies that are consistent with society's ultimate beliefs, rest upon individuals' attempts to make these fragmentary and tentative structures explicit. Because of the likelihood of inconsistencies and value-conflicts, Næss argues that individuals must strive to articulate fragments of their total views for the very purpose of trying to facilitate the type of policy agreement that Norton posits might be possible. In order for policy consensus not to be based upon tenuous pseudo-agreements or ruled-out a priori because of avoidable pseudo-disagreements, we must draw out the connections between our values, our tools for policy analysis, our policies, and our pragmatic policy justifications.[75]

Næss, NEPA, Norton, and Gore

The previous example suffices to prove that environmentalists' divergent value perspectives can lead to meaningful policy differences. It also demonstrates the relevance of establishing clear value priorities, highlights the consequence of deep problematizing, and confirms the significance of carefully tracing out the implications of prospective policies. There exist many other examples of radically contrasting policy proposals from environmentalists.[76] Another germane example is Gore's "Environmental Marshal Plan."[77]

While Gore's rhetoric throughout *Earth in the Balance* suggests that he has truly taken deep problematizing to heart, his concrete policy recommendations, admirable as many of them are, appear to rely too heavily upon efficiency improvements and market forces. Gore restricts his discussion of population to stabilization, he embraces the notion of economic growth instead of exploring reduced consumption and steady-state alternatives, and he fails to address biodiversity loss and wilderness preservation. While it seems unlikely that Gore falls into the trap Shrader-Frechette outlines (framing environmental problems as technical problems) he may be a victim of his own dilemma, "timidity of vision." His policy recommendations, while significant, represent only marginal improvements from the status quo. They are incompatible with the scale and magnitude of the environmental crises that he has gone to great effort to describe in his book. It appears as though Gore has somehow truncated the choice set of viable policy recommendations from the inception of his investigation.[78]

A final testimonial of this view that different policies may arise from different value prioritizations and different depths of intention is Lynton Caldwell's disappointment regarding the crippling of NEPA's provisions.[79] Even the most far-sighted and progressive environmental policy legislation will lie impotent and largely ignored as long as an appreciation of its provisions is wanting. For instance, if an environmentalist-legislator is a diehard technological optimist, NEPA's call to consider the negative side-effects of technologies may seem excessive. By facilitating the integration of values, ontological underpinnings, scientific information, semantics, argumentation, and individual responsibility, the DEA may help to improve policy by isolating issues that could lead to significant policy contrasts.

Norton's attempt to highlight the unity among environmentalists is a valiant but misguided effort at syncretism. Using Næss's terminology, it appears that Norton incorrectly assumes ostensible disagreements between environmentalists on policy matters are necessarily pseudo-disagreements and he assumes the ostensible agreements between environmentalists on policy matters are true agreements as opposed to pseudo-agreements. His "unity," while not to be totally discounted, appears much more fragile than he asserts.

A "common ground" may exist, but it is not adequate to bridge the very real and very serious disputes over policy goals and objectives. If Norton is truly willing to accept a strong pluralism at the level of worldviews, with their corresponding differences in ultimate values and ontological premises, he will have to relax his prescriptive thesis regarding policy confluence among environmentalists.[80] The debates over "sustainable development" (wilderness and growth, in particular) come to mind as one current example where a true rift in values and proposed policies exist. Such rifts are not likely to be bridged by the "shared" common goals of "growth" and "wilderness." Different values need not lead to opposing policies, but they often do. The critical point is that deep problematizing and the corollary commitment to thoughtfully consider all forms of social and political changes *do* often isolate meaningful distinctions, which sometimes lead to significant policy differences.

V. Næss's DEA:
A Fully Developed Approach to Policy Analysis?

The general rules are few and easily grasped, but the kinds of particular problematic situations are overwhelmingly rich and demand creativeness.[81]

Næss's DEA is sophisticated, subtle, and worked out in considerable philosophical detail. On the level of "general guidelines," the DEA has already made a significant and lasting contribution. It rests on firm philosophical foundations but, even by Næss's own account, it is incomplete and always "under way." I focus on three areas for future work: (1) how to motivate value priorities for ecological sustainability, (2) how to specify "vital needs" for different communities, and (3) how to "resolve" value-conflicts in environmental decision-making nonviolently.

A careful reading of not only the ecophilosophical literature, but also the general philosophical, social, and political literature is required to begin to draw out and piece together a coherent picture of the DEA. Comprehending Næss's total view concept is crucial to this understanding. A careful examination of the DEA, as a normative-derivational system, may offer significant insights but, ultimately, the success of the DEA hinges upon its ability to help motivate value priorities for ecological sustainability.

The dilemmas of attempting to stimulate these value priorities via duty and scientific naturalism have been highlighted. Given the immediacy of mounting a meaningful response to the ecological crisis, however, it is still unclear how Næss's "beautiful acts," deeds consistent with duties but motivated by inclination, can be fostered.[82] How can the all-sided maturity that Næss speaks of be cultivated when its ontological underpinnings may not have been inculcated? And how can we be sure that value priorities for nature will supersede other competing interests and obligations? While it has become all too clear how humans shape the world through technology and economic growth, it is much less clear how nature may work to shape the human mind and culture in positive ways. One possibility for inspiring Næss's ontological (wide identification) foundation for beautiful acts involves examining this second relationship, nature's potential to enlighten and instruct humans.[83]

The second area for future research involves elaborating Næss's notion of "vital needs." Næss appears to have introduced the expression to prompt us to reflect upon the limited correlation between consumption and quality of life.[84] George Brown, former Chairman of the House Science, Space, and Technology Committee, explains that:

> Basic human needs—elemental needs—are intrinsically different from other material needs because they can be satisfied. Other needs appear to be insatiable, as the consumption patterns of the United States clearly demonstrate. . . . Once basic human needs are met, satisfaction with our lives cannot be said to depend on the amount of things we acquire, use, and consume. . . . [M]ore technology based economic growth is not necessary to satisfy humanity's elemental needs, nor does more growth quench our thirst for consumption. In terms of the social contract, we justify more growth because it is supposedly the most efficient way to spread economic opportunity and social well-being. I am suggesting that this reasoning is simplistic and often specious.[85]

While Næss originally left the vital needs expression rather vague, to account for pluralism and diverse cultural beliefs, he expects considerable benefit to result from focusing detailed analysis, discussion, and debate toward clarifying what constitutes a "bundle" of vital needs for particular groups of people, in particular environments.[86] Additional benefit might also result from detailed elaboration of the "side effects" of excessive consumption and their impact upon others to satisfy their own vital needs.

An interesting example, which integrates both the idea of learning from nature and the issue of how to specify vital needs, comes from the decision by many Colombian Indians to abandon their government homes and return to their remote aboriginal homes along the Miriti River to practice their traditional lifestyles.[87] For a variety of reasons, the Colombian government has become amazingly supportive of these "reverse" migrations, setting aside more than one-quarter of the nation's land surface as permanently protected areas (*resguardos*). The "village" *capitans,* part shaman and part chief, were, however, faced with a profound philosophical dilemma: can a society selectively partake in the Western way of life without eroding its traditional lifestyle?

The *capitans* were clearly prepared to dissociate themselves from the vast majority of Western accouterments, but a few Western implements, particularly fishhooks and machetes, were found to be phenomenal labor savers. To obtain these minimal trade-goods would require earning what amounts to about several hundred dollars per year, per family. The *capitans* went through an independent, rigorous assessment of the tradeoffs associated with a wide variety of alternative schemes for earning cash. They did not want to export their canoes because it might deplete the best trees; they did not want to sell their sacred objects for religious reasons; and they did not want to market fish because of the possible long-term implications upon their fisheries and also because they did not want to address the implications of being "electrified," a requirement for protecting against spoilage. The *capitans* finally decided upon a scheme to raise and sell chickens, as the least onerous and compromising way to buy their fishhooks and machetes. What this example demonstrates is that the notion of vital needs, viewed non-trivially, can serve as a useful instrument for policy analysis.

Perhaps the most important area for future research involves establishing value priorities when conflicts arise not from misunderstandings, but because humans are constantly faced with complex choices that involve genuine trade-offs.[88] Næss himself points out:

> Identification with individuals, species, ecosystems and landscapes results in difficult problems of priority. What should be the relation of ecosystem ethics to other parts of general ethics?[89]

Asking "why" repeatedly may be effective for unearthing root causes by increasing our depth of intention, but in situations like this it cannot necessarily resolve the value-conflicts that arise both within individuals and between the members of society. In fact, as Lynton Caldwell suggests, the clarification of values may galvanize conflict.[90]

> No inference is warranted, however, that value clarification will reconcile interests. On the contrary, value analysis could lead to sharpened conflict.[91]

Where conflicts arise within or among individuals as a result of conflicting ultimate premises, or when conflicts arise on policy positions that have been reasoned consistently and coherently from fundamentals the DEA appears to offer scant recourse.

Pro-et-contra and *pro-aut-contra* surveys can be powerful heuristic aids for approaching such conflicts, but they do not represent realistic solutions for addressing complex, conflict-laden social decision problems.[92] Næss's surveys do, however, address the central philosophical issue that such conflicts can only be resolved by carefully weighing the qualitatively different implications of different alternatives. Modern environmental problems, with their complex trade-offs between ethical, ecological, scientific, political, legal, social, and economic considerations, demand an empirically and procedurally more sophisticated approach for systematically evaluating alternatives and assessing conflicts.[93]

Næss's DEA, like the far-sighted NEPA, makes an important contribution towards overcoming the environmental crises by calling attention to our false partitioning of science, ethics, and politics and by focusing on the need for methodical exploration of our perceptions, values, actions, and policies. Næss's emphasis upon deep problematizing and his focus on clarifying premise-conclusion statements highlights the important contrast between the deep ecology and reform environmental policy perspectives. While I agree with Norton that environmentalists share certain kinds of common goals at the most general level, for example, desiring clean land, air, and water, it is, nevertheless, consequential how they employ precization, specification, and elaboration to transform these general policy goals into policy perspectives and, ultimately, into particular concrete policy recommendations. When we ask how clean, where, how soon, and by what particular concrete policies, there are wide differences of opinion today and presumably these differences will persist. Gore has cogently pointed out how continuing to make decisions by relying upon narrow instrumental arguments and technological substitution may prolong the neglect of root causes, fail to address serious conflict, and, ultimately, generate catastrophic environmental consequences. But as the separation between Gore's policy perspective and concrete policy proposals underscores, the hope for overcoming the environmental crisis rests not in presumed unities, but in applying deep problematizing to generate tenable, justifiable policies.

Notes

This chapter is reprinted with minor revisions from Harold Glasser, "Næss's Deep Ecology Approach and Environmental Policy," *Inquiry* 39 (1996): 157–187. This is a special edition on the contributions of Arne Næss, edited by Andrew Light and David Rothenberg. The author thanks Peder Anker, Paul Craig, Alastair Hannay, Anthony Hainault, D. Jones, Richard Norgaard, Bryan Norton, Max Oelschlaeger, Terry Poxon, David Rothenberg, Thomas Seiler, George Sessions, Nina Witoszek, and Amanda Wolf for helpful discussions, comments, and encouragement. The author is indebted to Arne Næss and Andrew Light for their detailed review of, and insightful comments on, earlier drafts of this manuscript.

[1] Arne Næss, "The Shallow and the Deep, Long-Range Ecology Movement: A Summary," *Inquiry* 16 (1973): 95–100. This is the first published use of the term deep ecology. Næss actually introduced the English term in 1972 at the World Future Research Conference in Bucharest. Næss's radical views on preserving "free nature" date back to a 1965 article, "Nature Ebbing Out" (in Norwegian), which called for the protec-

tion of a wilderness, or rather free nature, area on the west coast of Norway (personal communication, 2/6/95).

[2] I discuss the DEA, not Næss's personal total view, Ecosophy T, formed by applying the DEA and not the deep ecology movement, the loose group of individuals who espouse support for the deep ecology platform.

[3] See for instance, Arne Næss, "The Connection of 'Self-realization!' with Diversity, Complexity and Symbiosis." Unpublished manuscript (1991a): 7 pages, 6.

[4] These six elements of the DEA are discussed in more detail in Harold Glasser, "Deep Ecology Clarified: A Few Fallacies and Misconceptions," *The Trumpeter Journal of Ecosophy* 12 (1995a): 138–142. I also plan to publish a more extensive, critical explication of the DEA from material cut from a previous draft of the present paper.

[5] Total views and our potential for comparing them and making them explicit is the central theme of Næss's *Hvilken verden er den Virkelige? (Which World is the Real World?)* (Oslo: Universitetsforlaget, 1969 and revised in 1982). *Which World* has recently been translated by Ingemund Gullvåg and is currently under revision by Næss and myself for inclusion in his upcoming *Selected Works*. See also Arne Næss, "Reflections About Total Views," *Philosophy and Phenomenological Research* 25 (1964): 16–29.

[6] The concept of normative-derivational systems and their use in action research is developed in Arne Næss, "Notes on the Methodology of Normative Systems," *Methodology and Science* 10 (1977): 64–79.

[7] For a listing of the eight points, with additional commentary, see Arne Næss, "The Deep Ecology Movement: Some Philosophical Aspects," *Philosophical Inquiry* 8 (1986a): 18–21 (hereafter referred to as Næss, 1986a). This paper is also reprinted in George Sessions, ed., *Deep Ecology for the Twenty-First Century* (Boston: Shambhala, 1995), 64–84.

[8] I originally pointed to the idea of intrinsic value representing an ultimate premise in an earlier unpublished manuscript, "The Distinctiveness of the Deep Ecology Approach to Ecophilosophy," (1991): 29 pages. I also mention the possibility of not embracing intrinsic value, but all other significant elements of the DEA, in "Demystifying the Critiques of Deep Ecology," *Rethinking Deep Ecology*, ed. Nina Witoszek, Nature and Humanities Series, (Oslo: Center for Development and the Environment, Oslo University, 1996).

[9] Arne Næss, *Ecology, Community, and Lifestyle: Outline of an Ecosophy,* translated and revised by David Rothenberg (Cambridge: Cambridge University Press, 1989), 38 (hereafter referred to as Næss and Rothenberg, 1989).

[10] Næss and Rothenberg, 1989, 36–8.

[11] Arne Næss, *Interpretation and Preciseness: A Contribution to the Theory of Communication* (Oslo: Jacob Dybwad, 1953), hereafter referred to as Næss, 1953, and Arne Næss, *Communication and Argument: Elements of Applied Semantics* translated by Alastair Hannay (Oslo: Universitetsforlaget/London: Allen and Unwin, 1966 and 1981) (hereafter referred to as Næss, 1981). For helpful clarification, see also Ingemund Gullvåg, "Depth of Intention" *Inquiry* 26 (1983): 31–83.

[12] For additional details on precization refer to the chapter, "Precization and Definition," in Næss, 1981, 37–72. For a more technical discussion of precization see, for instance, Næss, 1953, 56 and 77–79.

[13] For a more condensed version of a precization diagram see, Næss, 1953, 77.

[14] Næss, 1953, 64.

[15] Næss, 1953, 69–70.

[16] This discussion of depth in terms of premise-conclusion chains was suggested to me by Arne Næss (personal communication, 6/10/95).

[17] For the economic efficiency portion of this perspective see Terry Anderson, *Free Market Environmentalism* (Boulder, CO: Westview Press, 1991) and D. W. Pearce and R. K. Turner, *Economics of Natural Resources and the Environment* (Baltimore: Johns Hopkins University Press, 1990). For the industrial efficiency aspect of this argument see Jose Goldemberg, Thomas B. Johansson, Amulya K. N. Reddy, and Robert H. Williams, *Energy for a Sustainable World* (New Delhi: Wiley Eastern Limited, 1988); and R. Socolow, C. Andrews, F. Berkhout, and V. Thomas, eds., *Industrial Ecology and Global Change* (Cambridge, U.K.: Cambridge University Press, 1994).

[18] K. S. Shrader-Frechette, *Science Policy, Ethics, and Economic Methodology* (Dordrecht: D. Reidel, 1985), 106–111.

[19] For a discussion of the contrasting "deep" and "shallow" approaches to policies on pollution, resources, population, cultural diversity, technology, land and sea ethics, and education and scientific enterprise see Næss, 1986a, 18–21.

[20] Næss, 1986a, 21.

[21] Arne Næss, "Deepness of Questions and the Deep Ecology Movement," in George Sessions, ed., *Deep Ecology for the Twenty-First Century* (Boston: Shambhala, 1995), 205.

[22] Næss discusses his work in applied semantics and Gandhian communication in: *Gandhi and Group Conflict: An Exploration of Satyagraha* (Oslo: Universitetsforlaget, 1974); Næss, 1981; "Nonviolent Verbal Communication. The Gandhian Approach," unpublished manuscript (1993a): 9 pages; and Johan Galtung and Arne Næss, *Gandhis Politiske Etikk (Gandhi's Political Ethics)* (Oslo: Johan Grundt Tanum, 1955; 2nd edition 1968).

[23] Pseudo-agreement results when there appears to be propositional agreement, but this ostensible agreement is itself based upon miscommunication or misunderstanding. In this case, because individuals P and Q are talking about different things, their "agreement" cannot be judged to be propositional agreement. Pseudo-disagreement arises when there appears to be propositional disagreement, but this ostensible disagreement itself is based upon underlying miscommunication or misunderstanding. In this situation, because individuals P and Q are again talking about different things, their "disagreement" cannot be judged to represent propositional disagreement. For more details see, Næss, 1953, 123–126.

[24] For a discussion of this more sanguine rational skeptical view see, Arne Næss, *Skepticism* (London: Routledge and Kegan Paul/New York: Humanities Press, 1968).

[25] In Næss's terminology, we use "expressions" to convey the thought-content of "statements," which actually represent thoughts or concepts themselves. For instance, "Lundi," "Montag," "Måndag," and "Monday" are all expressions for the same statement, namely the first day of the typical work week.

[26] This approach for assessing *real* disagreements is outlined in "Surveys of Arguments for and against a Standpoint," Næss, 1981, 97–119.

[27] Arne Næss, "Self-Realization: An Ecological Approach to Being in the World." Reprinted in Sessions, 1995, 226 (hereafter referred to as Næss, 1995a).

[28] See Arne Næss, "The Function of Ideological Convictions," in *Tensions That Cause Wars (Common statement and individual papers by a group of social scientists brought together by UNESCO)*, ed. H. Cantril (Urbana, Illinois: University of Illinois Press, 1950a), 257–298; Arne Næss, "Nonmilitary Defense and Foreign Policy," in

Civilian Defense, ed. Adam Roberts (London: Peace News Pamphlet, 1964), 33–43; Arne Næss, "Civilian Defense and Foreign Policy," in *Civilian Defense: An Introduction*, ed. T. K. Mahadevan, et. al. (New Delhi, 1967), 102–116; Arne Næss, "Consequences of an Absolute *No* to Nuclear War," in *Nuclear Weapons and the Future of Humanity: The Fundamental Questions*, ed. Avner Cohen and Steven Lee (Totowa, New Jersey: Rowman and Allanheld, 1986b), 425–436.

[29] Arne Næss and Stein Rokkan, "Analytical Survey of Agreements and Disagreements," in *Democracy in a World of Tensions*, ed. Richard McKeon with the assistance of Stein Rokkan (Chicago: University of Chicago Press, 1951a), 447–512; Arne Næss, "Appendix I: The UNESCO Questionnaire on Ideological Conflicts Concerning Democracy," in *Democracy in a World of Tensions*, ed. Richard McKeon with the assistance of Stein Rokkan (Chicago: University of Chicago Press, 1951b) (hereafter referred to as Næss, 1951b), 513–521; and Arne Næss, Jens Christophersen, and Kjell Kva.lø, *Democracy, Ideology, and Objectivity: Studies in the Semantics and Cognitive Analysis of Ideological Controversy* (Oslo: Universitetsforlaget, 1956) (hereafter referred to as Næss, 1956).

[30] This issue is discussed in a documentary on Næss, "Crossing the Stones," by Norwegian Public Television.

[31] Næss's many articles on this issue are all in Norwegian. Two representative articles include: "0-vekst av null betydning?" ("Zero-growth of zero-importance?"), *Klassekampen* 4/6/92 and "Kulturelt mangfold trenger vern" ("Cultural Diversity needs protection") in *Rapport fra Konferansen Norske Kunstners og den Europeiske Union* (Oslo: Norges Kunstnersraad, November 1994), 7–13.

[32] Arne Næss, "Sustainable Development and Deep Ecology," in *Ethics of Environment and Development: Global Challenge, International Response*, ed. R. J. Engel and J. G. Engel (Tucson, AZ: The University of Arizona Press, 1990), 87–96; and Arne Næss, "Sustainability! The Integral Approach," in *Conservation of Biodiversity for Sustainable Development*, ed. O. T. Sandlund, K. Hindar, and A. H. D. Brown (Oslo: Scandinavian University Press, 1992), 303–310.

[33] Arne Næss, and Sigmund Kvaløy (translator), "Some Ethical Considerations with a View to Mountaineering in Norway," *Alpine Journal, The American Alpine Club* (1969): 230–233.

[34] Arne Næss, "The Tragedy of Norwegian Whaling: A Response to Norwegian Environment Group Support for Whaling," *North Sea Monitor* (December 1993b): 10–12.

[35] Arne Næss, "Self-realization in Mixed Communities of Humans, Bears, Sheep, and Wolves," *Inquiry* 22 (1979): 231–241 (hereafter referred to as Næss, 1979); Arne Næss and Ivar Mysterud, "Philosophy of Wolf Policies I: General Principles and Preliminary Exploration of Selected Norms," *Conservation Biology* 1 (1987): 22–34 (hereafter referred to as Næss and Mysterud, 1987); and Ivar Mysterud and Arne Næss, "Philosophy of Wolf Policies II: Supernational Strategy and Emergency Interim Management," unpublished manuscript (1990): 14 pages.

[36] Næss, 1995a, and Arne Næss, "The World of Concrete Contents," *Inquiry* 28 (1985a).

[37] The assertion is not that science is non-normative, but that in its status quo, "objective" context it is relatively neutral with respect to characterizing ecological problems and suggesting appropriate responses.

[38] Næss as quoted in Devall and Sessions, 1985, 74.

[39] For Næss's characterization of reform environmentalism see his "Deepness of Questions and the Deep Ecology Movement," reprinted in Sessions, 1995, p. 209.

[40] Although my discussion focuses upon NEPA, I might have also considered, for instance, the Wilderness Act or the Endangered Species Act. For a review of environmental policy legislation in the United States over the last twenty five years, see Norman J. Vig and Michael E. Kraft, "Environmental Policy from the Seventies to the Nineties: Continuity and Change," in *Environmental Policy in the 1990's: Toward a New Agenda*, eds. Norman J. Vig and Michael E. Kraft, 2nd edition (Washington, D.C.: Congressional Quarterly Press, 1994), 3-31.

[41] *Environmental Quality: The Twentieth Annual Report of the Council on Environmental Quality* (Executive Office of the President of the United States, 1990), 3.

[42] U.S. Congress, "Public Law 91-190 Jan. 1, 1970 (NEPA)." In *United States Statutes at Large: Containing the Laws and Concurrent Resolutions Enacted During the First Session of the Ninety-first Congress of the United States of America 1969 and Reorganization Plan, Recommendations of the President, and Proclamations* (Washington: United States Government Printing Office, 1970), 852–856. The succeeding quotations in this paragraph are from NEPA.

[43] Lynton K. Caldwell, "NEPA and the EIS—What We Should Have Learned," unpublished manuscript (1987), 1 (hereafter referred to as Caldwell, 1987).

[44] Næss and Rothenberg, 1989, 67.

[45] Al Gore, *Earth in the Balance: Ecology and the Human Spirit* (New York: Houghton Mifflin, 1992), 2 and 34–35 (hereafter referred to as Gore).

[46] Gore, 225.

[47] Gore, 11.

[48] Næss contends that the world is composed of subordinate and superordinate gestalts that are internally related. These contents *are* the world. For these contents, object, medium, and subject cannot be separated. The establishment of fact and value distinctions is precluded because they are all internally related through spontaneous experience. Abstract structures on the other hand, like scientific knowledge, are *of* the world. They are human creations that can enhance our understanding of contents. Human experiences are deciphered and interpreted through abstract structures, through multiple lenses that have the potential to both focus and distort. When individuals become alienated from the spontaneous experience of nature it becomes easier, Næss contends, to make false distinctions between the structures of reality and its contents. See Næss, 1985a: 417–428; Arne Næss, "The Basics of Deep Ecology," *Resurgence* 126 (1988): 4–7 (hereafter referred to as Næss, 1988); and Næss and Rothenberg, 1989.

[49] Bryan G. Norton, *Toward Unity among Environmentalists* (New York: Oxford University Press, 1991) (hereafter referred to as Norton). My discussion centers on Norton's argument, in "Interspecific Ethics," 220–243, that the distinction between deep and reform approaches is not consequential, not his general critique of deep ecology, which occurs in bits and pieces throughout his book. Although unacknowledged by Norton, his views appear consonant with the DEA in several critical areas, the importance of articulating basic assumptions and the idea that individuals embracing a wide plurality of worldviews might agree on particular policies. While Norton raises many important issues, his critique of deep ecology is riddled with misunderstandings in the form of pseudo-disagreements. He attempts to indict deep ecology for moral monism; he characterizes supporters of deep ecology as "environmental ethicists" (p. 91); he concludes that they share a single, monolithic worldview (p. 65); he asserts that concern over environ-

mental degradation arises from a perception that policies are "unjust" (p. 221); and, most importantly, he characterizes Næss's deep/shallow contrast as being over "values," not levels of problematizing (p. 11). Space limitations, unfortunately, preclude me from addressing these and many other issues. The crucial point here is that because there is not agreement on the content of the DEA it is premature to come to any conclusions regarding Norton's true evaluation of the DEA, beyond merely pointing out particular misunderstandings.

[50] Here we should bear in mind, however, that the statement "environmentalists are all interested in overcoming the ecological crisis," can be precisized, specified, and elaborated in a wide variety of ways. The word "overcoming," in particular, is open to a broad array of possible interpretations.

[51] Norton, 12.

[52] I take Norton's term, "worldviews," to be a T_0 or everyday, nontechnical expression from which Næss's more highly precisized concept of "total views" could be derived. In the following discussion I will treat the two terms as more or less synonymous.

[53] Norton, 229.

[54] Norton, 238.

[55] Norton, 240.

[56] While not asserting that humans are separate from nature, for the sake of argument I follow Norton's lead in assuming that the interests of humans and nature are separable.

[57] On plural rationalities and their relationship to environmental policy see John S. Dryzek, "Ecological Rationality," *International Journal of Environmental Studies* 21 (1983): 5–10, and John S. Dryzek, *Rational Ecology: Environment and Political Economy* (Oxford and New York: Basil Blackwell, 1987).

[58] Næss, 1986a, 21. The caveats include: (i) "Some policies based on successful homocentric arguments turn out to violate or compromise unduly the objectives of deeper argumentation"; (ii) "the strong motivation to fight for decisive change and the willingness to serve a great cause is weakened"; and (iii) "the complicated arguments in human-centered conservation documents as the World Conservation Strategy go beyond the time and ability of many people to understand and also tend to provoke interminable technical disagreements among experts." (pp. 21–22).

[59] Norton, 239.

[60] Norton, 201–204.

[61] Norton, 203.

[62] Richard B. Norgaard, "Environmental Science as a Social Process," *Environmental Monitoring and Assessment* 20 (1992): 96 (hereafter referred to as Norgaard).

[63] Norgaard, 109.

[64] The critical role of democratic, public participation in the formation of effective policy has been stressed by many others. See Jacques Ellul, "Technology and Democracy," in *Democracy in a Technological Society*, ed. Langdon Winner (Dordrecht and Boston: Kluwer Academic Publisher, 1992), 35–50; Stuart Hill, *Democratic Values and Social Choice* (Stanford, CA: Stanford University Press, 1992); Lewis Mumford, "Authoritarian and Democratic Technics," *Technology and Culture* 5 (1964): 1–8; Max Oelschlaeger, *Caring for Creation: An Ecumenical Approach to the Environmental Crisis* (New Haven, CT: Yale University Press, 1994); Robert Paehlke, "Democracy and Environmentalism: Opening a Door to the Administrative State" in *Managing Leviathan: Environmental Politics and the Administrative State*, eds. Robert Paehlke and Douglas

Torgerson (Peterborough, Ontario, Canada: Broadview Press, 1990), 35–55; John Pass-more, *Man's Responsibility for Nature* (New York: Scribner, 1974). The limitations along with the importance of democratic participation are discussed in Robin Eckersley, *Environmentalism and Political Theory: Toward an Ecocentric Approach* (New York: State University of New York Press, 1992).

[65] Norton, 237.

[66] Norton, 11.

[67] Norton, 4–13 and 237.

[68] Næss's use of these terms seems incompatible with Norton's more technical usage on page 235. Næss would not make Norton's clear distinctions between "anthropocentrism," "inherentism," and "incrementalism." Rather, he would argue, I think, that some entities have instrumental value, that the concept of "valuing" itself is dependent upon human consciousness, and that these entities may still have values independent of instrumental value and also independent of our ability to impute value to them. Norwegian versions of the eight points do not even use the terms "inherent" and "intrinsic" value, which appear in the English versions and are used as synonyms for the Norwegian term "egenverdi" (literally translated as "value in itself"), see Arne NæssW, *Ekspertenes Syn På Naturens Egenverdi (Expert Views on the Innate Value of Nature)* (Trondheim: Tapir Forlag, 1987), 11.

[69] Norton, 199.

[70] Norton, 37.

[71] Although I do suggest that articulating the basis for our policy conclusions is critical to the well-functioning of democracies. Such articulation is also a prerequisite for open, publicly-debated decision-making.

[72] Næss, 1988, 6.

[73] For a discussion of Muir's views on conservation and preservation see for instance, Steven Fox, *The American Conservation Movement: John Muir and His Legacy* (Madison, Wisconsin: University of Wisconsin Press, 1981).

[74] For insight into Pinchot's views on conservation and preservation see Gifford Pinchot, *The Fight for Conservation,* introduction by Gerald D. Nash eds., (Seattle: University of Washington Press, 1967).

[75] This is the primary focus of my Ph.D. dissertation, "Towards a Descriptive, Participatory Theory of Environmental Policy Analysis and Project Evaluation," Department of Civil and Environmental Engineering, University of California, Davis, 1995b (hereafter referred to as Glasser, 1995b).

[76] A few additional examples include: (1) Næss's work on clarifying the "sustainability notion," his work on wolf policy, and his arguments for not joining the European Union; (2) the Wildlands (Biodiversity) Project Proposal, *Wild Earth* (Special Issue), 1992; (3) Michael Soulé's critique of postmodern attempts to "reinvent" nature and his call for active management of wildlands based upon active caring as opposed to benign neglect, "The Social Siege of Nature," in *Reinventing Nature?: Responses to Postmodern Deconstruction,* ed. Michael Soulé, Gary Lease, and with illustrations by Alan Gussow, (Washington, D.C.: Island Press, 1995), 137–170; and (4) Paul Craig and Harold Glasser, "Transfer Models for 'Green Accounting': An Approach to Environmental Policy Analysis for Sustainable Development," in *NAS/NRC Report on Valuing Natural Capital.* National Research Council (Washington, D.C.: National Academy Press, 1994), 67–110.

[77] Gore, 295–360.

[78] For a discussion of how high level European policy makers in the field of global warming perceive a disjunction between their personal environmental values and their limited ability to reflect these values in their tools for evaluating policies see Harold Glasser, Paul Craig, and Willett Kempton, "Ethics and Values in Environmental Policy: The Said and the UNCED," in *Concepts, Methods, and Policy for Sustainable Development*, ed. Jan van der Straaten and Jeroen van den Bergh, (Washington, D.C.: Island Press, 1994), 80–103.

[79] Caldwell, 1987.

[80] This point was suggested to me by Andrew Light (personal communication, 7/11/95).

[81] Arne Næss, "Sets of Ultimate Philosophical Premises: Their Inevitable Plurality," unpublished manuscript (1991b): 13.

[82] Arne Næss, "Beautiful Action. Its Function in the Ecological Crisis," *Environmental Values* 2 (1993): 67–71.

[83] The possibilities for, and forms of, this "instruction" are only just beginning to be explored. Education might be gleaned indirectly from long periods of time working in community with natural systems, such as by farmers, game managers, foresters, or indigenous peoples. See for instance, the contrasts and similarities between Aldo Leopold, *Game Management* (New York: Charles Scribner's Sons, 1933) and Aldo Leopold, *A Sand County Almanac and Sketches Here and There* (New York: Oxford University Press, 1949). It might also occur more directly by analogizing observations. For example, contrasting nature's creations, and their often precarious dependence upon human generosity for habitat, with human creations might stimulate an appreciation for what we ourselves cannot make. Observing the efficiency of natural systems might arouse both an increased concern for the efficiency of human-managed systems as well as insights into how to make these systems themselves more efficient. Or alternatively, observing the tremendous pain and suffering caused by a predator attacking its prey might inspire an ambition to not bring about any unnecessary harm and suffering. The potential for drawing edification from nature has been considered in greater depth by, among others, Wendell Berry, *Home Economics* (San Francisco: North Point Press, 1987); Gary Snyder, *The Practice of the Wild* (San Francisco: North Point, 1990); David Abram, *The Spell of the Sensuous: Perception and Language in a More than Human World* (New York: Pantheon, 1996).

[84] Næss characterizes vital needs as broader than Brown's "basic needs." He contends that there is no definite, isolatable set of elemental needs. For instance, bears, sheep, and sheep-owners have complicated, interlinked, and conflicting needs in certain Norwegian communities. See, for instance, Næss, 1979, and Næss and Mysterud, 1987.

[85] George Brown, quoted in Philip H. Abelson, "Policies for Science and Technology," *Science* 260 (1993): 735. Brown was also one of the co-authors of the *Congressional White Paper on a National Policy for the Environment* (1968), that was the precursor of NEPA.

[86] Næss, 1979, initiates a preliminary analysis to consider the vital needs of humans living in northern Norway in mixed communities with bears, sheep, and wolves. Clearly much more work can be done along these lines.

[87] Adam Hochschild, "Amazon Nation: In the Heart of the Colombian Rain Forest, Indians Are Returning to Their Traditional Way of Life," *San Francisco Magazine* (July 23, 1995): 14–17, 26–32.

[88] This issue is addressed in Glasser, 1995b.

[89] Arne Næss, "Identification as a Source of Deep Ecological Attitudes," in *Deep Ecology*, ed. Michael Tobias (San Marcos, California: Avant Books, 1984), 262.

[90] This point is discussed in Næss, 1956.

[91] Lynton K. Caldwell, *"Quantifying Values: Four Intractable Problems,"* a discussion paper prepared for the Workshop on Environmental Values Research held at the Institute on Man and Science, Renssalaerville, NY, 1977, 6.

[92] In fairness to Næss, he points to the success of his UNESCO sponsored project that was able to induce both Communists and anti-Communists to soften and modify their positions through dialogue and debate, see Næss, 1951b. My argument is not so much that the approach itself has fundamental faults, but that it is an inadequate framework for considering both satisfying and trade-off criteria that can occur in a variety of qualitative and quantitative forms.

[93] The search for a framework for making environmental policy and project analysis decisions that is capable of considering both satisfying criteria and complex multicriteria trade-offs is taken up in Glasser, 1995b.

Chapter 45

Harold Glasser and the Deep Ecology Approach (DEA)

Arne Næss

It is of prime importance for the long-range usefulness of what theorists of a movement do that alternative formulations are at hand. Terminological idiosyncrasies are a strong factor, but I believe that following Gandhian rules of fair ("nonviolent") discussion assures that compromises are found in practical applications of theoretical concepts.

The article of Harold Glasser is a good example of a search for valuable reformulations. The new term "the deep ecology approach" (DEA) is certainly useful and there are other terminological novelties and slight "doctrinal" variations which also may be helpful for some. It would require much space to discuss them all. I shall in what follows only mention a very few points.

People whom we consider to be fairly integrated and who, mostly out of necessity, have to clarify where they stand in severe conflicts, have "total views" in my sense. Such views comprise what in untranslatable German is called *Lebens- und Weltanschauung*. They should not, as Glasser perhaps suggests, be thought of as a "system." Rather, they are attempts at a systematization. As such, they must include ethics and ontology and other areas Glasser mentions.

Because of my special background, it is natural and easy for me to work out systematization in terms of premise/conclusion relations. I leave to others elaborations in terms of cause/effect, and of the important forces of motivation. What is important is that DEA comprises a broad approach. Since "elements" 2 and 4 refer to my own, personal ecosophy, they should not be seen as necessary characteristics of DEA. I should perhaps add that even with normative "systems," we tend to be inconsistent and fallible. Values have as much to do with derivation as with feeling. If you agree to A, you feel you must also agree to B. If you are a materialist you feel you cannot accept a God. (Epicurus was an exception: he was a consistent materialist who accepted material God.)

It is a good thing that Glasser at least sometimes uses the term "deep problematization" instead of "deep questioning." We may pose questions without making them into personally felt problems—vital problems.

For me, extended care and solidarity depends upon what I call a "process of identification." Not all theorists of the deep ecology movement feel at home with this terminology. Perhaps "extended care" or "deepened care" would be an alternative: extended care for nonhumans and deepened care for suffering and deprived humanity? Or perhaps "extended solidarity and care?"

The formulation of the "8 points" is, for me, tentative, not "provisional," as suggested by Glasser. The latter term implies that we keep searching for a better, alternative formulation.

Instead of calling the 8 points "principles" I have since their first formulation liked somewhat longer terms, such as "points of expressing views which supporters of the deep ecology movement share on a fairly general and abstract level." There have been many analogous sets of formulations, such as Marxism for example, but the latter was not tentative, and its discussions did not even intend to follow the Gandhian rules of nonviolence. It aimed at confrontation, not at dialogue.

Glasser's heading: "The Depth Metaphor," might better read "Næss's notion of depth." As a slightly technical term in deep ecology, it is narrow, not broad. It is defined in terms of premise/conclusion chains. Suppose that something is taken as premise from which a conclusion is drawn. This premise may itself be a conclusion from another premise. In that case this other premise is, in my terminology, a "deeper" premise. If this deeper premise is itself the conclusion of a premise, then it is still deeper. Since we all start somewhere with regard to premises, the starting points are all called "ultimate premises." We normally stop at different levels of depth in our argumentation. Glasser adds: "The analytic origins of this broader 'depth' reference are in Næss's concept of levels of premise-conclusion chains. A premise-conclusion chain, $p>q$ and $q>r$ and $r>s$, can be formed from a series of premise-conclusion statements, p, q, r, and s, where $x>y$ symbolizes, from premise x, or set of premises x, follows conclusion y. Næss characterizes an argumentation pattern starting with q as 'shallower' than one starting from p. In the same sense, a problematization of s based upon p would be 'deeper' than one based upon q."

This is good. The only changes I propose is to leave out the word "characterizes" in favor of "defines." And "from premise x . . . follows conclusion y" should perhaps be qualified by: "follows in a fairly broad sense." The gist of the matter is that modern requirements in formal logic are so extremely strict that practically nothing of interest follows formally from anything else.

In an ecosophy the ultimates are supposed to be of philosophical or religious character. By contrast, in a philosophy, there may be chains of premise/conclusion relations. For the supporters of the deep ecology movement, ultimate premises have philosophical or religious components which partly underlie the social and political ones. That is, considerable changes in social life have some philosophical or religious implications for supporters of deep ecology. These have in part to do with their *Lebens- und Weltanschauung*.

To Glasser's careful analysis of Norton's position I wish to add that there presumably will be considerable differences within the ecological movement about its ultimate goal. The sides may eventually agree that there is an ecological crisis calling for vast resources. But what, in fact, is accomplished when some groups proclaim: "The crisis is overcome!"? Or that "The danger of future major ecological catastrophes is averted?" Or that "Strong international organizations are now monitoring the critical developments and have the power to do what must be done?" Or that "There is a global turn from increasing to decreasing ecological unsustainability"?

Supporters of the deep ecology movement will always push for more. Therefore Norton's convergence hypothesis will, I expect, be disconfirmed. The goal, as I see it, is often expressed through the optimistic slogan "full richness (abundance) and diversity of life on earth." It is only when we are on a (presumably) safe road towards such a condition on earth that we have overcome the ecological crisis. The deep ecology movement—or something along its lines—will have a mission long after less radical achievements have been accomplished. It should be unnecessary to add that it may well be that many activists in the shallow or reform movement will fight together with the supporters of the deep ecology movement to the last.

I fully endorse Glasser's conclusion to the effect that "a common ground" between various creeds and movements is a real possibility. It should not, however, make us underestimate very serious differences and disputes over policy goals and objectives. If Norton is truly willing to accept a strong pluralism at the level of worldviews with their corresponding differences in ultimate values and ontological premises, he will have to relax his prescriptive thesis regarding "policy confluence among environmentalists." But wherever possible, we will all support each other in spite of the limited "common ground."

Deep ecology strives for a change of attitudes to nature. Possible ways of bringing about such change are the main challenge: we have had research on conditions of religious conversions but very little on conditions of ecological conversions. It is ultimately not necessary that a majority of the population hold deep ecological views in order to make a change. What is important is that new generations learn about nature not only through botany and zoology but through experience of free nature—and through stories of landscapes, animals, and plants which make us love and respect nature.

Chapter 46

Convergence Corroborated:
A Comment on Arne Næss on Wolf Policies

Bryan Norton

I have argued elsewhere that Deep Ecology, understood as a social movement seeking to redress currently unacceptable environmental policies by embracing the belief that nature has intrinsic value, has failed to articulate policies that are both plausible and significantly different from the policies implied by a broad and long-sighted anthropocentric viewpoint.[1] The purpose of this "Comment" is to test that hypothesis through an examination of Arne Næss's thoughtful and interesting discussions of policies appropriate in "mixed communities"—communities that include both humans and large predators.[2]

If we are to understand the general importance of Deep Ecology, and especially its possible and likely contributions to policy, it is important to realize that the Deep Ecology philosophy of environmentalism, and the movement it has spawned, only make sense against a backdrop of empirical beliefs about environmentalists and their actions. I will call these background beliefs the "Divergence Theory of Environmentalism," for reasons that will become clear presently. The divergence theory is composed of two related elements. First, it includes a philosophical definition, elevated to the role of a metaphysical principle, marking the difference between anthropocentric and nonanthropocentric value systems. Second, the divergence theory uses this philosophical definition to explain the behavior and policy advocacy of environmentalists, positing that there are two competing movements with discernibly different policy programs clustered around these different and exclusively defined systems of ultimate values. The philosophical theory is attributed importance in policy discussions because it explains what is taken to be an observable phenomenon—the clustering of environmentalists around two exclusively definable paths of policy advocacy. Environmentalists gravitate toward ultimately incompatible policy programs, according to the divergence theory, because they are split between those who accept, and those who reject anthropocentrism.

Note that this is a distinctive application of the theory, originally due to the historian Lynn White, Jr., that Western societies have been so rough on the environment because our basic philosophical and religious assumptions are "anthropocentric."[3] Although White himself elaborated this point very little, philosophers, including Næss, have subsequently developed the theoretical distinction between anthropocentric and biocentric systems of value, and biocentric egalitarianism became a formative principle in Deep Ecology. According to White's argument, *the whole of Western society* has been anthropocentric (recognizing only a few outsiders in history such as St. Francis), and the philosophical distinction between anthropocentric and nonanthropocentric value systems was introduced to explain a society-wide phenomenon—that Western societies were failing to protect their environments. But the divergence theory's application of the anthropocentric/ nonanthropocentric distinction is not to explain the aggregated policy of the whole society, but rather to explain a difference in policy programs among factions within a relatively small subgroup of society—the environmentally active.[4] I am not saying this is a totally implausible application of White's hypothesis. It is arguable that Shallow Ecologists, though they call themselves environmentalists, advocate policies that are actually closer to those of advocates of unlimited economic growth than they are to the real advocates of environmental responsibility, the Deep Ecologists.[5] Indeed, there is historical precedent for this interpretation, in that early in the environmental movement in the United States there emerged two somewhat distinct groups—later labeled as "preservationist" versus "conservationist"—which advocated quite different policy programs.[6] So the divergence hypothesis remains arguable though I reject it for reasons summarized elsewhere.[7]

But my point here is that it is an assumption about the policy situation—an empirical belief that environmentalists can today reasonably be sorted into two categories exhibiting predictably different policy behaviors that must ultimately give interest to the Deep/Shallow distinction in the policy arena. If there is no clustering of the policy proposals of environmentalists into two, separable approaches advocated by reasonably stable groups of advocates who serve opposed ultimate values, then there is nothing for the Deep/Shallow distinction to explain, and the entire philosophical idea of separable and competing Deep and Shallow movements simply collapses for lack of interest. The question is not simply: Can we define, philosophically, a distinction between anthropocentric and nonanthropocentric value systems? The question is whether this distinction has a useful application to the environmental movement as it exists today. And if one believes, as I tried to show in *Toward Unity Among Environmentalists*, that it is false that American environmentalists today sort cleanly into two policy camps, the Deep/Shallow distinction collapses into a philosophical distinction looking for a policy difference to explain.

The divergence theory is not just an indirect expression of a false empirical hypothesis, however. The philosophical definition associated with it also implies a destructive heuristic—it urges us to address environmental problems by looking for differences between anthropocentrists and nonanthropocentrists. According to this heuristic, we enter policy discussions assuming that policies which are good for people will be damaging to the rest of nature, rather than assuming these are policies which would be better for both. And it encourages us to attempt to implement policies by attacking the ultimate values of opponents, rather than by seeking policies that support the whole range and plurality of environmental values.

By arguing against the divergence theory, I do not, of course, deny that environmentalists disagree on many specific policies in many situations. What I deny is that these disagreements are meaningfully or consistently explained by attributing opposed ultimate values to the shifting groups and coalitions that weigh in on various policy discussions. Further, I believe that, underlying the cacophonous voices of environmentalists in disarray, there is emerging a common policy voice, including common explanations and justifications, that can be shared by anthropocentrists and nonanthropocentrists, despite their differences about ultimate values. If either of these empirical beliefs is correct, it is simply not true—as advocates of the Deep/Shallow distinction must believe if their distinction is to be more than a philosophical curiosity—that the positions of anthropocentric environmentalists are closer to those of development-oriented economists than they are to those of deep ecologists and other nonanthropocentrists.

Given my very different understanding of the situation among activist environmentalists, I prefer the convergence theory, which states that, as anthropocentrists articulate more broadbased and long-term policies, these policies will converge with the policies of Deep Ecologists and other nonanthropocentrists, provided the latter adopt qualifications and clarifications necessary to achieve plausibility of their policy claims.[8] Admittedly, this theory has a somewhat curious status—it is both an empirically falsifiable predictive hypothesis about what will happen as environmentalists continue dialogue and advocacy and, on a deeper level, an article of faith that humans, being part of nature, share more common than divergent interests with the other elements of nature, and that the search for better policies will in fact benefit both humans and wild nature.[9] As an advocate of the convergence theory, I reject the divergence theorists' factual belief about environmentalists' behavior in the policy arena, so I find their philosophical definition/principle uninteresting as applied in the policy arena, because the empirical situation it is supposed to explain does not exist. It has the same validity as theories of witchcraft. Both are theories to explain the existence of groups of people who act according to behaviorally specifiable patterns; in both cases, however, attempts to establish empirically the existence of such behaviorally specified groups have failed.

Let us then proceed to test the two opposing theories/hypotheses by examining Næss's own recommendations for policies toward bear and wolves in mixed communities. If the divergence hypothesis is correct, it should be possible to describe distinct policies, one of which is supported by consistent application of Næss's philosophy/argument form, T, and another set of policies that are supported by appeal to anthropocentrists, and these policies should be clearly distinct and not overlapping. If, on the other hand, one finds a continuum of policy positions and a variety of philosophical viewpoints and justifications, along with a tendency to find compromise positions that may be acceptable to both anthropocentrists and nonanthropocentrists, then the example of Næss's wolf and bear policies tends to confirm the convergence hypothesis.

The policies advocated by Næss and Mysterud include (a) continued attempts to reduce mortality of livestock by carnivorous wild predators, including, where possible, subsidized cooperatives to watch sheep more closely than is economically feasible otherwise; (b) continued attempts to encourage local communities to find ways to gain economic advantage from the presence of wolf populations (because experience shows that local communities will tolerate otherwise hated animals if they have economic value), an (c) expanded programs to compensate particular farmers who suffer livestock losses, funded by the nationally based advocates of wolf protection. When all else fails, Næss and Mysterud recognize that it may be necessary to designate some areas as agricultural areas and others as nonagricultural, allowing wolves to be removed from agricultural areas. They would clearly regret it if this process resulted in the elimination of all wolf areas from Norway, but they nevertheless discuss whether this outcome is consistent with Norway living up to its international agreements: "Would norms of international solidarity to some degree be satisfied if Norway contributed heavily to the maintenance of protected European (e.g., Swedish or Finnish) wolf areas that have a significantly less dense human population inside wolf ranges? Our tentative answer is yes."

It seems to me (as an anthropocentric advocate of wolf protection and reintroduction) that these policies are about the best one can articulate, given the many conflicting values involved in these situations. One area where I would perhaps differ with Næss and Mysterud has to do with their rather lenient interpretation of international law. When an international treaty designates a species for protection it, in essence, declares special protection for that species, protection that should not be so easily balanced against other values, such as economic values or people's sensibilities toward sheep.[10] When international law declares a species for special protection, that special designation implies that further losses to that species are not "compensatable" across borders or across generations. I believe that the loss of wolves and bears from Norway would be a terrible loss to future Norwegians. Members of future generations of Norwegians, if they feel profoundly the loss of wilderness experiences, might judge harshly those who have sacrificed their birthright of wildness for a few sheep.

So the question of what to do to protect bears and wolves turns out to be far more complicated than deciding what has intrinsic value. Worse, determining that the suffering of both sheep and wolves is intrinsically bad does nothing to tell us what to do when human activities have made it inevitable that either sheep or wolves must suffer. This quibble aside, I believe Næss and Mysterud arrive at policies that could easily be supported by anthropocentrists—they are compromise policies which attempt to protect wolves while being as little disruptive of established human communities as possible. It will not matter, if I am correct in this interpretation, whether wolf advocates value wolves intrinsically, or if they value them for future generations, arguing that we ought not to destroy forever the possibility of humans having the experience of hearing a wild wolf howl.

Nevertheless, as Næss and Mysterud—probably correctly—conclude, we must give great weight to the psychological unfairness of preventing well-meaning and sensitive shepherds from protecting their highly valued sheep, sheep that are valued economically, but also as the main support for a distinctive, and valuable, human culture that has survived for centuries. At the same time, we must recognize that wildlife belongs not only to that particular "time-slice" of a community that currently occupies a place, but to a multigenerational community including persons not yet born. Here I think we can find a new common ground for the environmentalism of the future: the strongest element of Næss's work on wolf policies is his emphasis on human communities and the special status we must accord the sensitivities of traditional communities who have lived for generations—in this case, centuries—in a geographic region. This emphasis directs us toward the important issue of multigenerational communities and cultural institutions that create sustainable societies. As Næss realizes, there is an inherent tension between the attitude of more cosmopolitan populations, which value wolves while not having to live with the day-to-day consequences of sheep attacks—and who exert their environmental ideals through central governments—and local people. These locally developed sensibilities and deeply felt responsibilities to protect sheep must be treated with utmost respect, even by those who consider themselves as more progressive, more forward-looking, and more cosmopolitan in their values and attitude. Values and environmental problems understood in this way apparently reflect values that exist at different spatio-temporal scales of the society.[11]

Resolving these disagreements and tensions will not be easy—but my point is that these problems are unlikely to be resolved by reference to universal principles such as biospecies egalitarianism.[12] Despite my general respect for local values—shared with Næss and Mysterud—I would argue that in this case, the local people should—again, as Næss and Mysterud suggest—be pushed to change somewhat in the direction of wolf protection. My reasoning would not be based on equality of species, but on the importance of holding opportunities and options open for the future, and on the necessity in some cases for environmentalists to be advocates for people not yet born, when the interests of the future clash sharply with current attitudes of some communities. Too often, local communities have acted on the basis of short-term interests, only to learn that they have irretrievably deprived their children of something of great value.

So, as in the case of the temporarily depressed young adult who seeks to end his or her life, I would suspend the usual right of self-determination of local communities in the hope that a period of regulation and pressure from the centralized government—pressure to avoid irreversible outcomes like wolf extinction—will lead the local community to see the value of cohabiting with wolves. If the local community recognizes the value of wild wolves they may resolve to protect the full complement of their indigenous wildlife as treasures that should be passed on to future generations of the culture. During this period of regulation, agencies of the central government and national environmental groups can attempt, through public education and perhaps economic incentives to establish local support for predators.

So I conclude that Næss's position on wolf policy, despite the fact that the Deep/Shallow distinction suggests a strong divergence in policies of advocates of differing ultimate values, in fact converges with that of a broadly understood and long-sighted anthropocentrism. Næss's thoughtful policy proposals therefore corroborate my view that anthropocentrists concerned with the entire range of human values, over many generations, will converge with the viewpoints of nonanthropocentrists. The underlying source of this shared policy direction rests not in a revolutionary theory of intrinsic value, but in a concern for sustainable communities. If we believe in the wisdom of local cultures, and of their commitment to perpetuate their culture across time, then improving wolf policies—practically speaking, as Næss and Mysterud recognize—must be understood as a dialogue across generations, not between humans and nonhumans. The way to protect wolves in mixed communities is not to convince local sheep owners that the wolves have equal value with them or their sheep, but rather to convince them that the protection of wolves—and all the possibilities and options for experience and use of wolves that would be protected with them—will, in the true spirit of the "Deep, Long-Range Ecological Movement," be in the interest of their offspring and their evolving culture.

Notes

¹ *Toward Unity among Environmentalists* (New York: Oxford University Press, 1991). While I realize that the interpretation I offer and criticize is much more simplistic than the entire body of Arne Næss's writings, I believe it is not an unreasonable interpretation of Næss's original idea, outlined as a list of seven statements of principle in the classic paper, and introduced as follows: "A shallow, but presently rather powerful movement, and a deep, but less influential movement, compete for our attention." Næss proceeds to characterize the two competing movements with lists of principles. The second principle of Deep Ecology is *"biospherical egalitarianism* — in principle. (Quotation is from "The Shallow and the Deep, Long-Range Ecological Movement," this volume.) I take this principle to be, in an important sense, the defining one; if all species are morally equal, and humans have inherent value, natural objects have inherent value, as well. It is this expanded sense of value that changes one's value orientation, gives depth to the other principles, and inclines one to join the Deep Ecology movement rather than the Shallow Ecology movement.

I will not in this Comment address revisionist interpretations of deep ecology, such as that of Harold Glasser (this volume) who has argued that Deep Ecology is (a) consistent with the anthropocentric value position of the stewardship tradition and (b) that the term "deep" in "Deep Ecology" refers not to any substantive value position but to a specific technical methodology from Næss's distinctive theories of psycholinguistics and semantics, a method of "deep questioning." I do not address this revisionist interpretation because this is not the "philosophy" which has been injected into policy discussions, at least not in the United States.

When I speak of Deep Ecology here, as elsewhere, I therefore refer to a movement that would never have existed had its founder not advanced the idea that an important dichotomy exists among environmentalists—some of whom are "shallow" and some of whom are "deep"—and which implicitly criticizes environmentalists who employ a broadly anthropocentric analysis to environmental problems for their failure to attribute nonanthropocentric intrinsic value to nature. See, for example, Lester Milbrath's *Environmentalists: Vanguard for a New Society* (Albany: New York University Press, 1984) for an application of Deep Ecology's value categories in a multinational study of support for environmentalism. I argue in *Toward Unity* (pages 69–73) that Milbrath and other social scientists studying environmental attitudes have *imposed*, not found, a policy split between anthropocentrists and nonanthropocentrists. If Deep Ecologists mean only to say that there are many ways to question our current, abominable treatment of natural systems, and that we should strive to question as deeply as possible, then there is of course no controversy. But this version of Deep Ecology involves neither dichotomy nor exclusion. If Deep and Shallow Ecologies are not "competing" but complementary, most environmentalists would agree that we should think as deeply as possible, and necessary; so I guess it follows that all environmentalists are Deep Ecologists. I wish only that Deep Ecologists would—if that is all they mean to say—renounce (not just change labels of opponents from "shallow" to "reform") their exclusionary and insulting framework of analysis.

[2] I will refer, specifically, to Arne Næss, "Self-realization in Mixed Communities of Humans, Bears, Sheep, and Wolves," *Inquiry* 22 (1979): 231–241; and Arne Næss and Ivar Mysterud, "Philosophy of Wolf Policies I: General Principles and Preliminary Exploration of Selected Norms," *Conservation Biology* 1 (1987): 22–34. As far as I am aware, "Philosophy of Wolf Policies II" was never published.

[3] Lynn White, Jr., "The Historic Roots of the Ecological Crisis," *Science* 155 (10 March, 1967): 1203–1207.

[4] See Milbrath, *Environmentalists: Vanguard for a New Society*, for an argument that radical environmentalists and Deep Ecologists, who differ from the old-line wildlife and conservation organizations by having adopted nonutilitarian and nonanthropocentric values, form the "vanguard" of environmentalism and of a new society.

[5] As is argued, for example, by Bill Devall and George Sessions, *Deep Ecology: Living as if Nature Mattered* (Salt Lake City: Peregrine Smith Books, 1985), esp. 56–61, where modern "reform environmentalism" (Devall and Sessions's substitute term for "Shallow Ecology") is associated with the tradition of Gifford Pinchot, who advocated development of resources for human use, despite the fact that mainstream environmental groups have uniformly rejected Pinchot's developmental program as a failed set of policies.

[6] I have argued, however, that this split into two groups did not, even historically, correspond to the distinction, as suggested by the Deep Ecologists, between anthropocentric and nonanthropocentric value commitments. See "Conservation and Preservation: A Conceptual Rehabilitation," *Environmental Ethics* 8 (1986): 195–220. In general, the failure of Deep Ecologists and other nonanthropocentric environmental ethicists to recognize the

immense and important differences between a broad and long-term anthropocentrism and narrow, economism and consumerist anthropocentrism has perpetuated a misleading conception of the environmental movement.

[7] See *Toward Unity*, especially chapters 4 and 12.

[8] Næss himself makes the point that the principle of biospecies egalitarianism must be interpreted as an in-principle value only, and it should not be applied so as to rule out some exploitation. The "in principle" clause is inserted because any "realistic praxis necessitates some killing, exploitation, and suppression." (Quotation is from "The Shallow and the Deep, Long-range Ecological Movement.") In "Self-Realization in Mixed Communities," he says that strict application of this principle "is of course Utopian in the worst senses." So I take it that Næss accepts the necessary restrictions on biospecies egalitarianism. See *Toward Unity* for a more detailed discussion of the constraints placed on biospecies egalitarianism if it is to support practically employable policies.

[9] See my *Toward Unity*, and "Convergence and Contextualism: A Clarification and a Reply to Steverson," *Environmental Ethics*, forthcoming, for more detailed discussion.

[10] See Edith Brown Weiss, *In Fairness to Future Generations* (Tokyo and New York: The United Nations University and Transnational Publishers, Inc., 1988) for an interpretation of international environmental law as a trust for future generations.

[11] See B. G. Noon and B. Hannon, "Environmental Values: A Place-Based Theory," *Environmental Ethics*, forthcoming.

[12] A point that is made quite directly by Næss and Mysterud in "Philosophy of Wolf Policies I," 33: "Without the slightest doubt, we recommend wolves as members of the Nordic life community. But this clear theoretical acceptance of wolves on the basis of our philosophy of nature does not imply any definite practical wolf policy."

Part V

The Philosopher At Home

Figure 5. The Philosopher at Home.

Chapter 47

Value in Nature: Intrinsic or Inherent?

Jon Wetlesen

The First Principle of Deep Ecology

When Arne Næss and George Sessions proposed a common platform for the deep ecological movement in 1984, they formulated the first of its eight principles as follows:

> The well-being and flourishing of human and nonhuman Life on Earth have *value in themselves* (synonyms: *intrinsic value, inherent value*). These values are *independent of the usefulness of the nonhuman world for human purposes.*[1]

Implicit in this formulation are two ways in which things can have value: they may have value in themselves, i.e., "intrinsic value," which is taken to be synonymous with "inherent value"; or they may have "instrumental value," which is dependent on their usefulness for human purposes.

It may be objected that the wording of the first principle is somewhat unfortunate. This is due to the fact that value in itself is ascribed only to the well-being and flourishing of human and nonhuman life on earth, that is, to certain states of living beings (and possibly also to natural systems), rather than to these beings in their own right. Things are valued on account of their states or achievements, that is, on account of what they have, rather than on account of what they are. This way of ascribing value seems to favor one kind of normative ethical theory to the exclusion of other kinds; in brief it favors teleological rather than deontological ethics.[2]

To suggest this is not say that Næss and Sessions intended to formulate their first principle in such a way that a deontological ethic is excluded. That

405

would not really have served their purpose which was to find a formulation which could gain the adherence of different kinds of supporters of the deep ecological movement. What was needed was a common platform of formulations that allowed for an overlapping consensus, even though these formulations were justified from quite different kinds of comprehensive views: philosophical, religious, and ethical, the latter including both teleological and deontological approaches. As it stands, however, the formulation is open to the objection I mentioned. It may undermine its own purpose.

Perhaps this objection could be rebutted by pointing out that, although the present formulation attributes value in itself to certain states of living beings, this by itself does not exclude the possibility that value in itself could be ascribed to the living beings themselves. Although this is not explicitly expressed, it still remains an implicit possibility.

Even if we concede this point, it is nonetheless unfortunate that Næss and Sessions stipulate that the three terms of value should be used synonymously. It would surely have been much more lucid if the term "value in itself" had been used as a generic term, and "intrinsic value" and "inherent value" were employed as two of its specifications. In that case, "intrinsic value" could refer to certain states or achievements of living beings as understood within teleological ethics, and "inherent value" could be applied to these beings themselves as understood within deontological ethics. This, at least, is the thesis I shall argue for.

It should be noted, however, that there are certain variations in the formulation of this first principle. The formulation quoted above may be regarded as the standard version. It is to be found in most recent anthologies of environmental ethics or deep ecology.[3] There are other versions where the statement has been simplified, so that the three terms are reduced to one of them; either to "value in themselves,"[4] or "intrinsic value,"[5] or "inherent value."[6]

It must be admitted, however, that there is no consistent usage of these terms in ordinary language or in environmental literature. The expression "things have value in themselves" is a colloquial formulation, whereas "intrinsic value" and "inherent value" are somewhat more formal and artificial in nature. In the dictionaries they are often defined as synonymous, and indeed many authors do not distinguish between them.

Some authors, however, do make such a distinction. Frequently they will distinguish different interpretations of the term "value in itself," and reserve the terms "intrinsic value" and "inherent value" for these different conceptions. But even then we find little consistency in the literature. What one author calls "intrinsic value," another will call "inherent value," and vice versa.

Nevertheless, there has emerged a certain pattern of usage among contributors to deontological ethics which I find clarifying, and which it might be fruitful to follow. I have in mind especially the proposals of Tom Regan and Paul W. Taylor.[7] If we follow Regan, the term "inherent value" should be reserved for a moral status value which is ascribed to all and only those objects which are recognized to have a moral status, and therefore to be moral subjects towards whom moral agents have direct moral duties. When the term is used in this sense, value is ascribed to certain beings themselves on account of what they are. The underlying assumption is that if an object is a moral subject, it must have certain factual properties which are morally relevant as grounds for the ascription of moral status and inherent value. These factual properties may be inherent in the nature of the subjects. They serve as subvenient descriptive properties, which are used as grounds for the attribution of inherent value as a supervenient normative property. In addition the term "intrinsic value" can be ascribed in various ways to the states of these subjects. It can, for instance, be used as a moral achievement value, ascribed to persons with a good or holy will, or to persons of virtuous dispositions or to their states of well-being or flourishing; or it can be used as a term for an amoral state of value, such as the state of happiness in a hedonistic sense (pleasure and the absence of pain), or the state of preference satisfaction.

In order to avoid the objection of partiality, then, the first principle of deep ecology might be reformulated in a number of ways. One way of doing so, would simply be to omit the term "synonyms" and perhaps add "or" (intrinsic *or* inherent value). This would certainly be an improvement, but still it would not meet the objection that value in itself is ascribed only to the states of living beings (or their natural systems) and not to these beings (or systems) in their own proper right. Another way of amending the first principle of deep ecology might be the following:

Human and nonhuman Life on Earth have value in themselves (inherent value), and their states of well-being and flourishing also have value in themselves (intrinsic value). These values are independent of the instrumental value of the nonhuman world for human purposes.

I take it that the term curiously capitalized as "Life on Earth" should not be interpreted as a limitation of the scope of this principle. One imagines that if there are living beings and natural systems of such beings anywhere else in the universe, the principle should be extended to cover them as well.

This revised formulation might work to the satisfaction of some adherents of a deontological ethics, at least for those who accept a nonanthropocentric position on the question of who or what can have moral status. However, it might not be equally satisfactory to adherents of teleological ethics since it seems to be committed to one of the basic assumptions of deontological ethics: i. e., that we are duty-bound to have respect or reverence for moral persons and other moral subjects in their own right, and not only for their states or modes of being. Certainly, some people find it more appealing to act beautifully than to act dutifully, and perhaps base their actions on certain moral ideals or virtues. Even so, however, they may admit that people are bound by certain duties, especially if their inclinations are not so virtuous. Let us, then, explore possible alternatives to Næss's conception of value as formulated in the platform statement.

Inherent Value

I take it that in deontological ethics there is need for a special term for moral status value, and that the term "inherent value" is appropriate for this purpose. This term may be ascribed to all and only those objects which are attributed a moral status or moral standing, that is, the class of objects towards which moral agents are supposed to be bound by direct moral duties. The universe of objects, then, is divided into those which are moral subjects and those which are not. Inherent value is ascribed to the former, not to the latter.

It seems that we can distinguish two constitutive conditions for the ascription of inherent value to an object. Firstly, it is required that moral agents are bound by a direct moral duty towards the object. The notion of duty is presupposed here as a condition for the possibility of inherent value. This is the reason why this kind of value should be regarded as deontological: it is duty-based. It would not make any difference if we add that inherent value could also be constituted by the rights of the moral subject. In so far as we think about claim-rights, these will be correlated with duties anyway, so that the result will be the same. I believe we should stick to duties rather than rights, however. The notion of duty has been with us for a very long time. It can be found in deontological ethics of both a theological and a philosophical kind; by contrast the problematic of rights is historically quite recent. Besides, it is much more doubtful to ascribe rights to moral subjects other than human persons, whereas human agents may have direct duties towards such subjects even if these subjects are not ascribed rights.

Secondly, it is required that this differential treatment of objects which are subjects, and objects which are not subjects, can be justified by a morally relevant difference. That is, moral subjects must have some factual property which other objects lack, and this property must be morally relevant as a ground for ascribing moral status and inherent value to them. A factual property, in this sense, may be an empirical, theoretical, or metaphysical property. The assertion or denial that an object has such a property purports to have truth value. Furthermore, the ascription of inherent value is supervening on this factual (inherent) property.

Let us first address the question: what kind of objects can be moral subjects in this sense? Those who take an anthropocentric position assume that only humans can; either all humans or some humans. If this position is justified on the grounds that they belong to the biological species of mankind (*Homo sapiens*), we shall have a speciesistic justification. It is highly doubtful, however, that this is a morally relevant property, and hardly anyone attempts to justify an anthropocentric position on this basis.

Another ground is the property of being a moral agent or a moral person. It is commonly supposed that in order to be a moral agent, a person must have the ability to take moral responsibility for his or her actions, to be responsible or liable for them, and to defend them against objections from those who are affected by their consequences, for instance by way of justification or excuse.

This requires certain abilities, such as reason, linguistic competence and a free will. "Free will" in this case requires further elucidation as, for example that one is able to make decisions on the basis of the most convincing grounds, and to act on them without being completely determined by causes which are not rational grounds.

If these abilities are a necessary condition for being ascribed moral status as a moral subject with inherent value, many human beings will be denied this status. Minors, neonates, fetuses, the severely mentally retarded, the severely brain damaged, and the severely senile—all will have to be excluded. They simply lack the ability of being a moral agent. There remains, however, a possibility of including them by making a distinction between moral agents and moral persons. The notion of a moral person can be understood as a subject who has the capability or capacity of being a moral agent, whether this capability is an actual ability or not. It may be assumed that the capability is actually there, even if the ability is only potentially there, or perhaps if it is blocked because certain other conditions are lacking. And this actual capability may be taken as the ground for ascribing moral status and inherent value to all moral persons.[8]

According to this conception, the class of moral agents will be a subclass of moral persons and, as things are, this will include nearly all human beings, and probably only human beings. Speciesism is avoided, however, because it is not in principle excluded that some human beings are not moral persons on these grounds. Children born without a brain may be a case in point. Nor is it excluded that there could be moral agents or moral persons who are not human, for example extra-terrestrials.

In any case, if an anthropocentric position is justified on these grounds, all and only moral persons will be ascribed a moral status and inherent value; other moral subjects who are not moral persons will not be so recognized. A nonanthropocentric position, on the other hand, rejects this restriction and assumes that there may be other moral subjects in addition to moral persons. One possibility is that some or all individual living organisms (higher animals, all animals, plants, microorganisms) should be ascribed a moral status. Yet another possibility is that supra-individual wholes (species-populations, eco-systems) should be ascribed such status. How far we should go will depend on the justification given. I shall return to this point.

Let us next comment on the terminology of "inherent value" within the framework of deontological ethics. This can be done from a theological or a philosophical standpoint. In the Semitic religions it is commonly held that valid duties are grounded in the will of God; humans have a special moral status because God willed that they should be created in his image. Should this be interpreted in an anthropocentric sense? Those who understand it anthropocentrically assume that being created in the image of God is equivalent to being a moral person, and further that only moral persons have moral status. Other creatures are mere things with an instrumental value in relation to human purposes, and human beings are understood as despots in relation to the rest of nature. Those who understand it nonanthropocentrically assume that being created in the image of God is equivalent to being a moral agent, and hence of being accountable for one's actions. This corresponds with the idea of stewardship as a designator of man's role vis-à-vis nature. Each moral agent has a direct moral duty towards those things which God saw as good, that is, towards the rest of nature. In either case being created in the image of God is commonly understood as an ontological property, inherent in the nature of man and as a basis for a special moral status value which is ascribed to human beings (and sometimes also to other living beings). In a religious context one speaks about the holiness, sacredness or sanctity of human life, or even of all life. These terms have not only a religious, but also a moral import; they imply that the holy object is inviolable, untouchable, immune, shielded, protected, secure, set aside.

When we move from a religious to a philosophical context other terms are commonly employed to refer to moral status value. In Kant's ethics, for instance, the term "inner worth" is used for this purpose,[9] and in the modern International Bill of Human Rights the term "inherent dignity" is used for the moral status value of human beings or human persons.

As we said above, things may have value in themselves in several ways. One way is to have inherent value in a deontological sense. But there are other ways as well, and they should not be confused with each other. For one thing, it should not be confused with moral achievement value of a deontological kind. Kant, for instance, states that: "There is no possibility of thinking of anything at all in the world, or even out of it, which can be regarded as good without qualification, except a *good will.* "[10] Elsewhere he identifies this with a holy will. The goodness or holiness of a person's will should be interpreted as a moral achievement value, and as a kind of intrinsic value within a deontological framework. It may increase or decrease, but whatever its degree, this will not affect the inner or inherent value of the moral person, which is assumed to be constant and equal in all persons.

Intrinsic Value in Consequentialist Teleological Ethics

A fortiori inherent value, in the deontological sense, should not be confused with intrinsic values in teleological theories. Here we need to make an initial distinction between two kinds of teleological ethics: one consequentialist, the other holistic. They have different views on whether actions or persons may be ascribed intrinsic value in their own right. Typically the former denies, and the latter affirms, that they can.

In a consequentialist teleological ethics it is commonly assumed that intrinsic value can only be ascribed to certain states of affairs which may be produced as a result of human action. These may be mental states, such as pleasure and the absence of pain, or the satisfaction of preferences; or they may be other things such as wealth, power, prestige, etc. In this kind of ethics it is normally supposed that the point of a morally right action is to maximize intrinsic goods such as these. This concern may be particularistic or universalistic, depending on whether the interests to be maximized are those of some of the parties concerned, or all parties concerned. Utilitarianism embraces the latter conception.

In the utilitarian perspective, or more generally, in the consequentialist perspective, the relation between an action and its consequences is conceived as an external cause/effect relation. The action itself is not ascribed intrinsic value, but only instrumental value in so far as it is a means to the end in view.

The same argument applies to the agent. Typically, the agent as such is not ascribed either intrinsic or inherent value, but only instrumental value in so far as he or she is a causally necessary condition for bringing about a desired state of affairs. This is the receptacle view of a moral agent which Tom Regan has criticized so severely. Here the value of agents or other subjects is merely instrumental, valid in so far as they are receptacles of those mental states which are ascribed intrinsic value. This ascription affords no strong protection for the interest of the parties concerned. If happiness is maximized by sacrificing the interests of certain individuals or groups, that is what morally ought to be done. From a deontological viewpoint this seems to be an unacceptable scenario. It fails to recognize the inherent value of the individual moral person or other subjects involved.

According to classical utilitarianism, our basic moral duty is to choose actions which maximize the happiness or welfare of all parties concerned. If this is understood hedonistically, it amounts to maximizing the pleasure and minimizing the pain of those concerned in sum or on the average. From a non-anthropocentric viewpoint this has the advantage of taking into consideration not only the interests of humans, but also of sentient nonhumans. On the other hand, this extension of moral consideration does not apply very widely to the natural environment. It does not include insentient individual living organisms, and still less supra-individual wholes, such as species-populations or ecosystems. For this reason it has been found unsatisfactory by most adherents of deep ecology, land ethic, and other holistic approaches to environmental ethics.

Intrinsic Value in a Holistic Teleological Ethics

Holistic versions of a teleological ethics commonly assume that intrinsic value can be ascribed not only to those states of affairs which agents may bring about by means of their actions, but also to the actions and agents themselves. This can be done on the assumption that the highest good and final end of human actions is the good life and the good society as a whole. Happiness or welfare is not understood hedonistically but rather functionally: it is the well-functioning of a life-form as a whole and of the lives of its participants (each life is regarded as a whole and as a part of the commonwealth). In so far as actions and agents are understood as parts of this whole, they participate in the goodness of the whole, and their degree of intrinsic value will be proportional to the significance of their function in relation to the maintenance of this whole.

From the viewpoint of each individual agent the good and happy life may be characterized in terms of self-realization. According to Aristotle, this implies that the potentialities of human nature should be actualized so as to function at their best; and when that happens a person develops his or her virtues. Aristotle assumes that man can be understood as a rational animal. Aspects of human nature are to be found in non-rational animals, and in other parts of biotic and abiotic nature. When these capacities flourish at their best, they are constituted as moral virtues. Other aspects of human nature are specific to humans. When the rational faculties flourish, they form the intellectual virtues, which consist of practical reason (*phronesis*) or theoretical reason (*theoria*) or both. As for practical reason, it consists in a capacity of deliberation which is concerned with particular questions of action and of reasoning within the context of recognized opinions. (Aristotle, of course, argues that the best context for such opinions is the Greek city-state.)

This holistic conception of teleological ethics avoids the thoroughgoing instrumentalist view of actions and agents which is found in a consequentialist conception of teleological ethics. Within this framework it is possible to ascribe intrinsic value to a moral action, in so far as it is chosen for its own sake and not only as a means to something else and in so far as the decision is firmly grounded in the moral and intellectual virtues of the agent.

Moreover, this intrinsic value may be transferred from the action to the agent. Agents may also be ascribed intrinsic value, in so far as they have formed their attitudes and dispositions for action in a virtuous direction.

From the perspective of deontological ethics, these features of holistic teleological ethics are an improvement in relation to the consequentialist teleological ethics. Even so it is still a far cry from a holistic teleological conception of the intrinsic value of a person to a deontological conception of the inherent value of a person. If we compare Aristotle's and Kant's conceptions, we find two salient differences among others: Aristotle's lack of universalism and of egalitarianism in his conception of the value of each person.

For one thing, Aristotle has a particularistic conception about who can have intrinsic value, as against Kant who held to a universalistic conception about who can have inherent value. Aristotle assumes that intrinsic value can only be ascribed to free male citizens of a Greek city-state. This excludes all those who are not free citizens, such as women, free residential non-citizens, foreigners, and slaves. According to Aristotle, the latter are considered the "living instruments" of their owners and masters. Kant, on the other hand, assumes that all moral persons have inherent value.

Secondly, Aristotle has a hierarchical conception of the intrinsic value (concerning those who have such value), as against Kant who has an egalitarian conception of the distribution of inherent value. According to Aristotle's view, the worth or intrinsic value of a person is proportional to the virtue of that person. Some virtues can only be developed by free citizens of a Greek city-state; and they can be developed in different degrees depending on the roles and functions a person takes, and the significance of these roles and functions for the maintenance of the city-state as a whole. According to Aristotle's theory of distributive justice, political power should be distributed to each according to merit or worth (*kath'axían*).[11] Some are supposed to be more worthy than others, and some to be worthless.

Intrinsic Value in Deep Ecology

These deficiencies of the Aristotelian conception could be mitigated by enlarging the wholes in relation to which actions and agents are understood as parts. One expansion would be from the city-state (*polis*) to the world-state (*kosmopolis*), as was done, perhaps, by the Stoics not long after Aristotle. Another expansion could be from human communities to biotic communities, an expansion which has been proposed in our times by adherents of the deep ecology movement and of the land ethic.

According to the first principle of deep ecology, "The well-being and flourishing of human and nonhuman Life on Earth have value in themselves." If we follow the suggestion proposed above, this kind of "value in itself" should probably be interpreted as an intrinsic value understood in a holistic teleological ethics, and not as an inherent value understood in a deontological ethics. One reason for this is that according to this statement, value in itself or intrinsic value is primarily attributed to the well-being and flourishing of human and nonhuman life on earth. That is to say, in the present formulation it is attributed not to carriers of this value, but to their states of being or flourishing. According to one interpretation, this comes quite close to Aristotle's attribution of intrinsic value to certain actions or activities which are done for their own sake and not just for the sake of other things.

There is a further similarity. In Næss's version of deep ecology, this kind of flourishing is spelled out in terms of self-realization. The self to be realized is not the limited ego, but rather a comprehensive Self which is formed through wide cognitions and identifications with the communities of which one forms a part. There is a place here for identification with the local as well as wider human communities, including the human community as a whole, past, present, and future. But this is not the end of it, since there is also room for understanding oneself as part of wider biotic communities and ultimately as part of the biosphere on earth as a whole.

On the basis of this interpretation, intrinsic value is primarily ascribed to the flourishing and self-realization of living beings, in so far as their activities are understood as parts of such comprehensive wholes, both human and biotic. But secondarily, intrinsic value can also be transferred to the agents or other kinds of subjects who are the internal causes of this activity. This could be elaborated in terms of the notion of striving (conation) for self-preservation and self-realization. The notion of *conatus* is basic in the philosophy of Spinoza, and it is strongly related to similar notions in Stoic philosophy and the philosophy of Aristotle (cf. *entelecheia*). I mention this, since Spinoza's philosophy is certainly one of the main sources of inspiration for Næss's version of deep ecology. In this framework one can say that each real being endeavors to maintain itself and to realize its inherent nature. Whatever a being strives to achieve or maintain for its own sake—and not only for the sake of something else—is valued for its own sake. This is one way of understanding how intrinsic values are constituted. It can be applied reflexively to the striving itself. The reason why a being strives to maintain itself, is that it so strives. It is done without an external "why," since it has value and meaning in itself.[12] On this basis it can be assumed that each being attributes an intrinsic value to itself. This conception may make sense in the case of humans, although it must be admitted that it is more problematic when it is generalized to all kinds of real entities, not only sentient but also non-sentient; and not only individuals, but also supra-individual wholes in so far as they form natural dynamic systems. It appears to me that some of the deepest value intuitions in deep ecology have their roots in conceptions such as this.

Still, the notion of intrinsic value is different from the notion of inherent value mentioned above. It belongs to a holistic teleological ethics, and not a deontological ethics. Much solid ethical thinking can be done on this basis, involving among other things the weighing of competing interests and trade-offs between different parties concerned in decision making.

One weakness of an holistic ethic, however, is that it easily invites the accusation of being authoritarian, neglecting, for instance, human rights. According to certain interpretations of holism, there may be something to this charge; although on other interpretations it can easily be avoided. This point can most readily be made in relation to the criterion of rightness in the land ethic as formulated by Aldo Leopold:

A thing is right when it tends to preserve the integrity, stability, and beauty of the biotic community. It is wrong when it tends otherwise.[13]

If the first "when" in this statement is interpreted as "only if," then the whole statement invites an ecofascistic interpretation. This amounts to a replacement of other moral considerations and of giving priority to the biotic community. The consequences of this policy for the human use of natural resources, the deposit of wastes, and population policies might be drastic indeed. This kind of extremism may be avoided, however, by interpreting "when" as "if." In that case, the holistic criterion comes in as a supplementary consideration in addition to other moral standards. When there are conflicts these various considerations will have to be weighed. Environmental considerations will be one factor among others, and it will not automatically outweigh the others. But it will not be forgotten either.[14]

A similar defense can be made for deep ecology. This implies, however, that the holistic aspects of deep ecology should not be interpreted as a complete ethics by itself, but rather as a supplementary ethical consideration which should be added to other kinds of moral considerations. If this is accepted by adherents of deep ecology, one would suppose that they would be open to the necessity of assuming other kinds of ethics besides a holistic teleological ethics; and a deontological ethics may be just what is needed.

Extending Inherent Value to Subjects Who Are Not Persons

Deontological ethics may appear to be doubtful company from the viewpoint of deep ecology or the land ethic. One reason for this is that the prevailing position among adherents of a deontological ethics tends to be sharply anthropocentric. Moral status is ascribed to humans only, some or all, and denied to nonhuman beings, both individual and supraindividual.

This close association between deontological ethics and an anthropocentric position may well be one significant cause for the opposition found among many adherents of deep ecology and the land ethic to deontological ethics. Still, I believe we should not be too quick to assume that there is a necessary connection here. Perhaps it is entirely contingent and hence can be avoided? Perhaps moral status and inherent value can be extended beyond the range of human beings or moral persons, and to other kinds of moral subjects, individual or supraindividual?

For lack of space, I shall not develop this part of the argument in the present version of this paper. Elsewhere I attempt to do so, arguing casuistically by analogical extension from human agents to nonhuman beings, grounding the argument in the notion of conation.[15] In this conception conation is a basis for both intrinsic and inherent values, but in two different ways. It is the cause of evaluations which ascribe intrinsic value to certain activities or states, and it is the ground for ascribing inherent value to that being which has conation. It seems to me that deep ecology would have nothing to lose but much to gain by keeping the door open to this deontological possibility.

Notes

[1] Arne Næss and George Sessions, "Basic Principles of Deep Ecology," in Bill Devall and George Sessions, eds., *Deep Ecology. Living as if Nature Mattered* (Salt Lake City, Utah: Gibbs Smyth, 1985), 70.

[2] That is, an ethics which justifies what is morally right in terms of utility or virtue, rather than in terms of moral duties or moral rights.

[3] Arne Næss, "The Deep Ecological Movement: Some Philosophical Aspects," *Philosophical Inquiry* 8 (1986), 14. This has been reprinted in several recent anthologies, such as Michael Zimmerman, Baird Callicott, George Sesssions and Karen Warren, eds. *Environmental Philosophy: From Animal Rights to Radical Ecology* (Englewood Cliffs, N.J.: Prentice Hall, 1993), 197; Susan J. Armstrong, and Richard G. Boltzer, eds., *Environmental Ethics: Divergence and Convergence* (New York: McGraw-Hill Inc., 1993), 412. This version is also maintained by Bill Devall and George Sessions, "Deep Ecol-

ogy," in *Pojman* (1994), 115. Alan Drengson and Yuichi Inoue, eds. *The Deep Ecology Movement. An Introductory Anthology* (Berkeley, Ca: North Atlantic Books, 1995), 49.

[4] Bill Devall, "Deep Ecology and Radical Environmentalism," *Society and Natural Resources*, 4/1, 257; reprinted in Lori Gruen and Dale Jamieson, eds. *Reflecting on Nature. Readings in Environmental Philosophy* (New York: Oxford: Oxford University Press, 1994), 117.

[5] Arne Næss, *Ecology, Community and Lifestyle* (Cambridge: Cambridge University Press, 1989), 14.

[6] See the occurrence in Basic Principle 7 in Næss and Sessions 1985, p. 70: "appreciating *life quality* (dwelling in situations of inherent value)"; as well as Arne Næss, "Intrinsic Value: Will the Defenders of Nature Please Rise?" in *Conservation Biology*, eds. M. E. Soulé and B. A. Wilcox, (Sunderland MA: Sinauer Associates, 1986), 509; as well as in Arne Næss, "Deep Ecology and Ultimate Premises," *The Ecologist*, 18, 130. It would have been better to use the term "intrinsic value" instead of "inherent value" in these contexts.

[7] See for instance Tom Regan, *The Case for Animal Rights* (Berkeley: University of California Press, 1983), 235ff, 239ff, 242ff; and Paul W. Taylor, *Respect for Nature. A Theory of Environmental Ethics* (Princeton: Princeton University Press, 1986), 60, 71ff. On p. 75 Taylor introduces the term "inherent worth" in a way that is "essentially identical" to Regan's term "inherent value." My usage in the text will be rather close to this direction of interpretation. On page 73, however, Taylor proposes to use the term "inherent value" in a somewhat different sense.

[8] I follow Jens Saugstad's interpretation of Kant at this point. Jens Saugstad, *The Moral Ontology of the Human Foetus. A Metaphysical Investigation of Personhood.* Preliminary edition: Department of Philosophy, University of Oslo, 1993. Forthcoming: Olms Verlag, Hildesheim.

[9] Immanuel Kant, *Grundlegung zur Metaphysik der Sitten* (Riga, 1785), Second Section, 434ff.

[10] Kant, 1785, 393.

[11] Aristotle, *Nicomachean Ethics,* Book V, Chapter 3, 1131a24, in *The Basic Works of Aristotle* (New York: Random House, 1941).

[12] As for the notion of living for its own sake without an external "why," there is an interesting parallel with the mystical tradition of the Rhineland, going back to Meister Eckhart in the early fourteenth century, and Angelus Silesius (Johannes Scheffler) in the seventeenth century. This has been pointed out by John Caputo, *The Mystical Element in Heidegger's Thought* (Athens, Ohio: Ohio University Press, 1978), 60ff and 98ff. It seems that Heidegger has also taken up some elements from this tradition in his later philosophy, especially in his thinking about "the ground" (Martin Heidegger, *Der Satz vom Grund*, 5th ed. [Tübingen: Neske, 1965]), and about "releasement" (Martin Heidegger, *Gelassenheit* [Tübingen: Neske 1959]). There are many statements to this effect in the German writings of Meister Eckhart, for instance this one: "Ich lebe darum, dass ich lebe. Das kommt daher, weil das Leben aus seinem eigenen Grunde quillt; darum lebt es ohne Warum eben darin, das es (für) sich selbst lebt." ("I live because I live. This is so because life springs from its own ground; therefore it lives without a why just because it lives.") See Meister Eckhart, *Deutsche Predigten und Traktate.* Herausgegeben und übersetzt von Josef Quint, (München: Carl Hanser Verlag, 1963), 180. Angelus Silesius expressed a similar thought in the following verse: *"Die Ros' ist ohn' warum, sie blühet weil sie blühet, Sie acht't nicht ihrer selbst, fragt nicht, ob man sie siehet."* ("The rose is without why; it blooms because it blooms; It cares not for itself; asks not if it's seen.")

See Angelus Silesius (Johannes Scheffler), *Cherubinischer Wandersmann*, Vienna, 1675. (Hrsg Charles Waldemar: *Der Cherubinische Wandersmann*, München: Goodmann, 1960), 1: 289.

[13] Aldo Leopold, *A Sand Country Almanac and Sketches Here and There* (London/Oxford/New York: Oxford University Press, 1949), 224 f.

[14] This kind of defense is quite frequent in the literature. It has been made, for instance, by James Heffernan, "The Land Ethic: A Critical Appraisal," *Environmental Ethics* 4 (1982): 235–247; reprinted in Armstrong and Boltzer, 1993: 398–404; and by J. Baird Callicott, "The Search for an Environmental Ethic," in *Matters of Life and Death. New Introductory Essays in Moral Philosophy*, Tom Regan, ed., 3rd ed. (New York: Random House. 1993), 366 Tom Regan, ed., 1993:ff.

[15] A longer version of this paper is published in Nina Witoszek, ed., *Arne Næss and the Progress of Deep Ecology* (Oslo, SUM: University of Oslo, 1996). Further parts of the argument are also set out in my paper, "Who Has a Moral Status in the Environment?" in Nina Witoszek and Elisabeth Gulbrandsen, eds., *Culture and Environment: Interdisciplinary Perspectives*, Nature and Humanities Series, SUM (Oslo: Oslo University 1993), 98–129.

Chapter 48

Response to Jon Wetlesen

Arne Næss

The "8 points" of deep ecology were conceived as a *proposal* to formulate in untechnical language some important, fairly general and abstract views most supporters of the movement have in common.

Jon Wetlesen has, in a creative way, proposed that point 1 be "amended" in the following formulation:

> Human and nonhuman Life on Earth have value in themselves (inherent value), and their states of well-being and flourishing also have value in themselves (intrinsic value). These values are independent of the instrumental value of the nonhuman world for human purposes.

The best thing here is the use of "value in themselves." Actually my first versions relied on a Germanic term, *Eigenwert* and *egenverdi* in Norwegian. I tried to assure myself that people were acquainted with it; a minority answered "yes" to the question whether they sometimes used it themselves. And the term permits a delicate cloud of different interpretations in the sense of "perceptions," something of crucial importance for a successful consensus within a movement. When Jon Wetlesen introduces a philosophically excellent proposal for the consistent heteronymity of "inherent value" and "intrinsic value," he disturbs the cloud. Better use "value in themselves" and leave the proposal of the distinction in the comments. After all, any serious discussion of fairly common, abstract views needs *both* a short formulation as a point-of-departure *and* successively more precise and elaborate comments.

In short, what Jon Wetlesen calls the standard version of Point 1 is *unfortunate*. Like so many others, I had as a youngster been overwhelmed when looking at tiny creatures (in "unclean water") through a simple microscope and noticing how they approached some things and avoided others, and how they died when a drop of water dried out. An interesting expression in this connection is: "It makes sense to do something strictly for its own sake." It would suit me personally to let Point 1 read simply as follows: "Every living being has value in itself."

What Jon Wetlesen has to say about deontological and teleological ethics I agree with. Of course, the 8 points should be neutral in relation to the seemingly unending philosophical debate in this field. Personally, I belong to those who feel they may have direct duties towards animals. "Has Rollo (a kind, big black dog) got his breakfast?" Children in many families have the duty to ensure that a dog has got what is due to him or her. But others may of course have different opinions, defining or conceiving "duties" somewhat differently.

The careful clarification of terms like "inherent" and "moral subject" would be still better if Jon Wetlesen avoided the word "anthropocentric." How can humans be *centered* in their daily lives? Is my attention, concern, respect, valuation, really *centered* on the ecosystems, the biosphere as a whole, the planet earth? Many people, myself among them, don't like to think we have a clear-cut center. A short narrative: "Sorry Arne, I am hopelessly anthropocentric." What is the matter with this person? He spent thirty years in the arena of social work, caring for people. But incidentally he had been for just as long a time an activist fighting for the protection of patches of free nature. Accepting the 8 points? "Of course"—as if they were somewhat trivial. Many supporters of the deep ecology movement feel they cannot declare themselves to be ecocentric or even say yes to ecocentrism.

Chapter 49

Platforms, Nature, and Obligational Values

Per Ariansen

Many contributors to the ecophilosophical debate allude to Arne Næss's reluctance to probe the meaning of some key concepts of the deep ecology platform. The original article by Næss formed the concept of intrinsic value in order, among other things, to distinguish two approaches to environmental questions: one considered as deep and the other as shallow. These terms immediately signal an axiological scale, where what is "shallow" is not placed on a par with what is "deep."[1] Næss himself insists on the expression "adherents of the deep ecology approach" rather than "deep ecologists" to halt pejorative connotations. Even so, the very anxiety that one might belong to those endorsing a "shallow approach" keeps the deep ecology debate alive. As has been frequently noted, the attempt to find a more precise meaning in some of the key terms associated with the deep ecology platform is not always welcome. Arne Næss tends to be rather dismissive of serious attempts at exegesis, as this "would undermine the aim of the eight points."

This is, then, the paradox to be faced: a deep skepticism about the search for perceptions by the grand promoter of the theory of precizations. Not quite satisfied with the suggestions that the platform is meant as a broad discourse addressing popular contexts (McLaughlin), or that it aims to develop sensibilities that promote spontaneous attitudes and practices (Zimmerman), I wish to present a perspective on deep ecology (read "the deep ecological approach") which might elucidate some of the difficulties one often experiences when the platform—or key concepts of it—is taken as philosophically valid. Perhaps there is a way of reconciling certain difficulties and of "redeeming" deep ecology in the eyes of some of its critics? And perhaps an anthropocentric view of

420

value might prove a not too shallow approach?

What could be some possible motives behind the design of the deep ecology platform? A starting point might well be the belief that the technical fix approach, so dominant in Western culture, is overly optimistic. An immediate prudent response to this insight would be that we ought to curb technology by applying principles of precaution and sustainability. However, even if one could devise a set of actions that would be safe for humans, there might be other reasons for not performing them. There are, for instance, cases where desired goals cannot be reached because of moral limitations. We might realize, if we probe deep enough, that there are similar restrictions on our dealings with nature. Furthermore, according to old philosophical tradition, depth of understanding intensifies the quality of life, providing that one lives according to one's understanding. There is a double benefit in acknowledging morally protected values in nature: the prospect of a richer life *and* a greater chance to avoid the dangers of environmental collapse. Luckily views such as these are fairly widely held. The challenge is to devise a common platform for action.

Since deep ecology is a platform project—and a modern one at that—one will have to devise ways to deal with the diverse ideologies of post-fundamentalist society. In brief one would want to retain a plurality of views without opening the platform to just any kind of view. Some model of overlapping consensus is called for. Central to this model is that people need only share a basic minimum of views when deciding upon action. One's deeper convictions need not come up for debate. The Næssian "Level 1" of the deep ecology platform is devised to reconcile pluralism with the contours of a definite ideal. Further, the requirement that adherents *should* have some deep, Level 1–like conviction and that it should be integrated with one's other beliefs and guiding principles of action, will secure one element of what is sought, namely an integrated lifestyle with deep foundations.

So far the platform design has focused on form; what has not been addressed is the content. There are numerous lifestyles and integrated worldviews that would not fit the Næssian vision of depth and integration. Racists, Social Darwinists, moral egoists, etc., can all have deeply integrated outlooks and act from them. Hence one needs a platform declaration analogous to a manifesto to provide a beacon for congeniality of belief. The Næssian eight points have, of course, this function. Central to Næssian semantics, however, is the idea of a T_0 (T-zero) statement. A T_0 statement is a statement with an as yet unrefined meaning. When one uses a T_0 statement, one has not made a conscious choice between the range of its possible interpretations. Everyday language functions well at a T_0 level, although not in all cases: One of Næss' examples is that of a general who tells a colonel that the battle will start at seven o'clock the following day. The colonel asks whether it will be seven in the morning or in the evening. The general pauses: "Well, we never actually thought about that. . . ." Depending on situation and context, a statement may be interpreted in several directions.

The eight points could well be devised as a series of T_0 statements. As such they would not be void of meaning, but they would invite a variety of interpretations. One could, nevertheless, predict that the various interpretations that actually were made, would retain some family resemblance, so that the adherents at least would be able to unite in action against "unecological " practices and institutions. Thus the eight points as T_0 statements will "attract" people who accept the statements on the basis of their individual interpretations. These interpretations will tend to be integrated with (or possibly reform) their already existing views. If the integration is thorough, they will each have an ecosophy. From each person's point of view, the eight points will hold highly refined meanings and the person will have a motive for constant precization and deeper understanding. From a common platform perspective, however, an "official" precization would be counterproductive, as it would block the openness of the platform.

If the eight points were intended to function in the suggested manner, i.e., as T_0 statements, then this would explain the apparent lack of enthusiasm for attempts to proclaim what "intrinsic value," as articulated in the platform, *really* means. It also implies that the deep ecology platform is to a large extent a formal construct (integration of beliefs, structuring into levels) rather than a discourse with a definite, highly particular content. The presumption is that detailed and elaborate contents of various ecosophies rest with adherents/practitioners, although these ecosophies share deep ecology family traits. Næss's suggestion that one should act beautifully rather than dutifully is in this sense a part of deep ecology, even though the norm arises within his particular ecosophy. Jon Wetlesen's suggestion that some nonhumans have some form of moral status and that we have a duty to take that into consideration, would be yet another element which Wetlesen might claim (if he so wished) to be a part of a deep ecology outlook. After all, pluralism is what the movement promotes.

To formulate intentionally imprecise statements makes sense in several life-contexts. One is in situations of fraught negotiation, where differences of opinion are intentionally hidden under a smokescreen of imprecision. Ambiguous statements are no problem for those who collaborate in formulating them. And yet, imprecision may also give rise to what Næss calls *tendensiøs flertydighet*,[2] biased ambiguity. A given statement may draw support from those who see the intended meaning, but it may also draw support from those who see a different meaning in the statement and who would have rejected it had they read it according to the intended meaning.

My interpretation of deep ecology does not suggest that the impreciseness of statements at level 2 is part of a devious scheme. On the other hand, it should come as no surprise, especially for someone who has developed a theory of *tendensiøs flertydighet*, that a set of sentences, presented in a manifesto form, will easily lend themselves to be read as if they were intended to have a precise meaning even if they in fact were intended as T_0 statements. So, presenting a set of T_0 statements without overtly declaring their intended impreciseness is not likely to facilitate communication. This seems to be one crux of the debate on deep ecology.

So much for the platform design. The "content" of deep ecology hinges largely on the concept of intrinsic value. This concept naturally provokes disagreement regardless of its function in the platform. The general debate on the concept is muddled by a widespread confusion of terms and concepts.[3] Part of the environmentalist cultural critique lies in the charge that nature is considered as a mere means to humans. It has only instrumental value. In the Kantian tradition, the treatment of *humans* as a means is contrasted with treating humans as ends-in-themselves. Jon Wetlesen makes it convincingly clear that there are two alternatives to instrumental value: something may be enjoyed for its own sake and not (merely) instrumentally, and something may have a moral protection against being used (merely) instrumentally. The first of the two is properly termed intrinsic value. A less confusing term, used by Arne Næss in his work on the history of philosophy,[4] is *autotelic value*, the value something has in being sought as an end, not as a means. The relevant opposite of autotelic value would be *heterotelic value*, a suitable synonym of instrumental value.

From the point of view of a Kantian end-in-itself position—a position related profoundly to human obligations—it is clear that when there is a prohibition on treating humans instrumentally, it is not the instrumentality of the treatment per se that is essential. Eating a person to provide a protein diet reflects an instrumental valuation of the person. Eating the person for the joy of eating reflects her intrinsic value. Neither alternative is morally permissible. So it is not really treating the other instrumentally (heterotelically) which is the morally relevant opposite of treating the person as an end-in-herself; it is treating the other *with disregard for the person's autonomy*. It is the coercion, even slavery-like aspect of being treated as a mere instrument which makes the treatment morally offensive. The offense lies in the loss of autonomy.

In order to argue that the instrumental treatment of nonhuman beings is ethically relevant, one would have to explain how the instrumental treatment of such entities would offend them morally. Jon Wetlesen suggests that the term "inherent value" be used as a term for a moral status value that might be held by nonhumans. In employing the term "inherent," Wetlesen alludes to the second of the three meanings of intrinsic value in O'Neill's paper: Wetlesen's "inherent value" indicates that obligation somehow attaches to the inherent nature of some nonhuman beings and that an instrumental treatment of nonhumans might morally offend the inherent value. The immediate question is, then: which property carries this value and whence its moral status?[5] Wetlesen suggests that life (not *enjoying* life), or having the *conatus* of life, is a condition of a being's moral standing. Why should life give moral standing? Wetlesen indicates that he is ready to join those who have argued that life needs no "Why." If I wholly agree with him (as I do), my agreement only gives feeble support to his argument, partly because appeals to consensus do not suffice in these matters, and further because there is actually no consensus. A considerable number of people to whom life seems meaningless, persist in asking why. Such questions could hardly be deemed morally offensive.

If there is no convincing argument as to why a particular property confers inherent value, then the concept loses its moral explanatory power and motivating moral force and dwindles into a circular argument. Having inherent value gives no *reason* for moral obligation, it is merely another term for moral obligation.

Also, the very term "inherent" is unfortunate, in that it might suggest that obligation is a property that can inhere in objects, like magnetism or a positive electric charge. I would therefore prefer to talk about *obligational value* in connection with environmental philosophy. This term is easily distinguished from both intrinsic (autotelic) value and from instrumental (heterotelic) value; it is neutral on the issues of objectivity, and it suggests no particular locus for the source of obligation. Further, it may allow for other kinds of obligation than strictly ethical obligations. Above all, it directs attention to the crucial point in ethics—the source of obligation.

In order to investigate the interplay between inherent properties and obligationality, let us consider a chess piece. Superficially, one might hold to the idea that it is the particular shape (the inherent properties) of the tower-piece that obliges us to move it only in a certain manner. Clearly, the shape plays some part in the matter, but the real source of obligation is to be found, not in the inherent properties of the piece, but in the rules of the game. This may well provide an illuminating analogy to obligation in ethics. Alluding to the Kantian idea of self-legislation, I suggest that the realm of morality is constituted by rules in analogy with the way chess-rules constitute the world of chess, rules which decide what moves are permissible and what inherent shapes of the pieces are relevant to the game.

The rules constitute both the game and the player. Player autonomy is a tacit prerequisite of the game. No player should be coerced into making a particular move. No player should be cheated against. Players have player-rights that correspond to liberty-rights in ethics. Note that the rights of a player are not benefits that one distributes out of the goodness of one's heart. Player rights are constitutional requisites of the game-world. If one permits lies, coercion against one's will, unfairness, or disregard for the universality of moral rules, then moral space breaks down. To be true, morality, like any game, can survive a great deal of actual cheating, but it cannot accept that cheating be allowed. Permitting a person, for no relevant reason, to be denied the right to vote, amounts to cheating in the game of morality. One offends the player status—the end-in-itself status—of the person. Slavery is a moral offense even in cases where the slave suffers no pain or has no loss of material welfare. The moral damage is to the player-status of the enslaved person. The obligations to preserve the dignity of the player is in fact an obligation to the regime of morality.

In my opinion, it is fairly clear that nonhumans cannot be offended in the moral sense discussed above. This intuition is supported by the fact that we do not hold nonhumans morally responsible for their acts, and we would not blame them morally, no matter what they did to us. Respecting the dignity of moral players is, however, insufficient to give meaning to a full project of morality.

Why would anyone take an interest in a rules banning stealing, lying, and coercion if it were not for the fact that these things are relevant to suffering and joy? In a world where there is no suffering, although there are beings capable of rational discourse, it would be technically possible to tell a lie. One could merely willfully state something that is not the case. One would, however, be hard pressed to explain the moral relevance of this lie in such a world. A robbed person is offended on the moral aspect of property rights. But being deprived of the object, the person also suffers a welfare loss.

There can be no morality, then, without some concern for welfare issues. Such concern cannot be merely related to contracts of enlightened self-interest, since this would render acts of, say, stealing, morally neutral in cases where one would know that the loss would not be discovered or traced to theft. Thus ethics must incorporate some element of self-sacrifice for the purpose of preventing the suffering of others. Ethics is not merely about liberty rights, but also about obligations of beneficence. The source of obligation regarding liberty rights is explained by the analogy of a game. But with duties of beneficence there is a twofold problem: The first is to anchor them in ethics at all, and the second is to determine the extent of the duties involved. My suggestion regarding the first problem is that the issues of self-sacrifice and beneficence are already inscribed in human existence, before ethics as a system evolves. It is rooted in our animal nature and shows itself on that level as unmediated care for one's offspring. Further, caring can to various degrees be informed by conscious decision to protect others. The conscious decision is different from instinct as a motivational source. It represents a blend of instinctual impulse and rationality. This blend is what we term kindness. Ethics can be seen as a further rationalization of beneficence—bringing it under the constraints of rules or norms thereby making the concern for others an obligation. Instinct, love, and kindness can not on their own provide the universalistic perspective of distributional justice. From one perspective, then, caring precedes freedom and autonomy. The rationalization of compassion has proceeded from ideals of virtues (anchored in the alleged objective nature of ideals or essences) in ancient city states through medieval theological authorization to the modern, secular constitution where humans attempt to fuse compassion and rationality.

Since compassion precedes morality and, to a large extent, provides its raison d'être, disregard of the suffering of others mocks the project of rationalizing compassion. Being committed to morality implies sensitivity to the suffering of others. At this level it is not necessary that the object of our sensitivity (human or nonhuman) understands what is going on. It is sufficient that humans know what they are doing. A one-way morality towards nonhumans is therefore possible without positing an inherent value in the moral patient, as Jon Wetlesen suggests.

We are now faced with the second of the problems about welfare obligations in ethics: how far do they extend? The terms "suffering" and "compassion" might signal a full reintroduction of a utilitarian perspective. Pain gets its moral relevance from an ethics construed as a rationalization of compassion. Duties of minimizing suffering and maximizing pleasure arise. Pain extends through the living world. To demand its alleviation in all known occurrences is well-nigh absurd. However, one might question the moral relevance of pain. Perhaps pain needs to be informed by something else before it can take on a negative value. Pain, however excruciating, may even be appreciated as having a positive value, depending on circumstances. Kenneth Goodpaster suggests that pain might be considered value neutral information.[6] I suggest that the value aspect of pain enters when a state of pain is compared to other states, and the state of pain is not the preferred one, all taken into consideration. It takes an evaluative mind to understand values. Experienced pain is not, per se, a negative intrinsic value. The "all taken into consideration" rider is of decisive importance as it links experience with ontology. In many cases pain is a perfectly proper element of what *is*. It is quite proper that pain accompanies an athletic effort. In fact, the effort would lose its proper nature (be something else) if the pain part of it was eliminated, as the legislation against doping indicates.

Humans have a different relationship to painful experience than animals. Humans have learned to assess a vast spectrum of possible states and the possibility of bringing them about—often with the help of others. Even so, claims on others to alleviate a negative situation are informed by "social ontology" or social properness. One cannot claim the right to be carried by others unless one has a type of disability that makes such a claim justified. Further, with regard to humans as moral players, pain can arise with the disrespect for one's player status. Physical torture may not be more painful than what one experiences when tripping over a rock—but the suffering is far greater since human torture violates one's dignity as a player. This extra quotient of suffering is hard to imagine in the animal kingdom.

When positive or negative assessments of value and properness are actually made with regard to nonhumans, caring is called for when the negative experience of the patient is judged to be an improper state, all taken into consideration. Since there is no one else to turn to set the situation straight, the suffering of the patient will call on us to intervene. Occasionally a given situation may release a response of pre-moral kindness, as when the children bring home a bird with a broken wing. At other times we will feel a call of obligation which stems from the beneficence component of the ethical project, as with the treatment of domestic animals. Duty is triggered when a negative state in others is deemed improper according to standards of properness and obligation operative under a human, or rather a humane regime. Again, the component of impropriety is essential. When animals are brought under a human regime, their pains and pleasures are to a large degree in the hands of humans. We are obliged to commit ourselves to care. Thus, it is improper for humans to let animals in zoos go hungry, but it is not improper for humans to let animals in the wild go hungry.

Conscious decisions to help out in concrete situations, as well as existential decisions to commit oneself to general rules of conduct, all contribute to the creation of ourselves as individuals within a common culture. The level to which we respect the liberty rights of humans and the level to which we, as a common duty, respond to improper suffering in others contribute to the making of ourselves. The historic construction of humans as moral players has deemed it unconditionally improper to offend human beings as moral agents—even though we cheat at this game incessantly. The level of beneficence to which we are committed with regard to both humans and nonhumans is more open. Aside from the prudent bonuses in arrangements of mutual beneficence, the only reward for taking on duties of beneficence, whether towards humans or nonhumans is moral pride—a pride constantly contested by prospects of personal benefit at the expense of morality.

The commitment to respect nature is further promoted by the fact that the concepts we employ in inter-human relationships not merely could, but must lead us beyond the strictly human community, at least on some issues. Confronted with a sick animal in our custody, how can we avoid seeing the state of the animal as anything other than illness? It would simply be phenomenologically impossible to retain a category of illness if the state of the animal in question was not embraced by it. The same thing applies, not merely to suffering, but also to a wide number of concepts related to the loss of value: how could we avoid considering an eroded landscape a ruined landscape?[7]

The issue of properness is not limited to matters of suffering and compassion. Our chief concern is ontological rather that ethical: We are concerned that a wide spectrum of elements in nature should not lose their proper essence. This concern is vital because a valuational or essentialistic description of nature maintains a correspondingly valuational description of humans and of cultural activity. We operate within a tacitly acknowledged covenant or constitution that sets out the identity of humans and society on the one side and that of nature and nonhuman beings on the other. Nature holds a *constitutional value* [8] for humans. Our identity is reflected in and maintained by the identity we see in natural objects and processes and in the kind of arrangement we think proper between the two realms. A series of shifts in the description of nature reveals the historicity of this constitution. Wilderness, once discovered in retrospect as it was perceived to be endangered, is now dependent upon human efforts for its preservation. Surprisingly we find ourselves responsible for the continued life and well-being of our old adversary. What used to be the jungle—an infernal place—is now the rainforest—a natural cathedral.[9]

In this attempt to probe the intuitions behind the term "intrinsic value," we have arrived at a clearly anthropocentric position, one that hopefully maintains sound anchoring points for human obligation to the living and nonliving environment. To the extent that deep ecology is committed to nonanthropocentrism, this approach ought to be incompatible with the platform. However, if my interpretation of the eight points as widely open T_0 statements is viable, it would not surprise me if my application for enrollment be accepted, should I apply.

Notes

[1] Arne Næss, "The Shallow and the Deep, Long-Range Ecology Movements; A Summary," *Inquiry* 16 (1973): 95–100.

[2] Næss rehearses this concept in an analysis of how some uses of language may influence communication by incorporating elements of bias. The textbook with the relevant argument was used for decades by thousands of Norwegian university students. Arne Næss, *En del elementære logiske emner*, 11th edition (Oslo: Universitetsforlaget, 1982).

[3] J. O'Neill, "The Varieties of Intrinsic Value," *The Monist* 75 (1992): 119–138

[4] Arne Næss, *Filosofiens historie* (Oslo: Universitetsforlaget, 1967), 221.

[5] The question of moral status extends in two directions: One might ask the general question why there is a theme of morality in human life at all. This question may be impossible to answer. However, one might also ask why certain phenomena link to morality while others do not. The question is raised here in its second sense. Wetlesen takes as his point of departure that humans in general agree that there is such a thing as moral obligation, at least among and towards humans. One can then fruitfully search for the property/ies that this obligation links to. Life, or the *conatus* of life is, according to Wetlesen, a common denominator for all beings we actually grant a moral standing. Applying the principle of equal treatment of equal cases, he suggests an extension of moral membership to all beings that share this property. However, even if Wetlesen had correctly identified a common denominator, the question why this particular empirical trait contributes to—is a (partial) source of—moral obligation, remains unanswered. His use of the term inherent *value* suggests that not merely do the empirical properties inhere, so do in some sense the values in question.

[6] Kenneth Goodpaster "On Being Morally Considerable," in D. Scherer & T. Attig, eds., *Ethics and the Environment* (London: Prentice Hall, 1983).

[7] The game of morality is part of a wider "game" of rationalization: the project of building a world for humans to live in. Not only wanton pain, but also wanton destruction, offends this project. This is why Richard Routley's Last Man on Earth cannot freely destroy for pleasure. In doing so he offends the paragon identity of humans—even if he is the last one. R. and V. Routley, "Human Chauvinism and Environmental Ethics," in D. Mannison, ed., *Environmental Philosophy* (Australian National University, 1980).

[8] This concept has been analyzed more extensively in Per Ariansen, "The Non-utility Value of Nature, a Contribution to Understanding the Value of Biodiversity," *Ecological Economics* 24 (1998): 153-162.

[9] C. Slater, "Amazonia as Edenic Narrative," in W. Cronon, ed., *Uncommon Ground: Toward Reinventing Nature* (New York: Norton, 1995), 118.

Chapter 50

Platforms, Nature, and Obligational Values: A Response to Per Ariansen

Arne Næss

Per Ariansen's article opens in a way that could hurt me badly: "Many contributors to the ecophilosophical debate allude to Arne Næss's reluctance to probe the meaning of some key concepts of the deep ecology platform. The original article in Næss (1973) formed the concept of intrinsic value. . . ." I have spent many years to trying to make young Norwegians aware of the distinction between a verbal expression and its meanings. In a definite context where a designation has a fairly well delimited meaning, I propose that we say that it expresses a concept, otherwise it does not. The context of the 8 points is such that their designations, for instance, "intrinsic value," are deliberately not chosen as expressions of concepts. There is space for different concepts adjusted to moderately different theoretical points of views, and different practices.

Per Ariansen argues: "the attempt to find a more precise meaning in some of the key terms associated with the deep ecology platform is not always welcome." Yes, precise meanings, or better, precizations, have to be proposed, not found. "Precizations" refer to the level of verbal expression, not the level of meaning. If T_1 is a precization of T_0, the plausible interpretation of T_1 makes up a genuine subset of those of T_0. Through the subsets we reach for a level of formulations expressing concepts. Ecophilosophical *concepts*! Concepts in our ecosophies.

After airing my complaint, let me proceed to a passage of great practical import: "Since compassion precedes morality and, to a large extent, provides its raison d'être, disregard of the suffering of others mocks the project of rationalizing compassion. Being committed to morality implies sensitivity to the suffering of others. At this level it is not necessary that the object of our sensitivity (human or nonhuman) understands what is going on. It is sufficient that humans know what they are doing."

We need not "posit" inherent value in nonhumans in order to behave decently and with compassion! And, of course, some who say they are anthropocentric may well behave more in harmony with what supporters of deep ecology acknowledge as their goals, than some of the proclaimed deep ecologists themselves. But I expect Per Ariansen to use the word "compassion" in a very wide sense. Most theories of morality seem to hold that feelings and inclinations are morally irrelevant. If the *will* to obey, fundamental imperative is decisive, an authoritarian sadist may act in morally impeccable ways.

The concluding remarks of this article are worth considering. "In this attempt to probe the intuitions behind the term 'intrinsic value,' we have arrived at a clearly anthropocentric position . . . incompatible with the platform." But have we? The adjective "anthropocentric" has many meanings, and I do not see which one Ariansen has chosen. In this context, this adjective seems to do more harm than good.

Chapter 51

From Skepticism to Dogmatism and Back: Remarks on the History of Deep Ecology

Peder Anker

The word "deep" has created some confusion among deep ecologists and their critics. What does it mean to be "deep" and who is "shallow?" This dispute started when deep ecology moved from one philosophical culture and context to another, and when Næss's thoughts were adapted by Australian and American thinkers. I wish to suggest that the original ecological philosophy of Næss was first of all a critical project of asking deeper questions about modern materialistic society from a skeptical standpoint. When deep ecology evolved in the interaction with the English-speaking community, however, it turned into an often dogmatic philosophy which transformed questions about ecologically sustainable life into principles for living such life. This later version of constructive deep ecology has its own internal structural flaws and problems, some of which I will address in this essay. My main point, however, is to suggest that deep ecology's original core, the skeptical approach to modern industrial society, remains the most complex and the most stimulating contribution to the environmental debate.

Skepticism: A Way of Asking Deeper Questions

Early sources of Næss's ecological thought indicate that the main focus of his writings was to ask deeper questions concerning consumer society and human relations to nature. In 1968 Næss published his book on *Scepticism* which should, perhaps, be given more attention, not only within the deep ecology movement but in the philosophical community in general. In *Scepticism* Næss rejects the dominant interpretation of Scepticism as a philosophy that questions the possibility of knowledge, and advocates an even more radical Pyrrhonian-skepticism, which holds that a philosopher is doomed to seek truth knowing that truth cannot be found. According to Næss's interpretation of Sextus Empiricus' outline of Pyrrhonian skepticism, there are three possible philosophical positions embodied, respectively, by the Dogmatists who believe that truth can be found and that some truths are found, their opponents, the Academicians, who deny this, and finally the Skeptics who deny both possibilities. In a skeptical perspective, "those who claim that they have found at least one truth [are dogmatists], those who claim that truth cannot be found in any matter [are academicians], and those who neither claim that they have found at least one truth nor claim to know that truth cannot be found, but persist in their seeking [are skeptics]."[1] The skeptical way of life, Næss argues, follows eleven ways of announcing philosophical questions: (1) The skeptic philosopher reports as a chronicler, he does not affirm the truth of what he says, but only reports how things appear to him at the moment of writing. (2) The skeptic speaks, pronounces or "shows forth" and hence leaves his formulations open in a highly noncommittal way. (3) The skeptic will neither affirm nor deny facts of life, he will only accept in words what appears. (4) The skeptic speaks in "skeptical phrases"—and these make up either a subclass or a total class of his own formulations about non-evident things such as arguments. (5) He or she puts forward formulae for didactic purposes among skeptics. (6) The skeptic uses such words as "perhaps," "presumably," "it seems" out of standard context in order to remind the reader that nothing is taken for certain. (7) The skeptic says something indicative of his or her state of mind to show how she/he feels about things. (8) The skeptic is talking loosely in general terms. (9) He or she sends messages that leave the question of philosophical technique and mediation open. (10) The skeptic is saying things instead of "stating" or "asserting" things. Finally, (11) although the skeptic rejects probabilism, he or she has an inclination to believe one proposition rather than another.

The deep ecological scheme of thinking outlined in the classic 1970 article "Deepness of Questions and the Deep Ecology Movement," reveals a Pyrrhonic aspiration.[2] Næss does not claim to have found a truth, neither does he claim that truth does not exist; instead he is best described as "a seeker on the path." His famous chains of hypotheses and norms, premises and tentative conclusions are all influenced by the Phyrrhonic spirit and should not be taken for a dogmatic outline of philosophical truths.[3] This can be further illustrated by "The Apron" diagram, which is conceived in analogy with a hypothetical-deductive system.[4] This is not a strict logical system, but a general derivation. The numbers (1) through to (4) denote four logical levels, ranging from deeper premises (1) to a philosophical platform (2), via sociological description (3) to political action (4). A closer examination of these levels will reveal the skeptic endeavor:

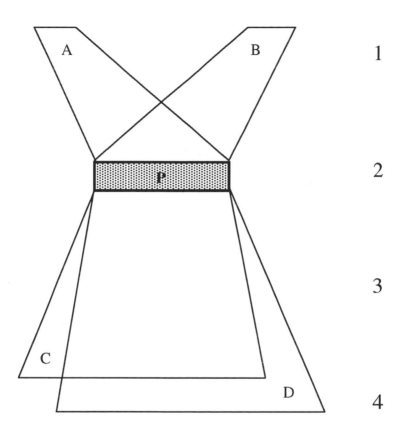

Figure 51.1. The Apron Diagram.

Level 1: In principle, deep ecology suggests and invites a large number of different ecosophies based on and inspired by different religions and philosophical traditions and systems. Every supporter of the movement is free to formulate his or her own version of an ecosophical understanding, assuming that his/her support for the deep ecology platform remains firm. Næss has designated his own version of ecosophy by the letter T.[5] Other contributors all recognize this metaethical pluralism. In the apron diagram, this pluralism is represented by the ecosophies A and B. These may be unsystematic fragments or comprehensive philosophical or religious worldviews. Næss's skepticism precludes a philosophical system based on a singular term or proposition. His basic premises do not start at a particular "point." This is because the deepest norms necessarily have to rest on an (unfounded) assertion, or on two mutually supportive assertions (which suggests a circular argument) or end up in an infinite regression. To avoid these logical problems the top of the diagram is flat. In Ecosophy T, Næss nevertheless proposes a starting "point" in the single norm "Self-realization!" I shall return to it later.

Level 2: The deep ecological movement is held together by shared views with regard to environmental problems. The different ecosophies support one or more of these ideas or a similar set of opinions. The transition from level 1 is not strictly logical, but is justified through a combination of loose formal logic and empirical hypotheses about actual states of affairs. Most deep ecology theorists are less concerned with the logical aspects and adhere to the platform on a more intuitive basis. In a skeptical fashion Næss "formulates, utters, puts forward and reports as a chronicler" what appears as environmental phrases or messages that most deep ecologists can generally support (as articulated by the platform P).[6] The platform is by no means a manifesto of dogmas a deep ecologist must endorse in order to be a member of the same club. The 8 points should rather be read in a Pyrrhonic spirit, as statements formulated in order to help environmentalists to ask deeper questions about the human relation to the earth and to assert their common goals. Næss stresses that (P) is only one of many possible ways of announcing an environmental position, and that he, as a skeptical philosopher, is only a supporter of deep ecology with the right to test counterpositions. In order to allow pluralism at level 1 and at the same time create consensus within the movement, central concepts at level 2 can be phrased in different ways: e.g., the chief idea that life on earth has "intrinsic value" can be reformulated as "inherent value" or "value in itself." But in spite of the diversity of ecosophies and respective metaphysical or religious positions at level 1, the platform does provide some sort of common ground. The impreciseness of the formulations allows for a high level of "overlapping consensus" about shared ideas in the movement.

Level 3: This level consists of an extensive description of social states of affairs as viewed by environmental interests and represents subsequent concretizations of the principles of the platform in the form of general (and not singular) specific norms of action.[7] The concretizations will be dependent on social context, i.e., they will take into account differences between societies and their value systems. For example, it has been documented that the population of Louisiana takes a more positive view of oil drilling than the population of California.[8] A general deep ecological norm of action would tend to be critical of oil drilling (because of pollution, CO_2-releases, etc.). Yet, given differing basic views in the two populations, a deep ecological norm of action might still be more critical of oil development in California than in Louisiana.

Level 4: This level refers to singular decisions made in concrete contexts of action guided by the level 3 descriptions and norms. Practical conclusions about particular issues will differ somewhat due to cultural, local, and philosophical differences (C and D). Conclusions reached at this level may lead to changes at other levels. The consequences of interventions at level 4 may in turn lead to changes in the norms of action at level 3. Thus interventions in society may ulti-mately lead to a change in sociological description belonging to level 3, which will in turn affect new norms of action. Practical conclusions may also lead to changes in the platform at level 2 or 1 itself, as the consequences of actions may raise a strong need for revising some ultimate norms or hypotheses.

It is difficult to criticize a skeptical strategy of reasoning. It is impossible to assault Pyrrho's notion of "truth" in view of the fact that Pyrrho neither claims that he has found at least one truth nor claims to know that truth cannot be found. By analogy, it is very hard to criticize Næss's *either-or* way of thinking since he reiterates that he is not a "deep ecologist" but a "supporter of deep ecology," one who persists in seeking ecological insights by asking deep ques-tions. This skeptical strategy of reasoning allows him to hold (P) and (not-P), while searching after (P). The skeptical way of formulating deep ecology makes it, then, an open philosophy. One can argue from a radical (A) or reformist po-sition (B), while holding a strict or modified version of (P), to finally reward deep ecological political action with multiple outcomes (C or D). In a political debate Næss can attack and retreat at the same time, offend and cajole, and finally score on all fronts.

Let us return to level 1 of the Apron in order to see how Næss poses deep questions within a deep ecological framework. Inspiration for Ecosophy T has been drawn from a number of sources, most importantly Benedict de Spinoza and Mahatma Gandhi.[9] Few readers of Næss's deep ecological writings have noted how Næss uses Pyrrhonism as a key to ask deep questions with regard to self-realization. His reading of Spinoza's holism and notion of God has the hallmarks of a Pyrrhonic search for truth. According to Spinoza, the power with which one struggles for self-preservation is an expression of the power of God in his active aspect,[10] so that those who realize themselves can be said to be living the life of God. Næss links this views with Gandhi's concept of self-reali-zation and the distinction between a "little self" (with a lower case s) and "The Big Self" (with a capital S).[11] God (synonymous with Self and Nature) is abso-lutely infinite and, by necessity, finding expression in all finite beings. Every act of self-expression is constitutive of the particular being's striving for self-actu-alization. Spinoza takes it to be a necessity, an operation by which God engen-ders the indispensable self-realization. It is human purpose to participate fully in the realization of the Self. Hence the call for "Self-realization!,"[12] that is, for a search of an understanding of the Being from which one's being proceeds: Na-ture.

It may be argued that religion is Næss's private affair. Still it is interesting to ask what it means that "God is Nature," if "Nature" can be interpreted in multi-farious ways. Christian, Hindu, atheist, Jewish, and pagan influences seem to mix and match in Næss. There are reasons to believe, however, that he distances him-self from any religious commitment. In skeptical wonder he moves playfully between systems. He shows great curiosity and respect, but seems to have little faith in any of them. With a mixture of pragmatic pietistic rationalism and mysti-cism, he repeats after Kepler that he is "attracted by the mysticism within mathematics, so to say, where I need not think of God or the divinity of numbers. One should never let the precision of science wear down the wonder within it."[13] "Infinite wonder" is perhaps the most apt description of what Næss understands by religion. Seen in this way, the concept of God becomes a matter of "asking deeper questions" or philosophical wonder about a strictly rationalist system. Similarly Ecosophy T is a skeptic's way of asking deep questions and tentative answers which should not be apprehended as truths but, rather, as possible interpretations of the lifeworld. Næss's skeptical model of Ecosophy T is a personal *Weltanshauung* that can not—and should not—be reduced to dogmatic announcements of truth. It is in the light of these qualifications that one must understand Næss's concept of the "self."

What consequences does all of this have for Næss's view of the individual? Ecosophic self-realization, as presented by Næss, is a recognition of biospheric participation in the Self. Everything is connected in an ecosocial unity; the individual is part of coexistence with Nature, a coexistence that is for the best of all concerned:

> [Life and death cooperate.] This presupposes that everything is connected and that "we" are fragments—not parts existing in isolation. . . . In order to be fragments of a greater whole, "we" are engaged in the formation of this unity. Through it, "we" take part in the greatness of the whole. To be a fragment is more than to be a part, in that we experience the whole and can base our lives on this awareness.[14]

Individuals realize themselves through identification with the extended Self or Nature. Self-realization is achieved through identification and symbolic coexistence with Nature. The sense of participating in a greater whole is basic to the individual's self-respect and self-esteem. If this greater context is destroyed by catastrophes, "nothing appears to remain [of the self]."[15] This does not, however, imply that self-realization is confined to particular societies. Inadequate self-recognition as an isolated ego independent of the deeper ecosocial unity is a misconceived and "shallow" self-recognition, as opposed to a "deep," adequate understanding of the self within biospheric interdependence.[16] Ecosophy assumes that an increase in recognition of biospheric togetherness is pleasurable, while a private ego-realization is tragic and full of sorrows. Which is not to say that private ego-realization is perceived as miserable; the individual in question may well experience happiness, but this happiness is passive and not active. These passive joys are like "the pleasures of slaves under the tyranny of passions."[17]

The human species has no right to decrease diversity through a standardization of nature, and any homogenization must be seen as a turn for the worse. Humankind, though unique, is not a privileged species, as all life subsists under the same, shared conditions.[18] The possession of reason, however, does place humans in a position whose singularity must not be underestimated: "Through not belonging in any particular place biologically, we are capable of making ourselves at home in all. We understand all of the more specialized forms of life."[19] All beings have moral value by virtue of their potential for self-realization, and human "speciesism" is thus reprehensible. An inadequate ego-realization implies a complete indifference to the potential for self-realization of other beings. The ethical goal is the achievement of identification and sympathy with other living beings, as the resultant symbiosis puts the emphasis on an interdependence for the common good.

Because the skeptical way of thinking refers also to ethics,[20] it poses problems when it comes to mobilizing an environmental movement. Næss admits as much, remarking that:

> I'm sorry to say, in some ways I feel miserable to be defending skepticism now [1974], because there is a very tragic conflict between the attitude I hold in my integrated and concentrated moments, which is more or less skeptical, and the requirement of consistent action. For instance, when we believe that we really must do something about some terrible pressing problem, we must somehow narrow down our perspective. The vast plurality of possible worlds—and how do we know in which world we live—are suddenly not only irrelevant, but contemplation of them undermines the willingness and capacity to act. Most people are only willing to act forcefully and consistently when they have a belief in the truth and close their minds to all else. The students say that we must get rid of particular textbooks of Næss because they undermine collective action now and over the next five years. And this is real; it is a tragedy, because they need rhetoric and dogmatism, I think. Scepticism breeds passivity. I do not feel that way, but the students do.[21]

There is a clear implication here that Næss's politically active students are unhappy with the skeptical approach because it "breeds passivity." In order to muster environmentalists, the students suggest that a philosopher needs to "narrow down our perspective" to a "belief in the truth" and to a rhetoric that can mobilize a collective action. Næss is prepared to persist in his skepticism though his confession explains some of his tolerance for the dogmatic adaptation of deep ecology in the English-speaking community.

Dogmatism: The Australian-American Adaptation of Deep Ecology

Due to a failure to understand Næss's skeptical way of tackling philosophical questions, many Australian and American philosophers within (and outside) the deep ecology movement have understood the ecosophy of "Self-realization!" in dogmatic terms. What started off in Norway as a way of problematizing environmental crisis, was understood as the way of responding to environmental problems.[22] When deep ecology moved from Norway to Australia and America, it moved from skepticism to a more rigid—and clear—position. Næss was attributed with the ability to derive truth from fundamentals. Two cases in point are the Australian philosopher Warwick Fox and the American philosopher Thomas Berry.

The assessment of Næss's thoughts by Fox illustrates a failure to understand Næss's way of asking deep skeptical questions about environmental problems. According to Næss, those who claim that they have found at least one truth are dogmatists. This is precisely how Næss is described in Fox's book *Towards a Transpersonal Ecology*. The principal question in Fox's book is: "Can it . . . be shown that asking deeper questions or deriving policies from fundamentals will always lead to ecocentric answers and policies?"[23] Næss's skeptical notion of "asking deeper questions" is here synonymous with the dogmatic thought of "deriving policies from fundamentals." What started in Bucharest in the early 1970s as a philosophy asking critical questions on environmental issues, has later turned into building constructive philosophy or moral paradigms based on the true ecological *Weltanshauung*. Fox ultimately treats Næss as if he had seen "the light" and knew all the answers with regard to how to live an ecologically responsible life. Deep ecology has become synonymous with the contemporary construction of ecotopias.

George Sessions's latest anthology on deep ecology is also instructive in this regard. A prototypical example is to be found in Thomas Berry's article "The Viable Human." Berry states that "The ecologist is offering a way of moving toward a new expression of the true wonderworld of nature as the context for a viable human situation."[24] He argues that ecology offers "expressions of the truth," which is exactly what Næss, in his work in favor of skepticism, tries to avoid. Furthermore, Berry writes about the "wonderworld of nature," as if the harmony in nature was the fact of nature. In the same article Berry writes about the universe in terms of "the Great Mother,"[25] and thus repeats the old stoic doxa of a natural, good greater union of things. The structural problems of Berry's romance with the earth is that a humanization of nature through elevating analogies and symbols demands censorship of the dark aspects of nature and of the human condition. Why not a symbol of the harsh stepmother,[26] unfolding her secret wisdom through radon gas or earthquakes in California? Humanization of nature in terms of "a Great Mother" or "a harsh stepmother" is, of course, part of an anthropocentric act of reading human ideas and values into nature. Anthropocentrism refuses to go away.

Skeptic Optimism and the Problem of Evil

In accordance with his skeptical way of thinking, Næss is critical of the current nominalistic legitimization of ethics. In his exchange with Genevieve Lloyd on Spinoza, he argues against a shift towards moralizing in order to find a satisfactory metaphysic of environmentalism. Consistently with his ontological Spinozism, Næss suggests that the only valid ethics should rely on intuitions.[27] One such "intuition" is an optimism and rationality with regard to nature and human possibilities: Nature is essentially good and Næss hopes that sometime in the future humanity will finally reconcile itself with the environment.

This poses problems. Despite his skepticism Næss seems to be of the opinion that all is for the best in the ecological world, and thus shares the optimistic view of humbler animals in the old Aristotelian tradition.[28] Even the most displeasing parts of nature have a hidden beauty:

> Even exquisitely "ugly" animals such as the Tasmanian devil . . . which seems to be unflinchingly aggressive toward humans and completely devoid of gratitude for whatever we do to satisfy its hunger and needs, elicit sympathy and respect not only when considered *sub specie aeternitatis*, as a natural wonder, part of the richness and diversity of life on this planet, but also as a symbol of our own aggressiveness and lack of gratitude. The Tasmanian devil permits us to laugh at ourselves.[29]

The Tasmanian devil has a value in itself and contributes to the richness, flourishing, and diversity of life. Furthermore, identification with the Tasmanian devil can be instructive on our way towards ecological self-realization: the devil is a mirror of our own stupid aggressiveness. Deep ecologists, we presume, require identification with all the other "ugly" parts of the household of nature: Species that act in a way that most humans find infinitely cruel, such as a snake slowly eating a living mouse, nature disasters that can be harmful to nature itself (thunderstorms, floods, or earthquakes), drastic changes in climatic conditions that create problems for human and animal welfare, and natural diseases, such as cancer, most humans could do without. All of these belong to the ecosystem with which we ideally should identify. The feeling of sympathy for other species suggests norms for moral and political action with regard to the environment. Evil is just a necessary shadow in an altogether harmonious nature. Since harmful nature is also part of the future sustainable society, the attitude of acquiescence vis-à-vis such nature is the only sensible strategy. It does not make sense to respond in punitive terms to demonstrate resistance against "natural" evil.

The inability to confront and deal with evil is especially conspicuous when it comes to disentangling evil from the human realm. Passivity vis-à-vis evil may lead to the extension of evil. Deep ecologists' support of green political ecology, that is politics inspired by ecological insights, entails a danger of conserving evil, whether metaphysical, physical, or moral. An example is to be found in Næss's article "Deep Ecology for the Twenty-Second Century."[30] Here Næss explains that he is "a convinced optimist when it comes to the twenty-second century," but first we will have to go through the catharsis of the twenty first. Depending on what we do today, Næss sketches four scenarios for deep ecology of the twenty-first century:

1. "ecologically strict policies, perhaps through undemocratic, and even brutal dictatorial military means";
2. breakdown and total chaos with harsh measures to fight it;
3. catastrophic events with "a turn towards sustainability, but only after enormous ecological devastation;"

4. Ecological enlightenment, with "drastic reduction in the quality of life" (no
    political regime is indicated, but let us assume that this scenario is demo-
    cratic).

Næss's hope is, of course, the last enlightenment scenario. Even if it is unclear
what a green heaven of the twenty-second century will look like, to some it may be
all too clear that deep ecology of the twenty-first century will be a walk through hell.
Næss's "optimism" is of a Ragnarok kind: envisioning one hundred evil years facing
humanity before a new mankind is reborn. The argument that evil in the twenty-first
century is necessary for the sake of tomorrow's bliss reveals structural similarities
with the eighteenth century optimism. Political use of force and violence is necessary in order to reach a higher goal in the future.

What sorts of ideas underpin deep ecological construction of the ecologically
sustainable society? First, the basis for sustainable politics is, according to Næss,
ecological sustainability: "Long-range, local, district, regional, national, and global
wide ecological sustainability is the criterion of ecologically responsible policies as a
whole."[31] Næss is silent on the question of whether, in order to cope with the crisis,
we will have to morally submit to ecological laws. It is doubtful whether mere
intuition and ecological empathy, sometimes advocated by Næss as a moral basis for
conflict-resolution in the "ideals of a Green society,"[32] will be a sufficient warrant
against crimes and misdemeanors. The Næss-inspired deep ecologist, T. O'Riordan,
argues that "Ecological (and other natural) laws dictate human morality."[33] If that is
the case, there is not much room for autonomy (or self-determination). It is legitimate to suggest that those few who know such laws will guide politics. The differ-
entiating factor will be the degree of ecological knowledge: deep, shallow, or none.
The membership of such an ecological community should be less the matter of
personal choice than of the dictates of the natural order.

Such perception of the ecological society, however qualified, is dangerously
close to Hannah Arendt's notion of radical evil. Arendt denigrates any politics that
takes its concerns from the household, whether the human household or the household of nature. Ecological politics seem to do precisely that. The notion of evil refers
to conditions of necessity in households that "transcend the realm of human affairs
and the potentialities of human power." In such conditions "men are unable to for-
give what they cannot punish and that they are unable to punish what has turned out
to be unforgivable."[34] Neither ecological science nor deep ecology specify any basis
for a morally inferred punitive action when natural evil breaks out.

The situation reveals a Job scenario discussed by Næss's famous student Peter
Wessel Zapffe.[35] Job, for no clear reason, was deprived of his family, his farm and
his health by God's omnipotence, covenant, and order. After Job's appeals for justice, God revealed himself in the shape of animal monsters and ordered Job to submit to his almighty will. The optimistic dogmatic ecosopher would have to join God
(or Nature) in this and preach along the same conservative paternalistic line: "Be
quiet, Job! Who do you think you are in the 'web of life'? You must remember Self-
realization (with capital S) and submit to the laws of ecology!"

To conclude. There are good reasons to mistrust totalizing visions put forward by some deep ecologists, and instead be more aware of the complexity and contradictions of the social organism. Therefore, in revaluing deep ecology it is worth rethinking the forgotten critical potential of this philosophy. Using the "skeptical deep ecology" against dogmatic "truths" current in ecological literature would reorient the environmental debate back to its primary track: the critique of progressive industrialism. Such a reorientation, however, would have to address the question of evil which keeps haunting nonanthropocentric ethics.

Notes

This chapter is reprinted with minor revisions from *Rethinking Deep Ecology*, Nature and Humanities Series, ed., Nina Witoszek (Oslo: Oslo University, Center for Development and the Environment, 1996). I am grateful to Nina Witoszek for her comments.

[1] Arne Næss, *Scepticism* (Oslo: Universitetsforlaget, 1968), 4, 7–12. See also Arne Næss, *A Sceptical Dialogue on Induction* (Assen, The Netherlands: Van Gorcum, 1984). Nicholas Rescher, *Scepticism: A Critical Reappraisal* (Oxford: Basil Blackwell, 1980).

[2] Arne Næss, "Deepness of Questions and the Deep Ecology Movement" (1970, revised in 1990), published in George Sessions (ed.), *Deep Ecology for the 21st Century* (Boston: Shambhala, 1995), 204–212.

[3] Arne Næss, "Finnes det objektive normer?" (Do objective norms exist?) in *Norsk Pedagogisk Årbok,* Oslo 1946–7, 7; Arne Næss, *Interpretation and Preciseness* (Oslo: Dybwad, 1953), chap. III and VII.

[4] Arne Næss, "Deep Ecology and Ultimate Premises," in *The Ecologist*, Vol. 18 Nos. 4/5 (1988): 131. Bill Devall and George Sessions, *Deep Ecology* (Salt Lake City: Gibbs M. Smith Inc., 1985), 226. An early version of the diagram is given in Arne Næss, "A Systematization of Gandhian Ethics of Conflict Resolution," *Conflict Resolution*, Vol. 2 no. 2 (1958): 141.

[5] T—as in the initial of Næss's "Tvergastein" cabin, located in the Norwegian mountains. The esoteric reference to Tvergastein illustrates the concrete ecological "rootedness" of Næss's ecosophic work in his own life. T can also be understood as short for *tolkning*—the Norwegian word for "interpretation," perhaps a cryptic reference to Næss's main work *Interpretation and Preciseness* (1953).

[6] See this volume, Chapter 20.

[7] Arne Næss, *Økologi, samfunn og livsstil* (Ecology, Society and Lifestyle), 5th edition (Oslo: Universitetsforlaget, 1976). (New identical edition 1992), 186.

[8] William R. Freudenberg and Robert Gramling, *Oil in Troubled Waters; Perceptions, Politics and the Battle over Offshore Drilling* (Albany: State University of New York Press, 1994).

[9] On Gandhi, see Arne Næss, "A Systematization of Gandhian Ethics of Conflict Resolution," in *Conflict Resolution*, Vol. 2 no. 2 (1958). Arne Næss: *Gandhi og atomalderen* (Gandhi and the Atomic Age), (Oslo: Universitetsforlaget, 1960), 28f. Johan Galtung and Arne Næss, *Gandhis politiske etikk* (Gandhi's political ethics), (Oslo: Tannum, 1955), (3rd edition, Pax Forlag, Oslo 1994), chap. 3. For reasons of space, I shall place less emphasis on Gandhi. None of which is to say that ecosophy is to be seen merely as

an interpretation of these sources—on the contrary, it is an independent philosophical system.

[10] Bendedict de Spinoza, *Ethics* E3P6Dem; E2P3Sch.

[11] Næss, *Ecology*, 1989, 84f.

[12] Næss, *Økologi*, 1976, 312; 1989, 197. As far as I can see, first formulated in Næss, *Conflict*, 1958, 142.

[13] David Rothenberg, *Arne Næss; Is it Painful to Think?* (Minneapolis:University of Minnesota Press, 1993), 73.

[14] Næss, *Økologi*, 1976, 276–277. My trans. *Ecology*, 1989, 173–4. The word "fragment" indicates a part that is torn loose, that is, torn apart from a greater whole. As can be seen, Næss uses "fragment" in an unusual (and possibly misguiding), sense: We are fragments (and not torn-off parts) of a whole. One possible interpretation of Næss's use of "fragment" is that the recognition of being part of a whole is a limited, that is, a fragmented, recognition of the infinite attributes of nature. Spinoza compares human "fragmented" understanding with that of a bloodworm living in its own blood-universe analogous to humans living with a fragmented perception of the whole. (Letter XV (XXXII) to Oldenburg). Yet such an interpretation of Ecosophy T may imply a problematic concept of the intrinsic value of living beings, so that it is the human anthropocentric, fragmented understanding of nature that implies the value of living things.

[15] Næss, *Økologi*, 1976, 320; *Ecology*, 1989, 173f.

[16] The term "shallow" is in inverted commas to show that it refers to the lack of deep questioning of the environmental crisis and not to "shallow people." It is this "shallow" anthropocentrism that Næss wishes to change. He does not say that the "shallow" ones cannot be "deep" when it comes to other issues. The term "shallow" seems to imply, and has in fact been taken to imply, that those outside the environmental movement are "one-sided" and "narrow-minded" in all areas. Though this view cannot legitimately be attributed to Næss, it is encoded in his use of words.

[17] Spinoza, E4P66Sch, E5P42Sch; the proposition follows from putting the two references together. Næss, *Ecology*, 1989, 85.

[18] Arne Næss, *Økologi og filosofi* (Ecology and Philosophy), (Oslo: Universitetsforlaget, 1972), 146; 1976, 271f, 296.

[19] Næss, *Økologi*, 1976, 266. See also page 271, note 4, 333. For purposes of later discussion, it is important to note that Næss distances himself from the pessimism of Peter Wessel Zapffe. Zapffe's opinion appears to be that man has no place in the biosphere; ontologically, we are tragic beings. We should apparently cease to exist voluntarily, before inevitable disaster befalls us. On Zapffe, see Peter Reed and David Rothenberg, *Wisdom in the Open Air* (Minneapolis: University of Minnesota Press, 1993), chap.2.

[20] Sextus Empiricus, *Against the Ethicists* (Cambridge: Loeb Classical Library, Harvard University Press, 1936).

[21] Næss in debate with A. J. Ayer, in Fons Elders, ed., *Reflexive Water: The Basic Concerns of Mankind* (London: Souvenir Press, 1974), 26.

[22] See Harold Glasser, "Deep Ecology Clarified: A Few Fallacies and Misconceptions," *The Trumpeter Journal of Ecosophy* 12 (1995): 138 -142.

[23] Warwick Fox, *Toward a Transpersonal Ecology* (Boston: Shambhala, 1990), 132, 93f. It appears that Fox has overlooked Næss's book on skepticism in notes 3f, p. 333f.

[24] Thomas Berry, "The Viable Human," in George Sessions, ed., *Deep Ecology for the 21st Century* (Boston: Shambhala, 1995), 11.

[25] Berry, "The Viable Human," 17.

[26] Following Pliny, who writes that "Nature appears to have created all other things [for man's sake]—though she asks a cruel price for all her generous gifts, making it hardly possible to judge whether she has been more a kind parent to man or more a harsh stepmother." Pliny, *Natural History* (Cambridge: Loeb Classical Library, Harvard University Press, 1942), Vol. II, Book VII, 507.

[27] Genevieve Lloyd, "Spinoza's Environmental Ethics," *Inquiry* 3 (1980): 293-311. Arne Næss, "Environmental Ethics and Spinoza's Ethics. Comments on Genevieve Lloyd's Article," *Inquiry* 23 (1980): 313–25. Sextus Empiricus, *Against the Ethicists*, 1936. George Sessions, "The Deep Ecology Movement: A Review," *Environmental Review* (Summer 1987), 117.

[28] Aristotle, *Parts of Animals*, 645a17–23.

[29] Arne Næss and Ivar Mysterud, "Philosophy of Wolf Policies: General Principles and Preliminary Exploration of Selected Norms," *Conservation Biology* 1 (1987): 23.

[30] Arne Næss, "Deep Ecology for the Twenty-Second Century," in Sessions, ed., *Deep Ecology*, 1995.

[31] Arne Næss, "Politics & the Ecological Crisis," in Sessions, ed., *Deep Ecology*, 1995, 447. (Næss's italics.)

[32] Arne Næss, "Politics & the Ecological Crisis," in Sessions, ed., *Deep Ecology*, 1995, 447. Næss, *Ecology*, 1989, 159.

[33] T. O'Riordan is quoted in David Rothenberg's introduction to Næss, *Ecology*, 1989, 15–17. Rothenberg refers to T. O'Riordan *Environmentalism* (London: Pion, 1981), 376.

[34] Hannah Arendt, *The Human Condition* (Chicago: The University of Chicago Press, 1958), 241.

[35] *The Bible*, Book of Job. See P. W. Zapffe, *Om det tragiske* [*On the Tragic*, 1941] (Oslo: Aventura, 1988), chap. 10., part 106, 478f.

Chapter 52

Response to Peder Anker

Arne Næss

The terms "shallow ecological movement" and "deep ecological movement" were originally introduced in a six-page summary of a lecture denied publication because of the restrictions imposed by the dictator Ceaušescu. The summary was to form part of the proceedings of the Third World Future Research Conference. It was not acceptable to the Romanian dictator.

The "shallow" movement was characterized as follows:

"Fight against pollution and resource depletion. Central objective: the health and affluence of people in the developed countries."

The remainder of the summary concerned the deep movement.

To my consternation, the term "deep ecologist" soon appeared. I felt compelled to insist that deepness must be defined in terms of total argumentation patterns, ones which supporters of the deep ecology movement would argue (in part) from ultimate premises, philosophical or religious.

Peder Anker writes in his introduction: "The word 'deep' has created some confusion among deep ecologists. What does it mean to be 'deep' and who is 'shallow'? This confusion arose when deep ecology moved from one philosophical culture and context to another and when Næss's thoughts were adapted by Australian and American thinkers."

First of all, let me repeat what I have always tried to make clear: the words "deep" and "shallow" are *NOT* applied to people, but to argumentation patterns. This makes it rather meaningless to pose a question like "Who is shallow?" True, my articles are numerous and often published in "obscure" periodicals. It is perhaps understandable that my attempts at depersonification do not reach every participant in the relevant debate.

444

Anker writes further: "I wish to suggest that the original ecological philosophy of Næss was first of all a critical project of asking 'deeper questions about modern materialistic society from a skeptical standpoint.' Sometimes I have argued that the essential difference between the two submovements, especially after 1973, is not well characterized by my summary: The deep movement *problematizes* every aspect of rich (industrial, developed) societies, all the way back to ultimate premises. Normally, however, English editors reject this important Germanic verb and insert the weaker verb: "to question." Further, the distinction between a definition of a term and a descriptive formulation of the essence of something, is too often neglected. The deep ecology movement is not defined through "asking deeper questions," and it would be very naive to say that if you question deeply enough you inevitably end joining the deep ecology movement. Plato or Zarathustra were not deep ecology supporters, though Plato did complain about ecological devastation. Anker does not make it sufficiently clear that relevant problematizing is conducted within the ecological movement itself. It has all to do with ecological sustainability, in short, "eco-sustainability." It is interesting to note that the problematizing of the democratic aspect of some industrial countries has never ended in a negative assessment: only democratic, essentially nonviolent processes have a chance to ensure ecological sustainability in an ethically acceptable way. And the so-called "Green political theorists" (usually distinguishing Green from merely green) agree on this. But this statement anticipates what I have to say later in my comments.

The way of thinking and feeling I have, perhaps unwisely, termed Pyrrhonic skepticism has been manifest in my writings since 1938. Its ethical aspect I found expressed by Gandhi: In severe conflicts *satyagraha* (nonviolence) is ethically required because you cannot ever be sure that the whole truth is on your side rather than that of your opponent. Even in the history of mathematics I found that so-called self-evident deductions have later been rejected as self-evidently false.

One way or the other, it is a pleasure to see Pyrrhonic skepticism being accepted as a guide when asking and answering deep questions. Anker does a timely, good job on this point. I shall not go into details, but merely mention point 8: "the skeptic is talking loosely when talking in general terms." As a member of a community, the skeptic must necessarily make use of the rhetorics of that community in order not to be misunderstood. Example: A person, R, is accused of having murdered somebody in city C. A skeptic Q, is subpoenaed as a witness and says: "I saw R in the city D, far from C, at the time of the murder." When asked "Are you quite sure?," the skeptic may well have the duty to answer "yes" if the way he feels is such that people would normally say "I am quite sure." The Pyrrhonic skeptic does not use "perhaps" in every sentence. He would not say "it seems to me that it was R I saw in the city D." He has a normal way of asserting things. If it is relevant, as in debates about different attitudes towards so-called knowledge, he explains his views more elaborately.

There are some utterances in Anker's article which I feel to be misleading. "One can argue from a radical (A) or reformist position (B)," Anker writes, "while holding a strict or modified version of (P),[1] to finally reward Deep Ecological political action with multiple outcomes (C or D). In political debate Næss can attack and retreat at the same time, offend and cajole, and finally score on all fronts."

In a political debate, as in other debates, I cannot attack and retreat at the same time. The Pyrrhonic way implies general fallibility—whatever x you are convinced is true or valid, may be false. If the word "radical" has two meanings M_1 and M_2, a participant in a debate may say, "I am radical if M_1 is meant, and reformist if M_2 is meant." From the point of view of semantics, the word "radical," like most important words, has no definite meaning, so it is often necessary to use the above if's. And even more important, there is little research done to date to map out different meanings through sets of precizations. One may, of course, at some stage of one's development change one's opinions, and, for instance, give up a radical position whether M_1 or M_2 is meant. This does not violate a reasonable norm of consistency. One does not necessarily hold incompatible views at a particular stage. Pyrrhonic skepticism does not make us free to be inconsistent. But if I assert "I am consistent in this debate," I may be wrong about that, and in a particular case, from feeling sure I have been consistent I may end up being sure I have been inconsistent. This follows from tentatively asserted general fallibility.

To be inclined to think as a Pyrrhonic skeptic is something rather special, and I am not sure that I recommend it to a social movement.[2] But there are less far-out ways of being undogmatic and open-minded in a debate. I assume that it is not a bad thing that nearly all supporters of the deep ecology movement are likely to believe that they have found some truths. They are dogmatists in the Pyrrhonic sense, but their way of communicating (and acting) may nevertheless be undogmatic in a very precious way. Some theorists of the deep ecology movement have sometimes been criticized for dogmatism in a vernacular, nontechnical sense, and that is serious, of course. Here a turn *in the direction of* Pyrrho may be good.

"The impreciseness of (P) allows for a high level of 'overlapping consensus' about shared ideas in the movement," Anker writes. The task of finding definitions of "the deep ecology movement" I leave to the lexicographers. A proper characterization of what the supporters stand for, might, I believe, be expressed in about 200–250 words. My tentative proposal I called "the 8 points of the deep ecology movement." Key terms are open to different interpretations. In this way they are, as Anker says, "imprecise," useful in establishing overlapping, but not complete, consensus about fairly general, important points of view.

When Anker goes on to describe my metaphysical views, Ecosophy T, etc., I tend to understand less of what he means and what he thinks I mean. "According to Spinoza, the power with which one struggles for self-preservation is an expression of the power of God in his active aspect, so that those who realize themselves can be said to be living the life of God. Næss links this with Gandhi's concept of self-realization and the distinction between a 'little self' (with a lower-case s) and 'The Big Self' (with a capital S)." I have used Spinoza as a great source of inspiration, but in my "reconstruction" of a small, but central part of his *Ethics* I neither introduce the term "God" (*Deus*), nor "necessity" (*necessitas*), nor God-or-Nature (*Deus siva Natura*). Nor have I employed terms such as "Self-realization" and "liberation" in the meaning Anker suggests. Anker does not refer to, or quote, what I say in my own book on Spinoza. (If he did, it would have perhaps made it easier to comment on what he says.)

About my norm "Self-realization!" and certain other norms (which he does not formulate), Anker says "The ultimate aim of these norms is a complete realization of N1 ('Self-realization!'): an 'ecosocial' utopia." I see a possibility of interpreting me in such a way. But a utopia for me is something, strictly speaking, *not* realizable. For me it makes little sense to think of a society of people realizing the big Self "completely," perhaps something more than Buddha or Gandhi have achieved.

Anyhow, I can accept one of Anker's conclusions: "Næss's skeptical model of Ecosophy T is a personal *Weltanschauung* that cannot—and should not—be enlarged to dogmatic announcement of truth. It is in the light of these qualifications that one must understand Næss's concept of the "self."

Of the many influences that temporarily have nearly made me a dogmatist in Pyrrhonic sense, is natural mysticism—oneness with nature and in nature, called by Ernst Mach (and others) "the oceanic feeling." But the metaphor of being a drop in the ocean could not really touch my heart, and the extreme philosophical holism even less. In *Ecology, Community and Lifestyle*, I write "From the identification process stems unity, and since the unity is of a gestalt character, the wholeness is attained." This is very abstract and vague! But it offers a framework for a total view, or better, a central perspective. A wholeness is attained, but temporarily, imperfectly.

The above seems to point in the direction of philosophical mysticism, but the fourth term, Self-realization, breaks in and reinstates the central position of the individual—even if the capital S is used to express something beyond narrow selves. The widening and deepening of the individual selves somehow never makes them into one "mass." Whatever the level reached in width and depth of the identification, individuality is not reduced. The sentence I used in the television discussion with A. J. Ayer—teasingly because he would detest it and wonder how an empiricist like myself could utter such woolly metaphysical stuff—is this: "Fundamentally all life is one," i.e., there is something fundamental which everything alive has in common (and which makes it possible to assert "every living being has the same right to live and blossom" or "every living being has value in itself"). And, of course, "we are more than our egos, and we are not fragments, hardly small and powerless." [3]

It is my impression that my emphasis on the individual, powerfully expressed by Ibsen and Gandhi, is typical of supporters of the deep ecology movement. Warwick Fox feels like a leaf on the tree of life, he has declared. To this I would say: It is not enough to be a leaf! Admittedly, no published version of point 1 of the 8 points makes the role of the individual clear. Unfortunately, the term "life form" very often will be interpreted to refer to species rather than specimens.

This leads me to a part of Anker's article where his expressed way of understanding deep ecologist positions differs most squarely from my own.

"Deep ecology movement and dogmas about the good, harmonious nature," is a simplification. But so is Anker's declaration to the effect that "When deep ecology moved from Norway to Australian and America, it moved from skepticism to dogmatism." Peder Anker knows my work on skepticism, and understands that what looks like a *dogmatic* assertion, may not be meant to be so:

> Fox ultimately treats Næss as if he had seen "the light" and knew all the answers with regard to how to live an ecologically responsible life. Deep ecology has become synonymous with the contemporary construction of ecotopias. George Sessions's latest anthology on deep ecology is also instructive in this regard. A prototypical example is to be found in Thomas Berry's article "The Viable Human." Berry states that "The ecologist is offering a way of moving toward a new expression of the true wonderworld of nature as the context for a viable human situation." He argues that ecology offers "expressions of the truth," which is exactly what Næss, in his work in favor of skepticism, tries to avoid.

An expression like "deriving policies from fundamentals" can be used by skeptics and dogmatics. In the former case, what is asserted is not truth but *derivability* from premises to conclusions. One does not assert the truth of premises and conclusions. To *offer* a way of moving *toward* something may be interpreted a little like my *proposal* to characterize the deep ecology movement through the 8 points (plus an invitation to offer alternatives to my proposal).

Worse in my view, or at least very much stranger, is to talk about the true "wonderworld of nature" without, broadly, "admitting" the existence of vast suffering and what we as humans see as unnecessary cruelty. The idea of minimizing interference in nature is not expressed by any supporter of the deep ecology movement I know of, though some readers of deep ecology literature may take it as implicit in deep ecology. "Harmony in nature" used by Thomas Berry may sometimes be a useful term. I found *his* use unwarranted at a memorable conference where I expressed both my intense intellectual interest in nature and the cosmos *and* my moral *disgust*. How did participants receive this message? I was smiling and they answered smiling.

Some literature on questions related to deep ecology exudes dogmatic optimism (in a broad sense). It is my feeling that it *offers* a way of seeing things that needs to be evaluated in a critical light by the reader. Such views, however, are not representative of opinions held by the majority of supporters of the deep ecology movement in the United States.

Since antiquity the term "to live according to what is natural," *kata fysin*, has been an eulogism. Never until now, however, has it been suggested that the few advocates of this kind of life have a tendency to join together and seek authoritarian regimes. Somewhat different is the influence of Rousseau's anti-civilization diatribes. There is a link between his nature eulogies and his very dangerous idea of "the will of the people." In conclusion Anker proposes to reorient the environmental debate back to its primary task, i.e., giving up the "totalizing visions put forward by some deep ecologists" and letting the "skeptical deep ecology" address "the question of evil—the question which keeps haunting nonanthropocentric ethics."

What are Anker's premises for such reorientation? Roughly speaking, they are as follows:

1. Deep ecology in its dogmatic form teaches that every natural process, including earthquakes and the formation of cancer ("natural evils") should not be resisted.
2. In a society which realizes the dogmatic deep ecology ideas must be a class-society where those who know ecological laws best determine policies and lifestyles.
3. Næss and others maintain that evil in the twenty-first century is necessary to reach bliss in the next, and political use of force and violence is necessary to reach that goal.

Since antiquity some authors have gone very far in the direction of taking what they call "natural" as guidelines for action. But I lack information of authors who make this a norm of passivity when faced with illnesses of the cruelty of cancer. Such an opinion deserves inclusion in the *Guinness Book of Records.* I have not met supporters of the deep ecology movement who profess, let alone "teach" such a norm. And nobody would accept norms from which it would follow that if you do not let "natural" illnesses develop, then you are *inconsistent.* Besides, I have not, in print or verbally advocated that "evil is necessary" to reach *any* goal.

The "primary task" of deep ecology should be, according to Anker, "criticism of progressive industrialism."

This I consider untenable. There is need for people whose work for the realization of eco-sustainable cultures springs from an integrated, deep outlook on life and reality. This implies deep questioning, touching their ultimate value priorities. Equally important is the work of those who join the general ecological movement but find they do not need any deep questioning. Pyrrhonic skepticism, which Anker finds so valuable, is a necessary corrective to both positions.

Notes

[1] "P" in the above quotation is shorthand for the so-called 8 points of the deep ecology movement.

[2] How did students react to the notion of Pyrrhonic scepticism? I did not have the opportunity to correct details in the published transcript of the debate with Ayer. There is a relevant passage quoted in Anker's article from the book edited by Fons Elders, *Reflexive Water: The Basic Concerns of Mankind* (London, 1974). The editing is misleading. I referred, in my discussion with Ayer, to a very special situation: how students

trying to instigate a "student revolution" in 1968 reacted when I told them I was going to give a semester's introduction to skepticism. The timing was completely wrong, they explained. Today students need strong beliefs, and fierce actions! And my textbooks were not adapted to the situation, of course. The student revolutionaries of 1968 were dissatisfied, sure! I asked them to work out their own list of obligatory readings. They proposed very heavy German and French works! They certainly did not, as students often do, ask for easy reading. All was "dialectical," including dialectical logic (Hegel).

[3] Arne Næss, *Ecology, Community and Lifestyle* (Cambridge: Cambridge University Press, 1989), 173.

Chapter 53

Arne Næss and the Norwegian Nature Tradition

Nina Witoszek

The Lineage of a Green Utopia

In 1984, on one of his many eco-trips round the world, Professor Arne Næss alighted at the University of Minnesota for an international conference. Conscious of, but unabashed by, the reputation of Norwegians as *Weltverbesserer* ("timeless world improvers"), he presented a paper in which he outlined the Green Utopia of Norway *anno* 2084.[1]

Næss imagines a group of visitors from Houston landing on an island near Bergen (islands are mandatory in Utopias—they so easily convert to versions of the self). The Houstonians encounter an egalitarian, self sufficient community riding around on bicycles. This community consists of humans, animals, plants, forests, and fjords coexisting in biotic bliss with one another. Technology has low visibility and is used with discernment. Odd atavisms from the twentieth century, however, remain. "The people are not willing to give up their wooden stoves, their telephones, their trains and their bicycles." There is even a counterculture of youths still infatuated with consumerism. "A not-too happy counterculture," obviously. Most strikingly, *Homo norvegicus futurus* does not require alcohol or drugs for the sufficient reason that he is rarely bored. The visitors from centers of decadence (such as Houston, Texas) are offered a pseudomathematical equation:

$$B = R / (F + D)^3$$

where boredom (B) is proportional to repetition (R) and inversely proportional to feeling (F) and discrimination (D) raised to the third power.

Significantly enough, there are only a few artists and scientists on the island. They feel that "Norway is too small for them and that they have little impact on the rest of the population. Apart from a few large centers of learning, most Universities and High Schools are small and interaction between them is less intense than a hundred years ago."[2]

This, in brief, is a utopia of the future ecocentric man: a logical extension in many ways of the principal strategies of Arne Næss's own deep ecology. It is moderately flexible (in that it allows for some concessions to the ancien régime) and moderately inconsistent—as indeed is Næss himself. If looked at carefully, it reveals an intimate connection, not just with contemporary ideas of environmental future, but with the indigenous nature tradition.

While discussing the nucleus of native inspiration in Næss's thought, Peter Reed and David Rothenberg have pointed to such matters as contemporary Norwegian philosophy (from Peter Wessel Zapffe to Sigmund Kvaløy); socio-ecological factors such as low population density, the salience of rural culture and indeed the very exuberance of nature itself; the robustness of *naturroman-tikken* in literature and painting from Wergeland to Finn Alnaes; the practice of everyday life fixated as it is on outdoor activities, and, finally, the ecopolitical strategies of both the Norwegian state and the radical native counterculture. [3]

While not disputing the relevance of these fairly evident factors, I wish to discuss in more detail the books, deeds, and people that have shaped the communal memory in which Næss's thought is immersed. For it is against the background of indigenous normative patterns and traditions of knowledge that we are struck, not by the radicalism, but the archaism of Næss's thought. These traditions reach far beyond contemporary green awakenings or a problematic Norwegian Romanticism; they draw heavily on the values of the Norwegian Enlightenment and, further, on the ancient wisdom encoded in the sagas. Næss, we might say, established a green canon for the twentieth century which resonates with modern sensibility, appeals to our intuitions and urges us to re-read and transform the status quo. But the canon itself is a theatre of memory, composed of preceding images, "places" and authors that have woven together a *mundus imaginalis*, a set of ethical standards and cognitive strategies which have been transmitted from generation to generation. The great strength of the canon assembled by Næss lies not merely in its power to colonize and challenge our minds but in its ability to assimilate and mobilize cultural energies which have their source in the cognitive-ethical fabric of Næss's native culture. Notwithstanding Næss's own insistence on the influence of Spinoza, Gandhi, and Advaita Vedanta on his work, there is an invisible tradition that nourishes deep ecology—invisible by virtue of the mere fact that Næss is so completely immersed in it and so unconsciously in dialogue with it. "Ideas," as Lord Acton once wrote, "have a radiation and development, an ancestry and posterity of their own, in which men play the part of godfathers and godmothers more than that of legitimate parents."[4]

From *Håvamål*
to the Pastoral Enlightenment to Næss

Central to Næss's ecological work is the notion of the proper cosmic humility of humankind. The systemic wisdom which represents humans as part of larger wholes sounds novel and "romantic" but is, of course, quite ancient. It is discernible in most cosmologies, including Western ones. The text of *Håvamål* in the *Poetic Edda* which, in the case of Norway, may be treated as just such an ancient ecological codex, taught one thing: keep measure, don't over-reach, survival is imperative. As the Jester would later put it in *King Lear*, "Have more than thou showest/ Speak less than thou knowest." In Norway the fascinating strategic opportunism of *Håvamål*—one that advocates a precarious equilibrium which avoids intolerable choices and desperate situations—has never been challenged by the Faustian mythos of the over-reacher. The old aristocratic code of suicidal honor, so typical of the sagas, died out with the Viking era and was never resuscitated as a national cultural ideal. It is the pragmatic, plebeian wisdom of *Håvamål* that, over the centuries, was elevated to the national ethos.

To a contemporary sensibility educated in hubris, the prescriptions of carefulness, caution, and moderation advocated by *Håvamål* sound like an uninspiring catechism of mediocrity. So too does Næss's Green Utopia. (So too does contemporary Norway, as some prejudiced observers insist.) The central injunction implicit in *Håvamål*: "Thou shalt not think (or show) thou art anybody special," is enlarged in Næss to read "We human beings should not think that we are special in the universe." In *The Edda*, we recall, this principle applies even to gods who have to pay for any excess of wisdom (Odin), beauty and goodness (Balder) or vitality (Thor). There is a remarkable continuity in this pattern of thought, an absence of those leaps and lacunas which would fracture or reorient the ancient template. The distance between *Håvamål* and Næss is nothing like the distance between, say *Beowulf* and Sir Alfred Ayer. It is as if in the Norwegian case the values of moderation and respect for the elements that have been incubating for centuries were simply recanonized by Næss—and with them, the pragmatic tradition that gives priority to action over the word, experience over fixed principle, practice over theory. Utterances like "the smaller we come to feel ourselves compared to the mountain, the nearer we come to participate in its greatness" are merely rhetorical adornments of an old wisdom designed to keep humans in their right place in the order of things.[5] So too the semi-Wordsworthian kinship with nature: "[f]rom about the age of eight a definite mountain became for me a symbol of a benevolent, equal-minded, strong 'father,' or of an ideal human nature"[6]—bears a particular cultural stamp. It articulates both an atavistic idea of nature as *ancestral* (in a literal rather than religious sense), and announces that undersocialized Norwegian self that prefers the simple relation to a cowslip to the necessarily intricate and fraught relation to a parent.

The Håvamålian, slightly a-social, commonsense pragmatism which underlies Næss's renowned inconsistency, is part of a culture that has been challenged less by other tribes and other scribes and more by the harshness of the elements. It bespeaks values that are resilient under stress and which, when it comes to Næss's most radical propositions, are qualified by the rhetorical adjunct "in principle." The "in principle" clause inserted into the programmatic article on biospherical egalitarianism, for example, is justified on the grounds that "any realistic praxis necessitates some killing, exploitation and suppression."[7] Concessions are unavoidable, dogmas are ductile, principles and practice diverge. That explains why, after thirty years of his deep ecological odyssey, it is still unclear how far Næss would go in demanding radical change from societies and individuals whose concerns about the environment are non-existent or based on "shallow" perceptions. The radical interpretation of deep ecological premises implies that "change" will necessitate a rejection of the liberal constitution through nonviolent action and the construction of a new society based on a biocentric worldview. The reformist interpretation, on the other hand, reduces deep ecology to a "therapeutic philosophy" attempting, within the existing political system, to raise people's consciousness in order to transform their ego-oriented self-realization into a proper, ecosophic one. Næss tends to tackle the problem contextually. If, in a discussion, one inquires about the reformist interpretation, the reply is that deep ecology is not a "reform movement." If, on the other hand, one criticizes the radical orientation, Næss retorts that deep ecology is by no means radical in a fundamentalist or totalitarian sense.[8] What looks like the strategy of a proverbial liberal, i.e., a man who cannot take his side in a debate, is, in fact, a gesture of pragmatic adjustment. For Næss, meaning is not a stagnant property inherent in an idea. Meaning *happens* to an idea which most feel to be right: it becomes true, is made true by events. Ultimately it is philosophizing-as-action that counts for Næss, a perpetual struggle of intelligent organisms to solve the problems created by their interaction with their natural environment.

There is one further element of the ancient semiosphere which has percolated into Næss's vision: Nordic eschatology. In *Voluspa*, which foretells the moral degeneration and the inevitable end of the world of gods and men, Ragnarok is to be followed by rebirth. A green world and a more benign race will populate the globe:

I see green again with growing things
the earth arise from out of the sea;
fell torrents flow, overflies them the eagle
on hoar highlands which hunts for fish.
[. . .]
On unsown acres the ears will grow
all ill grow better; will Baldr come then.
[. . .]
I see a hall than the sun more fair,
thatched with red gold, which is Gimle hight.

There will the gods all guiltless throne
and live forever in ease and bliss.[9]

Næss's version of this doomsday optimism is to be found in his "Deep Ecology for the Twenty Second Century."[10] As has been argued by Anker, though Næss declares himself a futurological optimist, he takes for granted that humankind has to go through a cathartic *rite de passage* first. Out of Næss's five extrapolations to the future ecological (dis)order, four are apocalyptic, envisioning breakdown and chaos followed by some form of ecological authoritarianism to impose order and stability. In short, Næss's predictions are all based on Voluspian optimism, one that envisions a hundred evil years before a new humankind is restored.

Just as it is erroneous to translate Næss's deep ecology into dogmatic or hierophantic terms (a tendency in American interpretations), so it misses the point to see him as an heir to European romanticism and the religion of nature. For the German and English Romantics, nature was imbued with meaning because it resonated with the selfhood of the poet or philosopher. Such meaning in turn reflected the glory of the numinous and the divinity of the world spirit. Not for Næss. In spite of his occasional references to a Greater Self, Næss's vision is a continuation of the Enlightenment agenda:

> Why should this philosophy [Kantianism] apply only to human beings? Are there no other beings with intrinsic value? What about animals, plants, landscapes, and our very special old planet as a whole?[11]

Shining through such declarations is not the sublime romanticism of Schiller or Emerson but the rationalist optimism of the Norwegian Enlightenment as it was practiced and preached by eighteenth and nineteenth century pastors. Næss's "Eight Points of Deep Ecology" read like an anti-manifesto resting as they do on rational rather than inflammatory propositions. His rhetoric eschews romantic affectation: "The universe is my universe, not my ego's but that of the great Self we have in common. This is metaphysics, but through philosophical research it can be developed in the direction of clarity and cognitive responsibility."[12]

In tune with the Enlightenment pastors, for whom rivers had tongues and the land was endowed with breasts and shoulders, Næss sees no discrepancy between rationalism and anthropomorphism. Characteristically, he attempts to rehabilitate the anthropomorphic imagination not on romantic-mystical, but on functionalist grounds. Thus the expression "the life of the river may be introduced in a scientific text by using the terminology of ecosystemics." And the slogan "'let the river live' has had an important function in situations of social conflict."[13] Clearly for Næss, being a pragmatist is not just a way of practicing philosophy and staying cheerful. It is part of that heritage of an optimistic and pre-technological enlightenment in which he is immersed and on which he continues to draw. Just as his native intellectual predecessors Martin Schweigaard and Niels Treschow, Næss stays ironically aware, even dismissive, of academicism and the pedantic abstractions of philosophy. The ancient imperative to excoriate elitism and to privilege an egalitarian populist self reasserts itself again and again in his work and public statements. So does the emphasis on practical action—a result of a peculiarly Norwegian obsession with the usefulness of art and philosophy. Hence "those who subscribe to the foregoing points have an obligation, directly or indirectly, to participate in the attempt to implement the necessary changes."[14]

Like Spinoza (but also like leading eighteenth and nineteenth century Norwegian writers, scientists, and philosophers such as Ludvig Holberg, Hans Strøm and Niels Treschow), Næsss seems to assume that the natural solution to any crisis, including the environmental one, is, in principle, discoverable by anyone, anywhere, and in any circumstances. If it has not been discovered, it must be due to immaturity, the clouding of reason, or perhaps bad luck:

> The rational solution of value conflicts is not something that is impossible to achieve. . . . I take it therefore to be an empirically testable hypothesis that the attainment of well-rounded human maturity leads to identification with all life forms in a wide sense of "life" and including the acknowledgment of the intrinsic values of all of these forms.[15]

There is a puzzle here. What seems at first sight like a utopian dimension to Næss's thought turns out to be a projection of the native *le bon sens* into a rescue package for environmentally exhausted civilization. The philosopher who has demanded: "Will the Defenders of Deep Ecology Please Rise?" speaks from a country in which the assertion of the inalienable right of the individual has constituted an almost unbroken tradition. It is a world in which the relative absence of urban culture, of reifying bureaucracy and wasteful aristocracy, of devastating wars and ethnic collisions could not but hatch some version of a philosophy which went beyond the human. The old Nordic imperative of *nøysomhet*, that untranslatable term which means contentedness in frugal but adequate circumstances, hardly needed to be invented or rediscovered. The older generation of Norwegians, for example, remembers a world in which parsimony and the ideal of Spartan austerity were synonymous with good citizenship. In some respects, deep ecology may be seen as possible and affordable due to a benign cultural blindness to the intractability and insolubility of conflicts in other semiospheres. In Norway the suppression of needs and the imaginative extension of individual worth and rights to all species are only partially innovatory ideas; fundamentally, they belong to an enduring indigenous tradition which emphasized the cult of virtuous simplicity and, well into the 1980s, opposed a materialistic concept of human felicity. Næss's vision is not a rootless abstraction, self-begotten and self-sustaining, severed from culture and history in the way other utopias have attempted to be. With deep ecology, Næss proffers an expanded version of values of the Norwegian rural Enlightenment to the rest of the globe.

It is this successful, rationalist-democratic worldview, one that was allowed to flourish in a culture largely spared the experience of social debasement and bestiality, which goes some way to explain the terrible beauty of deep ecology. When queried in the course of an interview as to the possible dangerous implications of a philosophy based on identification with the whole, Næss replied with his usual insouciance: "Everything really important is dangerous, so that's OK."[16] When pressed, however, he clearly opposed his philosophy to vitalism:

> I see an unconditional "cult of life" as being unethical. It is that strand that led in part to Nazism: You read nature in a certain way. You see the lions and their prey. You analogize to humans, a hierarchy emerges, with systems, totems of power. You begin to say yes to brutality, yes to exploitation. And among the humans, yes to sadism. One must be very careful, then, if one is to use "Life!" as the center of an ethic.[17]

These remarks reveal Næss's awareness of the problems intrinsic to a holistic approach. Still the belief that "Self-realization!" will be a sufficient warrant against totalitarian excesses springs from a culturally privileged faith in the peaceful coexistence of diverse species and the rational consensus-orientated dialogue between humans. It is difficult to imagine deep ecology being born in a latitude further south than Copenhagen: Its discourse and its worldview is, on the whole, rather wintry, unresponsive to the power of passion, the metaphysics of evil, and the lure of eroticism. Ultimately, it rests on a belief in a cosmic whole where every organism, from the king to your local friendly wolf is a good, self-restrained Protestant citizen.

Cultural "Radicalism" and
the Metaphysics of Authenticity

Cultural radicalism is a fetish phrase in the Norwegian history of ideas. Jon Elster, among others, has propounded the following definition:

> Cultural radicalism is a political and intellectual attitude. A cultural radical's commitment and indignation border on moralism. In his universe scandal is an important category. The analysis of economic and social causes is not his strong point. . . His motto has been formulated by Helge Krog: "If you are in doubt as to which standpoint to adopt vis a vis a concrete cause, choose the one which will harm you most.". . . . A cultural radical lives in the city. He is remote from mass movements on the periphery, be it language or the temperance cause, or low church ideas. . . . He takes the side of the weak, whether defined economically or culturally. . . . . Cultural radicalism is against Christianity but for women priests. . . .[18]

Given the comprehensiveness of this caricature, it is significant that Elster should overlook three important dimensions of radicalism *à la norvegienne.*

Firstly, although this radicalism is rational, intellectual, anti-clerical and anti-bourgeois, it is not the opposite of the eighteenth century provincial religious awakening but its continuation. It is principally a Norwegian *bud-dism* (from *bud* = "commandment"). Elster himself indicates that the deep structure of Norwegian counterculture reveals Manichaeism, moralism, fervent search for the truth and the ethics of social commitment—and these were the chief predilections of the eighteenth century priests. Secondly, cultural radicalism in Norway invokes, to a very large degree, nature as part of a ritual of resistance to bourgeois elitism or capitalist techno-worship. It is largely reactionary, in spite of its revolutionary pretensions. It appeals to values which have been central to Norwegian culture for a very long time: the ideal of egalitarian solidarity, the drive towards social betterment, democratic individualism, and the basically rationalist modus operandi. These values are hardly either "revolutionary" or new. What is new from the end of the nineteenth century on, is the obsessive, almost religious search for authenticity propelled by the shock of urban theatrics.

The rejection of the social mask and a resultant "truth pilgrimage" has been central to Norwegian writing from Ibsen, Bjørnson, and Hamsun to the socialist and Maoist apostles of the 1960s and 1970s. The great appeal of psychoanalysis and Marxism in Norway, if not in all of Scandinavia, had less to do with their revolutionary potential and more with their availability as techniques to unmask the social lie spawned by a nascent urban culture. *Det er bedre å snakke sant enn å snakke pent*, goes a Norwegian motto. ("It's better to talk truthfully than to talk beautifully.") If for Voltaire telling the truth was imperative only when one could not avoid it, for Norwegian writers and intellectuals truth telling has always been a cardinal commandment. For Ibsen, if truth and God had been separated, he would have chosen the truth. For socialist writers of the interwar period Hoel and Krogh, "the free writer has one and only one task: to tell the truth as he sees it, however uncomfortable it is."[19] The notion of society with its role-driven and role-ridden character, has always seemed false to the eco-existentialist on his way to the mountains. Freedom, liberty, equality, fraternity, justice, and natural rights—interpreted not as bourgeois ideas (as, say, in France) or aristocratic virtues (as in Poland)—have been mythologized into the original mores of the peasantry. Bourgeois freedom has been synonymous with "free trade, free selling and free buying" to use Marx's phrase.[20] Hence rebellion in the name of freedom and truth has always been rebellion in the name of nature.

"Feeling apart in many human relations, I identified with nature," confesses Næss—thus allying himself with the native *veritas* tradition.[21] The endless search for the naked, authentic individual with original opinions, free from clichés and received phraseology, has been part of both Næss's philosophy of nature and of language. His early study of *"Truth" as conceived by Those who are not Professional Philosophers*, is a typical example of the cultural radicalism of the 1930s, a search for the people's rather than the philosophers' truth.[22] It is also an anarchic countercultural lampoon of the pomposity of high science. Næss's progress thereafter has had a certain logical momentum to it—out of the entrapments of language and into the authenticity of nature. In some respects

Næss's deep ecology is a resolution of, and a therapy for, the cultural neuroses that troubled Ibsen, Hamsun, Sandemose, and countless other sensitive Norwegian souls.

Typically, Næss's radicalism of the truth is scarcely related to revolutionary radicalism in any of its usual forms. Fundamentally, it is a spectral radicalism that mimics the pragmatic strategies of the Norwegian prolonged enlightenment. Here is Arne Næss on this theme:

> Reform or revolution? I envisage a change of revolutionary depth and size by means of many smaller steps in a radically new direction. This essentially makes me belong to the political reformists, I suppose? Scarcely. *The direction is revolutionary, the steps are reformatory.*[23]

This, of course, should be nothing new to Næss's compatriots: it sounds like a *summa sumarum* of Norwegian radical-conservative politics up to the present.

What redeems Næss's restatement of the Norwegian *tao* with its fixation on the truth, the right way, the ethics of responsibility, commitment and struggle, is his ludic, skeptical intelligence. In a conversation with the British philosopher, Sir Alfred Ayer, Næss regretted his paradoxical, detached commitment: "I am sorry to say, in some ways I feel miserable to be defending skepticism now, because there is a very tragic conflict between the attitude I hold in my integrated and concentrated moments, which is more or less skeptical, and the requirements of consistent action. For instance, when we believe that we really must do something about some terribly pressing problem, we must somehow narrow our perspective."[24]

Though it may be a deeply felt conviction, consistency is, for Næss, as for Oscar Wilde, ultimately the last refuge of the unimaginative. Ultimately, Næss's exasperating plasticity points again to a pragmatic strategy of intellectual compromise, of fighting for a truth in the sense defined by Rorty: as something "good to believe in" rather than something that has a transcendental status.

Næssianic Predecessors and Interlocutors

The international influences on Næss's work are well defined and have been relatively well explored: Spinoza, Gandhi, and, of course, Socrates (Næss's proclaimed Socratic ambition is to be a "respectable pest"). Næss's principle of "Self-realization!" can be taken as inspired by the Hindu philosophy of the Greater Self—or as an extension of Marx's anticipation of a future in which "[i]n place of the old bourgeois society, with its class antagonisms, we shall have an association in which free development of each is the condition for the free development of all."[25] Similarly Næss's conception of the good life and his own modus vivendi bring to mind the early Marx who imagined a life in which it was "possible for me to do one thing today and another tomorrow, to hunt in the morning, fish in the afternoon, rear cattle in the evening, criticize (philosophize) after dinner, just as I have a mind, without ever becoming hunter, fisherman, shepherd, or critic."[26]

But there have been other influences at work. Peter Reed and David Rothenberg in the course of their compendium of native inspiration in Næss, mention such contemporary Norwegian philosophers and activists as Peter Wessel Zapffe, Nils Faarlund and Sigmund Kvaløy.[27] To these we might like to add a number of less obvious, but perhaps more significant, antecedents such as the eighteenth and nineteenth century thinker and philosopher Niels Treschow. Holism was an intrinsic dimension of Treschow's vision, which was also marked by an empirical bias uncontaminated by abstract speculation. All the furnishings of Treschow's philosophy—the monist inspiration of Spinoza and Leibniz, the attempt to "improve" on Kant's pure reason by inserting an empirical corrective, the socialist leanings, and the precursory evolutionism—are, from another perspective, a systematization and further development of a native "eco-humanism." Central to Treschow's vision is the idea of *Fuldkommenheds-Drivt* ("struggle for self-fulfillment," "self-realization"). All nature—both organic and nonorganic—is typified by a drive towards the realization of its individuality. "Moral, as well as physical fulfillment consists in the undisturbed harmony or, in other words, achievement of complete individuality, where all parts are so connected that no one is less essential or necessary than the other and no chance intervenes."[28] *Individuum est ineffabile,* and its suppression is the suppression of the richness and diversity of life. The characteristic melange of holism and individualism which figures so strongly in Treschow (and indeed in most eighteenth and nineteenth century strains of Norwegian thought), is also to be found in Næss's philosophy:

> There are two sorts of mysticism: in one of them you get completely absorbed in something much bigger than you, an organic whole or God, but on the other hand there is the mysticism you find in Spinoza, which tries to retain, after all has passed, the individual.[29]

Though it would be too much to call Treschow a "prototypal Næss," many of the leitmotifs of his nature philosophy will animate Næss's deep ecological thinking. Ultimately, however, both Treschow's and Næss's ideas build on the ancient wisdom as recorded in Snorre's *Edda*: a belief that "all is originally One," a strong sense of realism, and an assessment of reality through the prism of common sense and human experience:

> Almighty God created heaven and earth and all things in them, and lastly two humans from whom generations are descended. . . . He also gave them a portion of wisdom so that they could understand all earthly things and the details of everything they could see in the sky and on earth. They pondered and were amazed at what it could mean that the earth and animals and birds had common characteristics in some things. . . . Rocks and stones they thought of as equivalent to teeth and bones of living creatures. From this they reasoned that

the earth was alive and had life after a certain fashion, and they realized it was enormously old in count of years and mighty in nature.[30]

There is, finally, Henrik Wergeland, the only true Romantic among the nineteenth century Norwegian preachers of nature and nation. Again, it is less the romantic, demiurgic Wergeland, and more Wergeland the Enlightenment prankster and reformer, who can be rediscovered in Næss's thinking about humans and nature. The Wergelandian ecstatic identification with all beings—"I who read rapture in each petal of the hundred leafed rose"[31]—is given a more rationalist twist by Næss:

> Given our biological endowment, each of us has the capacity to identify with all living beings. . . . humans have the capacity to experience the intimate relations between organisms and the inorganic world—that is, between the biosphere and the ecosphere in general.[32]

Among more contemporary interlocutors, the most significant has undoubtedly been Peter Wessel Zapffe: Næss's philosophical opponent. There are, we might note, two schools of thinking about nature in the Norwegian cultural tradition exemplified, respectively, by Zapffe and Næss. The Næssian strain represents a culmination of Enlightenment optimism and rationalism combined with the folk tradition of Askeladdian resourcefulness and pragmatism. The second, more iconoclastic strain, figures in the work of Hamsun, Vigeland, and Zapffe. At its center there is nature conceived as *sacrum*, an incomprehensible, immoral God, awesome in its beauty and merciless in its mindless cruelty. If in the vision of the Norwegian Enlightenment there is less religion and more reason, in the apocalyptic school, religion (in its original pre-Christian sense) plays an enormous part. Here nature is God and, in the case of Zapffe, a dying God. "[It] shows neither morality nor reason;" its decline is inevitable, and nothing, not even man's most glorious accomplishments, can prevent final annihilation.[33]

For Zapffe, the human demand for meaning in a meaningless universe heading for an inevitable Ragnarok is the source of life-as-tragedy. No other existential genres are possible. Human beings are a "destructive environmental element" whose hapless role is to hasten the death of God. In his more torrid moments, Zapffe could see himself as a negative, ecological Christ, a "man who has grasped life in its cosmic context, and whose agony is the agony of the world."[34]

Per contra, at the center of Næss's deep ecology is a benign, rationally based hope, articulated in deep questions which curiously refuse to come to terms with the mystery of what it is to be human. In Zapffe's ecology, deep questions, when asked, unveil the cosmic rapaciousness of man and the awesome mortality of nature. Zapffian philosophy goes beyond the Nietzschean "Dare to lead the tragic life, and you will be redeemed,"[35] for it reaches to a bottomless void from which there is no exit.

Nature versus Culture

Irrespective of postmodern unmaskings of the cultural creation of nature, the *agon* between nature and culture has remained an enduring refrain in Norwegian texts until this very day. Its ultimate articulation is Norwegian ecophilosophical thought which, far from being anti-intellectual is, more or less unambiguously, anti-*Kultur* and anti-*Zivilisation* in orientation.[36] From the eighteenth century pastors and on to Ibsen, Hamsun, and contemporary *kulturradikaler*, Culture— conflated with a "high" culture of useless splendors and excesses—has been deprecated in Norway as a product of inhuman, mostly foreign, agencies and institutions. Hamsun, who always wanted to die "on the cowberry bog" ("Å dø paa en Tyttebærsmue") believed in the authority and the wisdom of the forest and simple folk.[37] As late as the 1980s the philosopher of *outdoor life*, Nils Faarlund, indicated an explicit conflict: "I prefer not to speak about man and culture but instead of nature and culture . . . and our present culture is on a colli- sion course with nature."[38] Yet another *friluftsliv* philosopher, Gunnar Breivik, makes an egalitarian claim which sounds so outrageous that it can only be Nor- wegian: "Hunting and trapping are equally good expressions of the relationship with nature as Grieg's music and Wergeland's poems."[39] Last but not least, the radical nature philosopher, Sigmund Kvaløy, has gone so far in his holy biocen- tric wrath as to oppose an ecophilosopher to a European:

> Ecophilosophy has become with us unmistakably Norwegian. In contrast to the urban, European, recreational perception of nature reserved for the upper classes, Norwegians have viewed closeness to nature as life necessity.[40]

Arne Næss has consistently derided such radical—if not fundamentalist— declarations. And yet, however we take it, his vision of Norway in 2084 signals an implicit skepticism with regard to both science and civilization. High culture, with its ideals based on elitist hierarchy and anthropocentric values, is part of a *hubris* scenario and therefore a nuisance in the deep ecological vision.[41] Sci- ence—not a very salient factor in the Green Utopia—has been berated by Næss in a separate work launching such commandments as "use imagination," "leave nature alone," "find alternative ways," "serve people!"[42]

The appeal of this anti-*Kultur* attitude can be traced back to long centuries of at-homeness in nature - and an exaggerated feeling of the threat posed by the *polis*. The Spartan impulse which inspired nineteenth century cultural national- ists to preach a way of life both simple and austere enough to make the agropo- lis genuinely self-sufficient, has never really died out in Norway. At the begin- ning of the nineteenth century Jacob Aall, the iron-master, complained bitterly of the contempt with which wealth was regarded by a large section of the Nor- wegian Parliament.[43] Næss's ideal, based as it is on a dream of an autarchic pastoral republic where small is beautiful and poor is dutiful, promulgates the old tradition. "We shall not be members of a rich man's club,"[44] is the battle cry of his protest against membership of the European Union. Though Næss himself would not want to own anything that would not fit in his coffin (or urn), his is a privileged, Midassian renunciation of all the gold (i.e., oil) which surrounds him. If his conservative radicalism has been inspiring (Norway, in effect, did not join the "rich men's club"), it is because it still resonates with a culture in which the old ideal of an austere, authentic, and independent existence remains part of the Norwegian dream. The dream has been summoned and amplified in the books and deeds of successive generations.

Ultimately, there is little to separate Næss's utopia of Norway in 2084 and Ludvig Holberg's subterranean state of "Potu," imagined in 1741.[45] In the latter, the Norwegian-born dramatist depicted a society of thinking trees, an enlightened state with an almost unlimited freedom of expression, immune from dogmas, spurning wealth, practicing deistic nature religion and full equality between the sexes. In Potu disputants are kept for public amusement, like gamecocks, and doctors of philosophy were called *Madiks*, the English equivalent of which is "worms." But above all, no one could become a professor who had not held some practical position.

Even if Næss never read Holberg, his personal life philosophy ultimately re-enacts the Holbergian ideal. According to the latter, the individual should "have only provisional opinions, and hence he should keep one door always ajar as a signal of his willingness to learn, his openness to instruction, and to the truth that might follow."[46]

Notes

This chapter was originally published in Norwegian in *Norske naturmytologier: Fra Edda til Økofilosofi* (Oslo: Pax, 1998). The author wishes to thank Professor Andrew Brennan's and Patrick Sheeran for valuable comments.

[1] Arne Næss, "The Green Utopia of 2084," unpublished paper presented at the University of Minnesota in 1984.

[2] Ibid. 8–13.

[3] Peter Reed and David Rothenberg, *Wisdom in the Open Air: The Norwegian Roots of Deep Ecology* (Minneapolis: University of Minnesota Press, 1993).

[4] *Letters of Lord Acton to Herbert Gladstone*, ed. Mary Paul (New York, 1955), 99.

[5] *The Mountain Spirit*, ed. Michael Tobias and Harold Drasdo (New York: Overlook Press, 1979), 13–14.

[6] "How My Philosophy Seemed to Develop," in *Philosophische Selbstbetrachtung, Philosophers on their Work*, ed. André Mercier and Maja Silvar (New York: Peter Land, 1983), 210–13.

[7] Arne Næss, "The Shallow and the Deep, Long-range Ecology Movements: a Summary," *Inquiry* 16 (1973), 95–6.

[8] To be more specific: During a debate with Karl Otto Apel on 18 July 1990 in Melbu, Norway, Næss rejected the radical interpretation in favor of the reformist one. Sometime later, however, in a lecture at the Center for Development and the Envi-

ronment at Oslo University (on 17 September 1991), he strongly emphasized that the deep ecology movement was a radical movement, not a reformist one. See Peder Anker, "From Scepticism to Dogmatism and Back," in *Rethinking Deep Ecology*, ed. Nina Witoszek (Nature and Humanities Series, Oslo University, 1996).

[9] *The Poetic Edda*, tranlated by Lee M. Hollander (Austin: University of Texas Press, 1962), 12.

[10] Arne Næss, "Deep Ecology for the Twenty-Second Century," in George Sessions (ed.) *Deep Ecology for the 21st Century* (Boston: Shambhala, 1995), 463–467.

[11] Arne Næss, "Intrinsic Value: Will the Defenders of Nature Please Rise?" in *Wisdom in the Open Air*, 71.

[12] Ibid., 225.

[13] Næss, "Intrinsic Value," 80.

[14] Næss, "Intrinsic Value," 76–77. One thinks immediately of Martin Schweigaard (the nineteenth century economist and the *spiritus movens* of the newly founded University in Christiania) and his famous declaration: "We will not, like Hegel, make revolution merely in words." See Gunnar Skirbekk, "Schweigaard og den norske tankerøysla: Kriminalhistoria om filosofiens påståtte død i Norge i 1830-åra," *Ord* (Oslo: Det Norske Samlaget), 140f.

[15] Næss, "Intrinsic Value," 71, 74.

[16] Reed and Rothenberg, *Wisdom in the Open Air*, 103.

[17] Reed and Rothenberg, *Wisdom in the Open Air*, 106.

[18] Jon Elster, "Cultural Radicalism," *Pax Lexicon*, Bind 4 (Oslo: Pax Forlag, 1980), 13.

[19] See Leif Longum, *Drømmen om det frie menneske* (Oslo: Universitetsforlaget, 1986), 93. See also A. G. Michaelsen, *Den gyldne lenke* (Oslo: Dreyer, 1977), 20.

[20] Marx, *The Communist Manifesto*, ed. S. Beer (New York, 1955), 25.

[21] Tobias and Drasdo, *The Mountain Spirit*, 210.

[22] Arne Næss, *Truth as Conceived by Those Who are Not Professional Philosophers* (Oslo: Det Norske Vitenskaps Akademi, Skrifter II, 1938).

[23] Reed and Rothenberg, *Wisdom in the Open Air*, 97.

[24] Alfred Ayer and Arne Næss, "The Glass Is on the Table: An Empiricist versus Total View," in *Reflexive Waters: The Basic Concerns of Mankind*, ed. Fons Elders (London: Souvenir Press, 1986), 26.

[25] Marx, *Communist Manifesto*, 32.

[26] Marx, *The German Ideology*, in ed. L. Feuer, *Basic Writings on Politics and Philosophy* (New York, 1959), 254.

[27] Reed and Rothenberg, *Wisdom in the Open Air*, passim.

[28] Niels Treschow, *Menneskeværd og Menneskevel* (Oslo: Johan Grundt Tanum Forlag, 1963), pp. 33–34. (trans. mine). Treschow called his system a "philosophy of identity" which distinguished three sources of truth: reason, experience, and revelation.

[29] Reed and Rothenberg, *Wisdom in the Open Air*, 103.

[30] See *Snorri Sturulson's Edda* (Cambridge University Press, 1954), 23–24.

[31] Henrik Wergeland, "Myself," in *H. Wergeland. Poems*, trans. I Grøndahl (Oslo: Gyldendal Norsk Forlag, 1929), 86.

[32] Næss, "Intrinsic Value," 73.

[33] Peter Wessel Zapffe, "Mysterium," in *Essays og Epistler* (Oslo: Gyldendal, 1967), 165. English version from *Wisdom in the Open Air*, 38.

[34] Peter Wessel Zapffe, "Den sidste Messias," in Peter Wessel Zapffe, *Essays*, utvalg ved Jan Brage Gundersen (Oslo: Aventura, 1992), 28. English version from *Wisdom in the Open Air*, 51.

[35] Frederik Nietzsche, *Birth of a Tragedy* (New York: Anchor, 1956), 60–61.

[36] See Næss's critique of science in *Anklagene mot vitenskapen* (Oslo: Universitetsforlaget, 1980).

[37] See Josef Wiehr, *Knut Hamsun, His Personality and His Outlook Upon Life*, Smyth Studies in Modern Languages, Vol. III, No.1–2 (Mass., 1922), 73.

[38] See Nils Faarlund, "Touch of the Earth: A Conversation with Nils Faarlund," in *Wisdom in the Open Air*, 233.

[39] See Gunnar Breivik, "To tradisjoner i norsk friluftsliv," in *Fra Fridtjof Nansen til våre dager*, eds. G. Breivik, H. Løvmo (Oslo, 1982), 10, trans. mine.

[40] Sigmund Kvaløy, "Økofilosofi versus New Age—Friluftsliv kontra kvantesprang," *Vitenskap og verdensbilder*, eds. Lars Gule and H. Laugerud (Bergen: Ariadne Forlag, 1989), 131, trans. mine.

[41] See Nina Witoszek, "Marx, Næss og Gaia—Hva med Kultur?," *Kontrast* (1991), 4.

[42] Arne Næss, *Anklagene mot vitenskapen* (Oslo, Universitetsforlaget, 1980), passim.

[43] "Wealth and property are a crime which must be castigated every day, and the favour of the great mob could be had only if complete economic equality—yes, equality of intellectual capacity—should be established." See Jacob Aall, *Breve fra Jernværkseier Jacob Aall til Sorenskriver (tilsidst Amtmand) G. P. Blom* (København, 1894), 4.

[44] Arne Næss, "Les traktaten om Europeisk Union!" *Nytt fra Natur og Ungdom* (NfNU) nr. 4 (1992): 3–5.

[45] Ludvig Holberg, *Nils Klims underjordiske Reise* (København, 1741).

[46] See Ludvig Holberg, *Epistler og Moralske Tanker,* utvalg ved Sigurd Højby (København: Gyldendals Uglebøger, 1945; rpt. 1973), 31–32.

Chapter 54

Is the Deep Ecology Vision a Green Vision or Is It Multicolored like the Rainbow? An Answer to Nina Witoszek

Arne Næss

I

In the political arena, the colors blue and red were already in use, and the ecological movement chose green. The key term "green" was a hit. But some metaphors are powerful and therefore dangerous. The pictures used by green parties and "prophets" tended to show innocent, plain, healthy people in a rustic, pastoral, or sylvan setting. It is understandable that industrialists and business people who basically accept the importance of the ecological movement ask questions like: "Must green societies be so boring?"

Nina Witoszek does not say that they must, but, if deep ecology supporters were *consistent*, then the suggestion is that they would indeed be green in an extremely narrow sense. I claim, on the contrary, that green societies and cultures may be diverse, or at least more diverse than the ones we have in Europe today. It is mainly the blue economy with its ever bigger markets, and ever more pressure towards material growth of the economy, that makes it difficult to maintain deeply different cultures.

Few philosophers are lucky enough to be the object of parodies of a high literary quality. But is "Arne Næss and the Norwegian Nature Tradition" *really* a parody?

It is unclear to me whether Nina Witoszek thinks that I expect "The Green Utopia" ever to be achieved. The supreme goal of ecologically sustainable policies is to protect and sustain full richness and diversity of life on earth. I

466

doubt this objective will ever be achieved. But I expect policies significantly more responsible than today, which will eliminate the threat of major ecological catastrophes. Not bliss, but certainly a *vision* of various eco-sustainable societies with at least as high a quality of life as the average in contemporary rich societies. The ultimate goal of the deep ecology movement is the full richness and diversity of life on the planet. It is my thesis that such a state still permits vast differences of noncoercive cultures and lifestyles. But it is not my thesis that this will ever happen. Visions are not predictions.

The primary, but not ultimate, aim of the deep ecology movement is to partake, together with the rest of the ecological movement, in the work for the *elimination of a crisis*. This is by definition a negative goal. The primary aim does not rule out vast creativity in the exploration of new and old lifestyles, fabulous new technologies and economic systems. But people living in a green society are not supposed to be some kind of new race. At least, humans will not be much different from what the God of the Old Testament knew Job to be. God arranged it so that Job had perhaps 4000 more sheep than the others, 3000 more camels than the others, and so on. In a green society there will be analogous, though hardly similar, possibilities: some will have more of the ecologically costly items. That is to say, deep ecology societies need not be green. They do not have to be agricultural or, as is often thought, reduced to activities which ensure satisfaction of basic needs. If we look carefully at what should be ruled out or tempered, it is really difficult to believe that the process need result in "mediocracy" and dull "egalitarianism."

II

Nina Witoszek uses hypotheses about my personal priorities in her argumentation. But outdoor life, in a sense that I presume is fairly common, has not played a major role in my life. "I belong to Tvergastein" is a meaningful sentence to me. But in most years at Tvergastein I have scarcely enjoyed outdoor life more than two hours a day on the average. Rather, I practice a sort of bioregionalism in the sense described by Gary Snyder. In the cabin at Tvergastein I regularly work more than in the city. Few colleagues (over some thirty years of my professorship) know that I tended to work on an average ten hours a day inside the cabin, and wrote most of my books there. I do not think there is anything peculiarly Norwegian about this indoor cabin life. If anything, it is more European. Once a visitor from one of the great cities looked through my cabin library—and saw the snow reaching all the way up to the window. Then he wrote a note to me about what he saw: Bibles in Norwegian, Sanskrit, and Greek, *The Cambridge Modern History*, the four–volumed superb and lovely L. Kieperts, *Differential und Integralrechnung*, Spinoza's *Opera*, Indian and Chinese philosophy, *Geschichte der Mathematics*, lots of Plato and Aristotle, and so on. The visitor did not expect these books high above the treeline. My ideal was to commute every year directly from this library to centers of learning—and to the desert, in search of unique spring blossoms.

Many people on hearing about the necessary changes of habit, exclaim: "I would rather go to hell first class!" Nobody should prevent them from doing this. The great question is: Does this or that good increase my quality of life to such a degree that it is worth all the necessary work? How much work is worth doing to possess this or that object or to travel by air?

Conspicuous consumption has always been a strong factor in the life of humans, and I do not expect a significant change. In a green society one may perhaps gain prestige from being seen in a five- or ten-horsepowered motorboat, whereas in contemporary rich countries this is nothing. Because "environmental" cost is taken into consideration, we shall hopefully get prestige from material splendors of other kinds than the present, largely unecological ones.

III

Is deep ecology reformatory or revolutionary? Is it modern or postmodern? There is a suggestion that I started by claiming that it was revolutionary, then I said it was reformatory, then again revolutionary, then both?

The point of departure in discussion is mostly at a level that is tentative or provisional from the point of view of empirical semantics. I call the employed formulations (sentences) T_0-formulations. Soon one feels that there may be pseudoagreements or disagreements in a prolonged debate. One has to consider the many different meanings of key terms. Gandhi supported what he and others called "nonviolent revolution," making extensive use of direct actions. But it was a step by step revolution. He insisted that one step at a time "is enough for me." If, and only if, the Gandhian terminology is accepted, then I would find it adequate to say that the deep ecology movement is revolutionary. If an action has to be violent in order to be called "revolutionary," then the movement is not revolutionary.

The use of "if" is perhaps too frequent in my writings; it certainly makes me more difficult to understand. (And of course, over the years, my opinions are not constant, and changes are not always explicit either.) May I add that I would find it a good thing if others used the condition-marking ifs more frequently. Speaking about "ifs," I think the distinction between "if" and "only if" is fruitful. "If x is a living being, then x has intrinsic value" does not imply "Only if x is a living being, then x has intrinsic value." Some have deplored the fact that, according to deep ecology, *only* living beings have intrinsic value, and they have then asked for a "deeper ecology" which would cover all natural beings. But there is nothing to prevent a supporter of the deep ecology movement from rejecting the proposition that only living beings have intrinsic value. Prolonged discussions make it necessary to specify different meanings of the expressions "living being" and "natural being."

So—is the deep ecology movement radical or reformist? If these two key terms were used for definite concepts—two fairly well delimited meanings shared by people engaged in social conflicts—answers could be straightforward. I certainly disagree with the suggestion that there is room for deep ecology "premises" which imply that change into ecosustainable societies "will necessitate the rejection of the liberal constitution" and a kind of "biocentric" system of justice. If unsustainability increases as outlined for instance in the new, well documented Club of Rome Report of 1992, there is a grave danger that some authoritarian or dictatorial regimes will take over in the next century—an unspeakable tragedy. If the deep ecology movement is revolutionary (in the agreed sense), I think social ecology may also be classed as revolutionary. Both ask for significant—perhaps also the word "essential" could be used here—changes in all aspects of society, and both focus primarily on the materially wealthy countries. The same holds for ecofeminism, or for some of the theoretical positions within ecofeminism: deep changes are called for, but not exactly identical with the ones contemplated by deep ecology theorists. Each movement has specific tasks.

How do supporters of the deep ecology movement view the likelihood of a complete success—ecological sustainability *and* full richness and diversity of life on earth? The term "full" is open to important differences of interpretations, but I personally think it will not be reached. This, of course, does not, or should not, hinder activism in favor of high levels of richness and diversity of living beings and cultures. I am optimistic about the twenty-second century, that is, I think it realistic to expect a turning of the tide: from increasing to decreasing ecological unsustainability. But from there to radical diminishing rates of extinction of species, to the establishment of large scale protected areas and of "bridges" between areas of free nature, the way seems very long, and "compromises" are likely. To be frank, I am astonished that people see inconsistency here. In short, deep ecology activism is compatible with the view that a complete realization of the goal is very unlikely. But as a philosopher, not as a politician, I have to take some "unlikely" futures seriously.

Ironic as Nina Witoszek is, it is difficult to guess whether she approves or disapproves of complex and inconsistent views. Among the "renowned inconsistencies" of Næss, she argues, none seems more glaring or blazing than that of proclaiming "biospherical egalitarianism" and then adding "in principle." Is not everything lost in this addition? In practice, one may always say: "Not equal in this case!" Obviously one cannot in a few words—or volumes—once and for all delimit norms of practice in, for instance, mixed communities. "Bears belong here, they have equal right to be here, but . . ." Since the French Revolution *egalité* has been an important, positive catchword among many groups, but the applications of the term have often been so disgusting or unwise that it also has been used as a dyslogism.

By "absolute" equalness in environmental concerns one might mean something covering the question of territory. One of the great difficulties for many mammals and birds is the steadily shrinking territories available. But what I have referred to is a value that living beings have, according to my intuition, in common. There are many words available for this common value (as I conceive it), but none are understood in the same way by everybody. I chose "intrinsic value," but "inherent value" is better. "Value in itself" is a less technical expression. For me a good criterion may be expressed in this way: "A being has inherent value if and only if it makes sense to do something strictly for its own sake." If a being has this kind of value, it should be respected, and instances of "killing, exploitation and suppression" (Næss 1973) need to be supported by ethical arguments. But this does not mean that "principles and practice deviate." In short, the expression "*x* and *y* are equal" does not imply that *x* and *y* are equal in every respect.

In the philosophy of law, the expression "guidelines" is important and the term "norm" is often avoided pointing as it does to tendencies of absolutism, categorical imperatives, and rigorism. My use of the absolutist term "norm" has been frequently criticized. At any rate, one has to walk along a narrow ridge with absolutism to the right and light-hearted, soft guidelines to the left.

Let me add that often when, in a definite situation, a person is said to be inconsistent and even agrees that she or he is inconsistent, there is usually no logical inconsistency but an inconsistency in relation to oversimplified, slogan-like formulations. Verbal formulations, except among great philosophers and authors, are oversimplifications also in those cases where one carefully chooses the words. Even so-called "dull persons," if given a chance and allowed to use an expert in codification and systematization, would reveal views of great significance and complexity. One would discover hundreds of factors operating even in everyday practical decisions (for instance, how to arrange a kitchen—the 600 or more things and their relations).

IV

As one of the theorists of the deep ecology movement, my life and preferences have been under scrutiny. What kind of green society would I, given my value priorities and preferences, look forward to? Certainly one respecting a high degree of self-determination, a high degree of individual choices, institutions that are open to personal initiative.

It is for me difficult to see any signs that there could possibly be a future authoritarian or dictatorial regime that would demand more respect for non-human living beings and their *Lebensraum* ("life space," a favorite National Socialist term). There may in the future be a majority who would, theoretically, say yes to the 8 points and similar sets of formulations. But fierce political struggles are likely to continue to center on issues remote from anything like those points. Any mild forms of ecosustainability, or better, policies preventing future catastrophic events, are likely to be burning political issues.

When reading about value priorities and ultimate normative premises, we read about structures. It is easy to get a feeling of being imprisoned in a kind of machinery if the ultimates are not said to be "happiness!" or "love!" But even if we start out with "love!" there will be dilemmas and norm-conflicts. The area of ethically neutral decision will be greater or smaller depending on how love gets implied in the workplace, in marriage, in educational efforts as parents. From the single (logical) ultimate "Self-realization!," as from "love!," one has to take into account the elaboration of the normative and descriptive content of an ecosophy.

Granted that ecologically sustainable societies are within reach, say in the twenty-second century, what is the range of possible *differences* of sustainable societies and, to use a broader terms, cultures? It has been noted that this question has rarely been discussed and that green utopias have resembled societies, or rather, communities, of marked rural character. If highly industrialized societies are dismantled, then it is often assumed we move towards rural societies of the kind we have known in the past. However, the view that supporters of the deep ecology movement are uniformly in favor of some sort of agrarian ecologically sustainable society is untenable. The term "green" is to some extent misleading, but of historical importance. The same holds for "society" and "culture." (As a substitute we may perhaps use "country" or "territory.") In the 1960s and 1970s it was difficult to envisage other negatives of the industrial, *black* societies. A useful slogan is "Industrial societies: *No*. Societies with industry: *Yes*." The "yes" does not imply that all thinkable ecosustainable ones *must* have industry, but I guess few would seriously shun living in a society without it.

What about "high culture"? Oppressive elitism is not implied by high culture. I do not find the high culture of the painter Munch "anthropocentric" in a way that would interfere with the goal of protecting full richness and diversity of life on the planet.

What about people with special interests? Can contemporary physical and astronomically oriented cosmology continue to blossom? The consumption of energy is formidable! There are millions of people interested in its continued development. One scenario: One community specializes in the continuation, but with a yearly energy consumption of, say, 10 percent of what is now spent in Europe on cosmological research. It *may* mean a development in ten years equal to the one we have now. But at this stage development is galloping at a pace that makes it impossible to keep up, except in minute areas within cosmology. Even within the 10 percent framework, the energy used would disturb the total energy balance. Why should people with no interest in cosmology have to use 1 percent less energy in order to satisfy a minority? Answer: "Polluters pay!"

A second scenario: There is a society where the total energy consumption is within proper limits, but where personal energy consumption per capita is 50 percent below proper limits. The rest goes to cosmology research and other research which is necessary in order to continue a ("slow") development within cosmology. The inhabitants might renounce some goods and services they would like to enjoy, their life would seem harsh to outsiders, but not to the seriously engaged. If, in addition, they lived in a small Switzerland surrounded by big, non-specialized societies, commuting would not require much energy. Family and children considered, one would not need to live all one's life in a "cosmo-land." In an eco-sustainable society with some forms of technology we today call "advanced," I would expect to find wood stoves, trains, and a lot of bicycles. (From an ecological point of view, the bicycle is an example of advanced transport technology.)

Like many others, I would like to live in such a country, that is, a society where many things now cheap would be expensive and/or restricted. The expense and/or restrictions should be severe only with regard to a small number of destructive (but sometimes desirable) goods and services.

Finale

Deep ecology formulates a program which may have been influenced by my own culture but which is not particularly new in the context of European tradition. Identification with and duties towards all living beings have been emphasized in European thought, starting with the technical and pragmatic Romans, such as Ovid:

> Take not away the life you cannot give:
> For all things have an equal right to live.

The acceptance of so-called "bioegalitarianism" in principle has been especially rich in British history. Important names: Edward Bancroft, Samuel Taylor Coleridge, William Wordsworth, William Blake, come to mind. Blake asserted that every thing that lives is holy:

> Am not I
> A fly like thee
> Or art not thou
> A man like me?

It has been rather common in English literature to stress the moral duties of man towards "the Brute Creation." Taking care of the self-realization potentials was suggested by Tryon (1683): We should assist beasts in "the obtaining of all the advantages their natures are by the great . . . creator made capable of." This is more radical than a norm against coercion of self-realization potentials! Coleridge talked about the fraternity of all living beings, "I hail thee brother."

The article by Nina Witoszek shows that it is more important than ever to focus on the cultural gains made possible through steps in the direction of maintaining richness and diversity. The generous estimation of nonhumans need not require any downgrading of the uniqueness of humans. I feel they are so unique in so many ways, that they need no "centering," whether anthropocentric or biocentric.

Postscript

Radical American Environmentalism Revisited

Ramachandra Guha

Editors' Note: This postscript arrived too late to include in the main part of the book. We are grateful to the publishers for delaying publication of the volume so that it could be included here.

I

The article which appears as Chapter 40 of the present volume was written at the end of an extended period of residence in the United States, which followed directly upon several years of research on the origins of Indian environmentalism. That background might explain the puzzlement and anger which, in hindsight, appear to mark the essay. To my surprise, the article evoked a variety of responses, both pro and con. The veteran Vermont radical, Murray Bookchin, himself engaged in a polemic with American deep ecologists, offered a short (three-line) letter of congratulation. A longer (thirty page) response came from Arne Næss. Næss felt bound to assume responsibility for the ideas I had challenged, even though I had distinguished between his emphases and those of his American interpreters. Other correspondents, lesser known but no less engaged, wrote in to praise or to condemn.[1] Over the years, the essay has appeared in some half dozen anthologies, as a voice of the "Third World," the token and disloyal opposition to the reigning orthodoxy's of environmental ethics.[2]

The essay having acquired a life of its own, I felt it prudent to print it here without any changes. This postscript allows me to expand and strengthen my case with the aid of a few freshly arrived examples.

II

Woodrow Wilson once remarked that the United States was the only idealistic nation in the world. It is indeed this idealism which explains the zest, the zeal, the almost unstoppable force with which Americans have sought to impose their vision of the good life on the rest of the world. American economists urge on other nations their brand of energy-intensive, capital-intensive, market-oriented development. American spiritualists, saving souls, guide pagans to one or other of their eccentrically fanatical cults, from Southern Baptism to Moral Rearmament. American advertisers export the ethic of disposable containers — of all sizes, from coffee cups to automobiles.

Of course, other people have had to pay for the fruits of this idealism. The consequences of the forward march of American missionaries include the undermining of political independence, the erosion of cultures, and the growth of an ethic of sheer greed. In a dozen parts of the world, those fighting for political, economic or cultural autonomy have collectively raised the question whether the American way of life is not, in fact, the Indian (or Brazilian, or Somalian) way of death.

One kind of U.S. missionary, however, has attracted virtually no critical attention. They are the ones who are worried that the rest of the world thinks their country has a dollar sign for a heart. The dress they wear is also colored green, but it is the green of the virgin forest. Deeply committed lovers of the wild, in their own country they have helped put in place a magnificent system of national parks. But they also have money and will travel. They now wish to convert other cultures to their gospel, to export the American invention of national parks worldwide.

My essay was one of the first attacks on an imperialism previously reckoned to be largely benign. After all, we are not talking here of the Marines, with their awesome firepower, or even of the World Bank, with its money, power and the ability to manipulate developing country governments. These are men (and more rarely, women) who come preaching the equality of all species, who worship all that is good and beautiful in Nature. What could be wrong with them?

I had suggested in my essay that the noble, apparently disinterested motives of conservation biologists and deep ecologists fueled a territorial ambition — the physical control of wilderness in parts of the world other than their own — that led inevitably to the displacement, and harsh treatment, of the human communities who dwelled in these forests. Consider in this context a recent assessment of global conservation by Michael Soulé, which complains that the language of policy documents has "become more humanistic in values and more economic in substance, and correspondingly less naturalistic and ecocentric." Soulé seems worried that in theory (though certainly not in practice!) some national governments and international conservation organizations (ICOs) now pay attention to the rights of human communities. Proof of this shift is the fact that "the top and middle management of most ICOs are economists, lawyers, and development specialists, not biologists." This is a sectarian plaint, a trade union approach to the problem spurred by an alleged "takeover of the international conservation movement by social scientists, particularly economists."[3]

Soulé's essay, with its talk of conspiracies and takeover bids, manifests the paranoia of a community of scientists which has a huge influence on conservation policy yet wants to be the sole dictator. A scholar acclaimed by his peers as the "dean of tropical ecologists" has expressed this ambition more nakedly than most. I have already quoted from a paper published by Daniel Janzen in the *Annual Review of Ecology and Systematics* which urges upon his fellow biologists the cultivation of the ability to raise cash so as to buy space and species to study. Let me now quote from are port he wrote on a new National Park in Costa Rica, whose tone and thrust perfectly complements the other, ostensibly "scientific," essay. "We have the seed and the biological expertise: we lack control of the terrain," wrote Janzen in 1986. This situation he was able to remedy for himself, by raising enough money to purchase the forest area needed to create the Guanacaste National Park. One can only marvel at Janzen's conviction that he and his fellow biologists know all, and that the inhabitants of the forest know nothing. He justifies the taking over of the forest and the dispossession of the forest farmer by claiming that

> Today virtually all of the present-day occupants of the western Mesoamerican pasture, fields and degraded forests are deaf, blind and mute to the fragments of the rich biological and cultural heritage that still occupies the shelves of the unused and unappreciated library in which they reside.[4]

This is an ecologically updated version of the White Man's Burden, where the biologist (rather than the civil servant or military official) knows that it is in the native's true interest to abandon his home and hearth and leave the field and the forest clear for the new rulers of his domain. In Costa Rica we only have Janzen's word for it, but elsewhere we are better placed to challenge the conservationist's paint of view. A remarkable book on African conservation has laid bare the imperialism, unconscious and explicit, of Western wilderness lovers and biologists working on that luckless continent. I cannot here summarize the massive documentation of Raymond Bonner's *At the Hand of Man*, so let me simply quote some of his conclusions:

> Above all, Africans [have been] ignored, overwhelmed, manipulated and out-maneuvered by a conservation crusade led, orchestrated and dominated by white Westerners.

> Livingstone, Stanley and other explorers and missionaries had come to Africa in the nineteenth century to promote the three C's — Christianity, commerce and civilization. Now a fourth was added: conservation. These modern secular

missionaries were convinced that without the white man's guidance the Africans would go astray.

[The criticisms] of egocentricity and neo-colonialism . . . could be leveled fairly at most conservation organizations working in the Third World.

As many Africans see it, white people are making rules to protect animals that white people want to see in parks that white people visit. Why should Africans support these programs? . . . The World Wildlife Fund professed to care about what the Africans wanted, but then tried to manipulate them into doing what the Westerners wanted: and those Africans who couldn't be brought into line were ignored.

Africans do not use the parks and they do not receive any significant benefits from them. Yet they are paying the costs. There are indirect economic costs — government revenues that go to parks instead of schools. And there an direct personal costs [i.e. of the ban on hunting and fuel-collecting, or of displacement].[5]

Banner's book focuses on the elephant, one of the half-dozen or so animals that have come to acquire "totemic" status among Western wilderness lovers. Animal totems existed in most pre-modern societies, but as the Norwegian scholar Arne Kalland points out, in the past the injunction not to kill the totemic species applied only to members of the group. Hindus do not ask others to worship the cow, but those who love and cherish the elephant, seal, whale or tiger try to impose a worldwide prohibition on its killing. No one, they say, anywhere, anytime, shall be allowed to touch the animal they hold sacred even if (as with the elephant and several species of whale) scientific evidence has established that small-scale hunting will not endanger its viable populations and will, in fact, save human lives put at risk by the expansion, after total protection, of the *lebensraum* of the totemic animal. The new totemists also insist that their species is the "true rightful inhabitant" of the ocean or forest, and ask that human beings who have lived in the same terrain (and with the animals) for millennia be taken out and sent elsewhere.[6]

I turn, last of all, to an ongoing controversy in my own bailiwick. The Nagarhole National Park in southern Karnataka has an estimated forty tigers, the species toward whose protection has been directed enormous amounts of Indian and foreign money and attention. Now Nagarhole is also home to about 6 000 people, who have been in the area for longer than anyone can remember, perhaps as long as the tigers themselves. The state Forest Department wants the people out, claiming they destroy the forest and kill wild game. The people answer that their demands are modest, consisting in the main of fuel wood, fruit, honey and the odd quail or partridge. They do not own guns, although coffee planters living on the edge of the forest do. Maybe it is the planters who poach big game? In any case the indigenous people ask the officials: if the forest is only for tigers, why have you invited India's biggest hotel chain to build a hotel inside it while you plan to throw us out?

Into this controversy jumps a green missionary passing through Karnataka. Dr. John G. Robinson works for the Wildlife Conservation Society in New York, for which he oversees 160 projects in 44 countries. He conducts a whistle-stop tour of Nagarhole, and before he flies off to the next project on his list hurriedly calls a press conference in the state capital Bangalore. Throwing the indigenous people out of the park, he says, is the only means to save the wilderness. This is not a one-off case but a sacred principle, for in Robinson's opinion "relocating tribal or traditional people who live in these protected areas is the single most important step towards conservation." Tribal people, he explains, "compulsively hunt for food," and compete with tigers for prey. Deprived of food, tigers cannot survive, and "their extinction means that the balance of the ecosystem is upset and this has a snowballing effect."[7]

One does not know how many traditional inhabitants Robinson met (none, is the likely answer). Yet the Nagarhole case is hardly untypical. All over India, the management of parks has sharply posited the interests of poor traditional inhabitants against those of wilderness lovers and urban pleasure-seekers who wish to keep parks "free of human interference" — that is, free of other humans. These conflicts are being played out in the Rajaji sanctuary in Uttar Pradesh, in Simlipal in Orissa, in Kanha in Madhya Pradesh and in Melghat in Maharashtra.[8]

Everywhere, Indian wild lifers have ganged up behind the Forest Department to evict the primary inhabitants and rehabilitate them far outside the forests. In this they have drawn sustenance from American biologists and conservation organizations, who have thrown the prestige of science and the power of the dollar behind the crusade to kick the spiritual owners of the forest out of their home.

Specious nonsense about the equal rights of all species hides the plain fact that green imperialists are possibly as dangerous and certainly more hypocritical than their economic or religious counterparts. For the American advertiser and banker hopes for a world in which everyone, regardless of color, will be in an economic sense an American — driving a car, drinking Pepsi, owning a fridge and a washing machine. The missionary, having discovered Jesus Christ, wants pagans also to share the discovery. The conservationist wants to "protect the tiger (or whale) for posterity," yet expects *other* people to make the sacrifice.

Moreover, the processes unleashed by green imperialism are well-nigh irreversible. For the consumer titillated into eating Kentucky Fried Chicken can always say, "once is enough." The Hindu converted to Baptism can decide later on to revert to his original faith. But the poor traditional inhabitants, thrown out of their homes by the propaganda of the conservationist, are condemned to the life of ecological refugees in a slum, a fate, for these forest people, which is next only to death.

III

The illustrations offered above throw serious doubt on Arne Næss's claim that the deep ecology movement is "from the point of view of many people all over the world, the most precious gift from the North American continent in our time."[9] For deep ecology's signal contribution has been to privilege above all other varieties of environmentalism the protection of wild species and wild habitats and to provide high-sounding, self-congratulatory but none the less dubious moral status for doing so. Treating "biocentric equality" as a moral absolute, tigers, elephants, whales, etc., will need more space to grow, flourish and reproduce, while humans — poor humans — will he expected to make way for them.

I by no means wish to see a world completely dominated by human beings, their mutualists, commensals and parasites. I have time for the tiger and the rainforest, and wish also to try and protect those islands of nature not yet fully conquered by us. My plea rather is to put wilderness protection (and its radical edge, deep ecology) in its place, to recognize it as a distinctively North Atlantic brand of environmentalism whose export and expansion must be done with caution, care, and above all with humility. For in the poor and heavily populated countries of the South, protected areas cannot be managed with guns and guards. Rather, conservation must take full cognizance of the rights of the people who lived in (and oftentimes cared for) the forest before it became a National Park or a World Heritage Site.[10]

Putting deep ecology in its place is to recognize that the trends it derides as "shallow" ecology might in fact be varieties of environmentalism that are more apposite, more representative, and more popular in the countries of the South. When Arne Næss says that "conservation biology is the spearhead of scientifically based environmentalism,"[11] I wonder why "agro ecology," "pollution abatement technology" or "renewable energy studies" cannot become the "spearhead of scientifically based environmentalism." For to the Costa Rican peasant or Ecuadorian fisherman, the Indonesian tribalor the slum dweller in Bombay, wilderness preservation can hardly be more "deep" than pollution control, energy conservation, ecological urban planning or sustainable agriculture.

Notes

[1] I refer to private communications. Published responses to my essay include David M. Johns, "The Relevance of Deep Ecology to the Third World: Some Preliminary Comments," *Environmental Ethics* 12, 2 (1990); J. Baird Callicott, "The Wilderness Idea Revisited: the Sustainable Development Alternative," *The Environmental Professional* 13, 2 (1991).

[2] These anthologies include Thomas A. Mappes and Jane S. Zembaty, eds., *Social Ethics: Morality and Public Policy* (fourth edition: New York: McGraw Hill, 1992);

Carolyn Merchant, ed., *Key Concepts in Critical Theory: Ecology* (N.J.: Humanities Press, 1994); Louis P. Pojman, ed., *Environmental Ethics: Readings in Theory and Application* (Boston: Jones and Bartlett, 1994); Lori Gruen and Dale Jamieson, eds., *Reflecting on Nature: Readings in Environmental Philosophy* (New York: Oxford University Press, 1994); Larry May and Shari Collins Sharriat, eds., *Applied Ethics: A Multicultural Approach* (Englewood Cliffs, N. J.: Prentice Hall, 1994); Andrew Brennan, ed., *The Ethics of the Environment* (Brookfield, Vt.: Dartmouth Publishers: 1995).

[3] Michael Soulé, *The Tigress and the Little Girl* (manuscript of a forthcoming book), Chapter VI, "International Conservation Politics and Programs"

[4] Daniel H. Janzen, *Guanacaste National Park: Tropical Ecological and Cultural Restoration* (San Jose: Editorial Universidad Estatal a Distancia, 1986). Also David Rains Wallace, "Communing in Costa Rica," *Wilderness* 181 (Summer 1988), which quotes Janzen as wishing to plan "protected areas in a way that will permanently accommodate solitude-seeking humans as well as jaguars, tapirs, and sea turtles." These solitude-seeking humans might include biologists, backpackers, deep ecologists, but not, one supposes, indigenous farmers, hunters or fishermen.

[5] Raymond Bonner, *At the Hand of Man: Peril and Hope for Africa's Wildlife* (New York: Alfred A. Knopf, 1993), pp. 35, 65, 70, 55, 221.

[6] Arne Kalland, "Seals, Whales and Elephants: Totem Animals and the Anti-Use Campaigns" in *Proceedings of the Conference on Responsible Wildlife Management* (Brussels: European Bureau for Conservation Development 1994). Also Arne Kalland, "Management by Totemization: Whale Symbolism and the Anti-Whaling Campaign," *Arctic* 46, 2 (1993).

[7] *The Deccan Herald*, Bangalore, 5 November 1995.

[8] A useful countrywide overview is provided in Ashish Kothari, Saloni Suri and Neena Singh, "Conservation in India: A New Direction," *Economic and Political Weekly*, 28 October 1995.

[9] Arne Næss, "Comments on the Article 'Radical American Environmentalism and Wilderness Preservation: A Third World Critique' by Ramachandra Guha," typescript (1989), page 23. Compare with Chapter 41 of the present volume.

[10] Recent writing by Indian scholars strongly disputes that conservation can succeed through the punitive guns-and-guards approach favored by many wildlife conservationists, domestic or foreign. For thoughtful suggestions as to how the interests of wild species and the interests of poor humans might be made more compatible, see Kothari et al. op. cit.; M. Gadgil and P. R. S. Rao, "A System of Positive Incentives to Conserve Biodiversity," *Economic and Political Weekly*, 6 August 1994; R. Sukuman, "Wildlife-Human Conflict in India: An Ecological and Social Perspective," in R. Guha, ed., *Social Ecology* (New Delhi: Oxford University Press, 1994).

[11] Arne Næss, *Ecology, Community and Lifestyle*, translated by David Rothenberg (Cambridge: Cambridge University Press, 1990), p. 45.

Index

Figure 6. The Philosopher on the Move.

Notes on Contributors

Arne Næss is emeritus professor of philosophy at the University of Oslo. His appointment in philosophy at the age of 27 marked him as the youngest full professor of philosophy in Norway's history. In the first part of his career he published articles and books on empirical linguistics, Spinoza and philosophy of science. He took early retirement to devote time to writing on the environmental crisis and to pioneering the ideas of deep ecology. His influential book *Ecology, Community and Lifestyle* was published in 1989. Næss is currently affiliated to the Center of Development and the Environment, Oslo University.

George Sessions teaches in the philosophy department of Sierra College, Rocklin, California. He is co-author of *Deep Ecology* (1985) and *Deep Ecology for the Twenty-First Century* (1995).

The late *Alfred Jules Ayer* was born in 1910, and spent a large part of his academic career at the University of Oxford. From 1946 to 1959 he was professor of philosophy at University College, London, and thereafter Wykeham Professor of Logic at Oxford. A fellow of the British Academy, he is the author of several outstanding books and numerous articles in the philosophy of language and philosophy of mind.

Fons Elders studied philosophy and history at the universities of Amsterdam, Paris and Leiden. He is a professor at the Academy of Physical Education, the Academy of Architecture, Rietveld Academy, and at the Theatre School in Amsterdam. He is presently a member of the Council of the University of Amsterdam. He has published on philosophy as science-fiction and on systematic philosophy.

Paul Feyerabend was born in 1924 and died in 1994. A distinguished philosopher of science, he was best known for his anarchic theories of knowledge. His most famous book, *Against Method*, was strongly influenced by the ideas of Thomas Kuhn, Karl Popper, and Imre Lakatos.

Bill Devall lectures in the Sociology Department, Humboldt State University, and is the co-author of *Deep Ecology* (1985).

Genevieve Lloyd is professor of philosophy at the University of New South Wales. She is the author of *The Man of Reason: "Male" and "Female" in Western Philosophy* (1993), *Being in Time: Selves and Narrators in Philosophy and Literature* (1993) as well as two recent books on Spinoza's ethics.

John P. Clark teaches philosophy at Loyola University, New Orleans, where he chairs the Environmental Studies Program. He has written and edited a number of books in social theory and ecological philosophy, including *The Anarchist Moment: Reflections on Culture, Nature and Power, Renewing the Earth: The Promise of Social Ecology,* and, *Equality, Geography: The Social Thought of Elisee Reclus.* Besides being an activist in the green movement he also works in ecological forestry.

Richard A. Watson is professor of philosophy at Washington University. His many publications include both scholarly work *(The Breakdown of Cartesian Metaphysics, The Longest Cave)* and novels *(Niagra, The Runner).*

William French teaches in the Theology Department of Loyola University, Chicago. His main research areas are in ecological ethics, Christian theology, and war and peace studies. He is also a member of the Chicago Center for Peace Studies.

Baird Callicott teaches philosophy at the University of North Texas. Although he originally specialized in ancient philosophy, he is now well-known for his numerous articles and books on environmental philosophy. His recent book, *Earth's Insights,* reviews many different environmental philosophies and defends Aldo Leopold's land ethic.

Warwick Fox teaches philosophy and is a member of the staff at the Centre for Professional Ethics, University of Central Lancashire, UK. He is the author of several articles on deep ecology and of the book *Toward a Transpersonal Ecology* (1990). He has wide research interests in ethics, worldviews, and philosophical counseling.

Andrew Brennan is professor of philosophy at the University of Western Australia. His early work was on philosophy of language and philosophy of mind. His books on the environmental philosophy include *Thinking About Nature* (1988) and an edited collection *The Ethics of the Environment* (1995).

Peter Reed held a Fulbright Scholarship in Norway from 1985–86 and then stayed on to work at the Council for Environmental Studies in Oslo. He died in an avalanche in the Jotunheimen in March 1987. He was co-editor, with David Rothenberg, of *Wisdom in the Open Air.*

Val Plumwood holds an Australian Research Council Fellowship and is author of the influential book *Feminism and the Mastery of Nature* (1993), as well as of numerous articles on environmental philosophy. She lives close to nature on Plumwood Mountain, New South Wales.

Kirkpatrick Sale is a journalist and writer who has published widely on politics and bioregionalism. His books include *Human Scale, Dwellers in the Land, The Conquest of Paradise: Christopher Columbus and the Columbian Legacy,* and *Rebels Against the Future: The Luddites and Their War on the Industrial Revolution.*

Michael Zimmerman has special interests in the philosophy of Heidegger and environmental ethics. He is the author of numerous articles and three books, including *Contesting Earth's Future* (1994). As well as teaching philosophy at Tulane University he is clinical professor of psychology at Tulane Medical School where he teaches a course on philosophy and psychotherapy.

Ariel Salleh is on the staff of the School of Social Ecology, the University of Western Sydney. She has a wide background in teaching environmental ethics and ecofeminism and was for a time the editor of the political theory journal *Thesis Eleven.* As a committed community activist, Salleh is an executive member of the New South Wales Conservation Council.

Karen J. Warren holds a chair of philosophy at Macalester College, St. Paul, Minnesota. She has edited two collections of essays on ecofeminism, but also has research interests in philosophical psychology and teaches philosophy and critical thinking to teachers and junior school students. Her recent studies include *Ecofeminism: A Philosophical Perspective on What It Is and Why It Matters.*

Patsy Hallen has been on the staff of Murdoch University, Western Australia, since 1975. Born in Canada, and a graduate of Boston University, she has a deep love of and attachment to the wilderness areas of Western Australia. She spends prolonged periods in the bush and in addition to writing on environmental ethics is a keen photographer and archivist of her experience of connection with the land.

Murray Bookchin has been a radical since his youth in the 1930s as a trade unionist, teacher, and author of some twenty books on ecology, politics, philosophy, history, and urban issues. His 1995 work, *Re-Enchanting Humanity,* elaborates on many of the themes taken up in the article printed in the present collection.

Andrew McLaughlin teaches philosophy at Lehman College, City University of New York. He has published several articles on deep ecology and is the author of *Regarding Nature: Industrialism and Deep Ecology* (1993).

Ramachandra Guha is a research fellow at the Ford Foundation and a full-time author and columnist. His publications include *The Unquiet Woods, Ecology and Equity,* and *Varieties of Environmentalism.* He lives in Bangalore, India.

Stephan Harding received his doctorate from Oxford University for his work on the ecology of the muntjac deer in Britain. He has worked as a conservation biologist and ecology teacher in various countries, including Costa Rica and India. He is currently based at Schumacher College in England, where he teaches deep ecology and Gaia theory.

Ivar Mysterud lectures in biology and ecology at the Biology Department, University of Oslo. He has for six years served as vice president of the International Association for Bear Research and Management. His recent publications include papers and reports on nature and carnivore management, mammal home range dynamics, and forest fire ecology.

Harold Glasser wrote his Ph.D. dissertation on deep ecology and environmental policy. He is currently working at the Foundation for Deep Ecology in San Francisco as general editor of *Selected Works of Arne Næss* to be published by Kluwer Academic Publishers.

Bryan Norton, a graduate of the University of Michigan, is professor of Environmental Public Policy, Georgia Institute of Technology. He has written widely on conservation biology and environmental ethics and much of his work focused on biological diversity. More recently he has been working on the definition of ecosystem health and how to determine parameters for sustainability. He is well known as the author of several books, including *Toward Unity Among Environmentalists* (1991).

Jon Wetlesen is a professor of practical philosophy at the University of Oslo, Norway. He studied under Arne Næss and wrote his doctoral dissertation on Spinoza. His subsequent work on Buddhist philosophy, *Self-knowledge and Liberation; A Buddhist Perspective*, was published in Norwegian in 1983. He is the author of several introductory texts on ethics, and has recently been working on Meister Eckhart's conception of becoming what you are.

Per Ariansen teaches in the Department of Philosophy, University of Oslo. He has been working in the field of environmental philosophy for several years and, in addition to his book *Miljøfilosofi* (Environmental Philosophy, 1992), he has published numerous articles on topics in environmental ethics.

Peder Anker is a graduate of the University of Oslo, and is now completing his Ph.D. in the history of ideas. His dissertation research is being conducted at the Department of the History of Science, Harvard University.

Nina Witoszek is associate professor at the Department of History and Civilization, European University, Florence, and is a senior research fellow at the Center for Development and the Environment, Oslo University. Her recent publications include *Talking to the Dead: A Study in Irish Traditions* (1997) and *Norwegian Nature Mythologies* (1998).